second edition

STRUCTURAL
STEEL DESIGN

Intext Series in Civil Engineering

consulting editor   RUSSELL C. BRINKER

Professor of Civil Engineering
New Mexico State University

Bouchard and Moffitt – SURVEYING, 5th ed.

Brinker – ELEMENTARY SURVEYING, 5th ed.

Clark, Viessman, and Hammer – WATER SUPPLY AND POLLUTION
CONTROL, 2d ed.

Ghali and Neville – STRUCTURAL ANALYSIS: A UNIFIED CLASSICAL
AND MATRIX APPROACH

Jumikis – FOUNDATION ENGINEERING

McCormac – STRUCTURAL ANALYSIS, 2d ed.

McCormac – STRUCTURAL STEEL DESIGN, 2d ed.

Meyer – ROUTE SURVEYING AND DESIGN, 4th ed.

Moffitt – PHOTOGRAMMETRY, 2d ed.

Salmon and Johnson – STEEL STRUCTURES: DESIGN AND BEHAVIOR

Ural – MATRIX OPERATIONS AND USE OF COMPUTERS IN
STRUCTURAL ENGINEERING

Wang – MATRIX METHODS OF STRUCTURAL ANALYSIS, 2d ed.

Wang and Salmon – REINFORCED CONCRETE DESIGN

Winfrey – ECONOMIC ANALYSIS FOR HIGHWAYS

second edition

STRUCTURAL
STEEL DESIGN

JACK C. McCORMAC
Associate Professor of Civil Engineering
Clemson University

Intext Educational Publishers

College Division of Intext

Scranton   *San Francisco*   *Toronto*   *London*

K-W-RC

LIBRARY OF CONGRESS CATALOG CARD NUMBER

75-160681

ISBN 0-7002-2342-8

TO

my wife, *Mary*

and

daughters, *Mary Christine* and *Ann Rebecca*

PREFACE
TO SECOND EDITION

In 1969 the American Institute of Steel Construction, the American Association of State Highway Officials, and the American Railway Engineering Association made substantial revisions to their specifications for structural steel. This edition has been prepared with the primary objective of updating its contents to agree with these new specifications.

In addition many sections have been rewritten and additional material included. The homework problems have been almost completely changed and their number greatly increased. Based on requests from students, answers are included for approximately half of the problems.

The author is very grateful to the many persons who have taken the time to write to him concerning various phases of the text and will continue to be extremely interested in hearing from anyone regarding any part of the book. He is especially grateful to Dr. Oktay Ural, University of Missouri–Rolla, for his helpful suggestions and review of the manuscript for this edition.

Jack C. McCormac

Clemson, South Carolina
May, 1971

PREFACE
TO FIRST EDITION

This book presents an elementary discussion of structural steel design. Its purpose is to set forth the fundamental theories necessary for the design of simple steel structures in such a manner as to create interest in the subject.

The design of individual members and their connections is discussed in Chapters 1 through 12. Chapters 13 through 20 treat designs for entire structures. Chapters 21 and 22 introduce the student to plastic analysis and design. A satisfactory background in the fundamentals of mechanics of materials and structural analysis is a prerequisite for this text.

It is strongly recommended that the student supplement the text by observing the actual erection of steel structures. If he develops an awareness of the details of steel construction, a large part of the purpose of this book will have been achieved, and the student will have made a long and important step toward becoming a structural designer.

Proficiency in the field of structures undoubtedly leads to many employment opportunities with appreciable economic rewards. Perhaps more important is the definite sense of accomplishment felt by the engineer in seeing the structures he has designed become reality and of service to the community.

Jack C. McCormac

Clemson, South Carolina
May, 1965

ACKNOWLEDGMENTS

The author gratefully acknowledges the aid he has received from several sources. He is indebted to R. C. Brinker, Dr. S. Maggard, Dr. C. Salmon, and I. A. Trively who have directly contributed to the preparation of the manuscript by their suggestions and criticisms, and to his own professors B. B. Williams and Dr. J. B. Wilbur who patiently instructed him in their design classes. The books used in their classes and in the classes taught by the author have naturally influenced the text material to some extent. These books include *Structural Design in Steel* by Thomas C. Shedd, *Design of Steel Structures* by E. H. Gaylord, Jr., and C. N. Gaylord, and *Structural Steel Design* by L. S. Beedle et al. Several organizations have kindly submitted photographs, acknowledgment for which is given with the pictures. Finally, thanks is due to Miss Lynn McMaster who typed the manuscript.

Jack C. McCormac

CONTENTS

chapter 10

BOLTED CONNECTIONS 230

Types of Bolts. Discussion of High-Strength Bolts. Advantages of High-Strength Bolts. Specifications for High-Strength Bolts. Installation of High-Strength Bolts. Shearing Resistance of Bolted Joints. Tension Loads on Bolted Joints. Prying Action. Bolts Subjected to Combined Shear and Tension. Problems.

chapter 11

WELDED CONNECTIONS 252

General. Advantages of Welding. Types of Welding. Welding Inspection. Classification of Welds. Welding Symbols. Butt Welds. Fillet Welds. Strength of Fillet Welds. AISC Requirements. Design of Simple Fillet Welds. Design of Fillet Welds for Truss Members. Shear and Torsion. Shear and Bending. Problems.

chapter 12

BUILDING CONNECTIONS 288

Selection of Type of Fastener. Types of Beam Connections. Standard Riveted or Bolted Beam Connections. Semirigid and Rigid Riveted or Bolted Connections. Types of Welded Beam Connections. Welded Web Angles. Design of Welded Seated Beam Connections. Welded Stiffened Beam Seat Connections. Welded Moment; Resistant Connections. Problems.

chapter 13

DESIGN OF STEEL BUILDINGS 321

Introduction. Types of Steel Frames Used for Buildings, Common Types of Floor Construction. Concrete Slabs on Open-Web Steel Joists. One-Way and Two-Way Reinforced Concrete Slabs. Composite Floors. Concrete-Pan Floors. Structural Clay Tile, Gypsum Tile, and Concrete-Block Floors. Steel-Decking Floors. Flat Slabs. Precast Concrete Floors. Types of Roof Construction. Exterior Walls and Interior Partitions. Design Live Loads (Vertical). Wind and Earthquake Loadings.

chapter 14

INTRODUCTION TO STEEL BRIDGES 344

General. Through, Deck and Half-Through Bridges. Erection Methods for Bridges. The Beam Bridge. The Plate Girder Bridge. Truss Bridges for Medium Spans. Subdivided Truss Bridges. Continuous Bridge Trusses. Cantilever Bridges. Steel Arches. Suspension Bridges. Miscellaneous Bridge Types. Summary of Bridge Types. Comparison of High Level Bridges and Low Level Movable Bridges. Movable Bridges. Selection of Bridge Type. Spacing of Piers and Abutments. Live Loads for Highway Bridges. Live Loads for Railway Bridges.

Composite Construction. Advantages of Composite Construction. Discussion of Shoring. Effective Flange Widths. Stress Calculations for Composite Sections. Shear Transfer. Proportioning Composite Sections. Design of Encased Sections. Design of Composite Sections Using AASHO Specifications. Miscellaneous. Problems.

Cover-Plated Beams. Introduction to Plate Girders. Comments on Specifications. Proportions of Plate Girders—AASHO and AREA. Cutting Off Cover Plates—AASHO, AREA, and AISC. Cover-Plate and Flange Connectors—AASHO, AREA, and AISC. Stiffeners—AASHO. Longitudinal Stiffeners—AASHO. Web Splices—AASHO, AREA, and AISC. Proportions of Webs—AISC. Proportions of Flange—AISC. Design of Stiffeners—AISC. Example Plate Girder Design—AISC. Problems.

Introduction. Types of Roof Trusses. Selection of Type of Roof Truss. Spacing and Support of Roof Trusses. Estimated Weight of Roof Trusses. Discussion of Roof Truss Analysis. Example Analysis of a Roof Truss. Design of a Roof Truss. Trusses for Industrial Buildings. Roof Truss Bracing. Problems.

Introduction. Bridge Floor System. Live-Load Truss Stresses. Truss Dead Loads. Selection of Truss Members. Lateral Bracing. Bridge-Truss Deflections. End Bearings for Bridges. Problems.

Mirror Lake Bridge, Wisconsin. (*American Bridge Division, U.S. Steel Corporation.*)

chapter 1

INTRODUCTION TO
STRUCTURAL STEEL DESIGN

1-1. ADVANTAGES OF STEEL AS A STRUCTURAL MATERIAL

A person traveling in the United States might quite understandably decide that steel was the perfect structural material. He would see an endless number of steel bridges, buildings, towers, and other structures—comprising, in fact, a list too lengthy to enumerate. After seeing these numerous steel structures he might be quite surprised to learn that steel was not made in the United States until 1856 and the first wide-flange beams were not rolled until 1908.

His assumption of the perfection of this metal, perhaps the most versatile of structural materials, would appear to be even more reasonable when he considered its great strength, light weight, ease of fabrication, and many other desirable properties. These and other advantages of structural steel are discussed in detail in the following paragraphs.

High Strength. The high strength of steel per unit of weight means dead loads will be small. This fact is of great importance for long-span bridges, tall buildings, and for structures having poor foundation conditions.

Uniformity. The properties of steel do not change appreciably with time as do those of a reinforced-concrete structure.

Elasticity. Steel behaves closer to design assumptions than most materials because it follows Hooke's law up to fairly high stresses. The moments of inertia of a steel structure can be definitely calculated while the values obtained for a reinforced concrete structure are rather indefinite.

Permanence. Steel frames that are properly maintained will last indefinitely. Research on some of the newer steels indicates that under certain conditions no painting maintenance whatsoever will be required.

Ductility. The property of a material by which it can withstand extensive deformation without failure under high tensile stresses is said to be its *ductility*. When a mild steel member is being tested in tension,

1

a considerable reduction in cross section and a large amount of elongation will occur at the point of failure before the actual fracture occurs. A material that does not have this property is probably hard and brittle and might break if subjected to a sudden shock.

In structural members under normal loads, high stress concentrations develop at various points. The ductile nature of the usual structural steels enables them to yield locally at those points, thus preventing premature failures. A further advantage of ductile structures is that when overloaded their large deflections give visible evidence of impending failure (sometimes jokingly referred to as "running time").

Additions to Existing Structures. Steel structures are quite well suited to having additions made to them. New bays or even entire new wings can be added to existing steel frame buildings, and steel bridges may often be widened.

Miscellaneous. Several other important advantages of structural steel are: (a) adaptation to prefabrication, (b) speed of erection, (c) weldability, (d) toughness and fatigue strength, (e) possible reuse after a structure is disassembled, and (f) scrap value even though not reusable in its existing form.

1-2. DISADVANTAGES OF STEEL AS A STRUCTURAL MATERIAL

In general steel has the following disadvantages:

Maintenance Costs. Most steels tend to corrode when freely exposed to air and must be periodically painted.

Fireproofing Costs. The strength of structural steel is tremendously reduced at temperatures which are commonly reached in fires. The steel frame of a building must be fireproofed to obtain an appreciable fire rating. It is to be remembered, however, that steel itself is not combustible.

Susceptibility to Buckling. The longer and slenderer compression members, the greater the danger of buckling. As previously indicated, steel has a high strength per unit weight and when used for steel columns is sometimes not economical because considerable material has to be used merely to stiffen the columns against buckling.

1-3. THE STRUCTURAL DESIGNER

The structural designer can take great pride in his part in the development of our country. Cities, farmlands, and industrial areas of the United States are filled with the amazing structures designed by members of his profession. But even this remarkable array of structures will be merely child's play compared to the structural endeavors of the next few generations. These structures of the future should provide endless opportunities in the structural field for young engineers.

The structural designer arranges and proportions structures and their parts so that they will satisfactorily support the loads to which they may feasibly be subjected. It might be said that he is involved with the following: the general layout of structures; studies of the possible structural forms that can be used; consideration of loading conditions; analysis of stresses, deflections, etc.; design of parts; and the preparation of design drawings. More precisely, the word *design* pertains to the proportioning of the various parts of a structure after the stresses have been calculated, and it is this process which will be emphasized throughout the text using structural steel as the material.

1-4. OBJECTIVES OF THE STRUCTURAL DESIGNER

The structural designer must learn to arrange and proportion the parts of his structures so that they have sufficient strength, reasonable economy, and the capability of being practically erected. These items are discussed briefly below:

Safety. Not only must the frame of a structure safely support the loads to which it is subjected, but it must support them in such a manner that deflections and vibrations are not so great as to frighten the occupants or cause unsightly cracks.

Cost. The designer needs to keep in mind the items causing lower cost without sacrifice of strength. These items which are discussed in more detail throughout the text include the use of standard-size members, simple connections and details, and the use of members and materials which will not require an unreasonable amount of maintenance through the years.

Practicality. Another objective is the design of structures which can be fabricated and erected without great problems arising. The designer needs to understand fabrication methods and should try to fit his work to the fabrication facilities available.

The designer should learn everything he can about the detailing, the fabrication, and the field erection of steel. The more he knows about the problems, the tolerances, and the clearances in shop and field the more probable it is that he will produce reasonable, practical, and economical designs. This knowledge should include information concerning the transportation of the materials to the job site (such as the largest pieces that can be practically transported by rail or truck), labor conditions, and the equipment available for erection. Perhaps the designer should ask himself the question, "Could I get this thing together if I were sent out to do it?"

Finally he needs to proportion the parts of the structure so that they will not unduly interfere with the mechanical features of the structure (pipes, ducts, etc.) or the architectural effects.

1-5. FACTOR OF SAFETY

The factor of safety of a structural member is defined as the ratio of strength of the member to its maximum anticipated stress. The strength of a member used in determining the factor of safety may be thought of as being the ultimate strength of the member, but often some lesser value is used. For instance, failure may be assumed to occur when the members become excessively deformed. If this is the case the safety factor might be determined by dividing the yield-point stress by the maximum anticipated stress. For ductile materials the safety factor is usually based on yield-point stresses while for brittle materials it is probably based on ultimate strengths.

The student may feel that it is quite foolish to build a structure with a strength of several times that which is theoretically required. As the years go by, however, he will learn that safety factors are subject to so many uncertainties that he may spend sleepless nights wondering if those he has used are sufficient (and he may join other designers in calling them "factors of ignorance" rather than factors of safety). Some of the uncertainties affecting safety factors are:

1. Material strengths may initially vary appreciably from their assumed values and they will vary more with time due to creep, corrosion, and fatigue.

2. The methods of analysis are often subject to appreciable errors.

3. The so-called beggaries of nature or acts of God (hurricanes, earthquakes, etc.) cause conditions difficult to predict.

4. The stresses produced during fabrication and erection are often severe. Workmen in shop and field seem to treat steel shapes with reckless abandon. They drop them. They ram them. They force the members into position to line up the bolt or rivet holes. In fact, the stresses during fabrication and erection may exceed those which occur after the structure is completed. The floors for the rooms of apartment houses and office buildings are probably designed for live loads varying from 40 to 80 psf (pounds per square foot). During the erection of such buildings the contractor may have 10 ft of bricks or concrete blocks or other construction materials or equipment piled up on some of the floors, causing loads of several hundred pounds per square foot. This discussion is not intended to criticize the practice (not that it is a good one), but rather to make the student aware of the things that happen during construction. (It is probable that the majority of steel structures are overloaded somewhere during construction but hardly any of them fail.)

5. There are technological changes which affect the magnitude of live loads. The constantly increasing traffic loads applied to bridges through the years is an illustration.

6. Although the dead loads of a structure can usually be estimated quite closely, the estimate of the live loads is more inaccurate. This is particularly true in estimating the worst possible combination of live loads occurring at any one time. For instance, in estimating the load supported by a column in the bottom level of a 30-story building— would 100 percent live load be assumed to exist on every one of the thirty floors at the same time or is some lesser percentage more realistic?

7. Other uncertainties are the presence of residual stresses and stress concentrations, variations in dimensions of member cross sections, etc.

The magnitude of the safety factors used will be affected by the preceding uncertainties and also by the answers to the following questions:

1. Is the structure to be permanent or temporary?

2. Is it a public or private structure?

3. What is the penalty for failure? Will there be loss of life or extensive property damage or great inconvenience while the structure is out of use?

4. Is a particular member a main one or a secondary one? (It may be reasonable to use high safety factors for the design of main members and low values for secondary members.)

1-6. FAILURES OF ENGINEERING STRUCTURES

Many people who are superstitious do not discuss flat tires or make their wills because they are afraid that by doing so they are tempting fate. These same people would probably not care to discuss the subject of engineering failures. Despite the prevalence of this superstition the author feels that an awareness of the items which have most frequently caused failures in the past is invaluable to experienced and inexperienced designers alike. Perhaps a study of past failures is more important than a study of past successes. Benjamin Franklin supposedly made the observation that "a wise man learns more from failures than from success."[1]

The designer of little experience particularly needs to know where he should give the most attention and where he may need outside advice. The vast majority of designers, experienced and inexperienced, select members of sufficient size and strength. The collapse of structures is usually due to insufficient attention to the details of connections, deflections, erection problems, and foundation settlements. Rarely if ever do

[1] Maurice J. Rhude, "Research Needed In Wood Structures," *Proc. ASCE*, vol. 93 no. ST2 (April, 1967), p. 79.

steel structures fail due to faults in the material; but rather to its improper use.

A frequent fault displayed by designers is that after carefully designing the members of a structure they carelessly select connections which may or may not be of sufficient size. They may even turn the job of selecting the connections over to draftsmen who may not have sufficient backgrounds to understand the difficulties that can arise in connection design. Perhaps the most common mistake made in connection design is to neglect some of the forces acting on the connection, such as twisting moments. In a truss for which the members have been designed for axial forces only, the connections may be eccentrically loaded, resulting in moments which cause increasing stresses. These secondary stresses are occasionally so large that they need to be considered in design.

Another source of failure occurs where beams supported on walls have insufficient bearing or anchorage. Imagine a beam of this type supporting a flat roof on a rainy night when the roof drains are not functioning properly. As the water begins to form puddles on the roof it tends to cause the beam to sag in the middle, causing a pocket to catch more rain which will cause more beam sag, etc. As the beam deflects it pushes out against the walls, causing possible collapse of walls or slippage of beam ends off the wall. Picture a 60-ft steel beam supported on a wall with only an inch or two of bearing when the temperature drops 50 or 60 degrees overnight. A collapse due to a combination of beam contraction, outward deflection of walls, and vertical deflection due to precipitation loads is not difficult to visualize; furthermore, actual cases in engineering literature are not difficult to find.

Foundation settlements cause a large number of structural failures, probably more than any other factor. Most foundation settlements do not result in collapse but they very probably cause unsightly cracks and depreciation of the structure. If all parts of the foundation of a structure settle equally, the stresses in the structure theoretically will not change. The designer, usually not able to prevent settlement, has the goal of designing foundations in such a manner that equal settlements occur. Equal settlements may be an impossible goal and consideration should be given to the stresses that would be produced if settlement variations occurred. The student's background in structural analysis will tell him that uneven settlements in indeterminate structures may cause extreme stress variations. Where foundation conditions are poor it is desirable, if feasible, to use determinate structures whose stresses are not appreciably changed by support settlements. (The student will actually learn in subsequent discussions that the ultimate strength of steel structures is affected only slightly by uneven support settlements.)

Some other sources of structural failures occur because inadequate attention is given to deflections, fatigue of members, bracing against swaying, vibrations, and the possibility of buckling of compression members or the compression flanges of beams. The usual structure when completed is sufficiently braced with floors, walls, connections, and special bracing, but there are times during construction when many of these items are not present. As previously indicated, the worst conditions may well occur during erection and special temporary bracing may be required.

1-7. SPECIFICATIONS

For most structures the designer is controlled by specifications. Even if not so controlled he will probably refer to them as a guide. No matter how many structures he has designed it is impossible for him to have encountered every situation, and by referring to specifications he is making use of the best available material on the subject. Engineering specifications are developed by various engineering organizations and present the best opinion of these organizations as to what represents good engineering practice. Examples of specifications that are referred to in detail in later chapters are:

American Institute of Steel Construction (AISC)
American Welding Society (AWS)
American Association of State Highway Officials (AASHO)
American Railway Engineering Association (AREA)
American Society for Testing and Materials (ASTM)

Municipal and state governments concerned with the safety of the public have established building codes by which they control the construction of various structures under their jurisdiction. These codes, which are actually ordinances, specify design loads, allowable stresses, construction types, material quality, and other factors. They vary considerably from city to city, a fact which causes some confusion among architects and engineers.

Several organizations publish recommended practices for regional or national use. Their specifications are not legally enforceable unless they are embodied in the local building code or made a part of a particular contract. Among these organizations are the AISC, AASHO, and others listed earlier in this section. Nearly all municipal and state building codes have adopted the AISC Specification and nearly all state highway departments have adopted the AASHO Specifications. These codes generally include some additional provisions pertaining to their local needs.

Many people feel that specifications prevent the engineer from thinking for himself—and there may be some basis for the criticism. They say that the ancient engineers who built the great pyramids, the Parthenon, and the great Roman bridges were controlled by few specifications, which is certainly true. On the other hand, it should be said that only a few score of these great projects were built over many centuries and they were apparently built without regard to cost of material, labor, or human life. They were probably built by intuition and by certain rules of thumb developed by observing the minimum size or strength of members which would just fail under given conditions. Their probably numerous failures are not recorded in history; only their successes endured.

Today, however, there are hundreds of projects being constructed at any one time in the United States which rival in importance and magnitude the famous structures of the past. It appears that if all engineers in our country were allowed to design projects such as these without restrictions there would be many disastrous failures. *The important thing to remember about specifications, therefore, is that they are not written for the purpose of restricting engineers but for the purpose of protecting the public.*

1-8. VARIATIONS IN DESIGNS

Designs of the same structures using the same specifications can be surprisingly different. The differences are primarily caused by the uncertainties mentioned in the preceding paragraphs which call for the application of the engineer's judgment. Two engineers designing a bridge might make entirely different estimates of future traffic, wind loads, snow loads, ice loads, etc. In selecting steel beams for a certain bending moment it will be discovered that there may possibly be several beams of entirely different dimensions and shapes which will support approximately the same moments.

Furthermore, different engineers will probably give different weight to what happens if the structure fails. For instance, in designing a line of power poles would the engineer design the poles to withstand twice the greatest wind force ever recorded anywhere on earth, or will he use some lesser loading condition, assuming that under very unusual storm conditions some poles may come down?

1-9. SLIDE-RULE COMPUTATIONS

A most important point which many students have difficulty in understanding is that structural design is not an exact science for which answers can confidently be calculated to six places. The reasons for this fact have already been discussed; the methods of analysis are based on

Hackensack River Bridge, New Jersey Turnpike (American Bridge Division, U.S. Steel Corporation).

partly true assumptions, the strengths of materials used vary appreciably, and maximum loadings can only be approximated. With respect to this last sentence, how many of the users of this book could estimate within 10 percent the maximum load in pounds per square foot that will ever occur on the building floor which they are now occupying? Calculations to more significant figures than obtainable with the slide rule are obviously of little value and may actually be harmful in that they mislead the student by giving him a fictitious sense of precision.

1-10. CHARTS AND TABLES

The use of various standards, tables, and charts provide a great deal of assistance in design. These devices give information about forms and details which are commonly used by the engineering profession and will thus help to provide economy both in the design office and in field construction.

It is probably undesirable, however, for the beginning engineer to make extensive use of most tables and charts until he has had some experience. One of the famous rules of engineering (and a very good one) is that the engineer should not use a table or chart which he does not understand sufficiently to reconstruct. He needs a sound knowledge of the basic principles of structural design in order to see the limitations of these devices. (The author would like to hedge a little on this subject by saying that he does not mean to imply that the young engineer going to work in a design office should refuse to use their design aids with which he is unfamiliar until he has worked them out on company time. They are in business to make money and need to have their personnel work as efficiently as possible.)

chapter 2

PROPERTIES OF
STRUCTURAL STEEL

2-1. STRESS-STRAIN RELATIONSHIPS IN STRUCTURAL STEEL

To understand the behavior of steel structures it is absolutely essential for the designer to be familiar with the properties of steel. Stress-strain diagrams present a valuable part of the information necessary to understand how steel will behave in a given situation. Satisfactory steel design methods cannot be developed unless complete information is available concerning the stress-strain relationships of the material being used.

If a piece of mild structural steel is subjected to a tensile force it will begin to elongate. If the tensile force is increased at a constant rate the amount of elongation will increase constantly within certain limits. In other words, elongation will double when the stress goes from 6,000 psi to 12,000 psi (pounds per square inch). When the tensile stress reaches a value roughly equal to one-half of the ultimate strength of the steel the elongation will begin to increase at a greater rate without a corresponding increase in the stress.

The largest stress for which Hooke's law applies or the highest point on the straight line portion of the stress-strain diagram is the *proportional limit*. The largest stress which a material can withstand without being permanently deformed is called the *elastic limit*. This value is seldom actually measured and for most engineering materials including structural steel is synonomous with the proportional limit. For this reason the term *proportional elastic limit* is sometimes used.

The stress at which there is a decided increase in the elongation or strain without a corresponding increase in stress is said to be the *yield point*. It is the first point on the stress-strain diagram where a tangent to the curve is horizontal. The yield point is probably the most important property of steel to the designer as the elastic design procedures are based on this value (with the exception of compression members where buckling may be a factor). The allowable stresses used in these methods are usually taken as some percentage of the yield point. Beyond

11

the yield point there is a range in which a considerable increase in strain occurs without increase in stress. The strain which occurs before the yield point is referred to as the *elastic strain*; the strain which occurs after the yield point, with no increase in stress, is referred to as the *plastic strain*. These latter strains usually vary from ten to fifteen times the elastic strains.

Yielding of steel without stress increase may be thought to be a severe disadvantage when in actuality it is a very useful characteristic. It has often performed the wonderful service of preventing failure due to omissions or mistakes on the designer's part. Should the stress at one point in a ductile steel structure reach the yield point, that part of the structure will yield locally without stress increase, thus preventing premature failure. This ductility allows the stresses in a steel structure to be readjusted. Another way of describing this phenomenon is to say that very

Newport Bridge between Jamestown and Newport, Rhode Island
(Bethlehem Steel Company).

high stresses caused by fabrication, erection, or loading will tend to equalize themselves. It might also be said that a steel structure has a reserve of plastic strain that enables it to resist overloads and sudden shocks. If it did not have this ability, it might suddenly fracture, like glass or other vitreous substances.

Following the plastic strain there is a range where additional stress is necessary to produce additional strain and this is called *strain-hardening*. This portion of the diagram is not too important to today's designer. A familiar stress-strain diagram for mild structural steel is shown in Fig. 2-1. Only the initial part of the curve is shown here because of the great deformation which occurs before failure. At failure in the mild steels the total strains are from 150 to 200 times the elastic strains. The curve will actually continue up to its maximum stress value and then

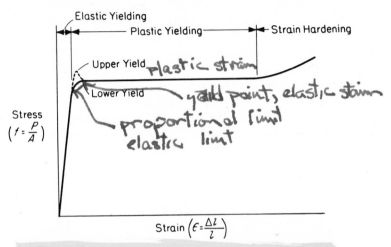

Fig. 2-1. Typical stress-strain diagram for a mild structural steel.

"tail off" before failure. A sharp reduction in the cross section of the member takes place (called "necking") followed by failure.

The stress-strain curve of Fig. 2-1 is typical of the usual ductile structural steel and is assumed to be the same for members in tension or compression. (The compression members must be short because long compression members subjected to compression loads tend to bend laterally and their properties are greatly affected by the bending moments so produced.) The shape of the diagram varies with the speed of loading, the type of steel, and the temperature. One such variation is shown in the figure by the dotted line which is marked *upper yield*. This shape stress-strain curve is the result when a mild steel has the load applied rapidly while the *lower yield* is the case for slow loading.

A very important property of a structure which has not been stressed beyond its yield point is that it will return to its original length when the loads are removed. Should it be stressed beyond this point it will return only part of the way to its original position. This knowledge leads to the possibility of testing an existing structure by loading and unloading and measuring deflections. If after the loads are removed the structure will not resume its original dimensions, it has been stressed beyond its yield point.

Steel is a compound consisting almost entirely of iron (usually over 98 percent). It also contains small quantities of carbon, silicon, manganese, sulphur, phosphorus, and other elements. Carbon is the material which has the greatest effect on the properties of steel. The hardness and strength increase as the carbon percentage is increased but unfortunately the resulting steel is more brittle and its weldability is adversely affected. A smaller amount of carbon will make the steel softer and more ductile but also weaker. The addition of such elements as chromium, silicon, and nickel produces steels with considerably higher strengths. These steels, however, are appreciably more expensive and are often not so easy to fabricate.

A typical stress-strain diagram for a brittle steel is shown in Fig. 2-2. Such a material shows little or no permanent deformation at fracture. Unfortunately, low ductility or brittleness is a property usually

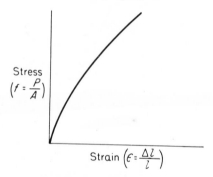

Stress $\left(f = \dfrac{P}{A}\right)$

Strain $\left(\epsilon = \dfrac{\Delta l}{l}\right)$

Fig. 2-2.   Typical stress-strain diagram for a brittle steel.

associated with high strengths in steels (although not entirely confined to high-strength steels). As it is desirable to have both high strength and ductility, the designer may have to decide between the two extremes or compromise between them. A brittle steel may fail suddenly without warning when overstressed, and during erection could possibly fail due to the shock of erection procedures.

2-2.   ELASTIC AND PLASTIC DESIGN METHODS DEFINED

The majority of steel structures designed in the past and of those being designed today are handled by the *elastic-design* methods. The designer estimates the "working loads," or loads which the structure may feasibly have to support, and proportions the members on the basis of certain allowable stresses. These allowable stresses are usually some fraction of the specified minimum yield point of the steel. Although the term "elastic design" is very commonly used to describe this method the terms *allowable-stress design* or *working-stress design* are definitely more appropriate. Many of the provisions of the specifications for this method are actually based on plastic or ultimate-strength behavior and not on elastic behavior.

The ductility of steel has been shown to give it a reserve strength and the realization of this fact is the theory behind *plastic design*. In this method the working loads are estimated and multiplied by certain factors and the members designed on the basis of collapse strengths. Other names for this method are *limit design* and *collapse design*. Although only a few thousand structures have been designed around the world by the plastic-design methods, the profession is definitely moving in that direction. This trend is particularly reflected in the latest specifications of the AISC.

The design profession has long been aware that the major portion of the stress-strain curve lies beyond the steel's elastic limit. Furthermore, tests through the years have made it clear that steels can resist stresses appreciably larger than their yield points, and that in cases of overload, indeterminate structures have the happy facility of spreading the load out due to the steel's ductility. On the basis of this information many plastic-design proposals have been made in recent decades. It is undoubtedly true that for certain types of structures, plastic design results in a more economical use of steel than does elastic design. Chapters 21 and 22 are devoted entirely to this subject.

2-3. STEEL SECTIONS

Structural steel can be economically rolled into a wide variety of shapes and sizes without appreciably changing its physical properties. Usually the most desirable members are those which have large section moduli in proportion to their areas. The I, T, and [shapes, so commonly used, fall into this class.

Steel sections are usually designated by the shapes of their cross sections. As examples, there are angles, tees, zees, and plates. It is necessary, however, to make a definite distinction between American standard beams (called S beams) and wide-flange beams (called W beams) as they are both I-shaped. The inner surface of the flange of a W section is either parallel to the outer surface or nearly so with a maximum slope of 1 to 20 on the inner surface, depending on the manufacturer.

Steel erection for the Chase Manhattan Bank
Building, New York City. (*Bethlehem Steel
Company.*)

The S beams, which were the first beam sections rolled in America, have a slope on their inside flange surfaces of 1 to 6. It might be noted that the constant, or nearly constant, thickness of W flanges as compared to the tapered S beam flanges may facilitate connections. Wide-flange beams comprise nearly 50 percent of the tonnage of structural steel shapes rolled today. The W and S sections are shown in Fig. 2-3 together with several other familiar steel sections. The uses of these various shapes will be discussed in detail in the chapters to follow.

Constant reference is made throughout this book to the *Manual of Steel Construction* published by the AISC. This manual, which provides detailed information for structural steel shapes, is referred to hereafter as the AISC Manual or the Steel Handbook. This manual, which provides detailed information for structural steel shapes, has been said to be the most used handbook ever produced by a single industry and over a million copies are now in circulation.[1] Reference is made herein to the

---

[1] Mace H. Bell, "Progress on the New AISC Manual—6th Edition," 1963 AISC Proceedings (New York: AISC, 1963) p. 7.

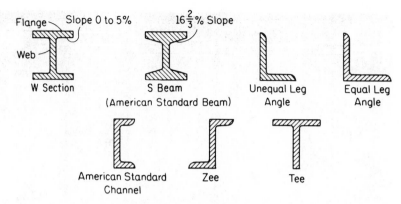

FIG. 2-3. Rolled-steel shapes.

7th edition of the handbook which is based on the February 1969 AISC Specification. Structural shapes are abbreviated by a certain system described in the handbook for use in drawings, specifications and designs. This system is standardized so that all steel mills can use the same identification for purposes of ordering, billing, etc. In addition so much work is handled today with computers and other automated equipment that it is necessary to have a letter and number system which can be printed out with a standard keyboard (as opposed to the old system where certain symbols were used for angles, channels, etc.). Examples of this abbreviation system are as follows:

1. A W 27 × 114 is a W section approximately 27 in. deep weighing 114 lb/ft.

2. An S 12 × 35 is an S section 12 in. deep weighing 35 lb/ft.

3. An HP 12 × 74 is a bearing pile section which is approximately 12 in. deep weighing 74 lb/ft. Bearing piles are made with the regular W rolls but with thicker webs to provide better resistance to the impact of pile driving.

4. An M 8 × 37.7 is a miscellaneous section approximately 8 in. deep weighing 37.7 lb/ft. It is one of a group of doubly-symmetrical H-shaped members which cannot by dimensions be classified as a W, S or HP section (see Fig. 2-3).

5. A C 10 × 30 is a channel 10 in. deep weighing 30 lb/ft.

6. An MC 18 × 58 is a miscellaneous channel which cannot be classified as a C shape by dimensions (see Fig. 2-3).

7. An L 6 × 6 × ½ is an equal leg angle, each leg being 6 in. long and ½ thick.

8. A WT 18 × 140 is a tee obtained by splitting a W 36 × 280. This type of section is known as a structural tee.

The student should refer to the AISC Manual for information con-

Structural shapes rolled at Bethlehem Steel Company's Bethlehem, Pa., plant. (*Bethlehem Steel Company.*)

cerning other rolled shapes, such as the distinction between bars and plates, designation of open web joists, etc. Additional sections will be mentioned herein as it becomes necessary.

Through the years there have been changes in the sizes of beam and column sections. For instance, there may be insufficient demand to continue rolling a certain shape; an existing shape may be dropped because a similar sized but more efficient shape has been developed; etc. Occasionally the engineer may need to know the properties of one of the discontinued shapes which are no longer listed in his edition of the Steel Handbook or in other tables normally available to him. As an example, it may be desired to add another floor to an existing building which was constructed with shapes no longer rolled. In 1953 the AISC published a book entitled *Iron and Steel Beams 1873 to 1952* which gives a complete listing of iron and steel beams and their properties rolled in the United States during that period.

2-4. MODERN STRUCTURAL STEELS

Most of the steel used in engineering structures in the United States is a structural carbon steel designated as A36 by the ASTM, but many other steels are available and demand for them is rising rapidly.

In recent decades the engineering and architecture professions have been continually requesting stronger steels, steels with more corrosion

Indiana Harbor Works, East Chicago, Ind. (*Inland Steel Company.*)

resistance, steels with better welding properties, and various other requirements. Research by the steel industry during this period has supplied several groups of new steels which satisfy many of the demands
and today there are quite a few structural steels designated by the ASTM
and included in the AISC Specification.

These steels can be grouped into three major classifications: the
carbon steels, the high-strength low-alloy steels and the heat-treated
constructional alloy steels. There are indeed other groups of high-strength
steels such as the heat-treated high-strength carbon steels (having yield
stresses in the 70,000 to 80,000 psi range) and the ultra high-strength
steels (having yield stresses in the 160,000 to 300,000 psi range) but these
are not included in this section because they are not today generally
covered by the ASTM and thus are not included in the AISC Specification.

Carbon Steels. These steels have as their principal strengthening
agents carefully controlled quantities of carbon and manganese. The
common everyday American steel, A36, which has a yield stress of 36,000
psi, is suitable for riveted, bolted or welded bridges and buildings. As
this is the most important steel today and may very well be for a good
many years to come it is used for the majority of the design problems in
this text. Other carbon steels include A500, and A501 (both applying
to tubing), and A529 (pertaining to some thinner plates and shapes).

Table 2-1 presents a brief summary of the various carbon and higher strength steels considered in the AISC Specification. The A242 and A588 steels are particularly corrosion resistant and are so entitled in Table 2-1.

High-Strength Low-Alloy Steels. There are a large number of high-strength low-alloy steels and they are included under several ASTM numbers. In addition to carbon and manganese these steels obtain their higher strengths and other properties by the addition of one or more alloying agents such as columbium, vanadium, chromium, silicon, copper, nickel, and others. Included are steels with yield stresses as low as 42,000 psi and as high as 65,000 psi. These steels (including A529, A242, A440, A441, A572, and A588) generally have much greater atmospheric corrosion resistance than the carbon steels.

Quenched and Tempered Steels. These steels have alloying agents in excess of those used in the carbon steels and they are heat-treated (by quenching and tempering) to obtain strong and tough steels. They are listed under the ASTM designation A514 and have yield stresses of 90,000 or 100,000 psi depending on thickness.

It is said that there are today more than 200 steels on the market which provide yield stresses in excess of 36,000 psi. The steel industry is now experimenting with steels with yield stresses varying from 200,000 to 300,000 psi and this may only be the beginning. Many people in the steel industry feel that steels with 500,000 psi yield strengths will be made available before the end of the 1970's. The theoretical binding force between iron atoms has been estimated to be in excess of 4,000,000 psi.[2]

Although the prices of steels increase with increasing yield points the percentage of price increase does not keep up with the percentage of yield-point increase. The result is that the use of the stronger steels will quite frequently be economical for tension members, beams and columns. Perhaps the greatest economy can be realized with tension members (particularly those without rivet or bolt holes). They may provide a great deal of saving for beams if deflections are not important or if deflections can be controlled (as by cambering, use of composite construction, etc.). In addition considerable economy can frequently be achieved with high-strength steels for short and medium length stocky columns. Another application which can provide considerable saving is in hybrid construction. In this type of construction two or more steels of different strengths are used, the weaker steels being used where stresses are smaller and the stronger steels where stresses are higher.

---

[2] L. S. Beedle, et al, *Structural Steel Design* (New York: The Ronald Press Company, 1964), p. 44.

Among the other factors which might lead to the use of high-strength steels are the following:

1. Superior corrosion resistance.
2. Possible savings in shipping, erection, and foundation costs caused by weight saving.
3. Use of shallower beams permitting smaller floor depths.
4. Possible savings in fireproofing because smaller members can be used.

The first thought of most engineers in choosing a type of steel is the direct cost of the members. Such a comparison can be made quite easily, but the economy of which grade to use cannot be obtained unless consideration is given to weights, sizes, deflections, maintenance, and fabrication. To make an accurate general comparison of the steels is probably impossible—rather it is necessary to have a specific job to consider.

2-5. FURNISHING OF STRUCTURAL STEEL

The furnishing of structural steel consists of the rolling of the steel shapes, the fabrication of the shapes for the particular job (including cutting to the proper dimensions and punching of holes necessary for field connections) and their erection. Occasionally a company will perform all three of these functions, but the average outfit performs only one or two of them. For instance, many companies fabricate structural steel and erect it while others may only be steel fabricators or steel erectors. There are approximately 400 companies in the United States which make up the fabricating industry for structural steel. Most of them do fabrication and erection.

Structural steel is said to be handled by mill or stock orders. The mill orders are the most economical as the fabricator orders the shapes to certain lengths directly from the rolling mill. The process of ordering directly, although requiring more time, saves handling costs and reduces the costs of storage because the material is not kept in stock for a time with the resulting interest and storage charges. Some fabricators carry certain sizes in stock. These sizes can be obtained immediately but will cost more because of the extra storage, interest, and handling costs previously mentioned.

The design of structural steel is usually made by an engineer in collaboration with an architectural firm. The designer makes design drawings which show member sizes, controlling dimensions, and any unusual connections. The company which is to fabricate the steel makes the detailed drawings which give all the information necessary to fabricate the members correctly. These details include all of the dimensions

TABLE 2-1

ASTM Designation	Type of Steel	Shapes Available	Recommended Uses	Yield Stress psi	Atmospheric Corrosion Resistance
A36	Carbon	Shapes and bars	Riveted, bolted or welded bridges and buildings, and other structural uses	36,000 up thru 8 in. (32,000 above 8 in.)	
A500	"	Cold-formed welded and seamless tubing	"	33,000 for Grade A / 42,000 for Grade B	
A501	"	Hot-formed welded and seamless tubing	Riveted, bolted and welded buildings, and related construction	36,000	
A529	"	PLs and bars up thru ½ in. and some light shapes		42,000	
A440	High-Strength	" " "	Riveted and bolted bridges and buildings, and other structural uses; not recommended for welding	50,000 up thru ¾ in. / 46,000 above ¾ in. thru 1½ in. / 42,00 above 1½ in. thru 4 in.	Approximately equal to two times that of structural carbon steel.
A441	High-Strength Low-Alloy	" " "	May be used for welded, riveted, and bolted structures but primarily intended for welded bridges and buildings	50,000 up thru ¾ in. / 46,000 above ¾ in. thru 1½ in. / 42,00 above 1½ in. thru 4 in. / 40,000 above 4 in. thru 8 in.	"

ASTM Designation	Type	Shapes/Plates	Use	Min. Yield Stress (psi)		Corrosion Resistance
A572	"	" " "	Grades 42, 45, and 50 especially intended for riveted, bolted or welded bridges, buildings, and other structures. Grades 55, 60, and 65 especially intended for riveted or bolted bridges, and for other structures which are riveted, bolted or welded	42,000 45,000 50,000 55,000 60,000 65,000	} varying thickness, chemical compositions, etc. (see ASTM)	
A242	Corrosion-Resistant High-Strength Low-Alloy	Shapes and bars	Welded, riveted or bolted construction; welding technique very important	50,000 up thru ¾ in. 46,000 above ¾ in. thru 1½ in. 42,000 above 1½ in. thru 4 in.		Approximately equal to four times that of structural carbon steel with copper
A588	"	" " "	May be used for welded, riveted or bolted construction but primarily intended for welded bridges and buildings; welding technique very important	50,000 up thru 4 in. 46,000 above 4 in. thru 5 in. 42,000 above 5 in. thru 8 in.		Approximately equal to four times that of structural carbon steel with copper
A514	Quenched and Tempered Alloy	PLs up thru 4 in.. and a limited number of shapes	Primarily intended for use in welded bridges and other structures; welding technique very important	100,000 up thru 2½ in. 90,000 above 2½ in. thru 4 in.		

Note: At this point the student should carefully examine pages 1-6 and 1-7 of the AISC Manual for more information regarding the different steels available. Particular attention should be given to the determination of yield stresses for the different grades of steels (for plates and bars see page 1-6, and for the rolled sections see page 1-7). Notice carefully the division of shapes into groups and the resulting effects on yield stresses.

for each member, the locations and sizes of holes, the position and sizes of connections, and the like.

The erection of steel buildings is more a matter of assembly than nearly any other line of construction work. Each of the members is marked in the shop with letters and numbers to distinguish them from the other members to be used. The erection is performed in accordance with a set of erection plans. These plans are not detailed drawings but are simple line diagrams showing the position of the various members in the building. Each of the lines shown has a number and letter on it which corresponds to the same designation on the fabricated steel. This lettering system enables the workmen in the field easily to find the position of each member. (The men performing the steel erection are called *ironworkers*, which is a name held over from the days before structural steel.)

2-6. DESIGN OF STEEL MEMBERS

The design of a steel member involves much more than a calculation of the properties required to support the loads and the selection of the lightest section providing these properties. Although at first glance, this procedure would seem to give the most economical designs, many other factors need to be considered. Among these are:

1. The designer needs to select steel sections of sizes which are usually rolled. Steel beams and bars and plates of unusual sizes will be difficult to obtain during boom periods and will be expensive during any period. A little study on the designer's part will enable him to avoid these expensive shapes. Steel fabricators are constantly supplied with information from the steel companies and the steel warehousemen as to the sizes of sections available. This information includes the section sizes as well as the standard lengths available. (Most structural shapes can be obtained in lengths from 60 to 90 ft depending on the producer, while it is possible under certain conditions to obtain some shapes up to 120 ft in length.)

The AISC Manual classifies the various sections as being regular or special. The regular ones are those in constant demand and are sold at the regular prices. The special ones are those for which the demand varies, such as zees. The designer will try to avoid the use of special shapes because they sell at an increased rate unless the order is very large.

2. A blind assumption that the lightest section is the cheapest one may be in considerable error. A building frame designed by the "lightest-section" procedure will consist of a large number of different shapes and sizes of members. Trying to connect these many-sized members and fit

them in the building will be quite complicated and the pound price of the steel will in all probability be rather high. A more reasonable approach would be to smooth out the sizes by selecting many members of the same sizes although some of them may be slightly overdesigned.

3. The beams usually selected for the floors in buildings will be the deeper sections because these sections for the same weights have the largest moments of inertia and the greatest resisting moments. As building heights increase, however, it may be economical to abandon this practice. As an illustration of this fact the erection of a 20-story building, for which each floor has a minimum clearance, is considered. It is assumed that the depths of the floor beams may be reduced by 6 in. without an unreasonable increase in beam weights. The beams will cost more but the building height will be reduced by 20×6 in. $= 120$ in. or 10 ft, with resulting savings in walls, elevator shafts, column heights, plumbing, wiring, and footings.

4. For larger sections, particularly the built-up ones, the designer needs to have information pertaining to transportation problems. The desired information includes the greatest lengths and depths that can be shipped by truck or rail, clearance available under bridges and power lines leading to the project, and allowable loads on bridges. It may be possible to fabricate a steel roof truss in one piece, but is it possible to transport it to the job site and erect it in one piece?

5. Sections should be selected which are reasonably easy to erect and which have no conditions present which will make them difficult to maintain. As an example, it is necessary to have access to all exposed surfaces of steel bridge members so that they may be periodically painted.

6. Buildings are often filled with an amazing conglomeration of pipes, ducts, conduits and other items. Every effort should be made to select steel members which will fit in with the requirements made by these items.

7. The members of a steel structure are often exposed to the public, particularly in the case of steel bridges and auditoriums. Appearance may often be the major factor in selecting the type of structure to be used as where a bridge is desired which will fit in and actually contribute to the appearance of an area. Exposed members may be surprisingly graceful when a simple arrangement and perhaps curved members are used, but other arrangements may create a terrible eyesore. The student has certainly seen illustrations of each case. It is very interesting to know that beautiful structures in steel are usually quite reasonable in cost.

chapter 3

TENSION MEMBERS

3-1. INTRODUCTION

Tension members are found in bridge and roof trusses, towers, bracing systems, and in situations where they are used as tie rods. The selection of a section to be used as a tension member is one of the simplest problems encountered in design. As there is no danger of buckling, the calculations simply involve the division of the load by the allowable tensile stress to give the net cross-sectional area required ($A_{req.} = P/F_t$) and the selection of a steel shape which furnishes the required area.

The type of member used may depend more upon the type of end connection than on any other factor. One of the simplest forms of tension members appears to be the circular rod, but there is some difficulty in connecting it to many structures. The rod has been used frequently in the past but has only occasional uses today in bracing systems, light trusses, and in timber construction. One important reason why rods are not popular with designers is that they have been used improperly so often in the past that they have a bad name; but if they are designed and installed correctly they are satisfactory for many situations.

The average size rod has very little stiffness and may quite easily sag under its own weight injuring the appearance of the structure. The threaded rods formerly used in bridges often worked loose and rattled. Another disadvantage of rods is the difficulty of fabricating them with the exact lengths required and the consequent difficulties of installation.

When rods are used in wind bracing it is a good practice to produce initial tension in them, as this will tighten up the structure and reduce rattling and swaying. To obtain initial tension the members may be detailed shorter than their required lengths, but a little thought on this method will reveal many situations where it will cause more troubles than it is worth. Perhaps a more practical method is to tighten the rods with some sort of sleeve nut or turnbuckle although their use increases costs.

The preceding discussion on rods should illustrate why rolled shapes such as angles have supplanted rods for most applications. In the early days of steel structures, tension members consisted of rods, bars, and perhaps cables. Today, although the use of cables is increasing for suspended-roof structures, tension members usually consist of single angles, double angles, tees, channels, wide-flange sections, or sections built up from plates or rolled shapes. These members look better than the old ones, are stiffer and easier to connect. Another type of tension section often used is the welded tension plate or flat bar which is very satisfactory for use in transmission towers, signs, foot bridges, and similar structures.

The tension members of steel roof trusses may consist of single angles as small as $2\frac{1}{2} \times 2 \times \frac{1}{4}$ for minor members. A more satisfactory member is made from two angles placed back to back with sufficient space between them to permit the insertion of plates for connection purposes. Where steel sections are used back-to-back in this manner, they should be connected every 4 or 5 ft to prevent rattling, particularly in bridge trusses. Single angles and double angles are probably the most common types of tension members in use. Structural tees make very satisfactory chord members for welded trusses because web members can conveniently be connected to them.

For bridges and large roof trusses tension members may consist of channels, W or S shapes, or even sections built up from some combination of angles, channels, and plates. Single channels are frequently used as they have little eccentricity and are conveniently connected. Although, for the same weight, W sections are stiffer than S sections, they may have a connection disadvantage in their varying depths. For instance, the W 12×79, W 12×72 and W 12×65 all have slightly different depths (12.38 in., 12.25 in., and 12.12 in. respectively), while the S sections of a certain nominal size all have the same depths. For instance, the S 12×50, the S 12×40.8, and the S 12×35 all have 12.00-in. depths.

Although single structural shapes are a little more economical than built-up sections, the latter are occasionally used when the designer is unable to obtain sufficient area or rigidity from single shapes. Where built-up sections are used it is important to remember that field connections will have to be made and paint applied; therefore, sufficient space must be available to accomplish these things.

Members consisting of more than one section need to be tied together. Tie plates (also called tie bars) located at frequent intervals or perforated cover plates serve to hold the various pieces in their correct positions. These plates serve to correct any unequal distribution of loads between the various parts. They also keep the slenderness ratios (to be discussed) of the individual parts within limitations and they may permit easier handling of the built-up members. Long individual members such as angles may be inconvenient to handle due to flexibility, but when four angles are laced together into one member as shown in Fig. 3-1, the member has considerable stiffness. None of the tie plates may be considered to increase the effective areas of the sections. As they do not theoretically carry portions of the stress in the main sections, their sizes are usually governed by specifications and perhaps by some judgment on the designer's part. Perforated cover plates (see Fig. 5-7) are an exception to this rule as part of their areas can be considered as being effective in resisting axial load.

FIG. 3-1. Types of tension members.

A few of the various types of tension members in general use are illustrated in Fig. 3-1. In this figure the dotted lines represent the tie plates or bars used to connect the shapes.

3-2. ALLOWABLE TENSILE STRESS

Until a few years ago allowable stresses were given in specifications for structural carbon steels only. Today, however, with the many high-strength steels available it is necessary for specifications to provide allowable values for several grades of steel. For buildings the AISC (Sec. 1.5.1.1.) permits allowable tensile values equal to 0.60 times the specified minimum yield points but not more than 0.5 times the specified minimum tensile strengths of the steels. These allowables are applicable to the net section of the members, except at pin holes, where the allowable tensile stress is reduced to 0.45 times the specified minimum yield point on the net section. Table 3-1 presents a summary of the AISC values.

The bridge specifications allow somewhat smaller allowable tensile values. The 1969 AASHO Specifications permit allowable tensions equal to $.55F_y$ for members without holes and the smaller of $.55F_y$ or $.46F_u$ (minimum tensile strength of steel) on net section for tension members with holes. The 1969 AREA Specifications permit 20,000 psi for allow-

TABLE 3-1

ALLOWABLE TENSILE STRESSES, AISC SPECIFICATION

Minimum Yield Point (ksi)	Allowable Tension on Net Section	
	Except at Pin Holes (ksi)	At Pin Holes in Eyebars, Pin-connected Plates or Built-up Members (ksi)
36.0	22.0	16.2
42.0	25.2	19.0
45.0	27.0	20.3
50.0	30.0	22.5
55.0	33.0	24.8
60.0	36.0	27.0
65.0	39.0	29.3
90.0	52.5*	40.5
100.0	57.5*	45.0

* Controlled by 0.5 times the specified minimum tensile strength.

able tension on net section for A36 steel and $.55F_y$ for higher strength steels.

It is not likely that stress fluctuations will be a problem in the average building frame because the changes in load in such structures usually occur only occasionally and produce relatively minor stress variations. Should there, however, be frequent variations or even reversals in stress the matter of fatigue must be considered. The result of such an investigation might very well be a reduction in allowable stresses. Reference should be made to the AISC Specification (Sec. 1.7 and Appendix B) for the reductions necessary when more than 20,000 stress fluctuations are anticipated during the life of the structure. (It would require two fluctuations each day for 25 years to equal 18,250 fluctuations.) The allowable stress reduction required by the AISC is controlled by the number of stress fluctuations, the range of the stress changes, the loading condition and the types of members.

Stress fluctuations and reversals are an everyday problem in the design of bridge structures. The AASHO Specifications present their requirements for determining allowable stresses for fatigue situations in their Article 1.7.3 while the AREA Specifications give their requirements in their Article 1.3.13.

3-3. NET SECTION

The presence of a hole obviously increases the unit stress in a tension member even if the hole is occupied by a rivet or bolt. (When high-strength bolts are used there may be some disagreement with this statement under certain conditions.) There is less area of steel to which the load can be distributed and there will be some concentration of stress along the edges of the hole.

Tension is assumed to be uniformly distributed over the net section of a tension member, although photoelastic studies show there is a decided increase in stress intensity around the edges of holes, sometimes equaling several times the stresses if the holes were not present. For ductile materials, however, a uniform stress distribution assumption is reasonable when the material is loaded beyond its yield point. Should the fibers around the holes be stressed to their yield point they will yield without further stress increase, with the result that there is a redistribution or balancing of stresses. At ultimate load it is reasonable to assume a uniform stress distribution. The subject of plastic theory will be discussed at length in later chapters. The importance of ductility on the strength of riveted or bolted tension members has been clearly demonstrated in tests. Tension members (with rivet or bolt holes) made from ductile steels have proved to be as much as one-fifth to one-sixth stronger than similar members made from brittle steels with the same ultimate strengths.

It is possible by a laborious mathematical process to consider stress concentrations occurring around holes and at other sudden changes in the dimensions of the cross section. The resulting stresses are quite approximate and it is doubtful if they are appreciably more valuable than those obtained by dividing the total load by the cross-sectional area after any holes are subtracted.

This discussion is applicable only for tension members subjected to relatively static loading. Should tension members be designed for structures subjected to fatigue-type loadings considerable effort should be made to minimize the items causing stress concentrations such as points of sudden change of cross section, sharp corners, etc. In addition as mentioned in Sec. 3.2 allowable stresses might have to be reduced.

The term "net cross-sectional area" or simply "net area" refers to the gross cross-sectional area of a member minus any holes, notches, or other indentations. In considering the area of such items as these it is important to realize that it is usually necessary to subtract an area a little larger than the actual hole. For instance, in fabricating structural steel which is to be connected with rivets or bolts the holes are usually punched $\frac{1}{16}$ in. larger than the diameter of the rivet or bolt. Furthermore, the punching of the hole is assumed to damage or even destroy $\frac{1}{16}$ in. more of the surrounding metal; therefore, the area of the holes subtracted is $\frac{1}{8}$ in. larger than the diameter of the rivet or bolt. The area of the holes subtracted is rectangular and equals the diameter of the hole times the thickness of the metal.

For steel much thicker than the rivet or bolt diameters it is difficult to punch out the holes to the full sizes required without excessive deformation of the surrounding material. These holes may be drilled or subpunched slightly smaller than the required sizes after which they are reamed to the required values. Very little material is damaged by this method as the holes are even and smooth and it is considered unnecessary to subtract the $\frac{1}{16}$ in. for damage to the sides. Even though the holes are subtracted (whether they are punched or subpunched and reamed) there will be unequal strains at or near the holes resulting in stress concentrations. Tests have shown that members with drilled holes are decidedly stronger than those with punched holes.

Example 3-1 illustrates the calculations necessary for determining the allowable tensile capacity of a plate-type of tension member.

Fig. 3-2

EXAMPLE 3-1. Determine the capacity of the $8 \times \frac{3}{8}$-in. plate shown in Fig. 3-2 if the allowable tensile stress is 22,000 psi. The plate is connected at its end with two lines of $\frac{3}{4}$-in. rivets.

Solution:

$$\text{Net area} = 8 \times \frac{3}{8} - (2)\ (\frac{3}{4} + \frac{1}{8})\ (\frac{3}{8}) = 2.34 \text{ sq in.}$$

$$\text{Allowable } P = (2.34)\ (22,000) = 51,480 \text{ lb}$$

The connections of tension members should be arranged so that no eccentricity is present. (An exception to this rule is permitted by the AISC for certain welded connections as described in Chap. 11.) If this arrangement is possible the stress is assumed to be spread uniformly across the net section of a member and the net area required equals the total load divided by the allowable stress. Should the connections have eccentricities, moments will be produced which will cause additional stresses in the vicinity of the connection. Unfortunately it is often quite difficult to arrange connections without eccentricity. Although specifications cover some situations, the designer may have to give consideration to eccentricities in some cases with estimates of his own.

The lines of action of truss members meeting at a joint are assumed to coincide. Should they not coincide, eccentricity is present and second-

FIG. 3-3

ary stresses are the result. The centers of gravity of truss members are assumed to coincide with the lines of action of their respective stresses. No problem is present in a symmetrical member as its center of gravity is at its center line, but for unsymmetrical members the problem is a little more difficult. For these members the center line is not the center of gravity, but the usual practice is to arrange the members at a joint so their gage lines coincide. If a member has more than one gage line, the one closest to the actual center of gravity of the member is used in detailing. Figure 3-3 shows a truss joint in which the gage lines of all the members pass through the same point.

3-4. EFFECT OF STAGGERED HOLES

Should there be more than one row of bolt or rivet holes in a member it is usually desirable to stagger them in order to provide as large a net area as possible at any one section to resist the load. In the preceding paragraphs tensile members have been assumed to fail transversely as along line AB in either Fig. 3-4(a) or (b). Part (c) of this figure shows a member in which a failure other than a transverse one is possible. The holes are staggered, and a failure along section $ABCD$ is possible unless the holes are a large distance apart.

To determine the critical net area in Fig. 3-4 (c), it might seem logical to compute the area of a section transverse to the member (as AE)

FIG. 3-4

less the area of one hole and then the area along section *ABCD* less two holes. The smallest value obtained along these sections would be the critical value, but this method is at fault. Along the diagonal line from *B* to *C* there is a combination of direct stress and shear and a somewhat smaller area should be used. The strength of the member along section *ABCD* is obviously somewhere between the strength obtained by using a net area computed by subtracting one hole from the transverse cross-sectional area and the value obtained by subtracting two holes from section *ABCD*.

Tests on joints show that little if anything is gained by using complicated and theoretical formulas to consider the staggered-hole situation, and the problem is usually handled with an empirical equation. The AISC and other specifications use a very simple method (suggested by V. H. Cochrane in 1922 in *Engineering News Record*) for computing the net width of a tension member along a zigzag section. The method is to take the gross width of the member regardless of the line along which failure might occur, subtract the diameter of the holes along the zigzag section being considered, and add for each inclined line the quantity given by the expression $s^2/4g$.

In this expression s is the longitudinal spacing (or pitch) of any two holes and g is the transverse spacing (or gage) of the same holes. The values of s and g are shown in Fig. 3-4(c). The AISC does not permit the computed net width along transverse or zigzag sections to exceed 85 percent of the transverse gross section because several decades of research have shown that a riveted or bolted joint seldom has an efficiency greater than 85 percent even if the holes represent a very small percentage of the gross area. There may be several paths any one of which may be critical at a particular joint. Each possibility should be considered and the one giving the least value should be used. Example 3-2 illustrates the method of computing the critical net area of a section which has three lines of bolts. (For angles, the gage for holes in opposite legs is considered to be the sum of the gages from the back of the angle minus the thickness of the angle.)

The problem of determining the minimum pitch of staggered bolts such that no more than a certain number of holes need be subtracted to determine the net section is handled in Example 3-3. The Steel Handbook has a chart entitled "Net Section of Tension Members," which can be used to determine the values of $s^2/4g$. This chart can also be used to handle the type of problem solved in Example 3-3.

EXAMPLE 3-2. Determine the critical net area of the $\frac{1}{2}$-in. thick plate shown in Fig. 3-5 using the AISC Specification (Sec. 1.14.3). The holes are punched for $\frac{3}{4}$-in. bolts.

Solution: The critical section could possibly be *ABCD, ABCEF,* or *ABEF.*

FIG. 3-5

Hole diameters to be subtracted are $\frac{3}{4} + \frac{1}{8} = \frac{7}{8}$ in. The net widths for each case are as follows:

$$ABCD = 11 - (2)\ (\tfrac{7}{8}) = 9.25 \text{ in.}$$

$$ABCEF = 11 - (3)\ (\tfrac{7}{8}) + \frac{(3)^2}{(4)\ (3)} = 9.125 \text{ in.} \qquad \text{(controls)}$$

$$ABEF = 11 - (2)\ (\tfrac{7}{8}) + \frac{(3)^2}{(4)\ (6)} = 9.625 \text{ in.}$$

Maximum width permitted by AISC = $(0.85)\ (11) = 9.35$ in. > 9.125 in.

Net area = $(9.125)\ (\tfrac{1}{2}) = 4.56$ sq in.   *Ans.*

EXAMPLE 3-3. For the two lines of bolt holes shown in Fig. 3-6 determine the pitch which will give a net area along *DEFG* equal to the one along *ABC*.

FIG. 3-6

The problem may also be stated as follows: determine the pitch which will give a net area equal to the gross area less one bolt hole. The holes are punched for $\frac{3}{4}$-in. bolts.

Solution:

$$ABC = 6 - (1)\ \left(\frac{7}{8}\right) = 5.125 \text{ in.}$$

$$DEFG = 6 - (2)\left(\frac{7}{8}\right) + \frac{s^2}{(4)\ (2)} = 4.25 + \frac{s^2}{8}$$

$$ABC = DEFG$$

$$5.125 = 4.25 + \frac{s^2}{8}$$

$$s = 2.65 \text{ in.} \hspace{4cm} Ans.$$

3-5. DESIGN OF TENSION MEMBERS

The preceding paragraphs have shown that the determination of the required net area for tension members is not difficult; however, it will be seen that the selection of the exact proportions of the members is not as simple. Although the designer has considerable freedom in the selection, the resulting members should have the following properties; (a) compactness, (b) dimensions which fit into the structure with reasonable relation to the dimensions of the other members, and (c) connections to as much as possible of the gusset plates so as to minimize stress concentrations.

The choice of member type is often affected by the type of connections used for the structure. Some steel sections are not very convenient to bolt or rivet together with the required gusset plates, while the same sections may be welded together with little difficulty. Tension members consisting of angles, channels, W or S sections will probably be used when the connections are made with bolts or rivets, while plates, channels, and structural tees might be used for welded structures.

Various types of sections are selected for tension members in the examples to follow and in each case where bolts or rivets are used some allowance is made for holes. Should the connections be made *entirely* by welding, no holes have to be added to the net areas to give the required gross areas. *The student should realize, however, that very often welded members may have holes punched in them for temporary bolting during field erection before the permanent field welds are made. These holes need to be considered in design.*

The slenderness ratio of a member is the ratio of its unsupported length to its least radius of gyration. Steel specifications give upper permissible values of slenderness ratios for both tension and compression members. The purpose of such limitations for tension members is to insure the use of sections with sufficient stiffness to prevent undesirable lateral deflections or vibrations. For tension members other than rods the AISC *recommends* maximum permissible slenderness ratios of 240 for main members and 300 for bracing and other secondary members.

The AASHO values are 200 and 240 respectively and are *mandatory*. The *mandatory* maximum for all tension members is 200 in the AREA.

It should be obvious to the student that the types of end conditions of tension members have an appreciable effect on their lateral stiffness. For instance, a pinned end member is freer to bend or vibrate laterally than is the same sized member with fixed end conditions. The AISC, therefore, recommends that an effective slenderness ratio Kl/r be used instead of just l/r. In this expression K is the effective length factor. It depends on the end conditions of the member, and when multiplied by l gives the estimated length of the member free to bend laterally. Recommended values of K are given in Table C.1.8.1 of the AISC Commentary (reproduced as Table 5-1 in this book).

The subject of effective lengths, which is of much greater significance for compression members than for tension members is discussed in detail in Chaps. 4, 5, and 8. By the time the student has studied those chapters he should have a thorough understanding of effective lengths. For the purposes of this chapter it is recommended that the student refer to the aforementioned table to obtain K values. For the usual tension member end condition, K will be considered equal to 1.0.

EXAMPLE 3-4. Select a W 12 shape to resist a 390 k tensile load using the AISC Specification and an allowable stress of 27,000 psi. The member is 30 ft long and is to be connected with ¾-in. bolts. Assume that there can be 4 bolt holes at any one cross section (two in each flange).

Solution:

$$\text{Net area required} = \frac{390}{27} = 14.43 \text{ sq in.}$$

Assuming flanges to be ⅝ in. thick after some study of the W tables in the Steel Handbook,

$$\text{Hole area} = (4)\,(\tfrac{7}{8})\,(\tfrac{5}{8}) = 2.18 \text{ sq in.}$$

$$\text{Gross area} = 14.43 + 2.18 = 16.61 \text{ sq in.}$$

Try W 12 × 58

Gross area	$= 17.10$ sq in.
Less holes $= (4)\,(\tfrac{7}{8})\,(0.641) =$	-2.24 sq in.
Net area provided	$= 14.86$ sq in. > 14.43 sq in. (OK)

$$\frac{Kl}{r} = \frac{1 \times 12 \times 30}{2.51} = 143 < 240 \qquad \text{(OK)}$$

Maximum permissible net area by AISC $= (0.85)\,(17.10) = 14.50$ sq in. > 14.43 sq in. required net area.   (OK)

Use W 12 × 58

EXAMPLE 3-5. Design a 9-ft single-angle tension member to resist a total tensile stress of 43,000 lb. The member is to be connected with ¾-in. bolts and only one bolt is assumed to be placed at any one section through the angle. Use the AISC Specification and an allowable stress of 22,000 psi.

Solution: This problem is one which can be conveniently handled with the use of a table and this procedure is followed here for a few angle sizes.

$$\text{Net area required} = \frac{43,000}{22,000} = 1.955 \text{ sq in.}$$

Angle Thickness (in.)	Area of One ⅞-in. Hole (sq in.)	Gross Area Required (sq in.)	Lightest Angles Available (Equal and Unequal Legs) and Their Areas (sq in.)
¼	0.219	2.174	6 × 3½ × ¼ (2.31)
5⁄16	0.273	2.228	4 × 3½ × 5⁄16 (2.25) 4 × 4 × 5⁄16 (2.40)
⅜	0.328	2.283	3½ × 3 × ⅜ (2.30) 3½ × 3½ × ⅜ (2.48)
7⁄16	0.383	2.338	3½ × 2½ × 7⁄16 (2.43) 3 × 3 × 7⁄16 (2.43)
½	0.438	2.393	3 × 2½ × ½ (2.50) 3 × 3 × ½ (2.75)

-Lightest section: L 4 × 3½ × 5⁄16

$$\frac{l}{r} = \frac{12 \times 9}{0.73} = 148 < 240 \qquad \text{(OK)}$$

Maximum net area by AISC = (0.85) (2.25) = 1.92 sq in. < 1.95 (N.G.)

Next lightest section: L 3½ × 3 × ⅜

$$\frac{Kl}{r} = \frac{12 \times 9}{0.625} = 173 < 240 \qquad \text{(OK)}$$

Maximum net area by AISC = (0.85) (2.30) = 1.96 > 1.95 (OK)

Use L 3½ × 3 × ⅜

A single-angle tension member was selected in Example 3-5 to resist a tensile load. Unless the end connections are made to both legs of the angle it will be eccentrically loaded and secondary bending stresses will be the result. For this situation some specifications such as the AASHO and the AREA require that the effective area of the unconnected leg be reduced by one-half regardless of whether the connection is bolted, welded, or riveted. A more desirable situation is created if a double-angle member is used with one angle on each side of the gusset plate as shown in

Each member consists
of 2 Ls with 1 L on
each side of gusset PL

Gusset PL

FIG. 3-7

Fig. 3-7. The resultant stress is supposedly kept in the plane of the gusset plate with this type of connection.

Based on a consideration of plastic behavior, the AISC does not deem it necessary to make a special reduction in the effective net area of an angle connected by one leg. Should a load be applied to an angle of this type the stress in the outside edge of the connected leg will quickly reach the yield point. Increases in the load will cause that part of the angle to yield with a consequent redistribution of the stresses throughout the remainder of the angle until the entire section has reached the yield stress. From this discussion it can be seen that the ultimate strength of the angle is not greatly affected by the type of connection (that is, to one leg or to two legs). This theory does not apply very well to fatigue type loadings.

Example 3-6 illustrates the design of a single-angle tension member connected by one leg using the AASHO Specifications and Example 3-7 illustrates the design of a double-angle tension member using the AISC Specification.

EXAMPLE 3-6. Select a single-angle tension member to resist a total force of 51,000 lb using the AASHO Specifications and an allowable stress of 20,000 psi. One leg of the angle is to be connected with $\frac{7}{8}$-in. bolts and it is assumed to be possible for two holes to occur at one section. The length of the member is 12 ft.

Solution:

$$\text{Net area required} = \frac{51,000}{20,000} = 2.55 \text{ sq in.}$$

Try L 7 × 4 × $\frac{3}{8}$

Gross area	=	3.98 sq in.
Less hole area = $-(2)$ (1) $(\frac{3}{8})$	=	$-$ 0.75 sq in.
Less 50% area of uncon. leg =		
$-(0.50)$ $(4 - \frac{3}{8})$ $(\frac{3}{8})$ =		$-$ 0.68 sq in.
Actual net area	=	2.55 sq in. = 2.55 sq in. (OK)

$$\frac{l}{r} = \frac{12 \times 12}{0.88} = 163 < 200 \qquad \text{(OK)}$$

Use 1 L 7 $\times$ 4 $\times$ $\frac{3}{8}$

EXAMPLE 3-7. Design a 20-ft double-angle tension member by the AISC
Specification to resist a tensile load of 105,000 lb. The member is to be connected with $\frac{3}{4}$-in. bolts and no more than 1 bolt hole in each angle is assumed
to occur at any one section. The allowable tension is 22,000 psi and a $\frac{3}{8}$-in.
gusset plate is used between the angles.

Solution:

$$\text{Net area required} = \frac{105,000}{22,000} = 4.77 \text{ sq in.}$$

Angle Thickness (in.)	Area of Two $\frac{7}{8}$-in. Holes (sq in.)	Gross Area Required (sq in.)	Lightest Pair Of Angles Available and Their Areas (sq in.)
$\frac{5}{16}$	0.546	5.32	6 $\times$ 3$\frac{1}{2}$ $\times$ $\frac{5}{16}$ (5.74)
$\frac{3}{8}$	0.656	5.43	5 $\times$ 3 $\times$ $\frac{3}{8}$ (5.72) 4 $\times$ 4 $\times$ $\frac{3}{8}$ (5.72)
$\frac{7}{16}$	0.766	5.54	4 $\times$ 3 $\times$ $\frac{7}{16}$ (5.74) 3$\frac{1}{2}$ $\times$ 3$\frac{1}{2}$ $\times$ $\frac{7}{16}$ (5.74)
$\frac{1}{2}$	0.876	5.65	3$\frac{1}{2}$ $\times$ 3 $\times$ $\frac{1}{2}$ (6.00) 3$\frac{1}{2}$ $\times$ 3$\frac{1}{2}$ $\times$ $\frac{1}{2}$ (6.50)

Lightest section: 2 Ls 4 $\times$ 4 $\times$ $\frac{3}{8}$

$$\frac{l}{r} = \frac{12 \times 20}{1.23} = \frac{240}{1.23} = 195 < 240 \qquad \text{(OK)}$$

$$\text{Maximum net area by AISC} = (2) \ (0.85) \ (2.86)$$
$$= 4.86 \text{ sq in.} > 4.77 \text{ sq in.} \qquad \text{(OK)}$$

Use 2 Ls 4 $\times$ 4 $\times$ $\frac{3}{8}$

Example 3-8 presents the review of a tension member built up from
two channels. Included in the problem is the design of the necessary tie
plates. The AISC Specification is used.

EXAMPLE 3-8. Two C 12 $\times$ 30s 12″ back-to-back (see Fig. 3-8) have
been selected to support a 328,000 lb tensile load. The member is 30 ft long, consists of A36 steel and has one $\frac{7}{8}$-in. bolt through each channel flange. Using the
AISC Specification determine if the member is satisfactory and design the necessary tie plates.

Solution:

$$\text{Net area required} = \frac{328,000}{22,000} = 14.90 \text{ sq in.}$$

Actual net area furnished:

$$.67" \rightarrow | \ \ | \leftarrow 5.33" \rightarrow |$$

c. g. of C

x —————————————— x 12.00"

2-C12 X 30s

$$\leftarrow \quad 12.00" \quad \rightarrow$$

FIG. 3-8

Gross area of 2 channels $=$ (2) (8.82) $=$ 17.64 sq in.
Less holes $=$ (4) (1.00) (.501) $=$ 2.00 sq in.
Actual net area furnished $=$ 15.64 $>$ 14.90 sq in.
                                                                  (OK)

Maximum net area permitted by
                    AISC $=$ (.85) (17.64) $=$ 15.00 $>$ 14.90 sq in.   (OK)

Slenderness ratio:

$$I_x = (2) \ (162) \qquad\qquad\qquad = 324 \text{ in.}^4$$
$$I_y = (2) \ (5.14) + (2) \ (8.82) \ (5.33)^2 \qquad = 508 \text{ in.}^4$$
$$r_x = \sqrt{\frac{324}{17.64}} = 4.29 \text{ in.}$$
$$\frac{Kl}{r} = \frac{(1.0) \ (12 \times 30)}{4.29} = 83.9 < 240$$
                                                                  (OK)

Design of tie plates (AISC Sec. 1.18.3.2):

Distance between lines of bolts $=$ 12.00 $-$ (2) (1¾) $=$ 8.50 in.
Minimum length of tie plates $=$ (⅔) (8.50) $=$ 5.67 in. (say 6 in.)
Minimum thickness of tie plates $=$(1/50) (8.50) $=$ .17 in. (say 3/16 in.)
Minimum width of tie plates (Sec. 1.16.5) $=$ 8.50 $+$ (2) (1½) $=$11.5 in.

Maximum permissible spacing of tie plates:

$$\text{Least } r \text{ of one C } = .763$$
$$\text{Max permissible } \frac{l}{r} = 240$$
$$\frac{12 \times l}{.763} = 240$$
$$l \qquad\qquad = 15.3 \text{ ft}$$

Use tie PLs 3/16 $\times$ 6 $\times$ 11½, maximum spacing 15 ft.

3-6. SPLICES FOR TENSION MEMBERS

A tension member splice has the purpose of replacing the member at the point where it is cut. At first glance the problem may seem to be an unusually simple one but there are several difficulties which can arise, primarily caused by eccentricities of loads.

Tension members are often more than large enough to resist the calculated maximum stress. This fact causes the following question to arise: "Should the splice be designed for the maximum calculated stress or for the actual strength of the member?" The AREA says that the splice must be made for the full strength of the member—that is, the full net effective area of the member must be replaced. The AASHO says a splice should be designed for the calculated maximum stress or 75 percent of the strength whichever is larger; while the AISC requires the design to be made for the calculated maximum stress or 50 percent of the member strength, whichever is larger.

Eccentricity of the loads is a common problem with splices as illustrated by the single-angle splice shown in Fig. 3-9. In this type of splice it may be possible to get the centers of gravities lined up in one direction as shown in part (a) of the figure but not in the other direction as shown in part (b) of the same figure.

Perhaps the usual practice in splice design is to neglect the effect of eccentricities, but the designer needs to be on the lookout for extreme cases so that he can allow for them. Actually the single-angle splice shown in the preceding figure with one plate is one of the worst types and should be avoided. In this regard it is desirable to splice all parts of tension members. For instance, if an angle is being spliced, each leg should be spliced. As described in Sec. 3-5, the AASHO permits the use of only one-half of the area of an unconnected angle leg in resisting stress. A specification such as this one was written to make a rough allowance for the effect of eccentricity.

FIG. 3-9. Single-angle splice (poor).

A few possible types of tension member splices are shown in Fig. 3-10.

FIG. 3-10

The rather poor method of splicing a single angle with a single plate is shown in part (a) of the figure. Part (b) shows a much better method (perhaps the best one) for splicing a single angle. In this method the splice is made with another angle. The splice angle has shorter legs and must therefore have a greater thickness than the angle being spliced to provide the same net area.

Sometimes a lug angle is used as shown in part (c) of the figure. This angle will reduce the eccentric bending stresses in the member and stiffen up the whole connection slightly. Splices may be butt splices or shingle splices. These types of splices are shown in parts (d) and (e) respectively of Fig. 3-10. In the butt splice a W shape or built-up member is cut entirely at one section and splice material must be added to make the splice. Probably the shingle splice for built-up sections is a little better in that it causes a reduction of stress concentrations by staggering the splices and also keeps the entire member from being cut at one point.

Sometimes it is necessary to use what is called an "indirect" splice. An indirect splice is one in which there is an intermediate plate between the part being spliced and the splice itself. Most specifications require an increase in the number or amount of connectors (rivets, bolts, or welds) when indirect splices are used. An increase of from one-fourth to one-third the number of connectors is usually required for each intermediate plate.

Many persons do not think that gusset plates should be used as splice plates or as part of them. The truth of the matter probably is that they should not be designed as gusset plates and then have the additional task of serving as splice plates without a proportionate increase in section. In other words, gusset plates which are used for such situations need to be designed for both tasks.

New Albany Bridge crossing the Ohio River between Louisville, Ky., and New Albany, Ind. (*The Lincoln Electric Company.*)

Rarely is it necessary to splice steel rods, as they are usually not of sufficient length to require splicing. Should splicing be necessary, however, turnbuckles may be used. These devices are also of advantage in putting initial tension in the rods and in getting them to fit properly as previously described in this chapter.

3-7. DESIGN OF RODS AND BARS

When rods and bars are used as tension members they may be simply welded at their ends, or they may be threaded and held in place with nuts. If the ends are threaded the net area is determined from the diameter at the root of the threads. The result is that the available area of the member is reduced. For many years it was considered good practice to select rods which had diameters, at the root of the threads, $\frac{1}{16}$ in. larger than theoretically required by stress. The purpose of this extra size was to account for stress concentrations at the roots of the threads.

Today, however, it has been found that due to the fact that the loads bear against the threads at some angle to the rod axis some additional strength is provided beyond that which would be calculated based on the area at the root of the threads. In Sec. 1.5.2.1 of the AISC Specification the threaded parts of bars are permitted an allowable tension of 0.60 F_y applied to an area equal to $0.7854 \left(D - \dfrac{0.9743}{n} \right)^2$ where D is the outside thread diameter and n is the number of threads per inch. The AISC says that this empirical area, which is in between the gross area and the area at the root of the threads, more closely predicts the allowable tensile strengths of threaded rods.

Sometimes upset bars are used where the ends are made larger than the regular bar and the threads placed in the enlarged section so that the area at the root of the thread is at least 20 percent larger than that of the regular bar. Upsetting permits the designer to use the entire area of the cross section despite stress concentrations. The use of upset bars is probably not economical unless a large order is being made and is usually avoided. They are not listed in the AISC Manual.

A common example of the use of tension rods occurs in steel-frame industrial buildings which have purlins running between their roof trusses to support the roof surface. These types of buildings will also frequently have girts running between the columns along the vertical walls. Sag rods may be required to provide support for the purlins parallel to the roof surface and vertical support for the girts along the walls. For roofs with steeper slopes than 1 vertically to 4 horizontally, sag rods are often considered necessary to provide lateral support for the purlins, particularly where the purlins consist of steel channels. Steel channels are commonly used as purlins but they have very little resistance to lateral bending. The section modulus needed to resist bending parallel to the roof surface is small but nevertheless an extremely large channel is required to provide such a modulus. The use of sag rods for providing lateral support to purlins made from channels is usually economical because of the bending weakness of channels about their y axes. For light roofs (as where trusses support corrugated steel roofs) sag rods will probably be needed at the one-third points if the trusses are more than 20 ft on centers. Sag rods at the midpoints are sufficient if the trusses are less than 20 ft on centers. For heavier roofs such as those made of slate, cement tile, or clay tile, sag rods will probably be needed at closer intervals. The one-third points will probably be necessary if the trusses are spaced at greater intervals than 14 ft and the mid points will be satisfactory if truss spacings are less than 14 ft. Some designers assume that the load components parallel to the roof surface can be taken by the roof, particularly if it consists of corrugated steel sheets, and that tie rods are unnecessary. This assumption, however, is open to some doubt and definitely should not be followed if the roof is very steep.

The designer has to use his own judgment in limiting the slenderness values for rods as they will usually be several times the limiting values mentioned for other types of tension members. A common practice of many designers is to use rod diameters no less than 1/500th of their lengths to obtain some rigidity even though stress calculations may permit much smaller sizes.

It is usually desirable to limit the minimum size of sag rods to $\frac{5}{8}$ in. because smaller rods than these are often injured during construction. The threads on smaller rods are quite easily injured by overtightening which seems to be a frequent habit of workmen. Sag rods are designed for the purlins of a roof truss in Example 3-9. The rods are assumed to support the simple beam reactions for the components of the gravity loads (roofing, purlins, snow and ice) parallel to the roof surface. Wind forces are assumed to act perpendicular to the roof surfaces and theoretically will not affect the sag rod stresses. The maximum stress in a sag rod will occur in the top sag rod because it must support the sum of the stresses in the lower sag rods. It is theoretically possible to use smaller rods for the lower sag rods but this reduction in size will probably be impractical.

EXAMPLE 3-9. Design the sag rods for the purlins of the truss shown in Fig. 3-11. Purlins are to be supported at their third points between the trusses which are spaced 21 ft on centers. Assume the specifications require a minimum size rod of $\frac{5}{8}$ in. and permit a tensile stress of 22,000 psi. It is further assumed that the required net section will be increased by $\frac{1}{16}$ in. to allow for stress concentrations. A clay tile roof weighing 16 psf of roof surface is used and supports a snow load of 20 psf of horizontal projection of roof surface. Details of the purlins and the sag rods and their connections are shown in Figs. 3-11 and 3-12. In these figures the dotted lines represent a common practice of using ties and struts in the end panels in the plane of the roof to give greater resistance to loads located on one side of the roof (a loading situation which might occur when snow is blown off one side of the roof during a severe windstorm).

Solution: Gravity loads in psf of roof surface are as follows:

$$\text{Purlins} = \frac{7 \times 11.5}{37.9} = 2.1 \text{ psf}$$

$$\text{Snow} = 20\frac{3}{\sqrt{10}} = 19.0 \text{ psf}$$

$$\text{Tile roofing} = \frac{16.0 \text{ psf}}{37.1 \text{ psf}}$$

$$\text{Component of loads parallel to roof surface} = \frac{1}{\sqrt{10}} \times 37.1 = 11.7 \text{ psf}$$

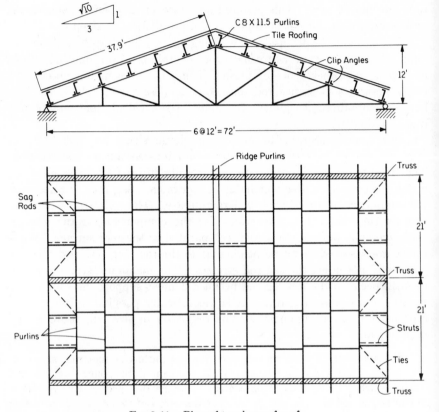

FIG. 3-11.   Plan of two bays of roof.

Load on sag rod $= (37.9)\ (7)\ (11.7)\ =\ 3{,}110$ lb

$$\text{Net area required} = \frac{3{,}110\ \text{lb}}{20{,}000} = 0.156\ \text{sq in.} \quad (\tfrac{5}{8}\text{-in. rod has } 0.226\ \text{sq in.})$$

<u>Use $\tfrac{5}{8}$-in. sag rod (minimum size permitted)</u>

Stress in tie rod between ridge purlins (stress in inclined sag rods assumed to be a component of this stress):

$$\text{Stress} = \frac{\sqrt{10}}{3} \times 3{,}110 = 3{,}270\ \text{lb}$$

$$\text{Net area required} = \frac{3{,}270}{22{,}000}\ 0.149\ \text{sq in.} \quad (\tfrac{5}{8}\text{-in. rod OK})$$

NOTE: The area calculated here is the required net area for a threaded rod unless an upset rod is used. In this case a threaded $\tfrac{5}{8}$-in. rod would be required

FIG. 3-12. Details of sag rod connections.

to supply the necessary area at the root of the thread. (See table, "Threaded Fasteners, Screw Threads" in Steel Handbook.)

3-8. EYE-BAR TENSION MEMBERS

Until the early years of the twentieth century nearly all bridges in the United States were pin-connected, but today they are used infrequently because of the advantages of riveted, welded, and bolted connections. One trouble with pin-connected trusses is the wearing of the pins in the holes causing looseness of the joints. Pin-connected eye bars are used occasionally today as tension members for long-span bridge trusses and as hangers for some types of bridges. These types of bridges are subjected to very large dead loads; and the eye bars are, therefore, prevented from rattling under traffic loads. The design of pin-connected members is substantially controlled by empirical specifications which are based on considerations for stress concentrations occurring near the pin holes.

Eye bars are formed by making a rectangular bar or plate with an enlarged head and boring a hole in this head to enable it to be pin-connected. Details of the bar as to the diameter of the head, etc., are probably not worked out by the designer and selection is made from the shapes available from the steel companies because of the high cost of other sizes. The truth of the matter is that eye bars are used infrequently and the cost of any size will be rather large and they will probably have to be specially ordered.

The large trusses for which eye bars are used require large members. Each member will probably be made up of several thicknesses of eye bars each being from 1 to 2 in. thick. From a safety standpoint it is desirable for failure to occur in the members rather than at the joints and the specifications usually require the net area of the bar at the pin to be larger than the net area of the body of the bar. An illustration is the AREA specification which requires a 40 percent increase in area at the pin.

PROBLEMS

3-1. (a) What is the allowable tensile load which a 6 × 4 × ⅝ L can support if it is connected with one line of ⅞-in. bolts and the allowable tensile stress is 20 ksi. Not AISC. (Ans. 104.8 k)

(b) Repeat the problem if two lines of ¾-in. bolts are present and A36 steel and the AISC Specification are used. (Ans. 104.9 k)

3-2. Determine the allowable tensile load which can be supported by a pair of 7 × 4 × ¾ Ls (long legs b to b) according to the AISC Specification if A36 steel is used. Assume that two rows of ⅞-in. bolts are used in the long legs and one row of ⅞-in. bolts in the short legs.

3-3. The member shown in the accompanying illustration is used to resist a tensile load of 1050 k. If the AISC Specification and A36 steel are used, is the member satisfactory? The member is 25 ft long and has pinned ends. Assume there are holes for four ⅞-in. bolts as shown. (Ans. Section is satisfactory; allowable $P = 1148\ k$, $\dfrac{Kl}{r} = 78.8$)

W 10 X 100 —

PL 1 X 16

PL 1 X 16

PROB. 3-3

3-4. Find the net area of the plate shown in the accompanying illustration. An 18 × ½ PL is used and the holes shown are for 1-in. bolts. AISC Specification.

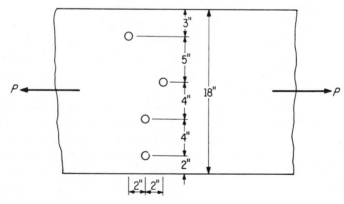

PROB. 3-4

3-5. Find the allowable tensile load which can be applied to the plate shown in the accompanying illustration if the allowable tensile stress is 20 ksi. The plate is 17 × ¾ and the holes shown are punched for ⅞-in. bolts. Not AISC Specification. (Ans. 202.5k)

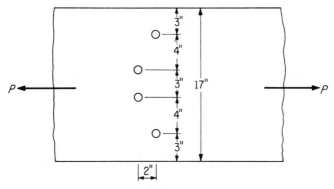

PROB. 3-5

3-6. A C10 × 15.3 is connected through its web with three gage lines of ⅞-in. bolts. The gage lines are 2½ in. on centers and the bolts are spaced 3 in. on centers along the gage line. If the center row of bolts is staggered with respect to the outer row determine the net cross-sectional area of the channel using the AISC Specification.

3-7. A single-angle tension member (7 × 4 × ⅝) has two gage lines in its long leg and one in the short leg for ¾-in. bolts arranged as shown in the accompanying illustration. Determine the allowable tensile load which the member can support if a steel with $F_y = 50$ ksi is used. AISC Specification. (Ans. 156 k)

PROB. 3-7

3-8. Determine the maximum permissible tensile load which can be supported by the pair of 5 × 5 × ⅞ Ls shown in the accompanying illustration if A440 steel and the AISC Specification are used. Standard gages are to be used as determined from the Steel Manual. Holes are for ¾-in. bolts.

PROB. 3-8

3-9. For the plate and bolts shown in the accompanying illustration find the minimum pitch s for which only two bolts need be subtracted at any one section. Bolts are $\frac{7}{8}$ in. (Ans. 2.45 in., say $2\frac{1}{2}$ in.)

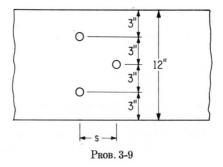

PROB. 3-9

3-10. Find the minimum pitch s in the plate of Prob. 3-9 so that only two and one half bolts need be subtracted at any one section.

3-11. An $8 \times 6 \times 1$ L is used as a tension member with one gage line of 1-in. bolts in each leg at the usual gage location.

(a)   What is the minimum amount of stagger necessary so that only one bolt need be subtracted from the gross area of the angle?

(b)   How would the use of the AISC "85 percent rule" affect this answer? (Ans. (a) 5.61 in., say $5\frac{5}{8}$ in.; (b) 2.9 in., say $2\frac{7}{8}$ in.)

3-12. An $8 \times 4 \times \frac{3}{4}$ angle is shown in the accompanying illustration.   Two

PROB. 3-12

rows of ⅞-in. bolts are used in the long leg and one in the short leg. Determine the stagger (or pitch s in the figure) necessary so that only two holes need be subtracted in determining the net area.

3-13. A W 10 shape is to be selected to support a tensile load of 280 k. The member is to be 28 ft long, have an allowable tensile stress of 20 ksi and is assumed to have two holes for ⅞-in. bolts in each flange. (Maximum l/r is 200.) Not AISC. (Ans. W 10 × 60)

3-14. Repeat Prob. 3-13 using A36 steel and the AISC Specification. Assume pinned ends.

3-15. Select the lightest American Standard channel which will safely support a tensile load of 175 k. The member is 18 ft long and is assumed to have a hole for a 1-in. bolt through each flange. A36. AISC. Ends are pinned. (Ans. C 15 × 33.9)

3-16. A welded tension member is to consist of two channels placed 12 in. back-to-back with the flanges turned in. Select the channels for a maximum tensile load of 450,000 lbs using A36 steel and the AISC Specification. The member is to be 30 ft long and is to have one end fixed and the other pinned.

3-17. The AISC Specification and A36 steel are to be used in selecting a single angle member to resist a tensile load of 42 k. The member is to be 12 ft long and is assumed to be connected with one row of ⅞-in. bolts. Assume pinned end connections. (Ans. 1 L 4 × 3½ × 5/16)

3-18. Repeat Prob. 3-17 selecting a pair of angles and using A36 steel. Assume angle legs are touching and assume one hole for ⅞-in. bolt in each angle.

3-19. Design member L_2L_3 of the truss shown in the accompanying illustration. It is to consist of a pair of angles with a ⅜-in. gusset plate at each joint. Use A36 steel, AISC Specification and assume $K = 1.0$. Assume two ¾-in. bolts in each angle. (Ans. Use 2 L 7 × 4 × ⅜ long legs b to b, total force in member 144 k)

Рrob. 3-19

. **3-20.** Select a single-angle tension member 12 ft long to support a load of 70 k if the allowable tension is 20 ksi and one leg of the angle is to be connected with a line of ¾-in. bolts. Use the AASHO provision that only one-half of the unconnected leg may be considered as being effective in resisting load. Maximum permissible l/r is 200.

3-21. Select a single angle member to resist a tensile load of 120 k. The member is 15 ft long and is assumed to be connected with two rows of ⅞-in. bolts.

52   TENSION MEMBERS

AISC Specification. $F_y = 65$ ksi. Pinned end connections. (Ans. 1 L 7 × 4 × ⅜)

3-22. Repeat Prob. 3-16 assuming that one ⅞-in. bolt passes through each flange. Design tie plates. AISC Specification.

3-23. A tension member is to consist of 4 equal leg angles arranged as shown in the accompanying illustration to support a tensile load of 560 k. The member is to be 30 ft long, have pinned ends and is assumed to have two holes for ⅞-in. bolts in each angle A36 Steel. AISC Specification. Design the member including the necessary tie plates. Ans 4 Ls 8 × 8 × ½ with ³⁄₁₆ × 6 × 1'-0" tie plates spaced at a maximum distance of 31.8 ft)

18"

|← 18" →|

Prob. 3-23

3-24. Select a threaded round rod as a hanger to resist a total tensile load of 12,000 lb. Use AISC Specification. A36 steel.

3-25. The horizontal thrust at the base of the three-hinge arch shown in the accompanying illustration is to be resisted by a tie rod of A36 steel. What size threaded round tie rod should be used if the AISC Specification is used? (Ans. 2¼ in. round rod-4½ UNC)

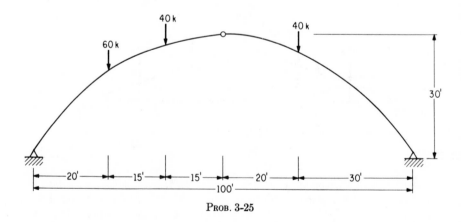

40 k

60 k

40 k

30'

|← 20' →|← 15' →|← 15' →|← 20' →|← 30' →|

|← 100' →|

Prob. 3-25

3-26. The roof trusses for a particular industrial building are spaced 21 ft on centers, have a roof covering weighing an estimated 6 psf of roof surface, and have purlins spaced as shown in the accompanying illustration and weighing an estimated 3 psf of roof surface. Design sag rods using A36 steel and the AISC Specification, assuming a snow load of 25 psf of horizontal surface. The sag rods are to be used at the one-third points.

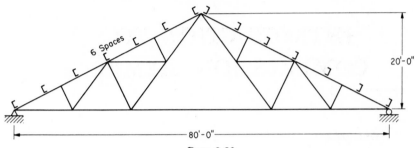

6 Spaces

20'-0"

80'-0"

PROB. 3-26

chapter 4

INTRODUCTION TO COMPRESSION MEMBERS

4-1. GENERAL

When a load tends to squeeze or shorten a member the stresses produced are said to be compressive stresses and the member is called a compression member. There are several types of compression members, the column being the best known. Among the other types are the top chords of trusses, bracing members, the compression flanges of rolled beams and built-up beam sections, and members which are subjected simultaneously to bending and compressive loads. Columns are usually thought of as being straight vertical members whose lengths are considerably greater than their thicknesses. Short vertical members subjected to compressive loads are often called struts or simply compression members; however, the terms *column* and *compression member* will be used interchangeably in the pages that follow.

There are two significant differences between tension and compression members. These are:

1. Whereas tensile loads tend to hold a member straight compressive loads tend to bend them out of the plane of the loads (a serious situation).

2. The presence of rivet or bolt holes in tension members reduces the area available for resisting loads; but in compression members the rivets or bolts are assumed to fill the holes (although there may be some very slight initial slippage until the bolts or rivets bear against the adjoining material) and the entire gross area is available for resisting load.

Tests on all but the shortest columns show that they will fail at P/A stresses well below the elastic limit of the column material because of their tendency to buckle or bend laterally. For this reason their allowable stresses are reduced in some relation to the danger of buckling. The longer a column becomes for the same cross section the greater becomes its tendency to buckle and the smaller becomes the load it will support. The tendency of a member to buckle is usually measured by the *slenderness ratio*, which has previously been defined as the ratio of the length

54

of the member to its least radius of gyration. The tendency to buckle is also affected by such factors as the types of end connections, eccentricity of load application, imperfection of column material, initial crookedness of columns, residual stresses from manufacture, etc.

The loads supported by a building column are applied by the column section above and by the connections of other members directly to the column. The ideal situation is for the loads to be applied uniformly across the column with the center of gravity of the loads coinciding with the center of gravity of the column. Furthermore, it is desirable for the column to have no flaws, to consist of a homogeneous material, and to be perfectly straight; but these situations are obviously impossible to achieve.

Guggenheim Laboratories, Princeton University, Princeton, N. J.
(*Bethlehem Steel Company.*)

Loads which are exactly centered over a column are referred to as axial or concentric loads. The dead loads may or may not be concentrically placed over an interior building column and the live loads may never be centered. For an outside column the loading situation is probably even more eccentric as the center of gravity of the loads will usually fall well on the inner side of the column. In other words, it is doubtful that a perfect axially loaded column will ever be encountered in practice.

The other desirable situations are also impossible to achieve because of the following: imperfections of cross-sectional dimensions, residual stresses, holes punched for rivets or bolts, erection stresses, and transverse loads. The result of all of these imperfections cannot be expressed in a formula and they truthfully require the use of high safety factors.

Slight imperfections in tension members and beams can be safely disregarded as they are of little consequence. On the other hand, slight defects in columns may be of major significance. A column which is slightly bent at the time it is put in place will have serious bending moments. Obviously a column is a more critical member in a structure than is a beam or tension member because minor imperfections in materials and dimensions mean a great deal. This fact can be illustrated by a bridge truss which has some of its members damaged by a truck. The bending of tension members probably will not be serious as the tensile loads will tend to straighten those members; but the bending of any compression members is a serious matter, as compressive loads will tend to magnify the bending in those members.

The preceding discussion should clearly show that column imperfections cause them to bend and the designer must consider stresses due to those moments as well as due to axial loads. Chapters 4 and 5 are limited to a discussion of axially loaded columns while members subjected to a combination of axial loads and bending loads are discussed in Chap. 8.

4-2. RESIDUAL STRESSES

In recent years research at Lehigh University has shown that residual stresses and their distribution are perhaps the most important factors affecting the strength of axially loaded steel columns. These stresses are of particular importance for columns with l/r values varying from approximately 40 to 120, a range which includes a very large percentage of practical columns. A major cause of residual stress is the uneven cooling of shapes after hot-rolling. For instance in a W shape the outer tips of the flanges and the middle of the web cool quickly while the areas at the intersection of the flange and web cool more slowly.

The quicker cooling parts of the sections when solidified resist further shortening while those parts which are still hot tend to shorten further as they cool. The net result is that the areas which cooled more quickly have residual compressive stresses while the slower cooling areas have residual tensile stresses. The magnitude of these stresses vary from about 10 to 15 ksi although some values greater than 20 ksi have been found.

When rolled-steel column sections are tested, their proportional limits are reached at P/A values of only a little more than half of their yield stresses and the stress-strain relationship is nonlinear from there up to the yield stress (see Fig. 4-1). Because of the early localized yielding occurring at some points of the column cross sections, buckling strengths are appreciably reduced. Reductions are greatest for columns with slenderness ratios varying from approximately 70 to 90 and may possibly be as high as 25 percent.[1]

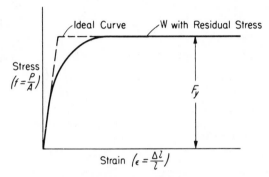

FIG. 4-1. Effect of residual stresses on column stress-strain diagram.

Residual stresses may also be caused during fabrication when cambering is performed by cold bending and due to cooling after welding. Welding can produce severe residual stresses in columns which actually can approach the yield point in the vicinity of the weld. Another important fact is that columns may actually be appreciably bent by the welding process decidedly affecting their load carrying ability. Figure 4-1 shows the effect of residual stresses due to cooling and fabrication on the stress-strain diagram for a hot-rolled W shape.

4-3. SECTIONS USED FOR COLUMNS

Theoretically an endless number of shapes can be selected to safely resist a compressive load in a given structure. From a practical viewpoint, however, the number of possible solutions is severely limited by such considerations as sections available, connection problems, and type of structure in which section is to be used. The paragraphs that follow are intended to give a brief resume of the sections which have proved to be satisfactory for certain conditions. These sections are shown in Fig. 4-2 and the letters in parentheses in the paragraphs to follow refer to the parts of this figure.

The sections used for compression members are usually similar to

---

[1] L. S. Beedle and L. Tall, "Basic Column Strength," *Proc. ASCE*, vol. 86 (July 1960), pp. 139–173.

those used for tension members with certain exceptions. The exceptions are caused by the fact that the strengths of compression members vary in some inverse relation to the l/r ratios and stiff members are required. Individual rods, bars, and plates are usually too slender to make satis-

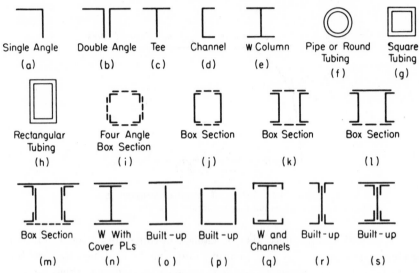

FIG. 4-2. Types of compression members.

factory compression members unless they are very short and lightly loaded.

Single-angle members (a) are satisfactory for bracing and compression members in light trusses. Equal-leg angles may be more economical than unequal-leg angles because their least r values are greater for the same area of steel. The top chord members of riveted or bolted roof trusses might consist of a pair of angles back-to-back (b). There will probably be a space between them for the insertion of a gusset plate at the joints necessary for connections to other members. An examination of this section will show that it is probably desirable to use unequal-leg angles with the long legs back to back to give a better balance between the r values about the x and y axes.

If roof trusses are welded, gusset plates may be unnecessary and structural tees (c) might be used for the top chord members because the web members can be welded directly to the stems of the tees. Single channels (d) are not satisfactory for the average compression member because of their almost negligible r values about their web axes. They can be used if some method of providing extra lateral support in the weak direction is available. The W shapes (e) are probably the most common shapes used for building columns and for the compression members of highway bridges. Their *r* values although far from being equal about the two axes are much more nearly balanced than for channels.

For small and medium loads, pipe sections or round tubing (f) are quite satisfactory. They are often used as columns in long series of windows, as short columns in warehouses, as columns for the roofs of covered walkways, in the basements and garages of residences, etc. Pipe columns have the advantage of being equally rigid in all directions and are usually very economical unless moments are large. The Steel Handbook furnishes the sizes of these sections and classifies them as being standard, extra strong, and double extra strong.

Bents fabricated from tubing sections in New Jersey. (*Bethlehem Steel Company.*)

Square and rectangular tubing (g) and (h) have not been used to a great extent for columns until recently. In fact, for many years only a few steel mills manufactured steel tubing for structural uses. Perhaps the major reason why tubing was not used to a great extent was the difficulty of making connections with rivets or bolts. This problem has been fairly well eliminated, however, by the advent of modern welding. The use of tubing for structural purposes by architects and engineers in the years to come will probably be greatly increased for several reasons. These include:

1. The most efficient compression member is one which has a constant

radius of gyration about its centroid, a property available in round tubing. Square tubing is the next most efficient compression member.

2. Their smooth surfaces permit easier painting.

3. They have excellent torsional resistance.

4. The surfaces of tubing are quite attractive.

5. When exposed the wind resistance of round tubing is only about two-thirds of that of flat surfaces of the same width.

A slight disadvantage which comes into play in certain cases is that the ends of tubing may have to be sealed to protect their inaccessible inside surfaces from corrosion. Although making very attractive exposed members for beams, tubing is at a definite weight disadvantage as compared to the regular rolled beam shapes. Their maximum section modulus is considerably less than for a rolled shape of the same weight per foot.

Where compression members are designed for very large structures it may be necessary to use built-up sections. Built-up sections are needed where the members are long and support very heavy loads and/or when there are connection advantages. Generally speaking, a single shape such as a W section is more economical than a built-up section having the same cross sectional area. With heavy column loads high strength steels can frequently be used with very economical results if their increased strength permits the use of W sections rather than built-up members.

When built-up sections are used they must be connected on their open sides with some type of lacing (also called lattice bars) to hold the parts together in their proper positions and to assist them in acting together as a unit. The ends of these members are connected with tie plates (also called batten plates or stay plates).

The dotted lines in Fig. 4-2 represent lacing or discontinuous parts and the solid lines represent parts that are continuous for the full length of the members. Four angles are sometimes arranged as shown in (i) to produce large r values. This type of member may often be seen in towers and in crane booms. A pair of channels (j) is sometimes used as a building column or as a web member in a large truss. It will be noted that there is a certain spacing for each pair of channels at which their r values about the x and y axes are equal. Sometimes the channels may be turned out as shown in (k).

A section well suited for the top chords of bridge trusses is a pair of channels with a cover plate on top (l) and with lacing on the bottom. The gusset plates at joints are conveniently connected to the insides of the channels and may also be used as splices. When the largest channels available will not produce a top chord member of sufficient strength a built-up section of the type shown in (m) may be used.

When the rolled shapes do not have sufficient strength to resist the column loads in a building or the loads in a very large bridge truss, their areas may be increased by adding plates to the flanges (n). In recent years it has been found that for welded construction a built-up column of the type shown in part (o) is a more satisfactory shape than a W with welded cover plates (n). It seems that in bending (as where a beam frames into the flange of a column) that it is difficult to efficiently transfer tensile force through the cover plate to the column without pulling the plate away from the column. For very heavy column loads a welded box section of the type shown in (p) has proved to be quite satisfactory. Some other built-up sections are shown in parts (q) through (s). The built-up section shown in parts (m) through (q) have an advantage over those shown in parts (i) through (m) in that they do not require the expense of the lattice work necessary in the former. Lateral shearing forces are negligible for the single column shapes and for the nonlatticed built-up sections, *but they are definitely not negligible for the built-up latticed columns.*

4-4. DEVELOPMENT OF COLUMN FORMULAS

The use of columns goes back before the dawn of history but it was not until 1729 that a paper was published on the subject by Pieter van Musschenbroek, a Dutch mathematician.[2] He presented an empirical column formula for estimating the strength of rectangular columns. A few years later in 1757 Leonhard Euler, a Swiss mathematician, published a paper of great value concerning the buckling of columns. He was probably the first person to realize the significance of buckling. The derivation of his formula, the most famous of all column expressions, is presented in Sec. 4-5.

Engineering literature is filled with formulas developed for ideal column conditions but these conditions are not encountered in actual practice. Consequently practical column design is based primarily on formulas which have been developed to fit with reasonable accuracy test-result curves. The reasoning behind this procedure is simply the fact that the independent derivation of column expressions does not yield formulas which give results comparing closely with test result curves for all ranges of l/r.

The testing of columns of various ranges of l/r results in a scattered range of values such as those shown by the broad band of dots in Fig. 4-3. The dots will not fall on a smooth curve even if all of the testing is done in the same laboratory because of the difficulty of exactly centering the

[2] L. S. Beedle et al., *Structural Steel Design* (New York: The Ronald Press Company, 1964), p. 269.

Test Result Curve

Fig. 4-3. Test result curve.

loads, lack of perfect uniformity of the materials, varying dimensions of the sections, end restraint variations, etc. The usual practice is to attempt to develop formulas which give results represented by an approximate average of the test results with an adequate safety factor applied. The student should also realize that laboratory conditions are not field conditions and column tests probably give the limiting values of column strengths.

4-5. DERIVATION OF THE EULER FORMULA

The Euler formula is derived in this section for a straight, concentrically loaded, homogeneous, long slender column with rounded ends. It is assumed that this perfect column has been laterally deflected by some means as shown in Fig. 4-4 and that if the concentric load P was removed the column would straighten out completely.

Fig. 4-4

The x and y axes are located as shown in the figure. As the bending moment at any point in the column is $-Py$ the equation of the elastic curve can be written as follows:

$$EI \frac{d^2y}{dx^2} = - Py$$

For convenience in integration both sides of the equation are multiplied by $2dy$ and the integration is performed.

$$EI\, 2\,\frac{dy}{dx}\, d\,\frac{dy}{dx} = -\,2\,Py\,dy$$

$$EI\left(\frac{dy}{dx}\right)^2 = -\,Py^2 + C_1$$

When $y = \delta$, $dy/dx = 0$, and the value of C_1 will equal $P\delta^2$ and

$$EI\left(\frac{dy}{dx}\right)^2 = -\,Py^2 + P\delta^2$$

The preceding expression is arranged more conveniently as follows:

$$\left(\frac{dy}{dx}\right)^2 = \frac{P}{EI}\,(\delta^2 - y^2)$$

$$\frac{dy}{dx} = \sqrt{\frac{P}{EI}}\,\sqrt{\delta^2 - y^2}$$

$$\frac{dy}{\sqrt{\delta^2 - y^2}} = \sqrt{\frac{P}{EI}}\,dx$$

Integrating this expression, the result is

$$\text{arc sin}\,\frac{y}{\delta} = \sqrt{\frac{P}{EI}}\,x + C_2$$

When $x = 0$ and $y = 0$, $C_2 = 0$. The column is bent into the shape of a sine curve expressed by the equation

$$\text{arc sin}\,\frac{y}{\delta} = \sqrt{\frac{P}{EI}}\,x$$

When $x = l/2$, $y = \delta$, resulting in

$$\frac{\pi}{2} = \sqrt{\frac{P}{EI}\,\frac{l}{2}}$$

In this expression P is the *critical buckling load* or the maximum load which the column can support before it becomes unstable. Solving for P

$$P = \frac{\pi^2\,EI}{l^2}$$

This expression is the Euler formula but is usually written in a little different form involving the slenderness ratio. Since $r = \sqrt{I/A}$ and $r^2 = I/A$ and $I = r^2 A$, the Euler formula may be written as

$$\frac{P}{A} = \frac{\pi^2\,E}{(l/r)^2}$$

The student should carefully note that the buckling load determined from the Euler equation is independent of the strength of the steel used. This equation is the only purely theoretical column formula of significance which has been developed to date, but is of value only when the end support conditions are carefully considered. The results obtained by application of the formula to specific examples compare very well with test results for centrally loaded, long slender columns with rounded ends. The engineer, however, does not encounter perfect columns of this type. The columns with which he works do not have rounded ends and are not free to rotate because their ends are bolted, riveted, or welded to other members. These practical columns have different amounts of restraint against rotation varying from slight restraint to almost fixed conditions. For the actual cases encountered in practice where the ends are not free to rotate, different length values can be used in the formula and more realistic values will be obtained.

Successfully to use the Euler equation for practical columns the value of l should be the distance between points of zero moment. This distance is referred to as the *effective length* of the column. For a pinned-end column (whose ends can rotate but cannot translate) the points of zero moment are at the ends a distance l apart. For columns with different end conditions the effective lengths may be entirely different.

Part (a) of Fig. 4-5 shows the type of bending considered in deriving

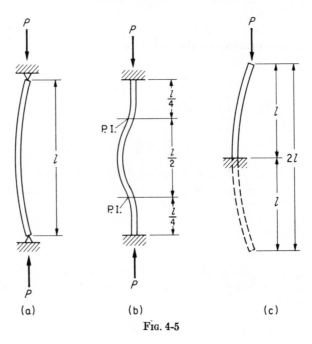

(a)   (b)   (c)

Fig. 4-5

the Euler Equation earlier in this section. [Actually Euler's 1757 publication presented only the so-called flagpole problem shown in Fig. 4-5(c) in which one end is built-in or fixed and the other end is free.] In part (b) of the same figure is shown a column whose ends are fixed. A fixed-end column has points of inflection (P.I.'s) at its one fourth points and the effective length or the distance between the points of inflection equals $l/2$. Obviously the smaller the effective length the greater the estimated strength obtained by substitution in the Euler expression. Although the effective length of the usual practical column falls in between these two values (l and $l/2$), it is possible for it to be greater than l. Should a column be completely free at one end and fixed at the other end its elastic curve will take the shape of the curve of a pinned-end column of twice its length and the effective length will be $2l$ as shown in part (c) of Fig. 4-5.

It might be interesting to note that for the column shown in part (b) of the figure the end moments actually restrain the column so as to decrease the deflection due to buckling. The result is that the effective length is less than l and the end moments may be thought of as actually strengthening the column. In columns of the type shown in part (c) the end moments actually weaken the column in that they increase the deflection due to buckling. Further discussions of effective lengths are made in Chaps. 5 and 8.

Research work in this field by Thomas H. Johnson showed that when practical end conditions were used entirely different values should be used for the Euler formula.[3] He found that when column ends were practically pin connected the value of the Euler formula should be

$$\frac{P}{A} = \frac{16E}{(l/r)^2}$$

For flat or nearly fixed ends he recommended the following:

$$\frac{P}{A} = \frac{25E}{(l/r)^2}$$

It is interesting to note that these values can be obtained by using effective lengths of $0.785l$ and $0.628l$ respectively in the original formula. These revised values of the Euler formula seem to give reasonable values for long slender columns with l/r *values* varying from approximately 120 to 200. The general practice, however, is to use very few members with the high slenderness ratios for which they are applicable. In fact some specifications prohibit the use of main members with l/r values

---

[3] "On the Strength of Columns," *Trans. ASCE*, vol. 15, (July 1886), p. 522.

in this range although they may permit such values for secondary members. One of the present AISC column expressions which will be discussed in Chap. 5 is the Euler formula divided by a factor of safety of 1.92 or 23/12. This formula can be written as

$$\frac{P}{A} = \frac{12\pi^2 E}{23 \ (l/r)^2}$$

A simple application of the Euler formula is given by Example **4-1**. It will be remembered that this expression was derived for stresses for which Hooke's law applies and, therefore, is not applicable to stresses above the proportional limit. This situation is encountered in Example 4-1.

FIG. 4-6

EXAMPLE 4-1. The wood column of Fig. 4-6 has a modulus of elasticity of 2,000,000 psi and a proportional limit of 5,000 psi. If the member is assumed to be pin connected, what are the critical axial loads it can support for unsupported lengths of 15 ft and 5 ft according to the Euler formula?

Solution: Properties of column:

$$A = (4) \ (6) = 24 \text{ sq in.}$$

$$I_x = (\tfrac{1}{12}) \ (4) \ (6)^3 = 72 \text{ in.}^4$$

$$I_y = (\tfrac{1}{12}) \ (6)(4)^3 = 32 \text{ in.}^4$$

Least $r = \sqrt{I/A} = \sqrt{32/24} = 1.155$ in.

Fifteen-foot column:

$$\frac{l}{r} = \frac{12 \times 15}{1.155} = 156$$

$$\frac{P}{A} = \frac{\pi^2 \ E}{(l/r)^2} = \frac{(\pi^2) \ (2,000,000)}{(156)^2} = 810 \text{ psi}$$

$$P = (810) \ (24) = 19,440 \text{ lb}$$

Five-foot column:

$$\frac{l}{r} = \frac{12 \times 5}{1.155} = 52$$

$$\frac{P}{A} = \frac{(\pi^2)\ (2{,}000{,}000)}{(52)^2} = 7{,}280 \text{ psi} > 5{,}000 \text{ psi proportional limit}$$

Euler formula not applicable.

4-6. REVISIONS TO EULER FORMULA

Engineers did not make great use of the Euler equation for a good many years after it was introduced. They felt the values obtained varied too much from test results. The derivation was based on a definite set of conditions (straight columns, concentric loads, etc.). When very careful tests are made under conditions approaching the assumed ones the results compare quite favorably as long as P/A does not exceed the proportional limit of the material. It should be noted here that tests of short columns show that they often fail at P/A stresses well above the proportional limit of the material.

Above the proportional limit the test values and the Euler values vary greatly. The reason for these variations can be understood when it is remembered that the method used to derive the Euler formula was satisfactory only for cases where stresses were proportional to strains. In other words, the modulus of elasticity is not constant outside of the elastic range. His formula with constant E is valid only for the elastic range and must be revised before it is applicable in the inelastic range. As time went by Euler's formula became fairly well accepted in the elastic range but in the inelastic range it was necessary to use certain empirical formulas (a practice still followed). Buckling at stresses above the proportional limit is referred to as *inelastic buckling*, while buckling at stresses below the proportional limit is referred to as *elastic buckling*.

In 1889 Friedrich Engesser proposed the so-called tangent-modulus theory[4] in which the moduli of elasticity for stresses above the proportional limit are determined from the slope of the stress strain curve. Engesser assumed that the column remained straight until failure and that the tangent modulus was constant for the entire cross section of a column. To plot a curve of the Euler equation above the proportional limit with the Engesser proposal it is necessary to assume certain values of P/A, find the tangent modulus for each from a stress-strain curve, and then use the Euler equation to determine the corresponding l/r values for plotting against P/A. The application of this method results in curves

---

[4] *Zeitschrift fur Architekur und Ingenieurwesen*, 1889.

which come much closer to test-result curves than does the use of the regular Euler expression.

Unfortunately the application of the tangent-modulus method is rather complex. A particular difficulty with the method is that the tangent modulus has to be determined with great care because in a small distance from the proportional limit to the elastic limit the modulus changes tremendously (from 29×10^6 psi to 0). The importance of determining the tangent modulus with extreme care is seen when it is realized that a great range of practical columns fall into this portion of the curve. The tangent-modulus method is not frequently used because of the difficulties mentioned in the preceding sentences.

During the last seventy years appreciation of the tangent-modulus theory by the engineering profession has made a full circle from considerable respect to little respect and back to considerable respect. After its introduction many engineers claimed that the theory was poor because a very important fact was not considered in its development. The fact supposedly neglected was that the strains on one side of the column were decreasing as were the stresses on that side, and that these changes were made in the range of the elastic modulus.

Based on this criticism Engesser revised his old theory and introduced the reduced-modulus or double-modulus theory in 1895. A reduced modulus somewhat greater than the tangent modulus is used and the estimated loads which a column can support are larger than those given by the original Engesser theory. For a good many years the double-modulus theory was accepted as being the correct theory of column action in the inelastic range, but in recent years considerable doubts have been voiced

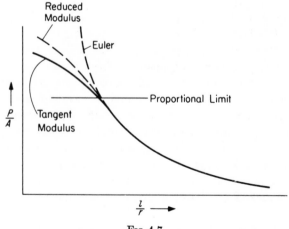

Fig. 4-7

about the double-modulus theory. Actual test results fall in between the values given by the two theories and in fact they tend to be closer to the tangent-modulus values than to the reduced-modulus values. Furthermore, the tangent-modulus values are on the safe side while the double-modulus values are on the unsafe side. F. R. Shanley presented a paper in 1947[5] which discussed the shortcomings of the double-modulus theory and showed that the original tangent modulus theory was the better of the two. Curves are presented in Fig. 4-7 showing the comparison of the results obtained by using these two formulas and also the Euler formula.

PROBLEMS

4-1. A 1-in. round steel bar serves as a pin-connected column. Using the Euler equation determine the critical load for the bar for lengths of 2 and 4 ft. $E = 29 \times 10^6$ psi. Proportional limit = 34,000 psi. (Ans. 24.3 k for 2 ft length, 6.08 k for 4 ft length)

4-2. Calculate the critical load for the pipe section shown in the accompanying illustration for lengths of (a) 40 ft, (b) 30 ft, and (c) 20 ft. Use the Euler equation with $E = 29 \times 10^6$ psi and a proportional limit equal to 33,000 psi.

$\frac{5}{8}$"

8"

PROB. 4-2

4-3. The two C 12 × 25s shown in the accompanying illustration serve as a 36 ft pinned-end column. Using the Euler equation determine the critical load

C 12 X 25

C 12 X 25

12"

PROB. 4-3

for the column if $E = 29 \times 10^6$ psi and the proportional limit is 34,000 psi. (Ans. 437 k)

[5] F. R. Shanley, "The Column Paradox," *J. Aeron. Sci.* (May 1947), p. 26.

70   INTRODUCTION TO COMPRESSION MEMBERS

4-4. A 14 ft column with pinned ends is made up of the angles shown in the accompanying illustration. The steel has a modulus of elasticity of 29 × 10⁶ psi and a proportional limit of 34,000 psi. Using Euler's equation
   (a) determine the critical load of the column
   (b) determine the critical load of one of the angles acting by itself

$$4 \text{ L s } 6 \times 4 \times \tfrac{3}{4}$$

PROB. 4-4

4-5. A W 8 × 40 is to serve as an 18 ft pin-connected column. What is the maximum allowable load it can support? Use the Euler expression, a proportional limit of 33,000 psi, $E = 29 \times 10^6$ psi and a safety factor of 2.5. (ANS. 119.6 k)

4-6. The pin-connected wooden column shown in the accompanying illustration is assumed to have an $E = 2 \times 10^6$ psi and a proportional limit of 3,000 psi. What is the allowable maximum axial load which it can support if a safety factor of 3 is used according to the Euler expression? Consider lengths of (a) 30 ft, (b) 25 ft, and (c) 20 ft.

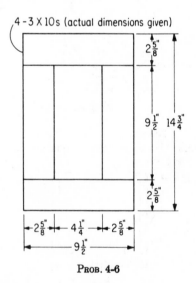

4 - 3 × 10s (actual dimensions given)

PROB. 4-6

4-7. An 8 ft pin-connected column has the cross section shown in the accompanying illustration. Using the Euler equation determine the allowable load which the column can support if the factor of safety is 2. $E = 29 \times 10^6$ psi. Proportional limit = 34,000 psi. (ANS. 52.2 k)

PROB. 4-7

4-8. A C 10 × 20 serves as a pin-connected column. Using the Johnson-re-vised Euler equation for pinned-end columns determine the critical load which it can support for a length of 10 ft. $E = 29 \times 10^6$ psi and the proportional limit is 34,000 psi.

4-9. A S 12 × 31.8 which serves as an 8 ft column has a proportional limit of 34,000 psi and an E of 29×10^6 psi. Using a factor of safety of 2 what is the maximum allowable load which it can support according to the Euler expression, if

(a) The column is assumed to be pinned at both ends thus having an effective length equal to l (Ans. 145 k)

(b) the column is assumed to have an effective length equal to $2l$ (Ans. 36.8 k)

4-10. Using the Euler expression, determine the required cross section for a square wooden column 20 ft long to support a load of 30 k. The modulus of elasticity is 1.76×10^6 psi, the proportional limit is 4,000 psi and a safety factor of 2.5 is to be used.

4-11. Using the Euler equation with a safety factor of 3 select a W 8 section to support a 60 k load for a 20 ft pin-connected column. $E = 29 \times 10^6$ psi. Proportional limit = 34,000 psi. Maximum permissible $l/r = 240$. (Ans. W 8 × 31)

4-12. A W 10 × 49 is to be used as a 34 ft pin-ended column but is braced at middepth in the weak direction. Using a safety factor of 3, $E = 29 \times 10^6$ psi and a proportional limit of 34,000 psi, determine the allowable total axial load which the column can support using the Euler equation.

chapter 5

DESIGN OF COMPRESSION MEMBERS

5-1. PRACTICAL DESIGN FORMULAS

Through the years hundreds of different column formulas have been developed with which their originators attempted to approximate test-result curves. Several general types of formulas have been developed such as the straight-line, the parabolic, the Rankine, and others. Some persons say there is no more variation in the results given by the various formulas than occurs in test results. These facts have probably led to the use of simpler formulas, since it is doubtful if the more complicated ones result in appreciably better designs. Several of the better-known column formulas are presented in this chapter.

5-2. STRAIGHT-LINE FORMULAS

The straight-line formulas are the simplest type of column expression which can be devised for a certain range of l/r. Although there is no theoretical reasoning behind these expressions they were in common use for many years particularly in bridge design. The straight-line formula was first proposed by W. H. Burr in 1882. In 1886 T. H. Johnson proposed a type of straight-line column formula in the *Transactions of the ASCE*.[1]

Straight-line formulas can be devised which will give values approaching test results for l/r values from about 50 to 120. These same formulas, however, give allowable stresses which are much too high when the slenderness ratio is below 50 and much too low when above 120. When load tests are made on short columns there is little decrease in strength as the slenderness ratio increases from zero until it exceeds a value of approximately 50 or 60. Some of the common straight-line formulas took this fact into account. One of these was the 1920 AREA

---

[1] "On the Strength of Columns," *Trans. ASCE*, vol. 15 (July 1886), p. 517.

formula (no longer applicable) which follows:

$$\frac{P}{A} = 15,000 - 50\frac{l}{r}$$

The AREA said the maximum value permissible was 12,500 psi regardless of the value obtained from the formula. In other words for l/r values from 0 to 50 the allowable compression stress was 12,500 psi and for higher l/r values the allowable stress was to be determined from the formula. At that time the AREA did not permit the use of main members with l/r values greater than 100 nor bracing with l/r values greater than 120.

Most of the straight-line formulas were developed during the early days of column tests when test results were quite inconsistent due to variations in testing conditions. During the past few decades these conditions have been greatly improved and column materials made more uniform. These factors have made better test results possible and the straight-line formulas are generally thought to be too inaccurate to represent the strength of steel columns. Consequently these formulas have been almost entirely replaced with parabolic expressions. Straight-line design formulas, however, are used today for some other structural materials. Example 5-1 illustrates the use of the 1920 AREA formula. To illustrate the trial-and-error nature of column design, a rather poor assumption is made for an allowable stress in this example.

EXAMPLE 5-1. Using the 1920 AREA formula, select a W section to support a 200 k load if the unsupported height of the column is 14 ft.

Solution: Assume that the allowable stress is 10,000 psi, and that the area required is $200,000/10,000 = 20$ sq in.

Try W 8 × 67 ($A = 19.70$ sq in. least $r = 2.12$)

Allowable $\dfrac{P}{A} = 15,000 - 50\dfrac{12 \times 14}{2.12} = 11,040$ psi

Allowable $P = (11,040)(19.70) = 218,000$ lb　　　　(overdesigned)

Area required $= \dfrac{200,000}{11,040} = 18.1$ sq in.

Try W 10 × 60 ($A = 17.7$ sq in., $r = 2.57$)

Allowable $\dfrac{P}{A} = 15,000 - 50\dfrac{12 \times 14}{2.57} = 11,730$ psi

Allowable $P = (11,730)(17.7) = 208,000$ lb

Area required $= \dfrac{200,000}{11,730} = 17.05$ sq in.

Try W 12 × 58 ($A = 17.1$ sq in., $r = 2.51$)

Allowable $\dfrac{P}{A} = 15{,}000 - (50)\left(\dfrac{12 \times 14}{2.51}\right) = 11{,}660$ psi

Allowable P = (11,660) (17-1) = 199,000 < 200,000

Use W 10 × 60 (although W 12 × 58 is probably OK)

5-3. PARABOLIC FORMULAS

Another group of fairly simple column expressions are the parabolic formulas. These empirical formulas, first proposed by J. B. Johnson,[2] can be made to represent test results fairly well for slenderness ratios varying from 0 to approximately 130 or 140. Above this range they give values which are much too conservative. The formulas which are given at the end of this paragraph are taken from the 1969 AASHO Specifications and are typical of parabolic column formulas. These particular expressions are given for concentrically loaded columns consisting of A36 steel and with l/r values not exceeding 130. It will be noted that most present-day U.S. specifications use F_a as the allowable axial compression stress instead of P/A.

$$F_a = \frac{P}{A} = 16{,}000 - 0.30\left(\frac{l}{r}\right)^2 \quad \text{(riveted ends)}$$

$$F_a = \frac{P}{A} = 16{,}000 - 0.38\left(\frac{l}{r}\right)^2 \quad \text{(pinned ends)}$$

EXAMPLE 5-2. Select a W 12 section to resist a compressive load of 150 k using the 1969 AASHO formula for pinned ends. The member is to be 20 ft long and consist of A36 steel.

Solution: Assume that the allowable P/A or F_a is 11,000 psi and that the area required is

$$\frac{150{,}000}{11{,}000} = 13.63 \text{ sq in.}$$

Try W12 × 50 ($A = 14.7$ sq in., $r = 1.96$)

$$\frac{l}{r} = \frac{12 \times 20}{1.96} = 122.5 < 130 \qquad \text{(OK)}$$

$$F_a = 16{,}000 - (0.38)\left(\frac{12 \times 20}{1.96}\right)^2 = 10{,}300 \text{ psi}$$

[2] J. B. Johnson, F. E. Turneaure, and C. W. Byran, *Modern Framed Structures* (New York: John Wiley & Sons, Inc., 1910), p. 47.

Allowable $P = (10,300) (14.7) = 151$ k > 150 k   (OK)

Use W12 × 50

Fig. 5-1

EXAMPLE 5-3.   Using the 1969 AASHO Specifications determine the allowable compressive load which the riveted member shown in Fig. 5-1 can support if it is 19 ft long and consists of A36 steel.

Solution:

$$A = (2) (12.6) + (20) (\tfrac{1}{2}) = 35.2 \text{ sq in.}$$

$$\bar{y} \text{ from top} = \frac{(25.2) (9.5) + (10) (0.25)}{35.2} = 6.86 \text{ in.}$$

$$I_x = (2) (554) + (25.2) (2.64)^2 + (\tfrac{1}{12}) (20) (\tfrac{1}{2})^3 + (10) (6.61)^2$$

$$I_x = 1723 \text{ in.}^4$$

$$I_y = (2) (14.4) + (25.2) (6.88)^2 + (\tfrac{1}{12}) (\tfrac{1}{2}) (20)^3$$

$$I_y = 1,553 \text{ in.}^4$$

$$\text{Least } r = \sqrt{\frac{1,553}{35.2}} = 6.64$$

$$\frac{l}{r} = \frac{12 \times 19}{6.64} = 34.3 < 130 \qquad \text{(OK)}$$

$$F_a = 16,000 - (0.30) (34.3)^2 = 15,650 \text{ psi}$$

Allowable $P = (15,650) (35.2) = 551,000$ lb

5-4. GORDON-RANKINE FORMULA

The preceding paragraphs have presented two empirical methods for estimating the reduction in strength of a column as the slenderness ratio increased. The straight-line formulas reduced the allowable stress in direct proportion to the slenderness ratio while the parabolic formulas reduced the stress by some squared value of the slenderness ratio. Another method of reducing the allowable stress with increasing slenderness is to divide the base stress by a number larger than one, which increases as l/r increases. The Gordon-Rankine expression is a formula of this type, has a fairly rational derivation and gives results in fairly close agreement with actual tests for l/r values from 120 to 200. For a good many years the AISC used the Gordon-Rankine expression to follow for the design of secondary members for l/r values from 120 to 200. (A *main member* is defined as a member of primary importance whose failure would be expected to cause immediate collapse of all or a large part of a structure. A *secondary member* is a member of secondary importance whose failure would not be so serious. It is further defined as a member which theoretically does not support dead loads other than its own weight nor live loads other than those caused by wind.)

$$\frac{P}{A} = \frac{18,000}{1 + \dfrac{(l/r)^2}{18,000}}$$

During the years when the AISC required this formula to be used for the design of secondary members, they also permitted its use for main members in the same l/r range if the formula was multiplied by 1.6 — $(l/r)/200$. This type of equation was developed by an English engineer, Lewis Gordon, but he used the square of the least side dimension instead of r^2. A famous Scottish engineer, W. J. M. Rankine, developed the equation in its present form.[3] For this reason it is commonly called the Rankine formula rather than the Gordon-Rankine formula. Example 5-4 illustrates the application of a Rankine formula to a bracing problem.

EXAMPLE 5-4. A 15-ft wind-bracing member is to be designed for a load of 35,000 lb. It is to consist of a pair of angles with a $\frac{3}{8}$-in. gusset plate between them. The following Rankine formula is to be used in the design:

$$\frac{P}{A} = \frac{18,000}{1 + \dfrac{(l/r)^2}{18,000}}$$

[3] W. J. M. Rankine, *A Manual of Civil Engineering* (London: Charles Griffin and Company 1883), pp. 522–523.

Solution: Assume that the allowable P/A is 8,500 psi and that the area required is $35,000/8,500 = 4.13$ sq in.

Try 2 Ls $4 \times 3 \times \frac{5}{16}$ ($A = 4.18$, $r = 1.27$) long legs back-to-back

$$\frac{l}{r} = \frac{12 \times 15}{1.27} = 142$$

Allowable $\dfrac{P}{A} = \dfrac{18,000}{1 + \dfrac{(142)^2}{18,000}} = 8,490$ psi

Allowable $P = (8,490)\,(4.18) = 35,500 > 35,000$ (OK)

Use 2 Ls $4 \times 3 \times \frac{5}{16}$

5-5. THE SECANT FORMULA

A rational type of formula which can be made to approximate test results for all values of l/r is the secant formula. Many investigators have worked with this type of column formula which is probably the most precise of all column expressions and which has fairly wide usage despite some difficulties of application. The results of all column formulas, no matter how complex, can be plotted on a graph or recorded in a table for practical use. On the other hand, the engineer may desire to substitute directly in the formula and for such cases the simpler formulas are probably more desirable.

The ASCE formed a committee for column research in 1923. In its reports this committee recommended the secant formula as being a very satisfactory expression for column design. The general form of the equation is as follows:

$$\frac{P}{A} = \frac{y}{1 + \dfrac{ec}{r^2}\,\sec\left(\sqrt{\dfrac{P}{AE}}\,\dfrac{l}{2r}\right)}$$

In this expression y is the yield point of the steel, c is the distance from the centroid to the extreme fiber, and e is the eccentricity of load application. This formula has a definite advantage in that it provides specifically for some eccentricity of load application. On the basis of studies of test results this committee recommended that a value for ec/r^2 (called the eccentric ratio) equal to 0.25 be used. This value supposedly provides for secondary stresses caused by bending and initial crookedness of columns.

The difficulty in using the secant formula is that while the goal is to obtain an allowable P/A stress for a particular column, P/A appears in both sides of the equation. The value of P/A, therefore, can be determined only with a trial-and-error process. The value finally obtained from the formula is actually the estimated load at which yielding begins in an eccentrically loaded column as its derivations made use of Hooke's law. The difference between the loads at which yielding begins and at which failure occurs may vary from only a few per cent to approximately 50 percent. The variation depends on such items as the slenderness ratio, direction of bending, shape of section, etc.

5-6. THE AISC FORMULAS

The AISC expressions were developed to incorporate the latest research information available concerning the behavior of steel columns. These formulas take into account the effect of residual stresses, the actual end restraint conditions of the columns, and the varying strengths of different steels. The important effect of residual stresses on the stress-strain curves was discussed in Sec. 4-2 and illustrated in Fig. 4-1. Different types of end restraints cause entirely different effective lengths and column strengths. A discussion of this subject was previously presented in Sec. 4-5 and is continued in Sec. 5-7 as it pertains to the AISC formulas.

The use of the AISC formulas results in more logical and economical designs than those given by the older expressions. Design by many other column formulas gives members which are appreciably overdesigned in the lower l/r range but the AISC formulas give fairly economical designs for all ranges of l/r. The expressions are rather complex to solve mathematically but as tables are available in the Steel Manual, designs can be made with little difficulty.

The AISC assumes that the upper limit of elastic buckling is defined by an average stress equal to $\frac{1}{2}$ of the yield point ($\frac{1}{2}F_y$). If this stress is equated to the Euler expression, the value of the slenderness ratio at this upper limit can be determined for a particular steel. This value is referred to as C_c, the slenderness ratio dividing elastic from inelastic buckling, and is determined as follows:

$$\frac{1}{2}\,F_y = \frac{\pi^2 E}{(L/r)^2}$$

$$= \frac{\pi^2 E}{C_c{}^2}$$

$$C_c = \sqrt{\frac{2\pi^2 E}{F_y}}$$

The values of C_c can be computed with little difficulty but the Steel

DESIGN OF COMPRESSION MEMBERS 79

Manual gives its values for each steel (126.1 for A36, 116.7 for the 42,000 psi yield point steels, etc.). For slenderness ratios less than C_c a parabolic formula (AISC Formula 1.5-1) is used. This is the Column Research Council equation for the ultimate strength of a centrally loaded column with a factor of safety applied.[4] In this expression F_a is the allowable axial stress (P/A) and K is the factor to be multiplied by the unsupported column lengths to give their estimated effective lengths (see Sec. 5-7).

$$Fa = \frac{\left[1 - \frac{(Kl/r)^2}{2C_c^2} \right] F_y}{\frac{5}{3} + \frac{3\,(Kl/r)}{8C_c} - \frac{(Kl/r)^3}{8C_c^3}} \qquad \text{(AISC Formula 1.5-1)}$$

For value of Kl/r greater than C_c the Euler formula is used. With a factor of safety of 1.92 (or 23/12) the expression becomes

$$F_a = \frac{12\pi^2 E}{23\,(Kl/r)^2} \qquad \text{(AISC Formula 1.5-2)}$$

Figure 5-2 shows the ranges in which the two AISC expressions are used.

FIG. 5-2

[4] Column Research Council, Engineering Foundation, *Guide to Design Criteria for Metal Compression Members*, B. G. Johnston (ed.), 2d ed. (John Wiley & Sons, New York, 1966).

Chase Building, Copley Square, Boston, Mass. (*Bethlehem Steel Company*.)

The denominator of Formula 1.5-1 is actually the factor of safety to be used and usually gives a value not much greater than the one used for axially loaded tension members. Tests have shown that short columns are not greatly affected by small eccentricities permitting the use of lower factors of safety. As columns become slenderer they become more sensitive to small imperfections and the factor of safety is increased up to 15 percent. It might also be noticed that the medium length columns are those in which residual stresses and initial column crookedness become quite important. The F. S. expression is a quarter sine wave which equals 5/3 when Kl/r is equal to zero and increases up to 23/12 when Kl/r equals C_c.

A third equation for compression members is given by the AISC for axially loaded bracing and secondary members when l/r exceeds 120.

$$F_{as} = \frac{F_a \text{ (by Formula 1.5-1 or 1.5-2)}}{1.6 - \dfrac{l}{200\,r}} \qquad \text{(AISC Formula 1.5-3)}$$

The AISC values given for bracing and secondary members are quite liberal because of the relative unimportance of these members. Another reason for the high allowable stresses available for the design of bracing and secondary members is that the persons writing the specifications took into account the appreciable end restraint which secondary members usually have. In other words, effective lengths have already been considered and *the designer should use the actual lengths of secondary and bracing members and not their effective lengths.* This discussion means that the secondary AISC column formulas should be used only for members which are fairly well braced against rotation and translation at the points where they are connected.

5-7. EFFECTIVE COLUMN LENGTHS

The value of Kl used in the AISC Specification is the *effective length* of the column which has previously been defined as the distance between the inflection points of the column. This distance was found to vary for different columns depending upon their types of end restraint. Should a column be perfectly fixed at each end [see Fig. 4-5 (b)] inflection points would occur at the quarter points when it is laterally deflected giving an effective length of $l/2$. Should the column be connected with

Column is in this position after sidesway and joint rotation

FIG. 5-3

frictionless pins [see Fig. 4-5(a)] the effective length would equal the actual length of the column.

Actually there are no perfect pin connections nor any perfect fixed ends, and the usual column falls in between the two extremes. This discussion would seem to indicate that column effective lengths always vary from an absolute minimum of $l/2$ to an absolute maximum of l, but there are exceptions to this rule. An example is given in Fig. 5-3 where a simple bent is shown. The base of each of the columns is pinned and the other end is free to rotate and move laterally (called sidesway). Examination of this figure will show that the effective length will exceed the actual length of the column as the elastic curve will theoretically take the shape of the curve of a pinned end column of twice its length. Table C 1.8.2 in the "Commentary on AISC Specification" in the Steel Handbook gives recommended effective lengths when ideal conditions are approximated. This table is reproduced here as Table 5-1 with the permission of the AISC. K is the theoretical value to be multiplied times the column length to give its theoretical effective length; however, more conservative values are recommended in the table for actual design practices.

TABLE 5-1

EFFECTIVE LENGTHS FOR MAIN MEMBERS ONLY*

	(a)	(b)	(c)	(d)	(e)	(f)
Buckled shape of column is shown by dashed line						
Theoretical K value	0.5	0.7	1.0	1.0	2.0	2.0
Recommended design value when ideal conditions are approximated	0.65	0.80	1.2	1.0	2.10	2.0
End condition code			Rotation fixed and translation fixed			
			Rotation free and translation fixed			
			Rotation fixed and translation free			
			Rotation free and translation free			

A heavy column showing base plate with
combination welded and high-strength
bolted connection. (*Bethlehem Steel
Company.*)

The use of these latter values will be illustrated in several design problems in the pages to follow and Kl will be referred to as the effective
length of the column.

The selection of the K value to be used for a particular column has
given practicing engineers as much trouble as any other part of the
AISC Specification. On many occasions K values have been selected
which are too large, resulting in overdesigned columns with resulting
economy losses. The difficulty seems to lie in distinguishing symmetrical
buckling from sidesway buckling. When sidesway buckling occurs a
smaller load can be supported.

When translation of the tops of the columns is clearly prevented as
by diagonal bracing, shear walls, attachment to adjacent buildings, etc.
(read Sec. 1.8.2 of the AISC Specification), symmetrical buckling will
occur. For such cases as these the column effective lengths can be no
greater than their actual lengths. Values of K equal to 1.0 can be conservatively assumed or lesser values estimated from parts (a), (b), or (d)

of Table 5-1 (AISC Table C.1.8.2) or by charts prepared for this purpose such as the "sidesway prevented" chart given by the Column Research Council in their publication *Guide to Design Criteria for Metal Compression Members*. A large percentage of the columns designed by the usual structural designer fall into this class.

It should be realized that most of the columns which the structural engineer has to design serve as members of frames and have effective lengths which are controlled by the amounts of restraint applied to their ends by the other members of the frame and by the walls of the structure itself. As no column ends are completely fixed or perfectly pinned, the designer may wish to interpolate between the values given in the table, the interpolation to be based on his judgment of the actual restraint conditions.

For most buildings, sidesway is substantially eliminated by masonry walls, but for buildings built with light curtain walls and large column spacings or for tall buildings built without a positive system of lateral bracing sidesway is appreciable. For such cases the bending stiffness of the structural frame provides most of the lateral support.[5] The effective lengths of columns for such laterally unsupported continuous frames are discussed in Chap. 8.

5-8. DESIGN OF COLUMNS WITH AISC FORMULAS

Examples 5-5 through 5-9 illustrate the design of different columns using the AISC expression. In part (a) of Example 5-5 the solution is made by substituting into the formulas but in the remainder of this example and in the other examples the Steel Handbook tables are used to simplify the calculations. It should be remembered that the yield points of several high-strength steels vary for different thicknesses (unless specially alloyed to keep values equal for thicker members); therefore, when these steels are involved it is necessary to carefully determine their yield stresses as described on pages 1-6 and 1-7 of the AISC Manual.

In part (b) of Example 5-6 a W section with cover plates is selected to support the column load. The steel mills roll a special shape, the W 14 × 320, which is called the column core section and is specifically designed for use with cover plates. It has wider and thinner flanges than some of the heavier W sections with the result that the cost of drilling flange holes is reduced.

EXAMPLE 5-5. Select a W section for the column and load shown in Fig. 5-4 using (a) A36 steel and (b) A441 steel.

---

[5] *Manual of Steel Construction* (New York: American Institute of Steel Construction, 1970). pp. 5-137 through 5-140.

600 k

15'

600 k

FIG. 5-4

Solution: (*a*) Using A36 steel:
Assume that the allowable F_a is 19.5 ksi and that the area required is $600/19.5 = 30.8$ sq in.

Try W 14 × 103 ($A = 30.3, r = 3.72$)

Effective length from Table 5-1 (or Table C 1.8.1. in AISC Specification Commentary)

$$Kl = (0.65) \ (15) = 9.75 \, \text{ft}$$
$$\frac{Kl}{r} = \frac{(12) \ (9.75)}{3.72} = 31.4$$

The value of F_a is taken from Table 1-36 in Sec. 5 of the AISC Specification as there is no need to laboriously substitute into AISC Formula 1.5.1.

$$F_a = 19.84 \, \text{ksi}$$

Allowable $P = (19.84) \ (30.3) = 601 \, \text{k} > 600 \, \text{k}$ \hfill (OK)

Use W 14 × 103

(*b*) Using A441 steel:
·Assume that the allowable F_a is 26 ksi and that the area required is $600/26 = 23.1$ sq in.

Try W 14 × 78 ($A = 22.9$ sq in., $r = 3.00$, Group 2 AISC; therefore, $F_y = 50,000$)

$$\frac{Kl}{r} = \frac{12 \times 9.75}{3.00} = 39$$

Allowable $F_a = 25.97$ ksi (from table)

Allowable $P = (25.97)\ (22.9) = 594$ k < 600 k

Use W14 $\times$ 78 (slightly overstressed)

EXAMPLE 5-6.　(a) Select a W section for the load and column shown in Fig. 515 using A441 steel.　(b) Using A36 steel and assuming a W 14 $\times$ 320 is on hand select PLs so the section will be satisfactory for the conditions of Fig. 5-5.

2,700 k

15'

2,700 k

FIG. 5-5

Solution: (a) Using A441 steel:

Assume that the allowable F_a is 22 ksi and that the area required is $2{,}700/22 = 122.8$ sq in.

Try W14 $\times$ 426 ($A = 125$, $r = 4.34$, Group 4 AISC; therefore, $F_y = 42{,}000$)

$$Kl = (1.0)\ (15) = 15\text{ ft}$$

$$\frac{Kl}{r} = \frac{12 \times 15}{4.34} = 41.4$$

Allowable $F_a = 21.94$ ksi

Allowable $P = (21.94)\ (125) = 2{,}740$ k $> 2{,}700$ k　　　　(OK)

Use W 14 $\times$ 426

(*b*) Using A36 steel:

Assume that the allowable F_a is 19 ksi and the area required is $2{,}700/19 = 142$ sq in.

Try W 14 $\times$ 320 column core section ($A = 94.1$ sq. in.)

DESIGN OF COMPRESSION MEMBERS 87

With 1 cover PL 20 $\times$ 1¼ each flange = 50.00 sq in.

Total area = 144.1 sq in.

$I_x = 4140 + (2) (25) (9.03)^2 = 8,201$ in.[4]

$I_y = 1640 + (\frac{1}{12}) (2.50) (20)^3 = 3,302$ in.[4]

$$r = \sqrt{\frac{3,302}{144.1}} = 4.79$$

$Kl = (1.0) (15) = 15$ ft

$$\frac{Kl}{r} = \frac{(12) (15)}{4.79} = 37.6$$

Allowable $F_a = 19.38$ ksi

Allowable $P = (19.38) (144.1) = 2,793$ k $> 2,700$ k

Use W 14 $\times$ 320 with 1 cover PL 20 $\times$ 1¼ each flange

EXAMPLE 5-7. Select a pair of unequal leg angles with a ⅜-in. gusset plate between them using A36 steel and the AISC Specification to support a 32-k load. The member is to be 19 ft long and is assumed to be secondary.

Solution: Assume that the allowable F_a is 6.5 ksi and that the area required is $32/6.5 = 4.92$ sq in.

Try 2 Ls 4 $\times$ 3 $\times$ ⅜ $(A = 4.97, r = 1.26)$

$$\frac{l}{r} = \frac{12 \times 19}{1.26} = 181$$

Using actual length and not the effective length for a secondary member.

Allowable $F_a = 6.56$ ksi

Allowable $P = (6.56) (4.97) = 32.6$ k > 32 k   (OK)

Use 2 Ls 4 $\times$ 3 $\times$ ⅜

EXAMPLE 5-8. Select a pair of channels for the column and load shown in Fig. 5-6. A36 steel and the AISC Specification are to be used. For connection purposes the back-to-back distance of the channels is to be 12 in.

Solution: Assume that the allowable F_a is 17.5 ksi and that the area required is $280/17.5 = 16.0$ sq in.

Try 2 C 12 $\times$ 30s $(A = 17.64, r_x = 4.29)$

$I_y = (2) (5.14) + (17.64) (5.33)^2 = 507$ in.[4]

$$r_y = \sqrt{\frac{507}{17.64}} = 5.37$$

$$Kl = (1) \ (20) \ = 20 \text{ ft}$$

$$\frac{Kl}{r} = \frac{(12) \ (20)}{4.28} = 56$$

Allowable $F_a = 17.81$ ksi

Allowable $P = (17.81) \ (17.64) = 314 \text{ k} > 280 \text{ k}$ (OK)

Use 2 C 12 × 30s

In the previous column examples the lesser value of the radius of gyration has been used. For some conditions it may be necessary to use the larger radius. Steel columns may be built into a substantial masonry wall in such a manner that the column is fully supported in the weaker direction. The designer, however, should be quite careful in assuming complete lateral support parallel to the wall, because a poorly built wall will not provide 100 percent lateral support.

Columns may often be supported at different intervals in one direction than in the other, as where girts running parallel to the exterior walls of a building frame into the sides of the columns. For such cases the columns are probably turned so that their stronger axes face the larger unsupported lengths. The design will be governed by the larger of the two slenderness ratios. Example 5-9 illustrates the design of a column which is braced at different intervals about its x and y axes. For another example the student is referred to Example 1 in the column section of the Steel Manual.

EXAMPLE 5-9. A W 12 column of A36 steel is to be designed to support an axial load of 400 k. The column is assumed to have an effective length with respect to its strong or major axis of 24 ft, and 18 ft for its weak or minor axis.

Solution: Assume that the allowable $F_a = 16$ ksi and that the area required is $400/16 = 25$ sq in.

Try W 12 × 85 ($A = 25.0$ sq in., $r_x = 5.38$, $r_y = 3.07$)

$$\frac{Kl_x}{r_x} = \frac{12 \times 24}{5.38} = 53.5$$

$$\frac{Kl_y}{r_y} = \frac{12 \times 18}{3.07} = 70.3$$

Allowable $F_a = 16.40$ ksi

Allowable $P = (16.4)(25.1) = 410\,k > 400\,k$ (OK)

Use W 12 × 85

5-9. LACING AND TIE PLATES

The necessity for built up compression members in large buildings and bridges has previously been discussed in Chap. 4. When members are built up from more than one section it is necessary for them to be connected or laced together across their open sides. The purpose of lacing or lattice work is to hold the various parts parallel and the correct distance apart and to equalize the stress distribution between the various parts. The student will understand the necessity for lacing if he considers a built-up member consisting of several sections (such as the four-angle member of Fig. 4-2) which supports a heavy compressive load. Each of the parts will tend to buckle laterally unless they are tied together to act as a unit in supporting the load. In addition to lacing it is necessary to have tie plates (also called stay plates or batten plates) as near the ends of the member as possible and at intermediate points if the lacing is interrupted. Parts (a) and (b) of Fig. 5-7 show arrangements of tie plates and lacing. Other possibilities are shown in parts (c) and (d) of the same figure.

The failure of several structures in the past has been attributed to inadequate lacing of built-up compression members. Perhaps the best-known example was the failure of the Quebec Bridge in 1907. Following its collapse the general opinion was that the lattice work of the compression chords was too weak and resulted in failure. This disaster brought home to the engineering profession the importance of carefully designed lacing.

Dimensions of tie plates and lacing are usually controlled by the specifications. The AISC (Sec. 1.18.3) says that the tie plates shall have a thickness at least equal to $\frac{1}{50}$ the distance between the connection lines

Fig. 5-7

of rivets, bolts or welds and shall have a length parallel to the axis of the main member at least equal to the distance between the connection lines.

Lacing usually consists of flat bars but may occasionally consist of angles, perforated cover plates, channels or other rolled sections. These pieces must be so spaced that the individual parts being connected will not have l/r values between connections which exceed the governing value for the entire built-up member. Lacing is assumed to be subjected to a shearing stress normal to the member equal to not less than 2 percent of the total compression in the member. The AISC column formulas are used to design the lacing in the usual manner. Slenderness ratios are limited to 140 for single lacing and 200 for double lacing. Double lacing must be used if the distance between connection lines is greater than 15 in.

Rather than using tie plates and lacing bars it is permissible to use continuous cover plates over the open sides of the built-up sections. Access holes are necessary, and these plates are referred to as perforated cover plates. Stress concentrations and secondary bending stresses are usually neglected but lateral shearing stresses must be checked as they must be for other types of lattice work. Perforated cover plates are becoming popular with an increasing percentage of engineers because they possess these advantages:

1. They are easily fabricated with modern gas cutting methods.

2. Some specifications permit the inclusion of their net areas in the effective section of the main members, provided the holes are made in accordance with their empirical requirements which have been developed on the basis of extensive research.

3. Painting of the members is probably simplified as compared to ordinary lacing bars.

Example 5-10 illustrates the design of lacing and end tie plates for the built up column of Example 5-8. Bridge specifications are somewhat different in their lacing requirements from the AISC but the design procedure is much the same.

EXAMPLE 5-10. Using the AISC Specification design bolted single lacing for the column of Example 5-8. Reference is made to Fig. 5-8.

FIG. 5-8

Solution: Distance between lines of bolts is 8.5 in. < 15 in.; therefore, single lacing OK.

Assume an inclination of 60° with axis of member. Length of channels between lacing connections is 8.5/cos 30° = 9.8 in., and l/r of 1 channel between connections is 9.8/0.77 = 12.7 < 56, which is l/r of main member.

Force on lacing bar:

Eversharp, Inc. building at Milford, Connecticut (*Bethlehem Steel Company*).

$$V = 0.02\,P = (0.02)\ (280) = 5.6\ \text{k}$$

$$\tfrac{1}{2}\,V = 2.8\ \text{k} = \text{shearing force on each plane of lacing}$$

Force on bar $= (9.8/8.5)\ (2.8) = 3.22\ \text{k}$

Properties of a flat bar:

$$I = \tfrac{1}{12}\,bt^3$$

$$A = bt$$

$$r = \sqrt{\frac{\tfrac{1}{12}\,bt^3}{bt}}$$

$$r = 0.288\,t$$

Design of bar:

$$\text{Maximum } \frac{l}{r} = 140$$

$$\frac{9.8}{0.288\, t} = 140$$

$$t = 0.243 \text{ in. (try } \tfrac{1}{4}\text{-in. flat bar)}$$

$$\frac{l}{r} = \frac{9.8}{(0.288)\,(0.250)} = 136$$

Allowable $F_a = 8.78$ ksi   (for secondary members)

$$\text{Area required} = \frac{3.22}{8.78} = 0.367 \text{ sq in. } (1.47 \times \tfrac{1}{4})$$

Minimum edge distance if $\tfrac{3}{4}$-in. rivet used $= 1\tfrac{1}{4}$ in.

Use $\tfrac{1}{4} \times 2\tfrac{1}{2}$ bar

Design of end tie plates:

Minimum length $= 8.5$ in.

With t not less than $\tfrac{1}{50}$ distance between rivet lines,

$$t = (\tfrac{1}{50})\,(8.5) = 0.17 \text{ in.}$$

Use $\tfrac{3}{16} \times 8\tfrac{1}{2} \times 11\tfrac{1}{2}$ end tie PLs

5-10. BASE PLATES FOR CONCENTRICALLY LOADED COLUMNS

The allowable compressive stress in a concrete or other type of masonry footing is much smaller than it is in a steel column. When a steel column is supported by a footing it is necessary for the column load to be spread over a sufficient area to keep the footing from being overstressed. Loads from steel columns are transferred through a steel base plate to a fairly large area of the footing below. (It will be noted that a footing performs a related function in that it spreads the load over an even larger area so that the underlying soil will not be overstressed.)

The base plates for steel columns can be welded directly to the columns or they can be fastened by means of some type of riveted or welded lug angles. These connection methods are illustrated in Fig. 5-9. A base plate welded directly to the column is shown in part (a) of the figure. For small columns these plates are probably shop-welded to the columns but for larger columns it may be necessary to ship the plates separately and set them to the correct elevations. The columns are then

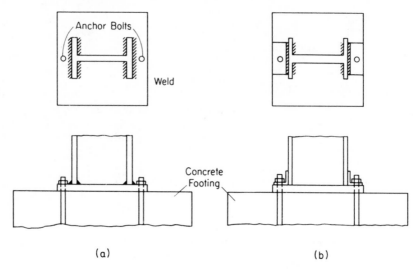

FIG. 5-9. Column base plates.

set and connected to the footing with anchor bolts which pass through the lug angles which have been shop-welded to the columns. This type of arrangement is shown in part (b) of the figure. Some designers like to use lug angles on both flanges and web.

The method of design suggested here is the one which is recommended by the Steel Manual. To analyze the base plate shown in Fig. 5-10 the column is assumed to apply a total load P to the base plate, and this load is assumed to be transmitted uniformly through the base plate to the footing below with a value of F_p psi (P/A). The footing will push back with a pressure of F_p psi and tend to curl up the cantilevered parts of the base plate outside the column as shown in Fig. 5-10. This pressure also tends to push up the part of the base plate between the flanges of the column, but the Steel Manual permits this bending to be almost ignored and the plate designed for the outside bending with points of maximum moment being assumed to occur near the contact of the flange with the plate.

With reference to Fig. 5-10 the Steel Manual suggests that maximum moments in a base plate occur at distances approximately 0.80b and 0.95d apart. The bending moment is calculated at each of these sections and the larger value used to determine the plate thickness needed. This method of analysis is only a rough approximation of the true conditions because the actual plate stresses are caused by a combination of bending in two directions.

FIG. 5-10

From Fig. 5-10 the following moment expressions can be written for the two critical sections considering in each case a 1-in. width of plate:

$$M = F_p n \, \frac{n}{2} = \frac{F_p n^2}{2}$$

$$M = F_p m \, \frac{m}{2} = \frac{F_p m^2}{2}$$

The section modulus of a 1-in. width of plate of t thickness is:

$$S = \frac{I}{C} = \frac{(\frac{1}{12}) \, (1) \, (t^3)}{t/2} = \frac{t^2}{6}$$

Since the stress is $Mc/I = M/S$, the required thickness of the base plate can be determined:

$$F_b = \frac{M}{S} = \frac{F_p \dfrac{m^2}{2}}{t^2/6}$$

$$= \frac{3F_p m^2}{t^2}$$

$$t = \sqrt{\frac{3\,F_p m^2}{F_b}}$$

Similarly in the other direction,

$$t = \sqrt{\frac{3\,F_p n^2}{F_b}}$$

Knowing the values of m and n, the thickness of plate required can be calculated. The example to follow illustrates the design of a column base plate. The allowable value of stress in a bearing plate by the AISC is $0.75F_y$ (27,000 psi for A36 steel). Before the final dimensions of the base plates are selected reference should be made to the Steel Manual so that standard sizes will be used. In this way the designer will be insured of economy and promptness of delivery. The Steel Manual includes a table entitled "Column Base Plates" which presents sizes of column base plates designed for the maximum column loads which various column sections can support. The plates in this table for each column section were selected for the highest probable load which the section could feasibly carry (i.e., the allowable column load with the smallest feasible Kl for the column). Selection of plates from these tables will normally give sizes which are decidedly overdesigned; therefore, it is recommended that they be individually designed as illustrated in Example 5-11.

Should the bases of the columns be transmitting moments, a situation normally occurring in mill buildings and in tier buildings designed to resist lateral forces, angles anchored to the footing which are designed for uplift forces can be used. Several excellent references are available for designing moment resisting base plates.[6,7]

EXAMPLE 5-11. Design a column base plate with A36 steel for a W 12 × 65 column and a load of 360 k. The column is to be supported by a concrete footing with an allowable bearing pressure of 750 psi. The dimensions are as shown in Fig. 5-11.

[6] William McGuire, *Steel Structures* (Englewood Cliffs, N.J.: Prentice-Hall, Inc., 1968), pp. 987–1004.
[7] John E. Lothers, *Design In Structural Steel*, 2d ed. (Englewood Cliffs, N.J.: Prentice-Hall, Inc., 1965), pp. 241–260.

FIG. 5-11

Solution:

$$\text{Area required} = \frac{360,000}{750} = 480 \text{ sq in. } (22 \times 22 \text{ PLs} = 484)$$

$$F_p = \frac{360,000}{484} = 744 \text{ psi}$$

$$n = 6.20 \text{ in.}$$

$$t = \sqrt{\frac{3F_p n^2}{F_b}} = \sqrt{\frac{(3)\ (744)\ (6.20)^2}{27,000}}$$

$$t = 1.78 \text{ in.}$$

Use $1\frac{7}{8} \times 22 \times 1' - 10''$ PLs

PROBLEMS

5-1. Using the 1920 AREA formula ($P/A = 15,000 - 50 \, l/r$, with a maximum value of 12,500 psi and a maximum l/r of 120) determine the allowable axial load for each of the following compression members:

(a) an 18 ft W 12 × 40 (Ans. 111 k)
(b) a 9 ft S 15 × 50 (Ans. 144 k)
(c) a 4 ft C 9 × 20 (Ans. 66 k)
(d) a 12 ft HP 14 × 73 (Ans. 268 k)

5-2. Using the AREA formula given in Prob. 5-1 determine the allowable axial compressive load which each of the following members can support:

(a) a 22 ft W 14 × 246
(b) a 15 ft WT 7 × 24
(c) a 7 ft L 4 × 3½ × ½
(d) a 4 ft M 12 × 11.8

5-3. Determine the allowable concentric load which each of the compression members shown in the accompanying illustration can support. Use the column formula given in Prob. 5-1.

PROB. 5-3

5-4. Select a W 14 section to support a 300 k axial load for an unsupported length of 16 ft using the column expression of Prob. 5-1.

5-5. Determine the allowable axial compressive load which can be supported by each of the sections shown in the accompanying illustration. Use the formula, $P/A = 15,000 - \frac{1}{4} (l/r)^2$.

PROB. 5-5

(c)   (Ans. 322 k)   (d)   (Ans. 740 k)

PROB. 5-5 (continued)

5-6. Select the lightest W12 section which will support an axial compressive load of 320 k for an unsupported length of 14'-6". Use the column formula $P/A = 15,000 - \frac{1}{4}(l/r)^2$.

5-7. A chord member of a bridge truss is to be 13 ft long and is to support an axial compressive load of 325 k. Using the column equation $P/A = 15,000 - \frac{1}{4}(l/r)^2$ select the lightest satisfactory W section. (Ans. W 14 × 78)

5-8. The following parabolic expression is to be used to select the most economical W12 column section to support a 250 k axial load

$$P/A = 17,000 - 0.40(l/r)^2$$

The column is to be 30 ft long and is to be laterally supported in the weak direction at the one-third points.

5-9. Select a W10 section to support an axial compressive load of 120 k. The unsupported length of the member is 30 ft and the Gordon-Rankine formula to follow is to be used

$$\frac{P}{A} = \frac{18,000}{1 + \dfrac{(l/r)^2}{18,000}}$$

(Ans. W 10 × 49)

5-10. Using the Gordon-Rankine formula of Prob. 5-9 determine the maximum axial compressive load which a W 12 × 50 with a $\frac{5}{8}$ × 12 cover plate bolted to each flange can support if it has an unsupported length of 34 ft.

5-11. Using the AISC Specification determine the allowable axial loads which the following columns can support:

(a) a W 8 × 40 with fixed ends, $l = 16'$-6", A36 steel (Ans. 202 k)

(b) a W 12 × 99 with pinned ends, $l = 20'$-0", A36 steei (Ans. 454 k)

(c) a W 10 × 60 with one fixed and the other pinned, $l = 24'$-6", $F_y = 45$ ksi (Ans. 280 k)

(d) a W 14 × 184 with fixed ends, $l = 22'$-0", $F_y = 45$ ksi (Ans. 1256 k)

(e) a Pipe 10 std. with pinned ends, $l = 20'$-0", A36 steel (Ans. 201 k)

(f) two $8 \times 8 \times \frac{3}{4}$ Ls separated $\frac{3}{8}''$ (for gueset PL at ends), pinned ends $l = 24'\text{-}6''$, A36 steel (Ans. 239 k)

5-12. Determine the allowable axial loads which the columns shown in the accompanying illustration can support. Use the AISC Specification and A36 steel.

(a)

(b)

(c)

(d)

PROB. 5-12

5-13. Several building columns are to be designed using A36 steel and the AISC Specification. Select the lightest available W sections for these columns which are described as follows:

(a) $P = 400$ k, $l = 16$ ft, fixed ends (Ans. W 12 × 72)

(b) $P = 180$ k, $l = 15$ ft, fixed at bottom, free at top (Ans. W 12 × 65)

(c) $P = 800$ k, $l = 20$ ft, pinned ends (Ans. W 14 × 158)

(d) $P = 2100$ k, $l = 16$ ft, fixed at bottom, pinned at top (Ans. W 14 × 370)

5-14. Using the AISC Specification and A36 steel select the lightest available rolled sections (W, HP, square, rectangular or round tubing) which are adequate for the following situations:

(a) $P = 100$ k, $l = 18$ ft, fixed ends

(b) $P = 275$ k, $l = 10$ ft, one end pinned the other fixed

(c) $P = 200$ k, $l = 14$ ft, pinned ends

5-15. Assuming axial loads only, select W sections for an interior column of the frame shown in the accompanying illustration. Use A36 steel and the AISC Specification. Each column section can be used for one or two stories before it is spliced, whichever seems advisable. Miscellaneous data: concrete weighs 150 lbs/ft³. LL on roof = 40 psf (includes roofing). LL on interior floors = 80 psf. Partition load on interior floors = 15 psf. All joints pinned. Frames 30 ft on center. (Ans. Several possible solutions such as W 14 × 61 top two stories and W 14 × 136 bottom two stories; or W 12 × 65 top two stories and W 12 × 133 bottom two stories; etc.)

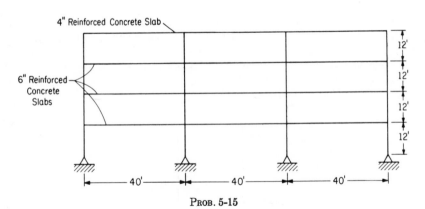

PROB. 5-15

5-16. A 27-ft column is laterally supported in the weak direction at its mid-depth. Select the lightest W section which can adequately support an axial load of 300 k. Allowable $P/A = 15,000 - \frac{1}{4} (l/r)^2$

5-17. A W section is to be selected to support an axial compressive load of 300 k. The member which is to be 24 ft long and is to be pinned top and bottom has lateral support (pinned) supplied in the weak direction at mid-depth. Select the section using A36 steel and the AISC Specification. (Ans. W12 × 58)

5-18. Repeat Prob. 5-17 if lateral support (pinned) is supplied in the weak direction at the one-third points.

5-19. Twenty-seven-ft steel columns for a building are to be braced at the one-third points for the minor axis. If the columns are to support axial loads of 90 k each and are to consist of A36 steel, select a C or MC section for each using the AISC Specification. Assume top and bottom supports are fixed and lateral supports are pinned. (Ans. MC 10 × 25.3)

5-20. Four 4 × 4 × ½ angles are used to form the member shown in the accompanying illustration. The member is 20 ft long, has pinned ends and consists of A36 steel. Determine the maximum allowable axial compressive load which the member can support according to the AISC. Design single lacing and end tie plates assuming connections are made to the angles with ¾-in. bolts.

18"

├──────18"──────┤

Prob. 5-20

5-21. Select a pair of channels to support an axial compressive load of 300 k. The member is to be 24 ft long with both ends pinned and is to be arranged as shown in the accompanying illustration. Use the AISC Specification, A36 steel and design single lacing and end tie plates assuming ¾-in. bolts are to be used for connections. (Ans. Use 2 C 12 × 30s with ¼ × 14 × 0'-11½" end tie plates and 11⁄32 × 2½ × 1'-4" single lacing bars at 45°)

├──8"──┤

Prob. 5-21

5-22. A W 12 × 53 supports an axial load of 180 k. Using the AISC Specification and A36 steel, design a base plate for the column if the supporting reinforced concrete footing has an allowable bearing pressure of 750 psi.

5-23. Design a column base plate for a W 14 × 111 supporting an axial load of 575 k. The supporting footing has an allowable bearing pressure of 750 psi. Use A36 steel and the AISC Specification. (Ans. Several plates can be selected, one which is satisfactory is 2⅜ × 28 × 2′ − 4″

5-24. An W 8 × 24 column supporting a 75 k axial load is bearing on a brick wall with an allowable bearing pressure of 500 psi. Design a base plate for the column using A36 steel and the AISC Specification.

5-25. A W 14 × 74 column has a 2 × 20 × 1′-8″ base plate which rests on a reinforced concrete spread footing with an allowable unit bearing pressure of 1125 psi. What is the maximum allowable axial load which this bearing plate can support? Use A36 steel and the AISC Specification. (Ans. 405 k)

chapter **6**

DESIGN OF BEAMS

6-1. TYPES OF BEAMS

Beams are usually said to be members which support transverse loads. They are probably thought of as being used in horizontal positions and subjected to gravity or vertical loads; but there are frequent exceptions— rafters, for example.

Harrison Avenue Bridge, Beaumont, Tex. (*Bethlehem Steel Company.*)

Among the many types of beams are joists, lintels, spandrels, stringers, and floor beams. *Joists* are the closely spaced beams supporting the floors and roofs of buildings, while *lintels* are the beams over openings in

104

masonry walls such as windows and doors. A *spandrel beam* supports the exterior walls of buildings and perhaps part of the floor and hallway loads. The discovery that steel beams as a part of a structural frame could support masonry walls is said to have permitted the construction of to-day's "skyscrapers." *Stringers* are the beams in bridge floors running parallel to the roadway, whereas *floor beams* are the larger beams in many bridge floors which are perpendicular to the roadway of the bridge and are used to transfer the floor loads from the stringers to the support-ing girders or trusses. The term *girder* is rather loosely used but usually indicates a large beam and perhaps one into which smaller beams are framed. These and other types of beams are discussed in the paragraphs to follow.

6-2. THE FLEXURE FORMULA

Included in the items which need to be considered in beam design are moments, shears, crippling, buckling, lateral support, deflection, and perhaps fatigue. Beams will probably be selected which satisfactorily resist the bending moments and then checked to see if any of the other items are critical. To select a beam for a given situation the maximum moment is calculated for the assumed loading and a section having that much resisting moment is selected from the AISC Manual.

The resisting moment of a particular section can be computed with the flexure formula $(F = Mc/I)$. This expression and the P/A expression are perhaps the most famous of all formulas to civil engineers. The fre-quency of their application is illustrated by the fact that some of the more modest structural designers often say, "All I know is P/A and Mc/I."

In the flexure formula f is the fiber stress in the outermost fiber a distance c from the neutral axis and I is the moment of inertia of the cross section. It should be remembered that this formula is limited to stress situations below the elastic limit because it is based on the usual elastic assumptions: a plane section before bending remains a plane sec-tion after bending; stress is proportional to strain, etc.

The value of I/c is constant for a particular section and is known as the section modulus. If a beam is to be designed for a particular bending moment M and for a certain allowable stress F the section modulus re-quired to provide a beam of sufficient bending strength can be obtained from the flexure formula as follows:

$$\frac{M}{F} = \frac{I}{c} = S = \text{the section modulus}$$

6-3. SELECTION OF BEAMS

The W shapes will normally prove to be the most economical beam sections and they have largely replaced channels and I beams for beam usage. Channels are sometimes used for beams subjected to light loads, such as purlins, and in places where clearances available require narrow flanges. They have very little resistance to lateral forces and need to be braced as illustrated by the sag rod problem in Chap. 3. The W shapes have more steel concentrated in their flanges than do S beams and thus have larger section moduli values for the same weights. They are relatively wide and have appreciable lateral stiffness. (The small amount of space devoted to S beams in the AISC Manual clearly shows how much their use has decreased from former years. They are today used primarily for special situations as where narrow flange widths are desirable, or where shearing forces are very high, or where the greater flange thickness next to the web may be desirable where lateral bending occurs as perhaps with crane rails.)

It is rare for beams to be made from bars, angles, or T sections because these shapes have low section modulus values in comparison to their weights and thus little resistance to bending.

A table is given in the AISC Manual entitled "Allowable Stress Design Selection Table." From this table steel shapes having sufficient section moduli can be quickly selected. Two important items should be remembered in selecting shapes. These are as follows:

1. These steel sections cost so many cents per pound and it is therefore desirable to select the lightest possible shape having the required section modulus (assuming that the resulting section is one which will reasonably fit into the structure). The table has the sections arranged in various groups having certain ranges of section moduli. The heavily typed section at the top of each group is the lightest section in that group and the others are arranged successively in the order of their section moduli. Normally the deeper sections will have the lightest weights giving the required section moduli, and they will be generally selected unless their depth causes a problem in obtaining the desired headroom, in which case a shallower but heavier section will be selected.

2. The section moduli values in the table are given about the horizontal axes for beams in their upright positions. If a beam is to be turned on its side the proper section modulus can be found in the detailed tables entitled "Properties For Designing" in the handbook. A W shape turned on its side may only be from 5 to 15 percent as strong as one in the upright position when subjected to gravity loads. In the same manner, the strength of a wood joist with the actual dimensions 2 × 10 in. turned on its side would only be 20 percent as strong as in the upright position (the percentage being based on the relative values of the section moduli).

The example problems to follow illustrate the design of steel beams whose compression flanges have lateral support, thus permitting the use of the same allowable stresses in the tension and compression flanges. Beams without sufficient lateral support for the compression flanges are considered in Secs. 6-5 and 6-6.

In each of these examples the weight of the beam to be selected must be included in the calculation of the bending moment to be resisted, as the beam must support itself as well as the external loads. The estimates of beam weight are very close here because the author was fortunately able to perform a little preliminary paperwork before making his estimate. The student is not expected to be able to glance at a problem and estimate exactly the weight of the beam required. Following the same procedure as did the author, however, he can do a little figuring on the side and make a very reasonable estimate. For instance, he could calculate the moment due to the external loads only, obtain the required section modulus, and select a beam having the required value. From this beam size he should be able to make a very good estimate of the weight of the final beam section which will often be a little larger than the trial beam size.

EXAMPLE 6-1. Select a beam section for the span and loading shown in Fig. 6-1, assuming full lateral support is provided for the compression flange by the floor above. Allowable bending stresses are 24,000 psi.

4.4 k/ft (not including beam weight)

FIG. 6-1

Solution: Assume beam weight = 61 lb/ft

$$M = \frac{wl^2}{8} = \frac{(4.461)(21)^2}{8} = 246 \text{ ft-k}$$

$$\text{Required section modulus} = \frac{(12)(246)}{24} = 123 \text{ in.}^3$$

The possible solutions include the following: (a) A W 21 × 62 is the section which has the closest S on the safe side. (b) But a W 24 × 61 is the most economical solution. (c) Should depth be restricted, W 18 × 70 or even a W 16 × 78 (very uneconomical) could be selected.

Use W 24 × 61

EXAMPLE 6-2. A 5-in. reinforced concrete slab is to be supported with steel beams 8 ft 0 in. on centers. The beams, which will span 20 ft, are assumed to be simply supported. If the concrete slab is designed to support a live load of 100 psf, determine the lightest steel section required to support the slab. The compression flange of the beam will be incorporated in the concrete slab and is thus laterally supported. The concrete weighs 150 lb/ft³ and the allowable bending stresses in the steel are 24,000 psi.

Solution:

$$DL: \quad Slab = (8)\left(\frac{5}{12}\right)(150) = 500 \text{ lb/ft}$$

Estimated beam weight $\quad= 30$

LL : $\quad 8 \times 100 \quad\quad\quad = 800$

Total uniform load $\quad\quad = \overline{1,330 \text{ lb/ft}}$

$$M = \frac{(1.33)\,(20)^2}{8} = 66.5 \text{ ft-k}$$

$$S_{req.} = \frac{(12)\,(66.5)}{24} = 33.2 \text{ in.}^3$$

Use W 14 × 26

The limiting moment permitted by the allowable stress method is the moment at which the stress in the outermost fibers first reaches the yield point. The true bending strength of a beam, however, is larger than this commonly used value because the beam will not fail at this condition. The outermost fibers will yield and the stress in the inner fibers will increase until they reach the yield stress, etc., until the whole section is plastified (see Sec. 21-3). It will be shown in Chap. 21 that before local failure will occur moments must be produced approximately 12 percent larger than those which will first produce the yield stress in the outermost fibers of W shapes.

The plastification process just mentioned is correct only if the beam remains stable in other ways: that is it must have sufficient lateral support to prevent lateral buckling of the compression flange (see Sec. 6-5) and it must have a sufficiently stocky profile to prevent local buckling.

The AISC gives different allowable bending stresses for different conditions. For most cases the allowable bending stress is as follows:

$$F_b = 0.66\, F_y$$

This expression can be used to determine the allowable bending stress in the extreme fibers of compact hot-rolled shapes and built-up members (not including members consisting of A514 steel which has $F_y = 90$ or 100 ksi nor girders built up with different yield stress steels called hybrid girders) which are symmetrical about and loaded in the plane of their minor axis and which meet the other requirements of Sec. 1.5.1.4.1 of the AISC.

A compact section is one which is capable of developing its plastic moment capacity before any local buckling occurs. To qualify as compact a section must meet the requirements of subparagraphs a through d of Sec. 1.5.1.4.1. Nearly all W and S shapes of A36 steel and a large percentage of those shapes made from higher strength steels are compact.

For noncompact laterally supported sections the AISC requires a reduction in F_b below 0.66 F_y while for laterally supported compact sections the allowable stress is equal to 0.66 F_y. The previously mentioned selection table has the shapes which are noncompact clearly identified by indicating the yield stresses above which they will be noncompact. Values are given for each shape for F_y' (the theoretical yield stress at which the shape becomes noncompact based on the flange proportion requirements) and F_y'' (the theoretical yield stress at which the shape becomes noncompact based on the web proportion requirements).

For a section to be compact the AISC says the half-flange width-to-thickness ratio should not exceed $52.2/\sqrt{F_y}$ (in which case, $F_b = 0.66\ F_y$, assuming the web is compact and the other provisions of Sec. 1.5.1.4.1 are met). If the ratio is greater than $95/\sqrt{F_y}$ it is noncompact and $F_b = 0.60$ F_y, but if it is in between the two values it is said to be *partially compact*. For partially compact sections a linear transition is provided between 0.66 F_y and 0.60 F_y by AISC Formula 1.5-5 as follows:

$$F_b = F_y \left[0.733 - 0.0014 \left(\frac{b_f}{2t_f} \right) \sqrt{F_y} \right]$$

The purpose of this formula is to avoid some of the abruptness of the transition from an allowable stress of 0.66 F_y to 0.60 F_y. If the yield stress of the steel being used is greater than F_y'' the allowable bending stress to be used is 0.60 F_y, but if it is less than F_y' the allowable bending stress is to be determined from AISC Formula 1.5-5.

To qualify for the 0.66 F_y allowable stress it is to be remembered that the lateral support requirements for the compression flange must also be met. A member is said to have lateral support when points of such support are located no further apart in inches than 76.0 b/F_y nor 20,000/$(d/A_f)\ F_y$. For substitution in these expressions b is the width of the compression flange, d is the total depth of the beam, A_f is the cross-sectional area of the flange (d/A_f values are given for the usual beam sections in the AISC Manual) and F_y is the yield stress in ksi. For A36 steel lateral support at distances no greater than 12.7 times the flange width will satisfy requirements for use of the 0.66 F_y allowable stress values. For the higher strength steels the distance limitation between points of lateral support varies in inverse proportion to $\sqrt{F_y}$.

6-4.   HOLES IN BEAMS

It is often necessary to have holes in steel beams. They are obviously required for the installation of bolts and rivets and sometimes for pipes, conduits, ducts, etc. If at all possible these latter type holes should be completely avoided. When absolutely necessary they should be placed through the web if the moment is large and through the flange if the shear is large. Cutting a hole through the web of a beam does not reduce its section modulus greatly or its resisting moment; but, as will be described in Sec. 7-1, a large hole in the web tremendously reduces the shearing strength of a steel section. When large holes are put in beam webs, extra plates are sometimes connected to the webs around the holes to serve as reinforcing against possible web buckling.

The presence of holes of any type in a beam certainly does not make it stronger and in all probability weakens it somewhat. The effect of holes has been a subject which has been argued back and forth for many years. The questions, "Is the neutral axis affected by the presence of holes?" and "Is it necessary to subtract holes from the compression flange which are going to be plugged with rivets or bolts?" are frequently asked.

The theory that the neutral axis might move from its normal position to the theoretical position of its net section when holes are present is quite questionable. A linear distribution of stress has been assumed in the preceding paragraphs of this chapter but when holes are present the situation is changed because there is considerable stress concentration around the holes.

Tests seem to show that flange holes for rivets or bolts do not appreciably change the location of the neutral axis. It is logical to assume that the location of the neutral axis will not follow the exact theoretical variation with its abrupt changes in position at rivet or bolt holes as shown in part (b) of Fig. 6-2. A more reasonable change in neutral axis location is shown in part (c) of this figure where it is assumed to have a more gradual variation in position.

It is interesting to note that flexure tests of steel beams seem to show that their failure is based on the strength of the compression flange even though there may be rivet or bolt holes in the tension flange. The presence of these holes does not seem to be as serious as might be thought particularly as compared to holes in a pure tension member. These tests show little difference in the strengths of beams with no holes and in beams with holes up to 15 percent of the gross area of either flange.

The AISC does not require the subtraction of holes in either flange provided the hole area in any one flange does not exceed 15 percent of the gross area of that flange, and then the deduction is only for the area in excess of 15 percent. Furthermore the AISC does not make a distinction between holes in the compression and tension flanges. Although the 15 percent value is permitted by the AISC, many specifications (notably the bridge ones) and a good many designers have not adopted the idea and follow the more conservative practice of deducting all holes.

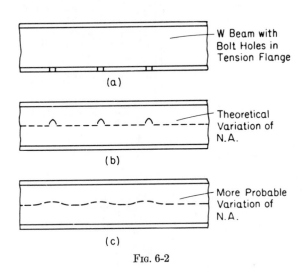

(a)

W Beam with
Bolt Holes in
Tension Flange

(b)

Theoretical
Variation of
N.A.

(c)

More Probable
Variation of
N.A.

Fig. 6-2

The AASHO and AREA require the calculation of two moments of inertia when holes are present. For compressive stresses the gross moment of inertia is to be used regardless of the presence of rivet or bolt holes. For tensile stresses the net moment of inertia is to be used. The neutral axis is assumed to remain at its normal position for both calculations. The effect of using the two different moments of inertia is to assume that rivets or bolt holes on the compression side of the beam have less effect than those on the tension side.

The usual practice is to subtract the same area of holes from both flanges whether they are present or not. For a section with two holes in the tension flange only, the properties of the section would be computed based on the subtraction of two holes from the tension flange and two holes from the compression flange. Example 6-3 illustrates this method. Again the author has made a few preliminary calculations in estimating the member size.

EXAMPLE 6-3. Redesign the beam of Example 6-1 assuming that it will be necessary to punch holes for two ¾-in. bolts in the tension flange. The AISC reduction is not to be permitted in this beam. Figure 6-3 shows a sketch of the assumed section.

Fig. 6-3

Solution: Assume beam weight $= 68$ lb/ft

$$M = \frac{(4.468)\ (21)^2}{8} = 246 \text{ ft-k}$$

$$\text{Net } S_{\text{req.}} = \frac{(12)\ (246)}{24} = 123 \text{ in.}^3$$

Try W 24 × 68 ($S = 153$ in.^{3})

Assuming two holes in each flange, I of holes about N. A. is

$$(4)\ (\tfrac{7}{8})\ (0.582)\ (11.57)^2 = 272 \text{ in.}^4$$

and S of holes is

$$\frac{272}{11.86} = 22.9 \text{ in.}^3$$

Actual net $S = 153 - 22.9 = 130.1$ in.^{3} > 123 in.^{3} (OK)

Use W 24 × 68

Should a hole be present in only one side of a flange of a W section, there will be no axis of symmetry for the net section of the shape. A correct theoretical elastic solution of the problem would involve the location of the principal axes, the calculation of the principal moments of inertia, etc. or substitution into the lengthy generalized equations for unsymmetrical bending presented in Sec. 7-5. Rather than following such lengthy procedures over a minor point it seems logical to assume holes in both sides of the flange. The results obtained will probably be just as satisfactory as those obtained by the more laborious methods mentioned.

6-5. LATERAL SUPPORT OF BEAMS

Probably the large majority of steel beams are used in such a manner that their compression flanges are restrained against lateral buckling. (Unfortunately, however, the percentage has not been quite as high as the design profession has assumed.) The upper flanges of beams used to support concrete buildings and bridge floors are often incorporated in these concrete floors. For situations of this type where the compression flanges are restrained against lateral buckling the allowable bending fiber stresses in the tension and compression flanges are considered to be equal.

Should the compression flange of a beam be without lateral support for some distance it will have a stress situation similar to that existing in columns. As is well known the longer and slenderer a column becomes the greater becomes the danger of its buckling for the same loading condition. When the compression flange of a beam is long enough and slender enough it may quite possibly buckle unless lateral support is provided.

There are many factors affecting the amount of stress which will cause buckling in the compression flange of a beam. Some of these factors are the properties of the material, the spacing and types of lateral support provided, the types of end support or restraints, the loading conditions, etc.

The tension in the other flange of a beam tends to keep that flange straight and restrain the compression flange from buckling; but as the bending moment is increased the tendency to buckle may become large enough to overcome the tensile restraint. When the compression flange does begin to buckle, twisting or torsion will occur, and the smaller the torsional strength of the beam the more rapid will be the failure. The W, S, and channel shapes so frequently used for beam sections do not have a great deal of resistance to lateral buckling and the resulting torsion. Some other shapes, notably the built-up box shapes, are tremendously stronger. These types of members have a great deal more torsional resistance than the W, S, and plate girder sections. Tests have shown that they will not buckle laterally until the strains developed are well in the plastic range. If they meet the requirements for compact shapes their allowable bending stresses are 0.66 F_y and if they are not compact their allowable bending stresses are equal to 0.60 F_y unless their compression flanges are not braced laterally for distances in excess of $2500/F_y$ times the transverse distance out-to-out of their webs (a very large distance).

In any case the width-thickness ratios of unstiffened projecting elements of the compression flange may not exceed $52.2/\sqrt{F_y}$, or if stiffened elements may not exceed $190/\sqrt{F_y}$ as described in the AISC Specification. F_y again is used in ksi. Stiffened compression elements are defined as those elements which have lateral support along both of the edges which are parallel to the direction of the compressive stress.

Some judgment needs to be used in deciding what does and what does not constitute satisfactory lateral support for a steel beam. A beam which is wholly encased in concrete or which has its compression flange incorporated in a concrete slab is certainly well supported laterally. When a concrete slab rests on the top flange of a beam, the engineer must study the situation carefully before he counts on friction to provide full lateral support. Perhaps if the loads on the slab are fairly well fixed in position, they will contribute to the friction and it may be reasonable to assume full lateral support. If on the other hand there is much movement of the loads and appreciable vibration, the friction may well be reduced and full lateral support should not be assumed. Such situations occur in bridges due to traffic, and in buildings with vibrating machinery such as printing presses.

Should lateral support of the compression flange not be provided by a floor slab, it is possible that such support may be provided with connecting beams or with special members inserted for that purpose. Beams which frame into the sides of the beam or girder in question and are connected to the compression flange can usually be counted on to provide full lateral support at the connection. If the connection is made primarily to the tensile flange, little lateral support is provided to the compression flange. Before support is assumed from these beams the designer should note if they themselves are prevented from moving. The series of beams represented with horizontal dotted lines in Fig. 6-4 provide questionable

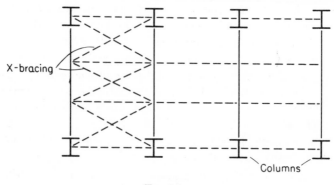

Fig. 6-4

lateral support for the main beams between columns. For a situation of this type some system of x-bracing may be desirable in one of the bays. Such a system is shown in Fig. 6-4. This one system will provide sufficient lateral support for the beams for several bays.

The corrugated sheet-metal roofs which are usually connected to the purlins with metal straps probably furnish only partial lateral support. A similar situation exists when wood flooring is bolted to supporting steel beams. At this time the student quite naturally asks, "If only partial support is available, what am I to consider to be the distance between points of lateral support?" The answer to this question is for him to use his judgment. As an illustration, a wood floor is assumed to be bolted every 4 ft to the supporting steel beams in such a manner that it is thought only partial lateral support is provided at those points. After studying the situation the engineer might well decide that the equivalent of full lateral support at 8-ft intervals is provided. Such a decision seems to be within the spirit of the specifications.

6-6. DESIGN OF LATERALLY UNSUPPORTED BEAMS

The general practice through the years has been to reduce the allowable stress in the fibers of the compression flange of a beam with little lateral support. As an illustration, the 1969 AASHO Specifications permit bending stresses of .55 F_y or 20,000 psi for A36 steel if full lateral support is provided. If lateral support is not provided, the allowable compressive stress is to be reduced in accordance with the following formula:

$$F_b = 20{,}000 - 7.5\left(\frac{l}{b}\right)^2$$

In this expression l is the distance in inches between points of lateral support and b is the flange width in inches. For higher strength steels the allowable values can be computed with similar expressions to be found in those specifications. Example 6-4 illustrates the use of the AASHO expression in the design of a beam. The application of lateral-support formulas is quite similar to that required for the various column expressions, and a section which can adequately resist the moment can quickly be found. It will be noted, however, that the determination of the lightest section which can adequately support the loads may involve quite a lengthy trial-and-error process, and for this reason curves such as those available in the AISC Manual and to be discussed later in this section are highly desirable.

EXAMPLE 6-4. Select a steel section for the loads and span of Fig. 6-5. The beam is to be designed with A36 steel and the 1969 AASHO Specifications. Lateral support is provided only at the beam ends.

Solution: Assume beam weight = 70 lb/ft

$$M = (20)\,(10) + \frac{(0.070)\,(20)^2}{8} = 203.5 \text{ ft-k}$$

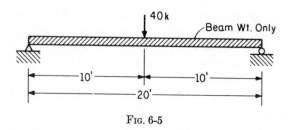

Fig. 6-5

Assume allowable fiber stress = 15 ksi

$$S_{req.} = \frac{12 \times 203.5}{15} = 163 \text{ in.}^3$$

Try W 24 × 76 (b = 8.985, S = 176)

$$F_b = 20,000 - 7.5\left(\frac{12 \times 20}{8.961}\right)^2 = 14.65 \text{ ksi}$$

$$\text{Resisting Moment} = F_b S = \frac{(14.65)\ (176)}{12} = 215 \text{ ft-k} > 203 \text{ ft-k}\quad\text{(OK)}$$

<u>Use W 24 × 76</u>

The AISC Specification presents three expressions (1.5-6a, 1.5-6b and 1.5-7) for determining the allowable bending fiber stresses in beams for which continuous lateral support is not provided. The expressions are applicable to rolled shapes, plate girders, and built-up members having an axis of symmetry in the plane of the web. Depending upon the proportions of the member and the unbraced length the designer will substitute in Formula 1.5-6a and 1.5-7 or into 1.5-6b and 1.5-7 and use the larger value so obtained provided the result is not greater than the maximum permissible value of 0.60 F_y.

The lateral buckling strength of a beam can be estimated by taking into account the torsional resistance of the beam about its longitudinal axis and the lateral bending resistance of the beam plus the resistance of the flange to torsion.[1-4] The resulting expression is, however, too complicated for practical engineering use.

For shallow thick-walled sections the resistance to torsion about the

[1] Karl De Vries, "Strength of Beams as Determined By Lateral Buckling," *Trans. ASCE*, vol. 112 (1947), pp. 1245–1271.

[2] G. Winter et al., "Discussion of 'Strength of Beams as Determined By Lateral Buckling,'" *Trans. ASCE*, vol. 112 (1947), pp. 1272–1320.

[3] G. G. Kubo, B. G. Johnston, and W. J. Eney, "Nonuniform Torsion of Plate Girders," *Trans. ASCE*, vol. 121 (1956), pp 759–785.

[4] K. Basler and B. Thürlimann, "Strength of Plate Girders In Bending," *Proc. ASCE*, vol. 87, no. 6 (August 1961), pp. 153–181.

longitudinal axis and the lateral buckling resistance are the most important factors. For these cases, AISC Formula 1.5-7 is considered to give a reasonable approximation of an allowable buckling stress. In this expression which follows, l is the distance between points of lateral support, d is the beam depth, and A_f is the flange area. Should the beam under consideration be a cantilever the unsupported length can be conservatively assumed to equal the actual length.[5]

The allowable bending compression stresses permitted by the AISC Specification for sections loaded in the plane of their webs and having an axis of symmetry in their webs equals the larger value computed by Formulas 1.5-6a or 1.5-6b and 1.5-7 as described in the following paragraphs except not more than $0.60\ F_y$. This procedure for determining allowable stresses also applies to compression on extreme fibers of channels bent about their major axes. When

$$\sqrt{\frac{102 \times 10^3\ C_b}{F_y}} \leqq \frac{l}{r_t} \leqq \sqrt{\frac{510 \times 10^3\ C_b}{F_y}}$$

$$F_b = \left[\frac{2}{3} - \frac{F_y\ (l/r_t)^2}{1530 \times 10^3\ C_b}\right]F_y \qquad \text{(AISC Formula 1.5-6a)}$$

When

$$\frac{l}{r_t} \geqq \sqrt{\frac{510 \times 10^3\ C_b}{F_y}}$$

$$F_b = \frac{170 \times 10^3\ C_b}{(l/r_t)^2} \qquad \text{(AISC Formula 1.5-6b)}$$

or, when the compression flange is solid and approximately rectangular in cross section and its area is not less than that of the tension flange

$$F_b = \frac{12 \times 10^3\ C_b}{ld/A_f} \qquad \text{(AISC Formula 1.5-7)}$$

Formula 1.5-7 gives allowable values which more nearly approach the shallow thick-walled sections but is somewhat conservative for a few deep thin W sections and nearly all plate girders. The designer could use the preceding formula and ignore the other one. His designs would be perfectly safe although considerably overdesigned for the cases mentioned. For these members the resistance of the flange to torsion is the predominant factor and AISC formulas 1.5-6a and 1.5-6b more clearly estimate the resistance of the flange of this item.

[5] S. Timoshenko and J. M. Gere, *Theory of Elastic Stability*, 2d ed. (New York: McGraw-Hill Book Company, Inc., 1961), pp. 257–262.

In this expression l is the unbraced length of the compression flange; r is the radius of gyration of the compression flange plus one-third of the compression web area taken about an axis in the plane of the web; and C_b is a bending coefficient determined as follows:

$$C_b = 1.75 + 1.05\left(\frac{M_1}{M_2}\right) + 0.3\left(\frac{M_1}{M_2}\right)^2 \leq 2.3$$

The end restraint conditions and the loading conditions may be such as to provide appreciable resistance to lateral buckling. C_b is a modifier which is given to estimate the effect of these items. In this expression for C_b, M_1 is the smaller and M_2 the larger of the bending moments at the ends of the unbraced length taken about the strong axis of the member. Should the moment at any point within the unbraced length be larger than the end moments, C_b shall be taken as 1. The ratio M_1/M_2 is considered positive if M_1 and M_2 have the same sign (reverse curvature bending) and negative if they have opposite signs (single curvature bending).

Example 6-5 illustrates the calculations necessary to determine the allowable stresses in a W section which has different unbraced lengths.

EXAMPLE 6-5. Determine the allowable bending stresses in a W33 × 130 (see Fig. 6-6) for simple spans of 10, 20, and 30 ft without lateral support. Use A36 steel and the AISC Specification.

FIG. 6-6

Solution: Computing properties of the section

$$A_f + \tfrac{1}{6} A_w = (11.510)\,(.855) + \left(\frac{1}{3}\right)\left(\frac{31.39}{2}\right)\,(.580) = 12.88 \text{ sq in.}$$

$$r_t = \sqrt{\frac{\frac{1}{2} \times 218}{12.88}} = 2.92 \text{ in.} \quad \text{(Available in AISC Manual)}$$

$$C_b = 1.0 \quad \text{when moment in span exceeds that at both ends}$$

(a) $l = 10$ ft

$12.7b = (12.7)(11.510) = 146 \text{ in.} = 12.1 \text{ ft} > 10 \text{ ft}$ (See L_c in AISC Manual)

$$\therefore F_b = 0.66\,F_y = 24 \text{ ksi}$$

(b) $l = 20$ ft

$$\sqrt{\frac{102 \times 10^3 \times 1.0}{36}} = 53 < \frac{l}{r_t} \text{ of } \frac{12 \times 20}{2.92} = 82.2 < \sqrt{\frac{510 \times 10^3 \times 1.0}{36}} = 119$$

$\therefore$ Use Formulas 1.5-6a and 1.5-7

$$F_b = \left[\frac{2}{3} - \frac{(36)\,(82.2)^2}{(1530)\,(10^3)\,(1)}\right]36 = 18.3 \text{ ksi} \leftarrow$$

$$F_b = \frac{12 \times 10^3 \times 1}{12 \times 20 \times 3.36} = 14.9 \text{ ksi}$$

(c) $l = 30$ ft

$$\sqrt{\frac{102 \times 10^3 \times 1.0}{36}} = 53 < \frac{l}{r_t} \text{ of } \frac{12 \times 30}{2.92} = 123.2 > \sqrt{\frac{510 \times 10^3 \times 1.0}{36}} = 119$$

$\therefore$ Use Formulas 1.5-6b and 1.5-7

$$F_b = \frac{170 \times 10^3 \times 1.0}{(123.2)^2} = 11.18 \text{ ksi} \leftarrow$$

$$F_b = \frac{12 \times 10^3 \times 1.0}{12 \times 30 \times 3.36} = 9.92 \text{ ksi}$$

Example 6-6 illustrates the design of a beam without full lateral support using the AISC Specification. The problem is very simple because the AISC Manual presents charts which show the allowable resisting moments of sections commonly used as beams which have varying unbraced lengths. These charts are entitled "Allowable Moments in Beams with Unbraced Lengths Greater Than L_u" (where L_u is the greatest unbraced length for which the allowable stress can be taken as 0.60 F_y). From these charts .it is possible to directly select the most economical rolled section for a beam which does not have full lateral support.

EXAMPLE 6-6. Select the lightest available steel section for the beam shown in Fig. 6-7 using the AISC Specification and A36 steel. Lateral support is provided at the ends only.

$$\text{F\scriptsize IG.}\ 6\text{-}7$$

Solution: Assume beam weight = 100 lb/ft

$$M = \frac{(7.1)\,(20)^2}{8} = 355\text{ft-k}$$

From Chart

Use W 30 × 99

Should it be necessary to design a beam without full lateral support when the charts cannot be used (as where charts are not available for the steel being used, or where the particular conditions do not fall on the chart, etc.) it will be necessary to use a trial and error solution. An allowable stress can be assumed, the required section modulus computed, a trial beam selected, the allowable stress determined for the trial beam size, etc. There, are however, several variables in the AISC formulas and although it's not difficult to find a section which will adequately support the load it is quite difficult to find the absolutely lightest section by trial and error.

The student should at this time carefully study the information presented in the AISC Manual on the subject of lateral support. The "Beam Load Tables" present for compact beam sections the allowable uniform load in kips for the spans for which they are practical. Although the information is primarily presented for A36 steel, factors are given to apply the information to beams made from higher strength steel. Also of particular interest are the values given for L_c and L_u for each shape. L_c is the maximum unbraced length of the compression flange of compact shapes for which the 0.66 F_y allowable bending stress is applicable, and L_u is the maximum unbraced length above which the allowable bending stress is less than 0.60 F_y. Use of this information can prevent a great deal of unnecessary substitution in the tedious lateral support expressions.

The student may quite logically ask the question, "What do I do if the beam in question has no compression flange?" Such a situation might very well occur in the bottom chord member of a truss subject to an intermediate load which causes bending in addition to the normal axial stress. Should the member consist of a pair of angles or a structural tee with the flanges on the tension side there will be no compression flange, only a web.

Girders for all-welded Connecticut expressway bridge. (*The Lincoln Electric Company.*)

The formulas presented in this section are for members which are symmetrical about both x and y axes, as W or S shapes. For other shapes more complicated expressions are needed for estimating the allowable stresses. For reference the student is referred to *Guide to Design Criteria for Metal Compression Members.*[6] A reasonable and very conservative practice is to assume $F_b = 0.60 \ F_y$ for all such situations, as long as the local buckling requirements of AISC Sec. 1.9.1 are satisfied.

6-7. DESIGN OF CONTINUOUS MEMBERS

The AISC Specification for the elastic design of continuous members leans definitely towards the plastic design theories. Both theory and tests show clearly that continuous ductile steel members meeting the requirements for compact sections have the desirable ability of being able to redistribute the moments caused by overloads. (The student is again referred to the introductory paragraphs of Chap. 21 for a detailed discussion of this subject.)

The continuous beam of Fig. 6-8 is considered in this paragraph. The magnitude of the load applied to this beam can be increased until it reaches a value above which there will be no increase in the support moments. (These moments, which are defined as plastic moments in Chap. 21, occur when the steel has been stressed to its yield point all the

[6] Column Research Council, B. G. Johnston (ed.), 2d ed. (John Wiley & Sons, New York, 1966).

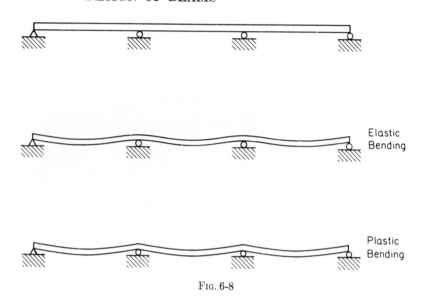

Elastic Bending

Plastic Bending

Fig. 6-8

way through the section at some point.) Should the load be increased further the beam will act as though there is no continuity over the interior supports. These points will act as though they are hinges so far as load increases go but will continue to transfer the plastic moments. Increases in load will cause increases in the positive moments out in the "simple beams" between supports but no increases at the supports. The result is that the negative and positive moments in the beam tend to equalize as the load is increased. The beam may be said to have a reserve of strength and will not fail until the load is decidedly increased above the value at which the outermost fibers of the steel were first stressed to its yield point.

The AISC says that for continuous compact sections the design may be made on the basis of $\frac{9}{10}$ of the maximum negative moments caused by gravity loads if the positive moments are increased by $\frac{1}{10}$ of the average negative moments at the adjacent supports. (The 0.9 factor is applicable only to gravity loads and not to lateral loads such as those caused by wind and earthquake. The factor can also be applied to columns which have axial stresses of less than 0.15 F_y.) This moment reduction does not apply to members consisting of A514 steel, hybrid girders nor to moments produced by loading on cantilevers. Example 6-7 (a) illustrates the design of a two-span beam falling into this class. Part (b) of this example illustrates the design of the same beam when the unsupported lengths exceed the maximum values permitted for compact sections.

EXAMPLE 6-7. (a)   A W 18 × 55 consisting of a steel with $F_y = 45$ ksi
is used for the span and loads of Fig. 6-9.   Is the section satisfactory according
to the AISC Specification if continuous lateral support is provided by a reinforced
concrete slab?   (b) Is the section satisfactory if lateral support is provided only
at beam supports and midspans?

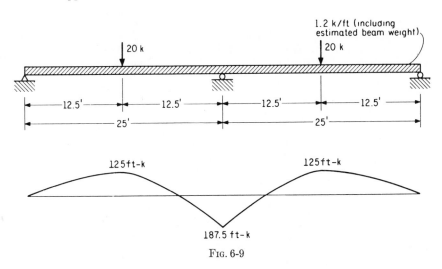

FIG. 6-9

Solution: (a) Continuous lateral support:

$$F_b = 0.66 \, F_y = 29.7 \text{ ksi}$$

Maximum negative M for design $= (0.9) \, (187.5) = 168.8$ ft-k

Maximum positive M for design $= 125 + (0.10)\left(\dfrac{0 + 187.5}{2}\right) = 134.4$ ft-k

FIG. 6-10

$$f_b = \frac{12 \times 168.8}{98.4} = 20.6 \text{ ksi} < 29.7 \text{ ksi} \qquad \text{(OK)}$$

(b) Lateral support at 12.5-ft intervals:

Considering the 12.5 ft at ends of beam:

$$C_b = 1.75 + (1.05)\left(\frac{0}{125}\right) + (0.3)\left(\frac{0}{125}\right)^2 = 1.75$$

$$A_f + \tfrac{1}{6} A_w = (7.532)(.63) + (\tfrac{1}{6})(16.86)(.390) = 5.83 \text{ sq in.}$$

$$r_t = \sqrt{\frac{\tfrac{1}{2} \times 45}{5.83}} = 1.98$$

$$\sqrt{\frac{102 \times 10^3 \times 1.75}{45}} = 62.9 < \frac{12 \times 12.5}{1.98} \text{ of } 75.7$$

∴ Use Formulas 1.5-6a and 1.5-7

$$F_b = \left[\frac{2}{3} - \frac{45(75.7)^2}{1530 \times 10^3 \times 1.75}\right]45 = 25.6 \text{ ksi}$$

$$F_b = \frac{12 \times 10^3 \times 1.75}{12 \times 12.5 \times 3.82} = 36.6 \text{ ksi} \leftarrow \text{Use } 0.60\,F_y = 27 \text{ ksi}$$

$$f_b = \frac{12 \times 125}{98.4} = 15.25 \text{ ksi} < 27 \text{ ksi} \qquad \text{(OK)}$$

Considering the interior 12.5-ft section:

$$Cb = 1.75 + 1.05\left(+\frac{125}{187.5}\right) + 0.3\left(+\frac{125}{187.5}\right)^2 = 2.58 > 2.30$$

$$C_b = 2.30$$

$$\sqrt{\frac{102 \times 10^3 \times 2.30}{45}} = 72.2 < \frac{12 \times 12.5}{1.98} \text{ of } 75.7$$

∴ Use Formulas 1.5-6a and 1.5-7

$$F_b = \left[\frac{2}{3} - \frac{(45)(75.7)^2}{1530 \times 10^3 \times 2.30}\right]45 = 27.3 \text{ ksi}$$

$$F_b = \frac{12 \times 10^3 \times 2.30}{12 \times 12.5 \times 3.82} = 48.2 \text{ ksi} \leftarrow \therefore \text{Use } 0.60\,F_y = 27 \text{ ksi}$$

$$f_b = \frac{12 \times 168.8}{98.4} = 20.6 \text{ ksi} < 27 \text{ ksi} \qquad \text{(OK)}$$

Section is satisfactory

PROBLEMS

Note: Consider moments only for the problems of this chapter.

6-1. Select the most economical section available for a 25 ft simple span if the beam is to support a uniform load of 4 k/ft. The beam is assumed to have full lateral support and an allowable bending stress of 20,000 psi. (Ans. W 24 × 84)

6-2. to 6-6. Select the most economical section available for each of the beams shown in the accompanying illustrations assuming full lateral support is provided for the compression flanges. Use A36 steel and the AISC Specification.

PROB. 6-2

30k   30k   4k/ft

(Ans. W24×94)

PROB. 6-3

12k   18k   2k/ft

PROB. 6-4

2.30 k/ft   (Ans. W12×14)

PROB. 6-5

3k/ft

PROB. 6-6

6-7. Select the most economical section for the beam shown in the accompanying illustration using a steel with an allowable bending stress of 30,000 psi. Full lateral support is assumed for the entire span. (Ans. W 36 × 150)

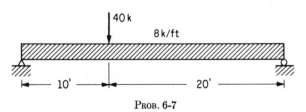

40k   8k/ft

PROB. 6-7

6-8. Select the most economical section available for a 32-ft simple span if the beam is to support a uniform load of 10 k/ft. Use A242 steel, the AISC Specification and assume that full lateral support is provided.

6-9. A W 24 × 68 consisting of A36 steel is used for a simple span of 30 ft. Using the AISC Specification and assuming full lateral support determine the maximum allowable uniform load which the beam can support in addition to its own weight. (Ans. w = 2.66 k/ft)

6-10. A beam consists of a W 16 × 45 with a ½ × 12 cover plate welded to each flange. If the allowable bending stress is 24,000 psi, determine the allowable uniform load which it can support in addition to its own weight for a 28-ft simple span.

6-11. Using the AISC Specification and A36 steel and assuming full lateral support determine the maximum allowable uniform load which the beam shown in the accompanying illustration can support in addition to its own weight for a 24-ft simple span. (Ans. 3.36 k/ft)

PROB. 6-11

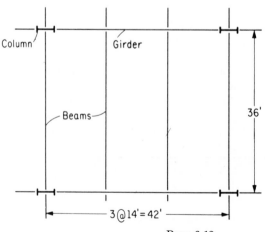

PROB. 6-12

6-12. The accompanying illustration shows the arrangement of beams and girders which are used to support a 6-in. reinforced concrete floor for a small industrial building. Using A36 steel and the AISC Specification design the beams and girders assuming they are simply supported. Assume full lateral support and a live load of 120 psf.

6-13. A 40-ft simple beam is to support two movable 20 k loads a distance of 12 ft apart. If the beam is to have full lateral support select a section to resist the largest possible bending moment. AISC. A36. (Ans. W 24 × 68)

6-14. Select the lightest C or MC section available to support a uniform load of 900 lbs/ft for an 18-ft simple span. A36. AISC. Full lateral support.

6-15. A W 27 × 94 with full lateral support is used for a 30-ft simple span and supports a 4 k/ft uniform load. There are assumed to be two holes for 1-in. bolts in each flange. Compute the maximum compressive stress using the gross section properties and the maximum tensile stress using the net section properties. Do not use the AISC Specification (Sec. 1.10.1) as regards the 15 percent rule of the gross flange area. (Ans. f_c = 22.8 ksi; f_t = 27.7 ksi)

6-16. The section shown in the accompanying illustration has two 1-in. bolts passing through each flange. Find the allowable uniform load which this section can support in addition to its own weight for a 24-ft simple span. Allowable bending stress = 18 ksi. Not AISC Specification.

$\frac{1}{2}$ X 18 PL

W 18 X 114

$\frac{1}{2}$ X 18 PL

PROB. 6-16

6-17. Rework Prob. 6-1 assuming two ¾-in. bolts pass through each flange of the section at the point of maximum moment. Not AISC. (Ans. W 27 × 94)

6-18. Rework Prob. 6-15 using the AISC Specification as regards the 15 percent of the gross flange area rule (Sec. 1.10.1).

6-19. It is desired to select a section to support a 2.5 k/ft load for an 18-ft simple span. If full lateral support is assumed and two ¾-in. bolts are needed in each flange, select a W section using A36 steel and the AISC Specification. (Ans. W 18 × 35)

6-20. Select a section for the span and loads shown in the accompanying illustration. Use an allowable F_b = 20 ksi and assume there are to be two holes for 1-in. bolts in the tension flange. Not AISC Specification.

PROB. 6-20

6.21. Using the 1969 AASHO expression for A36 steel ($F_b = 20{,}000 - 7.5$ $(l/b)^2$ select a W24 to support a 5 k/ft load for an 18-ft simple span if lateral support is provided at the beam ends only. (Ans. W 24 × 76)

6.22. Compute the allowable bending stresses in a W 21 × 55 for simple spans of 6, 12, and 25 ft if lateral support is provided at ends only. Use A36 steel and the AISC Specification.

6-23. A W 36 × 150 consisting of A36 steel is used for a simple span of 24 ft, and has lateral support at its ends only. What is the largest concentrated load which can be placed at the beam center line? AISC Specification. (Ans. 112.9 k)

6-24. The beam shown in the accompanying illustration has lateral support provided at points A and B only. Using A36 steel and the AISC Specification design the beam.

PROB. 6-24

6-25. Using a steel with $F_y = 65$ ksi and the AISC Specification what uniformly distributed load can a simply supported W 33 × 240 carry for a span of 40 ft when

    (a)   the compression flange is braced laterally   (Ans. 14.31 k/ft)

    (b)   the compression flange has lateral support only at its ends   (Ans. 5.36 k/ft)

6-26. What is the allowable uniform load which can be placed on a W30 × 99 (A 242 steel) which has lateral support provided at its ends only? The beam is simply supported and has a span of 30 ft. AISC Specification.

6-27. A W33 × 130 is used to support the loads and moment shown in the accompanying illustration. Using A36 steel and the AISC Specification and neglecting the dead weight of the beam, find if the beam is overloaded.

    (a)   if full lateral support is provided   (Ans. Beam is satisfactory, $M = 340$ ft-k, Resisting Moment $= 812$ ft-k)

PROB 6-27

(b) if lateral support is provided at the ends only   (Ans. Beam is satisfactory, $M = 340$ ft-k, Resisting Moment $= 377$ ft-k)

6-28. Repeat Prob. 6-19 if lateral support is provided at beam ends only.

6-29. A W30 × 99 with lateral support supplied at its ends only supports a concentrated load at the center of its 30-ft simple span. Using A242 steel and the AISC Specification determine the maximum permissible value of the load. (Ans. 25.3 k)

6-30. The architects specify that a beam no greater than 13.00 in. in depth be designed to support a uniform load of 10 k/ft for an 18-ft simple span. Design the beam with A36 steel and the AISC Specification assuming full lateral support.

6-31. Select the lightest available W section which will support the loads shown in the accompanying illustration using A36 steel the AISC Specification and assuming full lateral support is provided for the compression flange.   (Ans. W21 × 55)

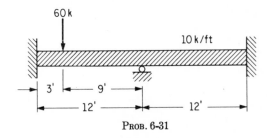

PROB. 6-31

6-32. Using A36 steel and the AISC Specification select the lightest available section for the beam shown in the accompanying illustration. The section is provided with full lateral support.

PROB. 6-32

6-33. Three methods of supporting a roof are shown in the accompanying illustration. Design the beam for each case using A36 steel and the AISC Specification if a 2 k/ft uniform load is to be supported. Assume full lateral support. (Ans. (a) W 24 × 76, (b) W 24 × 61, (c) W 24 × 61)

PROB. 6-33

chapter 7

DESIGN OF BEAMS
(CONTINUED)

7-1. SHEAR

The beam supporting transverse loads, shown in Fig. 7-1 (a), is sometimes said to be subjected to two types of shear—*transverse* and *longitudinal*. The first of these two shears is illustrated in part (b) of

Fig. 7-1

the figure where there is a tendency of the part of the beam to the left of section 1–1 to slide upward with respect to the part of the beam to the right of the section. Actually this type of shear failure will not occur in a regular steel beam because web crippling (discussed in next section)

131

will occur first. Transverse shear, however, can feasibly cause failure directly if the beam has been deeply coped as shown in part (c) of the figure.

The second type of shear is illustrated in part (d) of Fig. 7-1 and occurs due to the bending of the member which causes changes in lengths of the longitudinal fibers. For positive bending the lower fibers are stretched and the upper fibers are shortened while somewhere in between there is a neutral axis where the fibers do not change in length. Due to these varying deformations a particular fiber has a tendency to slip on the fiber above or below. The largest value of longitudinal or horizontal shear occurs at the neutral axis.

If a wooden beam was made by stacking boards on top of each other and not connecting them they would obviously tend to take the shape shown in part (d) of the figure. The student may have observed short heavily loaded timber beams with large transverse shears which split along horizontal planes.

This presentation may be entirely misleading in seeming to completely separate horizontal and vertical shears. In reality horizontal and vertical shear at any point are the same and may not be separated. Furthermore, one cannot occur without the other.

The tendency to slip is resisted by the shearing strength of the material. Although steel beam sizes are rarely controlled by shear it is wise to check them, particularly if they are short and heavily loaded. Maximum external shear usually occurs near the supports but shear is present throughout the beam. The average transverse shearing stress on the cross section of a beam at a certain point in the span equals the external shear divided by the cross-sectional area of the beam. The longitudinal shearing stress formula, however, shows that the shearing stress is not constant across a beam cross section but is zero at the outermost fiber and has its largest value at the neutral axis. The familiar formula, to follow, can be used to calculate the unit shearing stress at any point. (This formula applies to beams with open cross sections which are not subjected to torsion.)

$$v = \frac{VQ}{bI}$$

where V = external shear at the section in question

Q = statical moment of that portion of the section lying outside (either above or below) the line on which v is desired, taken about the neutral axis

I = moment of inertia of the entire section about the neutral axis

b = width of the section where the unit shearing stress is desired

When this expression is used to calculate the shear across the face of a W, M or S section the resulting values are very small in the flanges and quite large in the web. The values in the web are fairly uniform from top to bottom. Figure 7-2 shows the variation of shear on the cross section of a W 24 × 76 which is resisting an external shear of 60,000 lb.

FIG. 7-2

The common practice of assuming a uniform shearing stress variation in the web from top to bottom (using the full depth of the section) appears to be reasonable after examining Fig. 7-2. The shearing stress obtained in accordance with this assumption equals $60,000/(23.91)$ (0.440) $= 5,710$ psi which is not much smaller than the maximum theoretical value of 6,520 psi. The truth of the matter is that the allowable shearing stresses given by most specifications have been developed on the assumption that uniformly distributed shear calculations will be made. For most W, S and channel sections having fairly large flanges and thin webs the results obtained from this assumption are reasonable. For other shapes a few calculations may be necessary to see if the per cent error is appreciable.

A more conservative approach followed by some engineers is to use only the web depth in figuring the average shear. This method would give a result equal to $60,000/(22.51)$ $(0.440) = 6,050$ psi in the case being considered. Although some designers use the total beam depth and others only the web depth or even the depth between the toes of the fillets for rolled sections, they nearly all agree to use only the web depth for plate girders.

Generally these stresses are not a problem in steel beams because the webs of rolled shapes are capable of resisting quite large shearing stresses. Perhaps it is well, however, to list here the most common situations where shear might be excessive. These are as follows:

1. Should large concentrated loads be placed near beam supports they will cause large external shears without corresponding increases in bending moments. A fairly common example of this type occurs in tall buildings where on a particular floor the upper columns are offset with

respect to the columns below. The loads from the upper columns applied to the beams on the floor level in question will be quite large if there are many stories above.

2. Probably the most common shearing stress problem occurs where two members (as a beam and a column) are rigidly connected together so their webs lie in a common plane. In Sec. 1.5.1.2 of the *Commentary on AISC Specification,* formulas are given which show when the webs are overstressed in shear and how much they need to be thickened or reinforced when overstressed. This situation which commonly occurs at the junction of columns and beams (or rafters) in rigid frame structures is discussed in Chap. 22.

3. Where beams are notched or coped as was shown in Fig. 7-1(c) shear can be a problem. For this case shear stresses can be calculated for the remaining beam depth. A similar discussion can be made where holes are cut in beam webs for duct work or other items.

United States Pavilion, New York World's Fair. (*Bethlehem Steel Company.*)

4. Theoretically, very heavily loaded short beams can have excessive shears but practically this does not occur too often unless it is like case 1.

5. Shear may very well be a problem even for ordinary loadings

when very thin webs are used as in plate girders or in light gage cold formed steel members.

Should calculated shearing stresses exceed allowable values ($F_v = 0.40\ F_y$ in the AISC) shear plates can be connected to the webs in the zones of excessive stress.

7-2. WEB CRIPPLING

Beams which support heavy concentrated loads sometimes fail by web crippling or crushing unless the web is stiffened near the loads. Web crippling occurs due to the stress concentrations at the junction of the flange and the web, where the beam is trying to transfer compression in the relatively wide flange to the narrow web. Failure will occur when the metal begins to fail at the toe of the fillet in bearing and the flange and web have a tendency to fold over each other.

Most specifications assume the reaction or load spreads out from its place of application along a 45° plane (see Fig. 7-3). The toe of the

N = length of bearing, which cannot be less than k

k = distance from toe of fillet to outside of flange

t = thickness of web

R = reaction

$\dfrac{R}{t(N+k)}$ may not exceed $0.75\ F_y$

(AISC Formula 1.10-9)

Reaction

(a)

R = concentrated load

$\dfrac{R}{t(N+2k)}$ may not exceed $0.75\ F_y$

(AISC Formula 1.10-8)

Concentrated load

(b)

Fig. 7-3

fillet is the most dangerous location for failure because the resisting area has its smallest value there. The AISC does not permit the compression at this point in beams without web stiffeners to exceed $0.75\ F_y$. Should the allowable value be exceeded it is necessary to use stiffeners, or the bearing of the load or reaction must be spread over a greater length. The expressions for the length of bearing required are shown in Fig. **7-3**. The top flanges of a beam must have lateral support at the reaction points or the web crippling strength is greatly reduced.

The minimum bearing length at the end of a certain beam is calculated in Example **7-1**. For many beams the theoretical bearing length determined is too small to be practical and may even be negative. Should this be the case, the designer will select a reasonable value which will fit in with the construction requirements. For steel beams bearing on masonry a minimum bearing length of probably 4 in. should be used. It is to be remembered that a fairly large percentage of structural failures have occurred, particularly during erection, due to insufficient bearing. Another fact to keep in mind is that the bearing area should be large enough to keep the bearing stress from exceeding the allowable value of the supporting material. This subject is considered in Sec. 7-9 of this chapter.

EXAMPLE 7-1.   A W 33 × 130 consisting of A36 steel has been selected for the loading and span of Fig. 7-4. (*a*) Determine the minimum bearing length at the reactions. (*b*) The 50 k concentrated loads are applied to the beam over a width of 5 in. Is this sufficient?

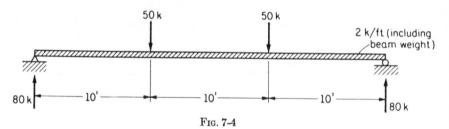

FIG. 7-4

Solution:

Properties of a W 33 × 130

$$\text{Web } t = 0.580 \text{ in.}$$

$$k = 1\tfrac{11}{16} \text{ in.} = 1.688 \text{ in.}$$

(*a*) Minimum bearing length required at the reactions:

$$\frac{R}{t\,(N+k)} = 0.75\,F_y$$

$$\frac{80{,}000}{(0.580)\,(N+1.688)} = (0.75)\,(36{,}000)$$

$$N = 3.43 \text{ in.}$$

(*b*) Web-crippling stress under concentrated loads:

$$\frac{R}{t\,(N+2k)} \text{ not to exceed } 0.75\,F_y$$

$$\frac{50,000}{(0.580)\,(6+2\times1.688)} = 9,200 \text{ psi} < 27,000 \text{ psi} \qquad \text{(OK)}$$

7-3. VERTICAL BUCKLING OF WEBS

The usual steel sections are rolled with proportions such that web crippling will occur before web buckling is possible. Although steel specifications at one time required the investigation of steel beams for web buckling, the requirement has been dropped; and they now only call for investigation of the possibility of web crippling. Built-up sections with high thin webs are a different matter and are considered in Chap. 16.

7-4. MAXIMUM DEFLECTIONS OF BEAMS

The deflections of steel beams are usually limited to certain maximum values. Among the several excellent reasons for deflection limitations are the following:

1. Excessive deflections may damage other materials attached to or supported by the beam in question. Plaster cracks caused by large ceiling joist deflections are one example.

2. The appearance of structures is often damaged by excessive deflections.

3. Extreme deflections do not inspire confidence in the persons using a structure although it may be completely safe from a strength standpoint.

4. It may be necessary for several different beams supporting the same load to deflect equal amounts.

Standard American practice for buildings has been to limit live-load deflections to approximately $\frac{1}{360}$ of the span length. This deflection is supposedly the largest value which ceiling joists can deflect without causing cracks in underlying plaster and is the value permitted by the AISC for beams and girders supporting plastered ceilings. The $\frac{1}{360}$ deflection is only one of many maximum deflection values in use because of different loading situations, different engineers and different specifications. For situations where precise and delicate machinery is supported maximum deflections may be limited to $\frac{1}{1,500}$ or $\frac{1}{2,000}$ of the span lengths. The 1969 AASHO Specifications limit deflections in steel beams and girders due to live load and impact to $\frac{1}{800}$ of the span. (For bridges in urban areas which are partly used by pedestrians the AASHO *recommends* a maximum value equal to $\frac{1}{1000}$ of the span lengths.)

Before substituting blindly into a formula which will give the deflection of a beam for a certain loading condition the student should thoroughly understand the theoretical methods of calculating deflections. These methods include the moment area, conjugate beam, and virtual work procedures. From these methods the centerline deflection expression for a uniformly loaded simple beam can be determined. Example 7-2 illustrates the application of this expression. In this problem all units are changed into pound and inch units. The conversion of the uniform load given in kips per foot to pounds per inch should be particularly noted.

$$\delta_\mathbb{C} = \frac{5wl^4}{384EI}$$

EXAMPLE 7-2. Determine the centerline deflection of the W 24 × 61 beam used in Example 6-1. Does the resulting value exceed $\frac{1}{360}$ of the span length? Assume $E = 29 \times 10^6$ psi and $I = 1{,}540$ in.^{4}.

Solution:

$$\delta_\mathbb{C} = \frac{(5) \left(\dfrac{4{,}461}{12} \right) (21 \times 12)^4}{(384)\ (29 \times 10^6)\ (1{,}540)}$$

$$\delta_\mathbb{C} = 0.436 \text{ in.}$$

Maximum allowable $\delta = \left(\dfrac{1}{360} \right) (12 \times 21) = 0.700$ in. > 0.436 in.   (OK)

Another deflection expression frequently used is the one giving the deflection at the centerline of a beam loaded with a concentrated load at the centerline.

$$\delta_\mathbb{C} = \frac{Pl^3}{48\,EI}$$

Some specifications handle the deflection problem by requiring certain minimum depth-span ratios. For example the AASHO suggests the depth-span ratio be limited to a minimum value of $1/25$. A shallower section is permitted but it should have sufficient stiffness to prevent a deflection greater than would have occurred if the $1/25$ ratio had been used.

A steel beam can be cold-bent or cambered an amount equal to the deflection caused by dead load or the deflection caused by dead load plus some percentage of the live load. Approximately 25% of the camber so produced is elastic and will disappear when the cambering operation is completed. Detailed information for particular shapes is given in the Steel Handbook in the section entitled "Standard Mill Practice." It should be remembered that a beam which is bent upwards looks much stronger and safer than one which sags downward (even a very small distance).

Ponding. A large percentage of modern buildings are constructed with flat roofs. During heavy rains water begins to accumulate on these roofs causing them to deflect into dish shapes which permit the retention of more water and thus more deflections, etc. This increase in water depths, which is referred to as ponding, is a serious matter as illustrated by the large number of flat roof failures during rain storms in the United States in recent decades.

Ponding will occur on almost any flat roof to a certain degree even though roof drains are present. The best method of preventing its occurrence is to have an appreciable slope on the roof (say a pitch of $\frac{1}{8}$ in. per foot or more) together with good drainage facilities.

Where ponding occurs the process of more water, increased deflections, more water, etc., continues until the successive deflections become smaller and smaller and equilibrium is reached *or* until the structure collapses.

Theoretical calculations for ponding are very complicated. The AISC requirements are based on work by F. J. Marino[1] in which he considered the interaction of a two-way system of secondary or sub-members supported by a primary system of main members or girders. Section 1.13.3 of the AISC Specification gives careful limitations for flat roofs to prevent ponding failures.

7-5. UNSYMMETRICAL BENDING

From mechanics of materials it is remembered that each beam cross section has a pair of mutually perpendicular axes known as the principal axes for which the product of inertia is zero. Bending which occurs about any axis other than one of the principal axes is said to be unsymmetrical bending. When the external loads are not in a plane with either of the principal axes or when loads are simultaneously being applied to the beam from two or more directions unsymmetrical bending is the result.

When the external loads are not in the principal plane the stresses can be determined by breaking the loads into components perpendicular to the principal axes, calculating the moments about each axis, and determining the maximum stresses caused by a combination of the two moments. The following expression can be written for the stress at any point in a beam subjected to unsymmetrical bending:

---

[1] F. J. Marino, "Ponding of Two-Way Roof System," *Engineering Journal* (New York: American Institute of Steel Construction, July, 1966) pp. 93–100.

$$f = \frac{M_x y}{I_x} \pm \frac{M_y x}{I_y} = \frac{M_x}{S_x} \pm \frac{M_y}{S_y}$$

It might be noted there that the longitudinal shearing stresses for a beam of this type can be calculated with a similar expression:

$$v = \frac{V_x Q_x}{b I_x} \pm \frac{V_y Q_y}{b I_y}$$

When a section has one axis of symmetry that axis is one of the principal axes and the calculations necessary for determining stress are quite simple. For this reason unsymmetrical bending is not difficult to handle in the usual beam section, which is probably a W, S, M, or C. Each of these sections has at least one axis of symmetry and the calculations are appreciably reduced. A further simplifying factor is that the loads are usually gravity loads and probably perpendicular to the x axis. For a case of this type the formula for stress is simply $f = Mc/I$.

Among the beams which must resist unsymmetrical bending are crane girders in industrial buildings and purlins for ordinary roof trusses. The x axes of purlins are parallel to the sloping roof surfaces while the large percentage of their loads (roofing, snow, etc.) are gravity loads. These loads do not lie in a plane with either of the principal axes of the inclined purlins and the result is unsymmetrical bending. Wind loads are generally considered to act perpendicular to the roof surface and thus perpendicular to the x axes of the purlins with the result that they probably do not cause unsymmetrical bending. The x axes of crane girders are usually horizontal but the girders are subjected to lateral thrust loads from the moving cranes as well as to gravity loads.

Should a compact, laterally supported beam be bent about its x axis only the allowable stress F_b will be 0.66 F_y using the AISC Specification. Should a similar shape be bent about its y axis only, F_b equals 0.75 F_y. Which allowable stress is to be used when both types of bending occur simultaneously? The AISC uses an allowable stress which is in effect a combination of the two allowable values. This is done by using the interaction equation to follow

$$\frac{f_{bx}}{F_{bx}} + \frac{f_{by}}{F_{by}} \lesssim 1.0$$

For compact laterally supported shapes the equation becomes

$$\frac{f_{bx}}{0.66\,F_y} + \frac{f_{by}}{0.75\,F_y} \lesssim 1.0$$

Examples 7-3 and 7-4 illustrate the design of beams subjected to unsymmetrical bending. To illustrate the trial-and-error nature of the problem the author did not do quite as much scratchwork as in the first example. The first design problems of this type which the student attempts may quite well take him several trials. Consideration needs to be given to the question of lateral support for the compression flange. Should the lateral support be of questionable nature the engineer should reduce the allowable compressive stresses by means of one of the expressions previously given for that purpose.

EXAMPLE 7-3. A certain beam is estimated to have a vertical bending moment of 120 ft-k and a lateral bending moment of 25 ft-k. These moments include the effect of the estimated beam weight. The loads are assumed to pass through the centroid of the section and the entire section modulus value is therefore available about each axis. Select a W shape which can resist these moments. Use A36 steel and the AISC Specification and assume full lateral support for the compression flange.

Solution:
First trial: The S required for vertical bending moments alone is $12 \times 120/24 = 60$ in.^{3}. Try a section with a larger section modulus.

Try W 24 $\times$ 61 ($S_x = 130, S_y = 9.76$)

$$f_{bx} = \frac{12 \times 120}{130} = 11.07 \text{ ksi}$$

$$F_{bx} = 0.66F_y = 24 \text{ ksi}$$

$$f_{by} = \frac{12 \times 25}{9.76} = 30.7 \text{ ksi}$$

$$F_{by} = 0.75\,F_y = 27 \text{ ksi}$$

$$\frac{f_{bx}}{F_{bx}} + \frac{f_{by}}{F_{by}} = \frac{11.07}{24} + \frac{30.7}{27} = 1.60 > 1.00 \qquad \text{(N.G.)}$$

Final trial:

Try W 14 $\times$ 74 ($S_x = 112, S_y = 26.5$)

$$f_{bx} = \frac{12 \times 120}{112} = 12.85 \text{ ksi}$$

$$f_{by} = \frac{12 \times 25}{26.5} = 11.32 \text{ ksi}$$

$$\frac{f_{bx}}{F_{bx}} + \frac{f_{by}}{F_{by}} = \frac{12.85}{24} + \frac{11.32}{27} = .95 < 1.00 \qquad \text{(OK)}$$

Use W 14 × 74
_____

It will be noticed in the solution for Example 7-3 that though the procedure used will yield a section which will adequately support the moments the selection of the absolutely lightest satisfactory section listed in the AISC Manual could be quite lengthy.

A further complication in the design of beams subject to unsymmetrical bending is caused by the fact that the loads often do not pass through the centroid of the section. For instance, the loads applied to a purlin are generally applied to its top flange and the result is a twisting moment or torsion in the inclined purlin. Rather than become involved in torsion calculations, a common design practice is to assume the lateral loads are carried only by the top flange of the beam. Only one-half of the section modulus about the y axis is considered effective and the value of f_{by} becomes $M_y/\frac{1}{2}S_y$. This rather poor design practice is used in Example 7-4.

EXAMPLE 7-4. Redesign the beam of Example 7-3 if the lateral loads are assumed to be applied to the top flange of the beam and thus do not pass through the centroid of the section. Reduce the effective modulus for the y axis by 50 percent.

Solution:

Try W 14 × 87 $(S_x = 138, S_y = 48.2)$
_____

$$f_{bx} = \frac{12 \times 120}{138} = 10.43 \text{ ksi}$$

$$f_{by} = \frac{12 \times 25}{\frac{1}{2} \times 48.2} = 12.44 \text{ ksi}$$

$$\frac{f_{bx}}{F_{bx}} + \frac{f_{by}}{F_{by}} = \frac{10.43}{24} + \frac{12.44}{27} = .894 < 1.0 \qquad \text{(OK)}$$

Use W 14 × 87
_____

In this example (7-4) the lateral moment was estimated to cause a stress of 12.44 ksi. Of this amount 6.22 ksi was thrown in to approximate the torsion effect. (Is this a precise engineering calculation?)

When a section does not have an axis of symmetry, the work required to locate the neutral axis, to calculate the principal moments of inertia, and to determine the necessary distances for a particular point are quite tedious. The expressions (from mechanics of materials) at the end of this paragraph can be used to locate the principal axes and calculate the principal moments of inertia. In these expressions I_{xy} is the product of inertia while the various other symbols used are shown in Fig. 7-5.

$$\tan 2\phi = \frac{I_{xy}}{I_y - I_x}$$

$$I_{x1} = \cos^2 \phi\, I_x + \sin^2 \phi\, I_y - 2\sin \phi \cos \phi\, I_{xy}$$

$$I_{y1} = \cos^2 \phi\, I_y + \sin^2 \phi\, I_x + 2\sin \phi \cos \phi\, I_{xy}$$

After the principal moments of inertia are determined the stresses can be obtained by breaking the loads into components perpendicular to each of the principal axes, calculating the moments about each, and substituting in the unsymmetrical bending expression. It will, however, be noted that the remaining calculations are still tedious particularly those involved in computing the perpendicular distances to each point (x and y in Fig. 7-5) from the principal axes.

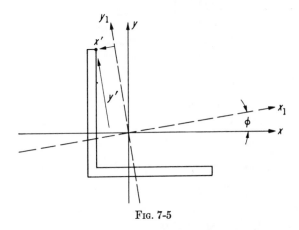

FIG. 7-5

The equation to follow may be more useful when the section in question has no axis of symmetry.

$$f = \frac{M_y I_x - M_x I_{xy}}{I_x I_y - I_{xy}^2}\, x + \frac{M_x I_y - M_y I_{xy}}{I_x I_y - I_{xy}^2}\, y$$

This general expression is applicable to any straight beam of constant cross section regardless of the shape and regardless of whether the section is open or closed. The x and y axes can be assumed in any convenient direction as long as they are perpendicular to each other and pass through the centroid of the cross section.

Example 7-5 illustrates the application of this expression. For substitution in the formula (as well as in the calculations for I_{xy}), x is considered to be positive for points to the right of the y axis and minus to the left, while y is positive for points above the x axis and minus below. A plus sign for the resulting stress indicates compression, and a minus sign indicates tension.

EXAMPLE 7-5. Determine the stress at points A, B, and C in the $6 \times 4 \times \frac{3}{4}$-in. angle shown in Fig. 7-6 due to gravity loads which cause a moment of 5 ft-k.

FIG. 7-6

Solution: Properties of section:

$$I_x = 24.5 \text{ in.}^4$$

$$I_y = 8.7 \text{ in.}^4$$

$$I_{xy} = (3.00) (+0.92) (-1.71) + (3.96) (-0.71) (+1.30)$$

$$= -8.37 \text{ in.}^4$$

Stress at A:

$$f = \frac{M_y I_x - M_x I_{xy}}{I_x I_y - I^2_{xy}} x + \frac{M_x I_y - M_y I_{xy}}{I_x I_y - I^2_{xy}} y$$

$$f_A = \frac{0 - (60,000) (-8.37)}{(24.5) (8.7) - (-8.37)^2} (-1.08) + \frac{(60,000) (8.7) - 0}{(24.5) (8.7) - (-8.37)^2} (+3.92)$$

$$= +10,620 \text{ psi (compression)}$$

Stress at B:

$$f_B = \frac{0 - (60,000) (-8.37)}{(24.5) (8.7) - (-8.37)^2} (-1.08) + \frac{(60,000) (8.7) - 0}{(24.5) (8.7) - (-8.37)^2} (-2.08)$$

$$= -11,350 \text{ psi (tension)}$$

Stress at C:

$$f_C = \frac{0 - (60,000) (-8.37)}{(24.5) (8.7) - (-8.37)^2} (+2.92) + \frac{(60,000) (8.7) - 0}{(24.5) (8.7) - (-8.37)^2} (-2.08)$$

$$= +2,700 \text{ psi (compression)}$$

7-6. DESIGN OF PURLINS

To avoid bending in the top chords of roof trusses, it is theoretically desirable to place purlins only at panel points. For large trusses, however, it is more economical to space them at closer intervals. If this practice is not followed for large trusses the purlin sizes may become so

Channel purlin
(a)

$$\frac{9}{512} w_y l^2 \qquad \frac{9}{512} w_y l^2$$

$$\frac{w_y l^2}{32}$$

$$\frac{3}{8}\frac{l}{2} \qquad \frac{3}{8}\frac{l}{2}$$

$$\frac{l}{2} \qquad \frac{l}{2}$$

Moment about web axis of purlins — sag rods at midspan
(b)

$$\frac{2w_y l^2}{225} \qquad \frac{1 w_y l^2}{360} \qquad \frac{2w_y l^2}{225}$$

$$\frac{w_y l^2}{90} \qquad \frac{w_y l^2}{90}$$

$$\frac{l}{3} \qquad \frac{l}{3} \qquad \frac{l}{3}$$

Moment about web axis of purlins — sag rods at one-third points
(c)

$$\frac{w_x l^2}{8}$$

Moment about X axis of purlin
(d)

Fig. 7-7

large as to be impractical. When intermediate purlins are used the top chords of the truss should be designed for bending as well as axial stress. Purlins are usually spaced from 2 to 6 ft apart depending on loading conditions, while their most desirable depth to span ratios are probably in the neighborhood of 1/24. Channels or S sections are the most frequently used sections but on some occasions other shapes may be convenient.

As previously described in Chap. 3, the channel and S sections are very weak about their web axes and sag rods are often necessary to reduce the span lengths for bending about those axes. Sag rods, in effect, make the purlins continuous sections for their y axes and the moments about these axes are greatly reduced, as shown in Fig. 7-7. These moment diagrams are developed on the assumption that the changes in length of the sag rods are negligible. It is further assumed that the purlins are simply supported at the trusses. This assumption is on the conservative side since they are often continuous over two or more trusses and appreciable continuity may be achieved at their splices. The student can easily reproduce these diagrams from his knowledge of moment distribution or other analysis methods. In the diagrams l is the distance between trusses, w_y is the load component *perpendicular* to the web axis of the purlin and w_x is the load component *parallel* to the web axis.

If sag rods were not used the maximum moment about the web axis of a purlin would be $w_y l^2/8$. When sag rods are used at midspan this moment is reduced to a maximum of $w_y l^2/32$ (a 75 percent reduction) and when used at one-third points is reduced to a maximum of $2w_y l^2/175$ (a 91 percent reduction). In the example problem to follow (Example 7-6), sag rods are used at the midpoints and the purlins are designed for a moment of $w_x l^2/8$ parallel to the web axis and $w_y l^2/32$ perpendicular to the web axis. To estimate the effect of torsion, the section modulus about the web axis is reduced by 50 percent.

FIG. 7-8

In addition to being of advantage in reducing moments about the web axes of purlins, sag rods can serve other useful purposes. First, they can provide lateral support for the purlins; secondly, they are useful in keeping the purlins in proper alignment during erection until the roof deck is installed and connected to the purlins.

EXAMPLE 7-6. Select a C6 purlin for the truss shown in Fig. 7-8. The trusses are 15 ft 0 in. on centers and sag rods are used at the midpoints between trusses. Full lateral support is assumed to be supplied from the roof above. Use A36 steel and the AISC Specification. Loads are as follows in terms of pounds per square foot of roof surface:

Snow	= 20 psf
Roofing	= 6 psf
Estimated purlin weight	= 4 psf
Total	30 psf
Wind pressure	= 10 psf $\perp$ to roof surface

Solution:

$$w_{\text{gravity}} = (4.42)\ (30) = 132.6\ \text{lb/ft}$$

$$w_{\text{wind}} = (4.42)\ (10) = 44.2\ \text{lb/ft}$$

$$w_x = 44.2 + \left(\frac{2}{\sqrt{5}}\right)(132.6) = 163\ \text{lb/ft}$$

$$w_y = \left(\frac{1}{\sqrt{5}}\right)(132.6) = 59.2\ \text{lb/ft}$$

$$M_x = \frac{(0.163)\ (15)^2}{8} = 4.58\ \text{ft-k}$$

$$M_y = \frac{(0.0592)\ (15)^2}{32} = 0.416\ \text{ft-k}$$

Try C 6 × 8.2 ($S_x = 4.38, S_y = 0.492$)

$$f_{bx} = \frac{12 \times 4.58}{4.38} = 12.55\ \text{ksi}$$

$$f_{by} = \frac{12 \times 0.416}{0.492} = 10.13\ \text{ksi}$$

$$\frac{f_{bx}}{F_{bx}} + \frac{f_{by}}{F_{by}} = \frac{12.55}{24} + \frac{10.13}{27} = 0.898 < 1.0 \qquad \text{(OK)}$$

Use C 6 × 8.2

7-7. THE SHEAR CENTER

The shear center is defined as the point on the cross section of a beam through which the resultant of the tranverse loads must pass so that the stresses in the beam may be calculated only from the theories of pure bending and transverse shear. Should the resultant pass through this point, it is unnecessary to analyze the beam for torsional moments. For a beam with two axes of symmetry the shear center will fall at the intersection of the two axes, thus coinciding with the centroid of the section. For a beam with one axis of symmetry the shear center will fall somewhere on that axis but not necessarily at the centroid of the section. This surprising statement means that to avoid torsion in some beams the lines of action of the loads should not pass through the centroid of the section.

The shear center is of particular importance for beams whose cross sections are composed of thin parts which provide considerable bending resistance but little resistance to torsion. Many common structural members such as the W, S, and C sections, angles and various beams made up of thin plates (as in aircraft construction) fall into this class and the problem has wide application.

The location of shear centers for several open sections are shown in Fig. 7-9. Sections such as these are relatively weak in torsion and for them and similar shapes the location of the resultant of the external loads can be a very serious matter. A previous discussion has indicated that the addition of one or more webs to these sections so they are changed into box shapes greatly increases their torsional resistance.

The average designer probably does not take the time to go through the sometimes tedious computations involved in locating the shear center

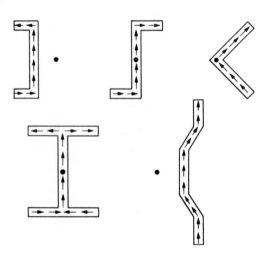

FIG. 7-9

and calculating the effect of twisting. He may instead just ignore the situation, or he may make a rough estimate of the effect of torsion on the bending stresses. An illustration of a rough estimate of the torsion effect in purlins was given in Example 7-4, where only one-half of S_y was considered effective when lateral loads were applied to the top flange. The large percentage of the total stress due to the rough estimate made in that example should keep the designer on the lookout for cases where his estimates might be too inaccurate.

Shear centers can be located quickly for beams with open cross sections and relatively thin webs. For other beams the shear centers can probably be found but only with considerable difficulty. The term *shear flow* is often used when speaking of thin-wall members although there is really no flowing involved. It refers to the shear per inch of cross section and equals the unit shearing stress times the thickness of the member. (The unit shearing stress has been determined by the expression VQ/bI and the shear flow can be determined by VQ/I if the shearing stress is assumed to be constant across the thickness of the section.)

Fig. 7-10

The channel section of Fig. 7-10(a) will be considered for this discussion. In this figure the shear flow is shown with the small arrows and in part (b) the values are totaled for each component of the shape and labeled H and V. The two H values are in equilibrium horizontally and the internal V value balances the external shear at the section. Although the horizontal and vertical forces are in equilibrium, the same cannot be said for the moment forces unless the lines of action of the resultant of the external forces passes through a certain point called the shear center. The horizontal H forces in part (b) of the figure can be seen to form a couple. The moment produced by this couple must be opposed by an equal and opposite moment which can only be produced by the two V values. The location of the shear center is a problem in equilibrium;

therefore moments should be taken about a point which eliminates the largest number of forces possible.

From this information the following equation can be written from which the shear center can be located:

$$Ve = Hh \quad \text{(moments taken about c.g. of web)}$$

Examples 7-7 and 7-8 illustrate the calculations involved in locating the shear center for two shapes. It will be noted that the location of the shear center is independent of the value of the external shear although V values are given in these examples.

EXAMPLE 7-7. The channel section shown in Fig. 7-11(a) is subjected to an external shear of 30 k. Locate the shear center.

(a)

Variation of shearing stresses

(b)

FIG. 7-11

Solution: Properties of section:

$$I_x = (\tfrac{1}{12})\,(3)\,(10)^3 - (\tfrac{1}{12})\,(2.7)\,(9.4)^3 = 63 \text{ in.}^4$$

$$v \text{ at } B = \frac{(30)\,(2.85 \times 0.3 \times 4.85)}{63} = 1.98 \text{ k/in.}$$

$$\text{Total } H = (\tfrac{1}{2})\,(2.85)\,(1.98) = 2.82 \text{ k}$$

Location of shear center:

$$Ve = Hh$$

$$30\,e = (2.82)\,(9.7)$$

$$e = 0.91 \text{ in. from } \text{₵ of web}$$

The student should clearly understand that shear stress variation across the corners, where the webs and flanges join, cannot be determined correctly with the mechanics of materials expression (VQ/bI or VQ/I for shear flow) and cannot be determined too well even after a complicated study with the theory of elasticity. The author as an approximation in the two examples presented here has assumed that shear flow continues up to the middle of the corners on the same pattern (straight line variation for horizontal members and parabolic for others). The values of Q are computed for the corresponding dimensions. Other assumptions could have been made such as assuming a shear flow variation continuing vertically for the full depth of webs and only for the protruding parts of flanges horizontally, or vice versa. Whichever of these assumptions is used the results will be approximately the same. It is rather disturbing to find that whichever assumption is used the values do not check out perfectly. For instance in Example 7-8 which follows the sum of the vertical shear flow values does not check out very well with the external shear.

EXAMPLE 7-8. The open section of Fig. 7-12 is subjected to an external shear of 20 k. Locate the shear center.

FIG. 7-12

Solution: Properties of section:

$$I_x = (\tfrac{1}{12}) \ (.25) \ (16)^3 + (2) \ (3.75 \times .25) \ (4.88)^2 = 129.8 \text{ in.}^4$$

Values of shear flow (labeled q):

$$q_A = 0$$

$$q_B = \frac{(20) \ (3.12 \times .25 \times 6.44)}{129.8} = 0.775 \text{ k/in.}$$

$$q_C = q_B + \frac{(20)\ (3.75 \times .25 \times 4.88)}{129.8} = 1.48 \text{ k/in.}$$

$$q_{\text{¢}} = q_C + \frac{(20)\ (4.88 \times .25 \times 2.44)}{129.8} = 1.94 \text{ k/in.}$$

These shear flow values are shown in Fig. 7-13(a) and the summation for each part of the member are given in part (b) of the figure.

FIG. 7-13

Taking moments about the center line of CD

$$- (4.22)\ (9.75) + (0.81)\ (3.75) + 20e = 0$$

$$e = 1.90 \text{ in.}$$

The theory of the shear center is a very useful one in design but it has certain limitations which should be clearly understood. For instance, the approximate analysis given in this section is only valid for thin sections. In addition steel beams often have variable cross sections along their spans with the result that the locus of the shear centers are not straight lines along those spans. The result is that if the resultant of the loads passes through the shear center at one cross section it might very well not do so at other cross sections.

7-8. LINTELS

Openings in brick or block walls which have relatively flat tops, such as windows and doors, require beams above them to support the masonry and other loads above. Although considerable arch action exists in the

masonry after the mortar has set, it is still necessary to support the
masonry while it is green to prevent settlement and possible destruction
of the arch action before it can develop. These supporting beams, called
lintels, may consist of any number of different shapes. For very small
openings, flat bars or plates may be used, whereas angles are convenient
for slightly larger openings. When the openings become quite large
structural tees, channels, S beams, W sections, or even built-up sections
may be necessary.

The amount of load which must be supported by a particular lintel
is quite uncertain and a good estimate can only be made after a careful
study is made of the particular situation. The window shown in Fig. 7-14

$$M_{\text{¢}} = \left(\frac{W}{2}\right)\left(\frac{l}{2} - \frac{1}{3}\frac{l}{2}\right) = \frac{Wl}{6}$$

(a)   (b)

Fig. 7-14

(a) is assumed to be located in a brick wall which is solid and continuous
above and around the sides of the window. It seems logical to assume
that the lintel will carry the triangular shaped portion of the wall above

Fig. 7-15

the window. This loading situation appears even more reasonable when it is known that examinations of old brick buildings often reveal cracks above the windows in approximately the shape of a triangle when the lintels have settled. In part (b) of the figure an expression is developed for the maximum moment in this type of lintel.

Figure 7-15 shows a group of windows located between two columns. A spandrel wall is located above the windows and as the figure shows the lintel will in all probability have to support the entire overhead wall.

Another loading condition for lintels which is often encountered in small buildings is shown in Fig. 7-16. The lintel shown there, which is

Fig. 7-16

placed above a series of windows on one floor, supports not only the walls above but also the reactions from the beams under the floor above.

The lintel selected for a particular wall must have dimensions which fit in reasonably well so that the brick or blocks can be placed without unusual difficulty. As it is desirable for the lintel not to be visible from one or both sides of a wall, it is usually buried in the wall. For this reason an inverted structural tee (⊥) or a pair of angles back to back (⅃L) are very satisfactory in many situations.

For many walls which consist of more than one thickness of brick or blocks (or combinations of bricks and blocks), the lintel may consist of two or more angles or other shapes or some combination of shapes one in each thickness which are not connected to each other. Should noncon-nected shapes be used an effort should be made to keep the deflections in each part equal. It is true that the window and door headers below might prevent the separate parts of the lintel from deflecting differently. Even if this is true, additional loads will probably be thrown on the lintel which tends to have the smallest deflection and cause it to be overstressed.

There is a great deal of information available as to the size of lintels which should be used for different size openings. One table suggests a $3\frac{1}{2} \times \frac{3}{8}$-in. flat bar for each 4-in. thickness of wall for openings of less than 2 ft; a $3\frac{1}{2} \times 3\frac{1}{2} \times \frac{5}{16}$-in. angle for each 4-in. thickness of wall for openings of 2 to 5 ft, etc. Despite the availability of this excellent information concerning lintel sizes consideration should be given to the particular loading conditions and member arrangements in the building under study to insure the selection of satisfactory sizes.

7-9. BEAM-BEARING PLATES

When the ends of beams are supported by direct bearing on concrete or other masonry construction it is frequently necessary to distribute the beam reactions over the masonry by means of beam bearing plates. The reaction is assumed to be spread uniformly through the bearing plate to the masonry and the masonry is assumed to push up against the plate

Fig. 7-17

with a uniform pressure equal to f_p psf. This pressure tends to curl up the plate and the bottom flange of the beam. The AISC Manual recommends that the bearing plate be considered to take the entire bending moment produced and that the critical section for moment be assumed to be a distance k from the centerline of the beam (see Fig. 7-17). The distance k is the same as the distance from the outer face of the flange to the web toe of the fillet given in the tables for each section (or it equals the flange thickness plus the fillet radius).

The determination of the true pressure distribution in a beam bearing plate is a very formidable task and the uniform pressure distribution assumption is usually made. This assumption is probably on the conservative side as the pressure is probably larger at the center of the beam than at the edges. The outer edges of the plate and flange tend to bend upwards and the center of the beam tends to go down concentrating the pressure there.

The required thickness of a 1-in.-wide strip of plate can be determined as follows:

$$M = f_p n \frac{n}{2} = \frac{f_p n^2}{2}$$

$$S = \frac{I}{C} = \frac{(\frac{1}{12})\ (1)\ (t)^3}{t/2} = \frac{t^2}{6}$$

$$\frac{M}{f} = S$$

$$\frac{f_p n^2}{2f} = \frac{t^2}{6}$$

$$t = \sqrt{\frac{3 f_p n^2}{F_b}}$$

Example 7-9 illustrates the calculations involved in designing a beam bearing plate. Notice that the distances B and C are desirably taken to the nearest full inch.

EXAMPLE 7-9. An W 18 × 70 beam ($b = 8.75$, $k = 1\frac{7}{16}$ in.) is to be end supported by a masonry wall which has an allowable bearing strength of 250 psi. Design a bearing plate for the beam with A36 steel and the AISC Specification. The end reaction is 40 k and the maximum length of bearing available is 12 in.

Solution: Minimum length of bearing for web crippling:

$$\frac{R}{t_w(N+k)} = 0.75\ F_y$$

$$\frac{40,000}{0.438\ (N + 1\frac{7}{16})} = (0.75)\ (36,000)$$

$$N = 1.95 \text{ in. (minimum permissible value of } C)$$

$$\text{Area required} = \frac{40,000}{250} = 160 \text{ sq in.}$$

$$B = \frac{160}{12} = 13.33 \text{ in.}$$

Try 12 × 14 in. PL

$$n = 7.00 - 1\frac{7}{16} = 5.56 \text{ in.}$$

$$f_p = \frac{40,000}{12 \times 14} = 238 \text{ psi}$$

$$t = \sqrt{\frac{3f_p n^2}{F_b}} = \sqrt{\frac{(3)\ (238)\ (5.56)^2}{27,000}}$$

$$= 0.905$$

Use 1 × 12 × 14 in. PL

On some occasions the beam flanges alone probably provide sufficient bearing area, but bearing plates are nevertheless recommended as they are useful in erection and insure an even bearing surface for the beam. They can be placed separately from the beams and carefully leveled to the proper elevations. When the ends of steel beams are enclosed by the concrete or masonry walls it is considered desirable to use some type of wall anchor to prevent the beam from moving longitudinally with respect to the wall. The usual anchor consists of a bent steel bar passing through the web of the beam and running parallel to the wall. These are called government anchors and details of their sizes are given in the AISC Manual. Occasionally clip angles attached to the web are used instead of government anchors. Should longitudinal loads of considerable size be anticipated, regular vertical anchor bolts may be used at the beam ends.

PROBLEMS

Note: Full lateral support is provided for all sections unless noted otherwise.

7-1. A W 24 × 68 has a maximum external shear of 75 k.

(a) Calculate the maximum theoretical shearing stress in the section. (Ans. 8,620 psi)

(b) Calculate the average shearing stress in the section using the full depth of the section. (Ans. 7,600 psi)

7-2. A W 18 × 45 has a maximum end shear of 35 k. Calculate the average shearing stress in the section (using the total depth of the section) and the actual maximum theoretical shearing stress.

7-3. Using A36 steel and the AISC Specification select the lightest section

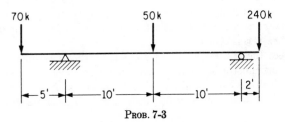

PROB. 7-3

for the span and loading shown in the accompanying illustration. Neglect beam weight in all calculations. (Ans. W 30 × 116)

7-4. Using the AISC Specification and A36 steel determine the maximum uniform load which can be placed on a W 14 × 34 which has a simple span of 6 ft 6 in.

7-5. A W 16 × 40 consisting of A36 steel is used as a simple beam for a span of 6 ft. Using the AISC Specification determine the maximum uniform load which the beam can support. (Ans. 23.69 k/ft)

7-6. A W 36 × 245 consisting of A36 steel is used as a simple beam for a span of 15 ft. Using the AISC Specification determine the maximum uniform load which the beam can support.

7-7. A W 33 × 220 is required for a certain span but, due to a strike in the steel mills, cannot be obtained on time, however an extra W 33 × 118 of sufficient length is available along with a good supply of plates. Select ⅞-in. thick cover plates to be welded to the flanges of the W 33 × 118 to provide a satisfactory substitute for the original beam. Use A36 steel and the AISC Specification. (Ans. W 33 × 118 with one ⅞ × 14 PL each flange)

7-8. A W 30 × 172 section has been specified for use on a certain job. By mistake, a W 30 × 124 section was shipped to the field. This beam must be erected today. Assuming that plates are obtainable immediately, select cover plates to be welded to the flanges to obtain the necessary section. Use A36 steel and the AISC Specification.

7-9. Repeat Prob. 7-7 if the original beam was to have been of a steel with $F_y = 50$ ksi and the substitute material is available only in A36 steel. Assume also that only 15/16-in. plates are available. (Ans. W 33 × 118 with 15/16 × 22 cover PL each flange)

7-10. Design a beam of A36 steel with a depth no greater than 12.00 in. to support a uniform load of 8 k/ft for a 20-ft simple span. Use AISC Specification.

7-11. A simply supported W 24 × 145 beam is 6 ft long and supports a concentrated load of 300 k 2 ft from the left end. If the length of bearing at the left support is 8 in. and at the concentrated load is 12 in., check the beam for bending, shear and web crippling. Use A36 steel and the AISC Specification. (Ans. Section is unsatisfactory as to web crippling)

7-12. A 30-ft beam is to support a moving concentrated load of 36 k. Using A36 steel and the AISC Specification select the most economical section. Also determine the maximum shearing stress in the section selected and compute the length of bearing required at each support from the standpoint of web crippling.

7-13. A 20-ft simple beam which supports a concentrated load of 20 k at mid-span, is laterally unsupported except at its ends and is limited to a maximum total deflection of $l/1000$. Select the most economical W section available using A36 steel and the AISC Specification. (Ans. W 18 × 55 or W 21 × 55)

7-14. Design a beam for a 24-ft simple span to support a 4 k/ft uniform load. The maximum permissible deflection is 1/1200th of the span and the allowable bending stress is 20 ksi.

7-15. Select the lightest available section for the span and loads shown in the accompanying illustration if the maximum permissible deflection is 1/1500th of the span. Neglect beam weight in all calculations and use A36 steel and the AISC Specification. (Ans. W 36 × 300 with ¼ × 7 PL each flange)

DESIGN OF BEAMS (CONTINUED)   159

Prob. 7-15

7-16. Select the lightest section available for the span and loads shown in the accompanying illustration if the maximum permissible deflection is 1/1000th of the span. Use A36 steel and the AISC Specification.

Prob. 7-16

7-17. The maximum permissible deflection in the beam shown in the accompanying illustration is 1/1200th of the span. Select the lightest available section using A36 steel and the AISC Specification. (Ans. W 36 × 194)

Prob. 7-17

7-18. Select the lightest available W section for the beam shown in the accompanying illustration. Lateral support is provided only at the 12-ft points and

Prob 7-18

a maximum deflection equal to 1/1500th of the 24 ft span is permitted. Neglect beam weight in all calculations and use A36 steel and the AISC Specification.

7-19. Select the lightest W section (A36 steel) which can support the loads shown in the accompanying illustration so the deflection will not exceed 1/1,200th of the span. Use the AISC Specification. (Ans. W 33 × 118)

6 k/ft

├─────30'─────┤├─────30'─────┤

PROB. 7-19

7-20. A W 21 × 62 serves as an 18-ft simple beam supporting a uniform gravity load of 2 k/ft. Compute the bending stresses at each corner of the beam if it is inclined as shown in the accompanying illustration. The loads are assumed to act through the c.g. of the section.

PROB. 7-20

7-21. Find the shear center for the section shown in the accompanying illustration. (Ans. $e = .93$ in. from web ₵)

PROB. 7-21

7-22. Find the shear center for the section shown in the accompanying illustration.

PROB. 7-22

7-23. Find the shear center for the section shown in the accompanying illustration. (Ans. $e = 1.03$ in.)

PROB. 7-23

7-24. Select a W 12 section to serve as a purlin between roof trusses 24 ft on centers. The roof is assumed to support a dead load of 20 psf of roof surface and a snow load of 20 psf of horizontal roof surface projection. The slope of the roof truss is 1 vertically to 2 horizontally and the purlins are to be spaced 12 ft on centers. Use A36 steel and the AISC Specification and assume loads pass through c.g. of section. Sag rods are assumed to be placed halfway between trusses.

7-25. Repeat Prob. 7-24 assuming lateral support for the purlins is provided at the 12-ft points only. (Ans. W 12 × 27)

7-26. Design an angle lintel to go over a 5-ft wide window in a 4-in. brick wall. The wall which is assumed to exist on the sides and over the window is assumed to weigh 120 lb/cu ft. Use A36 steel and the AISC Specification.

7-27. A lintel is to be located over a doorway in a brick building. The wall is 8 in. thick and weighs 125 lb/cu ft. The clear opening of the doorway is 12 ft 4 in. Select an inverted structural tee with a flange width of approximately 7 in. Use AISC Specification and A36 steel. (Ans. WT 7 × 15)

7-28. A 14-ft opening is to be constructed in a 12-in. brick wall. Using A36 steel and the AISC Specification design a lintel consisting of a structural tee and an angle. The parts should be selected so their deflections are approximately equal. The wall weighs 120 lb/cu ft.

7-29. Using the AISC Specification design a steel bearing plate of A36 steel for a W 21 × 68 beam with an end reaction of 62 k. The beam bears on a masonry wall having an allowable bearing stress of 500 psi. In a direction perpendicular to the wall the bearing plate may not be longer than 8 in. (Ans. Several sizes possible: one is a PL $1\frac{9}{16}$ × 8 × 16)

7-30. Design a steel bearing plate of A36 steel for a W 30 × 116 beam supported by a concrete wall. The allowable bearing on the concrete is assumed to be 750 psi and the maximum beam reaction is 105 k. Use the AISC Specification and assume the width of the plate perpendicular to the wall may not exceed 6 in.

7-31. Repeat Prob. 7-30 using a steel with $F_y = 45$ ksi steel for the beam and the bearing plate. Assume the allowable bearing pressure on the concrete is 1,125 psi. (Ans. Several sizes possible: one is a PL 2 × 6 × 16)

chapter **8**

BENDING AND AXIAL STRESS

8-1. OCCURRENCE

Structural members which are subjected to a combination of bending and axial stress are far more common than the student may realize. This section is devoted to listing a few of the more obvious cases. Columns which are part of a steel building frame must nearly always resist sizable bending moments in addition to the usual compressive loads. It is almost impossible to erect and center loads exactly on columns even in a testing lab and in an actual building the student can see that it is even more impossible. Even if building loads could be perfectly centered at one time they would not stay in one place. Furthermore, columns may be initially crooked or have other flaws with the result that lateral bending is produced. The beams framing into columns are quite commonly supported with framing angles or brackets on the sides of the columns. These eccentrically applied loads produce moments. Wind and other lateral loads cause columns to bend laterally, and the columns in rigid frame buildings are subjected to moments even when the frame is supporting gravity loads alone. The members of bridge portals must resist combined stresses as do building columns. Among the causes are heavy lateral wind loads, vertical traffic loads whether symmetrical or not, and the centrifugal effect of traffic on curved bridges.

The previous experience of the student has probably been to assume truss members axially loaded only. Purlins for roof trusses, however, are frequently placed in between truss joints, causing the top chords to bend. Similarly the bottom chords may be bent by the hanging of light fixtures, ductwork, and other items between the truss joints. All horizontal and inclined truss members have moments caused by their own weights, while all truss members whether vertical or not are subjected to secondary bending stresses. Secondary stresses are developed because the members are not connected with frictionless pins as assumed in the usual analysis, the member centers of gravities or those of their connectors do not exactly coincide at the joints, etc.

Inland Steel Building, Chicago, Ill. (*Inland Steel Company.*)

Moments in tension members are not as serious as those in compression members because tension tends to reduce lateral deflections while compression increases them. Increased lateral deflection in turn results in larger moments, which result in larger lateral deflections, etc It is hoped that members in such situations are quite stiff so as to keep the additional lateral deflections from becoming excessive.

8-2. CALCULATION OF STRESSES

Sometimes members are encountered which have as their most important loadings transverse bending moments but which are also subjected to axial loads. However, this is not nearly as common a situation as where the major loading is axial with some transverse bending occurring at the same time. The name *beam-column* is often given to members which have appreciable amounts of both axial compression and bending stresses. The stresses in members subjected to a combination of axial load and bending are difficult to obtain exactly and the stresses calculated in this chapter are truly approximate.

The stress at any point in a member subject to bending and direct stress is usually obtained from the familiar expression to follow. (This expression is said to be approximate because it does not include the effect of increased lateral deflections caused by moments and their subsequent effect on the moments and thus the stresses.)

$$f = \frac{P}{A} \pm \frac{Mc}{I}$$

Frequently bending occurs about some axis other than the x or y axis; that is, it occurs about both axes simultaneously. The corner columns of buildings may fall into this class. Stresses for members subjected to axial loads and bending about both axes are usually determined by the following expression:

$$f = \frac{P}{A} \pm \frac{M_x y}{I_x} \pm \frac{M_y x}{I_y}$$

Example 8-1 shows the calculations involved in computing the total stress in a member of a bridge truss due to its computed axial stress plus the flexure stress caused by its own weight. The calculations here are quite straightforward, but a few comments will probably be of value. First, it will be noted that although this is a riveted member the gross area of the section is used, because the rivet holes are at the ends of the member while the maximum bending is assumed to occur at the centerline. Secondly, the flexure stresses due to the weight of the member in this example are not very large, and as a matter of fact they are not very large in the average truss member. As truss members become unusually long and heavy the moments due to their own weights may become of appreciable magnitude.

The engineers who prepare the usual specifications used for the design of truss members have reduced the allowable axial stresses by approximately one-fourth to take into account the so-called secondary stresses. A similar discussion can be made for the magnitude of column flexure stresses due to column imperfections, slightly off-centered loads, and moments due to lateral deflections. This discussion shows that if the engineer went overboard theoretically, he would design all members, whether columns or beams or truss members, for axial load and bending. It is probable, however, that the decreased allowable stresses provide a sufficient margin to cover the usual case of off-center loads or otherwise imperfect columns and secondary truss member stresses. Unless the situation is severe the designer will probably not include the moments in his design. Specifications rarely mention the matter and it is up to the individual designer to use his own judgment. This discussion is not intended to apply to truss members which have transverse loads applied to them between the truss joints nor to columns which have appreciable moments applied as a part of a rigid frame structure.

EXAMPLE 8-1. A bottom chord of a riveted bridge truss is 22 ft long, has a maximum tensile stress of 310 k, and is made up of a 4 Ls, 6 × 4 × ½, arranged as shown in Fig. 8-1. Determine the maximum stress in the member due to the axial tension load plus the flexure stress due to the member's own weight.

4 Ls 6 X 4 X ½

FIG. 8-1

Solution: $(A_{gross} = 19$ sq in., $I_x = 43.8$ in.$^4)$

Weight of Ls $= \left(\dfrac{19}{144}\right)(490) = 64.8$ lb/ft

$$M = \frac{wl^2}{8} = \frac{(64.8)(22)^2}{8} = 3{,}920 \text{ ft-lb}$$

$$f = \frac{P}{A} + \frac{Mc}{I} = \frac{310{,}000}{19} + \frac{(12)(3{,}920)(4.00)}{43.8}$$

$$f = 16{,}300 + 4{,}290 = 20{,}590 \text{ psi}$$

Percent stress due to member's weight $= \dfrac{4{,}290}{20{,}590} = 20.8$ percent

8-3. SPECIFICATIONS FOR COMBINED STRESSES

The preceding paragraphs have shown how stresses due to flexure and axial load can be combined. As a matter of fact the calculations were quite simple, but the problems of establishing an allowable combined stress is a much more difficult problem. There are allowable stresses for pure bending and other allowable stresses for pure axial loads, but the two values given in one specification are probably appreciably different. What is the value to be used when the two types of stresses occur simultaneously? Most organizations use an allowable stress which is some combination of the two individual allowables. Expressions of this type are referred to as *interaction equations*. One interaction equation used by many specifications is as follows:

$$\frac{f_a}{F_a} + \frac{f_b}{F_b} \leq 1.0$$

In this expression f_a is the axial stress (P/A), F_a is the allowable stress if only axial stresses occurred, f_b is the flexure stress (Mc/I), and F_b is the allowable flexure stress if only bending stresses were present. For many years the AISC also used this expression for members subjected to a combination of the two types of stresses. Today the AISC permits its use only for certain conditions (to be described later in this chapter). This expression might be thought of as a percentage formula. For instance, if 60% of the allowable axial stress is used up by f_a/F_a, only 40 percent of the allowable flexure stress remains for the Mc/I stress. This expression has the affect of giving an allowable combined stress which will fall proportionately between the allowable individual values as each type of stress is to its allowable value. When the flexure stress is large with respect to the axial stress, the allowable combined stress will approach very nearly the allowable flexure stress. Similarly, when the axial stress is large in comparison to the flexure stress the allowable combined stress will be close to the allowable axial stress. Example 8-2 presents an illustration of the combination of the two types of stresses according to this commonly used expression.

Should bending occur about both axes, the following expression is used to consider the combined stress situation:

$$\frac{f_a}{F_a} + \frac{f_{bx}}{F_{bx}} + \frac{f_{by}}{F_{by}} \leq 1.0$$

EXAMPLE 8-2. A W 10×49 $(A = 14.40$ sq in., $S_x = 54.6$, $r = 2.54$ in.) is subjected to a moment of 40 ft-k and an axial compressive load of 100 k. The member is 15 ft long and has an allowable bending stress of 18 ksi and an allowable axial compressive stress to be determined from the formula $P/A = 15{,}000 - \frac{1}{4}(l/r)^2$. Is the member overstressed according to the $f_a/F_a + f_b/F_b \leq 1$ expression?

Solution:

$$f_a = \frac{100}{14.4} = 6.94 \text{ ksi}$$

$$F_a = 15{,}000 - \frac{1}{4}\left(\frac{12 \times 15}{2.54}\right)^2 = 13.75 \text{ ksi}$$

$$f_b = \frac{12 \times 40}{54.6} = 8.8 \text{ ksi}$$

$$F_b = 18 \text{ ksi}$$

$$\frac{f_a}{F_a} + \frac{f_b}{F_b} = \frac{6.94}{13.75} + \frac{8.8}{18} = 0.992 < 1 \qquad \text{(OK)}$$

8-4. DESIGN FOR AXIAL COMPRESSION AND BENDING

When the average designer is faced with the problem of selecting a member to resist combined stresses, he will probably estimate the size member required, after which he will check its combined stress in accordance with the requirements of the specification being used. Example 8-3 illustrates the design of a member of this type. To arrive at the assumed section in this example it was assumed that roughly one half of each allowable stress (F_a and F_b) was caused by the loads. The resulting axial stress value was divided into the total axial load to estimate the cross-sectional area required, and the flexure stress value was divided into the bending moment to estimate the required section modulus. A section was selected which had these proportions. Although the section selected by the method was satisfactory in this example it is usually necessary to make another trial or two to obtain an economical solution. The division of stresses was purely an estimate and some other division might be better. For instance if the axial load seems quite large in proportion to the bending moment, the designer might decide to estimate that 75 percent of the axial stress allowable is used and 25 percent of the bending stress allowable; or some other division. (Much more satisfactory methods are available for designing beam-columns, such as the one presented in Sec. 8-6 for the AISC Specification.)

EXAMPLE 8-3. Select a W10 beam-column to support an axial load of 120 k and a bending moment of 50 ft-k. The member has an unsupported length of 18 ft, has an allowable flexure stress of 18 ksi, and an allowable compressive stress of $P/A = 15,000 - \frac{1}{4}(l/r)^2$. The $f_a/F_a + f_b/F_b \leq 1.0$ expression is to be used in the design.

Solution: Estimated axial stress = 7 ksi

$$A_{req.} = \frac{120}{7} = 17.2 \text{ sq in.}$$

Estimated flexure stress = 9 ksi

$$S_{req.} = \frac{12 \times 50}{9} = 66.7 \text{ in.}^3$$

Try W 10 × 60 ($A = 17.7$ sq in., $S_x = 67.1$, $r = 2.57$)

$$f_a = \frac{120,000}{17.7} = 6,770 \text{ psi}$$

$$F_a = 15,000 - \frac{1}{4}\left(\frac{12 \times 18}{2.57}\right)^2 = 13,230 \text{ psi}$$

$$f_b = \frac{(12)(50,000)}{67.1} = 8,940 \text{ psi}$$

$$F_b = 18,000 \text{ psi}$$

$$\frac{f_a}{F_a} + \frac{f_b}{F_b'} = \frac{6,770}{13,230} + \frac{8,940}{18,000}$$

$$= 0.511 + 0.496 = 1.007 \text{ (slightly overstressed)} \qquad \text{(OK)}$$

8-5.   AISC REQUIREMENTS

For many years the AISC used the previously discussed $f_a/F_a + f_b/F_b \leq 1.0$ formula, but today they permit its use only under certain conditions. The present expressions are more conservative than the older expressions because a factor has been introduced in the equations to estimate the effect of additional moments caused by lateral displacements. As previously indicated a member subjected to a moment deflects laterally and an additional moment equal to the axial load times the lateral deflection is developed.

The present AISC Specification says that members subjected to a combination of axial compression and flexure stress must be proportioned to meet the requirements of both of the following expressions:[1]

$$\frac{f_a}{F_a} + \frac{C_{mx} f_{bx}}{\left(1 - \dfrac{f_a}{F'_{ex}}\right) F_{bx}} + \frac{C_{my} f_{by}}{\left(1 - \dfrac{f_a}{F'_{ey}}\right) F_{by}} \leq 1.0 \qquad \text{(AISC Formula 1.6-1a)}$$

$$\frac{f_a}{0.60 F_y} + \frac{f_{bx}}{F_{bx}} + \frac{f_{by}}{F_{by}} \leq 1.0 \qquad \text{(AISC Formula 1.6-1b)}$$

Should f_a/F_a be less than 0.15 the following formula can be used in lieu of the preceding ones.

$$\frac{f_a}{F_a} + \frac{f_{bx}}{F_{bx}} + \frac{f_{by}}{F_{by}} \leq 1.0 \qquad \text{(AISC Formula 1.6-2)}$$

Should bending occur about one axis only the appropriate term will drop out of these equations.

In these expressions f_a, f_b, F_a, and F_b are the same values which have been previously defined. F'_e is the Euler stress divided by a safety factor. Its value is given by the expression to follow in which l is the actual unsupported length in the plane of bending, r_b is the corresponding radius of gyration, and K is the effective length factor in the plane of bending.

$$F'_e = \frac{149,000,000}{(Kl/r_b)^2}$$

---

[1] For development of these formulas the student is referred to pages 364-369 in *Structural Steel Design* written by Beedle et al. (The Ronald Press Company, New York, 1964).

The value of F_e' can be increased by one-third for wind and seismic stresses according to the AISC Specification provided the section used is not overstressed (not counting the one-third increase) for the gravity dead, live and impact loads. In the first of the two AISC expressions $1 - f_a/F_e'$ is the *amplification factor* which has as its purpose the estimation of the increased moments caused by lateral deflection. The amplification factor is in the direction of greater conservatism as compared to the old $f_a/F_a + f_b/F_b$ expression. In fact for some conditions (depending on the actual slenderness ratios, axial loads, and moments involved) it is too conservative; and the formula has a *modification or reduction factor* to keep the estimated moments due to deflection from being too large.

For determining the value of the *modification factor*, C_m, Table C1.6.1.1. from the AISC Commentary is reproduced as Table 8-1 in this

TABLE 8-1

Category	Loanding Conditions ($f_a > 0.15F_a$)	f_b	C_m	Remarks
A	Computed moments maximum at end; joint translation not prevented	$\dfrac{M_2}{S}$	0.85	$M_1 < M_2$; $\dfrac{M_1}{M_2}$ negative as shown Check both Formulas (1.6-1a) & (1.6-1b)
B	Computed moments maximum at end; no transverse loading; joint translation prevented	$\dfrac{M_2}{S}$	$\left(0.6 \mp \atop 0.4 \dfrac{M_1}{M_2} \right)$ but not less than 0.4	Check both Formulas (1.6-1a) & (1.6-1b)
C	Transverse loading; joint translation prevented	$\dfrac{M_2}{S}$ Using Formula (1.6-1b) $\dfrac{M_3}{S}$ Using Formula (1.6-1a)	$1 + \psi \dfrac{f_a}{F_e'}$	Check both Formulas (1.6-1a) & (1.6-1b)

chapter with the permission of the AISC. This table shows the three separate categories used for determining the value of C_m. The formula numbers referred to in the table are the numbers given to them in the AISC Specification. These numbers were shown by the formulas earlier in this section.

Category A should be self-explanatory but a few notes are given here pertaining to the other categories. In category B, M_1/M_2 is the ratio of the smaller moment to the larger moment at the ends of the unbraced length. The ratio is negative if the moments cause the member to bend in single curvature ( ) or ( ) and positive if they bend the member in reverse curvature ( ) or ( ). It should be obvious that a member in single curvature has larger lateral deflections than a similar member bent in reverse curvature. With larger lateral deflections the moments due to the axial loads and thus the stresses will be greater. When a column is bent in single curvature substitution in the AISC formula will, therefore, give smaller allowable stresses.

Category C applies to members which are subjected to transverse loading between the joints and which are braced against joint translation in the plane of loading. The compression chord of a truss with a purlin load between its joints is a typical example of this category. The values of C_m for various cases of category C are shown in Table 8-2. This table is a reproduction of Table C1.6.1.2 from the AISC Commentary.

Most of the members encountered in actual practice which are subject to appreciable amounts of combined bending and axial stress are parts of a rigid frame structure, and the other members rigidly connected to the member in question have some appreciable effect on that member. This means that to determine the allowable axial stress the effective length of the member needs to be determined as previously described. From that previous discussion it is remembered that if sidesway is possible the effective length can be greater than the actual length, but if sidesway is prevented as by fairly heavy masonry walls the effective length will be less than the actual length.

In category A the effective lengths of the members are used in calculating F_a and it can never be less than the unbraced length and may even be greater. The effective length in the direction of bending is used in calculating F'_e. For the moment computations the actual unbraced length is used. In category B the columns have no sidesway nor transverse loading and the effective length is used for calculating F_a. It cannot be greater than the unbraced length and may be less. Again the effective length in the direction of bending is used in calculating F'_e. For the moment calculations the actual unbraced length is used. In category C the actual length of the members is usually used for all calculations or $K = 1.0$.

BENDING AND AXIAL STRESS

TABLE 8-2

Case	ψ	C_m
	0	1.0
	−0.3	$1 - 0.3\dfrac{f_a}{F'_e}$
	−0.4	$1 - 0.4\dfrac{f_a}{F'_e}$
	−0.2	$1 - 0.2\dfrac{f_a}{F'_e}$
	−0.4	$1 - 0.4\dfrac{f_a}{F'_e}$
	−0.6	$1 - 0.6\dfrac{f_a}{F'_e}$

Examples 8-4 and 8-5 illustrate the design of members subjected to combined bending and axial stress in accordance with the AISC Specification. It will be noted in these examples that f_b is the bending stress at the point of the member being considered. When there are no transverse loads the stress will be computed for the largest of the moments at the ends of the unbraced length. When a transverse load is applied the largest moment between the points of lateral support is used to compute f_b for substitution in the first of the two AISC expressions. For substitution in the second expression the largest moment at either of the supported points is used.

The joints of a truss are restrained from translation. For this reason it might seem reasonable to use an effective length for the compression members of a truss somewhat less than the actual lengths. The AISC, however, suggests that the use of $K = 1.0$ is wise when the ultimate load situation is considered. Should all of the members of a truss reach their ultimate load capacity at the same time the restraints against translation mentioned would be drastically reduced or eliminated.[2]

(a)

(b)

Fig. 8-2

EXAMPLE 8-4. For the truss shown in Fig. 8-2 (a) a W 8 × 31 is used as a continuous top chord member from joint L_0 to joint U_3. If the member consists of A36 steel, does it have sufficient strength to resist the loads shown in part (b) of the figure using the AISC Specification? Part (b) shows the portion of the chord from L_0 to U_1 and the 10 k load represents the effect of a purlin.

Solution:

Try W 8 × 31 ($A = 9.12$ sq in., $\dfrac{b_f}{2t_f} = 9.24$, $F'_y = 31.9$, $S_x = 27.4$, $r_x = 3.47$,

$r_y = 2.01, \dfrac{d}{A_f} = 2.31$)

$$f_a = \frac{125}{9.12} = 13.7 \text{ ksi}$$

Assuming that the member is fixed at L_0 and U_1 for the purpose of estimating moment:

$$M = \frac{Pl}{8} = \frac{(10)(13)}{8} = 16.25 \text{ ft-k}$$

---

[2] "Commentary on AISC Specification," *Manual of Steel Construction* (New York: American Institute of Steel Construction, Inc., 1970) pp. 5–140.

$$f_b = \frac{12 \times 16.25}{27.4} = 7.1 \text{ ksi}$$

Lateral support (pinned) is provided at 6.5-ft intervals.

$$L_c = 8.4' \text{ (from AISC Manual)} > 6.5 \text{ ft} < L_u = 20.0 \text{ ft}$$

But $F_y > F'_y$ ∴ $F_b = 36 \left[0.733 - 0.0014 \, (9.24) \sqrt{36} \right] = 23.6 \text{ ksi}$

$$F'_e = \frac{(12) \, (\pi)^2 \, (29 \times 10^3)}{23 \left[\left(\dfrac{0.65 \times 12 \times 13}{3.47} \right) \right]^2} = 175.2 \text{ ksi} \qquad \text{(can be looked up in AISC Manual, pp. 5–94)}$$

The member falls into category C:

$$C_m = 1 - 0.6 \, \frac{f_a}{F'_e} = 1 - 0.6 \, \frac{13.7}{175.2} = 0.953$$

Determining allowable value of F_a:

$$\frac{Kl}{r} = \frac{(0.8) \, (12) \, (6.5)}{2.01} = 31.1$$

$$F_a = 19.86 \text{ ksi (from AISC Manual)}$$

Substituting into AISC expressions:

$$\frac{f_a}{F_a} + \frac{C_m f_b}{(1 - f_a/F'_e)F_b} = \frac{13.7}{19.86} + \frac{0.953 \, (7.1)}{(1 - 13.7/175.2) \, 23.6} = 1.00 \qquad \text{(OK)}$$

$$\frac{f_a}{0.6 F_y} + \frac{f_b}{F_b} = \frac{13.7}{22} + \frac{7.1}{23.6} = 0.923 < 1$$

<u>Section is satisfactory.</u>

EXAMPLE 8-5. Select a W14 to resist the loads and moments shown in

500 k

220 ft-k

14'-0"

200 ft-k

500 k

FIG. 8-3

Fig. 8-3 if A36 steel and the AISC Specification are to be used. In the plane of loading there is no bracing and the column is subject to sidesway but has no transverse loading. An analysis of effective lengths has resulted in $K_x = 1.92$. In the perpendicular plane there is bracing and K_y has been estimated to equal 0.80.

   Solution:

Try W 14 × 158 ($A = 46.5$, $S_x = 253$, $r_x = 6.40$, $r_y = 4.00$, $L_c = 16.5$)

$$f_a = \frac{500}{46.5} = 10.75 \text{ ksi}$$

$$f_b = \frac{(12)\,(220)}{253} = 10.42 \text{ ksi}$$

$$\frac{K_x L_x}{r_x} = \frac{(1.92)\,(12)\,(14)}{6.40} = 50.3$$

$$\frac{K_y L_y}{r_y} = \frac{(0.80)\,(12)\,(14)}{4.00} = 33.6$$

$$F_a = 18.32 \text{ ksi}$$

$$L_c = 16.5 \text{ ft} > 14 \text{ ft}$$

Therefore,

$$F_b = 0.66\,F_y = 24 \text{ ksi}$$

and

$$F'_e = \frac{(12)\,(\pi)^2\,(29 \times 10^3)}{(23)\left(\dfrac{1.92 \times 12 \times 14}{6.40}\right)^2} = 58.9 \text{ ksi}$$

Member falls into category A, therefore

$$C_m = 0.85$$

Substituting into AISC expression:

$$\frac{f_a}{F_a} + \frac{C_m f_b}{(1 - f_a/F'_e)F_b} = \frac{10.75}{18.32} + \frac{(0.85)\,(10.42)}{(1 - 10.75/58.9)24} = 1.041 > 1.0 \quad \text{(N.G.)}$$

$$\frac{f_a}{0.6\,F_y} + \frac{f_b}{F_b} = \frac{10.75}{22} + \frac{10.42}{24} = 0.924 < 1.0$$

Section is unsatisfactory

Once again the student should note that allowable bending stresses vary for compact and noncompact sections. For a member subject to axial compression and bending the AISC (Sec. 1.5.1.4.1d) provides that the depth-thickness ratio of the web shall not exceed the following:

$$\frac{d}{t} = 412\,(1 - 2.33\,\frac{f_a}{F_y})/F_y \qquad \text{(AISC Formula 1.5–4)}$$

except that it need not be less than $257/\sqrt{F_y}$. From this expression F_y can be shown to equal $[257/(d/t)]^2$. For convenience this value (the theoretical yield stress at which the shape becomes noncompact) is given in the AISC manual for sections normally used as beams and is designated as F_y'''. Should F_y for the beam-column in question be greater than F_y''' the section will be noncompact; should it be between F_y'' and F_y''' it will be necessary to substitute in AISC Formula 1.5–4 to determine whether it is compact or noncompact.

8-6. DESIGN OF BEAM-COLUMNS-AISC

The design and analysis of a member subject to axial load and bending can be a very tedious and time-consuming affair involving a long trial and error procedure. If such a long process were to be used for all of the beam-columns in a large building an unbelievable amount of time would be required. For this reason (perhaps out of desperation) several quicker procedures have been devised.

For the purpose of this discussion it is desired to select a member which will adequately and economically support an axial load of 400 k and a maximum bending moment of 140 ft-k. One very satisfactory method of selecting the member is the "equivalent axial load method." For an illustration of the theory behind this method it is assumed that a section is selected for a fictitious axial load of 500 k and then is checked with the appropriate interaction equations for the real values $P = 400$ k and $M = 140$ ft-k.

If it is assumed that the column so selected does not satisfy the interaction equations it will be necessary to select a larger section based on a larger fictitious equivalent axial load. It is assumed that the process is repeated with a fictitious axial load of 600 k, but that the section selected is also unsatisfactory. It will be noted, however, that this second selection is closer to being satisfactory than was the first one.

Somewhere there is a fictitious column load which will yield a section which will satisfy the interaction equations for the P and M values given and it is the estimation of this fictitious equivalent load which is to be described. The value of this equivalent load is denoted as $P + P'_x$ herein where P'_x is the result of converting M_x into an equivalent axial load. This is the method presented in Sec. 3 of the AISC Manual. Should axial load plus bending be present about the axes (P plus M_x and M_y) an equivalent axial load for each of them is needed and the total equivalent load will be represented by $P + P'_x + P'_y$. The resulting equations are given as follows:

AISC Formula (1.6-1a)

$$P + P'_x + P'_y = P + \left[B_x M_x C_{mx} \left(\frac{F_a}{F_{bx}} \right) \left(\frac{a_x}{a_x - P(Kl_x)^2} \right) \right]$$
$$+ \left[B_y M_y C_{my} \left(\frac{F_a}{F_{by}} \right) \left(\frac{a_y}{a_y - P(Kl_y)^2} \right) \right]$$

AISC Formula (1.6-1b)

$$P + P'_x + P'_y = P \left(\frac{F_a}{0.6\,F_y} \right) + \left[B_x M_x \left(\frac{F_a}{F_{bx}} \right) \right] + \left[B_y M_y \left(\frac{F_a}{F_{by}} \right) \right]$$

AISC Formula (1.6-2) to be used in lieu of Formulas (1.6-1a) and (1.6-1b) when

$$\frac{f_a}{F_a} \leqq 0.15$$

$$P + P'_x + P'_y = P + \left[B_x M_x \left(\frac{F_a}{F_{bx}} \right) \right] + \left[B_y M_y \left(\frac{F_a}{F_{by}} \right) \right]$$

These equations which are very useful for preliminary design yield columns which are on the conservative size. Should bending occur about one axis only the equations are reduced by deleting the appropriate terms.

In these expressions B_x and B_y are the bending factors which are respectively equal to A/S_x and A/S_y. Their values which are tabulated in the Steel Manual vary from 0.18 to 0.25 for B_x while those for B_y vary from 0.443 to 2.25. The larger values occur with the smaller sections. A_x is a component of the amplification factor when bending is about the x axis and equals $0.149\,Ar_x^2 \times 10^6$. Similarly a_y is $0.149\,Ar_y^2 \times 10^6$ and both a_x and a_y are given for sections normally used as columns in the column section of the AISC Manual.

Example 8-6 illustrates the design of a beam-column using the equivalent axial load procedure. It will be noticed for the initial trials that only $P + P'_x = P + B_x M_x$ is used rather than the entire equations. Once a section is settled upon by this approximate procedure with the short equation the whole equations are used.

Example 8-6. Select a W14 for the column shown in Fig. 8-4 using A36 Steel and the AISC Specification. Assume $K = 1.0$ and $C_{mx} = 0.85$.

Solution: Noting $Kl = 15'$
Enter AISC tables with axial load only (400 k) try W 14 × 78 ($B_x = .190$)

$$P + P'_x = P + B_x M_x = 400 + (0.190)(12 \times 140) = 719 \text{ k}$$

Fig. 8-4

Enter tables with 719 k and try W 14 × 136 ($B_x = 0.186$)

$$P + P'_x = 400 + (0.186) (12 \times 140) = 712 \text{ k}$$

Enter tables with 712 k and try W 14 × 127 ($B_x = 0.185$)

$$P + P'_x = 710 \text{ k}$$

Try W 14 × 127 (allowable axial load = 692 k,[3] $A = 37.3$, $r_y = 3.76$, $L_c = 15.6$ ft $\therefore F_b = 24$ ksi, $B_x = 0.185$, $a_x = 220 \times 10^6$)

$$f_a = \frac{400}{37.3} = 10.72 \text{ ksi}$$

$$\frac{Kl}{r_y} = \frac{(1.0) (12 \times 15)}{3.76} = 47.9$$

$$F_a = 18.54 \text{ ksi}$$

$$\frac{f_a}{F_a} = \frac{10.72}{18.54} = 0.578 > 0.15 \qquad \therefore \text{ Must use Formula (1.6-1a) and (1.6-1b)}$$

Formula (1.6-1a)

$$P + P'_x = 400 + \left[(0.185) (12 \times 140) (0.85) \left(\frac{18.54}{24} \right) \right.$$

$$\left. \left(\frac{220 \times 10^6}{220 \times 10^6 - (400) (12 \times 15)^2} \right) \right]$$

$$= 617 \text{ k}$$

---

[3] These trial calculations overestimate the section size required $\therefore$ a little smaller section than seemingly required is tried.

Formula (1.6-1b)

$$P + P'_x = (400)\left(\frac{18.54}{22}\right) + \left[(0.185)\,(12 \times 40)\left(\frac{18.54}{24}\right)\right] = 577 \text{ k}$$

Reenter tables with equivalent axial load of 617 k use W 14 × 119

8-7. COMBINED AXIAL TENSION AND BENDING

The foregoing paragraphs and example problems have all pertained to members subjected to a combination of axial compression and bending. A less critical case but one which can occasionally be quite important occurs when a member is subjected to simultaneous axial tension and bending. Various specifications have different design requirements. For instance the AREA says that members subject to both axial tension and bending stress shall be so proportioned that the total axial tension plus the bending tension shall not exceed the allowable tension for axially loaded tensile members. (In addition they say that the compression caused by such bending may not exceed the allowable value for axially loaded compression members.)

The AISC requires a member subject to a combination of axial tension and bending to satisfy the expression which follows. In this expression f_b is the maximum tensile bending stress and F_b is the allowable bending tensile stress.

$$\frac{f_a}{0.60F_y} + \frac{f_{bx}}{F_{bx}} + \frac{f_{by}}{F_{by}} \leqq 1.0$$

A further requirement is that the computed bending compressive stress may not exceed the applicable value for allowable bending compressive stress.

8-8. FURTHER DISCUSSION OF EFFECTIVE LENGTHS OF COLUMNS

The subject of effective lengths was previously discussed in Chaps. 4 and 5. In fact Table 5-1 was presented to provide suggested effective lengths for columns with different degrees of end restraint. It is to be remembered that this table was developed for certain idealized conditions which might be entirely different from practical design conditions. This method is quite satisfactory for preliminary designs and for situations where sidesway is prevented by bracing.

Truthfully the effective length of a column is a property of the whole structure of which the column is a part. In the large majority of existing buildings it is probable that the masonry walls provide sufficient lateral support to prevent sidesway. Many modern buildings, however, are subject to sidesway. When light curtain walls are used, as they often are in modern bulidings, there is probably little resistance to sidesway. Sidesway is also present in tall buildings in appreciable amounts unless a definite diagonal bracing system is used. For these cases it seems logical to assume that resistance to sidesway is primarily provided by the lateral stiffness of the frame alone.

Perhaps a few explanatory remarks should be made at this point concerning the definition of sidesway as it pertains to effective lengths. In this discussion sidesway refers to a sidesway type of buckling. This not only includes sidesway as used in the analysis of indeterminate frames (where the frames deflect laterally due to the presence of lateral loads or unsymmetrical vertical loads) but also to columns whose ends could move transversely if the columns were loaded until buckling occurred.

For structures with sidesway the designer may make his own mathematical analysis of the structure to determine its effective length (although too lengthy to be practical for the average designer and design problem); he may on the basis of his judgment of the particular conditions interpolate between the values given in Table 5-1; or he may obtain effective lengths from the chart in the AISC Manual entitled "Alignment Chart for Effective Length of Columns in Continuous Frames." This chart is reproduced in Fig. 8-5 with the permission of the AISC.

The alignment chart is to be used to estimate the effective lengths of columns in frames where resistance to lateral movement is provided by the stiffness of the members of the frames. To use the chart it is necessary to obtain the sizes of the girders and columns framing into the column in question before its effective length can be determined. In other words, before the chart can be used a trial design has to be made of each of the members.

The effective lengths of each of the columns of a frame are estimated with the alignment chart in Example 8-7. (When sidesway is possible it will be found that the effective lengths are always greater than the actual lengths as is illustrated in this example. When frames are braced in such a manner that sidesway is not possible K will be less than 1.0.) An initial design has provided preliminary sizes for each of the members in the frame of Example 8-7. After the effective lengths are determined each column can be redesigned. Should the sizes change appreciably, new effective lengths can be determined, the column designs repeated, etc. Several tables are used in the solution of this example. These should be self-explanatory after the clear directions given by the AISC on the alignment chart are examined.

For most buildings the values of K_x and K_y should be examined separately. The reason for such individual study lies in the different possible framing conditions in the two directions. Many multistory

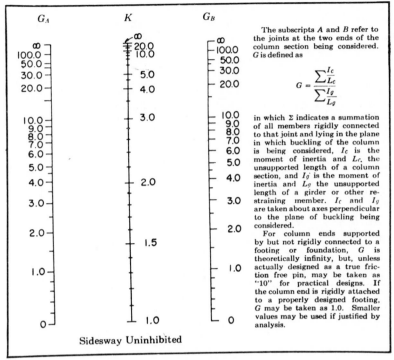

G_A K G_B

The subscripts A and B refer to the joints at the two ends of the column section being considered. G is defined as

$$G = \frac{\sum \dfrac{I_c}{L_c}}{\sum \dfrac{I_g}{L_g}}$$

in which Σ indicates a summation of all members rigidly connected to that joint and lying in the plane in which buckling of the column is being considered, I_c is the moment of inertia and L_c the unsupported length of a column section, and I_g is the moment of inertia and L_g the unsupported length of a girder or other restraining member. I_c and I_g are taken about axes perpendicular to the plane of buckling being considered.

For column ends supported by but not rigidly connected to a footing or foundation, G is theoretically infinity, but, unless actually designed as a true friction free pin, may be taken as "10" for practical designs. If the column end is rigidly attached to a properly designed footing, G may be taken as 1.0. Smaller values may be used if justified by analysis.

Sidesway Uninhibited

Fɪɢ. 8-5. Alignment chart for effective length of columns in continuous frames.

frames consist of rigid frames in one direction and conventionally connected frames with sway bracing in the other. In addition the points of lateral support may often be entirely different in the two planes. An examination of Example 8-5 will show that it is highly possible for the column action to be governed by K_y and for K_x to govern F'_e.

Fɪɢ. 8-6

EXAMPLE 8-7.   Determine the effective lengths of each of the columns of the frame shown in Fig. 8-6 using the AISC alignment chart given in Fig. 8-5.   The tentative sizes of each member are given in the figure.

Solution: Stiffness factors:

Member	Shape	I	L	I/L
AB	W8×24	82.5	144	0.572
BC	W8×24	82.5	120	0.687
DE	W8×40	146	144	1.015
EF	W8×40	146	120	1.220
GH	W8×24	82.5	144	0.572
HI	W8×24	82.5	120	0.687
BE	W18×50	802	240	3.34
CF	W16×36	447	240	1.86
EH	W18×96	1,680	360	4.66
FI	W16×58	748	360	2.08

G factors for each joint:

$$G = \frac{\sum \dfrac{I_c}{L_c}}{\sum \dfrac{I_g}{L_g}}$$

Joint	$\sum (I_c/L_c)/\sum (I_g/L_g)$	G
A	See FIG. 8-5	10.0
B	$\dfrac{0.572 + 0.687}{3.34}$	0.377
C	$\dfrac{0.687}{1.86}$	0.369
D	See Fig. 8-5	1.0
E	$\dfrac{1.015 + 1.220}{3.34 + 4.66}$	0.280
F	$\dfrac{1.220}{1.86 + 2.08}$	0.311
G	See Fig. 8-5	10.0
H	$\dfrac{0.572 + .687}{4.66}$	0.271
I	$\dfrac{0.687}{2.08}$	0.331

Column K factors from chart:

Column	G Values at Column Ends		K
AB	10.0	0.377	1.72
BC	0.377	0.369	1.12
DE	1.0	0.280	1.20
EF	0.280	0.311	1.10
GH	10.0	0.271	1.72
HI	0.271	0.331	1.10

Only one alignment chart is given in the AISC Commentary and that for frames in which sidesway is permitted. Another chart is available in the Column Research Guide[4] where sidesway is prevented. This chart is presented in Fig. 8-7. Examples 8-8 and 8-9 present two more beam-column problems and in these problems use is made of these effective length charts.

Sidesway Prevented

FIG. 8-7

[4] Column Research Council, Engineering Foundation, *Guide to Design for Metal Compression Members*, B. G. Johnston, (ed.), 2d ed. (John Wiley & Sons, New York, 1966).

EXAMPLE 8-8. Check the adequacy of the lower W8 × 40 column shown in Fig. 8-6 if it is assumed to have no bracing against sidesway in the plane of the frame. The member is assumed to be subjected to an axial load of 100 k and to have the moment diagram shown in Fig. 8-8. Assume $K = 1.0$ for the y direction and use A36 steel and the AISC Specification.

20 ft-k

30 ft-k

FIG. 8-8

Solution:

Using W 8 × 40 ($A = 11.8$, $S_x = 35.5$, $r_x = 3.53$, $r_y = 2.04$)

$$f_a = \frac{100}{11.8} = 8.44 \text{ ksi}$$

$$\frac{Kl_x}{r_x} = \frac{(1.20)(12 \times 12)}{3.53} = 48.8$$

(The value of $K = 1.20$ was obtained in Example 8-7)

$$\frac{Kl_y}{r_y} = \frac{(1.00)(12 \times 12)}{2.04} = 70.6 \leftarrow$$

$$F_a = 16.37 \text{ ksi}$$

$$\frac{f_a}{F_a} = \frac{8.44}{16.37} = 0.515 > 0.15 \qquad \therefore \text{Must use Formulas (1.6-1a) and (1.6-1b)}$$

$$f_b = \frac{(12)(30)}{35.5} = 10.15 \text{ ksi}$$

$$L_c = 8.6 \text{ ft and } L_u = 25.3 \text{ ft} \qquad \therefore F_b = 0.60F_y = 22 \text{ ksi}$$

$$C_m = 0.85$$

$$F'_e = 62.63 \text{ ksi} \qquad \text{for } \frac{Kl_x}{r_x} = 48.8$$

$$\frac{8.44}{16.37} + \frac{(0.85)\,(10.15)}{\left(1 - \dfrac{8.50}{62.63}\right)22} = 0.968 < 1.0 \qquad \text{Formula (1.6-1a)} \qquad \text{(OK)}$$

$$\frac{8.44}{22} + \frac{10.15}{22} = 0.844 < 1.0 \qquad \text{Formula (1.6-1b)} \qquad \text{(OK)}$$

Section is satisfactory

EXAMPLE 8-9. The columns in the frame shown in Fig. 8-9 are braced against sidesway in both directions. Check one of the upper columns which is subjected to an axial load of 180 k and the moments shown in the figure. Use A36 steel and the AISC Specification.

FIG. 8-9

Solution:

Using a W12 × 65 ($A = 19.1$, $I_x = 533$, $S_x = 88.0$, $r_x = 5.28$, $r_y = 3.02$, section is noncompact, $L_u = 27.7$ ft)

$$f_a = \frac{180}{19.1} = 9.42 \text{ ksi}$$

$$\frac{Kl}{r} = \frac{(1.0)\,(12 \times 15)}{3.02} = 59.6$$

$$F_a = 17.47 \text{ ksi}$$

$$\frac{f_a}{F_a} = \frac{9.42}{17.47} = 0.538 > 0.15 \qquad \therefore \text{Must use Formulas (1.6-1a) and (1.6-1b)}$$

$$f_b = \frac{(12)(75)}{88} = 10.22 \text{ ksi}$$

$$F_b = 22 \text{ ksi}$$

$$C_m = \left[0.60 + (0.40)\left(-\frac{66}{75} \right) \right] = 0.248 < 0.4$$

Use 0.4

Effective length factor in plane of bending determined as follows:

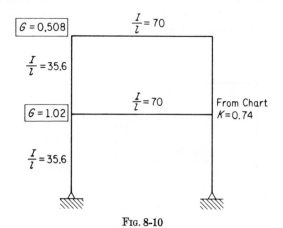

FIG. 8-10

$$\frac{Kl}{r_x} = \frac{(0.74)(12 \times 15)}{5.28} = 25.3$$

$$F'_e = 233.2 \text{ ksi}$$

$$\frac{9.42}{17.47} + \frac{(0.40)(10.22)}{\left(1 - \frac{9.42}{233.2} \right)(22)} = 0.733 < 1.0 \qquad \text{Formula (1.6-1a)} \qquad \text{(OK)}$$

$$\frac{9.42}{22} + \frac{10.22}{22} = 0.893 < 1.0 \qquad \text{Formula (1.6-1b)} \qquad \text{(OK)}$$

Section is satisfactory

PROBLEMS

8-1. Determine the maximum stresses in the compression chord of a roof truss caused by its own weight. The member is 24 ft 0 in. long and consists of two C 12 × 20.7's with a top cover plate ½ × 12 in. Assume the lacing and tie plates weigh 200 lb. (Ans. $f_t = + 1.18$ ksi, $f_c = - .648$ ksi)

8-2. The top chord of a roof truss is shown in the accompanying illustration. Determine the maximum stresses at the extreme fibers of this member if it is subjected to a moment of 50 ft-k and an axial compression of 400 k.

PL 1 X 20

C15 X 50 s

12"

Lacing

PROB. 8-2

8-3. An 18 ft W 14 × 87 is used to support an axial load of 300 k and a bending moment about its major axis of 60 ft-k. Is it adequate according to the following interaction formula and allowable stress values:

$$F_a = 15{,}000 - \tfrac{1}{4}\,(l/r)^2$$
$$F_b = 18{,}000 \text{ psi}$$
$$f_a/F_a + f_b/F_b \leqq 1.0$$

(Ans. Section unsatisfactory; interaction equation gives 1.12)

8-4. A column has a laterally unsupported length of 18 ft, an axial compression of 120 k and a bending moment of 40 ft-k. Select a W section for this member using the interaction formula and allowable stress values of Prob. 8-3.

8-5. A 12-ft column in a rigid frame building is subjected to an axial load of 300 k and to a moment of 80 ft-k. Using the interaction formula and the allowable stresses of Example 8-3 select a W shape. (Ans. W 14 × 103)

8-6. The column shown in Prob. 8-6 is to be designed to support an eccentric load of 120 k, located as shown in the figure. Select the lightest available W section using the design information of Prob. 8-3. Length = 16 ft.

Load

x ———————————————— x

3"

PROB. 8-6

PROB. 8-7

8-7. Same question as for Prob. 8-6 except the load is 100 k and is applied as shown in the accompanying illustration.   (Ans. W 12 × 72)

8-8. A column has a laterally unsupported length of 18 ft, an axial compression of 300 k and a bending moment of 60 ft-k.   Using the design formulas given in Prob. 8-3 select the most economical W section.

8-9. A column with an unsupported length of 28 ft must support an axial compressive load of 65 k and a moment of 65 ft-k.   Select a W section using the design formulas of Prob. 8-3.   (Ans. W 12 × 53)

8-10. A W10 × 39 pin-connected beam-column, which is subjected to sidesway, is 18-ft long.   A 120 k load is applied to the column at its upper end with an eccentricity of 2 in. so as to cause bending about the major axis of the section. Check the adequacy of the member with the AISC Specification if it consists of A36 steel.

8-11. Sidesway is prevented for the beam-column shown in the accompanying illustration.   If bending is about the major axis, is the member satisfactory?

PROB. 8-11

Use A36 steel and the AISC Specification. (Ans. Interaction equations yield 0.858 and 0.764 ∴ section is satisfactory)

8-12. A pin-connected W 10 × 45 consisting of A36 steel is used as a beam-column. If sidesway is possible and a load of 170 k is applied 1.50 in. off center at the upper end so as to cause bending about the y axis, is the member satisfactory according to the AISC Specification? Length = 12 ft.

8-13. Is the member shown in the accompanying illustration adequate? It is bent about its major axis and consists of A36 steel. Use the AISC Specification and assume sidesway is prevented. (Ans. Interaction equations yield 1.01 and 0.732 so probably satisfactory)

PROB. 8-13   PROB. 8-14

8-14. Select a W14 for the situation shown in the accompanying illustration. Use A36 steel, the AISC Specification and assume sidesway occurs.

8-15. Repeat Prob. 8-8 using the AISC Specification and A36 steel. The column is assumed to be pinned at both ends, to have no sidesway, and to have no transverse loading applied. The moments are maximum at the column ends and tend to bend the column in reverse curvature. (Ans. W 14 × 78)

8-16. Repeat Prob. 8-9 using the AISC Specification and A36 steel. The member is fixed at its ends and has no sidesway or transverse loading. The moments are maximum at the column ends and tend to bend the column in single curvature.

8-17. A 16-ft pinned-end column is subjected to a moment of 100 ft-k at one end and 120 ft-k at the other end such that it is bent in single curvature. There are no transverse loads, and joint translation is prevented. If the axial load is 150 k, select a W 14 section using the AISC Specification and A36 steel. (Ans. W 14 × 78)

8-18. Using the AISC Specification and A36 steel select a WT 7 for a 10 ft horizontal truss member with a 65 k axial compression load and a transverse uniform load of 75 lb/ft. The ends of the member are assumed to be pinned and joint translation is prevented.

8-19. Repeat Prob. 8-18 if the member ends are assumed to be fixed. (Ans. WT 7 × 15)

8-20. Repeat Prob. 8-18 if one member end is assumed to be fixed and the other pinned.

8-21. Repeat Prob. 8-7 using A36 steel and the AISC Specification. Assume the member is fixed at its ends and has no sidesway or transverse loading. The moments are maximum at the column ends and tend to bend it in single curvature. (Ans. W 14 × 68)

8-22. For the frame shown in the accompanying illustration select tentative beam and column sizes assuming moments at beam ends of $wl^2/10$ and the same values in the columns. Use the AISC Specification and A36 steel. The roof is to be designed to support a built-up roof weighing 6 psf plus a live load of 30 psf and the interior floor slab is to support a live load of 125 psf. Using the member sizes selected determine the column K values from the chart given in Fig. 8-5.

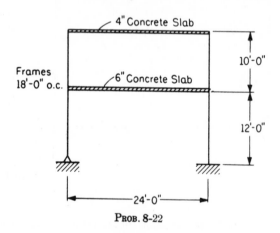

PROB. 8-22

8-23. Select a W 14 beam-column of A36 steel for an axial load of 200 k, $M_x = 50$ ft-k and $M_y = 30$ ft-k. Use AISC Specification and assume $Kl_x = Kl_y = 18$ ft and C_{mx} and $C_{my} = 0.85$. (Ans. W 14 × 84)

8-24. The frame of Prob. 8-22 is to be designed as a rigid frame structure. Use the tentative member sizes selected and distribute the moments. Select new member sizes using the K values determined in Prob. 8-23 in the column design. Determine the new column K values with the AISC chart.

chapter **9**

RIVETED CONNECTIONS

9-1. GENERAL

For many years the accepted method of connecting the members of a steel structure was by riveting. In recent years, however, the use of rivets has declined rapidly due to the tremendous upsurge of welding and more recently high-strength bolting. This chapter is devoted entirely to a discussion of riveted connections while Chaps. 10 and 11 are devoted to bolted and welded connections respectively. Standard types of connections with rivets, bolts, or welds are discussed in Chap. 12.

The rivets used in construction work are usually made of a soft grade of steel which will not become brittle when heated and hammered with a riveting gun to form the head. The usual rivet consists of a cylindrical shank of steel with a rounded head on one end. It is heated in the field to a cherry-red color (approximately 1800° F) inserted in the hole, and a head is formed on the other end probably with a portable rivet gun operated by compressed air. The rivet gun, which has a depression in its head to give the rivet head the proper shape, applies a rapid succession of blows to the rivet.

For riveting done in the shop the rivets are probably heated to a light cherry-red color and driven with a pressure type riveter. This type of riveter, usually called a "bull" riveter, squeezes the rivet with a pressure of perhaps as high as 50 to 80 tons and drives the rivet with one stroke. Because of this great pressure the rivet in its soft state is forced to fill the hole very satisfactorily. This type of riveting is much to be preferred over that done with the pneumatic hammer but no greater allowable stresses are allowed by riveting specifications. The bull riveters are built for much faster operation than are the portable hand riveters but the latter riveters are needed for places which are not easily accessible (i.e., field erection).

As the rivet cools it shrinks or contracts and squeezes together the parts being connected. The squeezing effect actually causes some transfer of stress between the parts being connected to take place by friction.

191

Handling hot rivets, Chicago, Ill. (*Inland Steel Company*).

The amount of friction is not dependable, however, and the specifications do not permit its inclusion in the strength of a connection. Rivets shrink diametrically as well as lengthwise and actually become somewhat smaller than the holes which they are assumed to fill.

Some shop rivets are driven cold with tremendous pressures. Obviously the cold-driving process works better for the smaller size rivets probably ¾ in. in diameter or less although larger ones have been successfully used. Cold-driven rivets fill the holes better, eliminate the cost of heating, and are stronger due to the fact that the steel is cold worked. There is, however, a reduction of clamping force since the rivets do not shrink after driving.

9-2. INSPECTION OF RIVETS

The use of experienced riveting crews for driving rivets is essential and even their work must be rigidly inspected. The inspectors should be sure the rivets are tight, have full-size heads, and are not overburned. Should bad rivets be found, they must be cut out. Although the riveting crews are not too happy about removing rivets, there is probably nothing which will improve their workmanship as much as the labor of cutting out a few bad rivets.

When holes for rivets are punched in structural steel, small burs will often be found on the under side of the holes. If these burs fall between two pieces to be riveted together, they should be removed. Members which are to be riveted need to be drawn up tightly with erection bolts before the riveting is performed. Where the members are not drawn closely together before riveting (as may be prevented by the presence of burs), the rivets may spread out, during driving, in the space between the members and prevent them from being pulled completely together.

Rivets must be properly heated and quickly driven before they cool. If they are driven when too cold (called overdriving) their heads can be knocked off quite easily. After they cool they should be carefully checked for tightness. The degree of tightness can be determined by placing a finger or a coin on one end of the rivet and hitting the other end with a light hammer. Should a rivet be loose, vibration will be felt. The sound produced when rivets are hit with a hammer will also tell an experienced inspector if the rivet is tight. Removal of rivets is rather hard work and too frequently riveters will check their own work. Upon finding loose rivets they will calk them with a cold chisel so that the hammer test by the inspector will not reveal looseness. Calking does not make a bad rivet good and the inspector needs to be on the lookout for calk marks.

Another item needing close inspection is the amount of burning of the rivets. Rivets which have been exposed to excessive temperatures or which have been reheated several times will have their strengths reduced. There is no doubt that riveting is one of the phases of construction requiring the closest inspection, perhaps requiring the full-time services of an inspector for as few as two or three riveting crews.

9-3. TYPES OF RIVETS

The sizes of rivets used in ordinary construction work are ¾ in. and ⅞ in. in diameter but they can be obtained in standard sizes from ½ in. to 1½ in. in ⅛ in. increments. The smaller sizes are used for small roof trusses, signs, small towers, etc., while the larger sizes are used for very large bridges or towers and very tall buildings. The use of more than one or two sizes of rivets on a single job is usually undesirable because it is expensive and inconvenient to punch different-size holes in a member in the shop, and the driving of different-size rivets in the field may be confusing. Some cases arise where it is absolutely necessary to have different sizes, as where smaller rivets are needed for keeping the proper edge distance in certain sections but these situations should be avoided if possible.

Rivet heads are usually round in shape, called button heads; but if clearance requirements dictate, the head can be flattened or even

194   RIVETED CONNECTIONS

countersunk and chipped flush. These situations are shown in Fig. 9-1.

The countersunk and chipped-flush rivets do not have a head large enough to develop full strength and should be discounted 50 percent in design. A rivet with a flattened head is to be preferred to a countersunk rivet but if a smooth surface is required the countersunk and chipped-flush rivet is necessary. This latter type of rivet is appreciably more expensive than the button head type in addition to being weaker and should not be used unless absolutely necessary.

Fig. 9-1. Types of rivets.

Various symbols are used on engineering drawings to represent the various types of rivets. Some of these symbols are shown in Fig. 9-2. The purpose of this figure is not to give a complete list of rivet symbols but rather to give an idea of their general appearance.

For a complete list the student can refer to the AISC Manual. He should particularly note the distinction between shop and field rivets in Fig. 9-2. The black circles representing field rivets should not be drawn

Description	Shop Rivets	Field Rivets
Button heads, both sides	○	●
Countersunk and chipped, near side		
Countersunk and chipped, far side	⊗	⊗
Countersunk and chipped, both sides		
Countersunk not over $\frac{1}{8}$ in. high, near side		

Fig. 9-2. Rivet symbols.

with diameters greater than one-half of those of the shop rivets, otherwise they will stand out so clearly as to be distracting on the drawing.

The two major ASTM classifications for structural steel application are described in the following paragraphs:

ASTM Specification A502, Grade 1. These rivets are used for most structural work (when rivets are used) including that done with the higher strength steels. They have a low carbon content of about 0.80 percent, are weaker than the ordinary structural carbon steel and have a higher ductility. The fact that these rivets are easier to drive than the higher strength rivets is probably the main reason that they are almost universally used regardless of the strength of the steel used in the structural members. (For many years they were listed as ASTM A141 rivets.)

ASTM Specification A502, Grade 2. The Grade 2 rivets have higher strengths than the Grade 1 rivets and were developed for the higher strength steels. They have more carbon and are harder than the Grade 1 rivets. Their higher strength permits the designer to use fewer rivets in a connection and thus smaller gusset plates. They are considerably more expensive than Grade 1 rivets and it might quite possibly be more satisfactory to use larger Grade 1 rivets after consideration is given to both economy and the increased difficulty of driving Grade 2 rivets. Their smaller ductility evidenced by the driving difficulty, probably results in somewhat smaller clamping forces and the higher strength advantage may be partially nullified.

9-4. TYPES OF JOINTS

The following paragraphs present a few of the elementary types of riveted joints subjected to axial forces. Eccentric connections are discussed in a later section of this chapter.

The Lap Joint. Figure 9-3(a) shows a lap joint in which two members are simply overlapped and connected together. The forces in the members of a lap joint tend to shear the connecting rivets off on the plane between the members and bear against the sides of the rivets as shown in the figure. These rivets are said to be in *single shear and bearing* (also called unenclosed bearing). Lap-joint rivets must have sufficient strength to satisfactorily resist these stresses and the members forming the joint must be strong enough to prevent the rivets from tearing through.

There is an eccentricity of load in the lap joint as the center of gravity of the stress in one member is not in line with the center of gravity of stress in the other member. A couple is present which causes an undesirable bending in the connection as shown in Fig. 9-3(a). For this reason the lap joint, which is desirably used only for minor connections, should be designed with at least two rivets in a line to minimize the possibility of a bending failure.

Lap joint

(a)

Butt joint

(b)

Fig. 9-3

The Butt Joint. A butt joint is formed when three members are connected as shown in Fig. 9-3(b). In this type of joint the rivets tend to be sheared off simultaneously on the two planes of contact between the members. Again the members are bearing against the rivets and the rivets are said to be in *double shear and bearing* (also called enclosed bearing). The butt joint is more desirable than the lap joint for two main reasons. These are:

1. The members are arranged so that the total shearing force P is split into two parts, causing the force on each plane to be only about one-half of what it would be on a single plane if a lap joint were used. From a shear standpoint, therefore, the load-carrying ability of a group of rivets in double shear is theoretically twice as great as the same number of rivets in single shear.

2. A more symmetrical loading condition is provided. (In fact the butt joint does provide a symmetrical situation if the outside members are the same thickness and have the same stress values.) The result is a reduction or elimination of the bending described for a lap joint.

The eccentricity of the lap joint connection causes the stresses to be unevenly distributed across the contact area between the rivets and the members being connected. For many years the AISC permitted a smaller allowable bearing stress for rivets in single shear than was allowed for rivets in double shear. In recent years, however, tests have shown that this distinction is probably unnecessary and today the AISC gives the same value for both cases.

Double-Plane Connections. The double plane connection is one in which the rivets are subjected to single shear and bearing but in which bending moment is prevented. This type of connection, which is shown for a hanger in Fig. 9-4(a), subjects the rivets to single shear on two different planes.

Fɪɢ. 9-4

Miscellaneous. Riveted connections generally consist of lap or butt joints or some combination of them but there are other cases. For instance there are joints in which more than three members are being connected and the rivets are in multiple shear as shown in Fig. 9-4(b). Several other types of riveted connections are discussed in this chapter. These include rivets in tension, rivets in shear and tension, etc.

9-5. FAILURE OF RIVETED JOINTS

Figure 9-5 shows several ways in which failure of riveted joints can occur. To be able satisfactorily to design riveted joints it is necessary to understand these possibilities. These are described as follows.

1. The possibility of failure in a lap joint by shearing of the rivet on the plane between the members (single shear) is shown in part (a).

(a) Failure by shearing of rivet

(b) Tension failure of plate

(c) Crushing failure of plate

(d) Shear failure of plate behind rivet

(e) Double shear failure of a butt joint

(f) Bending failure of rivet

FIG. 9-5

2. In part (b) the possibility of a tension failure of one of the plates through a rivet hole is shown.

3. A possible failure of the rivets and/or plates by bearing between the two is given in (c).

4. Part (d) shows another possibility in the shearing out of part of the member.

5. A butt joint is shown in (e) with the possibility of a shear failure of the rivets along two planes (double shear).

6. Should the rivets be quite long with respect to their diameter they may fail in bending before they do in shear or bearing. See part (f) of figure.

9-6. VARIATIONS FROM ACTUAL STRESSES

The usual methods of calculating rivet stresses which are described in this chapter may result in values which are appreciably different from the true stresses. Among the several factors which cause these variations are: friction between the members, bending of the rivets, stress concentrations around rivet holes, deformation of members being connected, and others.

Tests have shown that hot-driven rivets which are properly installed exert large clamping forces on the members being connected. These clamping forces multiplied by the proper coefficients of friction produce considerable friction between the members. Unless the shearing load at a particular joint exceeds the frictional resistance, no shear will be applied to the rivets. Should the shearing load exceed the frictional resistance, a little initial slippage will occur, and the load will be resisted by a combination of frictional resistance and by the rivets in shear and bearing.

The amount of clamping force produced by properly driven rivets has been measured to be around 30,000 psi, which is roughly the elastic limit of the rivet steel. Almost exactly the same value can be obtained theoretically by multiplying the cooling in degrees of the rivet times the coefficient of expansion of steel (0.0000065) times the modulus of elasticity, with a maximum value approximately equal to the elastic limit. Assuming a clamping force of 30,000 psi and a coefficient of friction of about 0.4, a frictional resistance of approximately 12,000 psi is obtained.

For average-length rivets it is probably permissible to neglect bending, but for rivets with very long grips it cannot be ignored. The specifications usually say that if a rivet exceeds a certain length its allowable load is reduced by a certain amount. For instance, the AISC requires the number of rivets in a group to be increased by 1 percent for each $\frac{1}{16}$ in. of grip beyond five diameters.

9-7. SPACING AND EDGE DISTANCES OF RIVETS

Before minimum spacings and edge distances can be discussed it is necessary for a few terms to be explained. The following definitions are given for a group of rivets in a connection and are shown in Fig. 9-6.

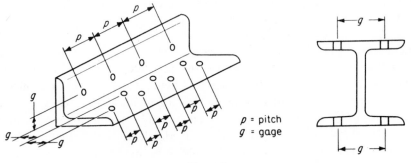

p = pitch
g = gage

Fig. 9-6

Pitch is the center-to-center distance of rivets in a direction parallel to the axis of the member.

Gage is the center-to-center distance of rivet lines perpendicular to the axis of the member.

The *edge distance* is the distance from the center of a rivet to the adjacent edge of a member.

The *distance between rivets* or rivet distance is the shortest distance between rivets on different rivet lines.

Rivets should be placed a sufficient distance apart to permit efficient installation and to prevent tension failures of the members between rivets. The AISC permits a minimum pitch of rivets equal to 2⅔ times the nominal rivet diameter with a preferred minimum of three diameters. On the other hand, it is desirable to place rivets reasonably close together in a connection to give compact joints and to reduce the amount of gusset-plate materials used.

Rivet holes should not be placed too near the edges of a member for two major reasons. The punching of holes too close to the edges may cause the steel opposite the hole to bulge out or even crack. The second reason applies to the ends of members where there is a danger of the rivet tearing through the metal. The usual practice is to place rivets a minimum distance from the edge of plates equal to from 1.5 to 2.0 times the rivet diameter so the metal there will have a shearing strength at least equal to that of the rivets. For more exact information it is necessary to refer to the specifications being used. The AISC has a set of minimum permitted edge distances. The values given depend on rivet size, stress conditions, whether material edges are rolled or sheared, etc. (The distances required are greater for sheared edges than for the edges of rolled shapes.)

Many specifications give maximum distances which rivets can be placed from the edge of a connection. The AISC maximum is 12 times the plate thickness but not to exceed 6 in. If rivets are too far from the edges openings may develop between the members being connected. Maximum spacings for rivets may also be given for compression members so that buckling will not occur between rivets.

The usual location of gage lines are given in the AISC Manual for the various steel sections. The designer should place rivets on these lines whenever possible to facilitate the punching of holes in the shop and the installation of rivets in shop and field. Holes cannot be punched very close to the web of a beam or the leg of an angle. They can be drilled but this rather expensive practice should not be followed unless there is an unusual situation. Even if the holes are drilled in these locations there will be considerable difficulty in driving the rivet and forming the head in the limited space.

9-8. STRENGTH OF RIVETED CONNECTIONS—RIVETS IN SHEAR

The factors determining the strength of a rivet are the rivet diameter and the thickness and arrangement of the pieces being connected. The actual distribution of stress around a rivet hole is difficult to determine, if it can be determined at all; and to simplify the calculations it is assumed to vary uniformly over a rectangular area equal to the diameter of the rivet times the thickness of the plate.

The strength of a rivet in bearing equals the allowable bearing unit stress of the rivet times the diameter of the shank of the rivet times the thickness of the member which bears on the rivet. The strength of a rivet in single shear is the allowable shearing unit stress times the cross-sectional area of the shank of the rivet. Should a rivet be in double shear its shearing strength is considered to be twice its single-shear value. No further increase beyond double shear is permitted for those rivets which are subjected to shearing forces on more than two planes.

For many years it was common for steel specifications to give different allowable bearing stresses depending on whether single shear or double shear was present. The feeling was that with single shear and bearing [see Fig. 9-3(a)] the eccentricity caused less uniform bearing stresses. Tests in recent years have shown that a distinction in the allowable bearing stresses between the two cases is not necessary. Even if there is a difference between the stress distributions (for the two cases) at small loads, the plastic behavior of the rivets at ultimate load makes a distinction unnecessary.

The effectiveness of a particular riveted joint is sometimes measured by the so-called efficiency of the joint. This term is usually defined as the ratio of the strength of the joint to the strength of the main members.

Examples 9-1 and 9-2 illustrate the simple calculations involved in determining the strength of riveted connections and the number of rivets required for a certain loading condition.

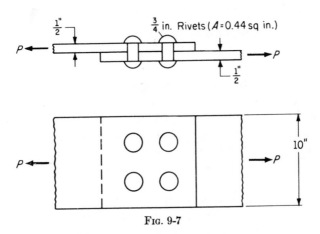

FIG. 9-7

EXAMPLE 9-1. Determine the allowable force P which can be applied to the plates shown in Fig. 9-7. The AISC Specification, A36 steel, and A502, Grade 1 rivets are used in the connection. (Allowable shear in rivets is 15,000 psi, allowable bearing in rivets is 48,600 psi, and allowable tension in steel plates is 22,000 psi.)

Solution: Rivets are in single shear and bearing:

Allowable shear in rivets $= (4)\ (0.44)\ (15,000) = 26,400$ lb

Allowable bearing in rivets $= (4)\left(\dfrac{3}{4}\right)\left(\dfrac{1}{2}\right)(48,600) = 72,900$ lb

Allowable tension in steel plates $=\left(10 - 2\times\dfrac{7}{8}\right)\left(\dfrac{1}{2}\right)(22,000) = 90,750$ lb

Maximum permissible load $P = 26,400$ lb

EXAMPLE 9-2.   How many $\frac{7}{8}$-in. A502, Grade 1 rivets are required for the connection shown in Fig. 9-8 if the plates are made from A36 steel?   Use AISC Specification.

47,000 lb

47,000 lb

94,000 lb

FIG. 9-8

Solution: Rivets in double shear and bearing on $\frac{1}{2}$ in.:

Allowable bearing per rivet $= (\frac{7}{8})\ (\frac{1}{2})\ (1.35\times 36,000) = 21,300$ lb

Allowable shear per rivet $= (2)\ (0.6)\ (15,000) = 18,000$ lb

Number of rivets required $= 94,000/18,000 = 5+$

Use six $\frac{7}{8}$-in. rivets

The assumption has been made that the loads applied to a riveted connection are equally divided between the rivets. For this distribution to be correct the plates must be perfectly rigid and the rivets perfectly elastic, but actually the plates being connected are elastic and have deformations which decidedly affect the rivet stresses. The effect of these deformations is to cause a very complex distribution of load in the elastic range.

Should the plates be assumed to be completely rigid and nondeform-ing, all rivets would be deformed equally and have equal stresses. This situation is shown in part (a) of Fig. 9-9. Actually the load resisted by the rivets of a group are probably never equal (in the elastic range) when there are more than two rivets in a line. Should the plates be deformable, the plate stresses and thus the deformations will decrease from the ends of the connection to the middle as shown in part (b) of Fig. 9-9. The result is that the highest stressed elements of the top plate

(a) Assuming nondeforming plates

(b) Assuming deformable plates

(c) Stepped joint (impractical)

FIG. 9-9

will be over the lowest stressed elements of the lower plate, and vice versa. The slip will be greatest at the end rivets and smallest at the middle rivets. The rivets at the ends will then have stresses much greater than those in the inside rivets.

The greater the spacing of rivets in a connection the greater will be the variation in rivet stresses due to plate deformation; therefore, the use of compact joints is very desirable as they will tend to reduce the variation in rivet stresses. It might be interesting to consider a theoretical (although not practical) method of roughly equalizing rivet stresses. The theory would involve the reduction of the thickness of the plate toward its end in proportion to the reduced stresses by stepping. This procedure which is shown in Fig. 9-9(c) would tend to equalize the deformations of the plate and thus the rivet stresses. A similar procedure would be to scarf the overlapping plates.

The calculation of the theoretically correct elastic stresses in a riveted group based on plate deformations is a tedious problem and is rarely handled in the design office. On the other hand the analysis of a riveted joint based on the plastic theory is a very simple problem. In this theory the end rivets are assumed to be stressed to their yield point. Should the total load on the connection be increased, the end rivets will deform without resisting additional load, the next rivets in the line will have their stresses increased until they too are at the yield point, and so forth. Plastic analysis seems to justify to a certain extent the assumption of rigid plates and equal rivet stresses which is usually made in design practice. This assumption is used in the example problems of this chapter.

When there are only a few rivets in a line the plastic theory of equal stresses seems to be borne out very well but when there are a large number of rivets in a line the situation changes. Tests have clearly shown that the end rivets will fail before the full redistribution takes place.[1]

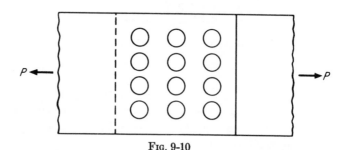

Fig. 9-10

EXAMPLE 9-3. The connection shown in Fig. 9-10 is to be made with A502, Grade 1 rivets, and the plates are to consist of A36 steel. Using the AISC Specification determine the diameter of rivets whose shearing strength will equal their bearing strength. (This diameter is sometimes referred to as the most economical diameter of the rivets for the thicknesses of materials involved.) What is the maximum allowable force P which can be applied to the connection if the most economical size rivets are used?

Solution: Equating double shear strength of one rivet to its bearing strength:

$$(2)\left(\frac{\pi d^2}{4}\right)(15,000) = (\frac{1}{2})(d)(48,600)$$

$$d = 1.03 \text{ in.}$$

[1] *Trans. ASCE*, vol. 105 (1940), p. 1193.

Use 1-in. rivets

Allowable capacity of connection:

   Shear in rivets $= (12)\ (2)\ (0.785)\ (15,000) = 282,000$ lb

   Bearing in rivets $= (12)\ (1.00)\ (0.50)\ (48,600) = 291,600$ lb

   Tension in plates $= (14 - 4 \times 1\frac{1}{8})\ (0.50)\ (22,000) = 104,500$ lb

   Maximum allowable load $= 104,500$ lb

Where cover plates are riveted to the flanges of W sections the rivets must carry the longitudinal shear on the plane between the plates and the flanges. With reference to the cover-plated beam of Fig. 9-11 the unit longitudinal shearing stress between a cover plate and the W flange can be determined with the VQ/bI expression. The total shear across the flange and for a 1-in.-length of the beam equals VQ/I.

The spacing of pairs of rivets in Fig. 9-11 can be determined by

FIG. 9-11

dividing the shear per inch at a particular section into the strength of the two rivets. The theoretical spacings will vary as the external shear varies along the beam. Example 9-4 illustrates the calculations involved in determining rivet spacings for a cover-plated beam.

EXAMPLE 9-4. At a certain section in the cover-plated beam of Fig. 9-11 the external shear is 190 k. Determine the required spacing of $\frac{7}{8}$-in. A502, Grade 1 rivets if the beam is rolled from A36 steel and the AISC Specification is to be used.

Solution:

$$I_x = 3,410 + (2) \ (16 \times \tfrac{3}{4}) \ (11.105)^2 = 6,360 \ \text{in.}^4$$

$$v = \frac{VQ}{I} = \frac{(190,000) \ (16 \times \tfrac{3}{4} \times 11.105)}{6,360} = 3,980 \ \text{lb/in.}$$

$$\text{Shear} = (2) \ (0.6) \ (15,000) = 18,000 \ \text{lb for 2 rivets}$$

$$\text{Bearing} = (2) \ (\tfrac{7}{8}) \ (\tfrac{3}{4}) \ (1.35 \times 36,000) = 63,700 \ \text{lb for 2 rivets}$$

$$p = \frac{18,000}{3,980} = 4.52 \ \text{in. (say } 4\tfrac{1}{2} \ \text{in.)}$$

9-9. RIVETS SUBJECTED TO ECCENTRIC SHEAR

Eccentrically loaded rivet groups are subjected to shears and bending moments. The student may feel such situations are rare but the truth is that they are much more common than he suspects. For instance, in a truss it is desirable to have the center of gravity of a member lined up exactly with the center of gravity of the rivets at its end connections. This feat is not quite as easy to accomplish as it may seem and connections are often subjected to moments.

Eccentricity is quite obvious in Fig. 9-12(a) where a beam is con-

(a)   (b)

Fɪɢ. 9-12

nected to a column. In part (b) of the figure a beam is connected to a column with a pair of web angles. For this connection it is obvious that even though no end moment is being considered the connection must resist some moment because the center of gravity of the load from the beam does not coincide with the reaction from the column.

The following several paragraphs are concerned with developing a method of calculating the forces in the rivets of an eccentric connection. For this discussion the rivets of Fig. 9-13(a) are assumed to be subjected to a load P which has an eccentricity of e from the c.g. (center of gravity) of the rivet group. To consider the force situation in the rivets an up-

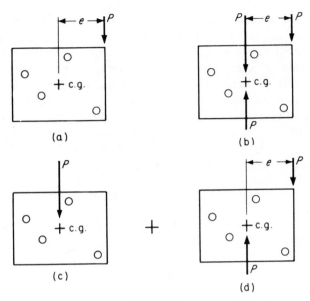

Fig. 9-13

ward and downward force, each equal to P, is assumed to act at the c.g. of the rivet group. This situation, shown in part (b) of the figure, in no way changes the rivet force. The force in a particular rivet will, therefore, equal P divided by the number of rivets in the group as seen in part (c), plus the force due to the moment caused by the couple shown in part (d) of the figure.

The magnitude of the forces in the rivets due to the moment Pe will now be considered. The distances of each rivet from the c.g. of the group are represented by the values d_1, d_2, etc. in Fig. 9-14. The moment

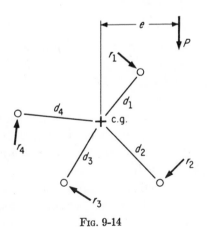

Fig. 9-14

produced by the couple causes the plate to rotate about the c.g. of the rivet connection with the amount of rotation or strain at a particular rivet being proportional to its distance from the c.g. (For this derivation the gusset plates are again assumed to be perfectly rigid and the rivets are assumed to be perfectly elastic.) Rotation is greatest at the rivet which is the greatest distance from the c.g. as will be the stress since stress is proportional to strain.

The rotation is assumed to produce forces of r_1, r_2, r_3, and r_4 respectively on the rivets in the figure. The moment transferred to the rivets must be balanced by resisting moments of the rivets as follows:

$$M = Pe = r_1 d_1 + r_2 d_2 + r_3 d_3 + r_4 d_4 \qquad (1)$$

As the force caused on each rivet is directly proportional to the distance from the c.g. the following expression can be written:

$$\frac{r_1}{d_1} = \frac{r_2}{d_2} = \frac{r_3}{d_3} = \frac{r_4}{d_4}$$

and writing each r value in terms of r_1 and d_1

$$r_1 = \frac{r_1 d_1}{d_1} \qquad r_2 = \frac{r_1 d_2}{d_1} \qquad r_3 = \frac{r_1 d_3}{d_1} \qquad r_4 = \frac{r_1 d_4}{d_1}$$

Substituting these values into equation (1) and simplifying:

$$M = \frac{r_1 d_1{}^2}{d_1} + \frac{r_1 d_2{}^2}{d_1} + \frac{r_1 d_3{}^2}{d_1} + \frac{r_1 d_4{}^2}{d_1}$$

$$= \frac{r_1}{d_1} (d_1{}^2 + d_2{}^2 + d_3{}^2 + d_4{}^2)$$

$$= \frac{r_1 \Sigma d^2}{d_1}$$

The force on each rivet can now be written as follows:

$$r_1 = \frac{M d_1}{\Sigma d^2} \qquad r_2 = \frac{d_2}{d_1} r_1 = \frac{M d_2}{\Sigma d^2} \qquad r_3 = \frac{M d_3}{\Sigma d^2} \qquad r_4 = \frac{M d_4}{\Sigma d^2}$$

Each value of r is perpendicular to the line drawn from the c.g. to the particular rivet. It is usually more convenient to break these down into vertical and horizontal components. In accomplishing this purpose reference is made to Fig. 9-15.

The horizontal and vertical components of the distance d_1 are represented by h and v respectively and the horizontal and vertical components

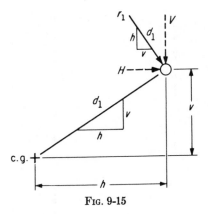

FIG. 9-15

of force r, are represented by H and V respectively in this figure. It is now possible to write the following ratio from which H can be obtained.

$$\frac{r_1}{d_1} = \frac{H}{v}$$

$$H = \frac{r_1 v}{d_1} = \left(\frac{M d_1}{\Sigma d^2}\right)\left(\frac{v}{d_1}\right)$$

$$= \frac{Mv}{\Sigma d^2}$$

By a similar procedure V is found to equal

$$V = \frac{Mh}{\Sigma d^2}$$

EXAMPLE 9-5. Determine the force in the most stressed rivet of the group shown in Fig. 9-16.

FIG. 9-16

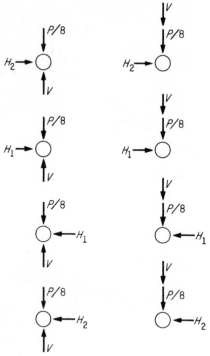

Fɪɢ. 9-17

Solution: A sketch of each rivet and the forces applied to it by the direct load and the clockwise moment are shown in Fig. 9-17. From this sketch the student will see that the upper right-hand rivet and the lower right-hand rivet are the most stressed and have equal stresses.

$$e = 6 + 1.5 = 7.5 \text{ in.}$$

$$M = Pe = (30)\,(7.5) = 225 \text{ in.-k}$$

$$\Sigma d^2 = \Sigma h^2 + \Sigma v^2$$

$$\Sigma d^2 = (8)\,(1.5)^2 + (4)\,(1.5^2 + 4.5^2) = 108$$

$$H = \frac{Mv}{\Sigma d^2} = \frac{(225)\,(4.5)}{108} = 9.38 \text{ k}$$

$$V = \frac{Mh}{\Sigma d^2} = \frac{(225)\,(1.5)}{108} = 3.13 \text{ k}$$

$$\frac{P}{8} = \frac{30}{8} = 3.75 \text{ k}$$

Force in lower right-hand rivet (equal to force in upper right-hand rivet) is determined as follows:

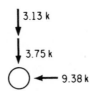

$$r = \sqrt{(6.88)^2 + (9.38)^2} = 11.64 \text{ k}$$

Should the eccentric load be inclined it can be broken down into vertical and horizontal components and the moment of each about the c.g. of the rivet group determined. Several design formulas can be developed which will enable the engineer to directly design eccentric connections but in all probability the process of assuming a certain number and arrangement of rivets, checking stresses, and redesigning is probably just as satisfactory.

This type of procedure for handling eccentrically loaded rivet groups has been used since at least 1870 and there has not been a great deal of experimental work supporting the method.[2, 3]

In the connection part of the AISC Manual a section entitled "Eccentric Loads on Fastener Groups" is presented. Should the student of this book attempt to use the tables and equations of the AISC Manual to solve the type of problems described in the last few pages he will obtain different answers from those obtained herein.

The conventional method described in this chapter is thought by many to provide a too conservative estimate of the allowable eccentric loads on rivet groups. The method described in this chapter omits two items affetcing the behavior of such connections. These are frictional resistance and the plastic redistribution of high fastener stresses. In the method presented in the AISC Manual the actual eccentric moment arm is reduced to an effective eccentric distance by an empirical formula resulting in a smaller calculated moment.[4]

9-10. RIVETS SUBJECTED TO COMBINED SHEAR AND TENSION

In the majority of framed connections for beams to beams and beams to columns the rivets are subjected to a combination of shear and tension.

2 William McGuire, *Steel Structures* (Englewood Cliffs, N.J.: Prentice-Hall, Inc., 1968), p. 813.

3 C. Reilly, "Studies of Iron Girder Bridges," *Proc. Inst. Civil Engrs.*, vol. 29 (London, 1870).

4 T. R. Higgins, "New Formulas for Fasteners Loaded Off Center," *Engr. News Record* (May 21, 1964).

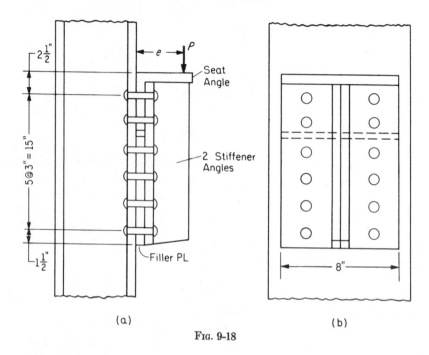

(a)   (b)

FIG. 9-18

This combination is true for the rivets in the bracket of Fig. 9-18 as well as for those in the connections shown in Figs. 12-1(a) and (b) and 12-3(a) and (b). In each of these connections the load being transferred tends to cause the connection to slide downward and this tendency is resisted by the shearing strength of the rivets. At the same time, the load is tending to rotate the connection, pulling the top rivets away from the column and pushing the lower part of the connection against the column.

The vertical shearing stress can be easily determined by dividing the vertical load by the cross-sectional area of the rivets involved; however, the stresses caused by bending are a little more difficult to compute. For this discussion the bracket connection of Fig. 9-18 with an eccentric load P is considered. The downward load and the upward shear in the rivets produce a couple. The distance between the two forces is assumed to be e and the moment produced Pe. An equal and opposite couple must be produced by the tension in the upper rivets and by the compression in the lower part of the connection.

An exact analysis of the rivet stresses produced by this situation is almost impossible; therefore, several different approximate methods have been developed by various designers. Perhaps the most common method is the one described in the paragraphs to follow.

In this method the initial tension in the rivets is neglected and the top of the connection is assumed to have pulled away from the column. Below the opening there is assumed to be a neutral axis above which the rivets are in tension and below which the connection angles are bearing against the column. It is assumed in this discussion that the bearing is spread over the full width of the angles. (Because of deformation of these angles the pressure at the outer edges is probably appreciably smaller than the pressure on the inside. For this reason many designers assume the compression is spread over some smaller width. It should be noted, however, that the varying widths used by different designers have little effect on the final tensile stresses determined in the top rivets.)

With the full-width assumption the neutral axis will usually lie about one-sixth to one-seventh of the depth of the connection above the bottom of the connection. From this information the location of the neutral axis can be estimated and its accuracy checked by taking moments about that location. After moments are taken it may be necessary to make a slight adjustment in the location. When the neutral axis is located the moment of inertia can be calculated and the stresses obtained by the flexure formula.

Tests on rivets subjected to combined shear and tension show that their ultimate strengths can be represented with an eliptical interaction curve. The curve has limits of F_t as the allowable stress if the rivet is stressed in tension alone and of F_v if stressed in shear alone. Such a curve is shown in Fig. C1.6.3.1 in the "Commentary on the AISC Specification" in the AISC Manual.

For A502, Grade 1 rivets the allowable combined stress permitted by the AISC is given by the following expression in which f_t is the calculated tensile stress and f_v is the calculated shearing stress:

$$F_t = 28,000 - 1.6\,f_v \leqq 20,000$$

In effect, this expression replaces the test result curve with three straight lines (also shown in Fig. C1.6.3.1 in the AISC Manual) and divides the values with appropriate factors of safety. The three straight lines are formed by the following conditions: (1) If $f_v < 5,000$ psi, $F_t = 20,000$ psi. (2) If $f_t < 4,000$ psi, $F_v = 15,000$ psi. (3) In between the limits $F_t = 28,000 - 1.6\,f_v$. Similar interaction formulas are given by the AISC for high-strength bolts and other types of rivets.

EXAMPLE 9-6.   Determine the maximum combined tensile and shearing stresses in the top rivets of the connection shown in Fig. 9-18. The stiffener angles are each $4 \times 4 \times \frac{1}{2}$ in.; the eccentric load is 75 k; the eccentricity is 3 in., and $\frac{7}{8}$ in. rivets are used. Does the resulting value exceed the AISC allowable for A502, Grade 1 rivets?

Solution: Assume neutral axis one-sixth of distance from bottom of connection:

$$(\tfrac{1}{6})\ (19\text{ in.}) = 3.166\text{ in. (say 3 in.) (see Fig. 9-19)}$$

FIG. 9-19

Check location of neutral axis:

$$(24) \ (1.5) = (2) \ (0.6) \ (1.5 + 4.5 + 7.5 + 10.5 + 13.5)$$

$$36 = 45 \qquad\qquad (N. \ G.)$$

Assume neutral axis 3.25 in. from bottom of connection (see Fig. 9-20):

FIG. 9-20

$$(8) \ (3\tfrac{1}{4}) \ (1.625) = (2) \ (0.6) \ (1.25 + 4.25 + 7.25 + 10.25 + 13.25)$$

$$42.2 = 43.5 \qquad\qquad (OK)$$

$$I = (\tfrac{1}{3}) \ (8) \ (3.25)^3 + (2) \ (0.6) \ (1.25^2 + 4.25^2 + 7.25^2 + 10.25^2 + 13.25^2)$$

$$= 91.4 + 422$$

$$= 513 \ in.^4$$

$$f_t = \frac{Mc}{I} = \frac{(225)\ (13.25)}{513} = 5.8\ \text{ksi}$$

$$f_v = \frac{75}{(12)\ (0.6)} = 10.4\ \text{ksi}$$

Allowable F_t for A502, Grade 1 rivets:

$$F_t = 28{,}000 - 1.6\,f_v \leq 20{,}000$$

$$= 28{,}000 - (1.6)\ (10{,}400)$$

$$= 11{,}300 \leq 20{,}000$$

Actual $f_t = 5.8\ \text{ksi} < 11.3\ \text{ksi (understressed)}$

AS previously indicated, there are other methods of estimating the stresses in rivets subjected to shear and tension. The method described here neglected any initial tension present in the rivets. If the rivets did have an initial tension (as they most certainly do) they would squeeze the connection against the column. Bending would serve to reduce the pressure at the top of the connection and, as before, there would be an increase in pressure at the bottom of the connection against the column. For this case the neutral axis could be assumed to lie at the middepth of the section. A very large moment is usually required before the initial pressure at the top of the connection can be overcome and cause pulling of the connection away from the column, causing in turn a change in the top rivet stress. This subject is discussed at length in Chap. 10 for high-strength bolts.

Another case where rivets are subject to a combination of shear and tension is shown in Fig. 9-21 and illustrated by the calculations of Example 9-7.

EXAMPLE 9-7. The tension member shown in Fig. 9-21 is connected to the column with eight ¾-in. A502, Grade 1 rivets. Is the connection satisfactory? Use A36 steel and the AISC Specification.

Solution:

$$f_v = \frac{48}{(8)\ (0.44)} = 13.65\ \text{ksi}$$

$$f_t = \frac{36}{(8)\ (0.44)} = 10.22\ \text{ksi}$$

$$F_t = 28.0 - 1.6\,f_v \leq 20.0$$

$$F_t = 28.0 - (1.6)\ (13.65) = 6.2\ \text{ksi} < 10.22\ \text{ksi} \qquad \text{(N.G.)}$$

∴ Connection is unsatisfactory

FIG. 9-21

9-11. RIVETS IN TENSION

Figure 9-22 (a) shows a connection in which the rivets are in tension. Perhaps one of the most common cases of tension rivets occurs in wind bracing for buildings. Many engineers have been very much opposed to the use of rivets in tension because of the fear that the rivet heads might be pulled off. This attitude might have been reasonable before 1930 but the results of tests published during that year[5] showed that improved riveting techniques produced rivets which were entirely capable of resisting tension loads.

Today the AISC permits their use in building design (giving an

FIG. 9-22

[5] W. M. Wilson and W. A. Oliver, *Tension Tests of Rivets,* University of Illinois Experiment Station, Bulletin, 210 (1930).

allowable tension of 20,000 psi for A502, Grade 1 rivets) ; but the AREA prohibits their use and the AASHO discourages their use. It should be noted in Fig. 9-22 (b) that if the members being connected are not fairly stiff, some prying action will occur which will increase the tension in the rivets. Should the members be fairly flexible, the designer should attempt to estimate the stresses caused by prying. A more detailed discussion of the action of tensile rivets including prying is presented in Chap. 12.

PROBLEMS

9-1. Determine the maximum allowable load P which can be resisted by the lap joint shown in the accompanying illustration if $7/8$-in. A502, Grade 1 rivets and the AISC Specification are used. Each of the plates is $5/8 \times 12$ and consists of A36 steel. (Ans. $P = 108$ k)

PROB. 9-1

9-2. Repeat Prob. 9-1 if the following allowable stresses are used. Allowable shear on rivets $= 13,500$ psi, allowable bearing on rivets $= 32,000$ psi for single shear and 40,000 psi for double shear and allowable F_t on plates $= 20,000$ psi.

9-3. The truss tension member shown in the accompanying illustration consists of a single angle $5 \times 3 \times 5/16$ in. and is made from A36 steel. The member is connected to a $1/2$-in. gusset plate with the $7/8$-in. A502, Grade 1 rivets shown. Using the AISC Specification determine the allowable value of P. (Ans. $P = 44.9$ k)

PROB. 9-3

9-4. Using the AISC Specification determine the number of $7/8$-in. A502, Grade 1 rivets required to develop the full strength of a $3/4 \times 14$-in. plate of A36 steel if two holes are to be deducted in computing the net section and the rivets are assumed to be in single shear.

9-5. Using the allowable stresses given in Prob. 9-2 determine the allowable value of P in the butt joint shown in the accompanying illustration if 1-in. rivets are used. (Ans. $P = 150$ k)

PROB. 9-5

9-6. The butt splice shown in the accompanying illustration is to be designed for a tensile load of 120 k. How many $7/8$-in. A502, Grade 1 rivets are required, using the AISC Specification and A36 steel?

PROB. 9-6

9-7. How many $7/8$-in. A502, Grade 1 rivets are required for the connection shown in the accompanying illustration if A36 steel and the AISC Specification are used. (Ans. *No.* = 15.55, say 16)

PROB. 9-7

9-8. For the connection shown in the accompanying illustration P equals 390 k. Determine the number of $7/8$-in. A502, Grade 2 rivets required. Use A36 steel and the AISC Specification.

PROB. 9-8

9-9. Determine the maximum allowable value of P for the connection shown in the accompanying illustration if 1-in. A502, Grade 2 rivets and the AISC Specification are used. The plates consist of A36 steel. (Ans. $P = 65.3$ k)

PROB. 9-9

9-10. Determine the number of ⅞-in. A502, Grade 1 rivets required by the
AISC Specification to develop the A36 truss members shown in the accompanying
illustration.

Prob. 9-10

9-11. The ½ × 11½-in. plates forming the lap joint shown in the accompanying illustration are made of A36 steel and are connected with ⅞-in. A502, Grade 1 rivets. Determine the pitch of the rivets (*s* in the figure) which will cause the strength of the plates to be equal to the strength of the rivets. The AISC Specification is to be used. (Ans. $s = 1.73$ in., say 1¾ in.)

Prob. 9-11

9-12. For the plates shown in the accompanying illustration determine the allowable value of P using 1-in. A502, Grade 1 rivets, A36 steel and the AISC Specification.

PROB. 9-12

9-13. For the beam shown in the accompanying illustration what is the required spacing of ¾-in. A502, Grade 1 rivets at a section where the external shear is 106 k. (Ans. $p = 4.59$ in., say 4½ in. on center)

PROB. 9-13

9-14. The cover-plated section shown in the accompanying illustration is used to support a 14.3 k/ft uniform load (including beam weight) for an 18-ft simple span. If ⅞-in. A502, Grade 1 rivets are used arranged as shown, work out a spacing diagram for the entire span. Assume the cover plates extend for the full span. A36. AISC.

$\frac{5}{16}$X 16 PL

W27 X177

$\frac{5}{16}$X 16 PL

Ls 8X4X$\frac{3}{4}$
(short legs back-to-back)

PL $\frac{1}{2}$ X 48

2$\frac{1}{2}$"

43$\frac{1}{2}$" 48$\frac{1}{2}$"

2$\frac{1}{2}$"

PROB. 9-14   PROB. 9-15

9-15. For the section shown in the accompanying illustration determine the required spacing of ¾-in. A502, Grade 1 rivets using A36 steel and the AISC Specification. $V = 220$ k. (Ans. $p = 3.49$ in., say 3½ in.)

PLs $\frac{1}{2}$X 20

Ls 8X8X$\frac{1}{2}$

PL $\frac{5}{8}$X 54

Note: rivets are not staggered

3"

3"

42$\frac{1}{2}$"

54$\frac{1}{2}$"

3"

3"

PROB. 9-16

9-16. For an external shear of 280 k determine the spacing of ⅞-in. A502, Grade 1 rivets for the condition shown in the accompanying illustration. A36. AISC Specification.

9-17. Determine the resultant load on the most stressed rivet in the eccentrically loaded connection shown in the accompanying illustration. (Ans. $R = 10.77$ k)

PROB. 9-17   PROB. 9-18

9-18. Determine the resultant load on the most stressed rivet in the eccentrically loaded connection shown in the accompanying illustration.

9-19. Determine the most stressed rivet and the magnitude of its load for the rivet group shown in the accompanying illustration. Determine also the size of rivets required for that load according to the AISC Specification. A502,

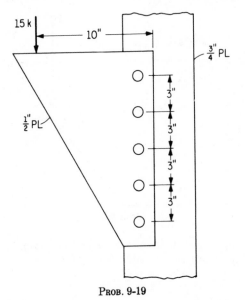

PROB. 9-19

Grade 1 rivets. A36 steel. Rivets in single shear. (Ans. $R = 10.44$ k, 1-in. rivets required)

9-20. Find the most stressed rivet and the magnitude of the force on that rivet for the connection shown in the accompanying illustration.

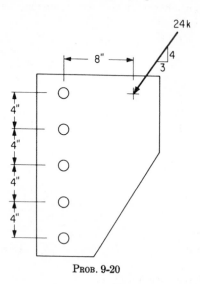

PROB. 9-20

9-21. The rivets shown in the accompanying illustration are 1-in. A502, Grade 2 and connect the ¾-in. plate to a ⅞-in. plate. Are the rivets of sufficient size? A36. AISC Specification. (Ans. No, $R = 16.7$ k, allowable $R = 15.7$ k)

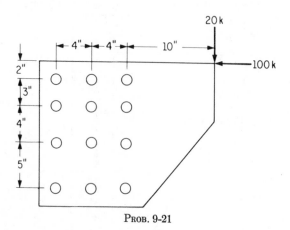

PROB. 9-21

9-22. Determine the rivet size for the connection shown in the accompanying illustration. A502, Grade 1 rivets. A36 steel. AISC.

PROB. 9-22

9-23. What is the allowable value of P in the accompanying illustration if the rivets are ⅞-in. A502, Grade 2 and are in double shear and bearing on ½ in.? A36. AISC Specification. (Ans. $P = 60.6$ k)

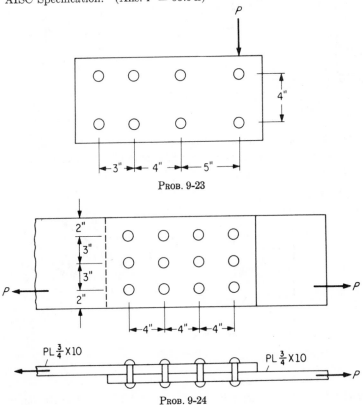

PROB. 9-23

PROB. 9-24

9-24. For the connection shown in the accompanying illustration determine the allowable value of P. It is assumed that the plates have sufficient capacity for the resulting value of P. Rivets are $\frac{7}{8}$-in. A502. Grade 1. A36. AISC Specification.

9-25. The MC 18 × 42.7 shown in the accompanying illustration consists of A36 steel. Using the AISC Specification determine the maximum permissible value of the eccentric load P if $\frac{7}{8}$-in. rivets are used. (Ans. $P = 46.8$ k)

PROB. 9-25

9-26. If the maximum allowable load on any one rivet in the rivet group shown in the accompanying illustration is 12 k determine the maximum permissible value of P.

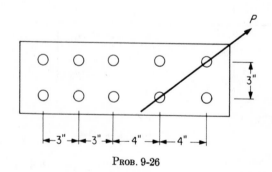

PROB. 9-26

9-27. The eccentric load P causes a total force of 8100 lbs on the most stressed rivet in the group shown in the accompanying illustration. Find the magnitude of P. (Ans. $P = 10,050$ lbs)

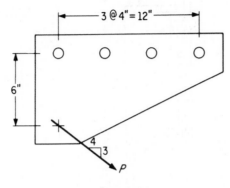

PROB. 9-27

9-28. Determine the most stressed rivet and the magnitude of the force applied to that rivet for the connection shown in the accompanying illustration. Note that rivet sizes are not the same throughout the connection (an undesirable situation).

PROB. 9-28

9-29. Using 1-in. A502, Grade 1 rivets determine if the connection shown in the accompanying illustration is satisfactory. A36. AISC Specification. (Ans. Connection is satisfactory, $f_t = 5.40$ ksi while $F_t = 13.4$ ksi)

PROB. 9-29

PROB. 9-30

9-30. Using the AISC Specification, A36 steel and ⅞-in. A502, Grade 1 rivets determine the permissible value of P for the connection shown in the accompanying illustration.

9-31. Is the connection shown in the accompanying illustration sufficient to resist the 60 k load which passes through center of gravity of the rivet group. A36. AISC Specification. (Ans. Unsatisfactory, $f_t = 13.65$ ksi $> F_t = 11.6$ ksi)

60 k

3
4

8-¾ in. A502, Grade 1 rivets

PROB. 9-31

9-32. If the load shown in the accompanying illustration passes through the center of gravity of the rivet group, how large can it be? A36. AISC Specification.

P

1
2

10-⅞ in. A502, Grade 1 rivets

PROB. 9-32

chapter 10

BOLTED CONNECTIONS

10-1. TYPES OF BOLTS

Bolting of steel structures is a very rapid field erection process which requires less skilled labor than does riveting or welding. These facts give bolting a distinct economic advantage over the other connection methods in the United States where labor costs are so very high. There are several types of bolts which can be used for connecting structural steel members. These include unfinished bolts, turned bolts, ribbed bolts, and high-strength bolts. Design calculations for the first three of these types are much the same as for rivets although the allowable stresses may be different. There are, however, a few differences for high-strength bolts and this chapter is primarily devoted to these differences. A few descriptive comments are presented in the following paragraphs about the various types of bolts.

1. *Unfinished bolts* (also called common, machine, ordinary, or rough bolts) are made of low carbon steel and are the cheapest type of connection available. They generally have square heads and nuts to reduce costs, but hexagonal heads are sometimes used as they have a little more attractive appearance, are easier to turn and easier to hold with the wrenches and they require less turning space. As they have relatively large tolerances in shank and thread dimensions their allowable stresses are appreciably smaller than those for rivets or turned bolts. They are primarily used in light structures subjected to static loads and for secondary members (such as purlins, girts, bracing, etc.) in larger structures. *The strength and advantages of unfinished bolts have usually been greatly underrated in the past.*

2. *Turned bolts* are probably formed from hexagonal stock and their threads cut with a die. They are machined to close tolerances to provide close fits in their holes, usually within $\frac{1}{50}$ in. Because of these close tolerances the holes must be very accurately made, probably necessitating reaming or drilling. With such close fitting they are much more satis-

factory in resisting shear than are unfinished bolts, however, they are used very infrequently for structural connections today. Some type of locknut is generally used with unfinished bolts.

3. *Ribbed bolts* are those which have standard rivet heads and raised fins or ribs spaced evenly around their shanks. The outside diameters of the ribs are a little larger than the hole diameters and they must be driven. The ribs cut grooves into the connected members insuring tight fits but making the bolts rather difficult to install—particularly when they are to pass through several thicknesses of steel because of the difficulty of perfectly lining up the holes. An appreciable amount of field reaming is probably the result. Ribbed bolts are usually assumed to have a strength equal to that of standard rivets of the same size.

4. *High-strength bolts* are made from medium carbon heat-treated steel and from alloy steel and have tensile strengths several times those of ordinary bolts. Although they are a relatively new type of fastener for structural steel they are today the most popular field connection method. High-strength bolts are being used for all types of structures, from small buildings to "skyscrapers" and monumental bridges. These bolts were developed to overcome the weaknesses of rivets—primarily insufficient tension in their shanks after cooling. The resulting rivet tensions may not be large enough to hold them in place during the application of severe impactive and vibrating loads. The result is that they may become loose and vibrate and may eventually have to be replaced. High-strength bolts are tightened until they have very high tensile stresses. The connected parts are clamped tightly together between the bolt and nut heads permitting loads to be transferred primarily by friction.

A recent addition to the bolt family is the so-called *interference bolt* which is made in accordance with the high-strength bolt specifications but which is also of the ribbed type. These bolts have knurled configurations with diameters a little larger than the holes in which they are

High-strength bolt.
(*Bethlehem Steel
Company.*)

to be placed. The usual tensioning methods with impact wrenches are not required, thus permitting their installation with ordinary spud wrenches. Because they can be installed with hand wrenches they are very useful in steel erection where the normal equipment for tightening is difficult to handle (such as for TV and transmission towers).

10-2. DISCUSSION OF HIGH-STRENGTH BOLTS

The joints obtained using high-strength bolts are superior to riveted joints in performance and economy and they have become the leading field method of fastening structural steel members. Structural steel connections made with high-strength bolts are a relatively new development but their acceptance has been nothing short of astounding. C. Batho and E. H. Bateman first claimed in 1934 that high-strength bolts could satisfactorily be used for the assembly of steel structures[1] but it was not until 1947 that the Research Council on Riveted and Bolted Structural Joints of the Engineering Foundation was established. This group issued their first specifications in 1951 and since that time high-strength bolts have been adopted by both building and bridge engineers for both static and dynamic loadings with amazing speed. They have not only quickly become the leading method of making field connections, but they also have been found to have many applications for shop connections. The construction of the Mackinac Bridge in Michigan involved the use of more than one million high-strength bolts.

Connections which were formerly made with ordinary bolts and nuts were not too satisfactory when they were subjected to vibratory loads because the nuts frequently became loose. For many years this problem was dealt with by using some type of locknut, but the modern high-strength bolts furnish a far superior solution.

10-3. ADVANTAGES OF HIGH-STRENGTH BOLTS

Among the many advantages of high-strength bolts partly explaining their rapid success are the following:

1. Smaller crews of men are involved as compared to riveting. Two two-man bolting crews can easily turn out over twice as many bolts in a day as the number of rivets driven by the standard four-man riveting crew. The result is quicker steel erection.

2. In comparison to rivets, fewer bolts are needed to provide the same strength.

3. Good bolted joints can be made by men with a great deal less

---

[1] C. Batho and E. H. Bateman, "Investigations on Bolts and Bolted Joints," H. M. Stationery Office, (London, 1934).

training and experience than is necessary to produce welded and riveted connections of equal quality. The proper installation of high-strength bolts can be learned in a matter of hours.

4. No erection bolts are required which may have to be later removed (depending on specifications) as in welded joints.

5. There is little noise as compared to riveting.

6. Cheaper equipment is used to make bolted connections.

7. No fire hazard is present and no danger present from the tossing of hot rivets.

8. Tests on riveted joints and bolted joints under identical conditions definitely show that bolted joints have a higher fatigue strength. Their fatigue strength is also equal to or greater than that obtained with equivalent welded joints.

9. Where structures are to be later altered or disassembled changes in connections are quite simple because of the ease of bolt removal.

10-4. SPECIFICATIONS FOR HIGH-STRENGTH BOLTS

High-strength bolts are of the A325 or the A490 types as classified by the ASTM. The A325 bolt is made from a medium carbon steel and gains its strength from heat treating by quenching, and tempering, while the A490 bolt gains its strength by alloying. Up until the present time the A490 bolt has not been used a great deal but its use will probably increase appreciably in the years to come for the new higher-strength steels.

The allowable shearing and tensile stresses permitted in the A325 and A490 bolts by the AISC are presented in Table 10-1. Allowable bearing stresses are equal to 1.35 times the yield point of the steel parts being connected.

The values given in the preceding table are for buildings. The AASHO and the AREA also gives recommended values for bridges. These values are in each case approximately 10 percent smaller than are the values for buildings.

Two allowable shearing stresses are given in this table, one for the friction-type connections where there is a high factor of safety against slippage and one for the bearing-type connections in which this factor of safety is substantially reduced. When high-strength bolts are used they clamp the plates being connected so tightly together that a great deal of friction is created between them. The shearing stress given for the friction-type connection is the maximum allowable shear before the friction is assumed to be overcome. This type of connection is to be used for structures where there is a great deal of impact and vibration with resulting

TABLE 10-1

RECOMMENDED ALLOWABLE STRESSES FOR HIGH-STRENGTH BOLTS FOR BUILDINGS

Fastener Description	Allowable Tension, F_t (psi)	Allowable Shear, F_v (psi)	
		Friction-Type Connection	Bearing-Type Connection
A325 and A449 bolts* when threading is not excluded from shear planes.	40,000	15,000	15,000
A325 and A449 bolts* when threading is excluded from shear planes.	40,000	15,000	22,000
A490 bolts, when threading is not excluded from shear planes.	54,000	20,000	22,500
A490 bolts, when threading is excluded from shear planes.	54,000	20,000	32,000

* The A325 specification covers quenched and tempered medium carbon steel bolts from ½ to 1½ in. (inclusive) in diameter, while the A449 specification covers medium carbon steel bolts and studs 3 in. and under for general applications.

stress variations or reversals or where any slippage is undesirable. Under ordinary circumstances no slippage is really expected in either type of connection.

The bearing allowable stress is considerably higher because of the smaller factor of safety against slippage. The higher allowable stress values for this case clearly show that it is the bearing-type connection which makes use of the high strengths of these bolts and gives the best economy.

There are other important items covered by the AISC Specification as they pertain to high-strength bolts. For new construction, high-strength bolts which are installed in a friction-type connection prior to welding may be considered as sharing the stress with the weld. Other types of bolts are not considered to share the stresses including high-strength bolts in bearing-type connections. Similarly in new work rivets and high-strength bolts both may be considered to share the stresses resulting from dead and live loads provided they are friction-type connections.

10-5. INSTALLATION OF HIGH-STRENGTH BOLTS

High-strength bolts are placed in holes $\frac{1}{16}$ in. larger in diameter than the bolts and they are usually tightened to a minimum tension equal to the *proofload* of the bolt. The proofload of a bolt is a lower boundary of the proportional or elastic limit and equals approximately 70 percent of the ultimate tensile strength of the A325 bolts. Table 10-2 gives the proofloads for various size A325 bolts as required by the Research Council Specification.

TABLE 10-2

Bolt Size (in.)	Minimum Bolt Tension (kips)
½	12
⅝	19
¾	28
⅞	39
1	51
1⅛	56
1¼	71
1⅜	85
1½	103

Although many engineers felt that there would be some slippage as compared to rivets (because of the fact that rivets more nearly filled the holes) the results seem to show that there is less slippage in high-strength bolted joints than in riveted joints under similar conditions.

It is interesting to note that the nuts used for high-strength bolts need no special provisions for locking. Once these bolts are installed and the nut sufficiently tightened to produce the tension required there is no tendency for the nuts to become loose even after millions of cycles of loading. In fact, there apparently is no case on record where nuts have worked loose on high-strength bolts which were properly installed.

During the first several years of appreciable use of high-strength bolts several different methods of trying to insure proper bolt tension were attempted. These methods included (1) applying a certain torque to each size bolt, (2) the use of automatic wrenches which stalled at a certain torque, and (3) turning the nut one full turn from the finger-tight position.

Great success in obtaining the proper tension was not obtained with any of these methods. One trouble with the methods of applying certain torques to the bolts was that different torques are required to tighten a bolt from the head than from the nut. For a time specifications called for bolts to be tightened to 90 percent of the proofload by using a certain torque. This specification was not completely successful because many users tried very hard not to go on the high side of the 90 percent figure. They were afraid that if they put the bolts into the plastic range, failure would occur. The result of their carefulness was that the bolts were frequently not tightened as high as the 90 percent figure desired.

In the "one turn of the nut" method slight differences in the nut and bolt threads, grit or dents in the threads, etc., made the so-called finger-tight position quite variable. Furthermore, the workmen standing around with torque wrenches didn't like to use their hands to tighten the nuts. (It has been said that this method was probably first developed for maintenance of, say, railroad bridges in remote areas where it was necessary to put in a few bolts here or there. The men had a fairly good rule to go by to obtain adequate tightening and they could do it with whatever equipment they might have with them.)

Today there are more satisfactory procedures for applying certain torques and a different "turn of the nut" method is used. Both methods are recommended without preference by the Research Council. In the calibrated wrench method at least three of each lot of bolts to be used on the job are tightened in a calibrating device and their tensions read. The wrenches are set to stall at the torque producing the desired tension. The calibration must be checked at frequent intervals to make sure proper tightening is being obtained.

In today's "turn of the nut" method, the nuts are spun on with an impact wrench until they are snug, the snug point being defined as the point at which the wrench begins to impact. (Supposedly this snug-tight position also corresponds to the tightening a man can achieve with his full strength with a spud wrench.) From the snug point the nuts are turned from $\frac{1}{2}$ to $\frac{2}{3}$ turns, depending on the lengths and diameters of the bolts. At the snug point a bolt will have a stress of several thousand pounds per square inch, and after turning the nut a stress in the plastic range is developed.

If the "turn of the nut" procedure is followed for A325 bolts no washers are required, but if the torque method is used a hardened washer is required under the part being turned. For an A490 bolt a hardened washer must be used under the end being tightened regardless of the tightening method. Washers are necessary at each end of A490 bolts when the material being connected has a specified minimum yield point less than 40 ksi. The reason for using a washer is to provide as uniform a friction as possible under the twisted ends of the various bolts.

For a while it was thought that the use of washers at each end would reduce the amount of "bolt relaxation" occurring due to the high stress concentrations under the head or nut. Tests, however, have shown that the actual losses without washers are less than approximately 5 percent and that about the same losses occur when washers are used at each end.

Another reason for specifying washers formerly was to prevent galling, which is injury to the metal during twisting due to friction, etc. It has been found, however, that any galling which takes place is not detrimental to the strength of the joints, whether static or fatigue loads are involved.

The Research Council does not specify a maximum bolt tension. (They do give a tolerance in the "turn of the nut" method of $\frac{1}{6}$ turn over and nothing under.) This means that a bolt can be tightened to the highest load that won't break it and the bolt will still do the job. Should the bolt break, another one is put in with no damage done. It might be noted that the nuts are stronger than the bolt and the bolt will break before the nut strips.

Torquing the nut for a high-strength bolt with an air-driven impact wrench. (*Bethlehem Steel Company*.)

The surfaces of joints including the area adjacent to washers need to be free of loose scale, dirt, burs, and other defects which might prevent the parts from solid seating. It is necessary for the surface of the parts to be connected to have slopes of not more than 1 to 20 with respect to the bolt axis unless beveled washers are used. For friction-type joints the contact surfaces must also be free from oil, paint, lacquer, or galvanizing. (There is now much evidence available which indicates that this prohibition of galvanization is not necessary in such structures as bridges.)[2,3]

About the only successful method of checking the tightness of high-strength bolts is with a torque wrench. The desired procedure is to check one or two of the bolts in a small connection and perhaps as many as 10 percent of those in a large connection. Should the torque required to tighten one or more of the bolts be less than the value required for installation, it will probably be necessary to check all of the bolts in that connection. Torque values higher than those specified are not sufficient cause for rejection.

10-6. SHEARING RESISTANCE OF BOLTED JOINTS

The loads transferred between members at riveted joints are generally assumed to be transferred by shear in the rivets, although it has been well known for many years that the transfer is made primarily by means of friction between the plates being connected. As rivets cool after being driven they shrink and cause a clamping action on the plates being connected, but the amount of clamping varies so much that it is not considered in design. High-strength bolts provide much higher and more dependable amounts of clamping, and it is therefore reasonable to assume that the loads in a bolted joint are also transferred by friction. Because a more uniform tension can be put in bolts, it is possible to obtain a more uniform shearing resistance with their use.

Tests have shown that A502, Grade 1 rivets have a maximum tensile stress due to contraction during cooling of about 30,000 psi, which for a 1-in. rivet equals a total tensile force of about 24,000 lb. (This value can be computed from the amount of cooling and the coefficient of contraction for steel, noting that the stress cannot very well exceed the elastic limit of the rivet steel of about 30,000 psi.) The minimum recommended total tension in a 1-in. high-strength bolt is 47,250 lb, which is twice as large as the best possible clamping force in a 1-in. rivet ($0.785 \times 30,000 = 23,550$ lb) under the most ideal conditions.

If bolts are tightened to their minimum tensile values there is very little chance of their bearing against the plates which they are connecting. In fact, tests show that there is very little chance of slip occurring unless there is a calculated shear of at least 50 percent of the bolt tension. This means that in the usual friction-type connection the bolts are not stressed

[2] J. R. Hall, "The Case for the Galvanized Bridge," *Civil Engineering* (November 1964) pp. 31–34.

[3] P. C. Birkemoe, and D. C. Herrschaft, "Bolted Galvanized Bridges—Engineering Acceptance Near," *Civil Engineering* (April, 1970) pp. 42–46.

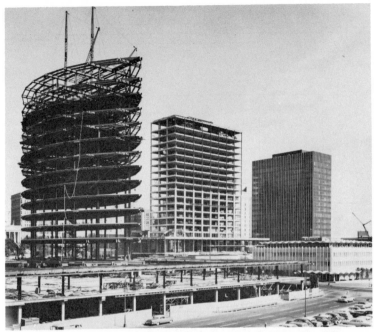

Three high-strength bolted structures in Constitution Plaza Complex, Hartford, Conn., using approximately 195,000 bolts. (*Bethlehem Steel Company.*)

in shear; however, the AISC gives an allowable bolt shear so that the connections may be proportioned by the same methods used for proportioning riveted connections subjected to shear.

The preceding discussion does not present the whole story because during erection the joints may be assembled with bolts, and as the members are erected their weights will often push the bolts against the side of the holes and put them in bearing and shear. Although it is probable that the tightening of the bolts produces enough friction to carry the loads, it is certainly not out of line to base the designs on the shearing strength of the bolts. Examples 10-1 and 10-2 illustrate the calculations involved in determining the different carrying capacities of a lap joint connected with friction bolts and bearing bolts.

EXAMPLE 10-1. The plates shown in Fig. 10-1, consisting of A36 steel, are connected with six $\frac{7}{8}$-in. A325 bolts. Determine the tensile capacity of the joint if the AISC Specification is used and no slippage can be tolerated (i.e., a friction-type connection).

Solution: Bolts in single shear (actually incorrect) and no bearing:

Allowable shear in bolts $= (6) (0.6) (15,000) = 54,000$ lb

FIG. 10-1

Allowable tension in PLs = [(12) (½) − (3) (½) (1)] 22,000 = 99,000 lb

<u>Allowable P = 54,000 lb</u>

EXAMPLE 10-2. Repeat Example 10-1 if a bearing-type connection is used.
Solution: Bolts in single shear and bearing on ½ in.:

Shear = (6) (0.6) (22,000) = 79,200 lb

Bear = (6) (½) (⅞) (1.35 × 36,000) = 127,500 lb

Allowable tension in PLs = [(12) (½) − (3) (½) (1)] 22,000 = 99,000 lb

<u>Allowable P = 79,200 lb</u>

10-7. TENSION LOADS ON BOLTED JOINTS

Bolted and riveted connections subjected to pure tensile loads have
been avoided as much as possible in the past by designers. The use of
tensile connections was probably "forced on" them more often for wind-
bracing systems in tall buildings than for any other situation. There are
some other locations where they have been used, however, such as hanger
connections for bridges, flange connections for piping systems, etc. Figure
10-2 shows a bolted connection where some of the bolts are subjected to
tensile loads.

Bolts in Tension

P

FIG. 10-2

Hot-driven rivets and tightened high-strength bolts are not free to shorten, with the result that large tensile forces are produced in them during their installation. These initial tensions are actually close to the yield points. There has always been considerable reluctance among designers to apply tensile loads to connectors of this type for fear that the external loads might easily increase their already present tensile stresses and cause them to fail. The truth of the matter, however, is that when external tensile loads are applied to connections of this type the connectors will experience little if any change in stress.

Hot-driven rivets which have cooled and shrunk or highly tightened bolts actually prestress the joints in which they are used against tensile loads. (To follow this discussion the student may like to think of a prestressed concrete beam which has external compressive loads applied at each end.) The tensile stresses in the connectors squeeze together the members being connected. If a tensile load is applied to this connection at the contact surface, it cannot exert any additional load on the bolts or rivets until the members are pulled apart and additional strains put on the bolts or rivets. The members cannot be pulled apart until a load is applied which is larger than the total tension in the connectors of the connection. This statement means that the joint is prestressed against tensile forces by the amount of stress initially put in the shanks of the connectors.

Another way of saying this is that if a tensile load P is applied at the contact surface it tends to reduce the thickness of the plates somewhat but at the same time the contact pressure between the plates will be correspondingly reduced and the plates will tend to expand by the same amount. The theoretical result then is no change in plate thickness and no change in connector tension. This situation continues until P equals the connector tension. At this time an increase in P will result in separation of the plates and thereafter the tension in the connector will equal P.

Should the load be applied to the outer surfaces there will be some immediate strain increase in the connector. This increase will be accompanied by an expansion of the plates even though the load does not exceed the prestress but the increase will be very slight because the load will go to the plate and connectors roughly in proportion to their stiffness. As the plate is much the stiffer it will receive most of the load. An expression can be developed for the elongation of the bolt based on the bolt area and the assumed contact area between the plates. Depending on the contact area assumed, it will be found that unless P is greater than the bolt tension its stress increase will be in the range of 10 percent. Should the load exceed the prestress the bolt stress will rise appreciably.

The preceding rather lengthy discussion is truthfully approximate but should explain why an ordinary tensile load applied to a riveted or bolted joint will not change the stress situation very much.

Recognizing the prestressing effect of high-strength bolts the Research Council and the AISC permit calculated tensile loads, independent of the tightening forces, to equal twice the allowable tensile stress given in the specifications.

10-8. PRYING ACTION

A further consideration that should often be given to tensile connections is the possibility of prying action. A tensile connection is shown in Fig. 10-3(a) which is subjected to prying action as illustrated in part (b) of the same figure. Should the flanges of the connection be quite thick

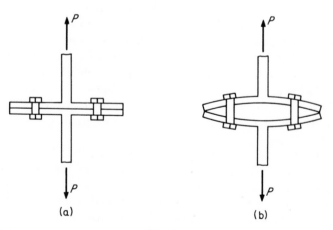

(a)   (b)

Fig. 10-3

and stiff the prying action will probably be negligible but not so if they are thin and flexible.

It is usually desirable to limit the number of rows of rivets or bolts in a tensile connection because a large percentage of the load is carried by the inner rows of multirow connections even at ultimate load. The tensile connection shown in Fig. 10-4 illustrates this point as the prying

Most of load is carried by inner lines of rivets or bolts if the flanges are flexible

Fig. 10-4

action will throw most of the load to the inner connectors, particularly if the plates are thin and flexible. For connections subjected to pure tensile loads estimates should be made of possible prying action and its magnitude.

10-9. BOLTS SUBJECTED TO COMBINED SHEAR AND TENSION

The bolts and rivets used for most structural steel connections are subjected to a combination of shear and tension. The combination is present even in the standard beam connections with the common web angles, to be described in Chap. 12. This stress condition is present in brackets and various types of moment-resisting connections, where the upper bolts or rivets are subjected to a vertical shear plus a tension caused by the fact that the beam end is trying to rotate downward and tends to pull the top portion of the connection away from the column or other member to which it is connected.

A high-strength bolted connnection for a tension member is reviewed in Example 10-3. The applied load in this example is subjecting the bolts to a combination of tension and shear. For such cases as this one the AISC says that the tensile stresses for bearing-type connections may not exceed the value given by the formula at the end of this paragraph. The

244   BOLTED CONNECTIONS

expression given is for the A325 bolt and f_v is the shearing stress produced by the applied loads.

$$F_t = 50{,}000 - 1.6f_v \leq 40{,}000$$

For A325 bolts used for friction-type joints, the AISC does not permit the shearing stresses caused to exceed the value given by the expression to follow. In this expression f_t is the tensile stress due to the applied load, T_b is the proofload of the bolt and A_b is the cross-sectional area of the bolt.

$$F_v = 15{,}000\left(1 - \frac{f_t A_b}{T_b}\right)$$

The problem of Example 10-3 is repeated in Example 10-4, except a friction-type connection is used. Although the connection is acting in shear and tension, friction prevents slippage of the bolt and consequent application of direct shear to the connectors.

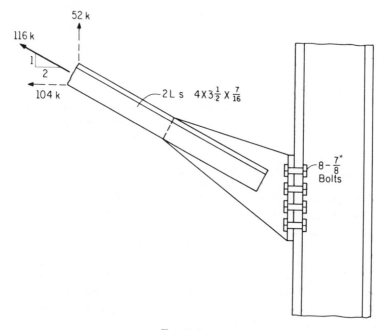

Fig. 10-5

EXAMPLE 10-3. The tension member shown in Fig. 10-5 is connected to the column with eight ⅞-in. A325 high-strength bolts in a bearing-type connection. Is this a sufficient number of bolts to resist the applied load according to the AISC Specification?

Solution: Shearing stress:

$$f_v = \frac{52}{(8)\ (0.6)} = 10.8 \text{ ksi} < 22 \text{ ksi} \qquad \text{(OK)}$$

Tension stress:

Allowable $F_t = 50 - (1.6)\ (10.8) = 32.7 \text{ ksi} < 40 \text{ ksi}$ (OK)

Actual $f_t = \dfrac{104}{(8)\ (0.6)} = 21.7 \text{ ksi} < 32.7 \text{ ksi}$ (OK)

Connection is satisfactory (perhaps overdesigned)

EXAMPLE 10-4. Rework Example 10-3 assuming that a friction-type connection is being used because no slip is permissible.
Solution:

$$f_t = \frac{104}{(8)\ (0.6)} = 21.7 \text{ ksi} < 40 \text{ ksi} \qquad \text{(OK)}$$

Allowable $F_v = 15 \left(1 - \dfrac{21.7 \times 0.6}{39.0} \right) = 9.99 \text{ ksi}$

Actual $f_v = \dfrac{52}{(8)\ (0.6)} = 10.8 \text{ ksi} > 9.99 \text{ ksi}$ (N.G.)

Connection is not satisfactory as friction type

Example 10-5 illustrates the calculations involved in determining the stress situation in the high-strength bolts in the bracket connection of Fig. 10-6. (The same procedure could be used for a riveted bracket

FIG. 10-6

if the rivets were assumed to have certain tensions after cooling.) The eccentric load on the bracket tends to bend the top of the bracket away from the column and push the bottom against the column. Unless the tendency to pull away from the column on the top is greater than the initial tension in the bolts there will be almost no change in bolt tension, as described in Sec. 10-7. It is felt that the calculations in this example problem are self-explanatory.

EXAMPLE 10-5.   Determine the stresses in the 1-in. A325 high-strength bolts shown in the eccentrically loaded connection of Fig. 10-6.

Solution: Stresses due to bolt tightening bearing the bracket against the column:

Proofload of 1-in. bolts is 51 k

Pressure on PLs when bolts tightened $= \dfrac{(10)\,(51)}{8 \times 20} = 3.19$ ksi

The stress diagram is shown in part (a) of Fig. 10-7.

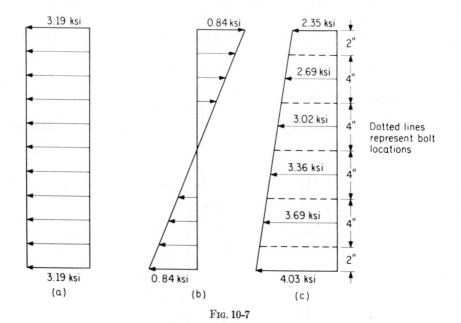

FIG. 10-7

Stresses due to eccentric load:

$$f = \frac{Mc}{I} = \frac{(150)\,(3)\,(10)}{(\frac{1}{12})\,(8)\,(20)^3} = 0.84 \text{ ksi}$$

The stress diagram is shown in part (b) of Fig. 10-7.

NOTE. The bolts going into this column cannot have an increase in stress unless the members start pulling apart, and the plates cannot pull apart unless the force applied exceeds the force bearing the pieces together.

Portion of the bolt tension caused by the moment (top bolts):

$$T \text{ due to moment} = 51 - \left(\frac{2.35 + 2.69}{2}\right)(4 \times 4) = 10.70$$

or

$$\frac{10.70}{0.785} = 13.62 \text{ ksi}$$

PROBLEMS

Note: The AISC Specification is to be used for all of the problems to follow.

10-1. If $\frac{7}{8}$-in A325 bolts are used in the connection shown in the accompanying illustration determine the tensile capacity of the joint (a) as a friction-type connection and (b) as a bearing-type connection. The plates are rolled from A36 steel. [Ans. (a) $P = 162$ k, (b) $P = 173.4$ k]

PROB. 10-1

10-2. Rework Prob. 9-5 using 1-in. A325 bolts in (a) a friction-type connection and (b) a bearing-type connection.

10-3. The truss member shown in the accompanying illustration consists of two C12 $\times$ 25s (A36 steel) connected to a 1-in. gusset plate. How many $\frac{7}{8}$-in. A325 bolts are required to develop the full tensile capacity of the member when it is used (a) as a friction-type connection and (b) as a bearing-type connection. [Ans (a) 15.28, say 16 bolts, (b) 10.42, say 12 bolts]

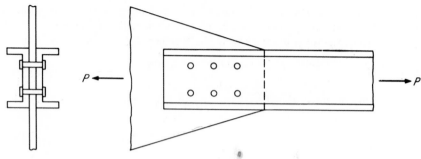

PROB. 10-3

10-4. Rework Prob. 10-3 if 1-in. A490 bolts and A242 steel are used.

10-5. For the connection shown in the accompanying illustration P equals 460 k. Determine the number of 1-in. A325 bolts required as (a) a friction-type connection and (b) as a bearing-type connection. A36 steel. [Ans. (a) 19.55, say 20 bolts; (b) 13.35, say 14 bolts]

PROB. 10-5

10-6. Rework Prob. 9-10 using $7\!/_8$-in. A325 bolts in a bearing-type connection.

10-7. For the beam shown in the accompanying illustration what is the re-

PROB. 10-7

quired spacing of $\frac{7}{8}$-in. A325 bolts in a bearing-type connection at a section where the external shear is 205 k.   A36.   (Ans. 5.52 in., say $5\frac{1}{2}$ in.)

10-8. Rework Prob. 9-14 using 1-in. A325 bolts in a bearing type connection.

10-9. The bracket plate shown in the accompanying illustration is connected to the column with four A325 bolts in a bearing-type connection.   Determine the size of the bolts required.   A36.   (Ans. 1-in. bolts)

PROB. 10-9

10-10. Determine the most stressed bolt in the connection shown in the accompanying illustration and determine the maximum force on that bolt.   Determine also the size of high-strength bolts (A490) required if a bearing-type connection is used.   A440 steel.

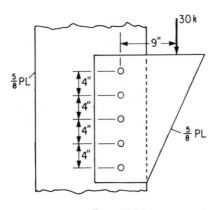

PROB. 10-10

10-11. For the bracket plate shown in the accompanying illustration $\frac{7}{8}$-in.

PROB. 10-11

A490 bolts are used in a bearing-type connection. Are they satisfactory? A36 steel. (Ans. Yes, $R = 15.64$ k while allowable $R = 19.2$ k)

10-12. Rework Prob. 9-23 using 1-in. A325 bolts in a bearing-type connection.

10-13. The connectors shown in the accompanying illustration are 1-in. A325 bolts used in a bearing-type connection. If A36 steel and the AISC Specification are used are the bolts sufficient? The $\frac{3}{4}$-in. plate is assumed to be connected to a 1-in. plate behind. (Ans. No. $R = 19.02$ k while allowable $R = 17.28$ k)

PROB. 10-13

PROB. 10-14

10-14. Determine the number of ¾ in. A325 bolts required in the angles and the flange of the W shape shown in the accompanying illustration if a bearing-type connection is used. Use A36 steel and the AISC Specification.

10-15. Repeat Prob. 10-14 if ⅞-in. bolts are used and no slip can be tolerated. (Ans. 12 bolts required in flange, 7 in angles)

10-16. Using A36 steel and ⅞-in. A325 bolts in a bearing-type connection check the adequacy of the connection shown in the accompanying illustration.

PROB. 10-16

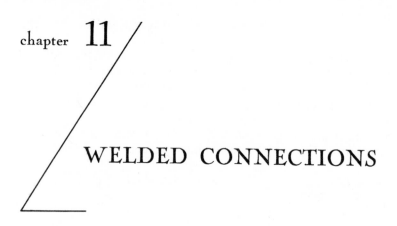

chapter 11

WELDED CONNECTIONS

11-1. GENERAL

Welding is a process in which metallic parts are connected by heating their surfaces to a plastic or fluid state and allowing the parts to flow together and join with or without the addition of other molten metal. It is impossible to determine when welding originated but it was several thousand years ago. Metalworking, including welding, was quite an art in ancient Greece at least three thousand years ago, but welding had undoubtedly been performed for many centuries before those days. Ancient welding was probably a forging process in which the metals were heated to a certain temperature (not to the melting stage) and hammered together.

Although modern welding has been available for a good many years, it has only come into its own in the last few decades for the building and bridge phases of structural engineering. The adoption of structural welding was quite slow for several decades because many engineers thought that welding had two great disadvantages—(1) that welds had reduced fatigue strength as compared to riveted connections and (2) that it was impossible to insure a high quality of welding without unreasonably extensive and costly inspection.

These negative feelings persisted for many years, although tests seemed to indicate that neither reason was valid. Regardless of the validity of these fears they were widely held and undoubtedly slowed down the use of welding, particularly for highway bridges and to an even greater extent for railroad bridges. Today most engineers agree that there is little difference between the fatigue strength of riveted and welded joints. They will also admit that the rules governing the qualification of welders, the better techniques applied, and the excellent workmanship requirements of the AWS specifications make the inspection of welding a much less difficult problem. Consequently welding is today permitted for almost all structural work other than for some bridges.

On the subject of fear of welding it is interesting to consider welded ships. Ships are subjected to severe impactive loadings which are difficult to predict and yet naval architects use all welded ships with great success. A similar discussion can be made for airplanes and aeronautical

Fabrication of plate girders for Connecticut expressway bridge. (*The Lincoln Electric Company.*)

engineers. The slowest adoption of structural welding has been for railroad bridges. These bridges are undoubtedly subjected to heavier live loads than highway bridges, larger vibrations, and more stress reversals; but are their stress situations as serious and as difficult to predict as those for ships and planes?

11-2. ADVANTAGES OF WELDING

Today it is possible to make use of the many advantages which welding offers, since the fatigue and inspection fears have been largely eliminated. Several of the many welding advantages are discussed in the following paragraphs:

1. To most persons the first advantage is in the area of economy, because the use of welding permits large savings in pounds of steel used. Welded structures allow the elimination of a large percentage of the gusset and splice plates necessary for riveted or bolted structures as well as the elimination of rivet or bolt heads. In some bridge trusses it may be

possible to save up to 15 percent or more of the steel weight by using welding. Welding also requires appreciably less labor than does riveting because one welder can replace the standard four-man riveting crew.

2. Welding has a much wider range of application than riveting or bolting. Consider a steel pipe column and the difficulties of connecting it to other steel members by riveting or bolting. A riveted or bolted connection may be virtually impossible but a welded connection will present no difficulties whatsoever. The student can visualize many other similar situations where welding has a decided advantage.

3. Welded structures are more rigid structures because the members are usually welded directly to each other. The connections for riveted or bolted structures are often made through connection angles or plates which deflect due to load transfer, making the entire structure more flexible. On the other hand, greater rigidity can be a disadvantage where simple end connections with little moment resistance are desired. In such a case the designer must be careful as to the type of joint he specifies.

4. The process of fusing pieces together gives the most truly continuous structures. It results in one-piece construction and because welded joints are as strong or stronger than the base metal no restrictions have to be placed on the joints. This continuity advantage has permitted the erection of countless slender and graceful steel statically indeterminate frames throughout the United States. Some of the more outspoken proponents of welding have referred to riveted and bolted structures, with their heavy plates and large number of rivets or bolts, as looking like tanks or armoured cars when compared to the clean, smooth lines of welded structures. For a graphic illustration of this advantage the student should compare the moment resisting connections of Fig. 12-4.

5. It is easier to make changes in design and to correct errors during erection (and at less expense) if welding is used. A closely related advantage has certainly been illustrated in military engagements during the past few decades by the quick welding repairs made to military equipment under battle conditions.

6. Another item which is often important is the relative silence of welding. Imagine the importance of this fact when working near hospitals or schools or when making additions to existing buildings. Anyone with close to normal hearing who has attempted to work in an office within several hundred feet of a riveting job will go along with this advantage.

7. Less safety precautions are required for the public in congested areas as compared to those necessary for a riveted structure where tossing of hot rivets is a necessity.

8. Fewer pieces are used and as a result time is saved in detailing, fabrication and field erection.

11-3. TYPES OF WELDING

Although both gas and arc welding are available almost all structural welding is arc welding. Sir Humphry Davy discovered in 1801 how to create an electric arc by bringing close together two terminals of an electric circuit of relatively high voltage. Although he is generally given credit for the development of modern welding, a good many years actually elapsed after his discovery before welding was actually performed with the electric arc. (His work was of the greatest importance to the modern structural world but it is interesting to know that many people say his greatest discovery was not the electric arc but rather a laboratory assistant whose name was Michael Faraday.) Several Europeans formed welds of one type or another in the 1880s with the electric arc, while in the United States the first patent for arc welding was given to Charles Coffin of Detroit in 1889.[1]

The figures to follow in this chapter show the necessity of supplying additional metal to the joints being welded to give satisfactory connections. In electric-arc welding the metallic rod which is used as the electrode melts off into the joint as it is being made. When gas welding is used it is necessary to introduce a metal rod known as a *filler* or *welding rod.*

In gas welding a mixture of oxygen and some suitable type of gas is burned at the tip of a torch or blowpipe held in the welder's hand or by an automatic machine. The gas used in structural welding is probably acetylene and the process is called oxyacetylene welding. The flame produced can be used for flame cutting of metals as well as for welding.

In arc welding an electric arc is formed between the pieces being welded and an electrode held in the operator's hand with some type of holder or by an automatic machine. The arc is a continuous spark which upon contact brings the electrode and the pieces being welded to the melting point. The resistance of the air or gas between the electrode and the pieces being welded changes the electrical energy into heat. A temperature of somewhere between 6,000 and 10,000°F is produced in the arc.[1] As the end of the electrode melts small droplets or globules of the molten metal are formed and are actually forced by the arc across to the pieces being connected penetrating the molten metal to become a part of the weld. The amount of penetration can actually be controlled by the amount of current consumed. Since the molten droplets of the electrodes are actually propelled to the weld, arc welding can be successfully used for overhead work.

A pool of molten steel can hold a fairly large amount of gases in solution and if not protected from the surrounding air will chemically

[1] Lincoln Electric Company, *Procedure Handbook of Arc Welding Design and Practice* (11th ed), 1957, Part I.

combine with oxygen and nitrogen. After cooling the welds will be relatively porous due to the little pockets formed by the gases. Such welds are relatively brittle and have much less resistance to corrosion. A weld can be shielded by using an electrode coated with certain mineral compounds. The electric arc causes the coating to melt and creates an inert gas or vapor around the area being welded. The vapor acts as a shield around the molten metal and keeps it from coming freely in contact with the surrounding air. It also deposits a slag in the molten metal, which has less density than the base metal and comes to the surface to protect the weld from the air while the weld cools. After cooling, the slag can easily be removed by peening and wire brushing (such removal being absolutely necessary before painting or application of another weld layer). A picture showing the elements of the shielded arc welding process is shown in Fig. 11-1. This figure is taken from the *Procedure*

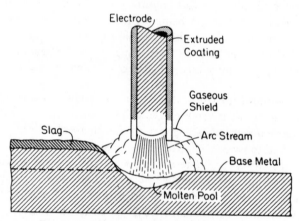

FIG. 11-1.   Elements of the shielded metal arc
welding process.

Handbook of Arc Welding Design & Practice published by the Lincoln Electric Company.

   The type of welding electrode used is very important as it decidedly affects the weld properties such as strength, ductility, and corrosion resistance. There are quite a number of different types of electrodes manufactured, the type to be used for a certain job being dependent upon the type of metal being welded, the amount of material which needs to be added, the position of the work, etc. The electrodes fall into two general classes—the *lightly coated electrodes* and the *heavily coated electrodes.*

   The heavily coated electrodes are normally used in structural welding because the melting of their coatings produces very satisfactory vapor shields around the work as well as slag in the weld. The resulting welds are stronger, more resistant to corrosion, and more ductile than are those produced with lightly coated electrodes. When the lightly coated electrodes are used, no attempt is made to prevent oxidation and no slag is formed. The electrodes are lightly coated with some arc stabilizing chemical such as lime.

Lincoln ML-3 Squirtwelder mounted on a self-propelled trackless trailer deposits this ¼-in. web-to-flange weld at 28 in. per minute. (*The Lincoln Electric Company.*)

11-4. WELDING INSPECTION

Three steps must be taken to insure good welding for a particular job. These are; (1) establishing good welding procedures, (2) use of prequalified welders, and (3) employment of competent inspectors in shop and field.

Section 1.17.1 of the AISC Specification says that welds can only be made by persons who have been qualified to perform the type of welding required by passing the tests prescribed in the *Code for Welding in Building Construction*, AWS D 1.0-69, of the American Welding Society.

When the procedures established by the AWS and AISC for good

258   WELDED CONNECTIONS

welding are followed and when welders are used who have previously been required to prove their ability, good results will probably be obtained. However, to make absolutely sure, well-qualified inspectors are needed.

Good welding procedure involves the selection of proper electrodes, current, and voltage; the properties of base metal and filler; and the position of welding, to name only a few factors. The usual practice for large jobs is to employ welders who have certificates showing their qualifications. In addition, it is not a bad practice to have each man make an identifying mark on each of his welds so that those persons frequently doing poor work can be located. This practice probably improves the general quality of work performed.

Visual Inspection. Another factor which will cause welders to perform better work is just the presence of an inspector whom they feel knows good welding when he sees it. For a man to make a good inspector it is desirable for him to have done welding himself and to have spent much time observing the work of good welders. From this experience he should be able to know if a welder is obtaining satisfactory fusion and penetration. He should be able to recognize good welds as to their shape, size, and general appearance. For instance the metal in a good weld should approximate its original color after it has cooled. If it has been overheated it may have a rusty and reddish-looking color. He can use various scales and gages to check the sizes and shapes of welds.

Visual inspection by a good man will probably give a good indication of the quality of welds but is not a perfect source of information as to the subsurface condition of the weld. There are several methods for determining the internal soundness of a weld. These include the use of penetrating dyes and magnetic particles, ultrasonic testing and radiographic procedures. These methods can be used to detect internal defects such as porosity, weld penetration and presence of slag.

Liquid Penetrants. Various types of dyes can be spread over weld surfaces and they will penetrate into surface cracks of the weld. After the dye has penetrated into the crack the excess surface material is wiped off and a powdery developer is used to draw the dye out of the cracks. The outlines of the cracks can then be seen with the eye. Several variations of this method are used to improve the visibility of the defects such as the use of flourescent dyes. After the dye is drawn from the cracks the cracks are made to stand out brightly by examination under black light.[2]

Magnetic Particles. In this method the weld being inspected is magnetized electrically. Cracks which are at or near the surface of the weld

[2] James Hughes, "It's Superinspector," *Steelways*, vol. 25, no. 4, (New York: American Iron and Steel Institute, September/October, 1969,) pp. 19–21.

cause north and south poles to form on each side of the cracks. Dry iron powdered filings or a liquid suspension of particles are placed on the weld. The patterns of these particles formed when many of them cling to the cracks show the locations of cracks and indicate their size and shape. A disadvantage of this method is that if multilayer welds are used the method has to be applied to each layer.

Ultrasonic Testing. In recent years the steel industry has applied ultrasonics to the manufacture of steel. Although the equipment is expensive the method is quite useful in welding inspection as well. Sound waves are sent through the material being tested and are reflected from the opposite side of the material. These reflections are shown on a cathode ray tube. Defects in the weld will affect the time of the sound transmission. The operator can read the picture on the tube and then locate flaws and learn how severe they are.

Radiographic Procedures. The more expensive radiographic methods can be used to check occasional welds in important structures. From these tests it is possible to make good estimates of the percentage of bad welds in a structure. The use of portable X-ray machines where access is not a problem and the use of radium or radioactive cobalt for making pictures are excellent but expensive methods of testing welds. These methods are satisfactory for butt welds (such as for the welding of important stainless steel piping at atomic energy projects) but are not satisfactory for fillet welds as the pictures are difficult to interpret. A further disadvantage of these methods is the radioactive danger. Careful procedures have to be used to protect the technicians as well as nearby workers. On the average construction job this danger probably requires night inspection of welds when only a few workmen are near the inspection area. (Normally a very large job would be required before the use of the extremely expensive radium or cobalt pills could be justified.)

11-5. CLASSIFICATION OF WELDS

There are three separate classifications of welds described in the following paragraphs. These classifications are based upon the types of welds made, positions of welds, and types of joints.

Type of Weld. The two main types of welds are the fillet welds and the butt welds (also known as groove welds). In addition there are plug and slot welds which are not too common in structural work. These four types of welds are shown in Fig. 11-2.

The fillet welds will be shown to be weaker than butt welds; however, most structural connections are made with fillet welds. Any person who has had experience in steel structures will understand why fillet welds are more common than are butt welds. Butt welds are used when the

Fillet Welds   Butt Welds

Slot Weld
Plug Welds
Fillet Weld

FIG. 11-2

members to be connected are lined up in the same plane. To use them in every situation would mean that the members would have to fit almost perfectly and unfortunately the average steel structure does not fit together in that manner. Many students have seen steel workers pulling and ramming steel members to get them in position. When members are allowed to lap over each other larger tolerances are allowable in erection and fillet welds are the welds used. Nevertheless butt welds are quite common for many connections such as column splices, butting of beam flanges to columns, etc.

A plug weld is a circular weld passing through one member to another and joining the two together. A slot weld is a weld formed in a slot or elongated hole which joins one member to the other member through the slot. The slot may be partly or fully filled with weld material. These two types of joints may occasionally be used when members lap over each other and the desired length of fillet welds cannot be obtained. They may also be used to stitch together parts of a member as the fastening of cover plates to a built-up member.

Position. Welds are referred to as being flat, horizontal, vertical, and overhead. They are listed in the preceding sentence in order of their economy with the flat welds being the most economical and the overhead welds being the most expensive. Although the flat welds can often be made with an automatic machine, most structural welding is done by hand. It has previously been indicated that the assistance of gravity is not necessary for the forming of good welds but it does speed up the process. The globules of the molten electrodes can be forced into the overhead welds against gravity and good welds will result but they are slow and expensive to make so it is desirable to avoid them whenever possible. These types of welds are shown in Fig. 11-3.

Type of Joint. Welds can be further classified according to the type of joint used as being: butt, lap, tee, edge, corner, etc. These joint types are shown in Fig. 11-4.

FIG. 11-3

Butt   Lap

Tee   Edge

Corner

FIG. 11-4

11-6. WELDING SYMBOLS

Figure 11-5 presents the method of making welding symbols, developed by the American Welding Society.[3] With this excellent shorthand system a great deal of information can be presented in a small space on engineering plans and drawings with a few lines and numbers. These symbols remove the necessity of drawing in the welds and making long descriptive notes. It is certainly desirable for steel designers and draftsmen to use this standard system. Should most of the welds on a drawing be of the same size, a note to that effect can be given and the symbols omitted, except for the off-size welds.

The purpose of this section is not to teach the student every possible type of symbol but rather to give him a general idea of the appearance of welding symbols and the information which they can show. He can easily

[3] Lincoln Electric Company, *Procedure Handbook of Arc Welding Design and Practice* (11th ed.), 1957. Courtesy of the publisher.

TYPE OF WELD							
Bead	Fillet	Plug or Slot	Groove				
			Square	V	Bevel	U	J
⌒	◺	⏖	||	∨	∨	⋃	⋃

Basic arc and gas weld symbols

Weld all Around	Field Weld	CONTOUR	
		Flush	Convex
○	●	—	⌒

Supplementary symbols

Finish Symbol
Contour Symbol
Root Opening, Depth of Filling for Plug and Slot Welds
SIZE: Size or Strength for Resistance Welds
Reference Line

Groove Angle, Included Angle of Countersink for Plug Welds
Length of Weld
Pitch (Center-to-Center Spacing) of Welds
Arrow Connecting Reference Line to Arrow Side of Joint, to Grooved Member, or Both

Specification Process or Other Reference
Tail (May Be Omitted when Reference Is not Used)
Basic Weld Symbol or Detail Reference

Field Weld Symbol
Weld All Around Symbol
Number of Spot or Projection Welds

FIG. 11-5

refer to the detailed information published by the AWS and reprinted in many handbooks (including the AISC Manual). At first glance the information presented in Fig. 11-5 is probably quite confusing to the student. For this reason a few very common symbols for fillet welds are presented in Fig. 11-6, together with an explanation of each.

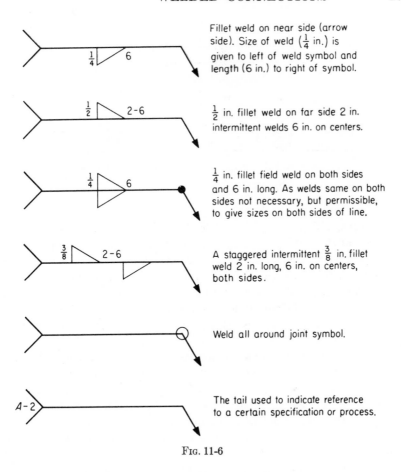

Fillet weld on near side (arrow side). Size of weld ($\frac{1}{4}$ in.) is given to left of weld symbol and length (6 in.) to right of symbol.

$\frac{1}{2}$ in. fillet weld on far side 2 in. intermittent welds 6 in. on centers.

$\frac{1}{4}$ in. fillet field weld on both sides and 6 in. long. As welds same on both sides not necessary, but permissible, to give sizes on both sides of line.

A staggered intermittent $\frac{3}{8}$ in. fillet weld 2 in. long, 6 in. on centers, both sides.

Weld all around joint symbol.

The tail used to indicate reference to a certain specification or process.

Fig. 11-6

11-7. BUTT WELDS

When complete penetration butt or groove welds are subjected to axial tension or axial compression the weld stress is assumed to equal the load divided by the net area of the weld. Three types of butt welds are shown in Fig. 11-7. The square butt joint, shown in part (a) of the figure, is used to connect relatively thin material up to roughly $\frac{5}{16}$ in. thickness. As the material becomes thicker it is necessary to use the single-vee butt welds and the double-vee butt welds illustrated in parts (b) and (c) respectively of Fig. 11-7. For these two welds the members are bevelled before welding to permit full penetration of the weld.

The butt welds shown in Fig. 11-7 are said to have *reinforcement*. Reinforcement is added weld metal which causes the throat dimension to be greater than the thickness of the welded material. Because of reinforcement or the lack of it, butt welds may be referred to as 100 percent,

FIG. 11-7

125 percent, 150 percent, etc., welds according to the amount of extra thickness at the weld. There are two major reasons for having reinforcement. These are: (1) reinforcement gives a little extra strength because the extra metal takes care of pits and other irregularities and (2) the welder can easily make the weld a little thicker than the welded material. He would have a difficult if not impossible task in making a perfectly smooth weld with no places which were thinner nor thicker than the material welded.

Reinforcement undoubtedly makes butt welds stronger and better when they are to be subjected to relatively static loads. When the connection is to be subjected to repeated and vibrating loads, however, reinforcement is not as satisfactory because stress concentrations seem to develop in the reinforcement and contribute to earlier failure. For such cases as these a common practice is to provide reinforcement and grind it off flush with the material being connected.

From the standpoints of strength, resistance to impact and stress repetition, and amount of filler metal required, butt welds are much to be preferred to fillet welds. From other standpoints, however, they are not so attractive and the vast majority of structural welding is fillet welding. Butt welds have higher residual stresses, and the preparations (such as the scarfing and veeing) of the edges of members for butt welds are expensive, but the major disadvantages probably lie in the problems involved in getting the pieces to fit together in the field. The advantages of fillet welds in this respect were described in Sec. 11-5. For these reasons field butt joints are not used very often, except on small jobs and where members may be fabricated a little long and cut in the field to the lengths necessary for precise fitting.

11-8. FILLET WELDS

Tests have shown that fillet welds are stronger in tension and compression than they are in shear, so the controlling fillet weld stresses given by the various specifications are shearing stresses. When practical, it is desirable to try to arrange welded connections so they will be subjected to shearing stresses only and not to a combination of shear and tension or shear and compression.

Fillet welds when tested to failure seem to fail by shear at angles of about 45° through the throat. Their strength is therefore assumed to equal the allowable shearing stress times the theoretical throat area of the weld. The theoretical throats of several fillet welds are shown in Fig. 11-8. The throat area equals the theoretical throat distance times the length of the weld. In this figure the root of the weld is the point

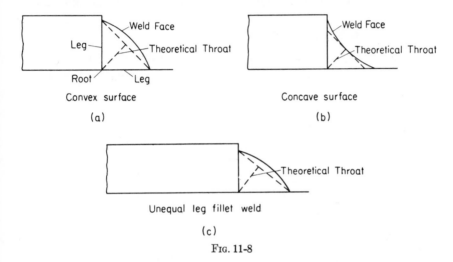

Convex surface

(a)

Concave surface

(b)

Unequal leg fillet weld

(c)

Fig. 11-8

where the faces of the original metal pieces intersect, and the theoretical throat of the weld is the shortest distance from the root of the weld to its diagrammatic face.

For the 45° or equal leg fillet the throat dimension is 0.707 times the leg of the weld, but it has a different value for fillet welds with unequal legs. The desirable fillet weld has a flat or slightly convex surface, although the convexity of the weld does not add to its calculated strength. At first glance the concave surface would appear to give the ideal fillet weld shape because stresses could apparently flow smoothly and evenly around the corner with little stress concentration. Years of experience, however, have shown that single-pass fillet welds of a concave shape have a greater tendency to crack, upon cooling and this factor has proved to be of greater importance than the smoother stress distribution of convex types.

When a concave weld shrinks the surface is placed in tension tending to cause cracks, whereas when the surface of a convex weld

shrinks it does not place the outer surface in tension ⌐◥. Rather as the face shortens it is placed in compression.

Another item of importance pertaining to the shape of fillet welds is the angle of the weld with the pieces being welded. The desirable value of this angle is in the vicinity of 45°. For 45° fillet welds the leg sizes are equal and such welds are referred to by the leg sizes (as a ¼ in. fillet weld). Should the leg sizes be different for a weld (not a 45° weld) both leg sizes are given in describing the weld (as a ⅜ by ½-in. fillet weld).

11-9. STRENGTH OF FILLET WELDS

For this discussion reference is made to Fig. 11-9. As previously indicated the stress in a weld is considered to equal the load P divided

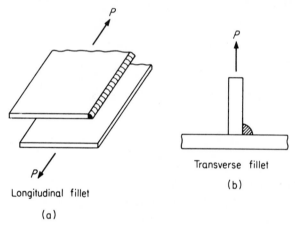

Longitudinal fillet

(a)

Transverse fillet

(b)

Fig. 11-9

by the throat area of the weld. This method of determining the strength of fillet welds is used regardless of the direction of load. Tests have shown that transverse fillets are without question about a third stronger than are longitudinal fillets, but this fact is not recognized by most specifications in order to simplify design calculations. One reason why transverse fillet welds are stronger is because they are more uniformly stressed for their entire length, while the longitudinal fillets are stressed unevenly due to varying deformations along the length of the weld. Another reason for their greater strength is given by tests which show failure occurs at an angle other than 45°, giving them a larger effective throat area.

11-10. AISC REQUIREMENTS

The allowable shearing stresses given by the AISC for various electrodes and base metals are given in Table 1.5.3 of the AISC Specification and are reproduced herein as Table 11-1. In this table the major ASTM classifications of electrodes as they affect structural steel design are shown. These include the E60XX, E70XX, E80XX, E90XX, E100XX and E110XX classifications, which are to be used with the differing grades of steels.

In this classification system the letter E represents an electrode while the first set of digits (as 80, 90 or 100) indicates the minimum tensile strength of the weld metal in ksi. The remaining digits designate the position, current and other necessary information which are to be employed with a certain electrode.

In addition to the allowable stresses given in Table 11-1 there are several other AISC provisions applying to welding. Among the more important are the following:

1. The minimum length of a fillet weld may not be less than 4 times the nominal leg size of the weld. Should its length actually be less than this value the weld size considered effective must be reduced to ¼ of the weld length.

2. The maximum size of a fillet weld for ¼ in. material is ¼ in. For thicker material it may not be larger than the material thickness less ⅟₁₆ in., unless the weld is specially built out to give a full throat thickness.

3. The minimum size fillet welds are given in Table 1.17.5 of the AISC Specification and vary from ⅛ in. for ¼ in. or less thickness of material up to ⅝ in. for material over 6 in. in thickness. The smallest practical weld size is about ⅛ in. and the most economical size is probably about ⁵⁄₁₆ in. The ⁵⁄₁₆-in. weld is about the largest size which can be manually made in one pass.

4. When practical, end returns should be made for fillet welds as shown in Fig. 11-10. The length of returns should not be less than twice the nominal size of the weld. When they are not used it is considered

FIG. 11-10

TABLE 11-1

Kind of Stress	Permissible Stress	Required Electrode	"Matching" Base Metal
Tension and Compression parallel to axis of any complete penetration groove weld	Same as for base metal		
Tension normal to effective throat of complete-penetration groove weld	Same as allowable tensile stress for base metal		
Compression normal to effective throat of complete or partial-penetration groove weld	Same as allowable compressive stress for base metal		
Shear on effective throat of complete-penetration groove weld	Same as allowable shear stress for base metal		
Shear stress on effective throat of fillet weld and partial-penetration groove weld regardless of direction of application of load; tension normal to the axis on the effective throat of a partial-penetration groove weld; and shear stress on effective area of a plug or slot weld. *The given stresses shall also apply to such welds made with the specified electrode on steel having a yield stress greater than that of the "matching" base metal.* The permissible stress, regardless of electrode classification used, shall not exceed that given in the table for the weaker "matching" base metal being joined.	18.0 ksi	AWS A5.1, E60XX electrodes AWS A5.17, F6X-EXXX flux-electrode combination AWS A5.20, E60T-X electrodes	A500 Grade A A570 Grade D
	21.0 ksi	AWS A5.1 or A5.5, E70XX electrodes AWS A5.17, F7X-EXXX flux-electrode combination AWS A5.18, E70S-X or E70U-1 electrodes AWS A5.20, E70T-X electrodes	A36 A53 Grade B A242 A375 A441 A500 Grade B A501 A529 A570 Grade E A572 Grades 42 to 60 A588
	24.0 ksi	AWS A5.5, E80XX electrodes Grade 80 Submerged Arc, Gas Metal-Arc or Flux Cored Arc Weld Metal	A572 Grade 65
	27.0 ksi	AWS A5.5, E90XX electrodes Grade 90 Submerged Arc, Gas Metal-Arc or Flux Cored Arc Weld Metal	A514 over 2½ in. thick
	30.0 ksi	AWS A5.5, E100XX electrodes Grade 100 Submerged Arc, Gas Metal-Arc or Flux Cored Arc Weld Metal	A514 over 2½ in. thick
	33.0 ksi	AWS A5.5, E110XX electrodes Grade 110 Submerged Arc, Gas Metal-Arc or Flux Cored Arc Weld Metal	A514 2½ in. and less in thickness

good practice by some designers to subtract 2 times the weld size from the effective weld length. End returns are useful in reducing the high stress concentrations which occur at the ends of welds, particularly for connections where there is considerable vibration and eccentricity of load. The AISC says (Sec. 1.14.7) that the effective length of fillet welds includes the length of the end returns used.

5. When longitudinal fillet welds are used alone for the connection of plates or bars, their length may not be less than the perpendicular distance between them. Furthermore, the distance between fillet welds may not be greater than 8 in. for end connections unless transverse bending is otherwise prevented.

11-11. DESIGN OF SIMPLE FILLET WELDS

The strength or design of several simple fillet welds is considered in the examples included in this section. A major point to remember in selecting welds is that it is desirable for the designer to select the simplest welds possible. The ability of the welder has a major effect on the strength of welds, particularly the difficult ones such as overhead or even vertical welds. An excellent welder is required to do a good job for these welds while the average welder can do good work with the simpler welds.

Examples 11-1, 11-2, and 11-3 illustrate calculations for simple fillet welds. In these and other problems, weld lengths are selected no closer than to the nearest $\frac{1}{4}$ in., because closer work cannot be expected in shop or field. There may be a question in the student's mind concerning the welds used in Example 11-3 and shown in Fig. 11-13. He may feel that there could be an unequal stress distribution in the welds if the plate thicknesses were different. A study of the figure, however, should show that the plates are held in position between the two welds and their elongations will be very nearly equal causing the welds to have approximately equal stresses.

The calculations for these problems can be slightly reduced if the strength of a $\frac{1}{16}$-in. fillet weld is computed for each of the two types of electrodes. The strength of a $\frac{7}{16}$-in. fillet weld can be obtained by merely multiplying 7 times the value computed for the $\frac{1}{16}$-in. weld thus eliminating a little slide rule work. For the E70 electrodes and A36 steel the strength of a $\frac{1}{16}$-in. fillet weld is equal to $(\frac{1}{16})$ (0.707) (21,000) or 925 lbs/in. Similarly a 1-in. weld has an allowable strength equal to (16) (0.925) = 14.8 k/in. These convenient values for fillet welds are used in several of the example problems of this chapter.

EXAMPLE 11-1. What is the allowable capacity of the connection shown in

Fig. 11-11 if A36 steel, the AISC Specification, and the E70 electrodes are used?
A $\frac{7}{16}$-in. fillet weld is used.

FIG. 11-11

Solution: Capacity per inch of a $\frac{7}{16}$-in. fillet weld is

$$(\tfrac{7}{16}) \ (0.707) \ (21,000) = 6,500 \ \text{lb}$$

Total capacity of weld $= (20) \ (6,500) = 130,000 \ \text{lb}$

Total capacity of 8 $\times$ $\frac{3}{4}$-in. bar $= (8) \ (\tfrac{3}{4}) \ (22,000) = 132,000 \ \text{lb}$

Capacity of connection $= 130,000 \ \text{lb}$

FIG. 11-12

EXAMPLE 11-2. Using A36 steel, the AISC Specification, and E70 elec-
trodes, design fillet welds to resist a full capacity tensile load on the $\frac{3}{8} \times$ 6-in.
bar shown in Fig. 11-12.
Solution:

$$P = (6) \ (\tfrac{3}{8}) \ (22,000) = 49,500 \ \text{lb}$$

Maximum weld size $= \frac{3}{8} - \frac{1}{16}$ in. $= \frac{5}{16}$ in.

Allowable load per inch for $\frac{5}{16}$-in. weld $= (5) \ (925) = 4,625 \ \text{lb/in.}$

Length of weld $= 49,500/4,625 = 10.7$ in.

Use end returns not less than $2 \times \frac{5}{16} = \frac{10}{16} =$ say 1 in. leaving 10.7 $-$

(2) (1.00) $= 8.7$ in. for side welds $=$ say $4\frac{1}{2}$ in. each side

Example 11-3. Design the fillet welds necessary for the lap joint shown in Fig. 11-13 if the AISC Specification, A36 steel, and E70 electrodes are used. The design is to be made to develop the full capacity of the plates shown.

Fig. 11-13

Solution:

Capacity of plates = (8) (½) (22,000) = 88,000 lb

Each $\frac{1}{16}$ in. of fillet weld can carry 925 lb.

Weld size required = 88,000/(16) (925) = ⅜-in.

On some occasions the lengths available for the usual longitudinal fillet welds are not sufficient for the load to be resisted. For the situation shown in Fig. 11-14 it may be possible to develop sufficient strength by

Fig. 11-14

welding along the back of the channel at the edge of the plate if sufficient space is available. The dashed lines shown in this figure show this weld.

Another possibility is the use of slot welds as illustrated in Example 11-4. There are several AISC requirements pertaining to slot welds which need to be mentioned here. This specification says that the width of a slot may not be less than the member thickness $+\frac{5}{16}$ in. (rounded off to the next greater odd $\frac{1}{16}$ in. since structural punches are made in odd 16th's diameters) nor may it be greater than $2\frac{1}{4}$ times the weld thickness. For members up to $\frac{5}{8}$ in. thickness the weld thickness must equal the plate thickness, and for members greater than $\frac{5}{8}$ in. thickness the weld thickness may not be less than one half the member thickness nor $\frac{5}{8}$ in. The maximum length permitted for slot welds is 10 times the weld thickness. The limitations given in specifications for the maximum sizes of plug or slot welds are caused by the detrimental shrinkage which occurs around these types of welds when they exceed certain sizes. Should holes or slots larger than those specified be used it is desirable to use fillet welds around the borders of the holes or slots.

Example 11-4 illustrates the design of the welds necessary to connect a channel to a plate. The calculations quickly show that the ordinary side and end fillet welds do not provide sufficient strength. It is decided that a slot weld will be used to resist the remaining load. The width of this weld is controlled by the specifications and its length can then be determined from the following:

$$\text{Allowable load} = \text{length} \times \text{width} \times \text{allowable stress}$$

EXAMPLE 11-4. Design welds to connect a C15 × 40 to the plate shown in Fig. 11-14. The load to be resisted is 250 k and E70 electrodes and the AISC Specification are to be used. As shown in the figure the channel may lap over the plate only 6 in. due to space limitations.

Solution:

Capacity of fillet weld:

Assume fillet weld size $= \frac{1}{2} - \frac{1}{16} = \frac{7}{16}$ in.

Capacity of $\frac{7}{16}$-in. fillet weld $= (7)(0.925)(6 + 6 + 15) = 175 \text{ k} < 250 \text{ k}$

Try a slot weld

Width of slot:

(a) $\frac{1}{2} + \frac{5}{16} = 1\frac{3}{16}$

(b) $(2\frac{1}{4})(\frac{1}{2}) = 1.12$ in.

Use $1\frac{5}{16}$ in.

Capacity of $\frac{7}{16}$-in. fillet weld $=$
$$(7)(0.925)(6 + 6 + 15 - 1\frac{5}{16}) = 169 \text{ k}$$

Load to be resisted by slot weld $= 250 - 169 = 81 \text{ k}$

Length of slot weld $= \dfrac{81}{(1\frac{5}{16})(21.0)} = 4.12$ in. (use $4\frac{1}{2}$ in.)

Maximum length permitted by AISC = (10) (½) = 5.00 in. > 4½ in. (OK)

<u>Use 4½ × $^{15}/_{16}$-in. slot weld</u>

Alternate Solution: Should space have been available on the back of the channel next to the plate a ⅜-in. fillet weld would carry (6) (0.925) (15) = 83.2 k.

11-12. DESIGN OF FILLET WELDS FOR TRUSS MEMBERS

Should the members of a welded truss consist of single angles, double angles, or similar shapes and be subjected to static axial loads only, the AISC permits their connections to be designed by the same procedures described in the preceding section. The designer can select the weld size, calculate the total length of the weld required and place the welds around the member ends as he sees fit.[4] (It would not be logical, of course, for him to place the weld all on one side of a member such as for the angle of Fig. 11-15 because of the rotation possibility. Example 11-5 illustrates the simple calculations involved in designing the welds for the ends of a truss member.

Fig. 11-15

EXAMPLE 11-5. Using the AISC Specification, A36 steel, and the E70 electrodes design side and end fillet welds for the full capacity of a 6 × 4 × ½-in. angle tension member with the long leg connected.

[4] *The Welding Journal,* January 1942, pp. 44–45.

Solution:

Tensile capacity of L = (4.75) (22) = 104.5 k

Maximum weld size = $\frac{1}{2} - \frac{1}{16} = \frac{7}{16}$ in.

Allowable load = (7) (0.925) = 6.48 k/in.

Length required = 104.5/6.48 = 16.15 in. (say 17 in.)

Place welds as shown in Fig. 11-15

The student should carefully note that the centroid of the welds and the centroid of the statically loaded angle do not coincide in the connection selected in Example 11-5 and shown in Fig. 11-15. Should a welded connection be subjected to repeated stresses (such as those occurring in a bridge member), it is considered necessary to place the welds so that their centroid will coincide with the centroid of the member. If the member being connected is symmetrical the welds will be placed symmetrically, but if the member is not symmetrical the welds will not be symmetrical.

The stress in an angle, such as the one shown in Fig. 11-16, is assumed to act along its center of gravity. If the center of gravity of weld re-

c. g. of Angle (must also be c. g. of welds)

L_1

L_2

FIG. 11-16

sistance is to coincide with the angle stress it must be asymmetrically placed, or in this figure L_1 must be longer than L_2. (When angles are connected by rivets or bolts there is usually an appreciable amount of eccentricity, but in a welded joint eccentricity can be fairly well eliminated.) The information necessary to handle this type of weld design can be easily expressed in equation form but only the theory behind the equations is presented here.

For the angle shown in Fig. 11-16 the force acting along line L_2 (designated here as P_2) can be determined by taking moments about L_1. The member stress and the weld resistance are to coincide and the moments of the two about any point must be zero. If moments are taken about L_1 the force P_1 (which acts along line L_1) will be eliminated from the equation and P_2 can be determined. In a similar manner P_1 can be determined by taking moments along L_2 or by $\Sigma\ V = 0$. Example 11-6 illustrates the design of fillet welds of this type. A similar problem is handled in Example 11-7 except an end fillet weld is included. The center of gravity and resistance of the end weld are known and can be easily included in the moment equations.

There are other possible solutions for the design of the welds for the angle considered in these two examples. Although the $\frac{7}{16}$-in. weld is the largest one permitted at the rounded edges of the $\frac{1}{2}$-in. angle and at its end, a larger weld could be used on the other side next to the outstanding leg. From a practical point of view, however, the welds should be the same size because different size welds slow the welder down in that he has to change electrodes to make different sizes.

EXAMPLE 11-6. Using the AISC Specification, A36 steel, and E70 electrodes design side fillet welds for the full capacity of the $5 \times 3 \times \frac{1}{2}$-in. angle tension member shown in Fig. 11-17. Assume the member is subjected to repeated stress variations, making any connection eccentricity undesirable.

FIG. 11-17

Solution: Tensile capacity of angle = (22,000) (3.75) = 82,500 lb. Taking moments about line L_1 to determine force P_2,

$$(82,500)\ (1.75) - 5\ P_2 = 0$$

$$P_2 = 28,875\ \text{lb}$$

$$P_1 = 82,500 - 28,875 = 53,625\ \text{lb}$$

Assuming welds size $\frac{1}{2} - \frac{1}{16} = \frac{7}{16}$ (capacity = $7 \times 925 = 6,475$ lb/in.),

$$L_2 = \frac{28,875}{6,475} = 4.45\ \text{in. (use } 4\frac{1}{2}\ \text{in.)}$$

$$L_1 = \frac{53,625}{6,475} = 8.28\ \text{in. (use } 8\frac{1}{2}\ \text{in.)}$$

Use end returns = $2 \times \frac{7}{16} = \frac{14}{16}$ in. (use 1 in.) This end return length can be subtracted from the side weld lengths reducing them to 3½ in. and 7½ in. respectively.

EXAMPLE 11-7.   Rework Example 11-6 using fillet welds along the sides and end of the angle.

Solution: Assuming $\frac{7}{16}$ in. welds (capacity = 6,475 lb/in.),

$$\text{Strength of end weld} = (5) \ (6,475) = 32,400 \ \text{lb}$$

Taking moments about the line L_1 to determine force P_2,

$$(82,500) \ (1.75) - (32,400) \ (2.5) - 5P_2 = 0$$

$$P_2 = 12,640$$

$$P_1 = 82,500 - 32,400 - 12,640 = 37,460 \ \text{lb}$$

$$L_2 = \frac{12,640}{6,475} = 1.95 \ \text{in.} \ \underline{(\text{use 2 in.})}$$

$$L_1 = \frac{37,460}{6,475} = 5.78 \ \text{in.} \ \underline{(\text{use 6 in.})}$$

11-13.   SHEAR AND TORSION

Fillet welds are frequently loaded with eccentrically applied loads with the result that the welds are subjected to either shear and torsion or to shear and bending. Figure 11-18 is presented in an attempt to show the student the difference between the two situations. Shear and torsion, shown in part (a) of the figure, is the subject of this section while shear and bending, shown in part (b) of the figure, is the subject of Sec. 11-14.

For this discussion the welded bracket of part (a) of Fig. 11-18 is considered. The pieces being connected are assumed to be completely rigid as they were in riveted connections. The effect of this assumption is that all deformation occurs in the weld. The weld is subjected to a combination of shear and torsion as was the eccentrically loaded rivet group considered in Sec. 9-9. The force caused by torsion can be computed from the following familiar expression:

$$f = \frac{Td}{J}$$

In this expression T is the torsion, d is the distance from the center of gravity of the weld to the point being considered, and J is the polar moment of inertia of the weld. It is usually more convenient to break the force down into its vertical and horizontal components. In the expressions to follow, h and v are the horizontal and vertical components of the distance d. (These formulas are almost identical to those used for determining stresses in rivet groups subject to torsion.)

$$f_h = \frac{Tv}{J} \qquad f_v = \frac{Th}{J}$$

These components are combined with the usual direct shearing stress which is assumed to equal the reaction divided by the total length of the welds. For design of a weld subject to shear and torsion it is convenient to assume a one inch weld and compute the stresses on a weld of that size. Should the assumed weld be overstressed a larger weld is required, if understressed a smaller one is desirable.

Although the calculations will in all probability show the weld to be overstressed or understressed the math does not have to be repeated as a ratio can be set up to give the weld size for which the load would produce

Welds subjected to shear and torsion

(a)

Welds subjected to shear and bending

(b)

Fig. 11-18

a stress exactly equal to the allowable. The student should note that the use of a 1-in. weld simplifies the units because 1 in. of length of weld is 1 sq in. of weld and the computed stresses can be said to be either kips per square inch or kips per inch of length. Should the calculations be based on some size other than a 1-in. weld the student will have to be very careful in keeping the units straight particularly in obtaining the final weld size. Example 11-8 illustrates the calculations involved in determining the weld size required for a connection subjected to a combination of shear and torsion. This kind of problem can be easily solved by using readily available tables. For instance this problem can be checked in the Steel Handbook by referring to the tables entitled "Eccentric Loads on Weld Groups."

EXAMPLE 11-8.   For the bracket shown in Fig. 11-19 (a), determine the fillet weld size required if E70 electrodes and the AISC Specification are used.

(a)   (b)

FIG. 11-19

Solution: Assuming a 1 in. weld as shown in part (b) of Fig. 11-19

$$A = 18 \text{ sq in.}$$

$$\bar{x} = \frac{(4)\ (2)\ (2)}{18} = 0.89 \text{ in.}$$

$$I_x = (\tfrac{1}{12})\ (1)\ (10)^3 + (2)\ (4)\ (5)^2 = 283.3 \text{ in.}^4$$

$$I_y = (2)\ (\tfrac{1}{3})\ (0.89^3 + 3.11^3) + (10)\ (0.89)^2 = 28.5 \text{ in.}^4$$

$$J = 283.3 + 28.5 = 311.8 \text{ in.}^4$$

Most stressed portions of weld are greatest distance from weld center of gravity [*A* and *B* in Fig. 10-19(b)].

$$f_h = \frac{Tv}{J} = \frac{(15 \times 11.11)\ (5)}{311.8} = 2.67 \text{ k/sq in.}$$

$$f_v = \frac{Th}{J} = \frac{(15 \times 11.11)\,(3.11)}{311.8} = 1.66 \text{ k/sq in.}$$

$$f_s = f_{\text{shear}} = \frac{15}{18} = 0.83 \text{ k/sq in.}$$

$$f_r = f_{\text{resultant}} = \sqrt{(1.66 + 0.83)^2 + (2.67)^2} = 3.65 \text{ k/sq in.}$$

Allowable stress on 1-in. fillet weld (E70 electrode) = (16) (0.925) = 14.8 k/in.

$$\text{Weld size required} = \frac{3.65}{14.8} = 0.247 \text{ in. (use } \tfrac{1}{4} \text{ in.)}$$

11-14. SHEAR AND BENDING

The welds shown in Fig. 11-18 (b) and in Fig. 11-20 are subjected to a combination of shear and bending.

FIG. 11-20

For short welds of this type the usual practice is to consider a uniform variation of shearing stress. If, however, the bending stress is assumed to be given by the flexure formula, the shear does not vary uniformly for vertical welds but as a parabola with a maximum value equal to 3/2 times the average value. These stress and shear variations are shown in Fig. 11-21.

The student should carefully note that the maximum shearing stresses and the maximum moment stresses occur at different locations. It is, therefore, probably not necessary to combine the two stresses at any one point. If the weld is capable of withstanding the worst shear and the worst moment individually it is probably satisfactory. In Example 11-9, however, a welded connection subjected to shear and bending is designed by the usual practice of assuming a uniform shear distribution in the weld and combining that value with the maximum bending stress. Again this problem may be checked by referring to the Steel Handbook tables entitled "Eccentric Loads on Weld Groups."

Vertical weld

Bending stress

Shearing stress

Fig. 11-21

EXAMPLE 11-9.   Using E70 electrodes and the AISC Specification determine the weld size required for the connection of Fig. 11-20 if $P = 30$ k, $e = 2\frac{1}{2}$ in., and $L = 8$ in.

Solution:

$$f_s = \frac{30}{(2)\ (8)} = 1.875 \text{ k/in.}$$

$$f = \frac{(30 \times 2.5)\ (4)}{(\frac{1}{12})\ (1)\ (8)^3\ (2)} = 3.51 \text{ k/in.}$$

$$f_r = \sqrt{(1.875)^2 + (3.51)^2} = 3.98 \text{ k/in.}$$

$$\text{Weld size required} = \frac{3.98}{14.8} = 0.269 \text{ in. (say } \frac{5}{16} \text{ in.)}$$

Should welds of the type shown in Fig. 11-22 be used for a W or S beam the web welds would probably be assumed to uniformly carry all of

Web Welds Assumed to Resist Shearing Forces

Flange Welds Assumed to Resist Bending Forces

Fig. 11-22

the shear and the flange welds all of the moment.   Chapter 12 presents more information on this subject.

PROBLEMS

11-1. A $5/16$-in. fillet weld is used to connect the members shown in the accompanying illustration. Determine the maximum load which can be applied to this connection according to the AISC if the steel is A36 and E70 electrodes are used. (Ans. $P = 49.5$ k)

Ꮲʀᴏʙ. 11-1

11-2. Rework Prob. 11-1 if A572 Grade 65 steel and E80 electrodes are used.

11-3. Design maximum size fillet welds to develop the full strength of the A36 bar shown in the accompanying illustration. Use E70 electrodes and the AISC Specification. (Ans. 8in. welds)

Ꮲʀᴏʙ. 11-3

11-4. Rework Prob. 11-3 using side welds and a vertical end weld at the end of the $1/2 \times 8$ bar. Also use A572 Grade 65 steel and ESO electrodes.

11-5. Rework Prob. 11-3 using side welds and welds at the end of the $1/2 \times 8$ PL at the connection. (Ans. Total $L = 13.6$ in., say 14 in.)

11-6. The $5/8 \times 8$-in. PL shown in the accompanying illustration consists of A36 steel and is to be connected to a gusset plate with $5/16$-in. fillet welds. Determine the length L required to develop the full strength of the bar if E70 electrodes and the AISC Specification are used.

PROB. 11-6

11-7. Design maximum size side fillet welds to develop the full tensile strength of a 6 ×4 × ½ L using E70 electrodes, A36 steel and the AISC Specification. The member which is connected on the 6 in. leg is subject to alternating stresses. (Ans. $\frac{7}{16}$ side welds 5½″ and 11″)

11-8. Rework Prob. 11-7 using side welds and a weld at the end of the angle.

11-9. Rework Prob. 11-8 using A514 steel and E110 electrodes. (Ans. side welds 6 and 15 in.)

11-10. One leg of an 8 × 8 × ¾ angle is to be connected with side welds and a weld at the end of the angle to a plate behind to develop the full capacity of the angle (A36). Balance the fillet welds around the center of gravity of the angle, use maximum weld size and assume the allowable stress in the welds is 11,500 psi.

11-11. It is desired to design the fillet welds necessary to connect a C10 × 30 made from A36 steel to a ⅜-in. gusset plate. End, side, and slot welds may be used to develop the full capacity of the channel. No welding is permitted on the back of the channel. Use E70 electrodes and the AISC Specification. It is assumed that due to space limitations the channel can lap over the gusset plate by a maximum of 10 in. (Ans. $\frac{5}{16}$ fillet welds and one $1\frac{1}{16}$ × $1\frac{1}{16}$ × 3 slot weld)

11-12. Rework Prob. 11-11 using A572 Grade 60 steel and E70 electrodes.

PROB. 11-13

11-13. Determine the maximum force per inch to be resisted by the fillet weld shown in the accompanying illustration. (Ans. 5.88 k/in.)

11-14. Determine the maximum force to be resisted per inch by the fillet weld shown in the accompanying illustration.

PROB. 11-14

11-15. Rework Prob. 11-14 if welds are used on the sides of the channel in addition to those shown in the figure. (Ans. 2.9 k/in.)

11-16. Determine the maximum force per inch to be resisted by the fillet welds shown in the accompanying illustration. Also determine the required weld thickness using A36 steel, E70 electrode and the AISC Specification.

PROB. 11-16

11-17. Determine the maximum eccentric load P which can be applied to the connection shown in the accompanying illustration if ¼-in. fillet welds are used. E70. A36. AISC Specification. (Ans. 10.9 k)

PROB. 11-17

11-18. Rework Prob. 11-17 if ⅜-in. fillet welds are used and the vertical weld is 10 in. high.

11-19. Determine the fillet weld size required for the connection of Prob. 11-13 if the load is increased to 30 k and the height of the weld is 12 in. A36. E70. AISC Specification. (Ans. 0.696 in., say ¾ in.)

11-20. Using E70 electrodes, A36 steel and the AISC Specification determine the fillet weld size required for the bracket shown in the accompanying illustration.

PROB. 11-20

11-21. Rework Prob. 11-20 if the load is increased from 18 to 30 k and the weld lengths increased from 6 to 8 in. (Ans. 0.637 in., say $1\frac{1}{16}$ in.)

11-22. Determine the fillet weld size required for the connection shown in the accompanying illustration. E70. A36. AISC Specification.

PROB. 11-22

11-23. Determine the fillet weld size required for the connection shown in the accompanying illustration. E70. A36. AISC Specification. What angle thickness should be used? (Ans. $\frac{3}{16}$ weld, $3 \times 3 \times \frac{1}{4}$ Ls)

PROB. 11-23

11-24. Determine the fillet weld size required for the connection shown in the accompanying illustration. A36. E70. AISC Specification.

W14×84

Beam reaction = 30 k

6"

L 6×4×¾

6"   8"

Prob. 11-24

11-25. Determine the allowable value of the load P which can be applied to the connection shown in the accompanying illustration if ⅜-in. fillet welds are used. E70. A36. AISC Specification. (Ans. 83.7 k)

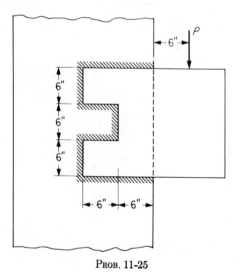

6"   P

6"

6"

6"

6"   6"

Prob. 11-25

11-26. Determine the length of ¼-in. fillet welds 12 in. on center required to connect the cover plates for the section shown in the accompanying illustration at a point where the external shear is 120 k. A36. E70. AISC Specification.

PL $\frac{3}{4}$ X 16

W21 X 62

PL $\frac{3}{4}$ X 16

PROB. 11-26

11-27. The welded plate girder shown in the accompanying illustration has an external shear of 480 k at a particular section. Determine the fillet weld size required to fasten the plates to the web. AISC Specification. E70. A36. (Ans. 0.267 in. required, AISC requires $\frac{5}{16}$ in. Sec. 1.17.5)

PL 1 X 16

Web $\frac{1}{2}$ X 48

PL 1 X 16

PROB. 11-27

12

BUILDING CONNECTIONS

12-1. SELECTION OF TYPE OF FASTENER

This chapter is concerned with the actual beam-to-beam and beam-to-column connections commonly used in steel buildings. Under present-day steel specifications four types of fasteners are permitted for these connections. These are rivets, welds, unfinished bolts, and high-strength bolts.

Selection of the type of fastener or fasteners to be used for a particular structure usually involves many factors, including requirements of local building codes, relative economy, preference of designer, availability of good welders or riveters, loading conditions (as static or fatigue loadings), preference of fabricator, and equipment available to him. It is impossible to list a definite set of rules from which the best type of fastener can be selected for any given structure. One can only give a few general statements which may be helpful in making a decision. These are listed as follows:

1. Unfinished bolts are often economical for light structures subject to small static loads and for secondary members (such as purlins, girts, bracing, etc.) in larger structures.

2. Field bolting is very rapid and involves less skilled labor than welding or riveting. The purchase price of high-strength bolts, however, is rather high.

3. If a structure is later to be disassembled, riveting and welding are probably ruled out, leaving the job open to bolts.

4. For fatigue loadings friction-type high-strength bolts are excellent, while welds and bearing-type high-strength bolts are very good.

5. Welding requires the smallest amounts of steel, probably provides the most attractive-looking joints and also has the widest range of application to different types of connections.

6. When continuous and rigid fully moment resisting joints are desired welding will probably be selected.

288

7. Welding is almost universally accepted as being satisfactory for shopwork. For fieldwork it is very popular in some areas of the United States while in others it is stymied by the fear that field inspection is rather questionable.

8. Rivets which can be rapidly installed in the shop with heavy riveters are nevertheless constantly losing ground to the ever-increasing use of welds and high-strength bolts.

9. For field work, rivets are rapidly becoming extinct except for some bridgework.

A most interesting article entitled "Choosing the Best Structural Fastener" by Henry J. Stetina appeared in the November 1963 issue of *Civil Engineering*. It would be well worth the student's time to read this article.

A valuable reference on the relative economy of various types of beam to beam and beam to column connections is given in a handbook published by the United States Steel Corporation in October 1963 entitled *Building Design Data*.

12-2. TYPES OF BEAM CONNECTIONS

According to their rotational characteristics under load, connections can be classified as being simple, semirigid and rigid. A connection which does not rotate at all or which has complete moment resistance is said to be a rigid connection while a connection which is completely flexible and free to rotate and has no moment resistance is said to be a simple connection. A semirigid connection is one whose resistance falls somewhere between the simple and rigid types.

From a practical standpoint, since there are no connections which are completely rigid or completely flexible, it is a common practice to classify them on a percentage of moment developed to complete rigidity or complete moment resistance. (A measure of the rotational characteristics of a particular connection cannot be practically obtained by a theoretical method and it is necessary to run tests and plot curves of the relationships between moments and rotations for each type of connection.) A rough rule is simple connections 0–20 percent, semirigid 20–90 percent, and rigid above 90 percent.

Each of these three general types of connections is briefly discussed in this section with little mention of the specific types of connectors used. The remainder of the chapter is concerned with detailed designs of these connections using specific types of fasteners. *In this discussion the author probably overemphasizes the semirigid and rigid type connections, because most of the building designs with which the average designer works will be assumed to have simple connections.* A few descriptive comments

(a) Framed simple connection (bolted or riveted)

(b) Seated simple connection (bolted or riveted)

(c) Framed simple connection (welded)

FIG. 12-1

are given in the following paragraphs concerning each of these three types of connections.

Simple Connections are quite flexible and are assumed to allow the beam ends to be substantially free to rotate downward under load as true simple beams should. Although simple connections do have some moment resistance (or resistance to end rotation) it is assumed to be negligible and they are assumed to be able to resist shear only. Several types of simple connections are shown in Fig. 12-1. More detailed descriptions of each of these connections and their assumed behavior under load are given in later sections of this chapter. In this figure each connection is shown as being made entirely with the same type of fastener while in actual practice two types of fasteners are often used for the same connection. For example, a very common practice is to shop-weld the web angles to the beam web and field-bolt them to the column or girder.

Semirigid connections are those which have appreciable resistance to end rotation thus developing appreciable end moments. In design practice it is quite common for the designer to assume all of his connections to be simple or rigid with no consideration given to those situations in between thereby simplifying the analysis. Should he make such an assumption for a true semirigid connection he may miss an opportunity for appreciable moment reductions. To understand this possibility the student is referred to the moment diagrams shown in Fig. 12-2 for a

(a) Simple connections (0%)   (b) Rigid connections (100%)

(c) Semirigid connections (50%)   (d) Semirigid connections (75%)

FIG. 12-2

group of uniformly loaded beams supported with connections having different percentages of rigidity. This figure shows that the maximum moments in a beam vary greatly with different types of end connections. For example, the maximum moment in the semirigid connection of part (d) of the figure is only 50 percent of the maximum moment in the simply supported beam of part (a) and only 75 percent of the maximum moment in the rigidly supported beam of part (b).

Actual semirigid connections are used fairly often but usually no advantage is taken of their moment reducing possibilities in the calculations. Perhaps one factor which keeps the design profession from taking advantage of them more often is the AISC Specification which says that consideration of a connection as being semirigid is permitted only upon presentation of evidence that they are capable of resisting a certain percentage of the moment resistance provided by a complete rigid connection.

A second deterring factor is the need for a method of analysis which falls in between analysis for simple beams and analysis for an indeterminate structure with completely rigid joints. The student can see that analysis of a building by moment distribution could be drastically affected if the end connections were assumed to have varying percentages of

A semirigid beam-to-column connection, Ainsley Building, Miami, Fla. (*The Lincoln Electric Company.*)

moment restraint. This subject is discussed in detail by Bruce Johnston and Edward H. Mount in a paper entitled "Analysis of Building Frames with Semi-Rigid Connection."[1] The student is also referred to Chap. 8 of *Advanced Design in Structural Steel* by John E. Lothers (Prentice-Hall, 1960) for an excellent discussion of this subject. Several types of semirigid connections are shown in Fig. 12-3.

(a) Web Ls with seat L and top L   (b) Structural tee connection

(c) Welded semirigid connection

Fɪɢ. 12-3

Rigid connections are those which theoretically allow no rotation at the beam ends and thus transfer 100 percent of the moment of a fixed end. Connections of this type may be used for tall buildings in which wind resistance is developed by providing continuity between the members of

[1] *Trans. ASCE,* vol. 107 (1942), p. 993.

the building frame.   Connections which provide almost 100 percent restraint are shown in Fig. 12-4.   In this figure the student might compare
the heavy, awkward riveted or bolted connections of parts (a) and (b)

(a) Structural tee connection   (b) Bracket connection

(c) Welded moment-resisting connection   (d) Welded moment-resisting connection

Fig. 12-4

of the figure with the welded types shown in parts (c) and (d).   From
the standpoint of appearance alone he might see why the welded moment
connections are more popular than the others.   The type of connection
shown in part (b) is becoming obsolete with only occasional use today.

In part (c) a welded connection is shown on one end of a beam
where the beam can be placed right up against the column.   Although
it is possible to butt one end of a steel beam against a supporting column
or girder, practical field dimensions in steel erection are not usually precise enough to permit such close fitting on the other end.   There it is
necessary to use some type of connection which permits a little variation
in fitting dimensions.   Part (d) of Fig. 12-4 presents such a connection.

12-3. STANDARD RIVETED OR BOLTED BEAM CONNECTIONS

Several types of standard riveted or bolted connections are shown in Fig. 12-5. These connections are usually designed to resist shear only, as testing has proved this practice to be quite satisfactory. Part (a) of

(a) Framed connection   (b) Framed connection

(c) Framed connection   (d) Seated connection

(e) Seated connection   (f) Seated connection with stiffener angles

FIG. 12-5

the figure shows a connection between beams with the so-called *framed connection*. This type of connection consists of a pair of flexible web angles probably shop connected to the web of the supported beam web and field connected to the supporting beam or column. When two beams are being connected it is frequently necessary to keep their top flanges at the same elevation, with the result that the top flange of one will have to be cut back (called *coping*) as shown in part (b) of the figure.

Simple connections of beams to columns can be either framed or seated as shown in Fig. 12-5. In part (c) of the figure a framed connection is shown in which two web angles are connected to the beam web in the shop, after which rivets or bolts are placed through the angles and column in the field. It is often convenient to have an angle, called an *erection seat*, to support the beam during erection. Such an angle is shown in the figure.

The seated connection has an angle under the beam similar to the erection seat just mentioned, which is shop-connected to the column. In addition, there is another angle probably on top of the beam which is field-connected to the beam and column. A seated connection of this type is shown in part (d) of the figure. Should space limitation prove a problem above the beam, the top angle may be placed in the optional location shown in part (e) of the figure. The top angle, at either of the locations mentioned, is very helpful in keeping the top flange of the beam from being accidentally twisted out of place during construction.

The amount of load which can be supported by the types of connections shown in parts (c), (d), and (e) of Fig. 12-5 is severely limited by the flexibility or bending strength of the horizontal legs of the seat angles. For heavier loads it is necessary to use stiffened seats such as the one shown in part (f) of the figure.

The majority of these connections are selected by referring to standard tables. The AISC Manual has excellent tables for selecting riveted, bolted or welded beam connections of the types shown in Fig. 12-5. After a rolled-beam section has been selected it is quite convenient to refer to these tables and select one of the standard connections, which will be suitable for the vast majority of cases. No numerical examples are given here because several examples together with a very good explanation are given in the AISC Manual. It is strongly suggested that the student study these examples very carefully and see if he can duplicate the shearing and bearing strengths given in the tables for the various connections.

In order to make these standard connections have as little moment resistance as possible the angles used in making up the connections are usually light and flexible. To qualify as simple end supports the ends of the beams should be free to rotate downwards. Figure 12-6 shows the manner in which framed and seated end connections will theoretically deform as the ends of the beams rotate downward. The designer does not want to do anything that will hamper these deformations.

For the rotations shown in Fig. 12-6 to occur there must be some deformation of the angles. As a matter of fact, if end slopes of the mag-

(a) Bending of framed-beam connection

(b) Bending of seated-beam connection

Fig. 12-6

nitudes which are computed for simple ends are to occur, the angles will actually bend enough to be stressed beyond their yield points. If this situation occurs, they will be permanently bent and the connections will quite closely approach true simple ends. The student should now see why it is desirable to use rather thin angles and large gages for the rivet or bolt spacing if flexible simple end connections are the goal of the designer.

These connections do have some resistance to moment. When the ends of the beam begin to rotate downward, the rotation is certainly resisted to some extent by the tension in the top rivets, even if the angles are quite thin and flexible. Neglecting the moment resistance of these connections will cause conservative beam sizes. If moments of any size are to be resisted, more rigid-type joints need to be provided than available with the framed and seated connection.

12-4. SEMIRIGID AND RIGID RIVETED OR BOLTED CONNECTIONS

The standard beam connections discussed in Sec. 12-3 are usually designed to transfer shear only. Although they do transfer moments, the amounts are very small due to the flexible angles used. When a frame is to be continuous or when resistance to wind or other lateral loads is to be provided by the joints, connections will be used which have much greater moment resistance.

Several types of semirigid and rigid connections were shown in Fig. 12-3 and 12-4. Perhaps the simplest semirigid connection type is the one shown in part (a) of Fig. 12-3, where a beam is connected to a column with a pair of standard web angles together with top and bottom clip angles. Usually the web angles are designed to resist the shears and are picked from the AISC Manual while the clip angles are designed to resist the moments. Another very satisfactory type of semirigid connection is the one shown in part (b) of Fig. 12-3. In this case the connection is made with a pair of structural tees and it is called a structural tee connection or a split beam connection.

In the riveted semirigid connection of Fig. 12-8 the end moment is resisted by an equal and opposite couple produced by the tensile force in the rivets in the top clip angles and a compressive force in the lower flange rivets. The rivets passing through the clip angle and the beam flange are placed in single shear by a force equal to the pull at the top of the connection. From this information the number of rivets can be easily determined.

To consider a method of determining the thickness of the clip angles in a connection of this type, Fig. 12-7 is presented showing the *assumed*

Point of Contraflexure

FIG. 12-7

bending condition of the top angle. The true bending condition of this angle is extremely complicated. An assumption is made here that no clamping force is provided by the rivet. It is further assumed that the angle bends in such a manner as to have a point of contraflexure midway between the top of the horizontal leg of the angle and the center of the rivet.

If this bending condition were correct, the bending moment in the angle could be estimated as being the force being transferred times the distance from the top of the horizontal leg or from the center of the rivet to the point of contraflexure. The angle thickness can be determined from the flexure formula using the moment estimated in the vertical angle leg. It is fairly common design practice to make some rough assumption as to the thickness of these clip angles without bothering to estimate the moment developed. The frequent result is angles which do not have sufficient thickness.

16.00"   W 16 X 40

Fig. 12-8

EXAMPLE 12-1.   Design a connection of the type shown in Fig. 12-8 to resist a moment of 30 ft-k and a shear of 25 k. Use $\frac{7}{8}$-in. A502, Grade 1 rivets, A36 steel, and the AISC Specification.

Solution: Design of web Ls to resist full shear:

From AISC Manual, "Framed Beam Connections" table:

Use 2 Ls $4 \times 4 \times \frac{1}{4} \times 8\frac{1}{2}$ in. with 3 rows of rivets

Selection of clip L rivets:

(a)   Rivets through column flange:

Allowable tension per rivet $= (0.6)\ (20) = 12$ k

Pull on rivets $= \dfrac{(12)\ (30)}{16.00} = 22.5$ k

Number of rivets required $= \dfrac{22.5}{12} = 1.87$ (say 2)

(b)   Rivets through beam flange:

Rivets in single shear and bearing on 0.503 in.

Single shear $= (0.6)\ (15) = 9$ k

Bearing $= (\frac{7}{8})\ (0.503)\ (1.35 \times 36) = 21.4$ k

$$\text{Number required} = \frac{22.5}{9} = 2.50 \text{ (say 4)}$$

Selection of clip ∟s:

Assume ∟s $7 \times 4 \times \frac{3}{4} \times 0$ ft 8 in. for rivets selected.

Distance from center of tension rivets to top of horizontal leg of ∟ $= 2\frac{1}{2} - \frac{3}{4} = 1.75$ in.

Moment in vertical leg of clip ∟ $= (22.5) (1.75/2) = 19.7$ in.-k

$$S = \frac{1}{6} bt^2 = \frac{M}{F_b}$$

$$t = \sqrt{\frac{6M}{b F_b}}$$

$$= \sqrt{\frac{(6) \ (19.7)}{(8) \ (27)}}$$

$$= 0.74 \text{ in.} < 0.75 \text{ in} \qquad\qquad \text{(OK)}$$

Use $7 \times 4 \times \frac{3}{4} \times 0$ ft 8 in. clip ∟

A split beam connection of the type shown in Fig. 12-3 (b) is designed in Example 12-2. This type of connection is the most rigid of the semirigid types. To understand its increased rigidity over the clip angle type the reader should compare the deformation diagrams for the tension sides of these two types of connections shown in Figs. 12-7 and 12-9. In Fig. 12-7 the tension part of the couple is acting eccentrically on the clip angle, while in Fig. 12-9 the structural tee is loaded axially and has less deformation.

With respect to Fig. 12-9, the pull is divided into $T/2$ times the

Fig. 12-9. Tension side of structural tee construction.

distance x. The other dimensions of the structural tee can be obtained from the space required to place the rivets. Another variation from the clip-angle problem is that no web angles are used to resist the shear, with the result that the rivets from structural tees to the columns are placed in a combination of shear and tension. In this discussion clamping force has again been very conservatively neglected. Truthfully, there are probably present rather large clamping forces. Another factor of importance is that on the compression side of the connection the rivets are pressed against the column and probably a large percentage of the total shear on the column is carried on that side by friction.

EXAMPLE 12-2. A split beam connection is to be designed for the W18 × 55 shown in Fig. 12-10 to resist a shear of 50 k and a moment of 60 ft-k. Design the connection if A36 steel, 1-in. A502, Grade 1 rivets, and the AISC Specification are used.

FIG. 12-10

Solution: Selection of rivets:

$$\text{Pull on tee} = \frac{(12)\ (60)}{18.12} = 39.7 \text{ k}$$

Rivets through beam flange in single shear and bearing on 0.630

Shear $= (0.785)\ (15) = 11.8 \text{ k}$

Bear $= (1)\ (0.630)\ (1.35 \times 36) = 30.7 \text{ k}$

$$\text{Number required} = \frac{39.7}{11.8} = 3.36 \text{ (say 4)}$$

Rivets through column flange in tension and shear

Assume 4 rivets in each tee.

$$f_v = \frac{50}{(8)\ (0.785)} = 7.96 \text{ ksi} < 15 \text{ ksi}$$

$$f_t = \frac{39.7}{(4)\ (0.785)} = 12.62 \text{ ksi}$$

Allowable F_t from AISC $= 28 - (1.6)\ (7.96) = 15.3 \text{ ksi} > 12.62 \text{ ksi (OK)}$

Selection of structural tee:

Assume gage of flange rivets $= 5\frac{1}{2}$ in.

After running through the following steps a few times on scratch paper, a WT 16.5 × 100 ($b_f = 15.75$, $t_f = 1.15$, $t_w = 0.715$, $d = 16.50$) is tried.

$$x = (\tfrac{1}{2})\ (5\tfrac{1}{2} - 0.715) = 2.39 \text{ in.}$$

$$M = \frac{39.7}{2}\ (2.39) = 47.5 \text{ in.-k}$$

Assuming length of ST $= 10$ in.,

$$t = \sqrt{\frac{6M}{bF_b}} = \sqrt{\frac{(6)\ (47.5)}{(10)\ (27)}} = 1.028 \text{ in.} \qquad \text{(OK)}$$

Use WT16.5 × 100 × 0 ft 10 in.

Space is not taken here to present the design of a rigid riveted or bolted connection because it is felt that all of the principles necessary to work such a problem are presented in this chapter and in Chaps. 9 and 11.

12-5. TYPES OF WELDED BEAM CONNECTIONS

The sections to follow present several methods of making welded connections between beams and girders and between beams and columns. These include web angles (Fig. 12-11), beam seats (Fig. 12-14), stiffened beam seats (Fig. 12-19), and moment-resistant connections (Fig. 12-22). The first three of these types are designed as simple connections and as such are expected to transfer end reactions while having no appreciable moment restraint. They are often referred to simply as *shear connections*. The moment-resistant connections provide resistance to both reactions and moments and are probably referred to as *moment connections*.

To design welded beam connections properly the designer must understand the stress conditions in the structure and how those stresses can be transmitted through welded connections. Two illustrations are as follows:

1. The majority of the bending stresses in beams occur in the flanges and if welds are to be designed to transfer these forces they should be primarily located at the beam flanges.

2. Similarly, most of the shearing forces in a beam occur in its web and welds designed to transmit these forces need to be primarily located on the webs.

Members may be welded directly to each other without the use of connecting plates and angles; however, such simple connections may have serious drawbacks. An illustration of this fact can be seen where a beam end is welded directly to another column or beam. If the designer uses a high vertical weld along the web, he will have a connection which can resist an appreciable moment whether that was his intention or not. The resulting fairly large moments will produce fairly large bending stresses. A previous discussion described the difficulties of getting members to fit together perfectly in the field as would be required for this type of connection.

12-6. WELDED WEB ANGLES

Beams for which simple end supports are desired are often connected with web angles as shown in Fig. 12-11. Web-angle connections are

Fig. 12-11

normally designed to transmit shear and as little moment as possible by minimizing rotation resistance. These angles are probably shop welded to the beam and may be field welded to the columns or girders. Perhaps a more common practice today is to shop-weld the angles to the beam and field connect them to the columns or girders with high-strength bolts. The angles extend out from the beam web by approximately ½ in., as shown in the figure. This distance is often referred to as the setback.

Erection bolts are usually necessary for erecting these beams. They are probably placed near the bottom of the angles so they will not appreciably reduce their flexibility. In some situations they may be necessary at the top of the angles to stabilize the joint during erection. Such bolts can be removed at a later date if it is felt that they provide too much restraint against rotation.

As previously described for riveted beam connections it is desirable to use the thinnest possible angles. Thin angles will deflect easily and let the beam ends rotate enough to approach the desired simple end conditions. As the load is applied to the beam, the beam end tends to rotate downward and the flexibility of the angles allows the top of the beam to move away from the column or girder. Three-inch legs are usually sufficient for connections to the beam web and the same or perhaps slightly longer legs are used for connections to the column or girder. The depth of the angle is limited by the beam depth and the space required for welding. The desired maximum weld depth equals the beam depth minus its width, but may be a little deeper. The thickness of the web angles will be $\frac{1}{16}$ to $\frac{1}{8}$ in. thicker than the weld size.

A good many designers assume that web angles are subject only to a vertical shear (equal to the end reaction) and no moment. Without question, however, the end reaction is eccentric with respect to both the shop and field welds and causes moment. For the field welds applied to the column or girder the load is transferred a distance e away, as shown in Fig. 12-12; and the moment in each weld equals $(R/2)(e)$. (Notice

FIG. 12-12

these vertical welds are returned about $\frac{1}{2}$ in. at the top of the angles because tests have shown such returns greatly strengthen the connection.)

These field welds are subject to a rotation effect which causes the web angles to be forced together against the beam web and pushed apart at the bottom, tending to shear horizontally the fillet weld. The usual practice is to consider that the neutral axis dividing the tension from the compression is located one tenth of the way down from the top of the angles. The horizontal shear is assumed to vary from zero at the one-tenth point to a maximum at the bottom of the angles.

The top pressure is assumed to be concentrated at the one-tenth point and as is seen in the figure the horizontal shear will be concentrated at the center of gravity of the triangle $0.3L$ from the bottom of the web angles. Since the couple produced by these forces must be equal and opposite to the external moment, the value of f_h can be determined as follows:

$$\left(\frac{1}{2}\right) (0.9L) \ (f_h) \ (0.6L) = \frac{R}{2} \ e$$

$$f_h = \frac{Re}{0.54 \ L^2}$$

The vertical shear (f_s) equals $R/2$ divided by the height of the weld and can be combined with f_h to obtain the maximum stress $(f_r = \sqrt{(f_h)^2 + (f_s)^2}\ )$ after which the weld size can be determined. Example 12-3 illustrates the calculations involved in the design of this type problem. The AISC Manual again has tables from which these values can be picked directly.

EXAMPLE 12-3. Design shop and field welds for the W21 $\times$ 68 beam shown in Fig. 12-13 using E70 electrodes and the AISC Specification. Assume web angles are 3 $\times$ 3 $\times$ $\frac{3}{8}$ $\times$ 0 ft 10 in. Beam reaction is assumed to be 44 k.

FIG. 12-13

Solution: Design of shop welds to beam web:

$$A = (2) \ (2.5) + 10 = 15 \text{ sq in.}$$

$$\bar{x} = \frac{(5) \ (1.25)}{15} = 0.42 \text{ in.}$$

$$I_x = (\frac{1}{12}) \ (1) \ (10)^3 + (2) \ (2.5) \ (5)^2 = 208.3 \text{ in.}^4$$

$$I_y = (2) \ (\tfrac{1}{3}) \ (1) \ (2.08^3 + 0.42^3) + (10) \ (0.42)^2 = 7.8 \text{ in.}^4$$

$$J = 208.3 + 7.8 = 216.1 \text{ in.}^4$$

$$f_h = \frac{(22) \ (2.58) \ (5)}{216.1} = 1.31 \text{ k/in.}$$

$$f_v = \frac{(22) \ (2.58) \ (2.08)}{216.1} = 0.545 \text{ k/in.}$$

$$f_s = \frac{22}{15} = 1.47 \text{ k/in.}$$

$$f_r = \sqrt{(0.545 + 1.47)^2 + (1.31)^2} = 2.40 \text{ k/in.}$$

Weld size required $= \dfrac{2.4}{14.8} = 0.162$ in. (say $\frac{3}{16}$ in.)

Design of shop weld to column:

$$f_h = \frac{Re}{0.54 \ L^2} = \frac{(44) \ (3)}{(0.54) \ (10)^2} = 2.44 \text{ k/in.}$$

$$f_s = \frac{44}{(2) \ (10)} = 2.2 \text{ k/in.}$$

$$f_r = \sqrt{(2.44)^2 + (2.2)^2} = 3.28 \text{ k/in.}$$

Weld size required $= \dfrac{3.28}{14.8} = 0.221$ in. (say $\frac{1}{4}$ in.)

12-7. DESIGN OF WELDED SEATED BEAM CONNECTIONS

Another type of fairly flexible beam connection can be obtained by using a beam seat such as the one shown in Fig. 12-14. Beam seats are

FIG. 12-14

obviously of advantage to the men performing the erection. The seat is probably shop welded to the column and field welded to the beams. Seat angles, which are also called shelf angles, may be punched for temporary erection bolts as shown in the figure. These holes can be slotted to permit easy alignment of the members.

In addition to the seat angle, a top angle is used which furnishes lateral support. As it is not usually assumed to resist any of the load, its size is probably selected by judgment. Fairly flexible angles are used which will bend away from the column or girder to which it is connected when the beam tends to rotate downward when under load [see Fig. 12-6(b)]. A common size angle selected is the $4 \times 4 \times \frac{1}{4}$-in. angle.

Unstiffened seated beam connections of practical sizes can support light loads up to only 50 or 60 k when A36 steel is used. For these light loads two vertical end welds on the seat are sufficient. The top angle is welded only on its toes so that as the beam tends to rotate this flexible angle will be free to pull away from the column.

The minimum length of bearing required by the AISC for the beam on the seat angle can be determined from the usual web crippling formula which was discussed in Chap 7. A length of from 3 to 4 in. is usually satisfactory. The beam reaction causes a bending moment in the horizontal leg of the seat angle. The critical section for bending (represented by section 1–1 in Fig. 12-15) is usually assumed to be at the edge of the

Fig. 12-15

fillet which is approximately $t + \frac{3}{8}$ in. from the back of the vertical leg for most angles and R (the beam reaction) is assumed to be concentrated at the center of the theoretical required bearing length.

Some designers, to obtain more flexible seats, use a higher allowable bending stress than normally permitted (an increase of approximately 20 percent being quite common). The resulting higher stress on the seat will cause it to rotate more and approach more nearly true simple end conditions. The length of the vertical leg of the seat angle can be determined from the weld size required. A depth can be assumed and the weld size required for that depth determined. After one trial a depth can probably be selected which will require a reasonable weld size.

There are many opinions concerning the stress variation in these vertical welds. Some designers assume that the neutral axis occurs at middepth, while others assume that the bottom third of the welds is in compression and the top two thirds in tension. The former method is used in the solution of Example 12-4. In this problem the author assumes there is a setback of ½ in. while the tables for seated beam connections in the AISC Manual are based on setbacks of ¾ in. to take care of the fact that beams may "underrun" a little. This causes a little difference in answers.

Fig. 12-16

EXAMPLE 12-4. Design an unstiffened beam seat for the simple beam shown in Fig. 12-16, using A36 steel, E70 electrodes, and the AISC Specification.

Solution: Length of bearing required:

$$\frac{R}{t\,(N+k)} = 0.75\,F_y$$

$$\frac{20{,}360}{0.299\,(N+1\ 1/16)} = 27{,}000$$

$$N = 1.46 \text{ in.}$$

Use a 4-in. horizontal leg

Fig. 12-17

Selection of seat angle:

Width of beam $= 6.99$ in.

Assume width of seat $\llcorner = 8.00$ in.

Assume thickness of $\llcorner = \frac{1}{2}$ in.

$$e = \frac{1.46}{2} + 0.50 - \frac{1}{2} - \frac{3}{8} = 0.36 \text{ in. (see Fig. 12-17)}$$

$$M = (20.36)\ (0.36) = 7{,}340 \text{ in.-k}$$

Using allowable $f = 0.75\ F_y = 27{,}000$ psi

$$f = \frac{Mc}{I}$$

$$27{,}000 = \frac{(7{,}340)\ (t/2)}{(\frac{1}{12})\ (S)\ (t^3)}$$

$$\underline{t = 0.43 \text{ in. (use } \frac{1}{2} \text{ in.)}}$$

Design of vertical welds (see Fig. 12-18):

Assumed stress variation
in vertical welds

Fig. 12-18

Assume welds are 6 in. deep

Moment on each weld $= (R/2)\ (e)$

$$e = \frac{1}{2} + 1.75 = 2.25 \text{ in.}$$

$$M = (2.25)\left(\frac{20.36}{2}\right) = 22.9 \text{ in.-k}$$

Resisting couple has a lever arm of $\frac{2}{3}\ L$ or 4 in.

$$(f_h \times 3 \times \frac{1}{2})\ (4) = 22.9$$

$$f_h = 3.81 \text{ k/in.}$$

$$f_v = \frac{20.36}{12} = 1.69 \text{ k/in.}$$

$$f_r = \sqrt{(3.81)^2 + (1.69)^2} = 4.17 \text{ k/in.}$$

Weld size required $= 4.17/14.8 = 0.282$ in. (use $\frac{5}{16}$ in.)

Use 6 $\times$ 4 $\times$ ½-in. seat ∟ $\times$ 0 ft 8 in. with 4 $\times$ 4 $\times$ ¼-in. top ∟

12-8. WELDED STIFFENED BEAM SEAT CONNECTIONS

When beam reactions become fairly large (above 40–60 k depending on steel used) the thickness required for the seat angles becomes excessive and it becomes necessary to use stiffened seats. Stiffened beam seats probably consist of a structural tee or of a couple of plates welded into the shape of a tee and their design is relatively simple. Figure 12-19 shows one type of stiffened beam seat.

Fig. 12-19

A stiffened beam seat must first provide sufficient bearing length for the beam from a web-crippling standpoint. After this length is determined it is necessary to estimate the position of the center of gravity of the beam reaction. When the beam is loaded and as its end begins to rotate, the center of gravity of the reaction tends to move towards the outer edge of the seat. The result is a larger eccentricity and a larger eccentric moment than would occur in a comparable unstiffened seat. Some designers assume that the center of gravity of the reaction is located at the center of the theoretical bearing length, while others assume it is located two thirds of the actual bearing length towards the outer edge. For this discussion the author assumes the reaction is centered a distance from the outer edge of the seat equal to one half of the theoretical bearing length required for web crippling.

The stems of beam seats usually are in little danger of buckling and they are not designed by a high-level theoretical method. In fact the usual practice followed is to make the stem thickness at least equal to the web thickness of the beam. Some more conservative designers limit the stem to certain maximum l/r ratios, and check it for axial load and bending. The depth of the stem is determined by the length of the weld required, and the width of the flange should be a little wider than the beam flange to permit reasonably simple field welds. On each side it is desirable for the seat to be at least twice the weld size wider than the beam flange.

Top flanges of beams connected by strap plates over a girder while lower flanges are butt-welded to the girder web—Ainsley Building, Miami, Fla. (*The Lincoln Electric Company.*)

Finally, the welds for the seat must be of sufficient size to adequately resist the shear and bending stresses applied to them. The vertical welds are close together and, therefore, have little resistance to transverse flexure. For this reason it is usually considered desirable to weld horizontally along the bottom of the top flange a distance equal to roughly one-fourth to one-half of the vertical web depth. These horizontal welds greatly increase the resistance of the connections to twisting. The horizontal weld can be made on top of the flange of the tee, but there is a slight possibility that such a weld may get in the way of the beam.

In the example problem to follow (Example 12-5) the stem is not considered to resist any of the moment as the weld is assumed to take it all. The maximum stress occurs at the bottom of the vertical welds and is determined by a combination of the shearing and flexure stresses. The weld dimensions are roughly estimated, and the size required for these dimensions is determined to see if the original dimensions are reasonable.

EXAMPLE 12-5. Design a structural tee stiffened seat for the reactions of the beam shown in Fig. 12-20. The design is to be made with A36 steel, E70 electrodes, and the AISC Specification.

6 k/ft

W 18 X 60 (t_w=0.416, $k=1\frac{3}{16}$, b=7.558)

16'

48.6 k   48.6 k

Fig. 12-20

Solution: Length required for bearing:

$$\frac{R}{t \, (N + k)} = 0.75 \, F_y$$

$$\frac{48,600}{(0.416) \, (N + 1.187)} = 27,000$$

$$N = 3.12 + 0.5 \text{ (set back)} = 3.62 \text{ in. (use 4 in.)}$$

$$e = 4 - \frac{3.12}{2} = 2.44 \text{ in.}$$

$$M = (48,600) \, (2.44) = 118,000 \text{ in.-lb}$$

Estimate weld length by dividing reaction by strength of a $\frac{3}{16}$-in. fillet weld

$$\text{Estimated length} = \frac{48.6}{2.77} = 17.52 \text{ in. (say 18 in.)}$$

Assume the welds shown in Fig. 12-21.

3"   3"

$L = 9"$

Fig. 12-21

$A = (2) \ (9 + 3) = 24 \ \text{in.}$

$y = \dfrac{(18) \ (4.5)}{24} = 3.37 \ \text{in.}$

$I_x = (\tfrac{1}{12}) \ (2) \ (9)^3 + (18) \ (1.13)^2 + (6) \ (3.37)^2 = 212.7 \ \text{in.}^4$

$f_v = \dfrac{48.6}{18} = 2.70 \ \text{k/in.}$ (neglecting shear carried by horizontal segments)

$f_s = \dfrac{(118) \ (5.63)}{212.7} = 3.12 \ \text{k/in.}$

$f_r = \sqrt{(2.70)^2 + (3.12)^2} = 4.13 \ \text{k/in.}$

Weld size required $= \dfrac{4.13}{14.8} = 0.279 \ \text{in.}$ (use $\frac{5}{16}$ in.)

Selection of structural tee:

The structural tee must have a stem thickness at least equal to that of the beam web (0.416 in.) and must be thick enough to support a $\frac{5}{16}$-in. weld. On page 4-50 of the AISC Manual it is recommended that the minimum stiffener plate thickness be at least equal to 2 times the required weld size when using A36 steel and E70 electrodes $(2 \times \frac{5}{16} = {}^{10}\!\!/_{16}$ in.). Its flange should be wider than that of the W18 $\times$ 60 by approximately $4 \times \frac{5}{16}$ in. to permit easy field welding. Its depth must also be at least 10 in.

Use WT 10.5 $\times$ 71 stiffened beam seat with a top L 4 $\times$ 4 $\times$ ¼ in.

12-9. WELDED MOMENT-RESISTANT CONNECTIONS

Perhaps the greatest efficiency in structural welding is reached in fully continuous structures. The two major reasons for this efficiency are:

1. The negative moments which are produced in the ends of continuous beams cause appreciable reductions in the positive moments out in the spans. These reduced moments permit the use of smaller members.

2. When overloads occur, they are more easily redistributed in fully continuous structures. The student will remember that the AISC recognizing this plastic redistribution permits the design of fully continuous structures for only $\frac{9}{10}$ of the maximum negative moments caused by gravity loads. This reduction is permissible if the positive moments are increased by $\frac{1}{10}$ of the average negative moments. (See Sec. 6-7.)

The welded beam connections discussed prior to this section were designed with the object of eliminating most of the moment resistance. For fully continuous structures the connections are designed to resist the full calculated moments. Figure 12-22(a) shows a common type of moment-resisting connection. In the connection shown the tensile force at the top of the beam is transferred by fillet welds to the top plate and by butt welds from the plate to the column. For easier welding the top plate is probably tapered as shown in part (b) of the figure. The student may have noticed such tapered plates used for facilitating welding in other situations.

Fig. 12-22

If the design is to be made for gravity loads alone the only forces (other than shear) which need to be considered are T in the top flange and C in the bottom flange. Should wind or other lateral forces be involved, it may become necessary to design all welds to resist tension as well as compression.

A common practice in moment-resisting welded connections is to butt weld the beam flanges flush with the column on one end and connect the beam on the other end with the type of connection just described. This practice is illustrated in Fig. 12-24, in Example 12-6.

If the column to which a beam is being connected bends appreciably at the connection the moment resistance of the connection is going to be reduced no matter how good the connection may be. Furthermore, if the top connection plate in pulling away from the column tends to bend the column flange as shown in part (a) of Fig. 12-23, the middle part of the weld may be greatly overstressed. For these reasons it is a desirable practice to reinforce the column with plates opposite the column flange as shown in part (b) of the same figure. This practice is somewhat

Top connection PL pulling
away from connection

May be cut back
to allow passage of
pipes, conduits, etc.

Weld is overstressed here

(a)   (b)

Fɪɢ. 12-23

objectionable to architects, for they like to run pipes and conduits up the
columns, but the plates can be cut back somewhat as shown in the figure.

The AISC says that stiffener plates have to extend only for half
of the column depth when a beam is framed in from only one side as
illustrated in Fig. 12-24. Should the beam be framed in from both sides,

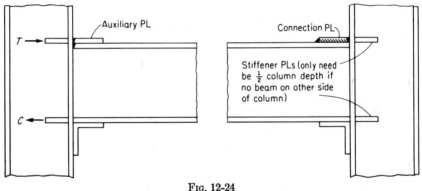

Auxiliary PL

Connection PL

T

Stiffener PLs (only need
be $\frac{1}{2}$ column depth if
no beam on other side
of column)

C

Fɪɢ. 12-24

the stiffener needs to extend for the full depth of the column as described in the preceding paragraph and shown in Fig. 12-23. Section
1.15.5 of the AISC Specification states when stiffeners shall be used and
gives the requirements for selecting their sizes. The design of a moment-
resistant connection is illustrated by Example 12-6.

Exᴀᴍᴘʟᴇ 12-6. Design moment-resistant connections of the type shown in
Fig. 12-22 for the ends of a W 18 × 45. The beam, which consists of A36 steel,
has end reactions of 42 k and end moments of 165 ft-k. The AISC Specification
and E70 electrodes are to be used. It is assumed that a 6 × 4 × ¾-in. seat L
has previously been selected.

Solution: Shear connection:

Try ¼-in. fillet welds on seat L

Depth required $= \dfrac{42}{2 \times 3.7} = 5.68$ in. (use 6 in. each side)

Moment connections on flush end:

Assuming a bevel butt weld for full flange width,

$\quad\quad T =$ force to be carried

$\quad\quad\quad =$ moment divided by c.-to-c. distance of flanges

$\quad\quad\quad = \dfrac{12 \times 165}{17.86 - 0.499} = 114.2$ k

Strength of butt weld in tension for full width of flange $= (7.477) \, (0.499)$ $(24) = 89.6$ k

Tension to be resisted by auxiliary PL $= 114.2 - 89.6 = 24.6$ k

Assuming a ⅜-in. thick PL, its width will equal

$$\frac{24.6}{⅜ \times 24} = 2.73 \text{ in. (say 3 in.)}$$

Assume a 3⁄16-in. fillet weld on auxiliary PL as shown in Fig. 12-25.

Fɪɢ. 12-25

Length of fillet weld $= \dfrac{24.6}{2.77} - 3 = 5.88$ in. (say 3 in. each side)

Allow 1 in. for bevel butt weld

Use auxiliary PL ⅜ × 3 × 4

Noᴛᴇ: Should wind moment be involved, a connection similar to this one would be designed for the lower flange; however, allowable stresses may be increased by one-third to resist wind forces, says AISC.

Moment connection at nonflush end:

Assuming T and C a distance apart equal to the beam depth,

$$T = \frac{12 \times 165}{17.86} = 111 \text{ k}$$

Assuming top connection has a width something less than the width of the beam flange (say 6½ in.), its thickness can be found as follows:

$$t = \frac{111,000}{6.5 \times 24,000} = 0.709 \text{ in. (say } \frac{3}{4} \text{ in.)}$$

Assume ⅜-in. fillet welds on PL

$$\text{Length of weld} = \frac{111}{5.55} = 20 \text{ in. (see Fig. 12-26)}$$

FIG. 12-26

NOTE: Diaphragm plates for the column should also be selected.

PROBLEMS

12-1. Determine the maximum end reaction which can be transferred through the web angle connection shown in the accompanying illustration if the moment produced by the connection is neglected. The steel is A36, the rivets are ⅞ in. A502, Grade 1, and the specification is AISC. Does the answer obtained agree with values given in the AISC Manual tables for framed beam connections? (Ans. 66.4 k)

12-2. Using the AISC Manual, select a pair of standard web angles for a W 33 × 240 with a maximum reaction of 180 k. The rivets are to be 1-in. A502, Grade 1 and the beam consists of A440 steel.

12-3. Repeat Prob. 12-2 if the maximum reaction is 250 k. (Ans. 7-row heavy framed connection)

12-4. Select a standard framed beam connection from the AISC Manual for a W16 × 40 with a maximum reaction of 50 k. The rivets are to be ⅞-in. A502, Grade 1 and the beam is made from A36 steel.

12-5. Select a pair of framed beam angles from the AISC Manual to connect a W21 × 68 beam (A36 steel) with a 44 k reaction to a column. The connection is to be made with ¾-in. A325 high-strength bolts, and a friction-type of connection is to be used. (Ans. 4-row framed connection)

12-6. Determine the resisting moment of the connection shown in the accompanying illustration if A36 steel, ⅞-in. A502, Grade 1 rivets, and the AISC Specification are to be used.

Clip L 7X4X⅞
2 Rivets
4 Rivets
W18X60

PROB. 12-6

12-7. A W16 × 36 beam with an end shear of 20 k and an end moment of 35 ft-k is connected to a W 12 × 58 column. Design an angle connection of the type used in Prob. 12-6 using ¾-in. A325 bearing type high-strength bolts and the AISC Specification. A36.

12-8. Rework Prob. 12-7 if a split beam connection of the type shown in Fig. 12-10 is to be used.

12-9. Design a structural tee connection of the type shown in Fig. 12-10 to develop one-third of the resisting moment of a W21 × 68 beam. Use A36 steel, ⅞-in. A325 bearing-type high strength bolts, and the AISC Specification.

12-10. Rework Prob. 12-2 using welded shop and field connections and E70 electrodes.

12-11. Rework Prob. 12-4 using welded shop and field connections and E70 electrodes.

12-12. Select a framed beam connection from the AISC Manual for a

W33 × 130 (A36) beam with a 120 k reaction. The web angles are to be shop-welded to the beam using E70 electrodes and are to be field-connected to the girder with ⅞-in. A325 bearing type high-strength bolts.

12-13. Rework Prob. 12-12 using welded shop and field connections.

12-14. Using the AISC Manual, select a seated beam connection using ¾-in. A502, Grade 1 rivets to support a 30 k reaction from a W16 × 40 (A36) beam. Assume col. gage = 5½" in col. web.

12-15. Rework Prob. 12-14 using a welded seated beam connection and E70 electrodes.

12-16. Using the AISC Manual, select a stiffened beam seat for a W24 × 84 (A36) beam for a reaction of 65 k using ¾-in. A325 bearing type high-strength bolts.

12-17. Rework Prob. 12-16 using a stiffened welded seat with E70 electrodes.

12-18. Design welded end connections for the ends of a W21 × 68 beam. The end moments produced are due to wind and are assumed to be equal to ⅔ of the moment resistance of the beam. Use E70 electrodes, the AISC Specification, and assume the column flanges to be 14 in. wide.

12-19. Design welded end connections for the ends of W 24 × 76 beam to resist gravity load moments equal to 50 percent of the moment resistance of the section. Use E70 electrodes, A-36 steel, and the AISC Specification. Assume the column flange to be 16 in. wide.

12-20. The beam shown in the accompanying illustration is assumed to be attached at its ends with completely rigid connections. Select the beam assuming full lateral support using A36 steel, and design welded connections using E70 electrodes and the AISC Specification.

PROB. 12-20

PROB. 12-21

12-21. The two W 16 × 40 beams shown in the accompanynig illustrations are to be made continuous across the supporting W 24 × 84 girder. If the end reactions of the beams are 20 k and their end moments are 40 ft-k, design the connection using E70 electrodes and the AISC Specification.

chapter 13

DESIGN OF STEEL BUILDINGS

13-1. INTRODUCTION

The material in this chapter generally pertains to the design of steel buildings from one to several stories in height, while the design of multistory buildings is presented in Chap. 20. The present discussion applies to apartment houses, office buildings, warehouses, schools, and institutional buildings which are not very tall with respect to their least

Coliseum in Spokane, Wash. (*Bethlehem Steel Company.*)

lateral dimensions. The separating factor between the buildings discussed here and those mentioned in the multistory chapter is the matter of wind stresses and not the actual height of the building in question. The usual rule of thumb is that if the height of the building is not greater than twice its least lateral dimension, provision for wind stresses is unnecessary. For buildings of these dimensions the walls and partitions probably provide sufficient resistance to wind forces except in unusual circumstances.

13-2. TYPES OF STEEL FRAMES USED FOR BUILDINGS

Steel buildings are usually classified as being in one of four groups according to their type of construction. These types are: bearing-wall construction, skeleton construction, long-span construction, and combination steel and concrete framing. More than one of these construction types can be used in the same building. Each of these types is briefly discussed in the following paragraphs.

Bearing-Wall Construction. Bearing-wall construction is the most common type of single-story light commercial construction. The ends of beams or joists or light trusses are supported by the walls which transfer the loads to the foundation. For taller buildings the walls by necessity must be thicker to provide sufficient strength and lateral stability. These increasing wall thicknesses usually establish an economical upper limit of roughly two or three stories for bearing-wall construction; although the method may occasionally be advantageous for parts of taller buildings.

The average engineer is not very well versed in the subject of wall-bearing construction with the result that he may often require complete steel or reinforced concrete frames where wall-bearing construction might have been just as satisfactory and at the same time more economical. Wall-bearing construction is not very resistant to seismic loadings and does have an erection disadvantage for buildings of more than one story. For such cases it is necessary to place the steel members floor by floor as the masons complete their work below thus requiring alternation of the masons and iron-workers.

Bearing plates are probably necessary under the ends of the beams or light trusses which are supported by the masonry walls because of the relatively low bearing strength of the masonry. Although theoretically the beam flanges may on many occasions provide sufficient bearing without bearing plates, the plates are almost always used—particularly where the members are so large and heavy that they must be set by a steel erector. The plates are probably shipped loose and set in the walls by the masons. Setting them in their correct positions and at the correct elevation is a very critical part of the construction. Should they not be properly set there will be some delay in correcting their positions. If a steel erector is used he will probably have to make an extra trip to the job.

When the ends of a beam are enclosed in a masonry wall, some type of wall anchor is desirable to prevent the beam from moving longitudinally with respect to the wall. The usual anchors consist of bent steel bars passing through beam webs. These are called *government anchors* and details of their sizes are given in the AISC Manual. Occasionally clip angles attached to the web are used instead of government anchors. Should longitudinal loads of considerable magnitude be anticipated, regular vertical anchor bolts may be used at the beam ends.

For small commercial and industrial buildings bearing-wall construction is quite economical when the clear spans are not greater than roughly 35 or 40 ft. If the clear spans are much greater it becomes necessary to thicken the walls and use pilasters to insure stability. For these cases it may often be more economical to use intermediate columns if permissible.

Skeleton Construction. In skeleton construction the loads are transmitted to the foundations by a framework of steel beams and columns. The floor slabs, partitions, exterior walls, etc. are all supported by the frame. This type of framing, which can be erected to tremendous heights, is often referred to as beam-and-column construction.

In beam-and-column construction the frame usually consists of columns spaced 20, 25, or 30 ft apart with beams and girders framed into them from both directions at each floor level. One very common method of arranging the members is shown in Fig. 13-1. The girders are placed in the longer direction between the columns, while the beams are framed

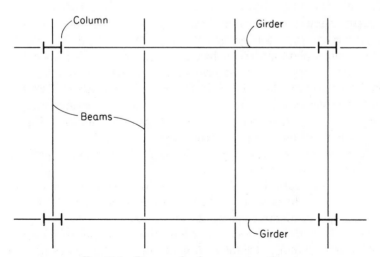

Fig. 13-1. Beam and column construction.

between the girders in the short direction. With various types of floor construction other arrangements of beams and girders may be used.

For skeleton framing the walls are supported by the steel frame and are generally referred to as *nonbearing* or *curtain walls*. The beams supporting the exterior walls are called *spandrel beams*. These beams,

FIG. 13-2. Spandrel beams.

which are illustrated in Fig. 13-2, can usually be placed so that they will serve as the lintels for the windows.

Long-Span Steel Structures. When it becomes necessary to use very large spans between columns as for field houses, auditoriums, theaters, hangars, or hotel ballrooms, the usual skeleton construction may not be sufficient. Should the ordinary rolled W sections be insufficient it may be necessary to use coverplated beams, plate girders, box girders, large trusses, arches, rigid frames, and the like. When depth is limited coverplated beams, plate girders or box girders may be called upon to do the job. Should depth not be so critical trusses may be satisfactory. For very large spans arches and rigid frames are often used. These various types of structures are referred to as long-span structures and most of them are discussed at length in the chapters to follow. Figure 13-3 shows a few of these types of structures.

Combination Steel and Concrete Framing. A tremendous percentage of the buildings erected today make use of a combination of reinforced concrete and structural steel. If reinforced-concrete columns were used in very tall buildings they would be extremely large on the lower floors and take up considerable space. Steel column shapes surrounded by and bonded to reinforced concrete are commonly used and are referred to as combination columns. Chapter 15 is devoted to the design of composite

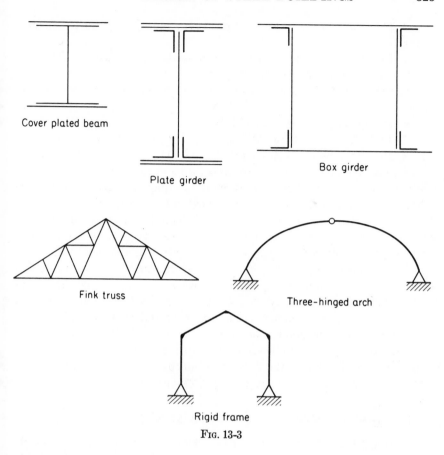

Cover plated beam

Plate girder

Box girder

Fink truss

Three-hinged arch

Rigid frame

FIG. 13-3

floors where steel beams and reinforced concrete slabs are bonded together in such a manner that they act compositely in resisting loads. Other systems will be mentioned in later chapters.

13-3. COMMON TYPES OF FLOOR CONSTRUCTION

Concrete floor slabs of one type or another are used almost universally for steel-frame buildings. Concrete floor slabs are strong, have excellent fire ratings and good acoustic ratings. On the other hand, appreciable time and expense is required for providing the formwork necessary for most slabs. Concrete floors are heavy, they need some type of reinforcing bars or mesh included, and there may be a problem involved in making them watertight. Among the many types of concrete floors used today for steel frame buildings are the following:

1. Concrete slabs supported with open-web steel joists (Sec. 13-4).

2. One-way and two-way reinforced concrete slabs supported on steel beams (Sec. 13-5).

3. Concrete slab and steel beam composite floors (Sec. 13-6).

4. Concrete-pan floors (Sec. 13-7).

5. Structural clay tile, gypsum tile and concrete block floors (Sec. 13-8).

6. Steel decking floors (Sec. 13-9).

7. Flat slab floors (Sec. 13-10).

8. Precast concrete slab floors (Sec. 13-11).

Among the several factors to be considered in selecting the type of floor system to be used for a particular building are: loads to be supported, fire rating desired, sound and heat transmission, dead weight of floor, ceiling situation below (to be flat or have beams exposed), facility of floor for locating conduits, pipes, wiring, etc.; appearance, maintenance required, time required to construct, and depth available for floor.

The student can obtain a great deal of information about these and other construction practices by referring to various engineering magazines and catalogues, particularly *Sweet's Catalog File.* The author cannot make too strong a recommendation for the student to examine these books to see the tremendous amount of data available therein which may be of use to him in his engineering practice. The sections to follow present brief descriptions of the floors mentioned in this section along with some discussions of their advantages and chief uses.

13-4. CONCRETE SLABS ON OPEN-WEB STEEL JOISTS

Perhaps the most common type of floor slab in use for small steel-frame buildings is the slab supported by open-web steel joists. The joists are really small parallel chord trusses whose members are often made from bars (from whence the common name *bar joist*) or small angles or other rolled shapes. A special paper reinforced with welded wire fabric is attached to the top of the closely spaced joists and a thin concrete slab is placed on top of the paper. This is probably the lightest type of concrete floor and comes very close to being the most economical one. A sketch of an open-web joist floor is shown in Fig. 13-4.

FIG. 13-4. Open-web joists.

Open-web joists are particularly well suited to building floors with relatively light loads and for structures where there is not too much vibration. They have been used a good deal for fairly tall buildings but generally speaking they are better suited for the shorter buildings. They are very satisfactory for supporting floor and roof slabs for schools, apartment houses, hotels, office buildings, restaurant buildings, and other similar low-level buildings.

Maximum open-web joist spacings center to center are about 24 in. for concrete floor slabs and 30 in. for concrete roof slabs. For floors and roofs with steel decking (to be described in Sec. 13-9) they can possibly be spaced as high as 7 ft on centers. Open-web joists can be obtained in standard depths from 8 to 24 in. in 2-in. increments. Each of the joists has a maximum span of about 48 ft for the deeper sections.

Open-web joists must be braced laterally to keep them from twisting

Short-span joists in the Univac Center of Sperry-Rand Corporation, Blue Bell, Pa. (*Bethlehem Steel Company.*)

or buckling and also to keep the floors from being too springy. Lateral support is provided by *bridging*, which consists of continuous horizontal rods fastened to the top and bottom chords of the joists or of diagonal cross bracing. Bridging is desirably used at spaces not exceeding 7 ft on centers.

Open-web joists are easy to handle and are quickly erected. If desired, a ceiling can be attached to the bottom of the joists or suspended therefrom. The open spaces in the webs are admirably suited for placing conduits, ducts, wiring, piping, etc. The joists should be either welded to supporting steel beams or well anchored in the masonry walls. When concrete slabs are placed on top of the joists they are usually from 2 to 2½ in. thick. Nearly all of the many concrete slabs on the market today can be used successfully on top of open-web joists.

There are also available joists in a longspan series varying in standard depths from 18 to 48 in. in 2-in. increments and also available with depths of 52, 56, or 60 in., and others. Maximum spans for which long-span joists can be used are as high as 120 ft.

13-5. ONE-WAY AND TWO-WAY REINFORCED CONCRETE SLABS

One-Way Slabs. A very large number of concrete floor slabs in old office and industrial buildings consisted of one-way slabs about 4 in. thick supported by steel beams 6 to 8 ft on centers. These floors were often referred to as concrete arch floors because at one time brick or tile floors were constructed in approximately the same shape, that is in the shape of arches with flat tops.

A one-way slab is shown in Fig. 13-5. The slab spans in the short

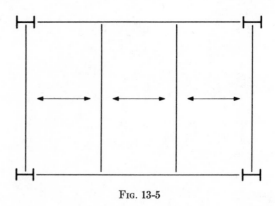

Fig. 13-5

direction shown by the arrows in the figure. One-way slabs are usually used when the long direction is two or more times the short direction. In such cases the short span is so much stiffer than the long span that almost all of the load is carried by the short span. The short direction is the main direction of bending and will be the direction of the main reinforcing bars in the concrete, but temperature and shrinkage steel is needed in the other direction.

A typical cross section of a one-way slab floor with supporting steel beams is shown in Fig. 13-6. When steel beams or joists are used to support reinforced concrete floors it may be necessary to encase them in

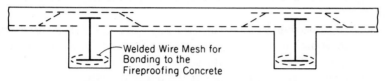

Welded Wire Mesh for
Bonding to the
Fireproofing Concrete

FIG. 13-6. One-way reinforced concrete slab.

concrete to provide the required fire rating. Such a situation is shown in the figure.

It may be necessary to leave steel lath protruding from the bottom flanges or soffits of the beam for the purposes of attaching plastered

The 104-ft steel joists for the Bethlehem Catholic High School, Bethlehem, Pa. (*Bethlehem Steel Company.*)

ceilings. Should such ceiling be required to cover the beam stems, this floor system will lose a great deal of its economy.

One-way slabs have an advantage when it comes to formwork in that the forms can be supported entirely by the steel beams with no vertical shoring needed. They have a disadvantage in that they are much heavier than most of the newer lightweight floor systems. The result is that they are not used as often as formerly for lightly loaded floors; but when a floor to support heavy loads is desired or a rigid floor or a very durable floor, the one-way slab may be a very desirable selection.

Two-Way Concrete Slabs. The two-way concrete slab is used when the slabs are square or nearly so and supporting beams are planned under all four edges. The main reinforcing runs in both directions. Other characteristics are similar to those of the one-way slab.

13-6. COMPOSITE FLOORS

Composite floors are those where the steel beams (rolled sections, coverplated beams, or built-up members) are bonded together with the concrete slabs in such a manner that the two act as a unit in resisting the total loads which the beam sections would otherwise have to resist alone. There can be a saving in sizes of steel beams when composite floors are used because the slab acts as part of the beam.

A particular advantage of composite floors is that they utilize concrete's high compressive strength as compared to its cost by keeping all or nearly all of the concrete in compression, and at the same time stress a larger percentage of the steel in tension than is normally the case in steel-frame structures (also advantageous). The result is less steel tonnage in the structure. A further advantage of composite floors is that they can permit an appreciable reduction in total floor thickness which is particularly important in taller buildings.

Two types of composite floor systems are shown in Fig. 13-7. The

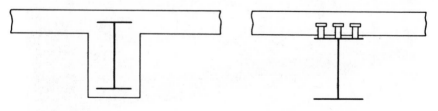

(a) Steel beam encased in concrete   (b) Steel beam bonded to concrete slab with shear connectors

Fɪɢ. 13-7. Composite floors.

One-piece metal dome pans. (*Gateway Erectors, Inc.*)

steel beam can be completely encased in the concrete and the horizontal shear transferred by friction and bond (plus some shear reinforcements if necessary). This type of composite floor is shown in part (a) of the

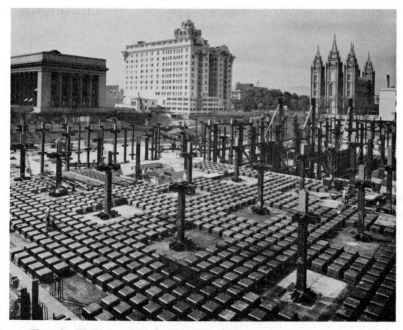

Temple Plaza parking facility, Salt Lake City, Utah. (*Ceco Steel Products Corporation.*)

figure. A second possibility is shown in part (b), where the steel beam
is bonded to the concrete slab with some type of shear connectors. Various types of shear connectors have been used during the past few decades
including spiral bars, channels, angles, studs, etc., but economic considerations usually lead to the use of round studs welded to the top flanges of
the beams in place of the other types mentioned. Typical studs are ½
to ¾ in. in diameter and 2 to 4 in. in length.

Cover plates may be welded to the bottom flanges of rolled steel
sections to give improved economy. The student can see that with the
slab acting as a part of the beam there is quite a large area available
on the compressive side of the beam. By adding plates to the tensile
flange a little better balance is obtained. Chapter 15 is devoted entirely
to the design of composite floors for buildings and bridges.

13-7. CONCRETE-PAN FLOORS

There are several types of pan floors which are constructed by placing
concrete on removable pan molds. (Some special light corrugated pans
are also available which can be left in place.) Rows of the pans are
arranged on wooden floor forms and the concrete is placed over the top
of them producing a floor cross section similar to the one shown in Fig.
13-8. Joists are formed between the pans, giving a tee-beam type floor.

Fig. 13-8. Concrete-pan floor.

These floors, which are suitable for fairly heavy loads are appreciably
lighter than the one-way and two-way concrete slab floors. Although
fairly light, they require a good deal of formwork including appreciable
shoring underneath the stems. Labor is thus higher than for many floors
but saving due to weight reduction and reuse of standard-size pans may
make them competitive. When suspended ceilings are required pan floors
will have a decided economic disadvantage.

Two-way construction is available—that is, with ribs or stems
running in both directions. Pans with closed ends are used and the
result is a waffle type floor. This latter type floor is usually used when
the floor panels are square or nearly so. Two-way construction can be

obtained for reasonably economical prices and makes a very attractive ceiling below and one which has fairly good acoustical properties.

13-8. STRUCTURAL CLAY TILE, GYPSUM TILE, AND CONCRETE-BLOCK FLOORS

Similar to the concrete-pan floors are the clay tile, gypsum tile, and concrete-block floors. These floors have approximately the same form-work and roughly the same effect as the metal-pan floors. They are not used very much today, as pan floors are more competitive costwise and provide a more attractive undersurface. Tile floors were at one time economical for spans up to 25 or 30 ft. A typical cross section of this type of floor is shown in Fig. 13-9.

FIG. 13-9. Tile or block floors.

This system does have an advantage over the metal-pan floors in that it gives a level ceiling underneath to which plaster can be applied directly without the necessity of hanging a ceiling. The lower tile surfaces are very satisfactory for bonding the plaster and no metal lath is needed except for the main steel beams at edges of the floor if they are to be fireproofed. When tile is used it is desirable to use tile of the same material under the concrete stems (as shown in Fig. 13-9); otherwise it is difficult to get an even color of plaster on the different material soffits.

A concrete slab roughly 2½ to 3 in. thick is cast monolithically with the supporting joists or stems spaced approximately 20 to 36 in. on centers. Among the standard tile sizes used are 12 × 12, 12 × 16 and 16 × 16 in plan with depths varying from 3 to 12 in. for the 12 × 12s and from 3 to 10 in. for the 12 × 16s and 16 × 16s. Tile floors have the advantage that conduits, wiring, piping, etc. can be conveniently placed through their cells. Should the panels be approximately square, joists can be used in both directions.

13-9. STEEL-DECKING FLOORS

Typical cross sections of steel-decking floors are shown in Fig. 13-10. Only two types are shown in the figure but several other variations are available. In recent years steel-decking floors have become quite popular for some applications particularly for office buildings. They are also

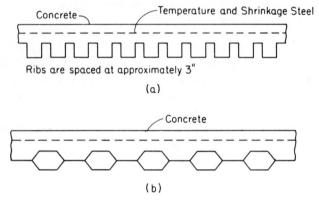

FIG. 13-10. Steel-decking floors.

popular for hotels and apartment houses and other buildings where the loads are not very large.

A particular advantage of steel-decking floors is that as soon as the decking is placed a working platform is available for the workmen. The light steel sheets are quite strong and can span up to 20 ft or more. Due to this considerable strength of the decking the concrete does not have to be particularly strong. This fact permits the use of lightweight concrete as thin as 2 or 2½ in.

The cells in the decking can be conveniently used for placing conduits, pipes, and wiring. The steel is probably galvanized and if exposed underneath can be left as it comes from the manufacturer or painted as desired. Should fire resistance be necessary, a suspended ceiling with metal lath and plaster will be used. The same is necessary if a flat ceiling is required below for the types of decking shown in Fig. 13-10, but decking is available with a flat soffit.

13-10. FLAT SLABS

Formerly flat slab floors were limited to reinforced concrete buildings but today it is possible to use them in steel-frame buildings. A flat slab is a slab which is reinforced in two or more directions and transfers its loads to the supporting columns without the use of beams and girders protruding below. The supporting concrete beams and girders are made so wide that they are the same depth as the slab.

Flat slabs are of great value when the panels are approximately square, when more headroom is desired than is provided with the normal beam and girder floors, when heavy loads are anticipated, and when it is desired to place the windows as near to the tops of the walls as possible. Another advantage is the flat ceiling produced for the floor below. Although the large amounts of reinforcing steel required cause increasing costs, the simple formwork cuts expenses decidedly. The significance of simple formwork will be understood when it is realized that over one half of the cost of the average poured concrete floor slab is in the formwork.

For the usual reinforced-concrete frame building with flat slab floors, it is necessary to flare out the tops of the columns forming column capitals and thicken the slab around the column with the so-called drop panels. These items are shown in Fig. 13-11.

Fig. 13-11. A flat slab floor for a reinforced-concrete building.

It is possible today in steel-frame buildings to use short steel cantilever beams connected to the steel columns and embedded in the slabs. These beams serve the purposes of the flared columns and drop panels in ordinary flat-slab construction. This latter arrangement is often called a *steel grillage* or *column head*. The flat slab is not a very satisfactory type of floor system for the usual tall building where lateral forces (wind or earthquake) are appreciable, because protruding beams and girders are desirable to serve as part of the lateral bracing system.

13-11. PRECAST CONCRETE FLOORS

Precast concrete sections are more commonly associated with roofs than they are with floor slabs but their use for floors is increasing. They are quickly erected and reduce the need for formwork. Lightweight aggregates are generally used in the concrete making the sections light and easy to handle. Some of the aggregates used make the slabs nailable and easily cut and fitted on the job. For floor slabs with their fairly

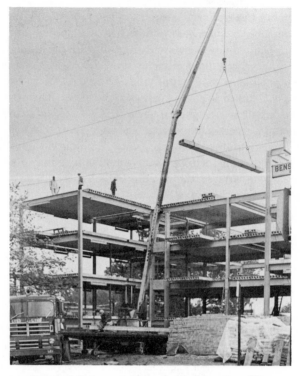

Interns' living quarters, Good Samaritan Hospital, Dayton, Ohio. (*The Flexicore Company, Inc.*)

heavy loads, the aggregates should be of a quality which will not greatly reduce the strength of the resulting concrete.

The reader is again referred to *Sweet's Catalog File* at this point. In these catalogs a great amount of information is available on the various types of precast floor slabs on the market today. A few of the common types of precast floor slabs available are listed after this paragraph and a cross section of each type mentioned is presented in Fig. 13-12. Due to slight variations in the upper surfaces of precast sections

Concrete Plank   Hollow-cored Slab   Prefabricated Concrete Block System   Channel Slab

FIG. 13-12. Precast concrete roof and floor slabs.

it is necessary to use a mortar topping of 1 to 2 in. before asphalt tile or other floor coverings can be installed.

1. *Precast concrete planks* are roughly 2 to 3 in. thick, 12 to 24 in. wide and are placed on joists up to 5 or 6 ft on center. They probably have tongue and groove edges.

2. *Hollow-cored slabs* are sections of roughly 6 to 8-in. depth and 12 to 18-in. widths which have hollow perhaps circular cores formed in them in a longitudinal direction thus reducing their weights by approximately 50 percent (as compared to solid slabs of the same dimensions). These sections which can be used for spans of from roughly 10 to 25 ft may be prestressed.

3. *Prefabricated concrete block systems* are slabs made by tying together precast concrete blocks with steel rods (may also be prestressed). They are generally 16 in. wide, 4 to 8 in. deep, and can be used for spans of roughly 8 to 32 ft.

4. *Channel slabs* are used for spans of approximately 8 to 24 ft. Rough dimensions of these slabs are given in Fig. 13-12.

13-12. TYPES OF ROOF CONSTRUCTION

The types of roof construction commonly used for steel frame buildings include concrete slabs on open-web joists, steel-decking roofs, and various types of precast concrete slabs. In addition, the other types mentioned in the preceding sections on floor types are occasionally used but they usually are unable to compete economically. Among the factors to be considered in selecting the specific types of roof construction are strength, weight, span, insulation, acoustics, appearance below, or type of roof covering to be used.

The major differences between floor-slab selection and roof-slab selection probably occur in the considerations of strength and insulation. The loads applied to roofs are generally much smaller than those applied to floor slabs, thus permitting the use of many types of lightweight aggregate concretes which may be appreciably weaker. Roof slabs should have good insulation properties or they will have to have insulation boards placed on them and covered by the roofing. Among the many types of lightweight aggregates used are wood fibers, zonolite, foams, sawdust, gypsum, expanded shale, etc. Although some of these materials decidedly reduce concrete strengths, they provide very light roof decks with excellent insulating properties.

Precast slabs made with these aggregates are light, quickly erected, have good insulating properties and usually can be sawed and nailed. For poured concrete slabs on open-web joists several lightweight aggregates work very well (zonolite, foams, gypsum, etc.), and in some cases the resulting concrete can easily be pumped up to the roofs, thereby facilitating construction. By replacing the aggregates with certain foams, concrete can be produced which is so light it will float in water. Needless to say the strength of the resulting concrete is quite low.

Steel decking with similar thin slabs of lightweight and insulating concrete placed on top make very good and economical roof decks. A competitive variation consists of steel decking with rigid insulation board placed on top followed by the regular roofing material. The other concrete-slab types are hard pressed to compete economically with these types for lightly loaded roofs. Should other types of poured concrete decks be used, the labor will be much higher. Furthermore, if an insulating type of lightweight aggregate is not used it will be necessary to place some type of insulating board on top of the slab before the roofing is applied.

13-13. EXTERIOR WALLS AND INTERIOR PARTITIONS

Exterior Walls. The purposes of exterior walls are to provide resistance to atmospheric conditions including insulation against heat and cold, satisfactory sound-absorption and light-refraction characteristics, sufficient strength and fire ratings. They should have satisfactory appearance and be reasonably economical.

For many years exterior walls were constructed of some type of masonry, glass, or corrugated sheeting. In recent decades, however, the number of satisfactory materials for exterior walls has increased tremendously. Available and commonly used today are precast concrete panels, insulated metal sheeting and many other prefabricated units. Of increasing popularity are the light prefabricated sandwich panels which consist of three layers. The exterior surface is made from aluminum, stainless steel, ceramic or plastic materials, and others. The center of the panel consists of some type of insulating material such as fiberglass or fiberboard, while the interior surface is probably made from metal, plaster, masonry, or some other attractive material.

Interior Partitions. The main purpose of interior partitions is to divide the inside space of a building into rooms. Their selection is based on appearance, fire rating, weight, or acoustical properties. Partitions are referred to as being bearing or nonbearing. These two types are described in the following two paragraphs.

1. *Bearing partitions* are those which support gravity loads in addition to their own weights and are thus permanently fixed in position. They can be constructed from wood or steel studs or from masonry units and faced with plywood, plaster, wallboard, or other material.

2. *Nonbearing partitions* are those which do not support any loads in

addition to their own weights and thus may be fixed or movable. Selection of the type of material to be used for a partition is based on the answers to the following questions: Is the partition to be fixed or movable? Is it to be transparent or opaque? Is it to extend all the way to the ceiling? Is it to be used to conceal piping and electrical conduits? Are there fire-rating and acoustical requirements? Perhaps the more common types are made of metal, masonry, or concrete. For design of the floor slabs in a building which has movable partitions, some allowance should be given to the fact that the partitions may be moved. Probably the usual practice is to increase the floor-design live load by 15 or 20 psf.

13-14. DESIGN LIVE LOADS (VERTICAL)

Floor Loads. The designer is usually fairly well controlled in the design live loads by the building code requirements in the particular area. The values given in these various codes unfortunately vary from city to city and the designer must be sure that his designs meet the requirements of that locality. The Steel Handbook presents a very detailed list of recommended live loads for various structures to which the student can conveniently refer. A few of the typical values for floor loadings from the handbook are listed in Table 13-1. The values in the

TABLE 13-1

TYPICAL BUILDING-DESIGN LIVE LOADS

Type of Building	LL (psf)
Apartment houses	
Corridors	60
Apartments	40
Public Rooms	100
Office buildings	
Offices	80
Lobbies	100
Restaurants	100
Schools	
Classrooms	40
Corridors	100
Storage warehouses	
Light	125
Heavy	250

AISC Manual were taken from the American Standard Building Code (American Standard A58.1-1955). In the absence of a governing code this one seems to be an excellent one to follow.

Roof Loads. The usual roof slab is designed for a minimum gravity load of 20 psf of horizontal projection of the roof whether the roof is sloping, curved, or flat. This live load does not include any wind or seismic effects which may also have to be considered. In some areas due to the shape of the roof (as it pertains to its snow-catching ability) and due to the particular climate, the designer may feel that 20 psf is not a sufficient load and he may increase it somewhat. Should the roof be used for other purposes than for supporting roofing, such as roof gardens or terraces, the live load should be increased to values ranging from 60 to 100 psf, or larger depending on the judgment of the designer.

Reduction in Design Live Loads. Each of the members of a building frame must be designed for the full dead loads which it supports, but it may be possible to design some members for lesser loads than their full theoretical live-load values. For example, it seems unlikely in a building frame of several stories for the absolutely maximum-design live load to occur on every floor at the same time. The lower columns in a building frame are designed for all of the dead loads above but probably for a percentage of live load appreciably less than 100 percent. Some specifications require that the beams supporting floor slabs be designed for full dead and live loads but permit the main girders to be designed under certain conditions for reduced live loads. (This reduction is based on the thought that it seems rather improbable that a very large area of a floor would be loaded to its full theoretical live-load value at any one time.) The AISC Manual presents some very commonly used reduction expressions (again taken from the American Standard Building Code). This information is listed as follows:

1. *Roofs.* No live load reduction is permitted.

2. *For live loads of 100 psf or less on floor slabs.* For live loads of 100 psf or less for any member supporting an area of 150 sq ft or more, the live load can be reduced by 0.08 percent per square foot of area supported except no reduction is permitted for places of public assembly. Furthermore the reduction may not exceed 60 percent nor the value given by the expression to follow for R (the percent reduction). DL and LL are the dead and live loads respectively in psf.

$$R = 100 \times \frac{DL + LL}{4.33\,LL}$$

3. *For live loads greater than 100 psf on floor slabs.* No reduction is permitted except for a 20 percent reduction in live loads used for column design.

13-15.   WIND AND EARTHQUAKE LOADINGS

Wind Forces.   A great deal of research has been conducted in recent years on the subject of wind forces.   Nevertheless a great deal more work needs to be done as the estimation of these forces can by no means be classified as an exact science.   The magnitudes of wind loads vary with geographical locations, heights above ground, types of terrain surrounding the buildings including other nearby structures, and other factors.

Wind pressures are assumed to be uniformly applied to the windward surfaces of buildings and are assumed to be capable of coming from any direction.   These assumptions are not quite accurate because wind pressures are not very even over large areas, the pressures near the corners of buildings being probably greater than elsewhere due to wind rushing around the corners, etc.   From a practical standpoint, therefore, all of the possible variations cannot be considered in design although today's specifications are becoming more and more specific in their requirements.

When the engineer working with large stationary buildings makes poor wind estimates the results are probably not too serious but this is not the case when tall slender buildings (or long flexible bridges) are being considered.   The usual practice for buildings is to ignore wind forces unless their heights are at least twice their least lateral dimensions.   For such cases as these it is felt that the floors and walls give the frame sufficient lateral stiffness to eliminate the need for a definite wind bracing system.   Should the buildings have their walls and floors constructed of very modern light materials or should they be located in areas of unusual wind conditions the 2 to 1 ratio will probably not be followed.   Building codes do not usually provide for estimated forces during tornadoes.   The forces created directly in the paths of these storms are so violent that it is not considered economically feasible to design buildings to resist them.

Wind forces act as pressures on vertical windward surfaces, pressures or suction on sloping windward surfaces (depending on the slope) and suction on flat surfaces and on leeward vertical and sloping surfaces (due to the creation of negative pressures or vacuums).   The student may have noticed this definite suction effect where shingles or other roof coverings have been lifted from the leeward roof surfaces of buildings.

The average building code in the United States makes no reference to wind velocities in the area or to shapes of the building or to other factors.   It just probably requires the use of some specified wind pressure in design such as 20 psf on projected area in elevation up to 300 ft with an increase of 2.5 psf for each additional 100-ft increase in height.   The values given in these codes are thought to be rather inaccurate for modern engineering design.

For a period of several years the ASCE Task Committee on Wind

Forces made a detailed study of existing information concerning wind forces. A splendid report of this information entitled *Wind Forces on Structures*[1] was presented by the committee in 1961. As stated in the report its purpose was to provide a compact source of information which could be practically used by the civil engineering profession.

In the report there is much information presented concerning wind-pressure coefficients for various types of structures, information concerning maximum wind velocities for particular geographical areas, and much additional data which can be of great value in realistically estimating wind forces. The estimated pressure in psf on a building can be obtained from the report by multiplying the dynamic pressure by the pressure coefficient. The dynamic pressure q can be determined from the following expression:

$$q = 0.002558 \ V^2$$

In this expression V is the estimated maximum velocity of the wind in miles per hour in the area and can be estimated from information presented in the report or from local weather bureau records. It is interesting to note that for the normal building with plane surfaces normal to the wind direction the pressure on the windward side plus the suction on the leeward side total 20 psf for a wind velocity of 77.8 mph.

The maximum wind and earthquake pressures for which design is made occur at large intervals of time and then last for only relatively short periods of time. It, therefore, seems reasonable to use higher allowable stresses (such as the one-third AISC increase) for lateral forces than for the relatively long-term gravity live loads.

Earthquake Forces. Many areas of the world, including the western part of the United States, fall in earthquake territory and in these areas it is necessary to consider seismic forces in design for tall or short buildings. During an earthquake there is an acceleration of the ground surface. This acceleration can be broken down into vertical and horizontal components. Usually the vertical component of the acceleration is assumed to be negligible but the horizontal component can be severe.

Most buildings can be designed with little extra expense to withstand the forces caused during an earthquake of fairly severe intensity. On the other hand, earthquakes during recent years have clearly shown that the average building which is not designed for earthquake forces can be destroyed by earthquakes that are not particularly severe. The usual practice is to design buildings for additional lateral loads (representing the estimate of earthquake forces) which are equal to some percentage

[1] *Trans. ASCE,* vol. 126, part II (1961), pp. 1124–1198.

(5 to 10 percent) of the weight of the building and its contents. An excellent reference on the subject of seismic forces is a publication by the Structural Engineers Association of California in July 1959 entitled "Recommended Lateral Force Requirements of Seismology Committee."

It should be noted that many persons look upon the seismic loads to be used in designs as being merely percentage increases of the wind loads. This thought is not really correct, however, as seismic loads are different in their action and as they are not proportional to the exposed area but to the building weight above the level in question.

chapter 14

INTRODUCTION
TO *STEEL* BRIDGES

14-1. GENERAL

The first bridge has been estimated to have been built as early as 15,000 B.C. In fact it has been said that man knew how to build bridges before he knew how to build houses. The first bridges probably consisted of stream crossings made with tree trunks or large flat stones laid across the streams. These latter bridges have been called *clapper bridges* because of the sound the loose stones made when being crossed.

Another type of bridge built before the dawn of history was the vine type of suspension bridge. A person first seeing the magnificent Golden Gate or Mackinac suspension bridges would be amazed to learn that the suspension bridge idea probably originated with the use of vines across gorges in the Himalayan Mountains many centuries ago. In the same vein, early man in the Southwest must have been amazed at the sight of the great natural stone arches there. It is useless to speculate on how much time elapsed before he got the idea of putting two large stones together in the shape of an inverted V to ford a small stream with an arch.[1]

The exact dates of construction of the first bridges are impossible to obtain. There is no question, however, that beam, arch, and suspension bridges have been built in some form for several thousand years. It is said that the oldest bridge still in use in the world is the Caravan Bridge over the river Meles at Smyrna, Turkey. Supposedly Homer and St. Paul both walked across this 40-ft stone-slab bridge many centuries apart.

Bridges built before 1840 in the United States were made of timber. In 1840 an all-iron bridge was built across the Erie Canal at Frankfurt, New York. The first bridge constructed with structural carbon steel was Ead's Bridge across the Mississippi River at St. Louis, begun in 1869 and

---

[1] H. S. Smith, *The World's Great Bridges* (New York: Harper & Row, 1953), p. 1.

completed in 1874. This bridge consists of three arches with a center span of 520 ft and end spans of 502 ft. It is well known for the tragic loss of life suffered during construction. Of 600 men who were employed in sinking the caissons there were 119 serious cases of the "bends" and 14 deaths.[2] This bridge was the essential link in the construction of the cross-continental railroad system and had a tremendous effect on the growth of the city of St. Louis.

During the last part of the nineteenth century and the early part of the twentieth the majority of bridges built were for railway traffic, but this is no longer the case. Due to various problems in the railroad industry today very few new railroad bridges are being built. On the other hand, the increase in highway traffic during the past few decades has caused a rise in highway bridge construction almost beyond belief. Today more than 6,000 bridges of all types are built each year in the United States.

14-2. THROUGH, DECK, AND HALF-THROUGH BRIDGES

The student has often seen highway bridges in which the trusses were on the sides. As he rode across the bridge he could see overhead lateral bracing between the trusses. This type of bridge is said to be a *through bridge*. The floor system is supported by floor beams which run under the roadway and between the bottom chord joints of the trusses.

In the *deck bridge* the roadway is placed on top of the trusses or beams. Deck construction has every advantage over through construction except for underclearance. There is unlimited overhead horizontal and vertical clearance, and future expansion is more feasible. Another very important advantage is that supporting trusses or beams can be moved closer together, reducing lateral moments in the floor system. Other advantages of the deck truss are simplified floor systems and possible reduction in the sizes of piers and abutments due to reductions in their heights. Finally, the very pleasing appearance of deck structures is another reason for their increasing popularity.

Should the roadway lie in between the top and bottom chords and should there be no room for overhead bracing, the bridge is said to be a *half-through* or a *pony bridge*. One major problem with the pony truss is the difficulty of providing adequate lateral bracing for the top chord compression members. This type of bridge is rarely practical today.

Today's bridge designer tries to prevent any sense of confinement for the users of his bridges. He will in trying to achieve this goal attempt to eliminate any overhead bracing or truss members which will protrude

---

[2] H. S. Smith, *op. cit.*, p. 84.

above the roadway level. The result is that the deck structure is again desirable unless underclearance requirements prevent their use or the spans are so large as to make them impractical.

14-3. ERECTION METHODS FOR BRIDGES

Before the various types of bridges are discussed it is felt that a few general comments should be made about the erection methods used for bridges of varying span lengths. A point that cannot be overemphasized is the necessity for carefully preparing an erection schedule. This schedule should actually be outlined before the final design is completed. Stresses may be caused in some members during erection in excess of those produced by the working loads; perhaps even more serious, the character of the stresses may be changed, as from tension to compression. Very large stresses may be caused by such things as heavy cranes moving on the trusses or by the forcing of parts to make them fit, as in getting opposite ends of a bridge to come together at the middle.

Swinging a plate girder into place on Goat Island Bridge across the Niagara River, Niagara Falls, N. Y. (*Bethlehem Steel Company.*)

The erection schedule should be developed showing the order of erecting various truss members. After this plan is made the joints can be designed showing which connections are to be field-made and which ones are to be shop-made. The gusset plates should be shop-connected to the correct members so they will be available in the proper order of erection.

In the paragraphs to follow a few comments are made about the common erection procedures used for short-, medium-, and long-span bridges.

Short-Span Bridges (Up to Approximately 125 ft). For these short spans it is usually possible to assemble the spans in the shop or at the job site and put them in place in one piece with crawler or truck cranes working from below or with a stiffleg derrick traveler. A traffic problem may be involved below (land or water) and it is important to limit the time of the interference to the absolute minimum.

Medium-Span Bridges (Approximately 125 to 400 ft). The usual procedure for medium spans is to use falsework, the temporary material used to support a structure until it is self-supporting. When falsework is used, erection stresses are kept at a minimum. In some cases deep fast-flowing water or deep gorges below may prevent the use of falsework and the cantilever erection procedure will probably be used. This method, which is particularly applicable to cantilever and continuous bridge trusses, is illustrated in Fig. 14-1. As shown in the figure, the end span

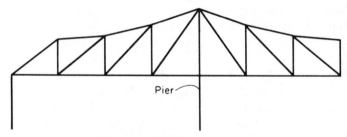

Fig. 14-1. Cantilever erection.

has been erected (probably on falsework) and the bridge is extended beyond the pier or tower, member by member with the use of small crane travelers. The truss is designed to be self supporting and the members are designed for the erection stress reversal that will occur. The same erection procedure will be followed from the opposite shore.

It should be realized that cantilever erection has the disadvantages of being more expensive and dangerous. Other erection methods which have been used for medium spans include floating the bridge section into place when water is being spanned, and the so-called *protrusion method* where the structure is rolled into place (illustrated in Fig. 14-2 for a girder).

Fig. 14-2. Protrusion method of erection.

Long Spans (Approximately 400 ft and Above). Falsework is usually not feasible for long-span bridges and the cantilever erection procedure will probably be used. Suspension bridges are erected from the cable and there is no interference with navigation. A few more comments about their erection is given in Sec. 14-11.

14-4. THE BEAM BRIDGE

The beam bridge, in which a concrete roadway slab is supported by W section beams, is very popular because of its simple design and construction. This type of span is economical for railroad spans up to roughly 50 ft and for highway spans of up to roughly 80 ft. It will be remembered from Chap. 7 that the AREA and the AASHO specify certain minimum depth-span ratios (1/15 and 1/25 respectively). Shallower beams can be used provided the deflections are limited to what they would have been if the design had been made using the recommended minimum ratios.

The W36×300, which is the deepest standard W section, has a total depth of 36.72 in. For the 1/15 AREA ratio the maximum span for which this section could be used is 45.9 ft and for the 1/25 AASHO ratio the maximum span is 76.5 ft. These values can be extended somewhat by using cover plates and/or limiting the deflections as required for smaller depth-span ratios. As previously described in Chap. 13, steel beams and concrete slabs may be constructed so they act together as composite sections. Simple-span composite highway spans have been economically used for spans as high as 120 ft.

14-5. THE PLATE GIRDER BRIDGE

For many years bridge trusses were quite commonly used for spans of from roughly 70 to 150 ft as well as for spans greater than 150 ft. Today, however, beam and plate girder bridges have almost completely captured the market for spans up to about 150 ft as well as for many larger spans. They are actually common for 200-ft spans and have been used for spans of well over 400 ft. The main span of the continuous Bonn-Beuel plate-girder bridge over the Rhine in Germany is 643 ft.

It is very difficult for trusses to compete with beam and plate-girder structures as long as the beams or girders can be shipped in one piece. Plate girders have been shipped in one piece for spans above 150 ft. The problems of fabrication, erection, and transportation usually limit built-up sections to maximum depths of roughly 10 or 12 ft. When deeper sections than these are required, trusses may prove to be competitive. Generally speaking, plate girders are very economical for railroad bridges from about 50 to 130 ft and for highway bridges from about 80 to 150 ft. They are frequently very competitive for much higher spans than these, par-

New York State Thruway crossing a railroad near Suffern, N. Y.
(*The Lincoln Electric Company.*)

ticularly where continuous spans are used. Actually simple spans greater than 100 ft are rarely economical. Chapter 16 is devoted to the design of plate girders.

14-6. TRUSS BRIDGES FOR MEDIUM SPANS

As spans become longer and loads heavier trusses will begin to be competitive. For spans greater than those economical for plate girders, truss bridges will probably prove to be economical. Although many bridge trusses are still in existence along the older highways, one-span, simply supported trusses are built quite infrequently today. A few types of bridge trusses which can be used for medium spans are shown in Fig. 14-3.

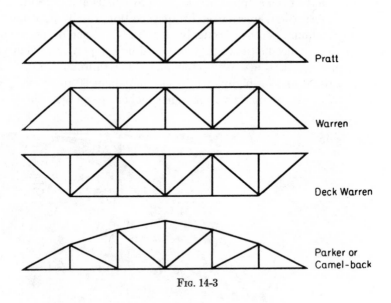

Pratt

Warren

Deck Warren

Parker or Camel-back

FIG. 14-3

The Pratt truss, which is reasonably economical for spans of 150 to 200 ft, has one advantage in that the diagonals are all in tension under dead loads. The end posts, however, are always in compression and the movement of live loads back and forth across the span may cause stress reversals in some of the diagonals.

The Warren truss is thought by many to have a little more attractive appearance than the Pratt and may be a little more popular for the same spans. It is probably used more as a deck truss than as a through truss because it is particularly economical when so used.

The deeper a truss is for the same size chord members the greater is its resisting moment. For longer spans it is economical to increase truss depths where the moments are larger. These varying depth trusses are definitely lighter than corresponding parallel chord trusses, but their fabrication costs are higher. Above approximately 180 to 200 ft the weight saving will more than cancel the extra fabrication costs and the so-called curved-chord trusses become economical. The Parker truss (also called a camel-back truss) is quite satisfactory for spans from roughly 180 to 360 ft. For long continuous and cantilever span trusses the depths are almost always varied with the moments. The greatest depths in these trusses will occur at the supports where the moments are largest.

14-7. SUBDIVIDED TRUSS BRIDGES

Various economic studies for truss bridges have shown that the diagonals should be kept at angles of approximately 45° with the horizontal and the depth to span ratios should vary from about 1/5 to 1/8 with the smaller ratios used for the larger spans. Should these recommendations be followed for spans much greater than 300 ft, the panel lengths will become excessive.

When panels are very long the compression member sizes get out of hand because of their excessive unsupported lengths. Furthermore, the floor system between panel points becomes unreasonably heavy and expensive for large panels. In fact floor beam spacings greater than 25 ft are not recommended.

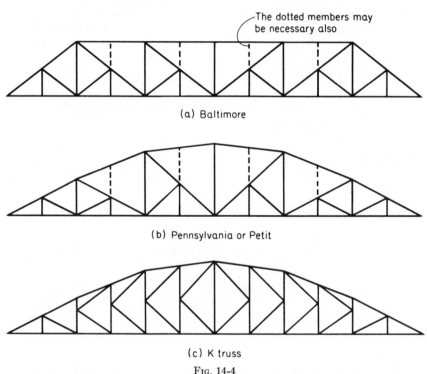

The dotted members may be necessary also

(a) Baltimore

(b) Pennsylvania or Petit

(c) K truss

Fig. 14-4

The subdivided trusses shown in Figs. 14-4(a) and (b) can be used to keep the panel lengths within the desired values for longer trusses while at the same time following economic requirements previously mentioned (diagonal slope and depth-to-span ratio). In part (a) of the figure the parallel chord Baltimore or subdivided Pratt truss is shown. Again it is usually more economical to use trusses which vary in depth with the moments and a curved chord Baltimore is shown in part (b) of the figure. This truss is usually called a Pennsylvania or Petit truss.

Subdivision introduces its own disadvantages. The trusses are usually not too attractive with their large number of members, their pound price is high due to the large number of connections and secondary stresses are often rather high. Another truss which accomplishes the same ends achieved with subdivision and without their disadvantages is the K truss shown in part (c) of Fig. 14-4. Simple-span bridges probably have an upper economical limit of roughly 600 ft although longer spans have been built.

14-8. CONTINUOUS BRIDGE TRUSSES

Continuous bridge trusses are normally economical for highway bridges for spans of from roughly 250 to 700 or 800 ft and for railroad bridges for spans of from roughly 450 to 700 or 800 ft. A very popular truss for continuous spans is the Warren, an example of which is shown in Fig. 14-5. For economic reasons continuous trusses may be subdivided

FIG. 14-5. Continuous Warren deck bridge.

as were the simple spans. Among the several advantages possessed by continuous bridge trusses as compared to simple-span trusses are the following:

1. There can be an appreciable saving of steel weight perhaps running as high as 10 to 20 percent with the higher values being possible for highway bridges. For railroad bridges the highest weight saving potential is probably in the range of 10 percent because of the more frequent stress reversals.

2. Fewer supports are required as longer spans are possible.

3. Continuous trusses are ideally suited for the cantilever type of erection.

4. Continuous bridges have been clearly shown to support higher ultimate loads than simple spans.

On the other hand, continuous trusses have some shortcomings. These include the following:

1. They are statically indeterminate to outer forces and are desirably used only where good foundation conditions are present.

2. There are more stress reversals in a continuous truss, with the result that part of the weight saving advantage is canceled.

3. An indeterminate structure is more difficult to analyze and design than is a determinate one.

14-9. CANTILEVER BRIDGES

Cantilever construction consists essentially of two simple spans each with an overhanging or cantilevered end (as shown in Fig. 14-6) and with

Fig. 14-6

another simple span in between, called the suspended span, supported by the cantilevered ends (as shown in Fig. 14-7).

Fig. 14-7

From Figs. 14-6 and 14-7 the student can see why these structures are sometimes referred to as see-saw construction because the bridge seems to see-saw over the main piers. In cantilever construction unsupported hinges or points of zero moment are introduced at each end of the suspended span. Figure 14-8 shows a sketch of a cantilever bridge truss showing one method of introducing the unsupported hinges.

Fig. 14-8

The method of forming the hinges should be carefully noted in this figure. The reader might claim that he has ridden over some cantilever bridges and has not noticed any missing truss members. Should the hinges be formed as shown in this figure, the missing members would probably be installed but would not be connected to resist stress. The purposes of their installation are for better appearance and for keeping the users of the bridge from being worried.

It is possible to locate the hinges in a cantilever bridge at such positions so as to obtain the same moments (and this roughly equivalent economy) as would occur in a continuous truss of the same spans so far as dead loads are concerned. This could be done by locating the hinges at points of zero moment or points of inflection in the center span of the continuous structure. Unfortunately such a situation does not apply to live loads. For long spans with their heavy dead loads, cantilever bridge trusses compare quite favorably with continuous construction, but in shorter spans continuous construction will probably prove to be more economical.

The cantilever bridge is said to have come into general use for long railroad bridges several decades ago because the suspension bridges of that time were not considered to be sufficiently rigid to withstand the heavy impact, nosing of locomotives, and other types of train loadings.

The usual economical cantilever spans range from approximately 500 to 1,800 ft for highway bridges and from 600 to 1,800 ft for railroad bridges. The longest cantilever bridge in the world is the Quebec Bridge which has an 1,800-ft center span. Perhaps the most famous cantilever bridge is the one which spans the Firth of Forth in Scotland. This bridge which was completed in 1890 was the first long railroad bridge built with steel. It has two 1,710-ft spans and is the second longest cantilever bridge in the world.

Among the several advantages possessed by cantilever bridges are the following:

1. Cantilever bridges can be used where foundation conditions are poor because they are statically determinate and pier settlement is not a serious matter as it affects stresses.

2. As they are statically determinate their analysis and design is simpler.

3. They are well adapted to cantilever erection.

The cantilever bridge does have several disadvantages including the following:

1. They are less rigid than continuous bridge trusses.

2. The construction of the hinges is expensive.

3. The reactions which have to be supplied at the supports can be disadvantageous. For example, there may be uplifts at the anchor piers while tremendously large reactions may have to be provided at the interior supports or main piers.

As to erection, the anchor spans are probably built on falsework and the interior spans by the cantilever erection method (previously illustrated in Fig. 14-1). The portion of the bridge truss between the interior hinges may often be floated to the site and lifted into position. It doesn't take much imagination to understand the importance of having an absolutely perfect check and recheck on dimensions for the final fitting.

During the construction of the Firth of Forth Bridge, calculations showed that a minimum temperature of 60°F was required to bring the bolt holes in position so as to get the lower chords to join for the final fitting. Construction was delayed due to various reasons until October and it appeared that the required temperature could not be obtained that year. To make the holes come in line, wood shavings and oily waste soaked in naphtha were laid along the chord and set on fire for 60 ft on either side of the connection, with the result that the required expansion was obtained and the connection was successfully completed. A similar but opposite situation was encountered during the construction of Ead's Bridge at St. Louis (an arch bridge previously mentioned in Sec. 14-1), when it was necessary to pack the chords in ice to reduce their lengths.[3]

14-10.   STEEL ARCHES

The arch is certainly one of the more attractive types of bridges. It is often defined by the structural engineer as a structure which under gravity loads tends to produce converging horizontal reactions. If the reader will examine the curved arch of Fig. 14-9, he will see that under

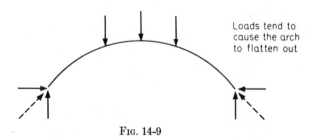

Loads tend to cause the arch to flatten out

Fɪɢ. 14-9

the vertical loads shown the arch will tend to spread or flatten out. The result is that large inward or converging reactions must be provided at the supports. Because of this fact there is a well-known expression about arches to the effect that "an arch never sleeps" because the horizontal thrust is always there, even due to the weight of the arch alone.

The horizontal reactions or thrusts tend to cause moments in an arch

---

[3] H. S. Smith, *op. cit.*, p. 126.

Henry Hudson Bridge over Harlem River, New York City. (*American Bridge Division, U. S. Steel Corporation.*)

which in turn tend to cancel the moments caused by the vertical reaction components. In other words, at a support the resultant of the vertical and horizontal reaction components (shown dotted in Fig. 14-9) tends to cause primarily axial compression in the arch. It is possible to construct

West End North Side Bridge, Ohio River, Pittsburgh, Pa. (*American Bridge Division, U. S. Steel Corporation.*)

an arch with a parabolic shape which when loaded with a uniform load will have no bending moment.

Arches are classified as being three-hinged, two-hinged, one-hinged (rare) or hingeless (fixed). They are further classified as being solid ribbed, tied, braced rib, or spandrel braced. These types are shown in Fig. 14-10. The solid rib steel arch is used more for highway bridges

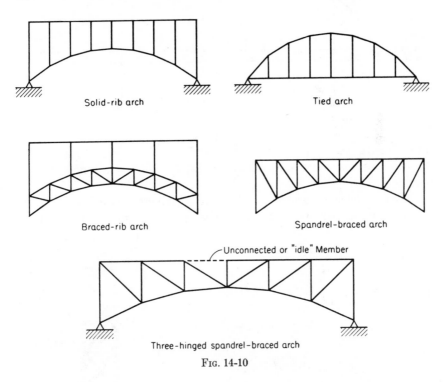

Solid-rib arch

Tied arch

Braced-rib arch

Spandrel-braced arch

Unconnected or "idle" Member

Three-hinged spandrel-braced arch

FIG. 14-10

than railroad bridges. Its upper economical limit is roughly 500 to 600 ft. The braced-rib arch, which is mainly used for highway bridges, is ideally suited for cantilever erection and is used for long spans with an upper economical limit of roughly 1,600 to 1,800 ft. The spandrel-braced arch is used primarily for railroad bridges. It has an upper economical limit of about 1,000 ft because it is heavier than the braced-rib arch and is not as well adapted to cantilever erection.

The longest arch bridge in the world is the 1,652-ft Kill van Kull highway bridge (a two-hinged, braced-rib arch) from Bayonne, N. J., to Staten Island. The Sydney Harbour, Australia, steel railway arch has a span of 1,650 ft and is also a two-hinged, braced-rib arch. The Lees' Ferry Bridge over the Colorado River in Arizona, which is a spandrel-braced arch with a 616-ft span, is 500 ft above the river level.

14-11. SUSPENSION BRIDGES

Probably the suspension bridge with its gracefully curving cables is the most beautiful of all bridge types. A suspension bridge is shown in Fig. 14-11. The bridge is supported by the cables which pass over the

FIG. 14-11

towers and are anchored at the bridge ends. The stiffening truss stiffens the cable against vibration caused by the live loads and holds it in its regular shape.

The suspension bridge provides an excellent method of reducing moments in long-span structures. The usual practice is to erect the

San Francisco-Oakland Bay Bridge. (*American Bridge Division, U. S. Steel Corporation.*)

structure with its weight being entirely carried by the cables. This is done by waiting to connect the stiffening trusses until all of the dead weight is carried by the hangers to the cables. The result is that these trusses carry none of the dead load and only a part of the live load. A large part of the live loads is transferred by the hangers to the cable, with the result that the amount of bending moment to be resisted by the trusses is tremendously reduced. The majority of the load on a suspension bridge is carried by the cable in tension, a very efficient and economical method.

The late Dr. D. B. Steinman said that suspension bridges were potentially economical for highway bridges for clear spans from 400 ft to 10,000 ft.[4] The longest existing suspension bridge until recently was the Golden Gate Bridge with its 4,200-ft suspended span. On November 21, 1964, however, this title was taken by the Verrazano-Narrows Bridge, which has a 4,260-ft suspended span across the entrance to New York's harbor from Brooklyn to Staten Island.

14-12. MISCELLANEOUS BRIDGE TYPES

There are several other types of steel bridges which are used, among them being rigid-frame bridges, orthotropic systems, Vierendeel trusses, and prestressed steel bridges. A brief discussion is made of each of these types in the following paragraphs.

Steel Rigid-Frame Bridges. A type of bridge which is quite often used for single spans is the steel rigid-frame bridge. This type of bridge which is very satisfactory for overpasses is economical for spans of from roughly 30 to 150 ft. The legs of the rigid frame serve as the abutments and provide continuity. The design of this type of structure can be handled in a manner quite similar to the method described for rigid frame buildings in Chap. 19.

Orthotropic Systems. In the usual types of bridges each of the parts (slab, stringers, floor beams, trusses, etc.) is assumed to perform a certain individual task without assistance by the other parts. In the orthotropic bridges the stringers and floor beams and main girders are rigidly connected together and a continuous deck plate is placed over them. The beams are welded to the underside of the plate to make the entire bridge a single unit in resisting loads. The various parts do not have clear-cut single functions—they all support the load together.

A paving surface (probably asphalt because of its light weight) is placed on the steel plate. Orthotropic bridges have been used primarily in Europe, the labor situation being a major factor. A great deal of labor

[4] D. B. Steinman, *A Practical Treatise On Suspension Bridges* (New York: John Wiley & Sons, Inc., 1929), p. 83.

is involved in constructing the bridges although there is a large saving in steel. The cheap labor and relatively expensive material situation makes them very competitive in Europe. In the United States, however, the very costly labor situation reduces their competitive position. Nevertheless these bridges seem to have great economic potential for the future in the United States.

Orthotropic bridges have been primarily used for spans of 200 ft or more, but they seem to have the potential for competing economically for spans of 100 ft or even less. One orthotropic plate girder bridge has a span of 856 ft. It is the Save River Bridge in Belgrade, Yugoslavia.[5] An excellent reference on the design of orthotropic bridges is the *Design Manual for Orthotropic Steel Plate Deck Bridges*, published in 1963 by the AISC.

Vierendeel Trusses. A type of truss which is uncommon in the United States but has had frequent application in Europe is the Vierendeel truss, developed by M. Vierendeel in 1896. This type of truss, illustrated in Fig. 14-12, is actually not a truss by the usual definition and requires

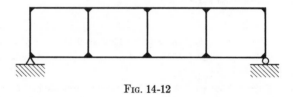

Fig. 14-12

the use of moment-resisting joints. Loads are supported by means of the bending resistance of its short heavy members. Although analysis and design are quite difficult, it is a fairly efficient structure.

Prestressed Steel Bridges. Another type of bridge construction which will probably be used a great deal in the future is the prestressed steel bridge. In a prestressed structure, stresses are introduced which are opposite in character to those that will be produced by the working loads. Another way of defining this process is to say that where the working loads cause positive moments, prestressing is introduced to produce negative moments, and vice versa.

Prestressing tends to counteract the effect of the working loads thus enabling the same structure to support increased loads or to be used for larger spans with the same loads. As an illustration of the prestressing idea the student is referred to Fig. 14-13. In part (a) of the figure the gravity loads shown tend to cause the truss to bend downwards, causing

[5] Jerry C. L. Chang, "Orthotropic-Plate Construction For Short Span Bridges," *Civil Engineering*, December 1961, p. 53.

(a)   (b)

FIG. 14-13

tension in the bottom chords and compression in the top ones (i.e., positive moments). In part (b) the bottom chord is compressed and the truss tends to bend upward (i.e., negative moments). One method of produc-

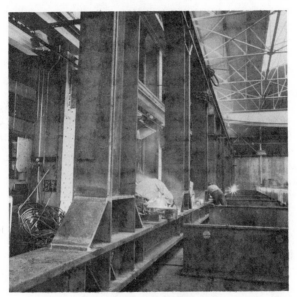

Shop fabrication of a Vierendeel truss. (*Bethlehem Steel Company.*)

ing the prestressing force in a truss is by tensioning a group of high-strength cables to very large initial stresses—perhaps as high as **175 ksi** —and attaching them to the bottom chord of the truss.

14-13. SUMMARY OF BRIDGE TYPES

A brief summary of the general types of steel bridges is given in Table 14-1, together with approximate economical spans. There are many variables involved in each of the values given. In this regard, notice that the table indicates that simple truss bridges may be economical for spans up to approximately 600 ft. This does not mean that any type

TABLE 14-1

SUMMARY OF BRIDGE TYPES AND SPANS

Type of Bridge	Approximate Range of Economical Spans	
	Highway Bridges	Railroad Bridges
W section (noncomposite)	0–80	0–50
W section (composite)	50–120	—
PL girder $\left(\begin{array}{c}\text{composite and}\\ \text{noncomposite}\end{array}\right)$	80–150	50–130
Simple truss	150–600	130–600
Continuous truss	250–800	450–800
Cantilever truss	500–1800	600–1800
Arch	100–1800	100–1000
Suspension	400–10,000	1500–10,000

of simple truss can be economical for this size of span. Obviously the subdivided and K trusses are the only ones which would be economical for such large spans. A similar argument can be made for arches. A few of the values in the table are only roughly estimated. For example, the 10,000 ft estimated economical span for suspension bridges has not even been approached.

14-14. COMPARISON OF HIGH LEVEL BRIDGES AND LOW LEVEL MOVABLE BRIDGES

Because our U. S. highways are subject to tremendous traffic volumes and to high-speed traffic, any kind of movable bridge on their routes is objectionable. The result is that the use of fixed high-level bridges furnishing the clearances required by the Corps of Engineers (which has jurisdiction over all structures crossing navigable streams) are usually desirable.

Nevertheless a bridge-design organization may be faced with the problem of spanning a navigable stream with a high bridge above the naval traffic or a low-level bridge with a movable span. (The discussion of tunnels, another feasible solution, is not considered in this text.)

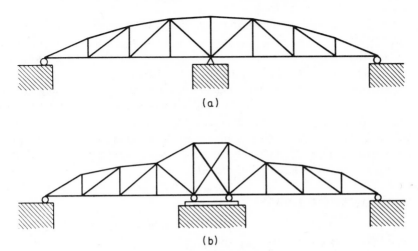

Fɪɢ. 14-14. Swing bridges.

Several types of low level movable bridges are shown in Figs. 14-14 and 14-15. Low-level bridges have smaller initial costs, take up less

Fɪɢ. 14-15. Vertical-lift bridge.

of the surrounding land areas at their ends, permit quicker crossing by vehicles (when a ship is not passing) and the operating costs of the crossing vehicles are reduced. This latter fact is of appreciable importance when railway traffic is involved. Low-level bridges may have some appreciable advantage when a high but narrow navigation channel is to be spanned.

On the other hand, low-level bridges with movable sections are always a nuisance to traffic above and below and are a real hazard for land traffic in cases of emergency use by fire engines, ambulances, etc. They require additional costs for the operators (24 hours per day seven days per week) for opening and closing of the bridges as well as the cost of the machinery and power for the opening and closing.

High-level bridges have much higher initial costs than low-level bridges, their long approaches damage or take up much of the surrounding area on the shores, they have steeper grades, and they may block off streets and through traffic for parts of urban areas.

The high-level bridge is probably selected for highway traffic or for a crossing in a rural area or for a location where the navigation channel to be spanned is wide. On the other hand, low-level movable bridges may be given serious consideration for railway traffic or for urban areas or for cases where an extremely high clearance (and probably narrow) is required over the navigation channel.

14-15. MOVABLE BRIDGES

The movable bridge may prove to be a satisfactory solution for crossing a waterway. It has the purpose of providing clearance for shipping without the expense of constructing high piers and raising the approach grades necessary for high level fixed bridges. The three main types of movable bridges are briefly described in the paragraphs to follow.

The Swing Bridge. The swing bridge is supported on a center pier and is rotated horizontally. The bridge can turn on a center pivot as shown in (a) of Fig. 14-14 or it can turn on a turntable as shown in (b) of the same figure.

With the swing bridge there is no problem with vertical clearance as it is unlimited but the center pier will serve as an obstruction to ships.

The Vertical Lift Bridge. As the name implies, the movable span is

George P. Coleman Bridge, Yorktown, Va. (*American Bridge Division, U. S. Steel Corporation.*)

lifted vertically above the navigational clearance area as shown in Fig. 14-15. This type of movable bridge is used where the horizontal clearance required is greater than the vertical clearance required.

Bascule Bridge. The bascule bridge is one in which the span is turned

Arthur Kill Bridge, Staten Island, N. Y. (*American Bridge Division, U. S. Steel Corporation.*)

Manasquan River highway bridge from Brielle to Point Pleasant, N. J. (*American Bridge Division, U. S. Steel Corporation.*)

up vertically at one end, usually by some type of counterweight system. It may prove to be a satisfactory solution when a narrow but high clearance is required.

14-16. SELECTION OF BRIDGE TYPE

Among the many factors which affect the choice of the type of bridge to be used for a given site are the following:

1. Span required.
2. Foundation conditions. (Poor foundation conditions may rule out indeterminate structures.)
3. Clearance required. (This factor can have a great effect on the erection method used and hence the type of structure.)
4. Probable erection methods required by conditions at the site.
5. Live loads to be supported.
6. First cost.
7. Operation and maintenance cost.
8. Harmony of bridge with surrounding terrain.

For a particular situation the designer could list all of the bridge types which might be economical for the span length involved. His next step might be to study the preceding factors 2 through 8 to determine if any of the possibilities were impractical. Should more than one possibility remain, preliminary designs and cost estimates for each may have to be made before a decision can be reached.

14-17. SPACING OF PIERS AND ABUTMENTS

This section is devoted to a discussion of the spacings of the piers and abutments for bridges. A well-known rule in bridge engineering on the subject of costs states that for best economy the cost of the superstructure should equal the cost of the substructure. Simply stated, the rule means that when foundation conditions are poor and thus substructure costs high per pier, it is desirable to use longer spans in order to reduce the number of piers.

For this rule to be completely applicable the pier depths, foundation materials, and other construction conditions must be the same at each pier. (It should be noted here that the cost of the superstructure varies roughly as the square of the span, whereas the cost of the piers varies roughly as the square of the depth below water level.) For uniform conditions the rule can be easily proved, as shown in several texts,[6] but space is not taken here for that purpose. Since the rule is perfect only

---

[6] E. H. Gaylord, Jr., and C. N. Gaylord, *Design of Steel Structures* (New York: McGraw-Hill Book Company, Inc., 1957), pp. 405–407.

for uniform conditions it should probably be taken in general as being an approximate rule of the greatest importance.

14-18.   LIVE LOADS FOR HIGHWAY BRIDGES

Although highway bridges must support several different types of vehicles, the heaviest possible loads are caused by a series of trucks. The AASHO specifies that highway bridges shall be designed for lines of motor trucks occupying 10-ft wide lanes. Only one truck is placed in each span for each lane. The truck loads specified are designated with an H prefix followed by a number indicating the total weight of the truck in tons. The weight is followed by another number indicating the year of the specifications. For example, an H20-44 loading indicates the 20-ton truck and the 1944 specifications. A sketch of the truck and the distances between axle centers, wheel centers, and other dimensions is given in Fig. 14-16.

H20-44
H15-44
H10-44

0.1W

0.4 W

0.1W

0.4 W

2'

6'   10' Lane Width

2'

14'-0"

Width of each rear tire
assumed to equal 1"
for each ton of total
truck load, as 20"
for H20-44.

Fig. 14-16

The selection of the particular truck loading to be used in design depends upon the bridge location, anticipated traffic, and related factors. These loadings may be broken down into three groups as follows.

Two-Axle Trucks, H20-44, H15-44, and H10-44. The weight of an H truck is assumed to be distributed two-tenths to the front axle (e.g., 4 tons, or 8 k, for an H20-44 loading) and eight-tenths to the rear axle. The axles are spaced 14 ft 0 in. on centers, while the center-to-center lateral spacing of the wheels is 6 ft 0 in. Should a truck loading varying in weight from these be desired, one that has axle loads in direct proportion to the standard ones listed here may be used. A loading as small as the H10-44 may be used only for bridges supporting the lightest traffic.

Two-Axle Trucks Plus One-Axle Semitrailer; HS20-44 and HS15-44. For today's highway bridges carrying a great amount of truck traffic, the two-axle truck loading with a one-axle semitrailer weighing 80 percent of the main truck load is commonly specified for design. The HS20-44 truck has 4 tons on the front axle, 16 tons on the rear axle, and 16 tons on the trailer axle. The distance from the rear truck axle to the semitrailer axle is varied from 14 to 30 ft, depending on which spacing will cause the most critical conditions.

Bridges for the new interstate highway system are designed in accordance with the AASHO Specifications using the HS20-44 loading. An alternative load can be used in place of the HS20-44 truck. This alternate system which consists of a pair of 24 k axle loads spaced 4 ft on center is critical for short spans only. This loading will produce maximum moments for simple spans from 11.5 to 37 ft and maximum shears for spans from 6 to 22 ft. For other spans the HS20-44 loading or its equivalent lane loading will be critical.

Uniform Lane Loadings. Computation of stresses caused by a series of concentrated loads, whether they represent two-axle trucks or two-axle trucks with semitrailers, is a tedious job; therefore, a lane loading which will produce approximately the same stresses is frequently used. The lane loading consists of a uniform load plus a single moving concentrated load. This load system represents a line of medium-weight traffic with a heavy truck somewhere in the line. The uniform load per foot is equal to 0.016 times the total weight of the truck to which the load is to be roughly equivalent. The concentrated load equals 0.45 times the truck weight for moment calculations and 0.65 times the truck weight for shear calculations. These values for an H20-44 loading would be as follows: 0.016×20 tons equals 640 lb/ft of lane; concentrated load for moment 0.45×20 tons equals 18 k; and concentrated load for shear 0.65×20 tons equals 26 k.

The lane loading is more convenient to handle but may not be used unless it produces stresses equal to or greater than those produced by the corresponding H or HS loading. It can be shown that the equivalent lane loading for the HS20-44 will produce greater moments in simple spans of 145 ft and above and greater shears for simple spans of 128 ft and above. Appendix A of the AASHO Specifications contains tables which give the maximum shears and moments in simple spans for the various H loadings or for their equivalent lane loadings whichever controls.

The possibility of having a continuous series of heavily loaded trucks in every lane of a bridge having more than two lanes does not seem as great as that for a bridge having only two lanes. The AASHO, therefore, permits the stresses caused by full loads in every lane to be reduced by a certain factor if the bridge has more than two lanes.

Impact. The truck and train loads on highway and railroad bridges are not applied gently and gradually but rather violently, causing stress increases. Additional loads, called impact loads, must be considered; these are taken into account by increasing the live-load stresses by some percentage, the percentage being obtained from purely empirical expressions. Numerous formulas have been presented for estimating impact. One example is the following 1949 AASHO formula for highway bridges, in which I is the percent of impact and L is the length of the span, in feet, over which live load is placed to obtain a maximum stress. The AASHO says that it is unnecessary to use an impact percentage greater than 30 percent, regardless of the value given by the formula. Notice that the longer the span length becomes the smaller becomes the impact.

$$I = \frac{50}{L + 125}$$

Wind loads. Wind can produce very large forces on bridges. On several occasions wind forces have been of sufficient magnitude to cause collapse. Accurately estimating the magnitude of these loads is very difficult because there are so many variables involved such as terrain, wind velocity, and sizes and shapes of members.

The present bridge specifications have been influenced appreciably by considerable testing of bridge models in wind tunnels.[7,8] The AASHO says that in applying wind loads the exposed area shall equal the sum of the areas of all floors, railing, members, etc., as seen in elevation. The loads they specify are estimated for a 100-mph wind but the values may be increased or decreased provided the designer can show good evidence for such changes. The magnitudes of the forces for different velocities are to be determined from the specified values in direct proportion to the squared values of the different velocities. A moving wind load is to be applied as follows:

For trusses and arches—75 psf
For girders and beams—50 psf

---

[7] John M. Biggs, Saul Namyet, and Jiro Adachi, "Wind Loads on Girder Bridges," *Proc. ASCE*, Sep. No. 587 (January 1955).

[8] John M. Biggs, "Wind Loads on Truss Bridges," *Proc. ASCE*, Sep. No. 201 (July 1953).

The total load so calculated may not be less than 300 lb per linear foot in the plane of the loaded chord nor 150 lb per foot in the plane of the unloaded chord for truss spans nor less than 300 lb per linear foot for girder spans.

When wind loads are combined with other loads the AASHO permits some increase in allowable stresses. For the dead load plus full wind load combination the allowable stresses can be increased by 25 percent. When wind loads are considered to be applied at the same time as dead load plus all of the other live loads, only 30 percent of the wind load is considered applied and the allowable stresses can be increased by 25 percent; however, a wind load must be included in this combination and applied to the live load 6 ft above the deck and equalling 100 lb per linear foot.

14-19. LIVE LOADS FOR RAILWAY BRIDGES

Railway bridges are commonly analyzed for a series of loads devised by Theodore Cooper. His loads, referred to as E loadings, represent two locomotives followed by a line of freight cars. A series of concentrated loads is used for the locomotives, while a uniform load represents the freight cars. Cooper introduced his loading system in 1894; it was the so-called E-40 load, pictured in Fig. 14-17. The train is assumed to have

Fig. 14-17. E-40 Cooper loading.

a 40-k load on the driving axle of the engine. Since his system was introduced, the weights of trains have been increased considerably, until at the present time bridges are designed on the basis of loads in the vicinity of an E-72 loading; and the use of E-80 and E-90 loadings is not uncommon.

Various tables that are obtainable present detailed information pertaining to Cooper's loadings such as axle loads, moments, and shears. If information is available for one E loading, the information for any other E loading can be obtained by direct proportion. The axle loads of an E-75 are 75/40 those for an E-40; those for an E-60 are 60/72 of those for an E-72. Tables used in conjunction with the maximum criteria presented later in this chapter greatly reduce the computations.

Cooper's loadings do not accurately picture today's trains, but they are still in general use despite the availability of several more modern and more realistic loadings such as Dr. D. B. Steinman's M-60 loading.[9]

Impact. Some AREA impact formulas are given at the end of this paragraph. The values given, which are to be applied vertically at the top of rails, are for open-deck bridges. For ballasted-deck bridges 90 percent of these values are to be used. In these expressions S is the distance between centers of longitudinal beams, girders or trusses, or the length, in feet, between the supports of floorbeams or transverse girders; L is the length, in feet, center to center of supports for stringers, transverse floorbeams without stringers, longitudinal girders and trusses or the length of the longer adjacent supported stringers, longitudinal beam, girder or truss for impact in floorbeams, floorbeam hangers, subdiagonals of trusses, transverse girders, etc. For rolling equipment without hammer blow (diesels, electric locomotives, tenders alone, etc.):

For L less than 80 ft $\qquad \dfrac{100}{S} + 40 - \dfrac{3L^2}{1600}$

For L 80 ft or more $\qquad \dfrac{100}{S} + 16 + \dfrac{600}{L-30}$

The AREA also specifies impact percentages for steam locomotives with hammer blow and for members receiving load from more than one track.

Wind Loads. The wind loads specified by the 1969 AREA Specifications are handled quite similarly to those required by the AASHO. A moving wind force of 30 psf is to be applied to 1½ times the vertical projections of leeward trusses which are not shielded by the floor system. The total values so determined may not be less than 200 lb per linear foot for the loaded chord or flange nor 150 lb per linear foot on the unloaded chord or flange. In addition a wind load is to be applied to the train equal to 300 lb per linear foot on the one track and applied 8 ft above the rail.

The AREA makes one further requirement as it pertains to load combinations. Should stresses computed for a 50-psf load applied as described in the preceding paragraph plus dead load be in excess of those caused by the wind loads also described in the last paragraph plus all other loads (dead, live, impact, and centrifugal), the members will be designed for the larger stresses.

[9] *Trans. ASCE*, vol. 86 (1923), pp. 606–636.

chapter 15

COMPOSITE DESIGN

15-1. COMPOSITE CONSTRUCTION

When a concrete slab is supported by steel beams and there is no provision for shear transfer between the two the result is a noncomposite section. There is no doubt in noncomposite construction but that the load causes the slab to deflect along with the beam, with the result that some of the load is carried by the slab. Unless, however, there is a great deal of bond between the two (as would be the case where the steel beam is completely encased in the concrete, or where a system of mechanical shear connectors is provided) the load carried by the slab is small and may be neglected.

For many years steel beams and reinforced-concrete slabs were used together with no consideration being made for any composite effect. In recent years, however, it has been shown that a great strengthening effect can be obtained by tying the two together to act as a unit in resisting loads. Steel beams and concrete slabs joined together compositely can often support a one-third or even greater increase in load than could the steel beams alone in noncomposite action.

Composite construction for highway bridges was given the green light by the adoption of the 1944 AASHO Specifications which approved the method. Since about 1950 the use of composite bridge floors has rapidly increased until today they are commonplace all over the United States. In these bridges the longitudinal shears are transferred from the stringers to the reinforced concrete slab or deck with shear connectors (to be described in Sec. 15-6) causing the slab or deck to assist in carrying the bending moments. This type of section is shown in part (a) of Fig. 15-1.

The first approval for composite building floors was given by the 1952 AISC Specification and today they are rapidly becoming popular. These floors may either be encased in concrete as shown in part (b) of Fig. 15-1 or be nonencased with shear connectors as shown in part (c) of the figure. The larger percentage of composite building floors being built today are

372

(a) Composite bridge floor with shear connectors

(b) Encased section for building floors

(c) Building floors with shear connectors

FIG. 15-1

of the nonencased type. If the steel sections are encased in concrete the shear transfer is made by bond and friction between the beam and the concrete and by the shearing strength of the concrete along the dotted lines shown in part (b) of Fig. 15-1. If more shearing strength is required, some type of steel reinforcing is provided along the sections indicated with the dotted lines.

15-2. ADVANTAGES OF COMPOSITE CONSTRUCTION

The floor slab in composite construction acts not only as a slab for resisting the live loads but also as an integral part of the beam. It actually serves as a large cover plate for the upper flange of the steel beam, appreciably increasing the beam's strength.

A particular advantage of composite floors is that they take advantage of concrete's high compressive strength as compared to its cost by putting all or almost all of the slab in compression. At the same time a larger percentage of the steel is kept in tension (also advantageous)

Bridge on John F. Kennedy Expressway, Chicago, Ill. (*Robert McCullough, Chicago, Ill.*)

than is normally the case in steel-frame structures. The result is less steel tonnage required for the same loads and spans (or longer spans for the same sections). Composite sections have greater stiffnesses than noncomposite sections and they have smaller deflections—perhaps only 20 to 30 percent as large. Furthermore, tests have shown that the ability of a composite structure to take overload is decidedly greater than for a noncomposite structure.

A further advantage of composite construction is the possibility of having smaller overall floor depths—a fact of particular importance for tall buildings. Smaller floor depths permit reduced building heights with the consequent advantages of smaller costs for walls, plumbing, wiring, ducts, elevators, and foundations. Another important advantage available with reduced beam depths is a saving in fireproofing costs for the beams. A disadvantage for composite construction is the cost of furnishing and installing the shear connectors. This extra cost will usually exceed the cost reductions mentioned for short, lightly loaded spans.

15-3. DISCUSSION OF SHORING

After the steel beams are erected the concrete slab is placed on them. The formwork, wet concrete, and other construction loads must, therefore, be supported by the beams or by temporary shoring. Should no shoring be used, the steel beams must support all of these loads as well as their own weights. Most specifications say that after the concrete has gained 75 percent of its 28-day strength the section has become composite and all loads applied thereafter may be considered to be supported by the composite section. When shoring is used it supports the wet concrete and the other construction loads. It does not really support the weight of the steel beams unless they are given an initial upward deflection (probably impractical). When the shoring is removed (after the concrete gains at least 75 percent of its 28-day strength) the weight of the slab is transferred to the composite section, not just to the steel beams. The student can see that if shoring is used it will be possible to use lighter and thus cheaper steel beams. The question then arises, "Will the saving in steel cost be greater than the extra cost of shoring?" Probably the answer is "No." The usual decision is to use heavier steel beams and do without shoring for several reasons. These include the following:

1. Apart from reasons of economy, the use of shoring is a tricky operation, particularly where settlements of the shoring is possible, as is often the case in bridge construction.

2. Tests have shown that the ultimate strengths of composite sections of the same sizes are the same whether shoring was used or not. If lighter steel beams are selected for a particular span because shoring is used, the result is a smaller ultimate strength.

3. Another disadvantage of shoring is that after the concrete hardens and the shoring is removed the slab will participate in composite action in supporting the dead loads. The slab will be placed in compression by these long-term loads and will have substantial creep and shrinkage parallel to the beams. The result will be a great decrease in the stress in the slab with a corresponding increase in the steel stresses. The probable consequence is that most of the dead load will be supported by the steel beams anyway and composite action will really apply only to the live loads as though shoring had not been used. A common practice when shoring is used is to reduce the calculated effective area of the concrete (as described in Sec. 15-5).

15-4. EFFECTIVE FLANGE WIDTHS

The portion of the slab or flange which can be considered to participate in the beam action is controlled by the specifications. For buildings the AISC permits the same method of computing effective flange widths as is permitted by the ACI for reinforced concrete tee beams. Reference is made here to Fig. 15-2.

The maximum effective flange width permitted by the AISC can be determined by computing the following values and will equal the least value of b so obtained.

1. b not greater than one fourth of the span of the beam.

2. b' not greater than one-half of the clear distance to the adjacent beam.

FIG. 15-2

3. b' not greater than eight times the slab thickness.

Should the slab exist only on one side of the beam, the following requirements control.

1. b not greater than one-twelfth of beam span.

2. b' not greater than one-half of the clear distance to the adjacent beam.

3. b' not greater than six times the slab thickness.

The AASHO requirements for maximum permissible flange widths are slightly different. The maximum flange width may not exceed one-fourth of the beam span, the distance center-to-center of the beams, nor twelve times the slab thickness. Should the slab only exist on one side of the beam the width may not exceed one-twelfth of the beam span, one-half of the distance center-to-center of the beams, nor six times the slab thickness.

15-5. STRESS CALCULATIONS FOR COMPOSITE SECTIONS

For stress calculations the properties of a composite section are computed with the transformed area method. In this method the cross-sectional area of one of the two materials has to be replaced or transformed into an equivalent area of the other. For composite design it is customary to replace the concrete with an equivalent area of steel, whereas the reverse procedure is used in reinforced-concrete design.

In the transformed area procedure the concrete and steel are assumed to be bonded tightly together so that their strains will be the same at equal distances from the neutral axis. The unit stress in either material can then be said to equal its strain times its modulus of elasticity (ϵE_c for the concrete or ϵE_s for the steel). The unit stress in the steel is then $\epsilon E_s / \epsilon E_c = E_s / E_c$ times as great as the corresponding unit stress in the concrete. The E_s / E_c ratio is referred to as the modular ratio n; therefore, n square inches of concrete are required to resist the same total stress as 1 sq. in. of steel; and the cross-sectional area of the slab (A_c) is replaced with a transformed or equivalent area of steel equal to A_c / n.

Should the neutral axis fall in the slab the concrete below may not be considered to contribute to the moment of inertia (except for deflection calculations) as this concrete is assumed to be cracked. In the example problems of this chapter, M_D is the dead-load moment which must be supported by the steel beam alone, M_L is the live-load moment applied to the composite section and M_d is the dead-load moment applied to the composite section.

Examples 15-1 and 15-2 illustrate the stress calculations for unshored composite sections using the AISC and AASHO specifications. As indicated in the discussion of shoring, tests have shown that the ultimate strengths of composite sections are the same whether shoring is used or not. On this basis the AISC says that all loads are to be considered as being applied to the composite section regardless of the use or nonuse of shoring.

For composite sections with no temporary shoring the AISC gives a maximum allowable bottom-flange steel stress of about 0.82 F_y. This allowable value is for the situation where all of the moments (M_D, M_d, and M_L) are assumed to be applied to the steel beam alone. This allowable value is checked by means of the expression given at the end of this paragraph for S_{TR}, the section modulus of the transformed composite section referred to the tension flange. When temporary shoring is not used, the value of S_{TR} may not exceed the value determined by substitution in this expression in which S_s is the section modulus of the steel beam alone referred to its tension flange. In applying the formula it is to be remembered that the loads supported by the steel beam before the concrete hardens may not cause the allowable stresses in the beam to be exceeded. Notice that M_L in this expression is the moment caused by all loads (*dead or live*) which are applied after the concrete has reached 75 percent of its 28-day strength.

$$S_{TR} = \left(1.35 + 0.35\,\frac{M_L}{M_D}\right) S_s$$

Stresses are calculated in Example 15-1 for a composite section using the AISC Specification and in Example 15-2 for another section in accordance with the AASHO requirements. In this latter example it is necessary to take into account the effect of creep in the concrete as it applies to the long-term loads. For the tension flange of the steel beam there will be stress due to M_D acting on the steel section alone, plus stress due to M_d acting on the composite section ($n = 30$), plus stress due to M_L acting on the composite section ($n = 10$). For the concrete no stress is caused by M_D, so the stress is caused by M_d acting on the composite section ($n = 30$), plus the effect of M_L acting on the composite section ($n = 10$).

EXAMPLE 15-1. Determine the stresses for the composite beam section shown in Fig. 15-3 according to the AISC Specification. Adequate shear connectors

FIG. 15-3

are assumed to be present and no shoring is used. Assume simple spans and the following data:

$$LL = 100 \text{ psf}$$

$$\text{Partition weight} = 18 \text{ psf}$$

$$4 \text{ in. concrete slab weighs } 50 \text{ psf}$$

$$f_c' = 3,000 \text{ psi}$$

$$f_c = 1,350 \text{ psi}$$

$$n = 9$$

$$\underline{\text{A36 steel}}$$

Solution:

Calculation of Moments

Loads applied before concrete hardens (75 percent of 28-day strength):

$$\text{Slab} = (8) (50) \qquad = 400 \text{ lb/ft}$$

$$\text{Beam} \qquad\qquad = 31 \text{ lb/ft}$$

$$\text{Total} \qquad\qquad = \overline{431 \text{ lb/ft}}$$

$$M_D = \frac{(0.431)(27)^2}{8} = 39.3 \text{ ft-k}$$

Loads applied after concrete hardens:

$$\text{Partitions} = (8)(18) \quad = 144 \text{ lb/ft}$$

$$\text{LL} \quad = (8)\ (100) = 800\ \text{lb/ft}$$

$$\text{Total} \quad = \quad \overline{944\ \text{lb/ft}}$$

$$M_L = \frac{(0.944)\ (27)^2}{8} = 85.9\ \text{ft-k}$$

$$M_T = 39.3 + 85.9 \quad = 125.2\ \text{ft-k}$$

Effective Width of Flange

(1) $b = (\tfrac{1}{4})\ (27 \times 12)$ $= 81$ in.

(2) $b' = (\tfrac{1}{2})\ (8 \times 12 - 5.525) = 45.24$ in.

     $b = (2)\ (45.24) + 5.525$ $= 96$ in.

(3) $b' = (8)\ (4)$ $= 32$ in.

     $b = (2)\ (32) + 5.525$ $= 69.525$ in.   (controls)

Properties of Composite Section

(Reference made here to Fig. 15-4)

$\dfrac{69.52''}{9} = 7.72''$

Transformed Area of Concrete Slab

4"

N.A.

15.84"

y_b

W 16 X 31

Fig. 15-4

$$A = 9.13 + (4)\ (7.72) = 40.01\ \text{sq in.}$$

$$y_b = \frac{(9.13)\ (7.92) + (30.88)\ (17.84)}{40.01} = 15.57\ \text{in.}$$

$$I = 374 + (9.12)\ (7.65)^2 + (\tfrac{1}{12})\ (7.72)\ (4)^3 + (30.88)\ (2.27)^2$$

$$= 1{,}106.6\ \text{in.}^4$$

Review of Stresses

Before concrete hardens:

$$f_s = \frac{(12)\ (39.3)\ (7.92)}{374} = 10.00\ \text{ksi} < 24\ \text{ksi} \qquad \text{(OK)}$$

$$S_{TR} = \frac{1,106.6}{15.57} = 71.1 \text{ in.}^3$$

Maximum permissible S_{TR} by AISC is

$$\left(1.35 + 0.35 \times \frac{85.9}{39.3}\right) 47.2 = 99.4 > 71.1 \qquad \text{(OK)}$$

After concrete hardens:

$$f_c = \frac{(12)\ (125.2)\ (4.27)}{(9)\ (1,106.6)} = 0.646 \text{ ksi} < 1.35 \text{ ksi} \qquad \text{(OK)}$$

$$f_s = \frac{(12)\ (125.2)\ (15.57)}{1,106.6} = 21.1 \text{ ksi} < 24 \text{ ksi} \qquad \text{(OK)}$$

EXAMPLE 15-2. Calculate the stresses in the composite section shown in Fig. 15-5 using the AASHO Specifications. Adequate shear connectors are as-

FIG. 15-5

sumed to be present and no shoring is used. Assume simple spans and the following data:

$$M_D = 300 \text{ ft-k}$$

$$M_d = 100 \text{ ft-k (due to curbs, railing, surface treatment, etc.)}$$

$$M_L = 450 \text{ ft-k}$$

$$M_T = 850 \text{ ft-k}$$

$$f_s = 18 \text{ ksi}$$

$$f_c = 1.2 \text{ ksi}$$

$$n = 10$$

Solution:

Properties of Composite Section

For $n = 10$:

$A = (^{66}\!/_{10})\ (6) + 41.6 = 81.2\ \text{sq in.}$

$y_b = \dfrac{(41.6)\ (16.66) + (39.6)\ (36.31)}{81.2} = 26.30\ \text{in.}$

$I = 7{,}460 + (41.6)\ (9.64)^2 + (^1\!/_{12})\ (6.6)\ (6)^3 + (39.6)\ (10.01)^2$

$= 15{,}390\ \text{in.}^4$

For $n = 30$:

$A = (^{66}\!/_{30})\ (6) + 41.60 = 54.8\ \text{sq in.}$

$y_b = \dfrac{(41.6)\ (16.66) + (13.2)\ (36.31)}{54.8} = 21.40\ \text{in.}$

$I = 7{,}460 + (41.6)\ (4.74)^2 + (^1\!/_{12})\ (2.2)\ (6)^3 + (13.2)\ (14.91)^2$

$= 11{,}340\ \text{in.}^4$

Final Stresses

$f_c = \dfrac{(12)\ (450)\ (13.01)}{(15{,}390)\ (10)} + \dfrac{(12)\ (100)\ (17.91)}{(11{,}340)\ (30)} = 0.516\ \text{ksi} < 1.2\ \text{ksi (OK)}$

$f_s = \dfrac{(12)\ (300)\ (16.66)}{7{,}460} + \dfrac{(12)\ (450)\ (26.30)}{15{,}390} + \dfrac{(12)\ (100)\ (21.40)}{11{,}340}$

$= 19.57\ \text{ksi} > 18.00\ \text{ksi}$ (N.G.)

15-6. SHEAR TRANSFER

The concrete slabs may rest directly on top of the steel beams or the beams may be completely encased in concrete for fireproofing purposes. The longitudinal shear can be transferred between the two by bond and shear and possibly some type of shear reinforcing if needed when the beams are encased. When not encased, mechanical connectors must transfer the load. Fireproofing is not necessary for bridges and the slab is placed on top of the steel beams. Bridges are subject to heavy impactive loads and the bond between the beams and the deck, which is easily broken, is considered negligible. For this reason shear connectors are designed to resist all of the shear between bridge slabs and beams.

Various types of shear connectors have been tried including spiral bars, channels, zees, angles, and studs. Several of these types of connectors are shown in Fig. 15-6. Economic considerations have usually led to the use of round studs welded to the top flanges of the beams. These studs are available in diameters from $\frac{1}{2}$ to 1 in. and in lengths from 2 to 8 in. but the most commonly used sizes are $\frac{3}{4}$ or $\frac{7}{8}$ in. and 2 to 4 in. in length. They actually consist of rounded steel bars welded on one end to the steel beams. The other end is upset to prevent vertical separa-

Fɪɢ. 15-6. Shear connectors.

tion of the slab from the beam. These studs can be quickly attached to the steel beams with stud-welding guns by semiskilled workers.[1]

Shop installation of shear connectors is initially more economical but there is a growing tendency to use field installation. There are two major reasons for this trend: the connectors may easily be damaged during transportation and setting of the beams, and they serve as a hindrance to the workmen walking along the top flanges during the early phases of construction.

AISC Requirements. The shear values permitted by the AISC for buildings for various types of connectors are presented in Table 15-1. This table is a reproduction of Table 1.11.4 from the AISC Specification. The values given for q are the ultimate strengths of the connectors reduced by a factor of 2.5 to obtain working load values.

The AISC requires that shear connectors have at least 1 in. of concrete cover in all directions. In addition unless they are located directly

[1] Ivan M. Viest, R. S. Fountain, and R. C. Singleton, *Composite Construction In Steel and Concrete* (New York: McGraw-Hill Book Company, Inc., 1958), pp. 50–51.

TABLE 15-1

Connector	Allowable Horizontal Shear Load (q) (kips) (Applicable only to concrete made with ASTM C33 aggregates)		
	f'_c (kips per square in.)		
	3.0	3.5	4.0
½″ diam. × 2″ hooked or headed stud	5.1	5.5	5.9
⅝″ diam. × 2½″ hooked or headed stud	8.0	8.6	9.2
¾″ diam. × 3″ hooked or headed stud	11.5	12.5	13.3
⅞″ diam. × 3½″ hooked or headed stud	15.6	16.8	18.0
3″ channel, 4.1 lb.	4.3w	4.7w	5.0w
4″ channel, 5.4 lb.	4.6w	5.0w	5.3w
5″ channel, 6.7 lb.	4.9w	5.3w	5.6w

w = length of channel in inches.

over the web their diameters shall not be greater than 2.5 times the flange thickness to which they are welded. Tests have shown if this rule is not met they will tend to tear out before their full shear-resisting capacity is reached.

Shear connectors must be capable of resisting both horizontal and vertical movement because there is a tendency for the slab and beam to

Channel-section shear connectors, Grand Rapids, Mich. (*The Lincoln Electric Company.*)

separate vertically as well as to slip horizontally. Most designers feel that because of the tendency to slip vertically the longitudinal spacing of connectors should not exceed approximately 2 ft. The upset heads of the common studs help to prevent vertical separation.

Careful attention should be given to the AISC method of determining the horizontal shear to be taken by the connectors. Rather than basing their designs on the shear computed by the VQ/I formula, shear is estimated at ultimate load conditions. When a composite beam is being tested, failure will probably occur with a crushing of the concrete. At that time it seems reasonable to assume that the concrete and steel have both reached a plastic stress condition.

For this discussion reference is made to Fig. 15-7. Should the neutral axis fall in the slab the maximum horizontal shear (or horizontal force

Fig. 15-7

on the plane between the concrete and the steel) is said to be $A_s F_y$; and if the neutral axis is in the steel section the maximum horizontal shear is considered to equal $0.85 f'_c A_c$. (For the student unfamiliar with the ultimate design theory for reinforced concrete the average stress at failure on the compression side of a concrete beam is usually assumed to be $0.85 f'_c$.)

From this information, expressions for V_h (the shear to be taken by the connectors) are written below. These values are divided by 2 to estimate conditions at working loads. The AISC says that the two expressions for V_h are to be solved and the smaller value used. V_h is the total shear to be resisted between the point of maximum positive moment in a simple span and the end of the beam. (For continuous beams, the wording would be "between the point of maximum positive moment and the point of contraflexure.") The number of shear connectors required on each side of the point of maximum positive moment can be determined by dividing V_h by q the strength of one connector of the size and type being used. As previously described the AISC permits a uniform spacing of connectors.

$$V_h = \frac{0.85\ f_c' A_c}{2}$$

$$V_h = \frac{A_s F_y}{2}$$

$$\text{Number of connectors} = \frac{V_h}{q}$$

Shear connectors are relatively flexible with the result that there is some slippage between the steel girders and the concrete slabs. Since slip does occur there is a redistribution of load between the connectors similar to that discussed for riveted connections in Sec. 9-8. Because of this redistribution of unequal connector loads the AISC permits, for the usual building with its design based on uniform loads, a uniform spacing of connectors between the points of maximum positive moment and the points of zero moment. However, for concentrated loads the AISC says that the number of connectors between the concentrated load and the nearest point of zero moment shall not be less than determined by the following formula:

$$N_2 = \frac{N_1\left(\dfrac{M\beta}{M_{max}} - 1\right)}{\beta - 1} \qquad \text{(AISC Formula 1.11-6)}$$

where M = moment (less than the maximum moment) at a concentrated load point

N_1 = number of connectors required between point of maximum moment and point of zero moment, determined by the relationship V_h/q or V'_h/q, as applicable

$\beta = \dfrac{S_{tr}}{S_s}$ or $\dfrac{S_{eff}}{S_s}$ as applicable

For continuous beams connectors may be spaced uniformly between the points of maximum negative moment and the points of zero moment says the AISC.

The resisting moment of a steel beam and concrete slab increases directly with the number of shear connectors used up to a maximum value when the required number of connectors for full composite action is used. At times it may not be feasible to use shear connectors, at other times it may be feasible or necessary to use only a part of the total number required thus providing only partial composite action. For this reason the AISC permits the use of full composite action and of partial composite action.[2]

For cases where the number of shear connectors required for full composite action is not used the AISC permits an effective section modulus to be determined by the following expression:

$$S_{eff} = S_s + \frac{V'_h}{V_h} (S_{tr} - S_s)$$

In this expression V_h is as previously defined and V'_h is the total shear developed between the steel and the concrete on each side of the point of maximum moment and equals q times the number of connectors furnished between the point of maximum moment and the nearest zero moment point.

AASHO Requirements. The AASHO requirements for the design of shear connectors are more conservative than those permitted for buildings by the AISC due to the nature of the highly impactive bridge loadings. The AASHO says that there shall be a minimum of 2 in. of concrete over the tops of shear connectors and the connectors must penetrate a minimum of 2 in. up from the bottom of the slab.

A maximum pitch of 24 in. is permitted except over the interior supports of continuous beams where it may be desirable to avoid placing them at points where tensile stresses are high in the flanges of the steel girders. The required number of connectors is still the same even if the pitch is modified in the negative moment region.

The AASHO says that shear connectors shall be designed for (a) Fatigue, and checked for (b) Ultimate Strength, and they may be spaced at regular or variable intervals.

(a) *Fatigue.* The shearing force to be taken per inch is to be calculated by the VQ/I expression where I is the regular transformed moment of inertia in the positive moment region, and in the negative moment region is the I of the steel girder including or excluding the steel reinforcing bars depending on whether sufficient shear connectors are used.

The required pitch of the connectors for fatigue at a particular cross-section is determined by dividing the shear to be taken per inch by the strength of the connectors used at one cross-section.

The AASHO allowable shear (lbs) for connectors, Z_r, is determined from the expressions to follow:

---

[2] R. G. Slutter and G. C. Driscoll, "Flexural Strength of Steel-Concrete Composite Beams" *Proc. ASCE*, vol 91, no. ST2 (April 1965), pp. 71–99.

(1) Channels:

$$Z_r = Bw$$

where w = length of channel shear connector measured in in. transverse to the steel girder

B = 4,000 for 100,000 cycles of loading, 3,000 for 500,000 cycles, 2,400 for 2,000,000 cycles

(2) Welded studs when H/d is equal to or greater than 4:

$$Z_r = \alpha\, d^2$$

where H = height of stud in in.

d = diameter of stud in in.

α = 13,000 for 100,000 cycles, 10,600 for 500,000 cycles, 7,850 for 2,000,000 cycles

Sec. 1.7.3 of the AASHO Specifications specifies the number of cycles of maximum stress to be considered for design depending on the types of highways, spans, etc.

(b) *Ultimate Strength.* After the connectors are designed for fatigue the AASHO says their number, N, used between the points of maximum moment and the end points or dead load points of contraflexure or between points of maximum negative moment and dead load points of contraflexure must be checked for ultimate strength by the expression to follow:

$$N = \frac{P}{\phi S_u}$$

where S_u = the ultimate strength of 1 shear connector in lbs.

ϕ = a reduction factor = 0.85

P = the force in the slab defined as P_1, P_2 or P_3 in the following:

For maximum positive moment points

$$P_1 = A_s F_y$$
$$P_2 = 0.85\, f'_c\, bc \qquad \text{or} \qquad 0.85\, f'_c A_c$$

For maximum negative moment points

$$P_3 = A_s^r F_y^r$$

where A_s^r = total area of longitudinal reinforcing bars at interior support within effective flange width of slab

F_y^r = yield stress of reinforcing steel

The AASHO ultimate strength value for a shear connector (S_u) is to be determined from the expressions to follow where t is the thickness of the web of the channel shear connector in in.

For channels

$$S_u = 550 \left(h + \frac{t}{2} \right) w \sqrt{f'_c}$$

For welded studs $(H/d \geqq 4)$

$$S_u = 930 \, d^2 \sqrt{f'_c}$$

Should the longitudinal reinforcing bars in negative moment regions not be used in computing section properties the AASHO presents another expression for computing the number of connectors to be used at the points of contraflexure.

Design of shear connectors in accordance with the AISC Specification is illustrated in Example 15-3 while AASHO spacing requirements are illustrated in Example 15-7.

15-7. PROPORTIONING COMPOSITE SECTIONS

Composite construction is of particular advantage economically when loads are heavy, spans are long, and beams are spaced at fairly large intervals. For steel-building frames, composite construction is economical for spans varying roughly from 25 to 50 ft, with particular advantage in the longer spans. For bridges, simple spans have been economically constructed up to approximately 120 ft and continuous spans 50 or 60 ft longer. Composite bridges are generally economical for simple spans greater than about 40 ft and for continuous spans greater than about 60 ft.

Usually cover plates are welded to the bottom flanges of steel beams with improved economy. The students can see that with the slab acting as part of the beam there is a very large compressive area available and by adding cover plates to the tensile flange a little better balance is obtained.

For best economy, thicker slabs and cover-plated beams are usually of advantage. An important point to realize is that the major cost of cover plates regardless of their size is in fabrication. The result is that heavy cover plates do not cost proportionately more than thin ones; it is logical, therefore, to use large cover plates or none at all from an economical standpoint. In fact the AISC Manual says that the use of a cover plate with an area of less than one-half that of the steel section is seldom justified. (See AISC Manual page 2-137.) Cover plates are not usually economical when light-weight concrete is used because the high modular ratios of such concrete greatly reduce the effective concrete areas.

In tall buildings where headroom is a problem it is desirable to use the minimum overall floor thickness possible. For buildings, minimum depth-span ratios of approximately 1/24 are recommended if the loads are fairly static and 1/20 if the loads are of such a nature as to cause appreciable vibration. The thicknesses of the floor slabs are known (from the concrete design) and the depths of the steel beams can be fairly well estimated from these ratios. For bridges the AASHO gives a desirable minimum ratio of 1/25 for total depth-to-span and 1/30 for steel-beam depth alone to span. Should shallower sections be used than these there is the usual requirement that the resulting deflections may not exceed those developed had the recommended ratios been followed.

Perhaps the greatest difficulty in composite design has been the selection of economical beam sizes as a lengthy trial-and-error process has been involved. In the past few years, however, a great deal of data has been published which appreciably abbreviates the problem. For example, the AISC Manual includes a set of tables for selecting sizes. These tables developed for building floors are given for 3,000 psi concrete, 36 and 50 ksi steels, and for 4, 4½, 5, and 5½ in. slabs.

An excellent method of estimating steel beam sizes for building or bridge composite floors is presented on page 104 of *Advanced Design In Structural Steel* by John E. Lothers (Prentice-Hall, Inc., 1960). Lothers suggests that the steel beams be designed as though they alone have to support all of the loads but using a higher allowable stress to account for the composite action. He presents a table of estimated allowable steel stress increases for varying values of n. The increases are as follows: 20 percent for $n = 15$, 24 percent for $n = 12$, 28 percent for $n = 10$, 33 percent for $n = 8$, and 37 percent for $n = 6$. Increases for n values in between the ones given are roughly proportional. In applying these values it must be remembered that the usual allowable steel stresses may not be exceeded by M_D alone. This information provides a very good initial trial section but another trial or two may still be necessary before a final selection is made.

Other information is available from several sources. The previously mentioned book by Viest, Fountain, and Singleton gives a great deal of information on the subject including design procedures, curves and tables of data. Additional data is contained in a book entitled *Properties of Composite Sections for Bridges and Buildings* published by the Bethlehem Steel Company (Bethlehem, Pa., 1962). Another excellent reference is Chaps. 3 and 11 and the accompanying nomograph of *USS Highway Structures Design Handbook* published by the United States Steel Corporation (Pittsburgh, Pa.).

Example 15-3 illustrates the design of a composite section with a cover plate on the bottom flange of the steel beam. The proportions of the section used in the problem were selected from the tables given in the Steel Handbook.

EXAMPLE 15-3. Design a composite section using A36 steel and the AISC Specification for the situation shown in Fig. 15-8. No shoring is to be used and

FIG. 15-8

simple spans are assumed. The following data are supplied:

$$\text{LL} = 120 \text{ psf}$$

$$\text{Ceiling weight} = 10 \text{ psf}$$

$$\text{Partition weight} = 15 \text{ psf}$$

$$\text{4-in. concrete slab} = 50 \text{ psf}$$

$$f'_c = 3,000 \text{ psi}$$

$$f_c = 1,350 \text{ psi}$$

$$n = 9$$

$$\underline{\text{A36 steel}}$$

Solution:

Calculation of Moments

Loads applied before concrete hardens:

$$\text{Slab} = (9)\ (50) \qquad = 450 \text{ lb/ft}$$

$$\text{Assumed beam weight} = \ \ 31 \text{ lb/ft}$$

$$\text{Total} \qquad\qquad = \overline{481} \text{ lb/ft}$$

$$M_D = \frac{(0.481)\ (27)^2}{8} = 43.8 \text{ ft-k}$$

Loads applied after concrete hardens:

$$\text{Ceiling} = (9)\,(10) = 90 \text{ lb/ft}$$
$$\text{Partitions} = (9)\,(15) = 135 \text{ lb/ft}$$
$$\text{LL} = (9)\,(120) = 1{,}080 \text{ lb/ft}$$
$$\text{Total} = \overline{1{,}305} \text{ lb/ft}$$

$$M_L = \frac{(1.305)\,(27)^2}{8} = 119 \text{ ft-k}$$

$$M_T = M_D + M_L = 162.8 \text{ ft-k}$$

$$\text{Required } S_b = \frac{(12)\,(162.8)}{24} = 81.4 \text{ in.}^3$$

Selection of trial section from Steel Handbook by interpolation

Try W 14 $\times$22 with $\frac{5}{8} \times 4$ cover PL

Properties of W 14$\times$ 22 with $\frac{5}{8} \times$ 4-in. cover PL

$$A = 6.49 + 2.50 = 8.99 \text{ sq in.}$$

$$y_b = \frac{(6.49)\,(7.48) + (2.5)\,(0.31)}{8.99} = 5.50$$

$$I = 198 + (6.49)\,(1.98)^2 + (2.5)\,(5.19)^2 = 291 \text{ in.}^4$$

$$S_s = \frac{291}{5.5} = 52.9 \text{ in.}^3$$

Properties of Composite Section from Steel Handbook by interpolation

$$y_b = 13.89 \text{ in.}$$
$$b = \text{effective width of flange} = 69.00 \text{ in.}$$
$$I_{TR} = 1{,}147 \text{ in.}^4$$
$$S_{TR} = 82.9 \text{ in.}^3 \text{ for tension flange}$$
$$S_{TR} = 258 \text{ in.}^3 \text{ for concrete flange}$$

Review of Section

Before concrete hardens:

$$f_s = \frac{(12)\,(43.8)\,(8.84)}{291} = 15.95 \text{ ksi} < 24 \text{ ksi} \qquad \text{(OK)}$$

Maximum permissible S_{TR} by AISC is

$$\left(1.35 + 0.35 \times \frac{119}{43.8}\right) 52.9 = 121.8 \text{ in.}^3 > 82.9 \text{ in.}^3 \qquad \text{(OK)}$$

After concrete hardens:

$$f_s = \frac{(12)\ (162.8)}{82.9} = 23.6 \text{ ksi} < 24.0 \text{ ksi} \qquad \text{(OK)}$$

$$f_c = \frac{(12)\ (162.8)}{(9)\ (258)} = 0.84 \text{ ksi} < 1.35 \text{ ksi} \qquad \text{(OK)}$$

Design of Shear Connectors

$$V_h = \frac{0.85\ f'_c\ A_c}{2} = \frac{(0.85)\ (3{,}000)\ (4 \times 69.00)}{2} = 352 \text{ k}$$

$$V_h = \frac{A_s F_y}{2} = \frac{(8.99)\ (36)}{2} = 162 \text{ k} \qquad \text{(controls)}$$

Assuming the $\tfrac{3}{4} \times 3$-in. headed stud which can resist 11.5 k (see Table 15-1),

$$\text{Number required} = \frac{162}{11.5} = 14.1 \text{ each side of } \textcent$$

Use 15 connectors on each side of $\textcent$ evenly spaced

The cover plate on the bottom flange of the steel beam is needed only for the sections of the span where the moment is largest. When the moment decreases to a value equal to the resisting moment of the slab and steel shape above, the cover plate can theoretically be cut off. The AISC and most other specifications state, however, that a cover plate should be extended some distance beyond its theoretical point of cutoff. The distance is that required for the connectors (rivets, welds, or bolts) to develop or transfer the portion of the flexural stresses taken by the plate at the theoretical point of cutoff. Example 15-4 illustrates the calculations required for determining cover-plate lengths.

Particular attention should be given to the design of the intermittent welds connecting the cover plate to the W shape. The student should be able to follow this design by reading the paragraph numbers referred to in the AISC Specification.

EXAMPLE 15-4. Determine the required length of the cover plate for the section designed in Example 15-3 if $\tfrac{1}{4}$-in. fillet welds, E70 electrodes, and the AISC Specification are used.

Solution: From AISC Manual:

$$y_b = 13.89 \text{ in.}$$

$$I = 1{,}147 \text{ in.}^4$$

S_{TR} for tension flange for section with cover PL $= 82.9$ in.^{3}

S_{TR} for section without cover PL $= 46.4$ in.^{3} (from AISC Manual)

Resisting moments:

M for section with cover PL $= \dfrac{(24)\ (82.9)}{12} = 165.8$ ft-k

M for section without cover PL $= \dfrac{(24)\ (46.4)}{12} = 92.8$ ft-k

Theoretical point of cutoff (see Fig. 15-9)

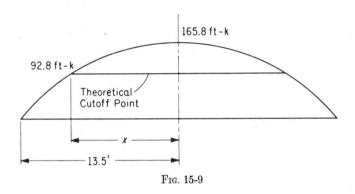

165.8 ft-k

92.8 ft-k

Theoretical Cutoff Point

x

13.5'

Fɪɢ. 15-9

For a uniformly loaded section with its parabolic moment diagram, the following expression can be written:

$$\frac{x^2}{(L/2)^2} = \frac{165.8-92.8}{165.8}$$

$$x = \sqrt{\frac{(13.5)^2\ (73.0)}{165.8}}$$

$$= 8.96 \text{ ft}$$

Total stress in plate at theoretical point of cutoff:

Total stress $\quad=$ average stress $\times$ PL area

Average stress $= \dfrac{(12)\ (92.8)\ (13.58)}{114.7} = 13.15$ ksi

Total stress $\quad= (13.15)\ (2.5) = 32.9$ k

Length of weld required:

Strength of $\frac14$ fillet weld $= 3.7$ k/in.

$L_{\text{req.}} = \dfrac{32.9}{3.7} = 8.86$ in

Use ¼-in. fillet welds on end of plate and for 8 in. on each side to conform to par. 1.10.4 of the AISC.

Total cover PL length = (2) (8.96 ft) + (2) (8 in.) = 19 ft 4 in.

Intermediate cover-plate welds:

Minimum length of intermittent welds (par. 1.17.7 AISC) = (4) (¼) = 1 in.

V at theoretical point of cutoff = (1.786) (13.5 − 4.54) = 16.0 k

$\dfrac{12\,Q}{I}$ (from Steel Handbook) = 0.34 by interpolation

$$v = \frac{VQ}{I} = \frac{(16.0)\,(0.34)}{12} = 0.453 \text{ k/in.}$$

Spacing of welds = $\dfrac{(1.5)\,(2)\,(3.7)}{0.453}$ = 24.5 in. c.-to-c.

Maximum spacing permitted (par. 1.18.3.1 AISC) = 24 t_f or 12 in. = (24) (0.34) = 8.16 in.

Use 8-in. spacing

15-8. DESIGN OF ENCASED SECTIONS

For fireproofing purposes the steel beams in building floors may be completely encased in concrete. Under certain conditions the horizontal shears between the slabs and beams can be considered to be transferred by natural bond and friction between the two. The AISC says that for this transfer to be permissible the encasing concrete must be placed integrally with the slab concrete and must cover the steel by at least 2 in. on the sides and bottom (or soffit). It is further required that the top of the steel section be at least 1½ in. below the top of the slab and 2 in. above the bottom of the slab. Finally, the encasing concrete must have adequate mesh or other reinforcing for its full depth and across the soffit of the beam.

The AISC says that encased beams with no shoring shall be able to resist M_D and in conjunction with the slab shall be able to resist $M_D + M_d + M_L$ without a steel stress exceeding 0.66 F_y. An alternative design method is permitted which says that the steel beam alone must be able to resist all moments without a steel stress exceeding 0.76 F_y. This value might be used where a reduction in calculations is desired. The higher allowable stress recognizes the fact that composite action permits the section to support more load than the steel beam could alone.

Should this latter method be used it is unnecessary to compute the properties of the composite section.

The critical sections for resistance to longitudinal shear in an encased beam are shown in Fig. 15-10. The total resistance to the longitudinal

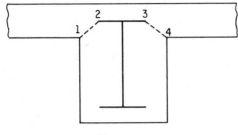

FIG. 15-10

shear can be estimated to equal the bond along the top of the steel shape (line 2–3 in the figure) plus the shearing resistance of the concrete along lines 1–2 and 3–4.

A typical value used for the allowable bond between the steel and concrete is $0.03\ f'_c$ while a common allowable shear in the concrete as along sections 1–2 and 3–4 is $0.12\ f'_c$. (A much smaller shear allowable is used in Example 15-5.) Should the longitudinal shear be greater than the sum of the shearing and bond resistance along the sections mentioned, some type of reinforcing will be necessary. The usual types of shear connectors on top of the beam flange will probably not be of much value because relatively large deformations will probably have to occur before much load can be applied to the connectors. By the time that much deformation occurs the natural bond between the steel and concrete will probably have broken. Some type of shear reinforcing placed along lines 1–2 and 3–4 will probably be the most effective method of increasing the shearing resistance. The longitudinal shear will have to be extremely large to require this shear reinforcing.

Example 15-5 illustrates the calculations involved in reviewing the design of an encased section. Notice in this problem that since no shoring is used the only longitudinal shear to be resisted is that produced by the loads applied after the concrete hardens. The ultimate-strength theory is today considered not to apply to these encased sections due to the lack of shear connectors, and longitudinal shears are computed by the familiar VQ/I expression.

Example 15-5. Using the AISC Specification review the encased beam section shown in Fig. 15-11 for longitudinal shear. No shoring is used and the following data are assumed:

Fig. 15-11

Allowable bond = 90 psi

Allowable shear = 180 psi

LL maximum external shear = 22 k

Effective flange width = 60 in.

$n = 9$

Solution:

Calculated Properties of Composite Section

Neglecting concrete area below flange,

$$A = 13.3 + \frac{(4)\,(60)}{9} = 39.96 \text{ sq in.}$$

$$y_b = \frac{(13.3)\,(10.44) + (26.66)\,(18)}{39.96} = 15.50 \text{ in.}$$

$$I = 584 + (13.3)\,(5.06)^2 + (\tfrac{1}{12})\,(\tfrac{60}{9})\,(4)^3 + (26.66)\,(2.5)^2$$
$$= 1{,}125 \text{ in.}^4$$

Q for area above section 1–2–3–4 in Fig. 15-12,

Fig. 15-12

$$Q = \tfrac{1}{9}\,[(4)(60)(2.5) - (7.04 \times 2.50)(1.75) - (2)(\tfrac{1}{2} \times 2.48 \times 2.5)(1.33)]$$
$$= 62.8 \text{ in.}^3$$

Checking Longitudinal Shear

$$v = \frac{VQ}{I} = \frac{(22,000)\,(62.8)}{1,125} = 1,230 \text{ lb/in.}$$

Allowable bond	$= (7.04)\,(90)$	$= 634 \text{ lb/in.}$
Allowable shear	$= (2)\,(3.52)\,(180)$	$= 1,270 \text{ lb/in.}$
Total shear resistance $=$		$\overline{1,904 \text{ lb/in.}} > 1,230 \text{ lb/in.}$

(OK)

For buildings continuous composite construction with encased sections is permissible. For continuous construction the positive moments are handled exactly as has been illustrated by the preceding examples. For negative moments, however, the transformed section is taken as shown in Fig. 15-13. The cross hatched area represents the concrete in

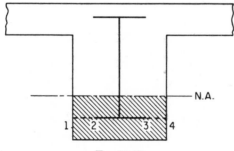

Fig. 15-13

compression and all concrete on the tensile side of the neutral axis (that is above the axis) is neglected. Notice also the fact that the resistance to longitudinal shear is provided along line 1–2–3–4 in the figure. Example 15-6 illustrates the review of a composite section for negative moment.

EXAMPLE 15-6. For the composite section shown in Fig. 15-14 and previously considered in Example 15-5 determine the bending stresses for negative moments of $M_D = 50$ ft-k and $M_L = 65$ ft-k assuming no shoring is used. If the maximum live load shear is 32 k, determine if extra shear reinforcing is needed in the negative moment region of the beam. Other data are the same as for Example 15-5.

Solution: Properties of section:

$$(1.33\,y_b)\left(\frac{y_b}{2}\right) = (13.3)\,(10.44 - y_b)$$

Fig. 15-14

where 10.44 is the distance from soffit to c.g. of **WF**.

$$y_b = 7.55 \text{ in.}$$

$$I_{TR} = 584 + (13.3)(2.89)^2 + (\tfrac{1}{3})(1.33)(7.55)^3 = 884 \text{ in.}^4$$

Review of Stresses

Before concrete hardens:

$$f_s = \frac{(12)(50)(8.06)}{584} = 8.28 \text{ ksi} < 24.0 \text{ ksi} \qquad \text{(OK)}$$

After concrete hardens:

$$f_c = \frac{(12)(115)(7.55)}{(9)(884)} = 1.31 \text{ ksi} < 1.35 \text{ ksi} \qquad \text{(OK)}$$

$$f_s = \frac{(12)(115)(10.95)}{884} = 17.1 \text{ ksi} < 24.0 \text{ ksi} \qquad \text{(OK)}$$

Check Shear

$$V = 32 \text{ k}$$

$$Q = (1.33)(2.38)\left(7.55 - \frac{2.38}{2}\right) = 20.2$$

$$v = \frac{VQ}{I} = \frac{(32,000)(20.2)}{884} = 732 \text{ lb/in.}$$

Allowable bond   = (7.04)(90)   =   634 lb/in.

Allowable shear   = (2)(2.48)(180) =   894 lb/in.

Total shear resistance   = 1,528 lb/in. > 732 lb/in. (OK)

15-9. DESIGN OF COMPOSITE SECTIONS USING AASHO SPECIFICATIONS

The AISC Specification for composite sections does not include cases where there are heavy moving loads with large vibrations and impact. Should loads of this nature be applied to a building floor, the designer might decide to use the AASHO Specifications. He might, however, reasonably decide to use higher allowable design stresses in both the steel beams and the shear connectors for his building than are permitted by the conservative AASHO.

There is little possibility of vertical separation between the slabs and steel beams in the usual building floor, but in bridges the heavy moving loads with their large impact will probably break the bond if shear connectors are not used. For this reason the only shear resistance permitted by the AASHO is to be provided by specifically designed shear connectors regardless of the arrangement of the beams and slabs.

Frequently a designer will not consider composite action for continuous bridge stringers but will in all probability use shear connectors in the negative-moment range because they give greater stiffness and prevent vertical separation and horizontal slipping between the slabs and stringers. Actually the AASHO says that for continuous spans the concrete on the tension side should be considered cracked and that if the

Continuous-welded plate girders in Henry-Jefferson Co., Iowa.
(*The Lincoln Electric Company.*)

reinforcing steel there not be used in computing the section, it will be unnecessary to use shear connectors.

Example 15-7 illustrates the design of a composite section using the AASHO Specifications. In bridge construction the top flange of the steel beam is usually encased in a concrete haunch as shown in Fig. 15-15.

FIG. 15-15

For simplicity, the effect of the haunch is not usually included in computing the properties of the composite sections. In this example fictitious values for maximum external shears applied to the composite section are assumed at three sections. These values are used to illustrate the design of shear connectors in accordance with AASHO requirements.

EXAMPLE 15-7. Using the AASHO Specifications and A36 steel design the simple composite section shown in Fig. 15-15 for the data given. No shoring is used and the following data are assumed:

$$\text{Span} = \ 40 \text{ ft}$$
$$M_D = 380 \text{ ft-k}$$
$$M_d = \ \ 80 \text{ ft-k}$$
$$M_L = 500 \text{ ft-k}$$
$$\overline{M_T = 960} \text{ ft-k}$$
$$f_s = \ \ 20.0 \text{ ksi}$$
$$f'_c = \ \ \ 3.0 \text{ ksi}$$
$$f_c = \ \ \ 1.2 \text{ ksi}$$
$$n = \ \ 10$$

Assumed maximum external shears due to live load and impact applied to composite section are 70 k at end, 52 k at 10 ft, and 36 k at 20 ft. An estimated 500,000 cycles of maximum stress is assumed to be applied to the shear connectors.

Solution:

FIG. 15-16

Trial Section (see Fig. 15-16)

Using Lothers' increased allowable stress method (28 percent increase for $n = 10$),

$$S_{req.} = \frac{(12)\ (960)}{(1.28)\ (20)} = 450 \text{ in.}^3$$

Try $W\ 36 \times 150$ ($A = 44.2, d = 35.84, t_f = 0.940, I = 9{,}030$)

Properties of Composite Section

For $n = 10$:

$$A = \left(\frac{68}{10}\right)(6) + 44.2 = 85.0 \text{ sq in.}$$

$$y_b = \frac{(40.8)\ (38.90) + (44.2)\ (17.92)}{85.0} = 28.00 \text{ in.}$$

$$I = 9{,}030 + (44.2)\ (10.08)^2 + (\tfrac{1}{12})\ (6.8)\ (6)^3 + (40.8)\ (10.9)^2 = 18{,}474 \text{ in.}^4$$

For $n = 30$:

$$A = (^{68}\!/_{30})\ (6) + 44.2 = 57.8 \text{ sq in.}$$

$$y_b = \frac{(13.6)\ (38.90) + (44.2)\ (17.92)}{57.8} = 22.90 \text{ in.}$$

$$I = 9{,}030 + (44.2)\ (4.98)^2 + (\tfrac{1}{12})\left(\frac{68}{30}\right)(6)^3 + (13.6)\ (16.00)^2 = 13{,}709 \text{ in.}^4$$

Review of Stresses

Before concrete hardens:

$$f_s = \frac{(12)\ (380)\ (17.92)}{9,030} = 9.06\ \text{ksi} < 20.0\ \text{ksi} \qquad \text{(OK)}$$

After concrete hardens:

$$f_s = 9.06 + \frac{(12)\ (80)\ (22.9)}{13,709} + \frac{(12)\ (500)\ (28.00)}{18,474} = 19.76\ \text{ks} < 20.0\ \text{ksi} \qquad \text{(OK)}$$

$$\text{(overstressed)}$$

$$f_c = \frac{(12)\ (80)\ (19.00)}{(30)\ (13,709)} + \frac{(12)\ (500)\ (13.9)}{(10)\ (18,474)} = 0.496\ \text{ksi} < 1.2\ \text{ksi} \qquad \text{(OK)}$$

Design of Shear Connectors

Assuming $3 - \frac{3}{4} \times 3$ headed studs ($H/d = 4.0$) at each section:

$$Z_r = \alpha d^2 = (10,600)\ (\tfrac{3}{4})^2 = 5,960\ \text{lb/stud}$$

$$S_u = (930)\ (\tfrac{3}{4})^2\ \sqrt{3,000} = 28,700\ \text{lb/stud}$$

Ultimate strength design:

$$P_1 = A_s F_y = (44.2)\ (36) = 1,590\ \text{k}$$

$$P_2 = 0.85\ f'_c bc = (0.85)\ (3.0)\ (68 \times 6) = 1040\ \text{k} \leftarrow$$

$$N = \frac{P}{\phi S_u} = \frac{1040}{(0.85)\ (28.7)} = 42.6\ \text{(say 43 each side of maximum moment point)}$$

Fatigue design:

$$Q = (6.8)\ (6)\ (10.9) = 445\ \text{in.}^3$$

$$v\ \text{at end} = \frac{(70)\ (445)}{18,474} = 1.69\ \text{k/in.}$$

$$\text{Spacing required} = \frac{3 \times 5.96}{1.69} = 10.6\ \text{in.}$$

$$v\ \text{at 10 ft} = \frac{(52)\ (445)}{18,474} = 1.25\ \text{k/in.}$$

$$\text{Spacing required} = \frac{3 \times 5.96}{1.25} = 14.3\ \text{in.}$$

$$v\ \text{at 20 ft} = \frac{(36)\ (445)}{18,474} = 0.866\ \text{k/in.}$$

$$\text{Spacing required} = \frac{3 \times 5.96}{0.866} = 20.65\ \text{in.}$$

Assuming the following spacing diagram (Fig. 15-17):

FIG. 15-17

Total number of shear connectors $= 3 \times 18 = 54$ each side of beam
$\mathfrak{C} > 43$ required by ultimate design. Use 54 connectors each side of $\mathfrak{C}$ with one placed at beam $\mathfrak{C}$. These can be spaced uniformly says AASHO.

15-10. MISCELLANEOUS

Continuous Spans. The AISC (Sec. 1.11.4) and the AASHO (Art. 1.7.100) permit the use of continuous composite design. If shear connectors are used as required by the applicable specification in the negative moment regions the reinforcing bars which are parallel to the steel girders and within the calculated effective width of the slab can be used in calculating the properties of the composite section.

The composite section properties are calculated by the elastic theory and any concrete in tension is neglected. The total cross-sectional area of a section in the negative moment region equals the area of the steel girder plus the area of the reinforcing bars plus the transformed area of any concrete which is in compression as in encased construction. The centroid of the section and its moment of inertia can be calculated by the usual methods.

Extra Reinforcing. For building design calculations the spans are often considered to be simply supported, but the steel beams do not generally have perfectly simple ends. The result of this situation is that some negative moment may occur at the beam ends with possible cracking of the slab above. To prevent or minimize cracking, some extra steel can be placed in the top of the slab extending 2 or 3 ft out into the slab. The amount of steel added is often roughly equal to the temperature and shrinkage requirements and is used in addition to those requirements.

Deflections. Deflections for composite beams may be calculated by the same methods used for other types of beams. The student must be careful to compute deflections for the various types of loads separately. For example, there are dead loads applied to the steel section alone (if no shoring is used), dead loads applied to the composite section, and live loads applied to the composite section. The deflections of the steel beam can be determined for the noncomposite loads and added to the deflections for the dead and live loads applied to the composite section.

To obtain reasonable results from deflection calculations, it is absolutely essential to use different moduli of elasticity (or different modular ratios) for long-term dead and live loads and short-term live loads applied to the slab. The common practice is to divide the modulus by 3 (or use $3n$ for the modular ratio in calculating the section properties) for the long-term loads. It is said that members designed by the AISC Specification with structural carbon steel will deflect from 10 to 20 percent more than the theoretically calculated values. Generally speaking, shear deflections are neglected although on occasion they can be quite large.[3] The steel beams can be cambered for all or only some portion of the deflection. It may be feasible in some situations to make a floor slab a little thicker in the middle than on the edges to compensate for deflection.

PROBLEMS

15-1. Using the AISC Specification, calculate the bending stresses for the section shown in the accompanying illustration. The section is used for a simple span of 24 ft and is to have a dead uniform load of 40 psf applied after composite action develops and a live uniform load of 150 psf. Assume no shoring and $n = 9$. (Ans. $f_s = 20.3$ ksi, $f_c = -0.64$ ksi)

Beams 6'-0" o.c.

4"

— W 14 X 30

Prob. 15-1

15-2. Rework Prob. 15-1 if a W 8 × 17 with an ½ × 8-in. cover plate on the tension flange is used instead of the W 14 × 30.

15-3. Rework Prob. 15-1 using the AASHO Specifications and $n = 10$. (Ans. $f_s = 23.3$ ksi, $f_c = -0.556$ ksi)

15-4. Rework Prob. 15-2 using the AASHO Specifications and $n = 10$.

15-5. Using the AISC Specification review the stresses in the encased section shown in the accompanying illustration if no shoring is used. The section is assumed to be used for a simple span of 30 ft and to have a dead uniform load of 30 psf applied after composite action develops and a live uniform load of 125 psf. Assume $n = 9$. (Ans. $f_s = 24.4$ ksi, $f_c = -1.05$ ksi)

[3] L. S. Beedle et al, *Structural Steel Design* (New York: The Ronald Press Company, 1964), p. 452.

PROB. 15-5

15-6. Using the AISC Manual, design a nonencased composite section for the simple span beams shown in the accompanying illustration assuming a 5-in. concrete slab and using A36 steel and 3,000-lb concrete. Use $n = 9$. Load applied after composite action $= 150$ psf. Assume no shoring. Use $\frac{3}{4} \times 3$-in. headed studs, assume full composite action and do not use cover plates on beam section. Maximum dead load deflection $= 1$ in. and maximum live load deflection $= \frac{1}{360}$ span.

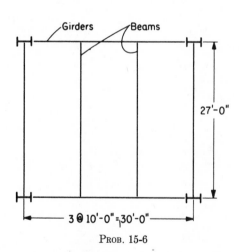

PROB. 15-6

15-7. For the floor plan shown for Prob. 15-6 design a nonencased section for the girders, assuming the floor plan is symmetrical on both sides of the girder. (Ans. W 24 × 94 with 87 $\frac{3}{4} \times 1$ studs)

15-8. Repeat Prob. 15-6 using an encased section.

15-9. Repeat Prob. 15-7 using an encased section.

15-10. Using the AASHO Specifications select a composite section for the following information: 6-in. concrete slab, $f_s = 20$ ksi, $f'_c = 3,000$ psi, $n = 10$, no shoring, beams spaced 6 ft 0 in. on centers, and each beam subjected to a live load caused by the movement of two 20-k loads 10 ft 0 in. on centers. Assume a simple span of 50 ft.

15-11. Rework Prob. 15-10 if shoring is used.

15-12. Design shear connectors for Prob. 15-1. Use $3\frac{1}{2} \times \frac{7}{8}$-in. headed studs. $f'_c = 3,000$ psi.

15-13. Design shear connectors for Prob. 15-1. Use $3 \times \frac{3}{4}$-in. headed studs and assume full composite action. $f'_c = 3,000$ psi. A36 steel. (Ans. 28 connectors)

15-14. Design shear connectors for Prob. 15-10. Use $3\frac{1}{2} \times \frac{7}{8}$-in. headed studs. $f'_c = 3,000$ psi.

15-15. Check to see if extra shear reinforcing is needed in the encased section of Prob. 15-5. $f'_c = 3,000$ psi. Assume allowable bond stress = 90 psi and allowable shear stress for concrete = 180 psi. (Ans. Calculated shear = 944 lb/in. < shear resistance = 1,710 lb/in.)

15-16. Determine the total deflection in Prob. 15-3 if the modulus of elasticity of the concrete is assumed to be 3×10^6 psi for short-term loads.

15-17. Calculate the total deflection in the section of Prob. 15-5 if $n = 9$ and $E = 3.16 \times 10^6$ psi for short-term loads. (Ans. 1.52″)

chapter 16

BUILT-UP BEAMS
AND PLATE GIRDERS

16-1. COVER-PLATED BEAMS

Should the largest available W section be insufficient to support the loads anticipated for a certain span, several possible alternatives may be taken. These include the use of the following: (1) two or more regular W sections side by side (an expensive solution), (2) a cover-plated beam, (3) a built-up section or plate girder, or (4) a steel truss. This section is concerned with the cover-plated beam alternative, and the remainder of the chapter is devoted to plate girders.

In addition to being practical for cases where the moments to be resisted are slightly in excess of those which can be supported by the deepest W sections, there are other useful applications for cover-plated beams. On some occasions the total depth may be so limited that the resisting moments of W sections of the specified depth are too small. For instance, the architect may show a certain maximum depth for beams in his drawings for a building. In a bridge, beam depths may be limited by clearance requirements. Cover-plated beams will nearly always prove to be the best solution for situations of these types. Furthermore, there can be economical uses for cover-plated beams where the depth is not limited and where there are standard W sections available to support the loads. A smaller W section than required by the maximum moment can be selected and have cover plates attached to its flanges. These plates can be cut off where the moments are smaller with resulting saving of steel. Applications of this type are quite common for continuous beams.

Should the depth be fixed and a cover-plated beam seem to be a feasible solution, the usual procedure will be to select the strongest standard section which has a depth leaving room for top and bottom cover plates, then select the coverplate sizes. A cover-plated beam is shown in Fig.

16-1.   If the section has been selected, the moment of inertia of the entire section equals the moment of inertia of the W section (I_s) plus the moment of inertia of the unknown plate sizes.   The moment of inertia of

Fɪɢ. 16-1

these plates about the x axis (neglecting the minute values about their own axes) equals Ad^2 for each plate.

If d represents the distance between the centers of gravities of the flange cover plates, the moment of inertia of the entire section can be expressed as

$$I_{\text{req.}} = I_s + 2A\left(\frac{d}{2}\right)^2$$

It is usually more convenient to work with section modulus values rather than with moments of inertia.   The section modulus required can be written approximately as follows (noting that $d/2$ is not exactly the correct distance to the outermost fiber of the plates):

$$S_{\text{req.}} = S_s + \frac{2A\,(d/2)^2}{d/2}$$

$$= S_s + Ad$$

From this last expression it is possible to estimate very closely the cover plate area required.   The value actually obtained will be very slightly on the small side due to the slightly incorrect distance between the outermost fibers used in the derivation.   A cover-plated beam design is illustrated in Example 16-1.   The connections between the cover plates and the W section of this example are not designed, as this matter will be discussed in the plate-girder design material to follow.   Actually a riveted connection of this type was illustrated previously in Example 9-4.

Eхамрle 16-1.   Select a beam limited to a maximum depth of 28 in. for the load and span of Fig. 16-2.   The beam is assumed to have full lateral support for its compression flange and to have an allowable bending stress of 20 ksi.

Fig. 16-2

Solution: Assume beam weight = 300 lb/ft.

$$M = \frac{(14.3)\,(24)^2}{8} = 1{,}030 \text{ ft-k}$$

$$S_{\text{req.}} = \frac{(12)\,(1{,}030)}{20} = 618 \text{ in.}^3$$

Try W 27 × 177 ($d = 27.31, b = 14.09, I = 6{,}740, S = 49.4$) (see Fig. 16-3)

Fig. 16-3

$$S_{\text{req.}} = S_s + Ad$$

$$618 = 494 + (A)\,(27.65)$$

$$A = 4.48 \text{ sq in.}$$

Flange width of W 27 × 177 = 14.09 in., therefore, assume 16 in. cover PL

Try 1 — 16 × ⁵⁄₁₆-in. cover PL each flange

Actual S furnished,

$$S = \frac{6{,}740 + (2)\,(16 \times \frac{5}{16})\,(13.81)^2}{13.97} = 619 \text{ in.}^3 > 618 \text{ in.}^3 \qquad \text{(OK)}$$

Use W 27 × 177 with 1—16 × ⁵⁄₁₆ cover PL each flange

16-2. INTRODUCTION TO PLATE GIRDERS

Plate girders are large I-shaped sections built up from plates and rolled sections. They have resisting moments somewhere between those

of rolled beams and steel trusses. Several possible plate girder arrangements are shown in Fig. 16-4. Possible riveted or bolted girders are
shown in parts (a) and (b) of the figure, while several welded types are

Riveted or bolted PL girders   Welded PL girders

Box girder

Fig. 16-4

shown in part (c) through (f). Nearly all plate girders constructed
today are welded, although they may frequently have bolted field splices.

The welded girder of part (d) of Fig. 16-4 is arranged to reduce
overhead welding as compared to the girder of part (c), but in so doing
may be creating a little worse corrosion situation if the girder is exposed
to the weather. A box girder, illustrated in part (g), is occasionally used
where moments are large and depths are quite limited. Box girders have
great resistance to torsion and lateral buckling.

Plates and shapes can be arranged to form plate girders of almost
any reasonable proportions. This fact may seem to give them a great
advantage for all situations, but for the smaller sizes the advantage is
usually canceled by the higher fabrication costs. For example, it is
possible to replace a W 36 with a plate girder roughly twice as deep
which will require considerably less steel and will have much smaller
deflections; however, the higher fabrication costs will almost always rule
out such a possibility.

Most steel highway bridges built today for spans less than about

80 ft are steel-beam bridges.   For longer spans the plate girder begins to compete very well economically.   Where loads are extremely large as for railroad bridges plate girders are competitive for spans as low as 45 or 50 ft.

The upper economical limits of plate girder spans depend on several factors, including whether the bridge is simple or continuous, whether a highway or railroad bridge is involved, the largest section which can be shipped in one piece, etc.   Generally speaking, plate girders are very economical for railroad bridges for spans from 50 to 130 ft and for high-way bridges for spans from 80 to 150 ft.   However, they are often very competitive for much longer spans, particularly when continuous.   In fact they are actually common for 200-ft spans and have been used for many spans in excess of 400 ft.

Buffalo Bayou Bridge, Houston, Tex.—a 270-ft span. (*The Lincoln Electric Company.*)

Plate girders are not only used for bridges.   They are also fairly common in various types of buildings where they are called upon to support heavy concentrated loads.   Frequently a large ballroom or dining room with no interfering columns is desired on a lower floor of a multi-story building.   Such a situation is shown in Fig. 16-5.   The plate girder shown must support some tremendous column loads for many stories above.   The usual building plate girder of this type is simple to analyze because it probably does not have moving loads, although some building girders may be called upon to support traveling cranes.

Fig. 16-5

The usual practical alternative to plate girders in the spans for which they are economical is the truss. In general plate girders have the following advantages with particular comparison made to trusses:

1. The pound price for fabrication is lower than for trusses but higher than for rolled beam sections.

2. Erection is cheaper and faster than for trusses.

3. Due to their compactness, vibration and impact are not serious problems.

4. Plate girders require smaller vertical clearance than trusses.

5. The plate girder has fewer critical points for stresses than do trusses.

6. A bad connection here or there is not as serious as in a truss where such a situation could spell disaster.

7. There is less danger of injury to plate girders in an accident as compared to trusses. Should a truck run into a bridge plate girder it would probably just bend it a little, but a similar accident with a bridge truss member could cause a broken member and perhaps failure.

8. A plate girder is more easily painted than a truss.

On the other hand, plate girders are usually heavier than trusses for the same spans and loads, and they have a further disadvantage in the large number of connections required between webs and flanges.

16-3. COMMENTS ON SPECIFICATIONS

At the present time (July 1971) there is an extreme difference between the design requirements given in the AISC Specification for buildings and those in the bridge specifications. Due to space limitations it is impossible to completely consider these different specifications.

The AISC Specification embodies the latest thoughts and research information pertaining to plate girders, with the result that design formulas are entirely different from those given in the bridge specifications. However, it is felt that in the near future the AASHO will adopt much of the theory now used by the AISC.

The next few sections describe some of the major design provisions of the AASHO according to which highway-bridge plate girders are designed today. Although it is highly possible that these specifications will soon be appreciably changed, the material will serve as a good background for plate-girder design with the AISC Specification. In the concluding sections of this chapter the AISC Specification is emphasized, as it is felt that this may very well be the material which the engineer will be working with in the near future in bridges as well as in buildings.

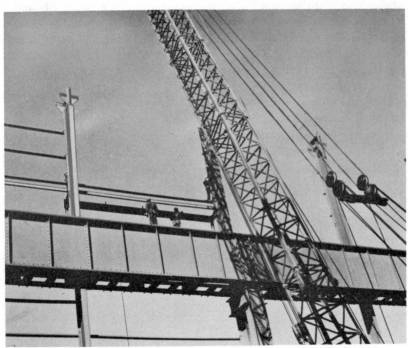

Indiana Harbor Works, East Chicago, Ind. (*Inland Steel Company.*)

Actually after the heading of each of the remaining sections of this chapter the specifications to which the general discussion is applicable are indicated (as AISC or AASHO and AREA).

16-4. PROPORTIONS OF PLATE GIRDERS—AASHO AND AREA

Depth. The depths of plate girders vary from about $\frac{1}{6}$ to $\frac{1}{15}$ of their spans with average values of $\frac{1}{10}$ to $\frac{1}{12}$, depending on the particular conditions of the job. One condition which may limit the proportions of the girder is the largest size which can be fabricated in the shop and shipped to the job. There may be a transportation problem such as clearance requirements which limit maximum depths to 10 or 12 ft along the shipping route.

The shallower girders will probably be used when the loads are light, and the deeper ones when very large concentrated loads need to be supported as from the columns in a tall building. If there are no depth restrictions for a particular girder it will probably pay the designer to make rough designs and corresponding cost estimates to arrive at a depth decision.

Web Size. After the total girder depth is estimated, the general proportions of the girder can be established from the maximum shear and the maximum moment. As previously described for S, M, and W sections in Sec. 7-1, the web of a beam carries nearly all of the shearing stress; this shearing stress is assumed by the AASHO to be uniformly distributed throughout the web. The web depth can be closely estimated by taking the total girder depth and subtracting a reasonable value for the depths of the flanges (roughly 2 in. each). The web depths are selected to the nearest even inch because these plates are not stocked in fractional dimensions.

For this discussion reference is made to Fig. 16-6 in which d is the

Fɪɢ. 16-6

total girder depth, h is the web depth, and t is the web thickness. In this figure it will be noted that the flange angles are placed so they extend about $\frac{1}{4}$ in. beyond the top and bottom of the web. If these clearances were not used, the small irregularities in depth of the web plate as it comes from the rolling mill might cause it to protrude slightly, resulting in expensive chipping or other leveling processes.

The web thickness can be determined from the expression to follow in which V is the maximum total shear and v is the allowable shearing stress given by the specifications:

$$t = \frac{V}{hv}$$

Shear is not the only factor that must be considered in selecting the web thickness. Where a large reaction or concentrated load is acting on the plate girder there is danger of buckling of the high thin web. To prevent such buckling the web can be stiffened with plates or angles at various intervals as described in Sec. 16-7.

Stress analysis shows that high, thin plate-girder webs may buckle due to a combination of bending and shearing stresses unless stiffeners are used at certain intervals. Tests have shown that for carbon steels there is little danger of buckling if the web thickness is at least $\frac{1}{60}$ of the unsupported depth of the web. Should a web be selected which is thinner than the value given by this ratio it will be necessary to provide stiffeners spaced no further apart than the clear web depth. It is usually more economical for bridge plate girders to use thinner webs with stiffeners than to use the thicker ones without stiffeners.

The AREA and AASHO specifications give minimum permissible ratios of web thickness to unsupported depths of $\frac{1}{170}$ for structural carbon steel regardless of the number and placing of stiffeners. Design by these specifications is, therefore, based on the so-called buckling strength of the girders. They do, however, recognize the fact that plate girders have considerable postbuckling strengths by using small safety factors.

From a corrosion standpoint the usual practice is to use some absolute minimum web thickness. For bridge girders, $\frac{3}{8}$ in. is a common minimum, while $\frac{1}{4}$ or $\frac{5}{16}$ in. are probably the minimum values for the more sheltered building girders.

Flange. After the web dimensions are selected the next step is to select the area of the flange. The goal, of course, is to select a flange of sufficient area which will not be overstressed in bending. For this discussion reference is made to Fig. 16-6. The total bending strength of the plate girder equals the bending strength of the web plus the bending strength of the flanges.

The moment of inertia of the entire plate girder equals the moment of inertia of the web about its own centroidal axis plus the area of each flange times the distance from its center of gravity to the centroid of the section squared (thus neglecting the very small moment of inertia of the flange about its own centroidal axis). To simplify the expression, the centers of gravity of the flanges are assumed to lie at the top and bottom of the web (a fairly good assumption).

The approximate gross moment of inertia of the plate girder can now be written as follows, where A_f is the area of one flange:

$$I = \frac{th^3}{12} + 2\,A_f\left(\frac{h}{2}\right)^2$$

It is usually more convenient to work with section modulus values in design as in ordinary beams. The gross section modulus of the girder can be written as

$$S = \frac{th^3/12}{h/2} + \frac{2\,A_f\,(h/2)^2}{h/2}$$

$$= \frac{th^2}{6} + A_f h$$

The required section modulus M/f is equated to S and the resulting expression is solved for A_f as follows:

$$\frac{M}{f} = \frac{th^2}{6} + A_f h$$

$$A_f = \frac{M}{fh} - \frac{th}{6}$$

The last term in this expression $th/6$ is referred to as the *web equivalent*. The AREA says that the web equivalent should be multiplied by 75 percent for bolted and riveted girders to estimate the effect of the holes in the web. There are undoubtedly a large number of holes in the webs of these girders where the stiffeners are connected. Should 1-in. holes be placed 4 in. on centers, one-fourth of the web will be theoretically cut out.

After the flange area formula is applied it is necessary to proportion the parts of the flange. For best economy it is desirable to place as large a proportion of the flange area in cover plates as possible. The plates are the greatest distance from the centroidal axis of the girder, and the larger their areas the greater the moment of inertia developed for the same total steel area. Cover plates can be conveniently cut off where moments are smaller, so another reason for putting more area in the cover plates is that by so doing more steel area can be cut off where moments are small. It has been found to be good economy to place from 40 to 60 percent of the total flange area in cover plates.

The flange angles selected will probably be unequal leg angles with the long legs horizontal to increase the moment of inertia and thus the resisting moment. Should a large number of rivets or bolts be needed to connect the angles to the web, equal leg angles may be necessary. Some small plate girders have only angles used for the flanges, but these are not too common. In fact, most specifications require at least one cover plate to run for the full girder length. A cover plate ties the flange angles together into a more compact unit and prevents water from collecting in the ¼-in. groove between the angles on top of the web and encouraging corrosion.

Suggestions as to proportioning the flange can usually be found in the specifications being used. For instance some specifications limit the maximum cover plate area to 70 percent of the flange area. It is often economical to use several cover plates because they can be cut off at the points where they are no longer required by moment (with the probable exception of the inside plate on each flange). It is probably reasonable to select plates which are all of the same widths and thicknesses. The specifications usually state that the plates may not be thicker than the flange angles and if of different thicknesses should decrease in thickness, going away from the centroid of the girder. As previously indicated, from a corrosion standpoint the cover plates should probably not decrease in

Arc-welded plate girders, Louisiana State Fair Grounds, Shreveport, La.
(*The Lincoln Electric Company.*)

width away from the centroid. (One exception to this statement was shown in Fig. 16-4 where the plates were so arranged as to reduce the amount of overhead welding.)

After the flanges are selected it is necessary to review the stresses to determine if the proportions selected are satisfactory. The method of computing the moment of inertia depends on the specifications being used. For instance, the AISC says the gross moment of inertia shall be used unless the holes in either flange exceed 15 percent of the flange area, in which case only the excess area is deducted. The AREA and AASHO require that the gross moment of inertia be used for calculating compressive stresses and the net moment of inertia be used for calculating tensile stresses. Both moments of inertia are to be calculated about the centroidal axis of the gross section. In either case when holes are being subtracted they are to be subtracted from both flanges—not just the tensile flange.

Example 16-2 illustrates the selection of the proportions of a plate girder and the review of stresses in the resulting section. The critical shears and moments for this highway bridge were assumed by the author. In Chap. 18 the calculations of critical shears and moments using the HS20-44 truck loadings are demonstrated.

EXAMPLE 16-2. Select proportions and review stresses for a riveted deck plate girder given the following data:

Specifications: 1969 AASHO

Steel: Structural carbon (A36)

Span = 100 ft

Maximum total moment = 8,200 ft-k

Maximum total shear = 330 k

Allowable shear in web = 12,000 psi

Allowable compression due to bending = 20,000 psi (assuming full lateral support for the compression flange)

Rivets: $\frac{7}{8}$-in. diameter A502, Grade 1
Solution:

Depth of Girder

Assume $d = \frac{1}{12}$ span = $(\frac{1}{12})$ (100 ft) = 100 in.

Size of Web

Web depth: $h = d - 4$ in. = 96 in.

Web thickness:

(1) For shear t $= \dfrac{330}{(12)\,(96)}$ 0.287 in.

(2) For corrosion minimum t = $\frac{5}{16}$ in.

(3) For diagonal compression $t = \frac{1}{170}$ of clear web depth

$= $ approx. $(\frac{1}{170})\,(84) = 0.494$ in.

Try $\frac{1}{2} \times$ 96-in. web   (See also Art. 1.7.71A)

Flange Area

Allowable bending stress in outermost fibers = 20 ksi

Approximate stress at top of web (or c.g. of flange) $= (\frac{48}{50})\,(20) =$ 19.2 ksi

$$A_f = \frac{M}{fh} - \frac{th}{6}$$

$$= \frac{(12)\,(8{,}200)}{(19.2)\,(96)} - \frac{(0.50)\,(96)}{6} = 45.3 \text{ sq in.}$$

Plus estimated area of rivet holes = 7.0 sq in.

Total flange area   = 52.3 sq in.

Flange Proportions

Placing approximately 40 percent of area in angles, try

2 Ls 8 × 6 × ¾ in.   = 19.88 sq in.

3 cover PLs ⅝ × 18 in.   = 33.75 sq in.

Total area   = 53.63 sq in.

Moments of Inertia (see Fig. 16-7)

Part	Area	Gross I
Web	48.00	36,864
Angles	19.88	86,700
Inside PL	11.25	53,100
Middle PL	11.25	54,400
Outside PL	11.25	55,900

$I_{\text{gross}} = 286{,}964$ in.^{4}

Fig. 16-7

Assuming holes for $\frac{7}{8}$-in. rivets spaced 4 in. on centers in web plus one line through vertical L legs and 2 lines through plates.

I holes:

$$\text{Web} = 2\,[(1)(\tfrac{1}{2})(4^2 + 8^2 + 12^2 + 16^2 + 20^2 + 24^2 + 28^2 + 32^2 + 36^2 + 40^2)] = 6{,}260$$

$$\text{Vertical L legs} = 2\,[(1)(2)(44.75)^2] \qquad = 8{,}000$$

$$\text{Cover PLs} = 2\,[(2)(1)(2.62)(48.81)^2] = 25{,}000$$

$$I \text{ holes} \qquad\qquad\qquad = 39{,}260 \text{ in.}^4$$

$$I \text{ net} = 286{,}964 - 39{,}260 = 247{,}704 \text{ in.}^4$$

Review of Stresses

$$f_c = \frac{(12)\,(8{,}200)\,(50.12)}{(286{,}964)} = 17{,}200 \text{ psi} < 20{,}000 \text{ psi} \qquad\qquad \text{(OK)}$$

$$f_t = \frac{(12)\,(8{,}200)\,(50.12)}{247{,}704} = 19{,}950 \text{ psi} < 20{,}000 \text{ psi} \qquad\qquad \text{(OK)}$$

16-5. CUTTING OFF COVER PLATES—AASHO, AREA, AND AISC

For those parts of the span where the bending moment has decreased sufficiently some cover plates may be cut off. Theoretically the resisting moment of the section with one plate cut off from each flange can be calculated, and for the parts of the beam where the moment is that small or smaller those plates can be eliminated. The resisting moment of the section can be calculated when two plates are cut off from each flange, etc. The usual practice, however, is to use a simpler method such as the one described in the following paragraphs.

Figure 16-8 shows the bending moment curve (here assumed to be parabolic) for a certain plate girder. For a plate girder subjected to

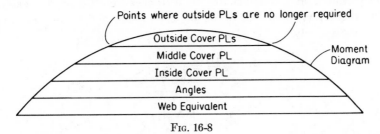

FIG. 16-8

moving loads, this curve should be a curve of the maximum possible moments throughout the beam. In this figure the moment is assumed to be resisted by the web equivalent, angles, and cover plates. Usually there is a little more area than theoretically required but this excess is conservatively neglected. Each square inch is assumed to resist an equal amount of the moment.

The points where the outside cover plate are no longer required, where the middle plates are no longer required, etc., can be accurately determined by scaling from a carefully plotted diagram. Perhaps a more common practice is to assume that the bending-moment curve is parabolic and write expressions for the cutoff points. Reference is made here to Fig. 16-9.

FIG. 16-9

In the expressions to be developed A_1 is the area of the outside plate, A_2 is the area of the middle plate, A_{FL} is the area of the flange plus the web equivalent, and x_1 and x_2 are the distances from the girder centerline to the theoretical points of cutoff of the outside plates and the middle plates respectively.

$$\frac{A_1}{A_{FL}} = \frac{x_1{}^2}{(l/2)^2}$$

$$x_1 = \frac{l}{2}\sqrt{\frac{A_1}{A_{FL}}}$$

Similarly,

$$x_2 = \frac{l}{2}\sqrt{\frac{A_1 + A_2}{A_{FL}}}$$

As previously described, the inside cover plate on each flange will probably have to extend for the full girder length. Should the moment diagram (neglecting the beam weight) consist of straight lines due to heavy stationary concentrated loads (as from columns in a multistory building), the theoretical points of cutoff can be found even more simply.

Most specifications require that cover plates be extended for some

Highway bypass bridge, Stroudsburg, Pa. (*Bethlehem Steel Company.*)

little distance beyond their theoretical points of cutoff. The plate is supposed to be carrying stress right up to its theoretical end, but it cannot do so unless there is some extra plate beyond the point connected to the girder for stress transfer. These extra distances depend on the individual designer and upon the specification being used. The AASHO Specifications say that if riveted cover plates are used the plate shall extend for a sufficient distance beyond its theoretical cutoff point to develop the capacity of the plate or it shall continue to a point where the computed stress equals the allowable fatigue stress, whichever extension is greater. In other words, there must be enough rivets through the plate outside of the theoretical cutoff point to have a shearing strength equal to the allowable tension or compression in the plate.

16-6. COVER-PLATE AND FLANGE CONNECTORS—AASHO, AREA, AND AISC

Cover-Plate Connectors. The rivets or bolts passing through the cover plates and flange angles must be of sufficient strength to resist the transfer of longitudinal shear between these parts. The cover-plate connectors shown in Fig. 16-10 are in single shear and bearing on the angle thickness

Fig. 16-10. Cover-plate connectors.

(or the sum of the cover plate thicknesses at the section, whichever is smaller). In the figure, p represents the pitch of the connectors, given two connectors every p inches. Each of the connectors must be able to resist half of the longitudinal shear for a distance of p inches.

In the expression to be developed, R is the allowable load on one connector under that condition. The allowable strength of the connector is equated to the load which it must carry and the theoretical pitch or spacing of the connectors can be determined as follows:

Longitudinal shear in pounds per inch of girder which must be resisted by the connectors equals

$$v = \frac{VQ}{I}$$

Shear to be resisted per connector equals

$$(\tfrac{1}{2}) \ (v) \ (p) = \frac{p \, VQ}{2 \, I}$$

$$R = \frac{p \, VQ}{2 \, I}$$

$$p = \frac{2 \, RI}{VQ}$$

In this expression for pitch of cover plate connectors I is the gross moment of inertia of the girder at the section being considered, V is the external shear at the section, and Q is the statical moment of the plates about the neutral axis.

Flange Connectors. The flange connectors are the rivets or bolts which pass through the angles and web. These horizontal connectors are in double shear and in bearing on the web thickness. They must have sufficient strength to resist the usual longitudinal shearing stress and they may also be required to resist a vertical shear due to loads applied to the top of the girder. The longitudinal shearing stress expression VQ/I is used in which Q is the statical moment of the flange about the neutral axis of the girder. The area involved is crosshatched in Fig. 16-11(a).

(a)   (b)

Fɪɢ. 16-11.   Flange connectors.

If a welded girder of the type shown in part (b) of the figure is used, the weld will be subjected to longitudinal shear only.

The strength of the connector R is equated to the horizontal shearing force to be resisted and the resulting expression is solved for p as follows:

$$R = \frac{VQ}{I}\, p$$

$$p = \frac{RI}{VQ}$$

Plate girders used in buildings are usually subjected to heavy concentrated loads. Stiffeners are placed under these loads and keep the flange connectors from being subjected to a direct vertical shear. In bridges, however, the wheel loads of trucks or trains move back and forth across the girders. It is not feasible to use continuous stiffeners all across the span, and the flange connectors are subjected to vertical shears due to the concentrated wheel loads. In Fig. 16-12 a uniform load of w lb/in. is assumed to be applied to the top of the girder and the vertical shear applied to each connector will equal wp. (For the moving

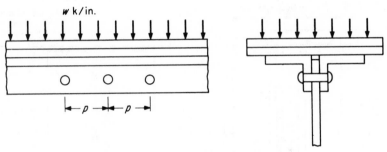

Fɪɢ. 16-12

concentrated loads the designer probably will make some assumed distribution of the concentrated wheel load to obtain the value of w described here. The AREA says that when the ties rest on the flanges a wheel load (including 80 percent impact) shall be spread over 3 ft. Sometimes the load may be assumed to be spread out at 45° in each direction through the roadway slab until it reaches the top of the girders.)

These connectors discussed are subjected to a combination of longitudinal and vertical shears and their allowable strength must be at least equal to the resultant of the two shears.

$$R = \sqrt{(wp)^2 + \left(p\,\frac{VQ}{I} \right)^2}$$

$$= p\sqrt{w^2 + \left(\frac{VQ}{I}\right)^2}$$

Solving this expression for the required pitch of the connector, the following expression is obtained:

$$p = \frac{R}{\sqrt{w^2 + (VQ/I)^2}}$$

16-7. STIFFENERS—AASHO

As previously described it is usually necessary to stiffen the high thin webs of plate girders to keep them from buckling. For riveted or bolted girders, angles are connected to the webs while for welded girders plates can be welded to the webs. Figures 16-13 and 16-14 show these types of stiffeners. Stiffeners are divided into two groups: the *bearing stiffeners* which transfer heavy reactions or concentrated loads to the full depth of the web, and the *nonbearing stiffeners* which are placed at various intervals along the web to prevent buckling due to diagonal compression.

(a) Angle bearing stiffeners   (b) Welded girder stiffeners

FIG. 16-13

FIG. 16-14

An additional purpose of bearing stiffeners is to transfer heavy loads to the web without putting all the load on the flange connectors.

Bearing Stiffeners. Bearing stiffeners should fit tightly against the flanges being loaded and should extend out toward the edges of the flange plates and angles as far as possible. In order to obtain a snug fit or good bearing between the flange and stiffeners it is desirable either to weld the stiffeners to the flanges or to mill their outstanding legs.

The usual specifications only allow the part of the stiffener legs outside of the fillets of the flange angles to be counted in supporting the load in pure bearing [see Fig. 16-13(a)]. The distance to the outside of the fillet can be found in the angle tables of the AISC Manual. The reaction or load is divided by the allowable bearing stress given by the specifications, and that much area must be provided outside of the flange-angle fillets. A riveted or bolted bearing stiffener is shown in Fig. 16-13(a) and a welded one in part (b) of the same figure. The stiffeners shown in this figure are cut off so they will fit in the corners of the fillet. Notice in part (a) of the figure how filler plates are needed between the web and the stiffeners. Riveted or bolted bearing stiffeners cannot be crimped as they can for nonbearing stiffeners as shown in Fig. 16-14.

Bearing stiffeners are really a special type of column which is difficult to analyze because it supports the load in conjunction with the web. The amount of support supplied by each is difficult to estimate. The specifications usually say that the load divided by the effective bearing area may not exceed the allowable bearing as previously described. Some specifications say in addition that P/A for the full stiffener area and some part of the web area may not exceed the allowable compression in a column of that size. For example, the AISC permits the use of a length of the web equal to 12 times its thickness plus the full stiffener area to act as a column for end-bearing stiffeners. The effective length to be used for the column (again difficult to estimate) is $\frac{3}{4}$ of the stiffener height, says the AISC. For interior bearing stiffeners they permit a length of web equal to 25 times the web thickness to be included in the effective column area.

Since bearing stiffeners cannot be crimped, they require the use of filler plates of thickness equal to that of the flange angle. Should the filler plates be held in place only by connectors which pass through the stiffeners, filler plates, and the web they are said to be *loose fillers*. *Tight fillers* are those which are connected by rivets or bolts passing through the stiffeners, filler plates, and web plus extra connectors passing through the filler plates (which are extended outside the stiffeners) and web, provided the number of extra connectors is equal to at least 50 percent of the number of connectors required by the stiffeners.

The usual procedure for determining the number of connectors required in bearing stiffeners is to divide the load or reaction by the connector strength. If loose fillers are used, the connectors are considered to be in double shear and bearing on the web thickness. Should tight fillers be used, the rivets are considered to be in double shear and bearing on a thickness equal to the web thickness plus that of the fillers or a thickness equal to that of the two stiffeners, whichever is the least. (A fairly common practice if loose fillers are used is to increase the number of connectors by 50 percent because it is felt that the connectors are subject to moment along with bearing and shear.)

Nonbearing Stiffeners. Nonbearing stiffeners are also called intermediate stiffeners or stability stiffeners. Tests have shown that if the ratio of the thickness of the web to its unsupported height is less than approximately 1/70 buckling due to diagonal compression is possible and intermediate stiffeners are required.

Very little effort is made to estimate the load applied to intermediate stiffeners. They are usually assumed to be subjected to no loads at all thus permitting the stiffener angles to be crimped as shown in Fig. 16-15.

FIG. 16-15. Intermediate stiffener.

The size of intermediate stiffeners is usually obtained by applying some empirical rule, or it may be definitely controlled by the specifications being used. The AASHO says that the length of the outstanding leg of a stiffener angle or a plate stiffener may not exceed 16 times its thickness nor be less than 2 in. + $\frac{1}{30}$ of the total girder depth and preferably shall not be less than $\frac{1}{4}$ the full width of the girder flange. An outstanding leg will probably be selected with a length equal to approximately $\frac{1}{30}$ of the girder depth plus 2 in. and with a thickness equal to approximately $\frac{1}{16}$ of the width but probably not less than $\frac{3}{8}$ in. The other leg of a stiffener angle need only be large enough to accommodate the connectors.

The spacing of intermediate stiffeners is also usually governed by specifications. The AASHO says intermediate stiffeners must be spaced at intervals not exceeding the least of the following:

1. The unsupported height of the web (so wrinkling or buckling cannot occur along a 45° line from the top to the bottom of the girder without encountering a stiffener).

2. The value given by the following expression in which f_v is the average unit shearing stress on the gross section of the web at the section being considered and t is the web thickness:

$$d = \frac{11,000}{\sqrt{f_v}} t$$

Art. 1.7.72 of the AASHO specifies a minimum I and other items for these stiffeners.

16-8. LONGITUDINAL STIFFENERS—AASHO

A web which is subjected to bending can most effectively be stiffened against buckling by means of horizontal or longitudinal stiffeners. The installation of transverse stiffeners does not greatly increase the buckling resistance of plate-girder webs, but longitudinal or horizontal stiffeners can provide a considerable increase in this resistance. If the buckling strength can be increased, thinner webs can be used, resulting in appreciable savings for some girders, particularly for very deep ones.

The AASHO says that the web thickness to unsupported web height ratio may not be less than 1/170 for structural carbon steel when only transverse stiffeners are used. Should a longitudinal stiffener be used in combination with transverse stiffeners, the minimum ratio is reduced to 1/340. (Other values are given for higher strength steels.) Since they do not require the longitudinal stiffener to be continuous, it can be cut off at the intersection with transverse stiffeners.

The best location for longitudinal stiffeners can be theoretically proved to lie approximately one-fifth of the distance from the compression flange to the tension flange. On this basis the AASHO says that the gage lines of longitudinal stiffeners are to be placed $\frac{1}{5}$ of D (where D is the clear distance between flanges) from the toe of the compression flange. The required moment of inertia of a longitudinal stiffener about the edge of the stiffener in contact with the web is required by these specifications to equal

$$I_E = Dt^3 \left(2.4 \frac{d_o^2}{D^2} - 0.13 \right)$$

In this expression D is the clear distance between flanges, d_o is the actual distance between transverse stiffeners, and t is the web-plate thickness. A one-sided stiffener (that is one side of the web only) designed by the AASHO Specifications is normally more economical than a two-sided one. The connection problem for a one-sided stiffener is only one-half what it is for a two-sided stiffener and the area required to furnish I_E is only about $\frac{5}{8}$ of the area required for a two-sided plate. The student can verify this figure by substituting for a given condition in the equation the required moment of inertia.

16-9. WEB SPLICES—AASHO, AREA, AND AISC

Splicing of plate-girder webs is not too desirable, if avoidable, but is frequently necessary for one or more of the following reasons:

1. The length of the girders may be so great that plates of the required length are not available from the steel mills.

2. Even if available extremely large plates are difficult to handle without their twisting out of shape. (A 100-ft web plate of the size selected in Example 16-2 would weigh 16,300 lb. Imagine the difficulties of handling a PL $\frac{1}{2} \times 96$ 100 ft long weighing over 8 tons without twisting it out of shape before the stiffeners are installed!)

3. The sizes of girders which can be transported over the highway and railroad routes to the job may be severely limited by clearances and other factors.

4. The equipment available to handle and erect the steel may also limit the sizes of girder sections.

Many engineers would not place a splice at the centerline of a simple span because of the large centerline moment even if only one splice is needed. They would probably use a pair of splices located at the stiffeners nearest the third points of the span. This practice is probably unnecessary because a single splice at the centerline is just as satisfactory from a strength standpoint, and is certainly cheaper than two separate splices. Also the moment at the third points is not substantially reduced from its value at the centerline.

For welded girders it is unnecessary to use splice plates because the webs can be joined by butt welding. Several possible splices are shown in Fig. 16-16 for riveted or bolted plate girders. The simplest and cheapest type of splice is the one shown in part (a) of the figure in which a single splice plate is used on each side of the web. This type of splice called a *single-plate splice* or *shear splice* is satisfactory but is definitely not as good as the other types shown in the figure. In part (b) a much stronger type of splice called the *triple-plate splice* or *moment splice* is shown.

Each of these first two types of splices have a disadvantage in that the plates do not run for the full depth of the web because the flange angles cover part of the web. In other words, the largest stress that occurs in the web in its outermost fiber is several inches away from the nearest

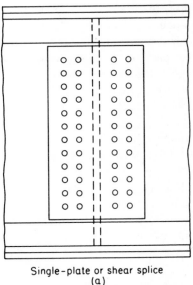

Single-plate or shear splice
(a)

Triple-plate or moment splice
(b)

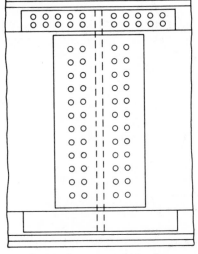

Triple-plate or moment splice
(c)

Fillers

Triple-plate splice with fillers
(d)

FIG. 16-16

part of the splice. It seems probable, therefore, that an appreciable portion of this maximum stress will be transferred over into the flange (at the break in the web), increasing the stress in the flange rather than going completely to the splice as desired.

The splices of parts (c) and (d) of Fig. 16-16 are probably the most desirable types from a theoretical standpoint. They consist of plates between the flanges (called shear plates) plus narrow plates over the vertical legs of the flange angles (called moment plates). In this type of splice the plates over the angle legs serve to splice the part of the web under the angles. Should the moment plate be deeper than the angle legs as shown in part (d), several filler plates will be needed. These plates are rather objectionable.

The common practice in designing a web splice is to select one that will replace the full moment resistance of the web and the maximum actual external shear at the section. Some engineers say that for determinate structures the splices should be designed only for the calculated maximum external shear, but for indeterminate structures they should be designed for the total shearing resistances of the webs. Their reasoning is that should plastic action occur in an indeterminate girder and the loads be redistributed, the splice would have a strength equal to that of the web.

The triple-plate splice has three plates on each side of the web, actually giving it a total of six plates. The top and bottom plates are referred to as the moment plates and are proportioned to have a resisting moment equal to that of the web. The resisting moment of the web equals fI/C or $\frac{1}{6} fth^2$ and can be said to equal one-sixth of the web area concentrated at the top and bottom of the web. An equivalent procedure was followed in developing the flange-area formulas in Sec. 16-4. The resisting moment of the splice plates is assumed to equal the area of one plate times its average stress, times the distance between the centers of gravities of the plates. The stress in a splice plate is in proportion to the stress in the outermost fiber of the web as are their respective distances from the neutral axis. For this discussion reference is made to Fig. 16-17.

FIG. 16-17

$$\text{Total force in moment plate} = \left(\frac{d}{h}f\right)(A_p)$$

Equating resisting moment of web to that of moment plates and solving for A_p

$$\left(\frac{fth}{6}\right)(h) = \left(\frac{d}{h}\right)(f)\ (A_p)\ (d)$$

$$A_p = \frac{th^3}{6\ d^2}$$

To use this expression it will be noted that d is not known. An excellent estimate of its value can be made, however, by assuming two or three horizontal rows of connectors in the moment plates. The widths of these plates necessary to include the connectors can be assumed; and the value of d, the distance center-to-center of the moment plates calculated. The area required for the moment plates can then be calculated. Since their width has already been assumed their thickness can be determined.

Finally, the length of the plates is established by the total number of rivets required. The connectors in the moment splice are designed for the total force to be carried by the plates fA_p (remembering that the stress in the moment plates is d/h times the stress in the outermost fiber of the web and using A_p as the theoretically required plate area). The number of connectors required equals the total stress in the plates divided by the strength of one connector. The connectors are in double shear and bearing on the web thickness or the sum of the two-splice plate thickness. The force that is developed by the connectors is also assumed to equal $(d/h)\ R$.

$$\text{Number of rivets} = \frac{(d/h)\ f\ A_p}{R}$$

The space available between the moment plates determines the depth of the shear plates using a clearance of about $\frac{1}{4}$ in. between the plates. The two shear plates (one on each side of the web) are selected to give an area sufficient to resist the total shear at the splice. The number of connectors used on each side of the web separation equals the external shear divided by the strength of one connector. The design of a triple-plate splice is illustrated by Example 16-3.

EXAMPLE 16-3. Design a triple-plate splice for the plate girder shown in Fig. 16-18 if the maximum calculated external shear is 175 k. Assume an allowable bending stress of 20 ksi and $\frac{7}{8}$-in. rivets with an allowable shear of 13.5 ksi and an allowable bearing of 44.0 ksi. Allowables shear in web = 12.0 ksi.

Solution: Design of moment plates:
Assuming three horizontal rows of $\frac{7}{8}$-in. rivets spaced 3 in. on centers and using $1\frac{1}{2}$-in. edge distance, depth of PLs= (2) (3) + (2) ($1\frac{1}{2}$) = 9 in.,

Fig. 16-18

$$d = 68.50 - (2) \ (\tfrac{1}{4}) - 9 = 59.00 \text{ in.}$$

$$A_p = \frac{th^3}{6 \ d^2} = \frac{(\tfrac{1}{2}) \ (80)^3}{(6) \ (59)^2} = 12.25 \text{ sq in. for 2 ₽s}$$

Thickness of ₽s $= \dfrac{12.25}{(2) \ (9)} = 0.681$ in. (say $1\tfrac{1}{16}$ in.)

R for rivets in double shear and bearing on $\tfrac{1}{2}$ in. $= (16.2) \ (\tfrac{59}{80}) = 11.95$ k each

Number of rivets $= \dfrac{(d/n) \ fA_p}{R} = \dfrac{(\tfrac{59}{80}) \ (20) \ (12.25)}{11.95} = 15.1$

<u>Use 15 rivets each side of web break</u>

Design of shear plates:

Depth of shear PLs $= 68.50 - (2) \ (\tfrac{1}{4}) - (2) \ (9) - (2) \ (\tfrac{1}{4}) = 49.50$ in.

$$A \text{ shear PLs} = \frac{175}{12} = 14.6 \text{ sq in. for 2 PLs}$$

$$t = \frac{14.6}{(2) \ (49.50)} = 0.147 \text{ in. (say } \tfrac{1}{4} \text{ in. minimum } t)$$

Rivets in double shear and bearing on $\tfrac{1}{2}$ in., $R = 16.2$ k

Number of rivets required $= \dfrac{175}{16.2} = 10.8$

<u>Use rivets spaced at 4 in. in shear PLs each side of web break giving more than required.</u>

Detail of the splice is shown in Fig. 16-19.

FIG. 16-19.   Detail of three-plate splice of
Example 16-3.

16-10.   PROPORTIONS OF WEBS—AISC

Buckling Considerations. The depths of plate girders have been previously discussed in Sec. 16-4 and were said to have average values varying from $\frac{1}{10}$ to $\frac{1}{12}$ of spans. After the total depth is assumed the web depth can be estimated to be from 2 to 4 in. less than the total depth and selected to the nearest inch. A plate-girder web must have sufficient thickness to prevent *vertical buckling of the compression flange.* As the compression flange of a simply supported beam deflects or curves downward it pushes against the web subjecting it to vertical compression. The amount of this downward force can be estimated to equal the total bending stress in the compression flange times the sine of the angle made by the curved flange with the horizontal.

The total load which can be applied to the web in this manner before the web buckles can be estimated by the Euler formula. Expressing this another way, the Euler formula can be used to determine a limiting height-to-thickness ratio to prevent buckling. Based on such a derivation (including an assumption for residual stress variation) the AISC (Sec. 1.10.2) says that the clear depth between flanges may not exceed the value computed by the expression given below. Substitution into this expression yields a value of $320t$ (where t is the web thickness) for **A36** steel.

$$\frac{14,000}{\sqrt{F_y(F_y + 16,500)}} t$$

The possibility of lateral buckling of the web may require a reduction in the allowable bending stress in the compression flange. It has been found that if the depth-to-thickness ratio of the web does not exceed $2,000/\sqrt{F_b}$ (equal to 162 for A36 steel) no reduction is necessary in the allowable flange stress.

For a trial girder section using A36 steel, a ratio of web depth to thickness somewhere between 162 and 320 will probably be selected, noting that the allowable bending stress in the flange will have to be reduced (to be described).

Web Shear. The AISC Specification for plate girders permits their design on the basis of postbuckling strength. Designs on this basis give better economy and provide a more realistic idea of the actual strength of a girder. Should a girder be loaded until initial buckling occurs, it will not collapse because of a phenomena known as tension field action.

After initial buckling a plate girder acts much like a truss. The web acts as a truss with tension diagonals and is able to resist additional shear. A diagonal strip of the web acts similarly to the diagonal of a parallel chorded truss (see Fig. 16-20). The stiffeners keep the flanges from coming together and the flanges keep the stiffeners from coming

Fig. 16-20. Tension field action in plate-girder web.

together. The intermediate stiffeners which before initial buckling were assumed to resist no load will after buckling resist compressive loads (or will serve as the compression verticals of a truss) due to diagonal tension. The result is that a plate-girder web can probably resist loads equal to two or three times those present at initial buckling before complete collapse will occur.

Until the web buckles initially, deflections are relatively small but after initial buckling the girder's stiffness decreases considerably and deflections may increase to several times the values estimated by the usual deflection theory.

The estimated total or ultimate shear which a panel (a part of the girder between a pair of stiffeners) can withstand equals the shear initially causing web buckling plus the shear which can be resisted by tension field action. The amount of tension field action is dependent on the proportions of the panels.

Based on a consideration of the ultimate shearing strength of a girder, AISC Formulas 1.10-1 and 1.10-2 were derived to estimate the maximum permissible shearing stresses in the webs. The average shearing stress f_v in the web of a girder can be computed by $V/t_w h_w$, where t_w and h_w refer to the thickness and height of the web respectively. The AISC says the values of the average shear (f_v) so computed may not exceed the values given by the following expression:

$$F_v = \frac{F_y}{2.89} (C_v) \leqq 0.4\, F_y \qquad \text{(AISC Formula 1.10-1)}$$

Alternately for girders, other than hybrid girders, with intermediate stiffeners designed as required by the AISC and if $C_v \leqq 1.0$ the allowable shear of Formula 1.10-2 may be used instead of that given by Formula 1.10-1.

$$F_v = \frac{F_y}{2.89} \left[C_v + \frac{1 - C_v}{1.15\sqrt{1 + (a/h)^2}} \leqq 0.4 F_y \right] \qquad \text{(AISC Formula 1.10-2)}$$

In these expressions a is the clear stiffener spacing. The definition of the other terms are given in AISC Sec. 1.10.5.2. The allowable values of the shear stress computed from these formulas are given in Table 3 in Appendix A of the AISC Manual for each of the steels.

Before an allowable shearing stress can be obtained for a particular girder it is necessary to try a stiffener spacing. Should the computed shearing stress not exceed the value given by these equations, no more intermediate stiffeners are required.

Using the AISC Specification overall economy can usually be obtained when unstiffened webs, or those which are sufficiently thick to carry shear without buckling, are used. Even though plate girders with unstiffened webs are heavier than those with intermediate stiffeners they usually cost less due to smaller fabrication costs. (In addition design calculations are reduced by about 50 percent.) The girder of Example 16-4 is proportioned with intermediate stiffeners to show how they are designed. An unstiffened girder would probably have been more economical.

Combined Bending And Shear. Another factor pertaining to the web design which needs to be investigated is the combined action of the shearing stress and the tension due to the moment in the plane of the web. The AISC says that the bending tensile stress in a plate girder web which depends upon tension field action subject to a combination of shear and tension cannot exceed 0.6 F_y nor the value given by the following expression in which f_v is the computed average shearing stress and F_v is the allowable shearing stress from AISC Formula 1.10-2.

$$\left(0.825 - 0.375\,\frac{f_v}{F_v}\right)F_y \qquad \text{(AISC Formula 1.10-7)}$$

The Commentary on AISC Specification says that plate-girder webs can be proportioned on the basis of bending stress alone if the shearing stress does not exceed 0.6 of its permissible value; or can be proportioned on the basis of shear alone when the bending stress does not exceed ¾ of its maximum value. Otherwise Formula 12 is to be applied.

16-11. PROPORTIONS OF FLANGE—AISC

The following expression for the area of the flange to resist a certain bending moment was developed in Sec. 16-4.

$$A_f = \frac{M}{fh} - \frac{th}{6}$$

It was assumed that there was an internal couple producing a resisting moment. Each force in the couple is equal to its flange area and web equivalent times a stress slightly less than the allowable stress in the extreme fiber. The lever arm is the distance between the centers of gravities of the forces.

Substitution into this expression gives the estimated flange area required from which the actual proportions of the flange can be decided. It will be remembered that the AISC (Sec. 1.9.1.2) to prevent local buckling of the compression flange says that the extended length of the flange divided by its thickness may not exceed $95.0/\sqrt{F_y}$. For A36 steel the protruding length may not be greater than $16t$, or it may be said that the maximum flange width is $32t$.

The usual beam theory says that the flexure stress in a plate girder varies proportionately with the distance from the neutral axis. Tests, however, have shown that the stress in the web on the compression side of the girder is less than this theory would indicate because the web deflects a small amount laterally. These lateral deflections cause the flange compression stresses to be in excess of those anticipated. The result is that nearly all of the compression stress is carried by the compression flange. On some occasions it is necessary to reduce the allowable bending stress in that flange. It has been found that if the web depth to thickness ratio exceeds $76.0/\sqrt{F_y}$ there is a slight buckling of the web. AISC Formula 1.10-5 is to be used when the ratio   is exceeded and the

AISC says that the allowable flange stress F'_b may not be greater than the following:

$$F'_b < F_b \left[1.0 - 0.0005 \frac{A_w}{A_f} \left(\frac{h}{t} - \frac{760}{\sqrt{F_b}} \right) \right] \qquad \text{(AISC Formula 1.10-5)}$$

In girders with sufficient lateral support F_b in the preceding expression is $0.60F_y$. Should sufficient lateral support not be available it is necessary to use the formula of Sec. 1.5.1.4.6a to obtain F_b.

16-12. DESIGN OF STIFFENERS—AISC

Bearing Stiffeners. The purpose and arrangement of bearing stiffeners was previously discussed in Sec. 16-7 and examples were shown in Figs. 16-13 and 16-14. The AISC says that the area of the stiffeners outside of the welds between the web and the flange [see Fig. 16-13 (b)] must be sufficiently large to keep the bearing stress from exceeding $0.90\ F_y$ (Sec. 1.5.1.5.1).

. The AISC says that bearing stiffeners should be reviewed as columns. For an end-bearing stiffener the "column" is assumed to consist of the parts of the stiffener outside of the web welds plus a length of the web equal to 12 times its thickness ($25t$ for intermediate bearing stiffeners). The stresses so obtained should not exceed the allowable column stress using an effective length equal to ¾ of the actual stiffener lengths. If the plate girder is securely fastened to columns at its ends by plates and/or angles end bearing stiffeners are usually unnecessary.

Intermediate Stiffeners. As previously described the post buckling behavior of a plate girder involving tension field action causes the stiffeners to act as compression members. AISC Formula 1.10-3 provides an area of intermediate stiffeners which is supposedly sufficient to withstand the compression so produced.

$$A_{st} = \frac{1 - C_v}{2} \left[\frac{a}{h} - \frac{(a/h)^2}{\sqrt{1 + (a/h)^2}} \right] Y\,Dht \qquad \text{(AISC Formula 1.10-3)}$$

The various terms included in this expression are given along with the formula in Sec. 1.10.5.4 of the AISC. Fortunately values of this rather complicated expression are recorded in the tables of the Appendix to the AISC Specification in the AISC Manual. The values given are expressed as percentages of the web area.

If a single plate or angle stiffener is used (instead of one angle or plate on both sides of the web), the AISC says the area obtained from Formula 1.10-3 should be multiplied by 1.8 if single-angle stiffeners are used and 2.4 if single-plate stiffeners are used. One-sided stiffeners are subject to moment in addition to axial load and it is necessary to increase their cross-sectional area to take into account their less efficient operation.

In Sec. 1.10.5.4 an expression is given to estimate the shear in pounds per inch which must be transferred between the intermediate stiffeners and web during shear transfer due to tension field action. This expression follows:

$$f_{vs} = h \sqrt{\left(\frac{F_y}{340}\right)^3} \qquad \text{(AISC Formula 1.10-4)}$$

If the actual web shear ($f_v = V/ht_w$) is less than the allowable shear at the point (Formula 1.10-2), the shear to be transferred can be reduced in direct proportion.

16-13. EXAMPLE PLATE GIRDER DESIGN—AISC

Example 16-4 illustrates the design of a welded plate girder supporting column loads at its one-third points using the AISC Specification. Since the girder is assumed to have full lateral support the allowable bending stress is 0.6 F_y or the value determined from Formula 1.10-5, which is the formula used when there is lateral buckling of the web on the compression side of the girder. For cases where full lateral support is not provided it is necessary to apply Formulas 1.5-6 and 1.5-7 in addition to Formula 1.10-5.

The cover-plate size can be reduced in those areas where the moments are smaller, the smaller plates being butt-welded to the larger plate. Space is not taken in this example to show such calculations. If the plates are changed in size, it is to be remembered that the smaller plates as well as the larger ones must meet the $95.0/\sqrt{F_y}$ requirement for their width-thickness ratios.

EXAMPLE 16-4. A welded plate girder is to be designed for a 54-ft simple span and is to support 150 k column loads at its one-third points together with a uniform load of 2 k/ft. The design is to be made with A36 steel, E60 electrodes, and the AISC specification, assuming that full lateral support is provided for the compression flange. For the convenience of the student, AISC section and formula numbers are shown throughout the example.

Solution: (a) Selection of web:

Assume girder depth = $\frac{1}{10} l = 65$ in.

Assume web depth = 62 in.

Maximum h/t ratio for no stress reduction in allowable flange stress = $760/\sqrt{22} = 162$ (Sec. 1.10.6).

Therefore, minimum t for no stress reduction = $62/162 = 0.383$ in.

Absolute maximum clear distance between flanges $= 322\ t$ (Sec. 1.10.2 and Appendix, p. 5-74).

Therefore, absolute minimum $t = 62/322 = 0.192$ in.

Try web PL $\frac{5}{8} \times 62$

(b) Shear and moment diagrams:

Area of web $= A_w = (62)\ (\frac{5}{16}) = 19.4$ sq in.

Weight of web $= (19.4/144)\ (490) = 66$ lb/ft

Estimated weight of flanges and stiffeners
(after some scratch-paper work)
$$= 200\ \text{lb/ft}$$
Total estimated girder weight $= \overline{266}$ lb/ft

Moment and shear diagrams are shown in Fig. 16-21.

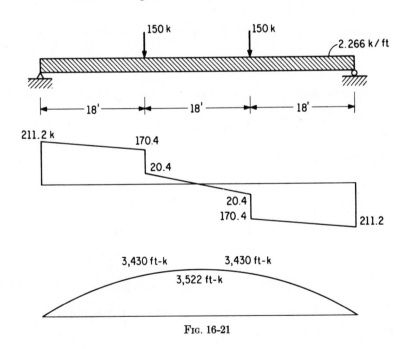

Fig. 16-21

(c) Flange selection:

Assume average flange stress $= (31.00/32.75)\ (22) = 20.9$ ksi

$$A_f = \frac{M}{fh} - \frac{1}{6}th = \frac{(12)\ (3,522)}{(20.9)\ (62.5)} - \left(\frac{1}{6}\right)\left(\frac{5}{16}\right)(62) = 29.2 \text{ sq in.}$$

Try PL $1\frac{1}{2} \times 20$ each flange $(A_f = 30.0$ sq in.$)$

Checking local buckling (AISC 1.9.1 and Appendix, p. 5-72)

$$\frac{10}{1.5} = 6.67 < 15.8$$

Review of flange stresses:

$$I = (\tfrac{1}{12})\,(\tfrac{5}{16})\,(62)^3 + (2)\,(30.0)\,(31.75)^2 \; = 66{,}700 \text{ in.}^4$$

$$f_b = \frac{(12)\,(3{,}522)\,(32.75)}{66{,}700} = 20.6 \text{ ksi}$$

Since $h/t = 62/\tfrac{5}{16} = 198 > 162$, allowable flange stress must be reduced from 22.0 ksi using AISC Formula 1.10-5.

$$F'_b = 22.0 \left[1.0 - 0.0005 \left(\frac{19.4}{30.0}\right) \left(198 - \frac{760}{\sqrt{22}}\right) \right]$$

$$= 21.7 \text{ ksi} > 20.5 \text{ ksi} \tag{OK}$$

(d) Location of first intermediate stiffener (AISC 1.10.5.2 and 1.10.5.3):

$$f_v \text{ at end} = \frac{211.2}{(62)\,(\tfrac{5}{16})} = 10.88 \text{ ksi}$$

$a =$ allowable spacing between stiffeners at end panels

$$= \frac{(11{,}000)\,(\tfrac{5}{16})}{\sqrt{10{,}880}} = 32.9 \text{ in.}$$

Tentatively place first intermediate stiffener 32 in. from end

$$\frac{a}{h} = \text{aspect ratio} = \frac{32}{62} = 0.516$$

$$\frac{h}{t} = \text{slenderness ratio} = \frac{62}{\tfrac{5}{16}} = 198$$

From which

$$\text{Allowable } F_v = 11.7 \text{ ksi} > 10.88 \text{ ksi} \tag{OK}$$

(AISC Formulas 1.10-1 and 1.10-2 and AISC Appendix Table 3-36)

(e) Spacing of other intermediate stiffeners:

Shear 2 ft 8 in. from end of girder $= 211.2 - (2.67)\,(2.266) = 205.1$ k

$$f_v = \frac{205.1}{19.4} = 10.55 \text{ ksi}$$

Intermediate stiffeners (AISC 1.10.5.3) not required if $h/t < 260$ and f_v < value permitted by Formula 1.10-2.

A bearing stiffener will be located under the column load 184 in. from the first intermediate stiffener.

For $a/h = 184/62 = 2.96$ and $h/t = 198$, $F_v < 10.55$ ksi.

Therefore, intermediate stiffeners are required.

Maximum value of $\dfrac{a}{h} = \left(\dfrac{260}{h/t}\right)^2$ (AISC 1.10.5.3)

From which maximum $a = (62)\left(\dfrac{260}{198}\right)^2 = 107$ in.

Try intermediate stiffener at $\frac{1}{2}$ point (at 92 in.)

$$\frac{a}{h} = \frac{92}{62} = 1.48$$

$$\frac{h}{t} = 198$$

Allowable F_v from AISC Table 3-36 = 7.63 ksi $<$ 10.55 ksi   (N.G.)

Try intermediate stiffeners at 1/6 points (at approx. 31 in.)

$$\frac{a}{h} = \frac{31}{62} = 0.5$$

$$\frac{h}{t} = 198$$

Allowable F_v from AISC Table 3-36 = 12.03 ksi $>$ 10.55 ksi   (OK)

Use approximately 31 in. spacing for 18 ft on each end of girder

Combined shear and bending at column loads:

$$f_v = \frac{170.4}{19.4} = 8.8 \text{ ksi}$$

Allowable bending stress F_b obtained from Formula 1.10-7 is

$$F_b = 0.6\, F_y = 22 \text{ ksi}$$

or

$$F_b = \left(0.825 - 0.375\,\frac{8.8}{11.12}\right)36 = 19.1 \text{ ksi}$$

$$f_b = \frac{(12)\,(3{,}430)\,(31.25)}{67{,}600} = 19.0 \text{ ksi} < 19.1 \text{ ksi} \qquad \text{(OK)}$$

Intermediate stiffeners between column loads:

$$f_v = \frac{20.4}{19.4} = 1.05 \text{ ksi}$$

BUILT-UP BEAMS AND PLATE GIRDERS

If no stiffeners are used, $a = (12)\ (18) = 216$ in.

$$\frac{a}{h} = \frac{216}{62} = 3.48$$

$$\frac{h}{t} = 198$$

Allowable F_v from AISC Table 3-36 $= 2.15$ ksi > 1.05 ksi   (OK)

Check web at $\mathcal{L}$ of center span to see if stiffener needed as per Sec. 1.10.10.2 and Formula 16. Assume construction prevents rotation of compression flange.

As described in Sec. 1.10.10.2 the calculated compression stress $= 2.266/(12 \times \frac{5}{16}) = 0.604$ ksi.

Allowable compression stress is

$$\left[5.5 + \frac{4}{(216/62)^2}\right] \frac{10,000}{(198)^2} = 1.49 \text{ ksi} > 0.604 \text{ ksi}   \text{(OK)}$$

Place stiffeners as shown in Fig. 16-24

(f) Design of bearing stiffeners (Sec. 1.10.5, 1.10.10 and 1.5.15.2):

Try 2—8 in. PLs

$$\text{Maximum } \frac{w}{t} \text{ ratio} = \frac{95.0}{\sqrt{36}}$$

$$\text{Minimum } t = \frac{8}{16} = 0.500 \text{ in.}$$

Checking bearing stress:

Allowable bearing $F_p = 0.90\ F_y = 33.0$ ksi (Sec. 1.5.1.5.1 and AISC Table 3-36).

Assuming $\frac{3}{8}$-in. welds between web and flange, $7\frac{5}{8}$ in. of PLs left to support load. Therefore,

$$f_p = \frac{150}{(2)\ (7\frac{5}{8})\ (\frac{1}{2})} = 19.7 \text{ ksi} < 33.0 \text{ ksi}   \text{(OK)}$$

Checking column action (Sec. 1.10.5):

"Column" area is shown in Fig. 16-22.

$$A_v = (7.8)\ (\frac{5}{16})   = 2.44 \text{ sq in.}$$

$$A \text{ PLs} = (2)\ (7\frac{5}{8})\ (\frac{1}{2}) = 7.62 \text{ sq in.}$$

$$A \text{ column}   = \overline{10.06 \text{ sq in.}}$$

$$I = (\tfrac{1}{12})(7.8)(\tfrac{5}{16})^3 + (2)(\tfrac{1}{12})\ (\tfrac{1}{2})(7\frac{5}{8})^3 + (2)(3.81)(4.34)^2 = 181 \text{ in.}^4$$

$$r = \sqrt{\frac{181}{10.06}} = 4.24$$

FIG. 16-22

Effective length $= Kl = \frac{3}{4} \times 62 = 46.5$ in. (Sec. 1.10.5)

$$\frac{Kl}{r} = \frac{46.5}{4.24} = 10.95$$

Allowable $F_a = 21.1$ ksi

Actual $f_a = \dfrac{150}{10.06} = 14.9$ ksi < 21.1 ksi   (OK)

<u>Use 2 PLs $\frac{1}{2} \times 8$ under column loads</u>

(g) Design of end bearing stiffeners:

Try 2—8 in. PLs

$$\text{Minimum } t = \frac{8}{16} = \frac{1}{2} \text{ in.}$$

Check bearing stress:

Allowable bearing $F_p = 0.90\, F_y = 33.0$ ksi

Assuming $\frac{3}{8}$-in. welds, $7\frac{5}{8}$ in. of PL left to support load. Therefore,

$$f_p = \frac{211.2}{(2)\,(7\frac{5}{8})\,(\frac{1}{2})} = 27.7 \text{ ksi} < 33.0 \text{ ksi} \qquad \text{(OK)}$$

Checking column action:

"Column" area is shown in Fig. 16-23.

$$A = (3.75)\,(\tfrac{5}{16}) + (2)\,(7\tfrac{5}{8})\,(\tfrac{1}{2}) = 8.80 \text{ sq in.}$$

$$I = 181 \text{ in.}^4$$

$$r = \sqrt{\frac{181}{8.80}} = 4.54$$

Effective length $= Kl = (\frac{3}{4})\,(62) = 46.5$ in.

$$\frac{Kl}{r} = \frac{46.5}{4.54} = 10.25$$

Allowable $F_a = 21.15$ ksi

Actual $f_a = \dfrac{211.2}{8.80} = 24.0$ ksi   (N.G.)

Subsequent calculations show $\frac{9}{16}$ stiffener satisfactory.

Use 2 PLs $\frac{9}{16} \times 8$ in. at girder ends

(h) Design of intermediate stiffeners:

Minimum required gross area of interior stiffener can be determined from AISC Formula 1.10-3, but values are recorded in AISC Table 3-36 for A36 steel.

For $h/t = 198$ and $a/h = 31/62 = 0.5$ minimum $A = (0.0277)(62)(\frac{5}{16})$ $= 0.527$

Try 2 PLs $\frac{1}{4} \times 4$

I about web $= (\frac{1}{3})\,(\frac{1}{4})\,(4)^3\,(2) = 10.67$ in.^{4}

Minimum I permissible (Sec. 1.10.5.4) $= \left(\dfrac{h}{50}\right)^4 = \left(\dfrac{62}{50}\right)^4 = 2.37 < 10.67$ (OK)

$$\frac{w}{t} = \frac{4}{\frac{1}{4}} = 16 \qquad\qquad\text{(OK)}$$

Intermediate stiffeners may be stopped a distance equal to four times the web thickness from the tension flange (Sec. 1.10.5.4).

$$L = 62.0 - (4)\,(\tfrac{5}{16}) = 60\tfrac{3}{4}$$

Use 2 PLs $\frac{1}{4} \times 4 \times 60\frac{3}{4}$ in. bearing on compression flange only

(i) Design of welds between web and intermediate stiffeners:

Total shear transferred $= f_{vs}$ (Sec. 1.10.5.4)

$$f_{vs} = h \sqrt{\left(\frac{F_y}{340}\right)^3}$$

$$= 62 \sqrt{\left(\frac{36}{340}\right)^3} = 2{,}150 \text{ lb/in. on two stiffener welds}$$

Assuming $\frac{3}{16}$ in. welds 3 in. long $= 1.8$ k/in. $\times 2 = 3.6$ k/in.

$$\text{Spacing} = \frac{(3)\ (3.6)\ (2)}{l} = 2.15$$

$$l = 10.05 \text{ in.}$$

Use $\frac{3}{16} \times 3$ welds 10 in. on centers

(j) Design of flange to web welds:

$$v = \text{horizontal shear between flange and web} = \frac{VQ}{I}$$

$$Q = (30)\ (32) = 960 \text{ in.}^3$$

$$v \text{ at girder end} = \frac{(211.2)\ (960)}{67,600} = 3.00 \text{ k/in.}$$

Minimum weld size $= \frac{5}{16}$ in. for $1\frac{1}{2}$ PL (AISC Table 1.17.5)

Assuming $\frac{5}{16}$ welds (E60 electrodes),

Allowable shear $= (2)\ (5)\ (0.6) = 6.0$ k/in.

Allowable shear on $\frac{5}{16}$ web $= (\frac{5}{16})\ (14.5) = 4.5$ k/in.

Minimum l of fillet welds $= (4)\ (\frac{5}{16}) = 1\frac{1}{4}$ in. (Sec. 1.17.6)

 Try $\frac{5}{16} \times 3$ welds located $(4)\ (4.5)/3.00 = 6$ in. on centers

Maximum spacing of compression flange to web welds (Sec. 1.18.3.1) is

$$24 \times \frac{5}{16} = 7.5 \text{ in.} > 6 \text{ in.} \qquad \text{(OK)}$$

Use $\frac{5}{16} \times 4$-in. welds 6 in. on centers

(k) Design of welds between bearing stiffeners and web:

Fɪɢ. 16-24

Use continuous welds both sides since bearing stiffeners are major load-carrying members.

Minimum weld size $= \frac{3}{16}$ (or 1.8 lb/in.)

Total strength furnished $= (2)\ (62)\ (1.8) = 223\ \text{k} > 211.2\ \text{k}$ (OK)

Use $\frac{3}{16}$ continuous fillet welds for all bearing stiffeners

(*l*) Design sketch of final girder design shown in Fig. 16-24.

PROBLEMS

16-1. A 50-ft plate girder consists of a $\frac{1}{2} \times 54$-in. web, $6 \times 6 \times \frac{1}{2}$-in. flange angles, and two $\frac{1}{2} \times 16$-in. plates on each flange. Determine the maximum tension and compression stresses for a bending moment of 2,400 ft-k. Assume 1-in. holes are placed in 4 in. on centers in the web and assume there are two cover plate rivets and one flange rivet at a section. AASHO Specifications. (Ans. $f_c = 17.6$ ksi, $f_t = 20.8$ ksi)

16-2. Repeat Prob. 16-1 assuming the girder to be welded.

16-3. Using the AASHO Specifications and structural carbon steel (A36), compute the maximum allowable bending moment for a riveted plate girder consisting of an $\frac{5}{8} \times 80$-in. web, $8 \times 6 \times \frac{3}{4}$-in. flange angles, and three $\frac{5}{8} \times 18$-in. cover plates on each flange. Assume holes of the size and distribution mentioned in Prob. 16-1. (Ans. 6,840 ft-k)

16-4. Determine the theoretical cutoff points of the outside and middle cover plates of the girder of Prob. 16-1 if it is assumed to be uniformly loaded.

16-5. Repeat Prob. 16-3 assuming the girder to be welded leaving off flange angles and assuming $F_b = 20$ ksi. (Ans. 5,550 ft-k)

16-6. Using the AASHO Specifications design end stiffeners for the girder of Prob. 16-3 if the maximum end reaction is 260 k.

16-7. Design a single-plate web splice for the girder of Prob. 16-3 if the external shear is assumed to be 150 k at the splice. (Ans. 2 PLs $\frac{9}{16} \times 25 \times 5'8''$ with 4 rows of rivets)

16-8. Design a triple-plate splice for the conditions described in Prob. 16-7.

16-9. Preliminary designs are to be made for a plate girder with A36 steel, the AASHO Specifications and $\frac{7}{8}$-in. bolts for a maximum bending moment of 3,000 ft-k and a maximum shear of 250 k. Proportion the girder with total depths of 48, 64, and 80 in. and compare the resulting cross-sectional areas. (Ans. 121.8, 96.5, and 104.5 sq in. respectively)

16-10. Rework Prob. 16-9 using a welded girder, A242 steel, and the AASHO Specifications.

16-11. Rework Prob. 16-9 using a welded girder, A36 steel, and the AISC Specification. (Ans. 80.0, 69.0, and 61.3 sq in. respectively)

16-12. If the external shear is 220 k at a section in the girder of Prob. 16-3, determine the theoretical spacing required for $\frac{7}{8}$-in. flange and cover-plate rivets using the AASHO Specifications and A36 steel. It is assumed that a 30 k concentrated load can be applied at the section. Assume this load is distributed over 12 in. by the time it reaches the girder and that rivets are arranged as in Fig. 16-10.

16-13. Repeat Prob. 16-12 if ⅞-in. A325 high-strength bearing bolts and the AISC Specification are used. (Ans. Theoretical values: flange bolts 7.67 in., cover plate-plate bolts 17.35 in.)

16-14. Design a bolted plate girder with A36 steel using the AISC Specification for the situation shown in the accompanying illustration. The girder is to be connected with ⅞-in. A325 high-strength bearing bolts. Full lateral support is assumed for the compression flange.

PROB. 16-14

16-15. Rework Prob. 16-14 using a welded girder and E60 electrodes.

16-16. Repeat Prob. 16-15 if lateral support for the compression flange is provided at the ends and column points only.

chapter 17

DESIGN OF ROOF TRUSSES

17-1. INTRODUCTION

Trusses may be defined as large, deep beams with open webs. They are usually formed by members arranged in triangles or groups of triangles, and the number of possible types is almost endless. The purposes of roof trusses are to keep the elements out (rain, snow, wind) and to support the loads connected underneath (ducts, piping, ceiling). While performing these functions they must also support the roofs and their own weight.

The engineer is often concerned with the problem of selecting a truss or a beam to span a given opening. Should no other factors be present, the decision would probably be based on consideration of economy. The smallest amount of material will nearly always be used if a truss is selected for spanning a certain opening; however, the cost of fabrication and erection of trusses will probably be appreciably higher than required for beams. For shorter spans the overall cost of beams (material plus fabrication and erection) will definitely be less but as the spans become greater, the higher fabrication and erection costs of trusses will be more than canceled by their weight saving. A further advantage of trusses is that for the same amounts of material they have greater stiffnesses than do beams.

On the subject of truss depths, it should be realized that the deeper a truss is made for a given span and loading the smaller will be the chord members, but that with deeper trusses the lengths of the web members increase. This fact means that the slenderness ratios of the web members may become a factor and require the use of heavier members.

It is impossible to give a lower economical span for steel trusses. They may be used for spans as small as 30 or 40 ft and as large as 300 to 400 ft. Actually they are not often used today for spans of less than 60 ft. Beams may be economical for some applications for spans much greater than the lower limits mentioned for trusses. The AISC Specifica-

450

tion permits the design of very thin webbed plate girders (see Chap. 16) which are quite competitive with roof trusses for many spans.

In the pages to follow the terms *pitch* and *slope* are often used. The pitch of a symmetrical truss is referred to as the rise of the top chord of the truss divided by the span. Should the truss be unsymmetrical, the numerical value of its pitch is not of much use. For such cases the slope

Truss for a Bethlehem Steel Company building at Lackawanna, N. Y., shipped upside-down. (*Bethlehem Steel Company.*)

of the truss on each side can be given. The slope is the rise of the top chord to its horizontal length often given as so many inches per horizontal foot. For symmetrical trusses the slope will equal twice the pitch.

17-2. TYPES OF ROOF TRUSSES

Roof trusses can be flat or peaked. In the past the peaked roof trusses have probably been used more for short-span buildings and the flatter trusses for the longer spans. The trend today for spans long or short, however, seems to be away from the peaked trusses and towards the flatter ones, the change being due to the appearance desired and perhaps more economical construction of roof decks.

Several of the commonly used types of roof trusses are shown in Fig. 17-1. A good many of these trusses have been named for the engi-

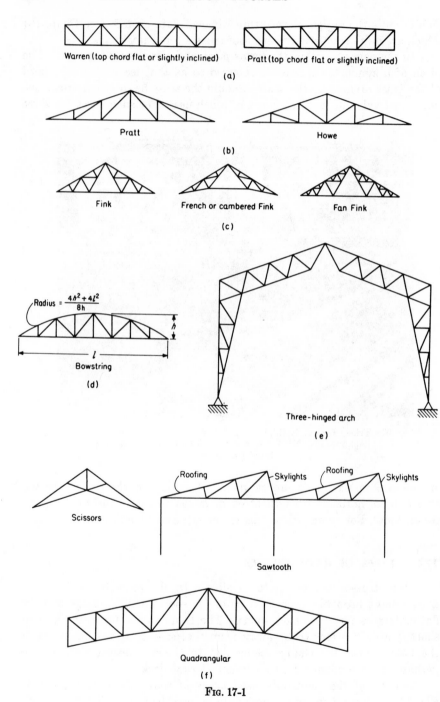

Warren (top chord flat or slightly inclined)

Pratt (top chord flat or slightly inclined)

(a)

Pratt

Howe

(b)

Fink

French or cambered Fink

Fan Fink

(c)

$$\text{Radius} = \frac{4h^2 + 4l^2}{8h}$$

h

l

Bowstring

(d)

Three-hinged arch

(e)

Scissors

Roofing   Skylights   Roofing   Skylights

Sawtooth

Quadrangular

(f)

FIG. 17-1

neers or architects who first developed them. A remark or two is made about each of these trusses in the paragraphs to follow. The letter at the beginning of each of these paragraphs corresponds to the letter in Fig. 17-1 beneath the type of truss being considered.

(a) The Warren and Pratt trusses have probably been used more for the flatter roofs (slopes of from $\frac{3}{4}$ to $1\frac{1}{4}$ in. per foot) where built-up roofing can be satisfactorily applied, than have the other types of trusses. These trusses can be economically used for flat roofs for spans of roughly 40 to 125 ft, although they have been used for spans as great as 200 ft. The Warren is usually a little more satisfactory than the Pratt.   The roofs may be completely flat for spans not exceeding 30 or 40 ft, but for longer spans the slopes mentioned are used for drainage purposes.

(b) The pitched Pratt and Howe trusses are probably the most common types of medium-rise trusses. The slopes intended here fall in between those given for (a) and (c). They have maximum economical spans of about 90 or 100 ft.

(c) For steep roofs (with slopes of 5 or 6 in. per foot) the Fink truss is very popular. The Pratt and Howe trusses may also be used for steep slopes but they are usually not as economical. The Fink truss has been used for spans as great as 120 ft. A fact which makes it more economical is that most of the members are in tension while those that are in compression are fairly short. The panel layout of a truss may be controlled by the purlin spacings. As it is usually desirable to have purlins placed at panel points only, the main panels may be subdivided. Fink trusses can be divided up into a large number of panels to suit almost any span or purlin spacing. The Fan Fink shown illustrates subdivision very well.

(d) If a curved roof is acceptable, the Bowstring truss can be used economically for spans of up to 120 ft, although on occasions it has satisfactorily been used for much longer spans. When properly designed, this truss has the unusual feature of having very small stresses in the web members. Despite the fact that there is some expense in bending the top chord, the Bowstring has proved quite popular for warehouses, supermarkets, garages, and small industrial buildings. A recommended radius of curvature for the top chord is given in the figure.[1]

(e) When spans appreciably above 100 ft are planned consideration might be given to using steel arches as they may provide the most economical solutions. The three-hinged arch is the only one shown here. As compared to the two-hinged and hingeless arches it has the following advantages:

[1] John E. Lothers, *Design In Structural Steel* (Englewood Cliffs, N.J.: Prentice-Hall, Inc., 1965), p. 348.

1. Analysis is easier as it is statically determinate.
2. Poor foundations are not such a serious matter as they might be for an indeterminate arch.
3. Erection is often simplified as the two halves of an arch can be erected separately and pinned together at the crown.

(f) In this part of the figure several miscellaneous types of trusses are shown. The scissors truss (which is so named because of its resemblance to a pair of scissors) may be satisfactory for supporting short span churches and other buildings with steep roofs. Sawtooth trusses may be used when adequate natural lighting is desired from skylights in wide buildings. Their steep faces support skylights and these faces usually face the north for more evenly diffused light. They are used when their numerous columns are not objectionable. A long-span roof truss which has been used for spans well over 100 ft is the Quadrangular truss. Near the centerline of this truss the diagonals are reversed for the purpose of keeping as many of them in tension as possible.

17-3. SELECTION OF TYPE OF ROOF TRUSS

The choice of the particular type of roof truss depends on a number of items including span, loading, preferred type of roof construction from architectural viewpoint, climate, lighting, insulation, and ventilation. The following paragraphs present a discussion of some of the more important factors which may affect the selection.

Pitch. The desired pitch of a roof truss to a great extent controls the selection of the type of truss to be used because, as described in Sec. 17-2, different types of trusses are economical for different slopes of roofs. For instance, the Fink truss is quite satisfactory for the steeper roofs.

Roof Coverings. The type of roof covering used has a great deal to do with the selection of the roof slope. For instance, the built-up tar-and-gravel roofs are probably unsatisfactory for slopes greater than 1 in. per foot, for the tar will tend to run downhill during the warm summer months despite the availability of the so-called steep-roofing tar or pitch. When built-up asphalt-and-gravel roofs are used somewhat steeper slopes are possible. The desirable slopes for slate roofs are about 7 in. per foot because water tends to work up under the slate on flatter slopes. Other desired slopes can be obtained from the manufacturers for the particular types of roof covering to be used.

Fabrication and Transportation Considerations. Fabrication and transportation difficulties need to be considered in selecting the type of truss to be used for a given situation. It is desirable economically to fabricate as much as possible of the truss in the shop—the whole truss if feasible —and to ship it to the job for erection. From a transportation standpoint the depth of the truss is often a controlling factor. As an example for a particular building it is assumed that the designer estimates that a 15-foot-deep truss will be the most economical, but the route along which the truss is to be shipped limits the maximum depths which can be transported to 12 ft. The truss may therefore be limited to a maximum depth of 12 ft, although it will be a little heavier, so that the whole truss can be assembled in the shop.

Tightening high-strength bolts. (*Bethlehem Steel Company.*)

Architectural Effect Desired. The ideas of the architect as to the aesthetic effect desired can quite well be the controlling factor. For example, he may want a flat roof and that will pretty well narrow the choice down to one or two trusses.

Climate. The climate in the particular area may be particularly important as to drainage, or retention of snow and ice.

17-4. SPACING AND SUPPORT OF ROOF TRUSSES

The spacing of roof trusses depends upon the type of roof construction, truss spans, and foundation conditions. The usual center-to-center spacings vary from 12 to 30 ft, the lower spacings used for the shorter spans and the larger spacings for the longer spans. For the 50- and 60-ft spans, spacings of roughly 12 to 20 ft on centers are common, while values of from 15 to 24 ft are common for 90- to 100-ft spans. For very long-span roof trusses, say more than 140 or 150 ft, the center-to-center spacings may be as great as 50 or 60 ft. The purlins for such large spacings are probably trusses themselves framing into the sides of the main trusses. These trusses will provide a large part of the lateral bracing needed. When poor soil conditions are present causing expensive foundations, the designer may use larger center-to-center truss spacings than he would under ordinary conditions.

The usual truss is supported on brick, block, or concrete walls or on steel or reinforced concrete columns. Trusses are usually attached at their ends to these walls or columns with anchor bolts. To provide for temperature expansion and contraction it is usually necessary to have the anchor bolts at one end set in a slotted hole in the bearing plate to permit the required shortening or lengthening. The estimated change in length of the truss equals the coefficient of expansion times the estimated temperature change times the span length plus the diameter of the anchor bolt plus a little margin. Some consideration should be given to the temperature at the time of erection as it pertains to placing the anchor bolt or positioning the slot. Should the truss be erected in the middle of the summer, it seems logical that the anchor bolt should be near the outer end of the slot as the truss will be expanded to a point near its greatest anticipated length. The dead and live loads supported by a truss also affect the length of the truss.

17-5. ESTIMATED WEIGHT OF ROOF TRUSSES

The usual loads to which roof trusses may be subjected were discussed in Chap. 13; therefore, the only discussion of loads in this chapter pertains to the estimated weights of the roof trusses themselves.

The weight of a roof truss can be estimated by the designer on the basis of his previous experience or by some reference to the various tables, curves, or formulas which have been developed for this purpose. An important fact to remember is that the designer certainly cannot estimate snow, ice or wind loads to the nearest 1 percent. Furthermore, he can only roughly estimate what the users of a building may hang on the trusses from below. These facts should show that it is unrealistic to expect him to estimate truss weights to the nearest 1 percent. In fact, estimates to the nearest 10 percent are probably quite reasonable.

One method of approximating the weight of a roof truss and its bracing is to estimate it to equal about 10 percent of the load it is to be required to support. For long spans the percentage probably should be increased a little. When the truss design is completed its weight should be roughly calculated and compared with the original weight estimate to see if that estimate was within reason.

Based on the previous experience of the design profession, the designer can estimate the weight of roof trusses as equaling so many pounds per square foot of roof surface. Dr. L. E. Grinter[2] recommends the following values, which vary somewhat with different spans and roof pitches:

1. For 40-ft spans and pitches varying from ⅓ to ¼ estimate truss weight equal to between 2 and 3½ lb for each square foot of roof surface.

2. For each 10 ft increase in span up to 80 ft the previous values should be increased by approximately 1 lb.

3. Increase the values by roughly ½ to 1 lb per square foot of roof surface for flat roofs.

4. Decrease the values by roughly ½ to 1 lb per square foot of roof surface for steeper roofs.

Through the years quite a few empirical formulas have been developed for estimating the weight of steel roof trusses. Nearly any of these expressions will give reasonable estimates if they are properly applied. One comment, however, should be made concerning expressions which are several decades old. Unless they take into account allowable stresses they will probably give estimated weights on the high side with today's steels, which have considerably higher allowable stresses than those used when the formulas were first presented.

One satisfactory expression for estimating the weight of steel roof trusses was presented in the *Engineering News Record* in 1919 in an article by Robins Fleming entitled "Weight of Roof Trusses By Empiric Formulas." This expression, which does include an allowable stress value, is as follows:

$$W = \sqrt{\frac{wa}{S}} \, (4 \, l^2 + 60 \, l)$$

where W = total roof truss weight

w = total gravity load supported per horizontal square foot

S = average allowable stress in psi used in design

a = center to center spacing of trusses

l = truss span in feet

17-6. DISCUSSION OF ROOF TRUSS ANALYSIS

Before the members of a roof truss can be selected it is necessary for the truss to be analyzed for the different types of loading which can occur. These loads include dead loads, snow and ice loads, and wind loads. In the more southern states a live load representing the roofers and their materials can be used in place of the snow loads.

A truss will probably be analyzed separately for each of the different types of loads because all of the different loads will probably not occur

[2] L. E. Grinter, *The Design of Steel Structures* (New York: The Macmillan Company, 1960), p. 284.

at the same time. As an illustration, it does not seem altogether logical to assume that a pitched roof will be covered with a full snow load when a 90-mph wind is blowing. Most engineers feel that the majority of the snow would blow off under such conditions, at least on the windward side. (Other engineers think that the snow may have crusted over and be substantially able to remain on the roof during the windstorm.)

There are several possible combinations of loads which may logically be applied at the same time to a roof truss. The three combinations listed at the end of this paragraph seem to cover the situation fairly well. The stresses for each member are computed for each of the different loads and combined for each of the combinations given, and the maximum stress for each member regardless of the combination from which it came is used for design. If a member is in tension for one combination and in compression for the other, it will have to be designed for both values.

1. Dead load + full snow load
2. Dead load + full wind load
3. Dead load + full wind load + ½ snow load

Another combination often used in addition to the preceding ones is a lesser wind (⅓ to ½) combined with dead load + full snow load assuming that such a wind would not blow off the snow.

In the following paragraphs are several further comments which may be of considerable importance for some cases as they pertain to the analysis of roof trusses.

1. The AISC Specification, which is used for a large percentage of steel roof truss designs in the United States, says that allowable stresses can be increased by one-third for stresses caused by wind or earthquake action alone or in combination with dead or live loads. This reduction is conveniently handled by multiplying the second and third load combinations (just given) for maximum stresses by ¾. This specification is followed in Example 17-1 which is presented in Sec. 17-7.

2. The procedure recommended today by the ASCE for estimating wind pressures results in suctions on the leeward sides of roof trusses and perhaps on the windward sides, depending on the slopes. Probably the large majority of designers neglect this suction in their designs.

3. If the AISC one-third reduction and the recommended ASCE wind forces are used for design, it will usually be found that the wind will not require any increases in the member sizes of roof trusses. Some engineers are not too happy about this situation as they feel the wind is another load and should cause greater stresses and thus require larger members. For this reason the Duchemin formula for estimating wind pressures is still occasionally used as it probably will cause stress increases.

4. Consideration may have to be given for the wind blowing from

both directions. If a truss has a roller support on one end and a hinge support on the other, wind from the left may produce different stresses in some members than wind from the right.

5. One further comment is made here concerning the computation of truss stresses, and this pertains to the actual types of end supports as they affect member stresses due to the wind loads. For fairly short trusses probably no provision is made for expansion. This type of truss would actually be statically indeterminate, but the usual practice is to assume that the horizontal load splits equally between the supports. As trusses become longer, expansion supports are used on one end. The designer may assume all the horizontal reaction is provided at the other support or he may more realistically assume that some proportion of the horizontal reaction (as $\frac{1}{4}$ or $\frac{1}{3}$) is actually provided at the expansion end. From this discussion it is obvious that there are several possible variations in the member stresses caused by the horizontal loads, depending on the assumptions made.

17-7. EXAMPLE ANALYSIS OF A ROOF TRUSS

Stresses are computed in this section for a roof truss with several possible loading conditions, and these various stresses are combined as described in the previous section to obtain the most critical values. The average designer might not go to quite as much detail for a small roof truss as was used here by the author.

The actual stress calculations are not shown in the figure, and only the answers are given. Stresses can be obtained algebraically or graphically, depending on the preference of the individual designer. Perhaps there is little advantage of one method over the other for gravity loads, but the graphical procedure can certainly be a time saver when lateral loads and complicated trusses are involved.

In Example 17-1 stresses are determined for a roof truss separately for dead load, full snow load, half snow load, and wind load. The full-snow and half-snow stresses can be determined by ratio from the dead-load stresses. The author has assumed that the half-snow-load situation consists of half the snow load all the way across the roof. He feels this is a more feasible condition with full wind blowing than assuming a full snow load on one side and none on the other as is often the practice.

The wind can blow from the left as it can from the right; therefore, in the maximum stress table of Example 17-1 the values of the wind stress in a member are given for both directions. To obtain the design stress shown in the final column of the table the most critical value of the wind stress is used. Should the wind or other loads cause stress reversal in a member, both values would be given in the design stress column. In the example problem presented here the dead-load plus snow load condition controlled for every member, but this definitely may not be true for other trusses.

Purlins are placed only at the joints in Example 17-1 to simplify the problem (although the resulting spacing is rather large) and it is unnecessary to consider bending in the top chord members due to intermediate loads. Should the top-chord panel lengths become exceptionally long, it may be economical to place purlins in between the joints. Another case where intermediate purlins might be used arises with certain types of roofing. Should the spacing of purlins not be greater than 4 or 5 ft, certain types of corrugated steel, gypsum tile, or other roofing can be placed directly on the purlins. Average purlins usually weigh from 2 to 5 psf of roof surface.

EXAMPLE 17-1. Determine the critical stresses for design for each of the members of the left-hand side of the truss of Fig. 17-2. Assume the following conditions:

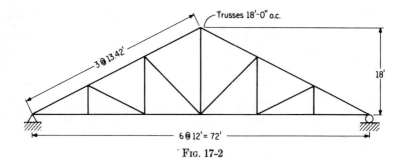

FIG. 17-2

1. Friction to be neglected at the expansion support.
2. Truss weight = 5 psf of roof surface and four purlins (10 WF 33) have been selected for each side of the truss.
3. Snow load = 20 psf of horizontal roof surface projection.
4. Wind loads as follows: 4.2 psf suction on windward side and 9 psf suction on leeward side as recommended by Committee 31 of the ASCE.
5. Roofing = 15 psf.

Solution: (a) Dead load stresses (Fig. 17-3):

$$\text{Truss weight} \quad = (5)\ (18)\ (13.42) = 1{,}205\ \text{lb}$$

$$\text{Roof covering} = (15)\ (18)\ (13.42) = 3{,}615\ \text{lb}$$

$$\text{Purlins} \qquad = (18)\ (33) \qquad\quad = \quad 594\ \text{lb}$$

$$\text{Full panel load} = \qquad\qquad\qquad\qquad\ \ 5{,}414\ \text{lb}$$

MAXIMUM STRESS TABLE

Member	Design Stresses Due to					Stress Combinations			Design Stresses
	Dead Load	Snow Load	Half Snow Load	Wind from Left	Wind from Right	DL+SL	(DL+WL) ¾	(DL+½SL +WL) ¾	
L_0L_1	+27.1	+21.6	+10.8	− 4.73	− 8.90	+48.7	+16.8	+24.9	+48.7
L_1L_2	+27.1	+21.6	+10.8	− 4.73	− 8.90	+48.7	+16.8	+24.9	+48.7
L_2L_3	+21.7	+17.28	+ 8.64	− 3.57	− 6.50	+39.0	+13.6	+20.1	+39.0
L_0U_1	−30.2	−24.1	−12.05	+ 7.25	+ 8.74	−54.3	−17.2	−26.2	−54.3
U_1U_2	−24.2	−19.3	− 9.65	+ 6.46	+ 7.10	−43.5	−13.3	−20.5	−43.5
U_2U_3	−18.2	−14.5	− 7.25	+ 5.76	+ 5.48	−32.7	− 9.5	−15.0	−32.7
U_1L_1	0	0	0	0	0	0	0	0	0
U_1L_2	− 6.1	− 4.8	− 2.40	+ 1.30	+ 2.73	−10.9	− 3.6	− 5.4	−10.9
U_2L_2	+ 2.7	+ 2.16	+ 1.08	− .58	− 1.22	+ 4.86	+ 1.6	+ 2.4	+ 4.9
U_2L_3	− 7.6	− 6.1	− 3.05	+ 1.66	+ 3.42	−13.7	− 4.5	− 6.8	−13.7
U_3L_3	+10.8	+ 8.64	+ 4.32	− 3.59	− 3.59	+19.44	+ 5.4	+ 8.7	+19.4

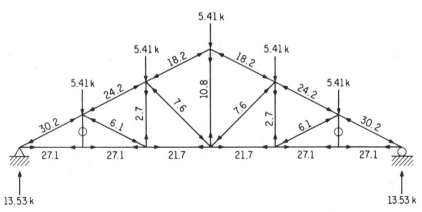

FIG. 17-3

(b) Stresses due to full snow load (Fig. 17-4):

Full panel load = (20) (12) (18) = 4,320 lb

Fig. 17-4

Fig. 17-5

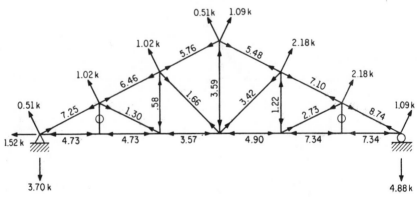

Fig. 17-6

Stresses determined by ratio from dead load stresses.

(c) Stresses due to half snow load (Fig. 17-5):

(d) Stresses due to wind from left (Fig. 17-6) (wind from right not shown):

Full panel load, windward side $= (4.2) (13.42) (18) = 1.02$ k

Full panel load, leeward side $\quad = (9) (13.42) (18) \quad = 2.18$ k

17-8. DESIGN OF A ROOF TRUSS

The members of the truss analyzed for various loading conditions in Example 17-1 are designed in this section, assuming welded connections are to be used. Before these designs are presented a few general remarks are made concerning the selection of the members of roof trusses. These are as follows:

1. For riveted and bolted trusses a pair of angles back-to-back is probably the most common type of member, but for short spans and lightly loaded trusses the single angle is sometimes used. It will be remembered from Sec. 3-5 that the single-angle tension member does have the disadvantage of eccentricity. Should the eccentric moments produced by the eccentricity be considered in the design of single-angle tension members, the resulting sections will probably be no more economical than if pairs of angles had been selected initially. For larger riveted or bolted roof trusses W, M, or S sections may be used for some of the members.

2. For welded roof trusses the chord members are usually made from structural tees, two angle sections or W sections.

3. The web members of roof trusses are commonly made from angles, channels or W sections regardless of the type of connections used.

4. A minimum size roof truss member may be required by the specifications being used or the designer may feel that members under a certain size are too flimsy for practical use. A minimum size member often specified consists of 2 Ls 2 $\times$ 2 $\times$ $\frac{1}{4}$.

5. An effort should be made to limit the width of truss members because it has been found that trusses with very wide members tend to have large secondary stresses.

6. The chord members of roof trusses often consist of one section which is continuous through several panel points. In the example problem given later in this section, the bottom chord is assumed to be continuous for half of the entire span while the top chord members run continuously from the support to the ridge. This means that each of these continuous sections will have to be designed for the maximum stress in any of its members. The result is that they will be overdesigned in some places where smaller stresses occur. This practice may seem to be uneconomical,

but if frequent splices are made to change member sizes where the stresses change the resulting savings in weight will probably be more than canceled by the cost of the splices. If splices have to be made at certain points for shipping or handling purposes, sizes may be economically changed at those points.

7. If purlins are spaced in between the joints of the top chord, moments will be produced and the members should theoretically be analyzed as continuous beams. Perhaps the most common procedure, however, is to assume each member has fixed ends as shown in Fig. 17-7.

FIG. 17-7

Another possibility is to analyze the top chord as a continuous member by moment distribution. Whichever method is used to determine the moments, the member should be designed for the resulting moments plus its direct stress as determined by the usual truss analysis. The design of members subject to bending and direct stress was discussed in Chap. **8**.

8. In Example 17-2 the tension and compression members are selected and shown in tables. The practicing engineer with the aid of various tables and other design data would probably not show his work in such detail, but it is felt that this detail may be of benefit to the student. The tables used are thought to be self explanatory. Perhaps a few comments will be helpful concerning the "minimum r" column in each of the tables. It will be remembered that the AISC permits maximum slenderness ratios of **240** and **200** respectively for main tension and compression members. The smallest permissible values of r are calculated for each of the members with their different lengths. This minimum value is of great assistance in preventing the designer from selecting members which are too slender, a fact he might not otherwise immediately discover. The minimum r values are of particular benefit in selecting members which have rather small stresses.

9. Should a member be subjected to stress reversal, a situation which does not occur in this example, it would have to be designed to resist both tension and compression.

EXAMPLE 17-2. Select member sizes for the truss analyzed in Example 17-1 assuming welded connections. Use A36 steel and the AISC Specification.
   Solution:

DESIGN OF TENSION MEMBERS

Member	Design Stress (k)	Area Required (sq in.)	Minimum Permissible r (in.)	Section Selected	Area Furnished (sq in.)	l/r
L_0L_1	+48.7	2.21	0.60	WT 3×8	2.36	171
L_1L_2	+48.7	2.21	0.60	WT 3×8	2.36	171
L_2L_3	+39.0	1.77	0.60	WT 3×8	2.36	171
U_2L_2	+ 4.9	0.22	0.60	2 Ls 2×2×¼	1.88	236
U_3L_3	+19.4	0.88	0.90	2 Ls 3×3×¼	2.88	232
U_1L_1	0	0	0.30	2 Ls 2×2×¼	1.88	118

DESIGN OF COMPRESSION MEMBERS

Member	Design Stress (k)	Minimum Permissible r, (in.)	Section Selected	l/r
L_0U_1	−54.3	0.81	WT 7×17	110
U_1U_2	−43.5	0.81	WT 7×17	110
U_2U_3	−32.7	0.81	WT 7×17	110
U_1L_2	−10.9	0.81	2 Ls 3×2×5⁄16 *	187
U_2L_3	−13.7	1.02	2 Ls 3½×2½×5⁄16 *	194

* Assuming ¼ in. spacing between Ls.

17-9. TRUSSES FOR INDUSTRIAL BUILDINGS

For many industrial buildings the roof is supported by a steel truss rigidly connected to supporting columns. Examples of this type of construction are shown in Fig. 17-8. For the arrangement shown in part (a) of the figure there is very little lateral rigidity unless knee braces (shown with dotted lines) are used. Knee braces are generally placed at angles of approximately 45°. Another type of industrial building truss is shown in part (b). It will be noted that knee braces are unnecessary for this type.

For a good many years one story industrial buildings were of the general type shown in Fig. 17-8. The name given to them was "mill buildings." These buildings, which provide large open areas, are quite

(a)   (b)

Fig. 17-8

economical to construct; but they are not especially attractive and lighting may be a problem. In recent years a large percentage of the market formerly taken by mill buildings has been taken over by rigid frame structures (considered in Chap. 19).

Mill buildings usually have exterior walls constructed from brick or block or perhaps some type of asbestos or metal siding or covering. The sheathing, which supports the roofing material, consists of wood, precast concrete slabs, some type of corrugated metal, etc. The sheathing is supported by the purlins which transfer the roof loads to the trusses as concentrated loads.

The trusses are supported by the columns and the walls are usually nonbearing. Although wind forces do not usually have a great effect on member sizes for one-story mill buildings, the installation of a good brac-

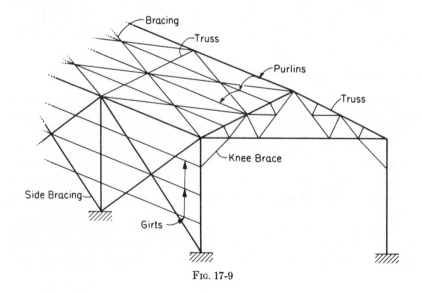

Fig. 17-9

ing system perpendicular to the trusses is important. A typical arrangement of the members of a mill building frame is shown in Fig. 17-9. More information is presented in Sec. 17-10 concerning the bracing of these and other roof truss systems.

17-10. ROOF TRUSS BRACING

Properly designed roof trusses or mill-building bents can satisfactorily resist horizontal and vertical loads applied to them in the plane of the truss, as shown in Fig. 17-10. However, to make a series of roof trusses or mill-building bents stable normal to the plane of the trusses, a definite system of lateral bracing has to be installed between the trusses.

Before these systems of lateral bracing are discussed it is necessary to make a comment or two about the erection of individual trusses. The

Fig. 17-10

usual size roof truss has very little lateral strength and the result is that its handling and erection may present something of a problem. Many designers, to ensure reasonable lateral stiffness, will not use a ratio of the width of the bottom chord to its total length less than a certain value ($\frac{1}{125}$ being common).

Small trusses are usually picked up at their peaks, causing the bottom chords to be put in compression. The result is that there is danger of lateral buckling of these members. A common practice among some steel erectors is to strap a timber (such as a 4 $\times$ 6) along the side of the truss to prevent it from bending laterally during erection. The steel erector probably sets the first truss and guys it off. After a few more trusses are erected the purlins can be installed and the structure begins to have appreciable lateral strength.

The bracing placed between roof trusses and mill-building bents

serves the purpose of transferring the lateral loads to the building foundation. The amount of bracing used varies a great deal from engineer to
engineer. In the paragraphs to follow a few general statements are made
about the various types of lateral bracing.

Complete bracing systems are not often required in both the planes
of the top and bottom chords; however, the presence of heavy moving
loads and considerable vibration (as caused by moving cranes) may
change the situation. Diagonal cross bracing should be used in the
planes of the upper chord members. These members tie the trusses together and with the assistance of the purlins (which act as struts) provide
the necessary upper chord bracing. The usual practice is to place upper
chord bracing only every three or four bays as shown in part (a) of
Fig. 17-11.

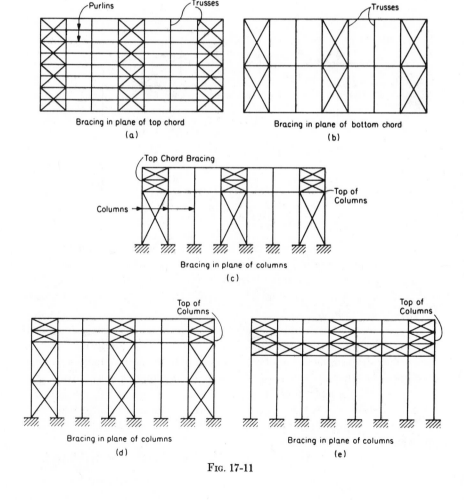

Bracing in plane of top chord
(a)

Bracing in plane of bottom chord
(b)

Bracing in plane of columns
(c)

Bracing in plane of columns
(d)

Bracing in plane of columns
(e)

Fig. 17-11

Diagonal bracing in the plane of the bottom chords is often omitted in small structures unless heavy vibrating type loads are anticipated in the building. For larger structures bracing is usually put in the plane of the bottom chords every three or four bays. A typical arrangement of this type of bracing is shown in part (b) of Fig. 17-11.

Longitudinal bracing is also needed in the plane of the columns. The wind acting against the end of the building is transferred by this bracing to the column bases. Examples of this type of bracing are shown in parts (c) and (d) of Fig. 17-11. An alternate method of providing this longitudinal bracing is shown in part (e). This latter bracing has the advantage that it gives little interference to the placement of windows.

The members of the three bracing systems described in the preceding paragraphs rarely have stresses of sufficient magnitude to affect their design and the usual practice is to select them on the basis of minimum sizes and controlling maximum slenderness ratios. To achieve tightly braced structures it is fairly common practice to detail the bracing members a little short so they will have to be slightly stretched to get them in place.

PROBLEMS

17-1. Using the load combinations suggested in Sec. 17-6 and the AISC Specification, determine the critical stresses in the members of the left-hand side of the Pratt truss shown in the accompanying illustration. Use the following data:

1. Snow = 24 psf of horizontal projection.
2. Wind = 11.5 psf pressure on windward side only.
3. Purlins = 3 psf of roof surface.
4. Roofing = 18 psf of roof surface.
5. Truss weight to be estimated by the *Engineering News Record* expression given in Sec. 17-5, assuming A36 steel is to be used.

Trusses 18'-0" o.c.

6 @ 15' = 90'

Prob. 17-1

17-2. Design the members of the left-hand side of the truss of Prob. 17-1. The members are to be welded using E70 electrodes.

17-3. Determine the design stresses for the members of one side of the Fink

PROB. 17-3

truss shown in the accompanying illustration, using the AISC Specification. Use the following data:

1. Snow = 20 psf of horizontal projection.
2. Wind = 9 psf suction on leeward surfaces and 4.1 psf suction on the windward side.
3. Purlins = 4 psf of roof surface.
4. Roofing = 20 psf of roof surface.
5. Truss weight to be estimated using Dr. Grinter's recommendations mentioned in Sec. 17-5.

17-4. Design the members of the truss of Prob. 17-3 using A36 steel. The members are to be welded using E70 electrodes.

17-5. Determine the design stresses in the members of the three-hinged arch shown in the accompanying illustration, using the AISC Specification and the following data:

1. Snow load = 20 psf of horizontal projection.
2. Wind = 15 psf pressure on sloping windward side, 7.5 psf suction on sloping leeward side, 20 psf pressure on vertical windward side, and 10 psf suction on vertical leaward side.
3. Purlins = 5 psf of roof surface.
4. Roofing = 15 psf of roof surface.
5. Truss weight to be estimated as in Prob. 17-1.

PROB. 17-5

chapter 18

DESIGN OF BRIDGES

18-1. INTRODUCTION

The general procedure for analyzing and designing steel bridges is quite similar to that used for steel buildings. The major differences between the two are caused by the different loading conditions. The analysis of bridges is greatly affected by heavy moving loads and the impact which they cause. Impact is usually a minor problem in the analysis of buildings, although it has to be considered in a few cases where it may be caused by such things as elevators, moving cranes, and vehicles in off-ground garages.

Bridge specifications are much more conservative than the AISC building Specification. Among the several reasons for this conservatism are:

1. Live loads make up a larger percentage of the total load applied to bridges than to buildings and they are more violently applied.

2. Steel bridge frames are nearly always exposed to the weather with consequent corrosion problems, while the structural steel used in buildings is usually enclosed and protected from the elements.

3. Perhaps another factor which may explain the higher allowable stresses in building design is the fact that the more liberal architectural profession has had considerable influence on building specifications.

A discussion of the various types of bridge trusses in common use was presented in Chap. 14 and will not be repeated here. This chapter is devoted to the design of a simple-span truss bridge using the AASHO Specifications.

Bridge specifications very clearly define the maximum loads to be applied to bridges for design purposes as well as spelling out the distribution of loads, values of impact, limiting depths, and various other specific design data. Example 18-1 illustrates the application of the AASHO Specifications in selecting the proportions of a 144 ft simple-span, through Pratt truss. Admittedly a plate girder might win out economically over

471

a truss for this span, but the purpose of this example is to illustrate briefly the steps involved in laying out a bridge truss. Subsequent examples in

Fort Duquesne Bridge, Pittsburgh, Pa. (*American Bridge Division, U.S. Steel Corporation.*)

this chapter will illustrate the design of the individual parts of this truss. The numbers in parentheses in this chapter refer to AASHO article numbers and are included for the student's benefit.

EXAMPLE 18-1. Select proportions for a two-lane, 144 ft through simple-span Pratt truss using the 1969 AASHO Specifications. Also determine roadway width and stringer spacing.

Solution: Layout of truss:

Minimum clearance   = 14 ft (Art. 1.1.7)

Minimum depth of sway bracing = 5ft (Art. 1.7.82)

Estimated floor depth   = 5 ft

Estimated minimum truss depth = 24 ft

Minimum preferable depth = $\frac{1}{10}$ span (Art. 1.7.11) = 14.4 ft < 24 ft (OK)

Assume diagonals at 45° as shown in Fig. 18-1.

Truss spacing and stringer layout:

Width of roadway   = 26 ft (Art. 1.1.7)

FIG. 18-1

Assume 1½-ft curbs each side = 3 ft

Assume truss widths   = 2 ft

Distance c.-to-c. trusses   = 31 ft

Assume outside stringers 2 ft 6 in. from center of trusses, placing them 26 ft 0 in. on centers.

Use stringers 6 ft 6 in. on centers as shown in Fig. 18-2.

FIG. 18-2

18-2. BRIDGE FLOOR SYSTEM

To understand the manner of application of loads to a supporting girder or truss it is necessary for the arrangement of the members of the floor system to be carefully studied. The most common type of bridge floor is supported by a series of beams parallel to traffic and running the length of each panel. These beams, called *stringers*, frame into and are supported by transverse beams, called *floor beams*. The floor beams frame into the panel points of the supporting trusses. This arrangement is shown in Fig. 18-3.

The slab may be bonded to the stringers with shear connectors to form composite construction (as described in Chap. 15), permitting the use of smaller stringers.

Stringers are usually conservatively assumed to be simply supported but actually they have some continuity in their construction. Sometimes they are specially designed to be continuous with connecting plates lapping over the flanges of the stringers and floor beams. There is probably more continuity present in the floor beams than in the stringers. They are usually quite rigidly connected to the truss verticals, thus appreciably adding to the lateral rigidity of the bridge. Despite this probably high degree of continuity, the floor beams are for simplicity assumed to have simple end supports.

Fig. 18-3

The design of simple-span stringers and floor beams is illustrated in Example 18-2 for the AASHO truck loadings. It is assumed that the concrete slab has previously been designed in accordance with the usual reinforced concrete principles and the requirements of Art. 1.3.2 of the AASHO.

A few explanatory remarks are made here concerning the application of the wheel loads. The truck is assumed to be centered in the middle of a 10-ft lane; thus no wheel load can be closer to the curb than 2 ft (Art. 1.2.5). Even though a wheel load is placed directly over an interior stringer it causes the adjacent stringers as well as the stringer in question to deflect due to the stiffness of the concrete slab. The obvious result is distribution of the load and the AASHO Specifications (Art. 1.3.1) attempt to estimate the effect of this distribution. They say the percentage of a wheel load to be taken is the center-to-center spacing of the stringers divided by a certain value which is determined from the type of floor, spacing of stringers, and number of traffic lanes. The outside stringers are assumed to support a portion of the wheel loads determined by assuming the flooring to act as a simple span between stringers.

It will be noted that the values for maximum live-load moments calculated in the example can be checked with tables in Appendix A of the AASHO Specifications. These tables are for axle loads and do not include effects of load distribution and impact.

EXAMPLE 18-2.   Design the stringers and floor beams for the bridge of Example 18-1 using the HS20-44 loading of the AASHO. Assume that an 8-in. concrete slab with a crown varying from 1 to 4 in. thick has previously been designed. The design is to be made with structural carbon steel (A36) and ⅞-in. A502, Grade 1 rivets. Assume the concrete weighs 150 lb per cubic foot.

Solution:

Design of Interior Stringers

Fraction of wheel load carried by each stringer (Art. 1.3.1.B) is

$$\frac{S}{5.5} = \frac{6.5}{5.5} = 1.18$$

Slab weight $= (1\,2\!/\!_{12})\,(150)\,(6.5) = 975$ lb/ft of stringer

Assume stringer weight $= 70$ lb/ft

$$\text{DL moment} = \frac{(1.045)\,(24)^2}{8} = 75.2 \text{ ft-k}$$

Place wheel loads as shown in Fig. 18-4 to cause maximum LL moment.

FIG. 18-4

LL moment $= (11.33)\,(8.5)\,(1.18) = 113.8$ ft-k (can be checked in Appendix A of AASHO).

$$I = \frac{50}{l + 125} = \frac{50}{24 + 125} = 33.6 \text{ percent}$$

[use 30 percent maximum (Art. 1.2.12.C)]

$$I \text{ moment} = (0.30)\,(113.8) = 34.1 \text{ ft-k}$$

Total moment $= 223.1$ k

$$S_{\text{req.}} = \frac{(12)\,(223.1)}{20} = 134 \text{ in.}^3$$

Use W 21 × 68

Design of Outside Stringers

Slab weight = (6.5) ($\frac{9}{12}$) (150) ($\frac{1}{2}$) = 366 lb/ft

Assumed weight of curbs, railings, etc. = 150 lb/ft

(Art. 1.3.1.B permits this load to be spread evenly to all stringers if placed after slab has cured.)

Assume stringer weight = 50 lb/ft

Total DL   = $\overline{566}$ lb/ft

DL moment = $\dfrac{(0.566)\ (24)^2}{8}$ = 40.8 ft-k

Part of wheel load supported by exterior stringers is 4.5/6.5 = 0.692 but not less than

$$\frac{6.5}{4.0 + \frac{1}{4} \times 6.5} = 1.16$$

(See Art. 1.3.1.B and Fig. 18-5.)

FIG. 18-5

Wheels arrangement for maximum moment same as for interior stringers.

LL moment = (11.33) (8.5) (1.16) = 112.0 ft-k

I moment = (0.30) (112.0) = 33.6 ft-k

Total moment = 186.4 ft-k

$$S_{req.} = \frac{(12)\ (186.4)}{20} = 112\ in.^3$$

Use W 24 × 55

Rivets Required Between Stringers and Floor Beams

Interior stringers:

DL shear $= (12)\ (975 + 68) = 12.50$ k

Place wheel loads as shown in parts (a) and (b) of Fig. 18-6 for maximum LL shear.

FIG. 18-6

Load going to stringer from part (a) of figure $= (2)\ (16) \left(\dfrac{5.0}{6.5}\right) = 24.6$ k.

These loads placed as shown in part (b) of figure.

Maximum LL shear $= 24.6 + \left(\dfrac{10}{24}\right) (16)\ (1.18) = 32.4$ k.

(Notice no slab distribution is assumed to occur for beams placed right at floor beam but distribution is assumed for the other wheel loads.)

$$I \text{ shear} = (0.30)\ (32.4) = 9.7 \text{ k}$$

$$\text{Maximum total shear} = 66.7 \text{ k}$$

Rivets from stringer to floor beam:

$$\text{Single shear value of rivets} = (0.6)\ (13.5) = 8.1 \text{ k}$$

$$\text{Number required} = \frac{66.7}{8.1} = 8.2 \qquad \text{(say 5 each side)}$$

Rivets from connection to web of stringer (web $t = 0.430$ in.):

$$\text{Double shear value of rivets} = (2)\ (0.6)\ (13.5) = 16.2 \text{ k}$$

$$\text{Bearing value} = \left(\frac{7}{8}\right) (0.430)\ (40) = 15.1 \text{ k}$$

$$\text{Number required} = \frac{66.7}{15.1} = 4.4 \quad \text{(say 5)}$$

Outside stringers: Rivet calculations not shown since they would merely be a repetition of those made for interior stringers.

Design of Floor Beams

Dead-load reactions from interior stringers = (24) (1.043) = 25.0 k

Dead-load reactions from outside stringers = (24) (0.578) = 13.9 k

These reactions are applied as concentrated loads to floor beams as shown in Fig. 18-7.

Fig. 18-7

Assume beam weight = 230 lb/ft

$$\text{DL moment} = (51.4)\,(15.5) - (25.0)\,(6.5) - (13.9)\,(13) + \frac{(0.23)\,(31)^2}{8}$$

$$= 480.6 \text{ ft-k.}$$

AASHO does not permit transverse distribution of wheel loads in slab for design of floor beams (Art. 1.3.1.C). Therefore, concentrated loads applied to floor beams from stringers are

$$16 + \left(\frac{10}{24}\right)(16) + \left(\frac{10}{24}\right)(4) = 24.34 \text{ k}$$

(See Fig. 18-8.)

Fig. 18-8

Truck loads placed in traffic design lanes of 13-ft width (Art. 1.2.6) and placed as shown in Fig. 18-9 to cause maximum LL moment:

$$\text{LL moment} = (48.68)\,(15.5) - (24.34)\,(2 + 8) = 512 \text{ ft-k}$$

$$I \text{ moment} = (0.30)\,(512) = 153.6 \text{ ft-k}$$

FIG. 18-9

Total moment $= 1{,}145.2$ ft-k

$$S_{req.} = \frac{(12)\ (1{,}145.2)}{20} = 688 \text{ in.}^3$$

Use W 33 $\times$ 220

Connections can be designed as previously described.

18-3. LIVE-LOAD TRUSS STRESSES

The live-load stresses are to be computed for the HS20-44 loading or the equivalent lane loadings, whichever causes the maximum values. It will be found that the equivalent lane loadings will control for moment when the loaded length exceeds 145 ft and for shear when the loaded length exceeds 128 ft. (These lengths are for the HS20-44 loading only.) Stresses can be computed with the aid of influence lines, by the panel-load method,[1] or by some other procedure.

In Example 18-3 influence lines are drawn for the members of the left-hand side of the truss under consideration in this chapter. From these influence lines it can be seen that the lane loadings control for all members except U_1L_1, U_1L_2, U_2L_2 and U_2L_3. The concentrated wheel loads are used for calculating the stresses in these latter members while the lane loadings are used for all other members.

The AASHO says the uniform lane loading is distributed across two 10-ft widths and is to be placed in design traffic lanes of 13-ft widths for a two lane roadway (Art. 1.2.6). As shown in Fig. 18-10, these two lane loadings are moved as close as possible to one of the trusses to cause maximum loads on that truss. From this figure the part of the live load going to the left truss can be seen to equal $17/31$ or 54.8 percent.

From the same AASHO article (Art. 1.2.6) the maximum percentage of the concentrated wheel loads can be determined as shown in Fig. 18-11. The maximum percentage in this case is the same as for the uniform lane

[1] J. C. McCormac, *Structural Analysis* (Scranton, Pa.: International Textbook Company, 1960), pp. 130–132.

Fig. 18-10

Fig. 18-11

loading case but can be slightly different for bridges of more than two lanes. The percentage is again 17/31 or 54.8 percent.

The impact percentage in the various truss members will be determined from the usual AASHO expression. This percentage is not constant for all members as it varies with the length over which the live load is placed to cause maximum stress.

EXAMPLE 18-3. Determine the maximum live-load stresses in each of the members of the truss selected in Example 18-1.

Solution: Drawing influence lines (Fig. 18-12).

Stress Calculations for Uniform Lane Loadings

Uniform lane loading to one truss $=$ (2) (0.640) (0.548) $=$ 0.703 k/ft

Concentrated load to one truss $=$ (2) (18) (0.548) $=$ 19.75 k

Impact percentage for 144-ft loaded length $= \dfrac{50}{144 + 125} = 18.6$ percent

L_0L_1 and L_1L_2:

    LL stress $=$ (0.703) ($+59.8$) $+$ (19.75) ($+.83$) $= +58.4$ k

    I stress $=$ (0.186) ($+58.4$) $= +10.8$ k

L_2L_3:

    LL stress $=$ (0.703) ($+96$) $+$ (19.75) ($+1.33$) $= +93.8$ k

    I stress $=$ (0.186) ($+93.8$) $= +17.4$ k

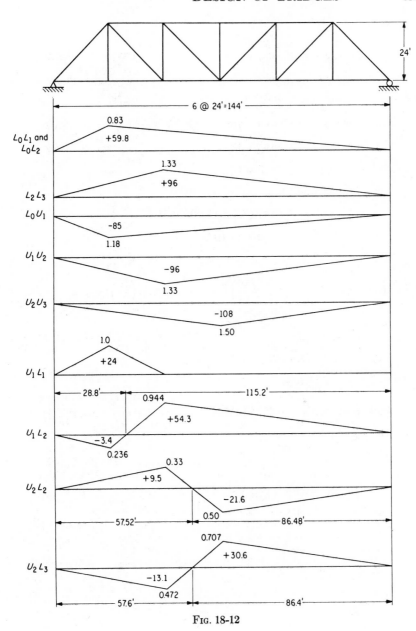

FIG. 18-12

$L_0 U_1$:

$$\text{LL stress} = (0.703)\,(-85) + (19.75)\,(-1.18) = -83.1\text{ k}$$

$$I \text{ stress} = (0.186)\,(-83.1) \qquad\qquad = -15.4\text{ k}$$

U_1U_2:

LL stress $= (0.703)\ (-96) + (19.75)\ (-1.33) = -93.8$ k

I stress $\quad = (0.186)\ (-161.3) \qquad\qquad\qquad = -17.4$ k

U_2U_3:

LL stress $= (0.703)\ (-108) + (19.75)\ (-1.50) = -105.4$ k

I stress $\quad = (0.186)\ (-105.4) \qquad\qquad\qquad = -\ 19.6$ k

Stress Calculations for Axle Loads

Concentrated wheel loads:

$$(2)\ (32)\ (0.548) = 35.1\ \text{k}$$

$$(2)\ (8)\ (0.548) = 8.8\ \text{k}$$

U_1L_1:

LL stress $= (35.1)\left[+1.0 + \left(\dfrac{10}{24}\right)(+1.0)\right] + (8.8)\left(\dfrac{10}{24}\right)(+1.0) = +53.3$ k

$$I = \frac{50}{48 + 125} = 28.9 \text{ percent}$$

I stress $= (0.289)\ (+53.3) = +15.4$ k

U_1L_2:

Positive LL stress $= (35.1)\left[0.944 + \left(\dfrac{82}{96}\right)(0.944)\right] + (8.8)\left(\dfrac{4}{19.2}\right)$
$(0.944) = +63.1$ k

$$I = \frac{50}{115.2 + 125} = 20.8 \text{ percent}$$

I stress $= (0.208)\ (+63.1) = +13.1$ k

Negative LL stress $= (35.1)\left[-0.236 + \left(\dfrac{10}{24}\right)(-0.236)\right] = -11.7$ k

$$I = \frac{50}{28.8 + 125} = 32.5 \text{ percent (maximum value is 30 percent)}$$

I stress $= (0.30)\ (-11.7) = -3.5$ k

U_2L_2:

Positive LL stress $= (35.1)\left[+0.33 + \left(\dfrac{34}{48}\right)(0.33)\right] = +19.8$ k

$$I = \frac{50}{57.52 + 125} = 27.4 \text{ percent}$$

I stress $= (0.274)\ (+19.8) = +\ 5.4$ k

Negative LL stress $= (35.1) \left[-0.50 + \left(\frac{58}{72}\right)(-0.50) \right] + (8.8)\left(\frac{0.48}{14.48}\right)$

$(-0.50) = -31.8$ k

$$I = \frac{50}{86.48 + 125} = 23.6 \text{ percent}$$

I stress $= (0.236)(-31.8) = -7.5$ k

U_2L_3:

Positive LL stress $= (35.1)\left[+0.707 + \left(\frac{58}{72}\right)(+0.707) \right] + (8.8)\left(\frac{0.4}{14.4}\right)$

$(+0.707) = +44.8$ k

$$I = \frac{50}{86.4 + 125} = 23.6 \text{ percent}$$

I stress $= (0.236)(+44.8) = +10.6$ k

Negative LL stress $= 35.1 \left[-0.472 + \left(\frac{34}{48}\right)(-0.472) \right] = -28.3$ k

$$I = \frac{50}{57.6 + 125} = 27.4 \text{ percent}$$

I stress $= (0.274)(-28.3) = -7.7$ k

18-4. TRUSS DEAD LOADS

The dead load of a truss bridge consists of the weight of the floor system, truss, and bracing. The weight of the floor system, which comprises a large percentage of the total weight, can be closely estimated by making a preliminary design of the floor. From the weight of the floor system the load applied to the truss can be determined. Before dead-load analysis can be made of the main trusses the weights of the trusses must be estimated.

To expedite the design procedure it is essential to make a good estimate of the truss weight. The designer can make a rough estimate, analyze and design the structure, calculate its weight, and revise his estimate, until his estimate and the design weight are reasonably close. This procedure can be rather time-consuming, particularly for long-span bridges, and a good truss weight estimate can definitely speed up the process.

The weight of the truss can be estimated by increasing the other dead loads by some percentage or by using some approximate formula. There is a great deal of published data available concerning the estimated weights of short- and medium-span bridges. There are, however, so many variables in the weight of a bridge such as different specifications, different floor types (as concrete or steel grid floors), different steels, etc., that it is necessary to check the weight of the designed structure to be sure the estimate was reasonable in each case.

Perhaps the most complete data on the weight of bridge structures was presented by J. A. L. Waddell in his book *Bridge Engineering* (Wiley, 1916) and revised in the *Transactions of the ASCE* in 1936.

Charles W. Hudson is credited with developing a formula (called the Hudson formula) for estimating the weight of a truss. In his formula, given at the end of this paragraph, W is the total weight of either a railway or bridge truss including its bracing, S is the maximum total tensile stress in the most stressed chord member, l is the length of the truss in feet and s is the allowable tensile stress. Since S is the maximum total tensile stress due to live load plus impact plus dead load, a value has to be assumed for the truss weight to apply the formula. If the largest tensile chord member is assumed to extend for the full length of the truss and its weight assumed to equal 20 percent of the weight of the entire truss and bracing, this formula can be derived.[2,3]

$$W = \frac{17\,Sl}{s}$$

Example 18-4 illustrates the application of the Hudson formula, the calculation of the dead-load stresses, and a summary of the maximum total stresses.

EXAMPLE 18-4. Estimate the weight of the truss considered in the previous examples of this chapter, compute the dead-load stresses and summarize the total stresses for all members.

Solution: Estimating truss weight by Hudson formula:

Member L_2L_3 is the largest stressed tensile chord member

DL floor beam reaction from Example 18-2 = 51.4 k

Adding 20 percent to this value to estimate truss weight = 61.7 k

Stress in L_2L_3 by taking moments at U_2 when a 61.7-k load is placed at each joint:

$$L_2L_3 = \frac{(48)\,(156.5) - (24)\,(61.7)}{24} = +250.4 \text{ k}$$

Estimated total stress in $L_2L_3 = +250.4 + 161.3 + 30.0 = +441.7$ k

$$W = \frac{(17)\,(441.7)\,(144)}{20} = 54{,}000 \text{ lb or 9 k at each joint}$$

[2] John E. Lothers, *Design In Structural Steel* (New York; Prentice-Hall, Inc., 1965).

[3] Thomas C. Shedd, *Structural Design In Steel* (New York: John Wiley & Sons, Inc., 1934).

Dead-load stresses (Fig. 18-13):

Dead-panel loads = 51.4 + 9   = 60.4

Fig. 18-13

Part of the estimated truss weight should theoretically be placed at the top-chord joints, but this refinement is considered unnecessary here.

Summary of maximum stresses (Fig. 18-14):

Fig. 18-14

Notice no stress reversals occurred and the stresses obtained in considering that possibility are not shown.

18-5.   SELECTION OF TRUSS MEMBERS

For a small truss bridge of the type being considered, it may be more economical to use W sections for nearly all of the members. For larger trusses, built-up sections will be used to provide the necessary stiffnesses for the compression members. For the truss being designed in this chapter W sections are used for all of the members.

When built-up sections are used, the upper chord of the truss will probably consist of one of the two arrangements shown in Fig. 18-15. In part (a) of the figure is shown an upper chord member built up from two channels and a cover plate. The gusset plates are attached to the

FIG. 18-15

back of the channels and the verticals fit between the gussets. A similar arrangement is shown in part (b) of the figure where the chord member is built up from four angles and three plates. For this type of riveted truss it is common practice to design the verticals first because the spacing between the aforementioned gusset plates is not known until the vertical member sizes are known.

After the verticals are designed in a truss with built-up members the upper chord members are designed, starting with the one with the greatest stress. The width of the cover plate for the compression chord is quite important because it appreciably affects the lateral stiffness of the compression flange and thus its allowable stress. In Art. 1.7.89 of the AASHO maximum width/thickness ratios for cover plates are provided, the values varying with F_y, f_a, etc. After the upper chord members are designed it is probably desirable to design the remaining web members (probably the compression members followed by the tension ones). The remaining tension members can be designed after which consideration is given to bracing, connections, supports, etc.

In Example 18-5 the members of the truss of Example 18-1 are designed using the maximum stresses previously obtained in Example 18-3, with W sections used for all of the members. The depth of these sections vary from member to member and it may be necessary in places to use filler plates to equalize depths. In designing the tension chord members two holes for $\frac{7}{8}$-in. rivets are assumed to be present in each flange and web. The web deduction was considered unnecessary for the tension diagonals and only flange holes were deducted.

Article 1.7.12 of the AASHO Specifications needs to be carefully studied before the truss members are selected. In this article the maximum permissible l/r ratios are presented. For main tension members 200 is the maximum value and 240 for bracing members. For compression members the comparable values permitted are 120 and 140 respectively. Sometimes r for a member is larger if part of the member is neglected in the calculations. In this regard the AASHO says any part of a member can be neglected in the calculations provided the strength of the remaining part (using the l/r value with the part neglected) and the strength of the whole section (using the true l/r value) are equal to or greater than the design stress.

EXAMPLE 18-5. Select W sections for each of the members of the truss of Example 18-1 using the maximum stresses obtained in Example 18-4. The members are to be designed with structural carbon A36 steel using the 1969 AASHO Specifications. Allowable tension $= 20,000$ psi on the net section and allowable axial compression $= 16,000 - 0.30 \, (l/r)^2$.

Solution:

DESIGN OF TENSION MEMBERS

Member	Design Stress	Length	Min. r	Net A Req.	Est. Hole A	Gross A Req.	Section Selected	Actual l/r	Actual Net A
L_0L_1	$+220.2$	24.0	1.44	11.01	3.30	14.31	W12×58	147	11.41
L_1L_2	$+220.2$	24.0	1.44	11.01	3.30	14.31	W12×50	147	11.41
L_2L_3	$+352.8$	24.0	1.44	17.64	3.54	21.18	W12×72	95	17.62
U_1L_1	$+129.1$	24.0	1.44	6.45	1.86	8.31	W12×31	196	7.26
U_1L_2	$+204.4$	33.9	2.03	10.22	2.30	12.52	W12×53	164	13.29
U_2L_3	$+ 98.1$	33.9	2.03	4.90	1.60	6.50	W12×53	164	13.29

Example design of L_0U_1:

Assume allowable $F_a = 10.75$ ksi

$$A_{\text{req.}} = \frac{312.5}{10.75} = 29.1 \text{ sq in.}$$

Try W 12 × 120 ($A = 35.3, r = 3.13$)

Allowable $F_a = 16,000 - (0.30)\left(\frac{12 \times 33.9}{3.13}\right)^2 = 10.93$ ksi

DESIGN OF COMPRESSION MEMBERS

Member	Design Stress	Length	Min. r	Section Selected	Allowable Load	Actual l/r
L_0U_1	−312.5	33.9	3.39	W12×120	−329	130*
U_1U_2	−352.8	24.0	2.40	W12×106	−419	92.5
U_2U_3	−396.8	24.0	2.40	W12×106	−419	92.5
U_2L_2	− 69.5	24.0	2.40	W12×40	− 72.2	148*

* l/r for L_0U_1 and U_2L_2 are greater than 120 but permissible under certain circumstances as described in AASHO Art. 1.7.12. See example design to follow.

Allowable $P = (35.3) (10.93) = 386 \text{ k} > 312.5 \text{ k}$

But $\dfrac{l}{r} = \dfrac{(12)(33.9)}{3.13} = 130 > 120$

If l/r of 120 used, allowable $F_a = 16{,}000 - (0.30)(120)^2 = 11.68 \text{ ksi}$

$$A_\text{req.} = \frac{312.5}{11.68} = 26.7 \text{ sq in.}$$

Effective area $= (35.3)\left(\dfrac{3.13}{3.39}\right)^2 = 30.1 \text{ sq in.} > 27.6 \text{ sq in.}$ \hfill (OK)

Allowable $P = (30.1)(10.83) = 329 \text{ k} > 312.5 \text{ k}$ \hfill (OK)

Design of U_3L_3:

Computed stress in this member is zero (although it truthfully has a total DL stress of 2 or 3 k due to the weight of the overhead members) and the smallest W12, a W 12 × 27, is used.

Figure 18-16 shows a sketch of joint U_2 of the truss being designed in this example.

Fig. 18-16. Joint U_2.

18-6.   LATERAL BRACING

A bridge truss must be braced laterally and longitudinally if it is to withstand lateral wind loads, vibrations from live loads, centrifugal forces on curves, nosing of locomotives, and the longitudinal forces produced by traffic loads when brakes are applied.   On the subject of braking forces imagine the effect on a bridge when the driver of a trailer truck going 60 mph suddenly applies the brakes while crossing the bridge.   As shown in Fig. 18-17, there are actually four distinct types of bracing systems

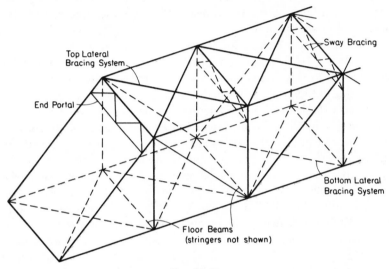

FIG. 18-17

in a through bridge.   These include the following:
1. A lateral bracing system in the plane of the top chord.
2. A lateral bracing system in the plane of the bottom chord.
3. A portal frame at each end of the bridge.
4. Intermediate sway frames.

Top and Bottom Lateral Trusses.   The wind forces are resisted by the top and bottom lateral bracing systems of a through bridge. These bracing systems usually consist of cross bracing desirably connected at their intersection points to reduce unsupported lengths.   The truss bracing is actually indeterminate but is probably analyzed by some approximate procedure.   One common method is to assume the shear divides equally between the diagonals and the members designed to take their respective stresses (the compressive stresses controlling sizes).   Another procedure is to assume the diagonals, which would ordinarily be in tension for a shear of that sign, resist the entire shear, after which the member is designed and checked for the case in which the shear is assumed to divide equally.

Members of the bottom lateral truss of a through bridge probably consist of single angles or double angles connected to the bottom flanges of the chords by means of gusset plates. The AASHO says the smallest angle which can be used for bracing is the $3 \times 2\frac{1}{2}$-in. angle and that no less than three rivets can be used for their end connections. The top lateral bracing is preferably (says the AASHO) connected to both flanges of the chord. Four angles arranged in an I shape with a depth equal to that of the chord and connected to the top and bottom flanges of the chord is an example. In addition to serving as wind bracing the top lateral system also serves to reduce the unsupported lengths of the top chord compression members.

The chord members of the lateral trusses are also the chords of the main trusses. It is therefore necessary to consider the combination of wind stresses in the chords as part of the lateral trusses with the stresses caused by dead load plus live load plus impact as part of the main truss.

When wind loads are combined with other loads the AASHO permits some increase in allowable stresses. For the dead load plus full wind load combination the allowable stresses can be increased by 25 percent. When wind loads are considered to be applied at the same time as dead load plus all the other live loads only 30 percent of the wind load is considered applied and the allowable stresses can be increased by 25 percent; however, a wind load applied to the live load 6 ft above the deck and equaling 100 lbs per linear foot must be included in this combination.

Sway Bracing and End Portals. The top lateral truss of a bridge (previously discussed) serves the purpose of resisting the wind forces along the top chords of the trusses. In addition to this bracing, however, intermediate sway frames and end portals are considered necessary to provide lateral stiffness and increase the torsional strength of the bridge. These systems were shown in Fig. 18-17.

The intermediate sway frames are difficult to analyze and are usually not designed for calculated stresses but are proportioned on the basis of l/r limitations. A different situation exists at the ends where the portals are located. The end posts of a through bridge are tied together with bracing and the result is called a *portal*. The purpose of this frame is to transfer the end reaction of the top lateral truss to the foundation. They are assumed to serve as the end supports for the top lateral trusses and as such must be able to resist half of the total top chord wind load. The deeper the bracing in the portals the smaller will be the bending in the end posts. Portals are actually indeterminate and are probably analyzed by some approximate method similar to the one used for mill buildings.[4]

---

[4] J. C. McCormac, *op. cit.*, pp. 216–223.

18-7. BRIDGE-TRUSS DEFLECTIONS

The deflections of bridge trusses are a very important subject to consider. Where underclearance is close it is essential to compute the deflections carefully. During cantilever erection, deflection calculations are even more critical because the various members must come together at exactly the right points for fitting. Even if underclearance is not a problem and the cantilever erection process is not being used, the appearance of a bridge truss is an important matter. Trusses with horizontal bottom chords will sag down in the middle, injuring their appearance and perhaps worrying the users of the bridge. These trusses should desirably be cambered to avoid such sagging.

Several methods are available for determining truss deflections. Perhaps the most practical one is the Williot-Mohr diagram with which the deflection of all truss joints can be obtained at the same time. Trusses can be cambered by one of the following methods.

1. The tension members can be made shorter and the compression members longer by the amounts they would theoretically lengthen or shorten respectively. After the loads are applied the truss would presumably return to its original theoretical dimensions. This method is generally followed for trusses roughly 300 ft or longer, while the second method described is probably used for the shorter trusses.

2. The second method used is to merely shorten the fabricated dimensions of the top chords. A common practice is to shorten these members by $\frac{1}{8}$ in. for each 10 ft of length.

The next question is "For what loads is camber to be made?" If the camber is made for all loads, the truss will probably be bowed up a little most of the time (perhaps not a bad situation). The usual practice is to camber bridge trusses for dead load plus some part of the live load. The AASHO merely says that camber shall be at least equal to the deflections produced by dead loads. A common practice for highway bridges, however, is to camber them for dead load plus live load but no impact. The AREA says that railroad bridges should be cambered for the deflections caused by dead load plus a uniform live load of 3 k per foot.

18-8. END BEARINGS FOR BRIDGES

This section is devoted to a discussion of the various types of bridge bearings which may be used by the bridge engineer. As for so many other subjects in this book the student can learn a great deal by taking time to stop at a few of the bridges in his locality and examine the bearings used. In general, bearings are classified as being of the expansion or fixed types. As the names imply, the expansion bearings are those that supposedly allow the bridge to freely expand or contract, and the fixed bearings are those that are fixed against longitudinal movement. The term fixed bearing is rather misleading because it does not necessarily mean the bearing is fixed against rotation as commonly intended in structural analysis. It instead means the position of bearing is fixed. These two types of end bearings are discussed briefly in the following paragraphs.

Expansion Bearings. Expansion bearings: (1) allow the bridge ends to freely move back and forth with temperature expansion and contraction, (2) allow the bridge to move freely at its ends with changes in the length of the bridge caused by the live loads, and (3) keep horizontal loads from being applied to some of the bridge supports where such forces may be undesirable.

Expansion bearings may be of the sliding type or of the roller or rocker types, depending on the spans and loads. For short spans a simple bearing plate can be used such as the one shown in Fig. 18-18 for a steel

Fıg. 18-18

stringer. In this arrangement the beam end is allowed to slide on a smooth metal plate. The expansion plates may be made from bronze with the sliding surfaces planed and polished, or from some copper alloy with smooth, true surfaces. Instead of following these requirements it is possible to use some type of bearing pad probably made from neoprene or rubber. These pads which are generally referred to as elastomeric pads are cheaper initially than the metal plates and require less maintenance.[5]

These kinds of bearing plates are not satisfactory for long spans where a large part of the reaction is caused by the live load. Downward deflections of the beam or truss cause the inside pressure for the plate to become excessive, with the result that the masonry support may be injured. It is, therefore, necessary to use some type of bearing that takes into account the deflections of longer span structures. The plate types

[5] H. E. Fairbanks, "Elastomeric Pads As Bearings For Steel Beams," *Proc. ASCE*, vol. 87, no. ST8 (December 1961).

of bearings also have considerable friction against temperature and stress-length changes. These items are more important for longer spans and the AASHO says plates can be used for spans of less than 50 ft. For spans greater than these it is necessary to use some type of support involving sliding plates, rockers or segmental rollers.

A sliding-plate type of expansion bearing which can be used for spans of up to 100 ft is shown in Fig. 18-19. In the first plate type of expansion

FIG. 18-19. Sliding expansion plates.

support the plate did not move as is the case for this sliding plate type of bearing.

For longer spans and heavier loads a more satisfactory type of bearing which can be used is the rocker type of bearing such as the one shown in Fig. 18-20. It can be seen in this figure that expansion and contraction is permitted by rolling on the curved surfaces of the rocker.

FIG. 18-20. Rocker expansion bearing.

Theoretically speaking, there is only a line of contact between a rocker and its bearing plate but application of load spreads out this contact. From various tests empirical formulas have been developed for rocker designs. These can be found in the specifications being used.

From this information it is obvious that for very large reactions the radius of the rocker required to provide the necessary bearing area and the length of the rocker will become impractical. To overcome this problem it may be necessary to use a series of segmental rollers of the types shown in Fig. 18-21. The segmental rollers are preferred to the round

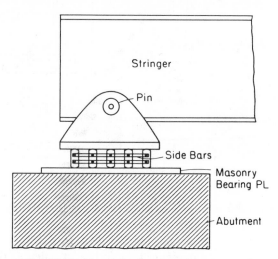

FIG. 18-21. Expansion bearing with segmental rollers.

ones because for the same diameter they require less space. A very important feature of this type of bearing is its ability to be cleaned to keep the bearing from binding. For this reason dust guards are often used and the rollers may have hour glass shapes to make the cleaning operation simpler.

Fixed Bearings. The AASHO permits the use of regular bearing plates connected to the abutment with anchor bolts for spans less than 50 ft. For spans greater than 50 ft it is considered necessary to use a bearing which takes into account the bridge deflection. Among the types of bearings that may be used are hinges, curved bearing plates, or some type of pin arrangement.

A hinge type of connection should allow end rotation of the members such as is provided by the pin of Fig. 18-22. When heavy loads are involved it may be necessary to provide the hinge with some type of lubrication system which will permit it to rotate freely and not wear quickly.

Actually, fixed bearings need to be designed for vertical and longi-

tudinal forces, but practically the vertical forces are so much larger than
the longitudinal ones that if they are designed for the vertical forces

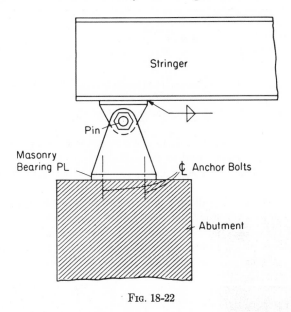

Fig. 18-22

they surely will be strong enough to take the others. In some cases the
specifications being used require the bearings to be designed for uplift,
whether there is any computed uplift or not.

PROBLEMS

18-1. A three lane, noncomposite, W section bridge has the cross section
shown in the accompanying illustration. Assuming a simple span of 54 ft, design
an interior beam using the 1969 AASHO Specifications, A36 steel, and the HS20-44
loading.

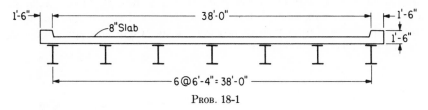

Prob. 18-1

18-2. The through highway bridge shown in the accompanying illustration
supports a three-lane roadway with the same cross section shown for Prob. 18-1
except that floor beams are also used. Design the stringers and floor beams for
this bridge assuming the curb and railing outside the outside stringer weigh

24'-0"

8 @ 22'-0"= 176'-0"

Prob. 18-2

180 lb per foot. Use the 1969 AASHO Specifications, A36 steel, and the HS20-44 loading.

18-3. Compute the design stresses in each of the members of the truss of Prob. 18-2.

18-4. Design the truss of Prob. 18-2 assuming the members are to be welded using the design stresses obtained in Prob. 18-3.

18-5. Repeat Prob. 18-4 assuming the members are to be connected with 1-in. rivets.

18-6. Establish the layout of a deck truss bridge of the type shown in the accompanying illustration using the 1969 AASHO Specifications. Also, establish the layout of the stringers. The bridge is to have four lanes of traffic and a 3 ft 0 in. sidewalk plus a handrail on each side. Assume the pavement is 8 in. thick and the curbing and sidewalk are 1 ft 6 in. thick.

160'-0"

Prob. 18-6

18-7. Design the stringers and floor beams for the layout selected in Prob. 18-6 using A36 steel and the HS20-44 loading.

18-8. Design the members of the truss selected in Prob. 18-6 using A36 steel and the HS20-44 loading.

18-9. A light highway bridge is to be designed for a private industry to support the H10-44 loading. The roadway is to be 20 ft 0 in. between curbs and is to have 1 ft 6 in. wide curbs on each side of the same total thickness. Assuming a 6-in. thick floor slab, establish layout for stringers and floor beams and design them. Also design a pony truss (Warren) for a 100 ft 0 in. span using A36 steel and the 1969 AASHO Specifications.

chapter 19

DESIGN OF RIGID FRAMES

19-1. INTRODUCTION

The rigid frame is a structure which has moment-resisting joints. The members are rigidly connected to each other at the joints to prevent relative rotation when the loads are applied. The advantages of these frames are economy, appearance, and saving in headroom. They can accomplish the same jobs which steel columns and trusses can accomplish and can do this without taking up nearly so much space. Rigid frames have proved to be very satisfactory for churches, auditoriums, field houses, armories, and other structures requiring large areas with no obstructions. Several of the more elementary types of rigid frames are shown in Fig. 19-1.

FIG. 19-1

A rigid frame has on occasion been defined as an arch wrapped around a clearance diagram. Figure 19-2(a) shows a parabolic arch. The area to be enclosed is assumed to be rectangular as represented by the dotted lines in the figure. In part (b) the arch is bent into a shape which just includes the clearance diagram. A similar situation is shown in parts (c) and (d) of the figure.

Rigid frames can be economical for spans of from 25 or 30 ft to 200 or more feet. They can be either single span or multispan and single story or multistory. This chapter is confined to single span single-story rigid frames. The frames are generally spaced from about 15 to 35 ft on centers, depending on loads, type of building, and spans.

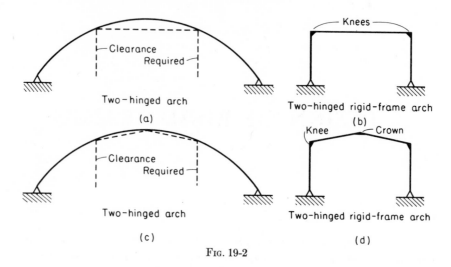

Fig. 19-2

19-2. SUPPORTS FOR RIGID FRAMES

Hinged Supports. The supports at the bases of rigid-frame columns can theoretically be either hinged or fixed. Practically speaking, the hinge is almost always used. This is the type of support represented by anchor bolts passing through a steel base plate into a concrete footing.

Coliseum of Oregon State University, Corvallis, Oreg. (*Bethlehem Steel Company*.)

To make the support act as close to a hinge as possible it is considered desirable to place the anchor bolts along a line corresponding to the neutral axis of the columns. Located on this line, which is perpendicular to the plane of the rigid frame, they will keep rotation resistance to a minimum. Should the bolts be placed near the corners of the bearing plate they would greatly increase the rotation resistance of the column base.

Although this type of hinge can supply a large vertical reaction component it can supply only a small horizontal one. When rigid frames of normal proportions have spans of approximately 60 to 80 ft or larger or when frames have small column height-to-span ratios, the horizontal reactions to be resisted become so large as to rule out the individual concrete spread footings. Either the footings (or the column bases) have to be tied together or the footings have to be supported by rock or some other rigid type of support. One solution which may be feasible for the smaller spans is to make use of the reinforcing bars in the floor slab by connecting them to the column bases.

A more common method is to use tie rods between the column bases to provide the necessary horizontal reaction components. These rods, which can be as large as 2 or 3 in. in diameter and which are generally connected to the column base plates are probably equipped with turnbuckles for adjusting them to the desired lengths. After the turnbuckles are adjusted to their proper positions the rods may be encased in concrete.

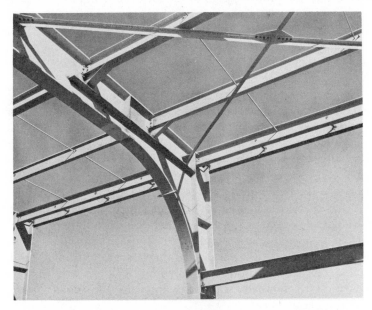

Penn Fruit Company Building, Bala-Cynwyd, Pa. (*The Lincoln Electric Company.*)

Tie rods are often initially tightened or prestressed to take (or counteract) the dead load reactions. Sometimes they are tightened by eye until the supports begin to give while on other occasions they may be tightened until attached gages show the stress has reached a certain value. In addition to taking the horizontal reaction components, the tie rods help resist overturning of the foundations due to lateral loads.

Fixed Supports. If a small concrete spread footing is used alone, it will probably rotate appreciably (thus approximating hinge behavior) no matter how rigidly the frame is connected to the footing. Unless a rigid frame is anchored in rock or in an extremely large and rigid concrete footing there is little chance of having a fixed support. For almost any other kind of support, including piling, there is probably settlement and rotation. If support settlement is feasible the support is not fixed and the designer will be wise to assume his supports are hinged.

For the rare case where a frame does have fixed supports there will be smaller deflections and moments. The design of rigid frames with fixed supports, however, is more difficult because there are more redundants, and the results may be more questionable because of the difficulty of really achieving fixed supports.

19-3. RIGID-FRAME KNEES

Probably the proper design of the knees of a rigid frame is the most critical part of the design because maximum moments occur at the knees. As a matter of fact they must be capable of carrying shear, thrust, and moment. The result is that they must be stronger than the columns and girders and they may be deepened or stiffened to provide the necessary strength.

Figure 19-3 shows several methods of making rigid joints or knees to give them greater moment resistance. Connections can be made by riveting, welding, or bolting but probably the cleanest-looking and most economical structures are obtained with welding. In designing rigid frames it is usually desirable to make as much use of standard rolled shapes as possible and to keep the large percentage of the welding (or other connections) in the region of the knees.

A deepened knee made with straight flanges is shown in part (a) of Fig. 19-3, while a knee with curved flanges is shown in part (b). Usually the straight-tapered knees are more economical than the other types because they are easier to fabricate and they may also be more rigid. Very careful and expensive cutting is required for the knees with curved flanges. The curved knee, however, is probably more attractive and for long spans can be quite economical.

In part (c) of Fig. 19-3 is shown a knee which involves no change

Fig. 19-3

in the W sections. The necessary strengthening is obtained by adding
plates to the flanges and web. This method of making up the knees is
rarely economical and then only for short spans. Greater depth is usually
required for economical knee design. A type of knee often used for steel
rigid frame bridges is shown in part (d) of the figure. It has the disadvantage that continuous welds are needed for the full height of the
column between the web and flanges.

19-4. APPROXIMATE ANALYSIS OF RIGID FRAMES

A two-hinged rigid frame or a rigid frame with fixed supports is statically indeterminate with the result that (as for any other indeterminate structure) the analysis is affected by the relative sizes of the members. Trial sizes or at least relative sizes need to be assumed for each of the members and the resulting structure analyzed to see if the assumed proportions were satisfactory. If the first size assumptions are poor, another set of sizes must be assumed and then checked, and so on. This trial-and-error process is referred to as design by successive approximations.

Unless fairly good initial member size assumptions are made, the problem can prove to be quite lengthy. There is, however, a good deal of published information on the analysis of rigid frames which should enable the designer initially to estimate very closely the moments in the frame he is designing. From these moments he can make some very good member-size assumptions which will greatly shorten the problem.

For this discussion the student is referred to the two-hinged rigid frame of Fig. 19-4. The vertical reactions for this frame can obviously

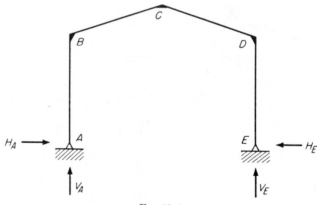

Fig. 19-4

be obtained by statics. Should the value of the horizontal reactions be available, the moment at any point in the frame can also be obtained by statics. Approximate expressions are available from which the values of these horizontal reactions can be estimated within a very few percent.

The published information is usually in the form of equations which give the values of H (the horizontal reaction components) for varying loading conditions. An example of this kind of information is shown in Fig. 19-5.[1]

[1] John D. Griffiths, *Single-Span Rigid Frames in Steel* (New York: American Institute of Steel Construction, 1948).

$$k = \frac{I_2 h}{I_1 m}$$

$$Q = \frac{f}{h}$$

$$N = 4(Q^2 + 3Q + k + 3)$$

(a)

$$H_A = H_E = \frac{wl^2}{8hN}(5Q + 8)$$

Uniform vertical load — entire span

(b)

$$H_A = H_E = \frac{wl^2}{16hN}(5Q + 8)$$

Uniform load — right span

(c)

$$H_E = \frac{wh}{4N}(5Q^3 + 20Q^2 + 30Q + 8Qk + 5k + 12)$$

$$H_A = w(h + f) - H_E$$

Uniform horizontal load — vertical and inclined surfaces

(d)

FIG. 19-5

From these equations the values of H can be estimated and the approximate moments at various points in the frame computed by statics. The member sizes can be estimated and will actually be the final sizes or very close to them if the equations are applied correctly. It should be noted that the values given for H by the formulas in Fig. 19-5 are actually good only for frames consisting of prismatic members. Practical rigid frames, however, will often be deepened at the knees. Deeper knees have greater moments with the result that the values of H are larger. Analysis also shows that these values vary with different column height-to-span ratios.

There is information available in several references which is helpful in estimating the increases in H for these factors. Martin P. Korn[2] suggests that H (as obtained by the formulas for constant section frames) be increased by 5 percent when the ratio of the frame height to span is 0.20 or more; by 10 percent when the ratio is 0.15; 15 percent for ratio of 0.12; etc. (The usual practice followed is not to increase the values of H when wind loads are involved.) In his book on rigid frames Korn presents tables which give values of the horizontal frame reactions as well as moments at the knees and crown for various loading conditions and different spans. Another valuable reference on the analysis and design of rigid frames is the *Procedure Handbook of Arc Welding Design & Practice* published by the Lincoln Electric Company.

19-5. "EXACT" ANALYSIS OF RIGID FRAMES

After the member sizes are estimated it is necessary to analyze the frame by one of the so-called exact methods. The student has probably been exposed to slope deflection, moment distribution, column analogy, and other methods and he may want to know which one to use. The answer is probably the method in which he has the most confidence.

It is not the purpose of this section to explain several methods of analyzing indeterminate rigid frames, as such information can be found in several excellent textbooks on statically indeterminate structures. Only one general method of analysis is included and its application is limited to one-span hinged rigid frames. For this discussion the frame of Fig. 19-6 is considered.

Under load the distance from A to D represented by l in the figure changes because the roller at D moves slightly one way or the other. The amount of this deflection can be obtained by taking moments about D

[2] Martin P. Korn, *Steel Rigid Frames Manual Design and Construction* (Ann Arbor, Mich.: J. W. Edwards, Inc., 1953), p. 15. A person doing rigid-frame design would be wise to obtain a copy of this well-written and interesting book.

Fig. 19-6

of the M/EI diagram from A to D (the second moment-area theorem) where y is the vertical distance from a horizontal axis through the hinges.

$$\delta_L = \sum \frac{My}{EI}\, ds$$

It is now desired to analyze the hinged frame shown in Fig. 19-7, which is statically indeterminate to the first degree.

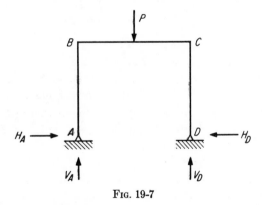

Fig. 19-7

The moment diagram for this frame equals the "simple beam" moment diagram plus the moment diagram due to the redundant force H. These moment diagrams are shown in Fig. 19-8 and are drawn as M/EI diagrams for deflection considerations. As is the usual practice for frames of this type, the moment diagrams are shown on the sides of the members on which tension occurs.

After examining Fig. 19-8, an expression can be written for the change in span length from A to D in the frame. In this expression, which equals zero, M' represents the "simple beam" moment at any point. It will be

Fig. 19-8

noted from Fig. 19-8 that if M' is considered positive the moment due to H will be of the opposite sign. The resulting expression is solved for H.

$$\sum \frac{My}{EI} \, ds = \sum \frac{M'y}{EI} \, ds + \sum \frac{(-Hy)\,(y)}{EI} \, ds = 0$$

$$H = \frac{\Sigma \, (M'y/EI) \, ds}{\Sigma \, (y^2/EI) \, ds}$$

The student familiar with column analogy will see that the preceding expression is the same as the column-analogy expression for hinged frames. The value of the numerator of this expression equals the moment of the area of the M'/EI diagram about the axis through the hinges. The denominator $\Sigma \, (y^2 ds/EI)$ is actually the "moment of inertia" of the frame about an axis through the hinges except that the width of each member is $1/EI$.

Examples 19-1 and 19-2 briefly illustrate the analysis of two frames consisting of prismatic members. In these two problems the "moments of inertia" of the columns about the axis through the hinges are obtained with the usual expression for the moment of inertia about the base of a rectangle ($\frac{1}{3} \, bh^3$). For the horizontal girder in Example 19-1 the "moment of inertia" is obtained by merely using the transfer expression (Ad^2). Its moment of inertia about its own axis is considered negligible. For the inclined girders or rafters of Example 19-2 it is considered necessary to include the "moments of inertia" of the girders about their own axes. These values are computed by using the expression shown in Fig. 19-9 which was taken from the AISC Manual.

Should a member be nonprismatic and thus have varying moments

$$I_x = \frac{bd\,(b^2 \sin^2 \alpha + d^2 \cos^2 \alpha)}{12}$$

FIG. 19-9

of inertia along its cross section, it will be necessary to divide it up into sections of convenient ds lengths to make the necessary computations. The values of M' and I would be the average values for those ds lengths. Should small ds lengths be used the "moment of inertia" of the segments about their own axes can be neglected in computing the $\Sigma\,(y^2 ds/EI)$ values. If E is constant it can be omitted from these calculations as it will be canceled. As a part of Example 19-3 a frame with deepened knees, and thus varying moments of inertia, is analyzed.

Welded rigid frame foundry, Bay City, Mich. (*The Lincoln Electric Company.*)

EXAMPLE 19-1. Determine the value of H_D for the rigid frame shown in Fig. 19-10 (a). The "simple beam" M'/EI diagram is drawn in part (b) of the figure.

Frame

(a)

M'/EI Diagram

(b)

FIG. 19-10

Solution:

$$\sum \frac{M'y}{EI}\, ds = \text{moment of area of "simple beam" } M'/EI \text{ diagram about}$$

axis through hinges is

$$\left(\frac{2,500}{EI}\right)(15) = \frac{37,500}{E2} = \frac{18,750}{E}$$

$$\sum \frac{y^2}{EI}\, ds = \text{"moment of inertia" of the frame of } 1/EI \text{ width about}$$

axis through hinges is

$$\left(\frac{1}{3}\right)\left(\frac{1}{E1}\right)(15)^3\,(2) + \left(\frac{20}{E2}\right)(15)^2 = \frac{4,500}{E}$$

$$H = \frac{\Sigma\,(M'y/EI)\, ds}{\Sigma\,(y^2/EI)\, ds} = \frac{18,750/E}{4,500/E} = 4.16 \text{ k}$$

EXAMPLE 19-2. Determine the value of H_E for the gabled frame shown in Fig. 19-11 (a) for which all members are assumed to have the same moments of inertia. The simple beam M'/EI diagram is shown in part (b) of the figure.
Solution:

Fig. 19-11

TABLE FOR $\sum \dfrac{M'y}{EI} \, ds$

Member	y	ds	$\dfrac{M'}{EI} \, ds$	$\dfrac{M'y}{EI} \, ds$
AB	—	15	—	—
BC	25	25	$125/E$	$3,125/E$
CD	25	25	$125/E$	$3,125/E$
DE	—	15	—	—
				$\Sigma = 6,250/E$

TABLE FOR $\sum \dfrac{y^2}{EI} \, ds$

Member	I_0	Ad^2	$\dfrac{y^2}{EI} \, ds$
AB	—	—	$1,125/E$
BC	833	12,650	$13,483/E$
CD	833	12,650	$13,483/E$
DE	—	—	$1,125/E$
			$\Sigma = 29,216/E$

$$H = \frac{\Sigma \ (M'y/EI) \ ds}{\Sigma \ (y^2/EI) \ ds} = \frac{6{,}250/E}{29{,}216/E} = 0.214 \ \text{k}$$

19-6. PRELIMINARY DESIGN

Example 19-3 illustrates the preliminary design of a rigid-frame structure. The following paragraphs provide a brief discussion of some parts of the design which may need explanation.

Purlins. After the span, center-to-center spacings, and other dimensions have been selected for a frame, the purlins can be designed. Space is not taken to review their design which was previously considered in Sec. 7-6. Perhaps, however, the two major services which they perform should be repeated. In addition to supporting the roofing they provide lateral support for the girders.

Purlins rest on, or frame into, the sides of the top flanges of the girders. They are probably much shallower than the girders and do not provide lateral support for the bottom girder flanges. Near the center of the frames, the top flanges of the girders are in compression due to positive moments and lateral support is provided by the purlins at their connection points. Near the knees of the frame, however, there will usually be negative moments, and the ordinary depth purlins will not extend down a sufficient distance to provide lateral support for the bottom (now compression) flanges. For this reason some type of deepened purlin is needed.

Several methods of providing the necessary lateral support in the negative moment regions are shown in Fig. 19-12. In part (a) of the figure the very end of the purlin is deepened, while in part (b) braces are run from the purlins to the bottom of the girder. Another possibility is shown in (c) where a small truss with depths at its ends equal to the girder depths is used as the purlin. Outside purlins may very well be located just to the inside of the columns so they can be used to provide bracing to the inside flange.

Approximate Analysis of Frame. An approximate analysis of the frame can be made using formulas of the type given in Fig. 19-5. Any feasible load combinations which might be critical should be considered in the analysis. In Example 19-3 five different loading conditions are considered. In some frames there are other load combinations which should be considered in addition to the ones mentioned here such as crane loads or equipment loads. The AISC one-third allowable stress increase when wind loads are involved is again used by multiplying the combinations which include wind forces by $\frac{3}{4}$. The loading conditions considered here are as follows:

1. DL + SL
2. DL + drift (or snow on one half of the roof)

(a)

(b)

PL or L for
Connection to
Girder

2 Ls or Cs

2 Ls

2 Ls

2 Ls

(c)

Fig. 19-12

3. ¾ (DL + ½ SL + WL)
4. ¾ (DL + drift + WL)
5. ¾ (DL + SL + ½ WL)

The DL + SL combination is very often the controlling condition and some designers may not even make the calculations for the other combinations. This combination is not always the critical one and before the student starts omitting some of the feasible possibilities he should have a good deal of experience with frames. After such experience he may be able to recognize some load situations which do not have to be considered.

Drawing up the Knee. After the approximate analysis is made tentative moments can be calculated for the sizing of the members. For this design example a circular deepened knee is to be used. The greatest moments in the frame occur at the knees whereas the greatest moments in the columns and girders occur at their points of tangency with the knees. These points of tangency can be roughly estimated at this time and column and girder sizes estimated for the moments at those points. The exact sizes of the members are not desired at this time, only their approximate depths, so that the knees can be drawn.

After the member depths are estimated the proportions of the knee can be established. Knee proportions are often established more on the basis of what is attractive than on the basis of structural needs. Korn (previous reference) recommends that a minimum radius of 2½ times the depth of the column or girder (whichever is larger) be used for circular knees. He also says that from the standpoint of appearance there is too much knee if its depth exceeds 2½ times the depth of the column or girder (whichever is larger).

Preliminary Design of Members. After the knee dimensions are established, the critical moments at the points of tangency in the columns and girders can be calculated. The columns and girders must be able to resist moments, shears, and axial forces. Although the shears and axial forces are usually quite small in relation to the moments they are of such magnitude that they need to be considered in design. It will be remembered from Chap. 8 that when the AISC Specification is used for such cases the designs are to be made with their interaction formulas, Formulas 1.6-1a, 1.6-16, and 1.6-2, as applicable.

Using the AISC Specification it is also necessary to estimate effective lengths to calculate allowable stresses. For the design of the columns and girders it is assumed here that the effective lengths are equal to the unbraced lengths (thus $K = 1.0$). This assumption which seems quite reasonable is made for the following two reasons:

1. Axial loads are relatively small in these frames.

2. There is no doubt but that the effective lengths of the members in the plane of the frames are greater than their lengths ($K > 1.0$) because of sidesway. The actual values depend on the overall stiffness of the frame as discussed in Chap. 8; however the use of $K = 1.0$ yields very reasonable results because the least r is for the y axis (which is laterally braced).

For a detailed discussion of this subject the student is referred to Beedle et al., *Structural Steel Design* (New York: The Ronald Press Co., 1964), pp. 668-675.

"Exact" Analysis of Frame. After the tentative member sizes are selected the stresses are reviewed by an exact procedure such as the one described in Sec. 19-5. If the approximate formulas have been carefully applied it will probably be unnecessary to revise the design. The approximate formulas are so good that many designers just omit this step. The only objection the author has to this omission is caused by the fact that inadvertently foolish math mistakes are often made and this procedure provides an independent check.

Example 19-3. Make a preliminary design of the frame shown in Fig. 19-13 using A36 steel and the AISC Specification. The frames are 18 ft 0 in on centers and there are assumed to be seven equally spaced purlins on each side which

FIG. 19-13

provide lateral support for both flanges of the girders. The loads for which design is to be made are as follows:

DL (not including frame weight) = 16 lb/horizontal sq ft

Assume girder weight   = 80 lb/horizontal ft

Snow load   = 30 lb/horizontal sq ft

Wind load   = 20 lb/horizontal sq ft

Analysis is to be made for each of the five load combinations mentioned earlier in this section.

Solution:

Determining Approximate Values of H Using Equations of Fig. 19-5

Assuming $I_1 = I_2$ in Fig. 19-13,

$h = 20.0$ ft

$f = 15.0$ ft

$m = \sqrt{(15)^2 + (45)^2} = 47.4$ ft

$k = \dfrac{I_2 h}{I_1 m} = \dfrac{20.0}{47.4} = 0.422$

$Q = \dfrac{f}{h} = \dfrac{15.0}{20.0} = 0.75$

$N = 4\,(Q^2 + 3Q + k + 3) = 4\,(0.75^2 + 3 \times 0.75 + 0.422 + 3) = 24.94$

(a) DL + SL (see Fig. 19-14):

Value of H increased by 5 percent in accordance with Korn's recommendations.

$$H_A = H_E = 1.05\,\frac{wl^2}{8hN}\,(5Q + 8) = (1.05)\left(\frac{908 \times 90^2}{8 \times 20 \times 24.94}\right)(5 \times 0.75 + 8)$$

$$= 22{,}750 \text{ lb}$$

$w=80+(16+30)(18)=908\ \text{lb/ft}$

Fɪɢ. 19-14

$w=(18)(30)=540\ \text{lb/ft}$

Fɪɢ. 19-15

(b) Drift load (see Fig. 19-15):

Value of H increased by 5 percent in accordance with Korn's recommendations.

$$H_A = H_E = 1.05 \, \frac{w\,l^2}{16\,hN}\,(5Q+8) = (1.05)\left(\frac{540 \times 90^2}{16 \times 20 \times 24.94}\right)(5 \times 0.75 + 8)$$

$$= 6{,}740 \text{ lb}$$

(c) Wind load (see Fig. 19-16):

$w=(18)(20)$
$=360\ \text{lb/ft}$

Fɪɢ. 19-16

Usual practice is not to increase the value of H for wind load to take into account effect of deepened knee.

$$H_E = \frac{wh}{4N}\,(5Q^3 + 20Q^2 + 30Q + 8Qk + 5k + 12)$$

$$= \frac{(360)\ (20)}{(4)\ (24.94)}\ (5 \times 0.75^3 + 20 \times 0.75^2 + 30 \times 0.75$$
$$+ 8 \times 0.75 \times 0.422 + 5 \times 0.422 + 12)$$
$$= 3{,}790\ \text{lb}$$

$$H_A = w\ (h + f) - H_E = (360)\ (20 + 15) - 3{,}790 = 8{,}810\ \text{lb}$$

Estimating Frame Moments

(a) DL + SL (see Fig. 19-17):

FIG. 19-17

$M_{\text{knee}} = (22.75)\ (20) = 455\ \text{ft-k}$

$M_{\text{crown}} = (40.9)\ (45) - (22.75)\ (35) - (45)\ (0.908)\ (22.5) = 120\ \text{ft-k}$

(b) DL + drift:

$$M_{\text{knee}} = 320\ \text{ft-k}$$
$$M_{\text{crown}} = 87\ \text{ft-k}$$

(c) ¾ (DL + ½ SL + WL)

$$M_{\text{knee}} = 294\ \text{ft-k}$$
$$M_{\text{crown}} = 48\ \text{ft-k}$$

(d) ¾ (DL + drift + WL)

$$M_{\text{knee}} = 297\ \text{ft-k}$$
$$M_{\text{crown}} = 46\ \text{ft-k}$$

(e) ¾ (DL + SL + ½ WL)

$$M_{\text{knee}} = 399\ \text{ft-k}$$
$$M_{\text{crown}} = 78\ \text{ft-k}$$

Moment Diagram for Critical Moments (DL + SL) (see Fig. 19-18)

Preliminary Design of Frame

455 ft-k   120 ft-k   455 ft-k

Fig. 19-18

(*a*) Laying out knee:

Assuming $R = 7.00$ ft and computing the angles and distances shown in Fig. 19-19. Preliminary calculations show that W24 sections can be reasonably used for column and girders.

Fig. 19-19

(*b*) Trial column design:

Maximum moment (from Fig. 19-17) $= (22.75)(14.24) = 324$ ft-k

$$\text{Maximum thrust} = V_A = 40.9 \text{ k}$$

Try W 24 × 94 ($A = 27.7$, $d/A_f = 3.07$, $S_x = 221$, $r = 1.98$)

$$f_a = \frac{40.9}{27.63} = 1.48 \text{ ksi}$$

$$\frac{Kl}{r} = \frac{(1)(12)(14.24)}{1.98} = 86.2$$

$$F_a = 14.65 \text{ ksi}$$

$$\frac{f_a}{F_a} = \frac{1.48}{14.65} = 0.101 < 0.150 \text{ (use Formula 1.6-2 AISC)}$$

$$f_b = \frac{(12)(324)}{221} = 17.58 \text{ ksi}$$

$$F_b = \frac{12,000,000}{(12)(14.24)(3.07)} = 22.8 > 22.0 \text{ (use 22.0 ksi)}$$

$$\frac{f_a}{F_a} + \frac{f_b}{F_b} = \frac{1.48}{14.65} + \frac{17.58}{22.0} = 0.900 < 1.00 \qquad \text{(OK)}$$

(c) Trial girder design:

Maximum moment from Fig. 19-19 is

$$- (22.75)(21.62) + (40.9)(5.46) - (5.46)(0.908)(2.73) = -282 \text{ ft-k}$$

$$\text{Maximum } T = (22.75)(\sin 71° 35')$$
$$+ (40.9 - 5.46 \times 0.908)(\cos 71° 35') = 32.9 \text{ k}$$

Try W24 × 68 ($A = 20.00$, $b_f = 8.961$, $S_x = 153$, $r = 1.87$)

$$f_a = \frac{32.9}{20.0} = 1.645 \text{ ksi}$$

$$\frac{Kl}{r} = \frac{(1)(12)(7.67)}{1.87} = 49.3$$

$$F_a = 18.41 \text{ ksi}$$

$$\frac{f_a}{F_a} = \frac{1.645}{18.41} = 0.893 < 0.15 \text{ (use Formula 1.6-2 AISC)}$$

$$f_b = \frac{(12)(282)}{153} = 22.1 \text{ ksi}$$

$$L_c = 9.5 > 7.67 \text{ ft (use 24.0 ksi)}$$

$$\frac{f_a}{F_a} + \frac{f_b}{F_b} = \frac{1.645}{18.41} + \frac{22.1}{24.0} = 1.01 > 1.00 \text{ (slightly overstressed)}$$

Segment	Section	x	y	M' Due to DL+SL	ds	I of Section (ft⁴)	$\dfrac{ds}{I}$	$\dfrac{M'yds}{I}$	$\dfrac{y^2ds}{I}$
1	W 24 × 76	0	7.12	0	14.24	0.129	110.5	0	5,600
2	Flange PLs ¾ × 9 and ½ web	0.16	16.90	6.5	5.25	0.193	27.2	2,990	7,760
3	"	3.03	20.80	120	"	"	"	67,800	11,780
4	W 24 × 94	8.76	22.92	323	6.94	0.101	68.6	508,000	36,000
5	"	15.35	25.12	521	"	"	"	899,000	43,400
6	"	21.94	27.31	676	"	"	"	1,265,000	51,300
7	"	28.53	29.51	796	"	"	"	1,615,000	59,800
8	"	35.12	31.71	878	"	"	"	1,910,000	69,000
9	"	41.71	33.90	918	"	"	"	2,140,000	78,800

$$\tfrac{1}{2}\,\Sigma = \frac{363,440}{E}$$

$$\tfrac{1}{2}\,\Sigma = \frac{8,407,790}{E}$$

(d) Trial knee section:

To reasonably fit in with the W 24 × 94 column and the W24 girder flange and web dimensions, try ⅞ × 9-in. flange plates and ½-in. web plates.

$$H = \frac{\Sigma\,(M'ds/EI)}{\Sigma\,(y^2ds/EI)} = \frac{(2)\,(8,407,790)/E}{(2)\,(363,440)/E} = 23.1 \text{ k}$$

A check on column and girder sizes for the moments caused by an H of 23.1 k shows that they are satisfactory though girder is slightly overstressed.

19-7.   FINAL DESIGN AND DETAILS

Knee Design.   An exact theoretical determination of the stress distribution in the knees of a rigid frame is quite a complex problem because the stress variation is decidedly different from that in a straight beam subject to bending.   The neutral axis does not fall at the middepth of the section because the compressive stresses accumulate going around the inside of the knee and the large percentage of the knee cross section will be placed in tension.   The neutral axis for a rounded knee is roughly 25 percent of the distance from the bottom. This value varies a few percent with different roof pitches.

The usual designer will probably not go to a great deal of trouble in attempting to determine precise stresses in the knee. He will probably just use some approximate method for checking stresses. As the compressive stresses are rather high all around the inside curved surface and actually a little beyond the points of tangency, the usual practice is to place stiffeners at the points of tangency and at the knee.

It is probably desirable to additionally stiffen the compression flanges of the knee to prevent local buckling. These stiffeners which can be triangular in shape need only to extend for about one-third of the web depth. They are usually placed at distances on centers equal to about 2½ or 3 times the flange width.

Allen County War Memorial, Fort Wayne, Ind.
(*The Lincoln Electric Company.*)

Lateral Bracing. The student may have seen rigid frames where there was no bracing between the knees of the frame. He may think that the roof and the purlins provide sufficient lateral bracing and that the addition of special bracing is unnecessary. He must, however, be very careful because if the frame is not laterally stable, it may fail at very low computed stresses.

A plastic analysis of rigid frames will show that plastic hinges will form at the knees, after which there will be a redistribution of moments to other parts of the frame. For this redistribution to take place, however, it is essential for satisfactory lateral bracing to be provided in the vicinity of the plastic hinges. Bracing is also necessary for resisting wind loads perpendicular to the plane of rigid frames.

Cross bracing is usually not too satisfactory because it can interfere with the windows in the vertical walls. One type of bracing shown in Fig. 19-20 is frequently very satisfactory. This bracing, which might be

Fig. 19-20

connected to the diagonal stiffeners at the corners, is similar to the end portals in a through bridge and is often called *knee bracing*.

In the plane of the roof cross bracing is very satisfactory. Looking at the building from the side, the bracing might very well be arranged as shown in Fig. 19-21. Probably each of these members will be designed

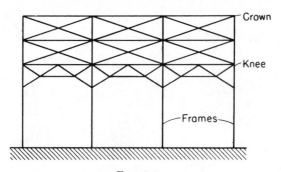

Fig. 19-21

as a tension member capable of carrying the entire wind shear in its panel.

Design of Tie Rods. The net cross-sectional area of the tie rod can be determined by dividing the maximum horizontal reaction H by the allowable tie rod stress. In selecting the tie rods there are several items to be considered. It is necessary to provide a rod whose net area at the root of the threads equals the required value. Should the rods not be encased in the concrete it may be well to provide a little extra diameter to estimate the effect of corrosion. Incidentally the base plates can be made with the connections for the rods built into them.

Temperature Stresses. For the usual span, rigid-frame temperature stresses are not normally considered as they are probably negligible unless spans in excess of about 200 ft are involved.

19-8. PLASTIC DESIGN OF RIGID FRAMES

The plastic design of rigid frames is felt to be a little beyond the scope of this book. The student, however, should realize that the plastic procedure will not only simplify analysis but will also provide considerable opportunities for economy. The AISC has published a booklet[3] which includes the design of single-span rigid frames by this method. The use of this excellent publication produces very realistic designs and abbreviates greatly the rather laborious elastic design procedure described in this chapter.

PROBLEM

19-1. Design the rigid frame shown in the accompanying illustration using the AISC Specification and A36 steel. The frames are assumed to be spaced 20 ft 0 in. on centers and are subjected to a wind load of 20 psf of vertical projection and a snow load of 20 psf of horizontal projection.

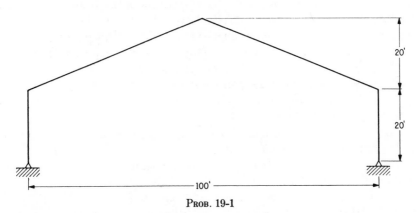

PROB. 19-1

[3] *Steel Gables And Arches* (New York: American Institute of Steel Construction, 1963).

chapter 20

MULTISTORY BUILDINGS

20-1. INTRODUCTION

Space is not taken in this introductory text to discuss the design of multistory buildings in detail. The material of this chapter is presented merely to give the student a general idea of the problems involved in the design of such buildings and not to present elaborate design examples.

Office buildings, hotels, apartment houses, and other buildings of many stories are quite common in the United States and the trend is towards an even larger number of tall buildings in the future. Available land for building in our heavily populated cities is becoming scarcer and scarcer and costs are becoming higher and higher. Tall buildings require a smaller amount of this expensive land to provide required floor space. Other factors contributing to the increased number of multistory buildings are new and better materials and construction techniques.

There are, on the other hand, several factors that may limit the heights to which buildings will be erected. These include the following:

1. Certain city building codes prescribe the maximum heights to which buildings can be constructed.

2. Foundation conditions may not be satisfactory for supporting buildings of many stories.

3. Floor space may not be rentable above a certain height. Someone will always be available to rent the top floor or two of a 250-story building, but floor numbers 100 through 248 may not be so easy to rent.

4. There are several cost factors which tend to increase with taller buildings. Among these factors are elevators, plumbing, heating and air conditioning, glazing, exterior walls, wiring, etc.

Whether a multistory building is used for an office building, a hospital, a school, an apartment house, or whatever, the problems of design are generally the same. The construction is probably of the skeleton type in which the loads are transmitted to the foundation by a framework of steel beams and columns. The floor slabs, partitions, and exterior walls

522

are all supported by the frame. This type of framing which can be erected to tremendous heights may also be referred to as beam-and-column construction. Bearing-wall construction is probably not used for buildings of more than a few stories although it has on occasion been used for buildings up to 8 or 10 stories. The columns of a skeleton frame are probably spaced 20, 25, or 30 ft on centers with beams and girders framing into them from both directions (see Fig. 13-1). On some of the floors, however, it may be necessary to have much larger open areas between columns for dining rooms, ballrooms, etc. For such cases very large beams (perhaps plate girders) may be needed to support column loads for many floors above.

It is usually necessary in multistory buildings to fireproof the members of the frame with concrete, gypsum, or some other material. The exterior walls are probably constructed with concrete or masonry units although an increasing number of modern buildings are being erected with large areas of glass in the exterior walls.

For these tall and heavy buildings the usual spread footings may not be sufficient to support the loads. If the bearing strength of the soil is high, steel grillage footings may be sufficient, but for poor soil conditions pile or pier foundations may be necessary.

For multistory buildings the beam-to-column systems are said to be

Broadview Apartments, Baltimore, Md. (*The Lincoln Electric Company.*)

superimposed on top of each other story by story or tier by tier. The column sections can be fabricated for one, two, or more floors with the two-story lengths probably being the most common. Theoretically, column sizes can be changed at each floor level but the costs of the splices involved usually more than cancel any savings in column weights. Columns of three or more stories in height are difficult to erect. The result is that the two-story heights work out very well most of the time.

20-2. COLUMN SPLICES

Column splices are usually placed 2 or 3 ft above floor levels to keep from interfering with the beam and column connections. Typical column splices are shown in Fig. 20-1. As shown in the figure, the column ends are usually milled so they can be placed firmly in contact with each other for purposes of load transfer. When the contact surfaces are milled a large part of the axial compression (if not all) can be transferred through the contacting areas. It is obvious that splice plates are necessary even though full contact is made between the columns and only axial loads are involved. They are even more necessary when consideration is given to the shears and moments existing in practical columns subjected to off-center loads, lateral forces, moments, etc.

There is obviously a great deal of difference between tension splices and compression splices. In tension splices all load has to be transferred through the splice, whereas in splices for compression members a large part of the load can be transferred directly in bearing between the columns. The splice material is then needed to transfer only the remaining part of the load.

The amount of load to be carried by the splice plates is difficult to estimate. Should the column ends not be milled, the plates should be designed to carry 100 percent of the load. When the surfaces are milled and axial loads only are involved, the amount of load to be carried by the plates might be estimated to be from 25 to 50 percent of the total load. If bending is involved perhaps 50 to 75 percent of the total load may have to be carried by the splice material.

The bridge specifications spell out very carefully splice requirements for compression members but the AISC does not. For example, the AREA says that compression member splices shall be designed to carry at least one-half of the total load. They further specify that compression members be spliced on all four sides.

Part (a) of Fig. 20-1 shows a splice which may be used for columns with the same nominal depths. The student will notice in the AISC Manual that wide-flange shapes of the same series (as W12)

Fig. 20-1

generally have the same inside distances between flanges although their total actual depths may vary as much as several inches (8.72 in. from a W 14 × 730 to a W 14 × 22). The type of splice shown in part (b) of the figure which has filler plates is used when the nominal depth of the top column is more than 2 in. less than that of the lower column.

Part (c) shows a type of splice which can be used for columns of equal or different nominal depths. For this type of splice the butt plate is shop-welded to the lower column and the clip angles used for field erection are shop-welded to the upper column. In the field the erection

Welded column splice for Colorado State Service Building, Denver, Colo. (*The Lincoln Electric Company.*)

bolts shown are installed and the upper column is field-welded to the butt plate. The horizontal welds on this plate resist shears and moments in the columns.

Part (d) shows welded splices made on all four sides of the columns. The web splices are bolted in place in the field and field-welded to the column webs. The flange splices are shop-welded to the lower column and field welded to the top column. The web plates may be referred to as *shear plates* and the flange plates as *moment plates*.

20-3. DISCUSSION OF LATERAL FORCES

For tall buildings, lateral forces must be considered as well as gravity forces. The usual practice is to consider wind forces in a building-frame design when the height is two or more times the least lateral dimension. The usual framing of buildings with a smaller height-width ratio has sufficient stiffness to resist forces of large magnitude without any special design provisions. Perhaps the common 2-to-1 ratio is a little high, however, for some modern buildings with their large areas of glass in the exterior walls.

High wind pressures on the sides of tall buildings produce overturning moments. These moments are probably resisted without difficulty by the axial strengths of the columns but the horizontal shears produced on each level may be of such magnitude as to require the use of special bracing or moment-resisting connections.

Unless they are fractured, the floors and walls of tall buildings provide a large part of the lateral stiffness of tall buildings. Although the amount of such resistance may be several times that provided by the lateral bracing, it is difficult to estimate and may not be reliable. Today so many modern buildings have light movable interior partitions, glass exterior walls, and lightweight floors that the steel frame should be assumed to provide all of the required lateral stiffness.

A building must not only be braced sufficiently laterally to prevent failure but also prevented from deflecting so much as to injure its various parts. Another item of importance is the provision of sufficient bracing to give the occupants a feeling of safety. They might not have this feeling in tall buildings which have a great deal of lateral movement in times of high winds. There have actually been tales of occupants of the upper floors of tall buildings complaining of seasickness on very windy days.

Many areas of the world, including the western part of the United States, fall in earthquake territory; and in those areas it is necessary to consider seismic forces in design for tall or low buildings. During an earthquake there is an acceleration of the ground surface. This acceleration can be broken down into vertical and horizontal components. Usually the vertical component of the acceleration is assumed to be negligible but the horizontal component can be severe.

Most buildings can be designed with little extra expense to withstand the forces caused during an earthquake of fairly severe intensity. On the other hand, earthquakes during recent years have clearly shown that the average building which is not designed for earthquake forces can be destroyed by earthquakes that are not particularly severe. The usual practice is to design buildings for additional lateral loads (representing the estimate of the earthquake forces) which are equal to some percentage (5–10) of the weight of the building and its contents.

Many persons look upon the seismic loads to be used in design as being merely percentage increases of the wind loads. This is not altogether correct, however, as seismic loads are different in their action and are not proportional to the exposed area but to the building weight above the level in question.

The effect of lateral forces is to require the use of more steel. If the AISC Specification is used, however, it will be remembered that allowable stresses can be increased by one-third when wind or seismic loads are being considered alone or in combination with dead or live loads.

Chase Manhattan Bank Building, New York City.
(*Bethlehem Steel Company.*)

Despite this increase in allowable stresses the lateral forces will probably require the addition of bracing or moment-resistant connections as described in the following section.

20-4. TYPES OF LATERAL BRACING

A steel building frame with no lateral bracing is shown in Fig. 20-2 (a). Should the beams and columns shown be connected together with the standard ("simple beam") connections, the frame would have little resistance to the lateral forces shown. Assuming the joints to act as frictionless pins, the frame would be laterally deflected as shown in part (b) of the figure.

To resist these lateral deflections, the best, simplest, and most economical method from a theoretical standpoint is the insertion of full diagonal bracing as shown in part (c) of Fig. **20-2**. From a practical

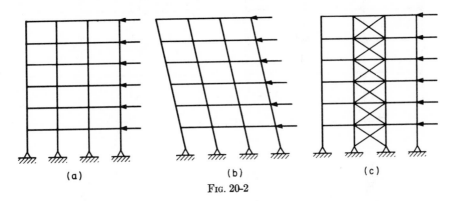

(a)   (b)   (c)

FIG. 20-2

standpoint, however, the student can easily see that in the average building full diagonal bracing would often be in the way of doors, windows, and other wall openings. Furthermore, many buildings have movable interior partitions and the presence of interior cross bracing would greatly reduce this flexibility. As diagonal bracing is the most direct, efficient, and economical it should be used whenever conditions permit. Usually it will only be convenient in solid walls in and around elevator shafts, stairwells, and other walls in which few or no openings are planned.

The most common method of providing resistance to lateral forces in tall buildings is the use of moment-resistant connections as illustrated in Fig. 20-3(a). This type of bracing is referred to as *bracket type bracing*. Various types of moment-resistant connections are discussed in Sec. 20-6 and shown in Fig. 20-5.

Other types of lateral bracing are shown in parts (b), (c), and (d) of Fig. 20-3. Each of these bracing types has the disadvantage that it is not very satisfactory for exterior walls which are largely glass. The result is an increased use of the bracket type bracing. The term *braced bent* is usually given to bents which are braced regardless of the method.

Knee braces shown in part (b) of the figure can be used in exterior walls unless the glass area is extremely large. They are also quite satisfactory for use in interior walls because they do not interfere with normal openings. The K bracing shown in part (d) can be used to advantage only where small openings are present in the walls. It might be noted that in the upper floors of a building the shearing forces are smaller and it may be possible to dispense with some or all of the lateral bracing on these levels.

Since the lateral forces are usually assumed to be equal in intensity

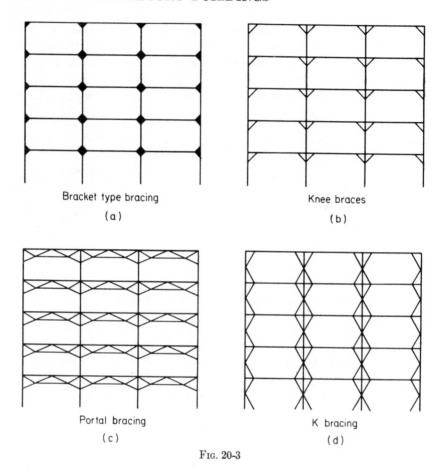

Bracket type bracing

(a)

Knee braces

(b)

Portal bracing

(c)

K bracing

(d)

Fig. 20-3

against all sides of the building, the student may ask, "Should the same bracing be used in both directions of a building?" If the building is square or nearly square the answer is probably yes. When the length of a building is several times its least lateral dimension it is highly possible that the bracing will be left out in the long direction because the wind forces will be spread over so many columns that sufficient resistance will be present without bracing. For buildings in between these two extremes the designer will have to use his judgment.

In the usual building the floor system (beams and slabs) is assumed to be rigid in the horizontal plane and the lateral loads are assumed to be concentrated at the floor levels. Floor slabs and girders acting together also provide considerable resistance to lateral forces. Investigation of steel buildings which have withstood high wind forces have shown that the floor slabs distribute the lateral forces so that all of the columns on a particular floor have equal deflections. When rigid floors are present they spread the lateral shears to the columns or walls in the building. When lateral forces are particularly large, as in very tall buildings or where seismic forces are being considered, certain specially designed walls may be used to resist large parts of the lateral forces. These walls are called *shear walls*.

It is not necessary to brace every panel in a building. Usually the bracing can be placed in the outside walls with less interference than in the inside walls where movable partitions may be desired. Probably the bracing of the outside panels alone is not enough and some interior panels may need to be braced. It is assumed that the floors and beams are sufficiently rigid to transfer the lateral forces to the braced panels. Three possible arrangements of braced panels are shown in Fig. 20-4. A

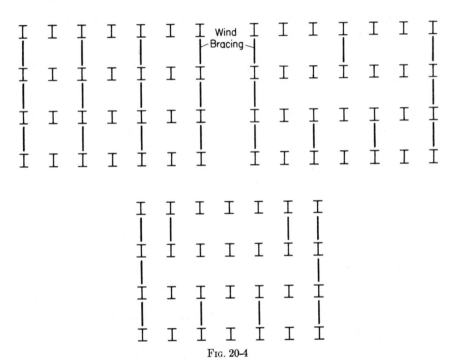

FIG. 20-4

symmetrical arrangement is probably desirable to prevent uneven lateral deflection in the building and thus torsion.

The AISC Specification permits three types of construction for steel building frames. These are listed as follows with a brief comment about each pertaining to bracing.

1. Type I construction is the type of construction which has rigid

moment-resisting joints. Its use is permitted unconditionally by the AISC.

2. Type II construction is the type of construction in which the beam and girder ends are simply supported. Larger beams and girders are required because of the large simple-beam moments, but these simple end connections produce smaller column moments. To provide resistance to lateral forces it is necessary to use one of the types of bracing previously discussed.

3. Type III construction is the type of construction where the member ends have semirigid connections and have the ability to resist certain moments in between the values of types I and II. The AISC says this type of construction will be permitted only if evidence is presented supporting the minimum values of restraint used in the design.

20-5. ANALYSIS OF BUILDINGS WITH DIAGONAL WIND BRACING FOR LATERAL FORCES

Full diagonal cross bracing has been described as being the best and most economical type of wind bracing for tall buildings. Where this type of bracing cannot practically be used due to interference with windows, doors, or movable partitions, moment-resisting brackets are often used. Should, however, very tall narrow buildings (with height-to-least-width ratios of 5.0 or greater) be constructed, lateral deflections may become a problem with moment-resisting joints. The joints can satisfactorily resist the moments but the deflections may be excessive.

Should maximum wind deflections be kept under 0.002 times the building height there is little chance of injury to the building, says ASCE Subcommittee 31.[1] The deflection is to be computed neglecting any resistance supplied by floors and walls. To keep lateral deflections within this range it is necessary to use deep knee bracing or full diagonal cross bracing when the height-to-least-width ratio is about 5.0; and for greater values of the ratio, full diagonal cross bracing is essential.[2]

The student may often see bracing used in buildings in which he would think wind stresses were negligible. Such bracing stiffens up a building appreciably and serves the useful purpose of plumbing the steel frame during erection. Before bracing is installed the members of a steel building frame may be twisted in all sorts of directions. Connecting the diagonal bracing should pull them into their proper positions.

---

[1] "Wind Bracing In Steel Buildings," *Trans. ASCE*, vol. 105 (1940), pp. 1713–1739.

[2] L. E. Grinter, *Theory of Modern Steel Structures* (New York: The Macmillan Company, 1962), p. 326.

When diagonal cross bracing is used it is desirable to introduce initial tension into the diagonals. This prestressing will make the building frame tight and reduce its lateral deflection. Furthermore, the prestressed members can support compressive stress by reductions in the initial tensions. Since the pretensioned members can resist compression, the horizontal shear to be resisted will be assumed to split equally between the two diagonals. For buildings with several bay widths, equal shear distribution is usually assumed for each bay.

Should the diagonals not be initially tightened rather stiff sections should be used so they will be able to resist appreciable compressive stresses. The direct axial stresses in the girders and columns can be found by joints from the shear stresses assumed in the diagonals. Usually the girder axial stresses so computed are too small to consider but the values for columns can be quite important. The taller the building becomes the more critical are the column axial stresses caused by lateral forces.

For types of bracing other than cross bracing similar assumptions can be made for analysis. The student is referred to pages **333–339** of *Theory of Modern Steel Structures* by L. E. Grinter (New York: Macmillan, **1962**) for discussion of this subject.

20-6. MOMENT-RESISTING JOINTS

For a large percentage of buildings under 8 to 10 stories in height the beams and girders are connected to each other and to the columns with simple end framed connections of the types previously described in Chap. 12. As buildings become taller it is absolutely necessary to use a definite wind-bracing system or moment-resisting joints. Moment-resisting joints may also be used in lower buildings where it is desired to take advantage of continuity and the consequent smaller beam sizes and depths and shallower floor construction. Moment-resisting brackets may also be necessary in some locations for loads which are applied eccentrically to columns.

Several types of moment-resisting connections which may be used as wind bracing are shown in Fig. 20-5. The design of connections of these types was also presented in Chap. 12. The average design outfit through the years will probably develop a file of moment-resisting connections from their previous designs. When they have a wind moment of such and such a value they merely refer to their file and select one of their former designs which will provide the required moment resistance.

In the following paragraphs a few comments are made about each of the types of connections shown in Fig. 20-5. The letter preceding each of these paragraphs corresponds to the letter in the figure for that connection.

(a) The top-angle and seat-angle connection shown, sometimes called an *angle bracket*, provides the minimum acceptable type of wind connection. Even if web angles, shown dashed, are added, the moment resistance is not appreciably increased. This type of wind connection is not satisfactory for very tall buildings.

(b) The split-beam bracket is probably the most common type of wind connection used in multistory buildings. When large girder reactions have to be transferred by this excellent type of connection the seat may have to be stiffened as showed by the dashed line.

(c) This heavy bulky connection may be used to resist very large

Angle bracket
(a)

Split-beam connection
(b)

Heavy bracket
(c)

Welded moment-resisting joint
(d)

Fig. 20-5

moments. Although it can reduce girder moments decidedly, its high fabrication cost probably cancels the saving in girder weight.

(d) In this figure a very good welded type of connection for resisting wind moments is shown. The simple clean lines of this connection and much smaller amounts of connection steel used should be noted. Although the connections of parts (a) and (b) of Fig. 20-5 are shown to be riveted or bolted, they can also be satisfactorily welded.

20-7. ANALYSIS OF BUILDINGS WITH MOMENT-RESISTING JOINTS FOR LATERAL LOADS

Approximate methods have been very popular for many years for analyzing multistory buildings for lateral forces. Among the several reasons for this popularity have been the following:

1. Large building frames are statically indeterminate to a very high degree and their analysis by an "exact" method is a lengthy and difficult problem.

2. The resistance to lateral forces supplied by the walls and floors in a tall building is difficult to estimate accurately and the results of analysis by an "exact" method are therefore not very precise.

3. Before the members of an indeterminate structure can be designed their stresses have to be determined, but these stresses are dependent upon their sizes. Application of an approximate analysis should yield stresses from which very good estimates of member sizes can be made for preliminary design.

The analysis of multistory buildings is a very difficult problem, and past practice has been to use one of the several approximate methods of analysis available. Today, however, with the availability of the digital computers it is feasible to make exact analyses in appreciably less time than required to make the approximate analyses (without the use of computers). The more accurate values obtained permit the use of smaller members. The results of computer usage are money-saving in analysis time and in the use of smaller members. In an excellent reference on this subject it is claimed that a frame with over 1,400 degrees of freedom was solved in just over 8 min on the computer and that as of that time (1964) the computer cost would have been just over $80.[3]

In the pages that follow a brief review of the portal and cantilever approximate methods is presented. No consideration is given in either of these methods to the elastic properties of the members. These omissions can be very serious in unsymmetrical frames and in very tall buildings.

---

[3] Ray W. Clough, Ian P. King, and Edward L. Wilson, "Structural Analysis of Multistory Buildings," *Proc. ASCE*, vol. 90, no. ST3 (June 1964).

To illustrate the seriousness of the matter, the changes in member sizes are considered in a very tall building. In such a building there will probably not be a great deal of change in beam sizes from the top floor to the bottom floor. For the same loadings and spans the changed sizes would be due to the large wind moments in the lower floors. The change, however, in column sizes from top to bottom would be tremendous. The result is that the relative sizes of columns and beams on the top floors are entirely different from the relative sizes on the lower floors. When this fact is not considered it causes large errors in the analysis.

If the height of a building is roughly five or more times its least lateral dimension, it is generally felt that a more precise method of analysis should be used than the portal or cantilever methods. There are several excellent approximate methods which make use of the elastic properties and which give values closely approaching the results of the "exact" methods. These include the Factor method, the Witmer method of K percentages, and the Spurr method. Should an exact method be desired, the slope deflection and moment distribution methods are available. If the slope deflection procedure is used, the designer will have the problem of solving a large number of simultaneous equations. The problem is not so serious, however, if he has access to a digital computer.

The Portal Method. The most common method of analyzing tall building frames for lateral loads is the portal method. The chief advantage of this method, which is said to be satisfactory for most buildings up to 25 stories,[4] is its simplicity. A detailed description of this method, including the basis for the assumptions made, can be found in most structural analysis books. Only a brief listing of the steps involved in its application is given in this section. These steps are as follows:

1. The horizontal shears on each level are arbitrarily distributed between the columns. One commonly used procedure is to assume the shear divides between the columns in the ratio of one part to exterior columns and two parts to interior columns. Another common distribution (and the one used in the illustrative problem to follow) is to assume the shear V taken by each column is in proportion to the floor area which it supports.

2. The moment M in each column is assumed to equal the column shear times half the column height (thus assuming a point of contraflexure at middepth).

3. The girder moments M are determined by joints by noting the sum of the girder moments at any joint equals the sum of the column moments at that joint. These calculations are easily made by starting at the upper

---

[4] "Wind Bracing in Steel Buildings," *Trans. ASCE*, vol. 105 (1940), p. 1723.

left joint and working joint by joint across to the right; after which the next level is handled left to right, etc.

4. The shear V in each girder is assumed to equal its moment divided by half the girder length.

5. Finally, the column axial stresses S are determined by summing up the beam shears and other column axial stresses at each joint. These calculations are again handled conveniently by working from left to right and from the top floor down.

In Fig. 20-6 a building frame is shown which is to be analyzed

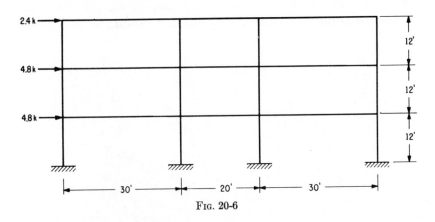

Fig. 20-6

by the portal method. The frames are assumed to be placed 20 ft 0 in. on centers and the exterior walls are assumed to be subjected to a wind pressure of 20 lb per vertical square foot. From this data the horizontal loads shown at each floor level are calculated.

This frame is analyzed in Fig. 20-7 by the portal method. The arrows

Fig. 20-7. Frame analysis by the portal method.

shown on the figure give the direction of the girder shears and the column axial stresses.   The student can visualize the stress condition of the frame if he assumes the frame is tending to be pushed over from left to right by the wind, stretching the left exterior columns and compressing the right exterior columns.

The Cantilever Method.   Another simple method of analyzing building frames for lateral forces is the cantilever method.   This method is said to be a little more desirable for high narrow buildings than the portal method and may be used satisfactorily for buildings with heights not in excess of 25 to 35 stories.[5]   It is not as popular as the portal method.

Instead of initially assuming the horizontal shears to be divided be-

Expansion of Southern Bell Telephone Company Building, Atlanta, Ga. (*Bethlehem Steel Company.*)

[5] *Op. cit.*

tween the columns on each level in some proportion, the first assumption in the cantilever method pertains to the column axial stresses.   The axial stress in a particular column is assumed to vary in direct proportion to its distance from the center of gravity of the group of columns on that level.   With the wind blowing from left to right, the columns to the left of the center of gravity will be in tension while those to the right will be in compression.   The steps involved in analyzing a building frame for lateral forces by the cantilever method are as follows:

1. To obtain the column axial stresses moments are taken above an assumed plane of contraflexure through the middepth of the columns on each level.   As an illustration of this procedure, moments are taken here to determine the axial stresses in the columns on the top level of the building frame of Fig. 20-5.   A free body is drawn in Fig. 20-8 of the

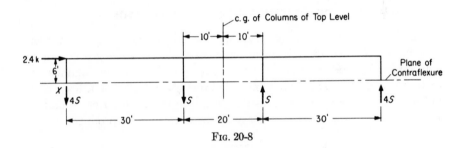

FIG. 20-8

part of the building above the assumed plane of contraflexure on the top level.   The following equation is written:

$$\Sigma \, M_x = 0$$

$$(2.4) \ (6) + (30) \ (S) - (50) \ (S) - (80) \ (4S) = 0$$

$$S = 0.0424$$

2. The girder shears are determined by joints from the column axial stresses.

3. The girder moments are determined by multiplying the girder shears by the half girder lengths.

4. The column moments are found by joints from the girder moments.

5. The column shears are obtained by dividing the column moments by the half-column heights.

The analysis of the frame of Fig. 20-6 by the cantilever method is illustrated in Fig. 20-9.   Arrows representing the directions of the column axial stresses and the girder shears are again shown for the benefit of the student.

FIG. 20-9. Frame analysis by the cantilever method.

20-8. ANALYSIS OF BUILDINGS FOR GRAVITY LOADS

Simple Framing. If simple framing is used, the design of the girders is quite simple because the shears and moments in each girder can be determined by statics. The gravity loads applied to the columns are relatively easy to estimate but the column moments may be a little more difficult. If the girder reactions on each side of the interior column of Fig. 20-10 are equal, no moment will theoretically be produced in the

FIG. 20-10

column at that level. This situation is probably not realistic because it is highly possible for the live load to be applied on one side of the column and not on the other or at least be unequal in magnitude). The results will be column moments. If the reactions are unequal the moment produced in the column will equal the difference between the reactions times $d/2$ of the column.

When computing the moments in exterior columns there may often be moments due to spandrel beams opposing the moments caused by the floor loads on the inside of the column. Nevertheless, gravity loads will generally cause the exterior columns to have larger moments than the interior columns.

To estimate the moment applied to a column above a certain floor it is probably reasonable to assume that the unbalanced moment at that level splits evenly between the column above and below. In fact, such an assumption is often on the conservative side as the column below may be larger than the one above.

Rigid Framing. For buildings with moment-resisting joints it is a little more difficult to estimate the girder moments and make preliminary designs. If the ends of each girder are assumed to be completely fixed, the moments for uniform loads are as shown in Fig. 20-11 (a). Conditions of

Fixed-end beam

(a)

Simple beam

(b)

Fig. 20-11

complete fixity are probably not realized, with the result that the end moments are smaller than shown in part (a) of the figure. There is a corresponding increase in the positive centerline moments approaching the simple moment ($w\ l^2/8$) shown in part (b) of the figure. Probably a moment diagram somewhere in between the two extremes is more realistic. Such a moment diagram is represented by the dotted line of Fig. 20-11 (a). A reasonable procedure is to assume a moment in the range of $\frac{1}{10}\ w\ l^2$, where l is the clear span.

When the beams and girders of a building frame are rigidly connected to each other a continuous frame is the result. From a theoretical standpoint an accurate analysis of such a structure cannot be made unless the entire frame is handled as a unit.

Before this subject is pursued further it should be realized that in the upper floors of tall buildings the wind moments will be small and the framed and seated connections described in Chap. 12 will provide sufficient moment resistance. For this reason the beams and girders of the upper floors may very well be designed on the basis of simple beam moments, while those of the lower floors may be designed as continuous members with moment-resistant connections because of the larger wind moments.

For the design of beams and girders it is necessary to consider two loading conditions: (DL + LL) and (DL + LL + WL) ¾. In this latter expression WL represents lateral forces whether due to wind or wind and earthquake and the ¾ factor represents the AISC one-third increase in allowable stresses when lateral forces are involved. For the upper floors the wind moments will not increase the girder sizes because of the allowable stress increase but on lower floors they will begin to cause increased sizes.

From a strictly theoretical viewpoint there are several live loading conditions which need to be considered to obtain maximum shears and moments at various points in a continuous structure. For the building frame shown in Fig. 20-12 it is desired to place live loads to cause

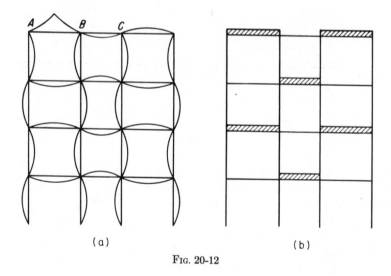

(a)   (b)

Fig. 20-12

maximum positive moment in span *AB*. A qualitative influence line for positive moment at the centerline of this span is shown in part (a) of the figure. This influence line shows that to obtain maximum positive moment at the centerline of span *AB* the live loads should be placed as shown in part (b) of the figure.

To obtain maximum negative moment at point *B* or maximum positive moment in span *BC*, other loading situations need to be considered. With the increased availability of the digital computers more of this detailed type of analysis is being done every day. The student, however, can see that unless the designer has access to a computer he probably will not have sufficient time to go through all of these theoretical situations. Furthermore, it is doubtful if the accuracy of our analysis methods would justify all of the work anyway. It is, however, often feasible to take out two stories of the building at a time as a free body and analyze that part by one of the "exact" methods such as the successive correction method of moment distribution.

Before such an "exact" analysis can be made it is necessary to make an estimate of the member sizes, probably based on the results of analysis by one of the approximate methods.

20-9. DESIGN OF MEMBERS

Girders. The girders can be designed for the two load combinations mentioned in Sec. 20-8, (DL + LL) and (DL + LL + WL) ¾. For the top several floors the second condition will not control design, but further down in the building it will control the sizes. As previously described in Chap. 13, the specifications may permit some considerable reduction in the live loads assumed to be supported by the girders.

Should simple framing be used the girders will be proportioned for simple beam moments plus the moments caused by the lateral loads. For continuous framing the girders will be proportioned for $w \ l^2/10$ (for uniform loads) plus the moments caused by the lateral loads. An interesting comparison of designs by the two methods is shown in pages 717–719 of Beedle et al., *Structural Steel Design* (New York: Ronald, 1964). It may be necessary to draw the moment diagram for the two cases (gravity loads and lateral loads) and add them together to obtain the maximum positive moment out in the span. The value so computed may very well control the girder size in some of the members.

A major part of the design of a multistory building is involved in setting up a column schedule which shows the loads to be supported by the various columns story by story. The gravity forces can be estimated very well while the shears, axial stresses, and moments caused by lateral forces can be roughly approximated for the preliminary design from some approximate method (portal, cantilever, or factor).

If both axes of the columns are free to sway, the column effective lengths theoretically must be calculated for both axes as described in Chap. 8. If diagonal bracing is used in one direction, thus preventing sidesway, the K value will be less than 1.0 in that direction. When frames are braced in the narrow direction it is reasonable to use K = 1.0 for both axes.

MULTISTORY BUILDINGS

After the sizes of the girders and columns are tentatively selected for a two-story height, an "exact" analysis can be performed and the members redesigned. The two stories taken out for analysis are often referred to as a *tier*. This process can be continued tier by tier down through the building. Many tall buildings have been designed and are performing satisfactorily in which this last step (the two-story "exact" analysis) was omitted.

chapter 21

PLASTIC ANALYSIS

21-1. INTRODUCTION

All designs performed in the previous chapters of this book were based on the elastic theory. The maximum load which a structure could support was assumed to equal the load which first caused a stress somewhere in the structure to equal the yield point of the material. Engineering structures have been designed for many decades by this method with satisfactory results. The design profession, however, has long been aware that ductile materials do not fail until a great deal of yielding occurs after the yield stress is reached. These final chapters (Chaps. 21 and 22) are devoted to a consideration of the behavior of ductile steel structures in the plastic range.

When the stress at one point in a ductile steel structure reaches the yield point, that part of the structure will yield locally, permitting some readjustment of the stresses. Should the load be increased, the stress at the point in question will remain approximately constant, thereby requiring the less stressed parts of the structure to support the load increase. It is true that statically determinate structures can resist little load in excess of the amount that causes the yield stress to first develop at some point. For statically indeterminate structures, however, the load increase can be quite large; and these structures are said to have the happy facility of spreading out overloads due to the steel's ductility.

As early as 1914 a Hungarian, Dr. Gabor Kazinczy, recognized that the ductility of steel permitted a redistribution of stresses in an overloaded indeterminate structure.[1] In the United States Prof. J. A. Van den Broek introduced his plastic theory which he called limit design. This theory was published in a paper entitled "Theory of Limit Design" in February 1939 in the *Proceedings of the ASCE*.

In the plastic theory, rather than basing designs on the allowable-

---

[1] Lynn S. Beedle, *Plastic Design of Steel Frames* (New York: John Wiley & Sons, Inc., 1958), p. 3.

stress method the problem is handled by considering the greatest load which can be carried by the structure acting as a unit. The resulting designs are quite interesting to the structural engineer as they offer several advantages. These include the following:

1. When the plastic-design procedure is used there can be considerable savings in steel (perhaps as high as 10 or 15 percent for some structures) as compared to a similar design made by the elastic procedure. The necessary continuity connections required in plastic design may reduce the actual money savings somewhat.

2. Plastic design permits the designer to make a more accurate estimate of the maximum load that a structure can support enabling him to have a better idea of the actual safety factor of the structure. The elastic method works very well for computing the stresses and strains for loads in the elastic range, but gives a very poor estimate of the actual collapse strength of a structure.

3. For many complicated structures plastic analysis is easier to apply than is elastic analysis.

4. Structures are often subjected to large stresses which are difficult to predict such as those caused by settlement, erection, etc. Plastic design provides for such situations by permitting plastic deformation.

Despite these several important advantages the acceptance of plastic design has been rather slow. Until recent years there has not been a great deal of information available concerning the ductility of steel. If a particular steel is brittle the plastic theory does not apply. A few decades ago when the design profession was just becoming interested in this theory there were several disastrous brittle failures of welded tanks and ships. (That also was the time when welded structures were beginning to gain popularity.) The acceptance of plastic design was slowed down to a walk for a long time, but in recent years much research has been performed in these areas, and plastic design is today gaining some acceptance.

Despite the great progress made in the field of plastic design the method still has some disadvantages with which the designer should be completely familiar. These include the following:

1. Plastic design is of little value for the high strength brittle steels. (The method is just as applicable to high-strength steels as it is to those of lower strength structural grade steels as long as the steels have the required ductility.)

2. Plastic design today is not satisfactory for situations where fatigue stresses are a problem.

3. Columns designed by the plastic theory provide little savings.

4. Although for many indeterminate structures plastic analysis is

simpler than elastic analysis, it should be realized that unstable plastic structures are more difficult to detect than are unstable elastic structures.

21-2. THEORY OF PLASTIC ANALYSIS

The basic theory of plastic design has been shown to be a major change in the distribution of stresses after the stresses at certain points in a structure reach the yield point. The theory is that those parts of the structure which have been stressed to the yield point cannot resist additional stresses. They instead will yield the amount required to permit the load or stresses to be transferred to other parts of the structure where the stresses are below the yield stress and thus in the elastic range and able to resist increased stress. Plasticity can be said to serve the purpose of equalizing stresses in cases of overload.

For this discussion the stress-strain diagram is assumed to have the idealized shape shown in Fig. 21-1. The yield point and the proportional

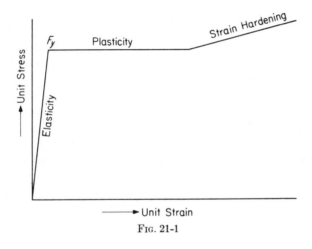

Fig. 21-1

limit are assumed to occur at the same point for this steel, and the stress-strain diagram is assumed to be a perfectly straight line in the plastic range. Beyond the plastic range there is a range of strain hardening. This latter range could theoretically permit steel members to withstand additional stress, but from a practical standpoint the strains occurring are so large that they cannot be considered.

21-3. THE PLASTIC HINGE

As the bending moment is increased at a particular section of a beam there will be a linear variation of stress until the yield stress is reached in the outermost fibers. An illustration of stress variation for a rectangular beam in the elastic range is shown in part (b) of Fig. **21-2**. The

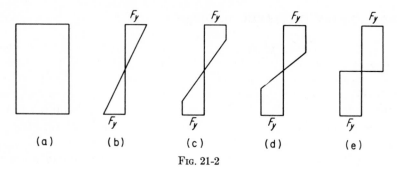

Fɪɢ. 21-2

yield moment of a cross section is defined as the moment which will just produce the yield stress in the outermost fiber of the section.

If the moment is increased beyond the yield moment the outermost fibers which had previously been stressed to their yield point will continue to have the same stress but will yield, and the duty of providing the necessary additional resisting moment will fall on the fibers nearer to the neutral axis. This process will continue with more and more parts of the beam cross section stressed to the yield point as shown by the stress diagrams of parts (c) and (d) of the figure, until finally a fully plastic distribution is approached as shown in part (e). When the stress distribution has reached this stage a *plastic hinge* is said to have formed because no additional moment can be resisted at the section. Any additional moment applied at the section will cause the beam to rotate with little increase in stress.

The *plastic moment* is the moment which will produce full plasticity in a member cross section and create a plastic hinge. The ratio of the plastic moment M_p to the yield moment M_y is called the *shape factor*. The shape factor equals 1.50 for rectangular sections and varies from about 1.10 to 1.20 for standard rolled-beam sections.

This paragraph is devoted to a description of the development of a plastic hinge in the simple beam shown in Fig. 21-3. The load shown is applied to the beam and increased in magnitude until the yield moment

Fɪɢ. 21-3

is reached and the outermost fiber is stressed to the yield point. The magnitude of the load is further increased with the result that the outer fibers begin to yield. The yielding spreads out to the other fibers away from the section of maximum moment as indicated in the figure. The length in which this yielding occurs away from the section in question is dependent on the loading conditions and the member cross section. For a concentrated load applied at the ₵ of a simple beam with a rectangular cross section, yielding in the extreme fibers at the time the plastic hinge is formed will extend for one third of the span. For a W shape in similar circumstances yielding will extend for approximately one eighth of the span. During this same period the interior fibers at the section of maximum moment yield gradually until nearly all of them have yielded and a plastic hinge is formed as shown in Fig. 21-3.

Although the effect of a plastic hinge may extend for some distance along the beam it is assumed to be concentrated at one section for analysis purposes. For the calculation of deflections and for the design of bracing the length over which yielding extends is quite important.

When steel frames are loaded to failure, the points where rotation is concentrated (plastic hinges) become quite visible to the observer before collapse occurs.

21-4. THE PLASTIC MODULUS

The yield moment M_y can be defined as equalling the yield stress times the elastic modulus. The elastic modulus equals I/c or $bd^2/6$ for a rectangular section and the yield moment equals $F_y\, bd^2/6$. This same value can be obtained by considering the resisting internal couple shown in Fig. 21-4.

The resisting moment equals T or C times the lever arm between them, as follows:

$$M_y = \left(\frac{F_y\, bd}{4}\right)\left(\frac{2}{3}\, d\right) = \frac{F_y\, bd^2}{6}$$

The elastic section modulus can again be seen to equal $bd^2/6$ for a

Fɪɢ. 21-4

Fig. 21-5

rectangular beam. The resisting moment of a rectangular section at full plasticity can be determined in a similar manner (see Fig. 21-5).

$$M_p = \left(F_y \frac{d}{2} b\right)\left(\frac{d}{2}\right) = \frac{F_y bd^2}{4}$$

The plastic moment is said to equal the yield stress times the plastic modulus. From the foregoing expression for a rectangular section, the plastic modulus Z can be seen to equal $bd^2/4$. The shape factor, which equals M_p/M_y, $F_y Z/F_y S$, or Z/S, is $(bd^2/4)/(bd^2/6) = 1.50$ for a rectangular section.

A study of the plastic modulus determined here shows that it equals the statical moment of the tension and compression areas about the neutral axis. Unless the section is symmetrical, the neutral axis for the plastic condition will not be in the same location as for the elastic condition. The total internal compression must equal the total internal tension. As all fibers are considered to have the same stress (F_y) in the plastic condition, the areas above and below the neutral axis must be equal. This situation does not hold for unsymmetrical sections in the elastic condition. Example 21-1 illustrates the calculations necessary to determine the shape factor for a tee beam and the ultimate uniform load w_u which the beam can support.

EXAMPLE 21-1. Determine M_y, M_p, and Z for the steel tee beam shown in Fig. 21-6. Also calculate the shape factor and the ultimate uniform load (w_u) which can be placed on the beam for a 12-ft simple span. $F_y = 36$ ksi.

Fig. 21-6

Solution: Elastic calculations:

$A = (8) (1\frac{1}{2}) + (6) (2) = 24$ sq in.

$\bar{y} = \dfrac{(12) (0.75) + (12) (4.5)}{24} = 2.625$ in. from top flange

$I = (\frac{1}{3}) (2) (1.125^3 + 4.875^3) + (\frac{1}{12}) (8) (1\frac{1}{2})^3 + (12) (1.875)^2$

$= 122.4$ in.^{4}

$S = \dfrac{I}{C} = \dfrac{122.4}{4.875} = 25.1$ in.^{3}

$M_y = F_y S = \dfrac{(36) (25.1)}{12} = 75.3$ ft-k

Plastic calculations:

Neutral axis is at base of flange.

$$Z = (12) (0.75) + (12) (3) = 45 \text{ in.}^3$$

$$M_p = F_y Z = \dfrac{(36) (45)}{12} = 135 \text{ ft-k}$$

$$\text{Shape factor} = \dfrac{M_p}{M_y} \quad \text{or} \quad \dfrac{Z}{S} = \dfrac{45}{25.1} = 1.79$$

$$M_p = \dfrac{w_u l^2}{8}$$

$$w_u = \dfrac{(8) (135)}{(12)^2} = 7.5 \text{ k/ft}$$

The values of the plastic moduli for the standard steel beam sections are tabulated in the Steel Handbook in the "Plastic Design Selection Table." These values will be frequently used in the pages to follow.

21-5. FACTORS OF SAFETY AND LOAD FACTORS

The factor of safety used in designing a particular structure should probably be selected only after a study is made of the uncertainties present in the design (a subject previously discussed in Chap. 1). Perhaps the usual practice, however, is to use a value which seems reasonable from the standpoint of past experience as expressed in the specifications being used. The usual safety factor considered to be present in elastic design is the one obtained by dividing the yield point of the steel by its working stress. For compact laterally supported beams of A36 steel this safety factor equals $36/24 = 1.50$ using the AISC Specification.

If the safety factor is multiplied times the shape factor, the result is referred to as the *load factor*. For a typical W section the load factor equals the safety factor 1.50 times an average shape factor of W sections of about 1.12 equals 1.68 (say 1.70). In plastic design the working loads are multiplied by the load factor to give the estimated ultimate loads and members are proportioned with these loads on the basis of plastic or collapse strengths. This procedure is illustrated in the design examples of Chap. 22. In actual practice, load factors varying from roughly 1.70 to 2.00 are used depending on the individual designer's judgment of the particular conditions. The minimum values for load factors permitted by the AISC for design purposes are presented in Sec. 22-2.

21-6.   THE COLLAPSE MECHANISM

A statically determinate beam will fail if one plastic hinge develops. To illustrate this fact, the simple beam of constant cross section loaded with a concentrated load at midspan shown in Fig. 21-7 (a) is considered.

Fig. 21-7

Should the load be increased until a plastic hinge is developed at the point of maximum moment (underneath the load in this case) an unstable structure will have been created as shown in part (b) of the figure. Any further increase in load will cause collapse.

The plastic theory is of little advantage for statically determinate beams and frames but it may be of decided advantage for indeterminate beams and frames. For an indeterminate structure to fail it is necessary for more than one plastic hinge to form. The number of plastic hinges required for failure of indeterminate structures will be shown to vary from structure to structure, but may never be less than two. The fixed-end beam of Fig. 21-8 cannot fail unless the three plastic hinges shown in the figure are developed.

Although a plastic hinge may have formed in an indeterminate structure, the load can still be increased without causing failure if the geometry of the structure permits. The plastic hinge will act like a real hinge insofar as increased loading is concerned. As the load is increased

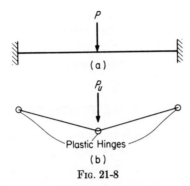

(a)

Plastic Hinges
(b)

FIG. 21-8

there is a redistribution of moment because the plastic hinge can resist
no more moment. As more plastic hinges are formed in the structure
there will eventually be a sufficient number of them to cause collapse.
Actually some additional load can be carried after this time before collapse occurs as the stresses go into the strain hardening range, but the
deflections which would occur are too large to be permissible.

The propped beam of Fig. 21-9 is an example of a structure which

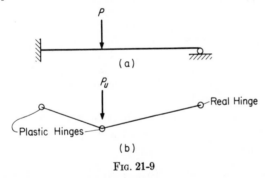

(a)

Real Hinge

Plastic Hinges
(b)

FIG. 21-9

will fail after two plastic hinges develop. Three hinges are required for
collapse but there is a real hinge on the right end. In this beam the
largest elastic moment caused by the design concentrated load is at the
fixed end. As the magnitude of the load is increased a plastic hinge will
form at that point.

The load may be further increased until the moment at some other
point (here it will be at the concentrated load) reaches the plastic moment. Additional load will cause the beam to collapse. The arrangement
of plastic hinges and perhaps real hinges which permit collapse in a structure is called the *mechanism*. Parts (b) of Figs. 21-7, 21-8, and 21-9
show mechanisms for various beams.

After observing the large number of fixed-end and propped beams
used for illustration in this text, the student may form the mistaken idea

that he will frequently encounter such beams in engineering practice. These types of beams, truthfully, are difficult to find in actual structures but are very convenient to use in illustrative examples. They are particularly convenient for introducing plastic analysis before continuous beams and frames are considered.

21-7. PLASTIC ANALYSIS BY THE EQUILIBRIUM METHOD

The method of plastic analysis known as the *equilibrium method* will be illustrated in this section for several beams. The analysis includes the computations of the plastic moments, the consideration of load redistribution after plastic hinges have formed, and the calculation of the ultimate loads which exist when the collapse mechanism is created.

As the first illustration the fixed-end beam of Fig. 21-10 is considered.

FIG. 21-10. Elastic moment diagram.

This beam is assumed to support a load of 6.5 k/ft, including its own estimated weight. A beam is selected by the elastic procedure using A36 steel and assuming full lateral support.

$$M = \frac{wl^2}{12} = \frac{(6.5)\ (18)^2}{12} = 175.5 \text{ ft-k}$$

$$S_{\text{req.}} = \frac{(12)\ (175.5)}{24} = 87.8 \text{ in.}^3$$

Use W 18 × 50 ($S = 89.1$ in.³)

It is desired to determine the value of w_u, the ultimate uniform load which this W section can support before collapse.

The maximum moments in a uniformly loaded fixed-end beam in the elastic range occur at the fixed ends as shown in Fig. 21-10. If the magnitude of the uniform load is increased, plastic moments will eventually be developed at the beam ends as shown in Fig. 21-11 (b). Although the plastic moment has been reached at the ends and plastic hinges

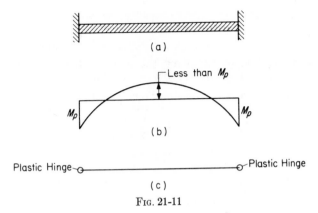

(a)

Less than M_p

M_p M_p

(b)

Plastic Hinge   Plastic Hinge

(c)

Fig. 21-11

formed, the beam cannot fail as it has, in effect, become a simple end-supported beam for further load increase as shown in part (c) of the figure.

The load can now be increased on this "simple" beam; and the moments at the ends will remain constant; but the moment out in the span will increase as it would in a uniformly loaded simple beam. This increase is shown by the dotted line in Fig. 21-12 (b). The load may be

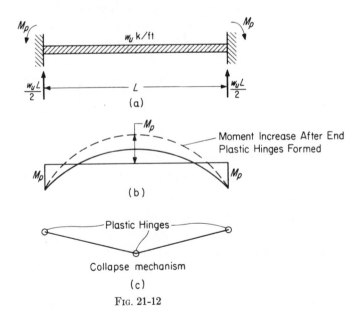

M_p w_u k/ft M_p

$\frac{w_u L}{2}$ L $\frac{w_u L}{2}$

(a)

M_p Moment Increase After End
Plastic Hinges Formed

M_p M_p

(b)

Plastic Hinges

Collapse mechanism

(c)

Fig. 21-12

increased until the moment at some other point (here the beam center line) reaches the plastic moment. When this happens a third plastic hinge will have developed and a mechanism will have been created permitting collapse.

One method of determining the value of w_u is to take moments at the centerline of the beam (knowing the moment there is M_p at collapse). Reference is made here to Fig. 21-12 (a) for the beam reactions. The value of Z was obtained from the Steel Handbook.

$$M_p = -M_p + \left(w_u \frac{l}{2}\right)\left(\frac{l}{2} - \frac{l}{4}\right)$$

$$= \frac{w_u\, l^2}{16}$$

$$w_u = \frac{16\, M_p}{L^2}$$

$$M_p = F_y\, Z = \frac{(36)\,(101)}{12} = 303 \text{ ft-k}$$

$$w_u = \frac{(16)\,(303)}{(18)^2} = 14.95 \text{ k/ft}$$

The plastic safety factor equals $14.95/6.50 = 2.30$. This value appears to be a more realistic value for a ductile steel structure than the one computed on the basis of the yield stress (about 1.5).

The same values could be obtained by considering the diagrams shown in Fig. 21-13. From structural analysis the student will remember

FIG. 21-13

that a fixed-end beam can be replaced with a simply supported beam plus a beam with end moments. Thus the final moment diagram for the fixed-end beam equals the moment diagram if the beam had been simply supported plus the end-moment diagram.

FIG. 21-14

For the beam under consideration the value of M_p can be calculated as follows after studying Fig. 21-14:

$$2\,M_p = \frac{w_u\,l^2}{8}$$

$$M_p = \frac{w_u\,l^2}{16}$$

The propped beam of Fig. 21-15 (a) has been designed by the elastic

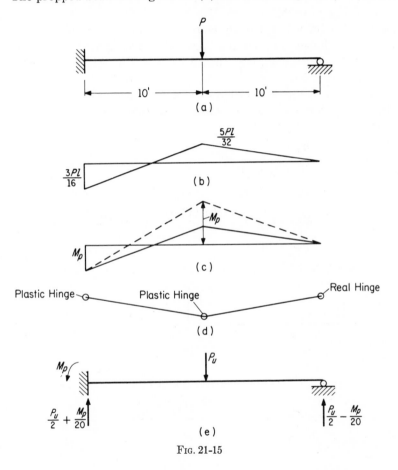

FIG. 21-15

method to support a 50-k concentrated load at mid-span. The W 18 × 55 ($S = 98.4$ in.^{3}, $Z = 112$ in.^{3}) beam of A36 steel selected is now to be considered as a second illustration of plastic analysis. The elastic moment diagram for a propped beam loaded with a concentrated load P at midspan is shown in part (b) of the figure. From this diagram the maximum moment can be seen to occur at the fixed end. The concentrated load is assumed to be increased until the plastic moment is reached at the fixed end and a plastic hinge formed.

After this plastic hinge is formed the beam will act as though it is simply supported insofar as load increases are concerned, because it will have a plastic hinge at the left end and a real hinge at the right end. An increase in the magnitude of the load P will not increase the moment at the left end but will increase the moment out in the beam as it would in a simple beam. The increasing simple beam moment is indicated by the dotted line in part (c) of Fig. 21-15. Eventually the moment at the concentrated load will reach M_p and a mechanism will form, consisting of two plastic hinges and one real hinge as shown in part (d).

The value of the maximum concentrated load P_u which the beam can support can be determined by taking moments to the right or left of the load. Part (e) of Fig. 21-15 shows the beam reactions for the conditions existing just before collapse. Moments are taken to the right of the load as follows:

$$M_p = \left(\frac{P_u}{2} - \frac{M_p}{20}\right)(10)$$

$$= 3.33\,P_u$$

$$P_u = 0.3\,M_p$$

$$M_p = F_y Z = \frac{(36)\,(112)}{12} = 336 \text{ ft-k}$$

$$P_u = 100.8 \text{ k}$$

The other method described for handling the plastic analysis of a

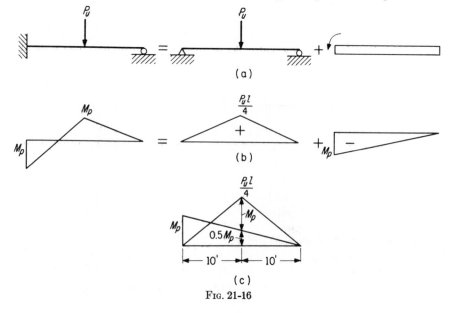

Fig. 21-16

structure involved the drawing of the plastic-moment diagram on the structure after the structure had been made determinate by the creation of a sufficient number of plastic hinges and the equating of the resulting diagram to the simple-beam moment diagram. This procedure is repeated in Fig. 21-16 for the beam previously considered in Fig. 21-15.

From part (c) of Fig. 21-16 the following expression can be written for the moment at the centerline of the beam:

$$M_p + 0.5 \, M_p = \frac{P_u \, l}{4}$$

$$P_u = 0.3 \, M_p$$

Another example is handled by a similar procedure in Fig. 21-17.

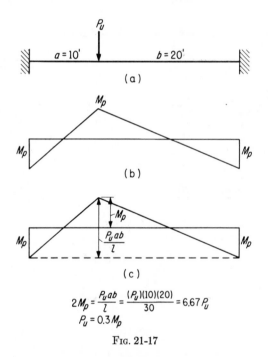

$$2M_p = \frac{P_u ab}{l} = \frac{(P_u)(10)(20)}{30} = 6.67 \, P_u$$

$$P_u = 0.3 \, M_p$$

Fig. 21-17

A propped beam with two concentrated loads is shown in Fig. 21-18 (a). Design was performed by the elastic procedure for the 30-k and 50-k loads shown and a W24 × 84 ($S = 197$ in.³, $Z = 224.0$ in.³) was selected. It is now desired to determine the ultimate values of the two concentrated loads if they are increased at such a rate that they remain in the same proportion to each other. In part (b) of the figure the larger load at collapse is said to equal P_u and the smaller one 0.6 P_u.

As the loads are increased, the plastic moment will first be reached at the left end. After this plastic hinge forms the structure will be determinate since the right end is a real hinge. The loads may be increased until eventually another plastic hinge forms out in the span at one of the two concentrated loads. The point where the second plastic hinge will form is not obvious and it will be necessary to consider both possibilities.

Should the second plastic hinge be assumed to form at the point of

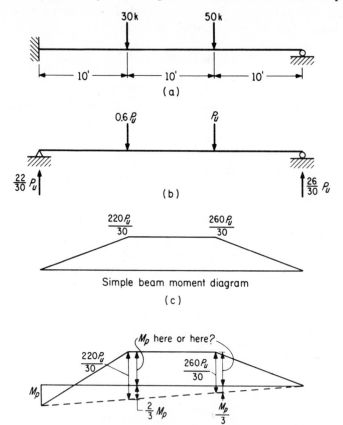

Fig. 21-18

application of the 0.6 P_u concentrated load [see Fig. 21-18 (d)] the values of M_p and P_u can be determined as follows:

$$M_p + \frac{2}{3} M_p = \frac{220\, P_u}{30}$$

$$M_p = 4.4\, P_u$$

$$P_u = 0.227\, M_p$$

If the second plastic hinge is assumed to form at the point of application of P_u, the values of M_p and P_u would be as follows:

$$M_p + \frac{M_p}{3} = \frac{260\,P_u}{3}$$

$$M_p = 6.5\,P_u$$

$$P_u = 0.154\,M_p$$

The moment at the concentrated load P_u will obviously be greater than the moment at the concentrated load $0.6\,P_u$ and the second plastic hinge will occur at P_u. The numerical value of P_u and the factor of safety for plastic can now be calculated.

$$M_p = F_y\,Z = \frac{(36)\ (224)}{12} = 672 \text{ ft-k}$$

$$P_u = (0.154)\ (672) = 103.5 \text{ k}$$

$$\text{F.S.} = \frac{103.5}{50} = 2.07$$

The purpose of this problem is to show the student what to do when

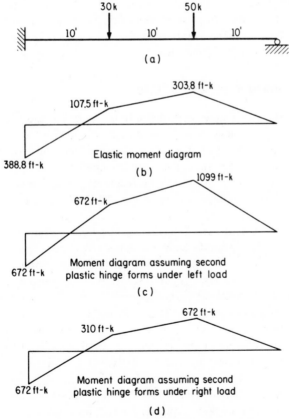

(a)

303.8 ft-k

107.5 ft-k

388.8 ft-k

Elastic moment diagram

(b)

1099 ft-k

672 ft-k

672 ft-k

Moment diagram assuming second
plastic hinge forms under left load

(c)

672 ft-k

310 ft-k

672 ft-k

Moment diagram assuming second
plastic hinge forms under right load

(d)

Fɪɢ. 21-19

there is more than one feasible way in which a structure may collapse. The procedure involves the comparison of the various possibilities by making the necessary mathematical calculations for each. Actually there are some other combinations of hinges which might cause collapse for the beam of Fig. 21-18. Although these other cases are not critical for this particular beam the student will need to learn to consider all collapse possibilities. This same beam is analyzed in Sec. 21-8 by the much simpler virtual work method and all of the possible mechanisms are considered. (The author felt that a consideration of all of the possibilities for the first example of this type using the equilibrium method would be confusing to the student and he only presented the two most obvious collapse possibilities to show how they would be compared to each other to determine which was the more critical.)

If there be any doubt in the student's mind as to whether he has selected the correct location of the second plastic hinge, he can plot the moment diagrams for the two possibilities as shown in Fig. 21-19. Should he have selected the wrong location the moment somewhere will exceed the calculated value of M_p. This situation is shown in part (c) of the figure where the assumed location of the second plastic hinge under the left load is shown to be impossible.

21-8. THE VIRTUAL-WORK METHOD

As the beams or frames become more complex the equilibrium method becomes more and more tedious to apply. A method is introduced in this section, called the *virtual-work method*, which will usually prove to be simpler and quicker than the equilibrium method. This procedure will be used to rework the problems previously considered in Sec. 21-7 and will be further illustrated in Chap. 22 for continuous beams and frames.

The structure is assumed to deflect through a small additional displacement after the ultimate load is reached. The work performed by the external loads during the displacement is equated to the internal work absorbed by the hinges. As a first illustration the uniformly loaded fixed-ended beam of Fig. 21-10 is considered. This beam and its collapse mechanism are redrawn in Fig. 21-20. Owing to symmetry, the rotations at the end plastic hinges are equal and they are represented by θ in the figure; thus the rotation at the middle plastic hinge will be 2θ.

The work performed by the total external load $(w_u l)$ is equal to $w_u l$ times the average deflection of the mechanism. The average deflection equals one-half the deflection at the center plastic hinge ($\frac{1}{2} \times \theta \times l/2$). The external work is equated to the internal work absorbed by

Fig. 21-20

the hinges or to the sum of M_p at each plastic hinge times the angle through which it works. The resulting expression can be solved for M_p and w_u as follows:

$$M_p \left(\theta + 2\theta + \theta\right) = w_u \, l \left(\theta \times \frac{l}{2} \times \frac{1}{2}\right)$$

$$= \frac{w_u \, l^2}{16}$$

$$w_u = \frac{16 \, M_p}{l^2}$$

For the 18-ft span used in Fig. 21-10 these values become

$$M_p = \frac{(w_u) \, (18)^2}{16} = 20.25 \, w_u$$

$$w_u = \frac{M_p}{20.25}$$

Plastic analysis can be handled in a similar manner for the propped beam of Fig. 21-15. This beam is redrawn in Fig. 21-21 together with its

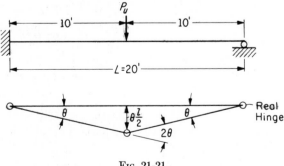

Fig. 21-21

collapse mechanism. Again the end rotations are equal and are assumed to equal θ.

The work performed by the external load P_u as it moves through the distance $\theta\, l/2$ is equated to the internal work performed by the plastic moments at the hinges, noting that there is no moment at the real hinge on the right end of the beam.

$$M_p\,(\theta + 2\theta) = P_u\left(\theta\,\frac{l}{2}\right)$$

$$M_p = \frac{P_u l}{6} \quad \text{(or 3.33 } P_u \text{ for the 20-ft beam shown)}$$

$$P_u = \frac{6\,M_p}{l} \quad \text{(or 0.3 } M_p \text{ for the 20-ft beam shown)}$$

The fixed-end beam of Fig. 21-17 is redrawn in Fig. 21-22 together

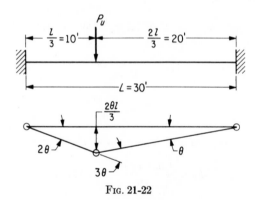

FIG. 21-22

with its collapse mechanism and the assumed angle rotations. From this figure the values of M_p and P_u can be determined by virtual work as follows:

$$M_p\,(2\theta + 3\theta + \theta) = P_u\left(2\theta \times \frac{l}{3}\right)$$

$$M_p = \frac{P_u\, l}{9} \quad \text{(or 3.33 } P_u \text{ for this beam)}$$

$$P_u = \frac{9\,M_p}{l} \quad \text{(or 0.3 } M_p \text{ for this beam)}$$

A person beginning the study of plastic analysis needs to learn to think of all the possible ways in which a particular structure might collapse. Such a habit is of the greatest importance when he begins to analyze more complex structures such as the frames of Chap. 22. In this light the plastic analysis of the propped beam of Fig. 21-18 is considered by the virtual-work method. The beam with its two concentrated loads is shown in Fig. 21-23 together with four possible collapse mechanisms

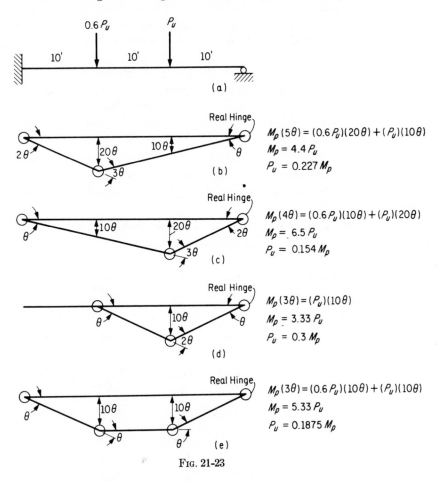

$M_p(5\theta) = (0.6 P_u)(20\theta) + (P_u)(10\theta)$
$M_p = 4.4 P_u$
$P_u = 0.227 M_p$

(b)

$M_p(4\theta) = (0.6 P_u)(10\theta) + (P_u)(20\theta)$
$M_p = 6.5 P_u$
$P_u = 0.154 M_p$

(c)

$M_p(3\theta) = (P_u)(10\theta)$
$M_p = 3.33 P_u$
$P_u = 0.3 M_p$

(d)

$M_p(3\theta) = (0.6 P_u)(10\theta) + (P_u)(10\theta)$
$M_p = 5.33 P_u$
$P_u = 0.1875 M_p$

(e)

Fig. 21-23

and the necessary calculations. It is true that the mechanisms of parts (b), (d) and (e) of the figure do not control, but such a fact is not obvious to the average student until he makes the virtual work calculations for each case. Actually the mechanism of part (e) is based on the assumption that the plastic moment is reached at both of the concentrated loads simultaneously (a situation which might very well occur).

The value for which the collapse load is the smallest in terms of M_p is the correct value (or the value where M_p is the greatest in terms of P_u). For this beam the second plastic hinge forms at the P_u concentrated load and P_u equals $0.154 M_p$.

21-9.   LOCATION OF PLASTIC HINGE FOR UNIFORM LOADINGS

There was no difficulty in locating the plastic hinge for the uniformly loaded fixed-end beam, but for other beams with uniform loads, such as propped or continuous beams, the problem is rather difficult. For this discussion the uniformly loaded propped beam of Fig. 21-24(a) is considered.

The elastic moment diagram for this beam is shown in part (b) of the figure. As the uniform load is increased in magnitude, a plastic hinge will first form at the fixed end. At this time the beam will, in effect, be a "simple" beam with a plastic hinge on one end and a real hinge on the other. Subsequent increases in the load will cause the moment to change as represented by the dotted line in part (b) of the figure. This process will continue until the moment at some other point (a distance x from the right support in the figure) reaches M_p and creates another plastic hinge.

The virtual work expression for the collapse mechanism of this beam shown in part (c) of Fig. 21-24 is written as follows:

$$M_p \left(\theta + \theta + \frac{l-x}{x} \theta \right) = (w_u l) \ (\theta) \ (l-x) \left(\frac{1}{2} \right)$$

Solving this equation for M_p, taking $\dfrac{dM_p}{dx} = 0$ the value of x can be calculated to equal $0.414\,l$. This value is also applicable to uniformly

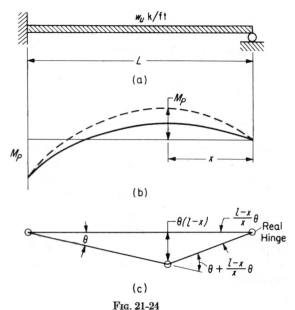

(a)

(b)

(c)

Fɪɢ. 21-24

Fig. 21-25

loaded end spans of continuous beams with simple end supports as will be illustrated in Chap. 22.

The beam and its collapse mechanism are redrawn in Fig. 21-25 and the following expression for the plastic moment is written using the virtual-work procedure:

$$M_p \, (\theta + 2.414 \, \theta) = (w_u l) \, (0.586 \, \theta \, l) \, (\tfrac{1}{2})$$
$$M_p = 0.0858 \, w_u l^2$$

PROBLEMS

21-1 to 21-10. Find the values of S, Z and the shape factor about the x axes for the sections shown in the accompanying illustrations.

(Ans. 198.4, 234, 1.18)

Prob. 21-1

Prob. 21-2

(Ans. 197.5, 248, 1.255)

PROB. 21-3

PROB. 21-4

(Ans. 114.6, 208.2, 1.82)

PROB. 21-5

PROB. 21-6

(Ans. 218, 254.6, 1.17)

PROB. 21-7

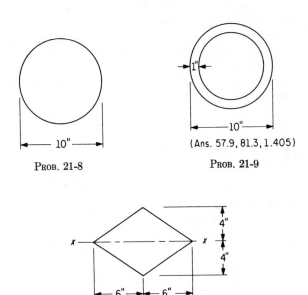

PROB. 21-8   (Ans. 57.9, 81.3, 1.405)

                              PROB. 21-9

PROB. 21-10

21-11 to 21-17. Determine the values of S, Z and the shape factor about the x axes for the situations described.

21-11. A W 30 × 172. (Ans. 521, 594, 1.13)

21-12. A W24 × 100 with one ¾ × 16 in. PL on each flange.

21-13. Two 8 × 6 × ⅝-in. Ls long legs vertical and back-to-back. (Ans. 19.7, 35.8, 1.82)

21-14. Two C 10 × 30s back-to-back.

21-15. Four 8 × 8 × ¾ in. Ls arranged as shown in the accompanying illustration.   (Ans. 64.5, 104.5, 1.62)

PROB. 21-15

21-16. The section of Prob. 5-5 (b).

21-17. The section of Prob. 5-12 (b).   (Ans. 226, 267, 1.18)

21-18. Rework Prob. 21-2 considering the y axis.

21-19. Rework Prob. 21-12 considering the y axis.   (Ans. 91.9, 153, 1.67)

21-20. Rework Prob. 21-14 considering the y axis.

21-21 to 21-31. Select beam sections for the situations shown using the elastic theory, A36 steel, the AISC Specification, and assuming full lateral support. Calculate the factors of safety for the resulting beam sections according to the elastic and plastic theories.   The loads shown in each figure are assumed to include the estimated beam weight.

(Ans. With .9 rule: W16 X 40, 1.45, 2.18
without .9 rule: W18 X 40, 1.54, 2.35)

PROB. 21-21

PROB. 21-22

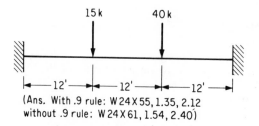

(Ans. With .9 rule: W24 X 55, 1.35, 2.12
without .9 rule: W24 X 61, 1.54, 2.40)

PROB. 21-23

PROB. 21-24

20 k   30 k   40 k

|← 10' →|← 10' →|← 10' →|← 10' →|

(Ans. With .9 rule: W24X84, 1.43, 2.24
without .9 rule: W27X84, 1.54, 2.44)

PROB. 21-25

24 k

|← 12' →|← 18' →|

PROB. 21-26

20 k   40 k

|← 20' →|← 10' →|← 10' →|

(Ans. With .9 rule: W24X84, 1.43, 2.52
without .9 rule: W27X84, 1.54, 2.74)

PROB. 21-27

12 k   20 k   18 k

|← 12' →|← 8' →|← 10' →|← 10' →|

PROB. 21-28

2.4 k/ft

|← 24' →|

(Ans. With .9 rule: W21X44, 1.42, 2.41
without .9 rule: W18X50, 1.54, 2.55)

PROB. 21-29

20 k

3.6 k/ft

|← 15' →|← 15' →|

PROB. 21-30

2 k/ft

|← 10' →|← 20' →|← 10' →|

(Ans. Using .9 rule: W21X49, 1.52, 2.16
without .9 rule: W21X49, 1.52, 2.16)

PROB. 21-31

chapter 22

PLASTIC ANALYSIS AND DESIGN

22-1. INTRODUCTION TO PLASTIC DESIGN

The shape factor multiplied by the safety factor was defined as the *load factor* in Chap. 21 and was shown to have an average value of approximately 1.70 for beams. To design a beam by the plastic method, the estimated working load is multiplied by the load factor; the plastic moment is calculated and a member is selected which furnishes the required plastic modulus ($Z = M_p/F_y$). Example 22-1 presents a comparison of elastic and plastic designs for a uniformly loaded fixed-end beam.

EXAMPLE 22-1. Design the beam shown in Fig. 22-1 by the plastic and elastic methods. The uniform load is 3 k/ft and includes the estimated beam weight. Use A36 steel, the AISC Specification, and assume full lateral support.

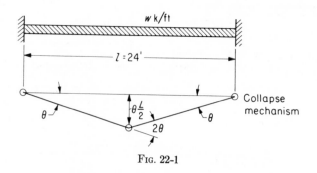

FIG. 22-1

Solution: Plastic analysis:

$$M_p \left(\theta + 2\theta + \theta \right) = (w_u L) \left(\frac{1}{2} \theta \frac{l}{2} \right)$$

$$= \frac{w_u \, l^2}{16}$$

Plastic design:

$$w_u = (1.70) \ (3) = 5.1 \text{ k/ft}$$

$$M_p = \frac{(5.1) \ (24)^2}{16} = 183.6 \text{ ft-k}$$

$$Z_{\text{req.}} = \frac{(12) \ (183.6)}{36} = 61.2 \text{ in.}^3$$

Use W 18 × 35

Elastic design:

$$-M = \frac{wl^2}{12} = \frac{(3) \ (24)^2}{12} = -144 \text{ ft-k}$$

$$+M = \frac{wl^2}{24} = \frac{(3) \ (24)^2}{24} = +72 \text{ ft-k}$$

$-M$ for design $= (0.9) \ (-144) = -129.6 \text{ ft-k}$

$+M$ for design $= 72 + (0.10) \left(\dfrac{144 + 144}{2} \right) = +86.4 \text{ ft-k}$ $\Bigg\}$ (AISC Sec. 1.5.1.4.1)

$$S_{\text{req.}} = \frac{(12) \ (129.6)}{24} = 64.8 \text{ in.}^3$$

Use W 18 × 40

Percent weight saving by plastic design $= \frac{5}{40} = 12.5$ percent

Plastic design is permissible for statically determinate structures but has little if any economic advantage. To illustrate this fact, the design of a simply supported beam by the two methods is presented in Example 22-2. The shape factor advantage (about 12 percent) has already been substantially used in the 10 percent higher allowable bending stress permitted by the AISC for compact laterally supported sections. As only one plastic hinge is needed to cause a statically determinate structure to be unstable, there is no redistribution of load after the hinge forms.

EXAMPLE 22-2. The beam shown in Fig. 22-2 is assumed to support a uniform load of 4 k/ft (including the estimated beam weight). Design the beam by the plastic and elastic methods using A36 steel, the AISC Specification, and assuming full lateral support.

Solution: Plastic analysis:

$$M_p \ (2\theta) = (w_u \, L) \left(\frac{1}{2} \, \theta \, \frac{L}{2} \right)$$

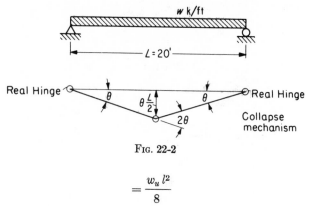

FIG. 22-2

$$= \frac{w_u \, l^2}{8}$$

Plastic design:

$$w_u = (1.70) \ (4) = 6.8 \, \text{k/ft}$$

$$M_p = \frac{(6.8) \ (20)^2}{8} = 340 \, \text{ft-k}$$

$$Z_{\text{req.}} = \frac{(12) \ (340)}{36} = 113.3 \, \text{in.}^3$$

<u>Use W 21 × 55</u>

Elastic design:

$$M = \frac{(4) \ (20)^2}{8} = 200 \, \text{ft-k}$$

$$S_{\text{req.}} = \frac{(12) \ (200)}{24} = 100 \, \text{in.}^3$$

<u>Use W 21 × 55</u>

If all of the plastic hinges needed to produce the collapse mechanism for an indeterminate structure form at the same time, plastic design will yield the same section as will elastic design. For such situations there is no load redistribution after the first hinge forms. This same situation was shown to occur in statically determinate structures where the formation of one plastic hinge was sufficient to cause collapse (see Example 22-2).

Three plastic hinges are required to form a mechanism for a fixed-end beam, but the elastic moment diagram shown in Fig. 22-3 shows that if such a beam is loaded with a concentrated load at its centerline the hinges will all theoretically form at the same time. Example 22-3 illustrates the design of this beam. The student does not have to worry about overlooking a situation where there is no redistribution or where all of the plastic hinges form simultaneously. The virtual-work pro-

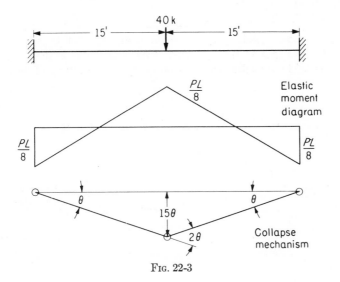

FIG. 22-3

cedure will yield the correct expression for M_p regardless of the order in which the hinges are formed.

Example 22-4 presents the design of a fixed-end beam loaded with a concentrated load at a point other than midspan. For this beam there is appreciable load redistribution after the first and second hinges form.

EXAMPLE 22-3. Design the beam shown in Fig. 22-3 by the plastic and elastic methods using A36 steel, the AISC Specification, and full lateral support. Assume the load given takes into account the estimated beam weight.

Solution: Plastic analysis:

$$M_p \ (\theta + 2\theta + \theta) = P_u \ (15\theta)$$
$$= 3.75 \ P_u$$

Plastic design:

$$P_u = (1.70) \ (40) = 68 \text{ k}$$
$$M_p = (3.75) \ (68) = 255 \text{ ft-k}$$
$$Z_{\text{req.}} = \frac{(12) \ (255)}{36} = 85 \text{ in.}^3$$

<u>Use W 21 × 44</u>

Elastic design (no advantage in 0.9 rule in AISC Sec. 1.5.1.4.1):

$$M = \frac{(40) \ (30)}{8} = 150 \text{ ft-k}$$

$$S_{req.} = \frac{(12)\ (150)}{24} = 75 \text{ in.}^3$$

Use W 21 × 44

EXAMPLE 22-4. Design the beam shown in Fig. 22-4 by the plastic and elastic methods using A36 steel, the AISC Specification, and assuming full lateral support. Assume the load given takes into account the estimated beam weight.

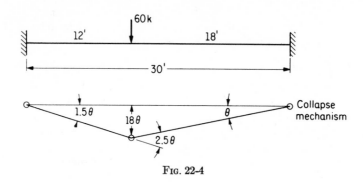

FIG. 22-4

Solution: Plastic analysis:

$$M_p\ (1.5\theta + 2.5\theta + \theta) = (P_u)\ (18\theta)$$
$$= 3.6\ P_u$$

Plastic design:

$$P_u = (1.70)\ (60) = 102 \text{ k}$$
$$M_p = (3.6)\ (102) = 367.2 \text{ ft-k}$$
$$Z_{req.} = \frac{(12)\ (367.2)}{36} = 122.4 \text{ in.}^3$$

Use W 21 × 55

Elastic design:

Drawing of elastic moment diagram is shown in Fig. 22-5.

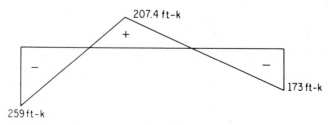

FIG. 22-5

$$-M \text{ for design} = (0.9)\,(-259) = -233.1 \text{ ft-k}$$

$$+M = +207.4 + (0.10)\left(\frac{259 + 173}{2}\right) = +229 \text{ ft-k}$$

$$S_{\text{req.}} = \frac{(12)\,(233.1)}{24} = 116.6 \text{ in.}^3$$

Use W 24 × 61

Percent weight saving by plastic design $= ^6\!/_{61} = 9.8$ percent

22-2. AISC REQUIREMENTS FOR PLASTIC DESIGN

Several of the more important requirements of the AISC Specification pertaining to plastic design are presented as follows:

1. Plastic design is permissible for simple and continuous beams, one and two-story rigid frames and for braced multistory rigid frames. In addition portions of structures rigidly constructed so as to be continuous over at least one interior support can be designed plastically.

2. The plastic design procedure can be used for steels having specified yield points up to 65 ksi (A572, Grade 65).

3. The load factors used in design may not be less than 1.7 for the given dead and live loads nor less than 1.3 for those loads acting in conjunction with a load factor of 1.3 for any wind or seismic forces. (The 1.3 value is obtained by making use of the one-third increase in allowable stresses for wind and seismic loadings provided in AISC Section 1.5.6 This is the same thing as multiplying the load by ¾ or in this case the load factor.)

4. The webs of beams and girders or columns which are not stiffened in some manner (as with diagonal stiffeners or doubler plates) shall be designed so that the ultimate shear, V_u, in kips does not exceed $0.55F_ytd$ where t is the web thickness and d is the member depth.

5. The members of a plastically designed structure must be prevented from local and lateral buckling until the plastic hinges develop. To prevent such buckling the AISC provides minimum width-thickness ratios for the flanges of S, W and similar built-up shapes as well as maximum permissible depth-thickness ratios for the webs of such members.

The minimum width-thickness rations $(b_f/2t_f)$ are given in Sec. 2.7 of the AISC Specification and equal 8.5 for $F_y = 36$ ksi, 8.0 for $F_y = 42$ ksi, etc. In addition the width-thickness ratio of the flange plates in box sections and cover plates are not permitted to be greater than $190/\sqrt{F_y}$.

The depth-thickness ratio of the webs of members subject to plastic bending may not exceed the values given by the equations to follow.

$$\frac{d}{t} = \frac{412}{\sqrt{F_y}}\left(1 - 1.4\frac{P}{P_y}\right) \qquad \text{(AISC Formula 2.7-1a)}$$

when

$$\frac{P}{P_y} \leqq 0.27$$

$$\frac{d}{t} = \frac{257}{\sqrt{F_y}} \qquad \text{(AISC Formula 2.7-1b)}$$

when

$$\frac{P}{P_y} > 0.27$$

6. To prevent lateral and torsional displacements at the plastic hinge locations associated with the collapse mechanism the members must be braced in those locations and at distances from the hinges not exceeding the value l_{cr} given by the following equation.

$$\frac{l_{cr}}{r_y} = \frac{1,375}{F_y} + 25 \qquad \text{(AISC Formula 2.9-1a)}$$

when

$$+ 1.0 > \frac{M}{M_p} > - 0.5$$

$$\frac{l_{cr}}{r_y} = \frac{1,375}{F_y} \qquad \text{(AISC Formula 2.9-1b)}$$

when

$$- 0.5 > \frac{M}{M_p} > - 1.0$$

where r_y = the r of the member about its weak axis
 M = smaller moment at the ends of the unbraced length
M/M_p = end moment ratio which is positive when the member is bent in reverse curvature and negative when bent in single curvature

These requirements do not have to be followed in the vicinity of the last hinge to form but the lateral bracing requirements for elastic design must be met.

7. Web stiffeners are frequently required at plastic hinges to prevent hinges forming in a member at its point of connection to another member. For such situations it may be necessary to use web stiffeners as required by Sec. 1.15.5 of the AISC Specification.

8. If the edges of structural steel members in the vicinity of the plastic hinges are sheared, the edges should be ground, chipped, or planed

smooth. Furthermore, holes in similar locations must be drilled or sub-punched and reamed to full size.

9. There are several other AISC requirements for plastic design which refer in detail to columns, haunched members, connections, etc.

Example 22-5 illustrates the design of a uniformly loaded propped beam using the AISC Specification. The W section selected in this problem is a compact shape, but the ratios required for such shapes are checked to illustrate their application.

EXAMPLE 22-5. Design a section for the span and loading shown in Fig. 22-6 using A36 steel and the AISC Specification. Lateral support is assumed to be provided at 4-ft intervals.

FIG. 22-6

Solution:

Plastic Analysis

$$M_p \, (\theta + 2.414\theta) = (w_u) \, (24) \, (14.06\theta) \, (\tfrac{1}{2})$$
$$= 49.4 \, w_u$$

Plastic Design

$$w_u = (1.70) \, (3) = 5.1 \, \text{k/ft}$$
$$M_p = (49.4) \, (5.1) = 252 \, \text{ft-k}$$
$$Z_{\text{req.}} = \frac{(12) \, (252)}{36} = 84 \, \text{in.}^3$$

Try W 21 × 44 ($A = 13.0$, $d = 20.66$, $b_f = 6.500$, $t_f = 0.451$,

$t_w = 0.348$, $r_y = 1.27$)

Checking AISC Requirements

Shear and moment diagrams just before collapse shown in Fig. 22-7.

1. Shear:

$$0.55 \, F_y \, td = (0.55) \, (36.0) \, (0.348) \, (20.66) = 142.5 \, \text{k} > 73.1 \, \text{k} \quad \text{(OK)}$$

FIG. 22-7

2. Local buckling:

$$\frac{b_f}{2t_f} = \frac{6.500}{(2)\,(0.451)} = 7.2 < 8.5 \qquad\qquad \text{(OK)}$$

$$\frac{P}{P_y} = \frac{0}{P_y} \text{ since no axial load} \qquad \therefore \text{Use AISC Formula 2.7-1a}$$

$$\frac{d}{t} = \frac{20.66}{0.348} = 59.5 < \frac{412}{\sqrt{36}}\left(1 - 1.4\,\frac{0}{P_y}\right) = 68.8 \qquad\qquad \text{(OK)}$$

3. Lateral buckling:

  Plastic hinge at support

$$\frac{M}{M_p} = -\frac{34}{285.9} = -0.119 > -0.5 \qquad \therefore \text{Use AISC Formula 2.9-1a}$$

$$\frac{l_{cr}}{r_y} = \frac{4 \times 12}{1.27} = 37.8 < \frac{1,375}{36} + 25 = 63.2 \qquad\qquad \text{(OK)}$$

Interior plastic hinge is the last one to form (∴ see AISC Sec. 1.5.1.4.1)

$$\left.\begin{array}{c} \dfrac{76.0 \times 6.50}{\sqrt{36}} = 82.3 \\[2ex] \dfrac{20.000}{7.05 \times 36} = 78.8 \end{array}\right\} \qquad \text{Both} > 4 \times 12 = 48'' \qquad\qquad \text{(OK)}$$

22-3. CONTINUOUS BEAMS

Continuous beams are very common in engineering structures. Their continuity causes analysis to be rather complicated in the elastic theory, and even though one of the complex "exact" methods is used for analysis, the resulting stress distribution is not nearly so accurate as is usually assumed.

Plastic analysis is applicable to continuous structures as it is to one-span structures. The resulting values definitely give a more realistic picture of the limiting strength of a structure than can be obtained by elastic analysis. Continuous statically indeterminate beams can be handled by the virtual-work procedure or the equilibrium procedures as they were for the single-span statically indeterminate beams. All of the example problems of this chapter are handled by the virtual-work procedure. As an introduction to continuous beams Examples 22-6 and 22-7 are presented to illustrate two of the more elementary cases. These designs should be checked for shear, local buckling, etc., as was Example 22-5, but space is not taken to show the calculations.

EXAMPLE 22-6. Select a steel shape for the two-span beam shown in Fig. 22-8 using A36 steel, the AISC Specification, and assuming full lateral support.

FIG. 22-8

Solution: Plastic analysis:

$$M_p (2\theta + \theta) = (P_u) (10\theta)$$
$$= 3.33 P_u$$

Plastic design:

$$P_u = (1.70) (40) = 68 \text{ k}$$
$$M_p = (3.33) (68) = 226.7 \text{ ft-k}$$
$$Z_{req.} = \frac{(12) (226.7)}{36} = 75.6 \text{ in.}^3$$

Use W 18 × 40

EXAMPLE 22-7. Select a section for the beam shown in Fig. 22-9. Use A36 steel, the AISC Specification, and assume full lateral support.

FIG. 22-9

Solution: Plastic analysis:

$$M_p\,(2.414\theta + \theta) = (w_u)\,(24)\,(14.06\theta)\,(\tfrac{1}{2})$$

$$= 49.4\,w_u$$

Plastic design:

$$w_u = (1.7)\,(4) = 6.8\;\text{k/ft}$$

$$M_p = (49.4)\,(6.8) = 336\;\text{ft-k}$$

$$Z_{req.} = \frac{(12)\,(336)}{36} = 112\;\text{in.}^3$$

Use W 18 × 55, or W 21 × 55, or W 24 × 55

Additional spans have little effect on the amount of work involved in the plastic design procedure. The same cannot be said for elastic design. Example 22-8 illustrates the design of a three-span beam which is loaded with a concentrated load on each span. The student from his knowledge of elastic analysis can see that plastic hinges will initially form at the first interior supports and then at the centerlines of the end spans, at which time each end span will have a collapse mechanism.

EXAMPLE 22-8. Select a steel section for the beam and loading shown in Fig. 22-10 using A36 steel, the AISC Specification, and assuming full lateral support.

Solution: Plastic analysis:

$$M_p\,(2\theta + \theta) = P_u\,(15\theta)$$

$$= 5\,P_u$$

FIG. 22-10

Plastic design:

$$P_u = (1.70) \ (30) = 51 \text{ k}$$

$$M_p = \ (5) \ (51) \ = 255 \text{ ft-k}$$

$$Z_{\text{req.}} = \frac{(12) \ (255)}{36} = 85 \text{ in.}^3$$

Use W 21 × 44

A uniformly loaded two-span beam with equal spans was designed in Example 22-7. A two-span uniformly loaded beam with unequal spans is designed in Example 22-9. If the same size section is used for both spans, the longer span will obviously collapse first, and the shorter span will be decidedly overdesigned. Nevertheless this procedure is used in this example.

FIG. 22-11

EXAMPLE 22-9. Select a section for the beam shown in Fig. 22-11 using A36 steel, the AISC Specification, and assuming satisfactory lateral support.

Solution: Plastic analysis:

$$M_p \ (\theta + 2.414\theta) = (24 \ w_u) \ (14.06\theta) \ (\tfrac{1}{2})$$

$$= 49.4 \ w_u$$

Plastic design:

$$w_u = (1.70)\ (6) = 10.2\ \text{k/ft}$$

$$M_p = (49.4)\ (10.2) = 504\ \text{ft-k}$$

$$Z_{\text{req.}} = \frac{(12)\ (504)}{36} = 168\ \text{in.}^3$$

Use W 24 × 68

It may be more economical to select a section for the shorter span with its smaller moment and run it through both spans. Cover plates can be added in the longer span where the moment is greater than the plastic resisting moment of the section selected. The procedure is illustrated in Example 22-10 for the beam designed in Example 22-9. In the example a W21 × 44 with a plastic moment resistance of 285.9 ft-k is selected for the shorter span. The moment diagram for this beam (Fig. 22-13) shows that cover plates are needed for 15.70 ft in the right-hand span where the moment exceeds 285.9 ft-k.

This paragraph is devoted to the derivation of an expression for determining cover-plate sizes and is almost identical with the derivation presented in Sec. 16-1. For this discussion Z is the required plastic modulus for the entire moment, Z_s the plastic modulus for the section selected for the shorter span, d the depth of the section selected for the shorter span, t_p the thickness of one cover plate and A_p is the area of one cover plate. An approximate expression for A_p can be written as follows:

$$Z = Z_s + 2A_p \left(\frac{d}{2} + \frac{t_p}{2} \right)$$

$$A_p = \frac{Z}{d + t_p} - \frac{Z_s}{d + t_p}$$

The cover plates should probably be extended a little distance beyond their theoretical points of cutoff. Some designers extend the plates 6 to 12 in. on each end, while others extend them until half of the strength of the plates is developed by the welds connecting them to the beam.

From a standpoint of economy some consideration should be given to using the W 24 × 68 (selected for the 24-ft span in Example 22-9) for both spans. Its weight for the two spans totals 2,856 lb while the weight of the W21 × 44 with the cover plates in the longer span (selected in Example 22-10) weighs 2,138 lb. The use of cover plates saved 718 lb of steel but their connection costs may have exceeded the cost of 718 lb of structural steel.

EXAMPLE 22-10. Select a section for the 18-ft span of the beam of Example 22-9 (see Fig. 22-12) and design the necessary cover plates for the 24-ft span.

FIG. 22-12

Solution: Plastic analysis for 18-ft span:

$$M_p (2.414\theta + \theta) = (18\, w_u)\, (10.55\theta)\, (\tfrac{1}{2})$$
$$= 27.8\, w_u$$

Plastic design for 18-ft span:

$$w_u = (1.70)\, (6) = 10.2\, \text{k/ft}$$
$$M_p = (27.8)\, (10.2) = 284\ \text{ft-k}$$
$$Z_{\text{req.}} = \frac{(12)\, (284)}{36} = 94.5\ \text{in.}^3$$

Use W 21 × 44 $(Z = 95.3\ \text{in.}^3, d = 20.66)$

$$\text{Actual } M_p = \frac{(36)\, (95.3)}{12} = 285.9\ \text{ft-k}$$

Drawing of moment diagram is shown in Fig. 22-13.

Design of cover plates for long span:

$$Z_{\text{req.}} = \frac{(12)\, (600)}{36} = 200\ \text{in.}^3$$

Assuming $t_p = \tfrac{1}{2}$ in.,

$$A_p = \frac{200}{20.66 + 0.50} - \frac{95.3}{20.66 + 0.50} = 4.95\ \text{sq in.}$$

Try 10 × ½-in. cover plates $(A_p = 5.0\ \text{sq in.})$

$$Z = 95.3 + (2)\, (5.0)\, (10.58) = 201.1\ \text{in.}^3 > 200\ \text{in.}^3 \qquad \text{(OK)}$$

Use ½ × 10-in. cover plates 17.0 ft long

FIG. 22-13

22-4. PLASTIC ANALYSIS OF FRAMES

The pin-supported frame of Fig. 22-14(a) is statically indeterminate to the first degree. The development of one plastic hinge will cause it to become determinate while the forming of a second hinge can create a mechanism. There are, however, several possible mechanisms which might feasibly occur in the frame. A possible beam mechanism is shown in part (d) of the figure, a sidesway mechanism is shown in part (d) and a possible combination beam and sidesway mechanism in part (e). The critical condition is the one which will cause the smallest value of P_u.

Example 22-11 presents the plastic analysis of the frame of Fig. 22-14. The distances through which the loads move in the virtual-work procedure should be carefully studied. The solution of this problem shows that superposition does not apply to plastic analysis, a point of major significance. The situation shown in part (c) of Fig. 22-14 added to the situation of part (d) does not equal that of part (e). In other words the effects of different loads cannot be determined separately and added together as they can in elastic analysis. The three-fourth AISC rule, representing a one-third increase in allowable stresses when lateral loads are involved, is used in this problem.[1]

[1] The AISC Specification reflects the ¾ reduction by permitting the load factor of 1.7 for frames to be reduced to 1.3 when lateral loads are involved. Using these load factors in design it is unnecessary to use the ¾ value as done in Examples 22-11 through 22-13.

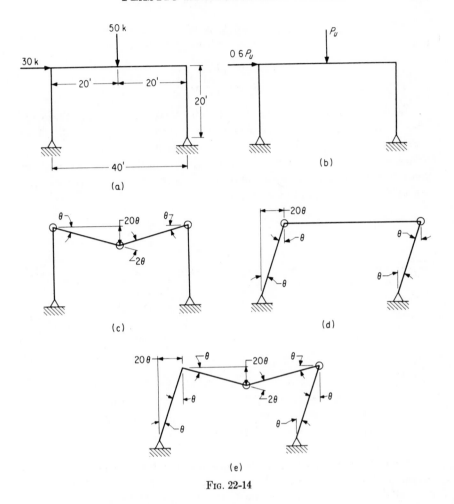

Fig. 22-14

EXAMPLE 22-11. Determine an expression for the plastic moment in the frame of Fig. 22-14.

Solution: Case (c) of figure:

$$M_p \, (\theta + 2\theta + \theta) = P_u \, (20\theta)$$
$$M_p = 5 \, P_u$$

Case (d) of figure:

$$M_p \, (\theta + \theta) = (\tfrac{3}{4}) \, (0.6 \, P_u) \, (20\theta)$$
$$M_p = 4.5 \, P_u$$

Case (e) of figure:

$$M_p \, (2\theta + 2\theta) = (\tfrac{3}{4}) \, (0.6 \, P_u) \, (20\theta) + (\tfrac{3}{4}) \, (P_u) \, (20\theta)$$
$$M_p = 6 \, P_u \qquad \text{(controls)}$$

Critical value is the smallest value of P_u (or the largest value of M_p in terms of P_u).

$$M_p = 6\,P_u$$

$$P_u = 0.167\,M_p$$

Example 22-12 is similar to Example 22-11 except that there are even more possible collapse mechanisms. Parts (a), (b), and (c) of Fig. 22-16 show possible beam collapse mechanisms, while part (d) shows a sidesway mechanism. Parts (e) and (f) of the figure show possible combination sidesway and beam mechanisms. Study carefully the angles used for parts (e) and (f).

FIG. 22-15

EXAMPLE 22-12. Determine the critical value of P_u for the frame shown in Fig. 22-15.

Solution: Possible collapse mechanisms are shown in Fig. 22-16.

Critical value of $P_u = \frac{1}{16.25}\,M_p$

Example 22-13 illustrates the analysis of a frame with fixed supports. The fact that the frame has two more redundants than the hinged frames of the last two examples in no way makes its plastic analysis more difficult.

EXAMPLE 22-13. Determine the critical value of P_u for the frame shown in Fig. 22-17.

Solution: Possible collapse mechanisms are shown in Fig. 22-18.

Critical value of $P_u = \frac{1}{15}\,M_p$

For many frames the locations of the plastic hinges are not obvious.

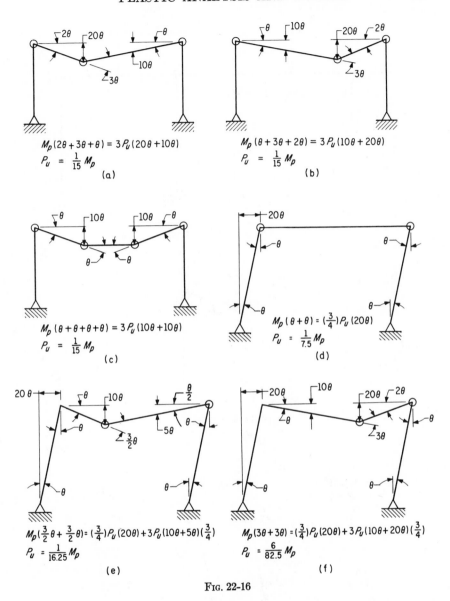

$$M_p(2\theta + 3\theta + \theta) = 3P_u(20\theta + 10\theta)$$
$$P_u = \frac{1}{15}M_p$$

(a)

$$M_p(\theta + 3\theta + 2\theta) = 3P_u(10\theta + 20\theta)$$
$$P_u = \frac{1}{15}M_p$$

(b)

$$M_p(\theta + \theta + \theta + \theta) = 3P_u(10\theta + 10\theta)$$
$$P_u = \frac{1}{15}M_p$$

(c)

$$M_p(\theta + \theta) = \left(\frac{3}{4}\right)P_u(20\theta)$$
$$P_u = \frac{1}{7.5}M_p$$

(d)

$$M_p\left(\frac{3}{2}\theta + \frac{3}{2}\theta\right) = \left(\frac{3}{4}\right)P_u(20\theta) + 3P_u(10\theta + 5\theta)\left(\frac{3}{4}\right)$$
$$P_u = \frac{1}{16.25}M_p$$

(e)

$$M_p(3\theta + 3\theta) = \left(\frac{3}{4}\right)P_u(20\theta) + 3P_u(10\theta + 20\theta)\left(\frac{3}{4}\right)$$
$$P_u = \frac{6}{82.5}M_p$$

(f)

Fig. 22-16

The usual procedure for such cases is to assume a mechanism and compute the value of M_p. Should the correct hinge location have been assumed, the value of M_p will be the correct value. If the wrong hinge location was assumed the value of M_p will be too small.

Several other mechanisms can be assumed and M_p quickly computed for each. The largest value of M_p computed will be the one used. Al-

Fig. 22-17

$$M_p(4\theta) = (6P_u)(10\theta)$$
$$P_u = \frac{1}{15} M_p$$

(a)

$$M_p(4\theta) = (\tfrac{3}{4})P_u(20\theta)$$
$$P_u = \frac{4}{15} P_u$$

(b)

$$M_p(6\theta) = (\tfrac{3}{4})P_u(20\theta) + 6P_u(10\theta)(\tfrac{3}{4})$$
$$P_u = \frac{1}{10} M_p$$

(c)

Fig. 22-18

though the mechanism finally used may not be exactly the right one, it will be satisfactory for all practical purposes. (It might be noted that the moment diagram can be drawn as a check for any one of the assumed conditions. If the moment at no point in the frame exceeds the calculated value of M_p, the correct mechanism has been used.)

For a frame supporting concentrated and uniform loads, the expected positions of the plastic hinges will be at the concentrated loads. When a structure supports only uniform loads there will be a large (actually unlimited) number of possible hinge locations. After a few mechanism locations have been assumed and M_p determined for each, it is possible to narrow down the "critical hinge" location within a foot or two.

Shear stresses are often high within the boundaries of the rigid connection of two or more members whose webs lie in a common plane. Such a situation occurs at the rigid frame knee in part (a) of Fig. 22-19. Since most of the moment in a beam is resisted by the flanges, an internal resisting couple is assumed to be located at the centers of the flanges with a lever arm of $0.95d_b$ as shown in part (b) of the figure. The magnitude of each of these forces V can be determined as $V = M_p/\overline{0.95d_b}$.

This force is applied perpendicularly to the column as a shearing force. The column must have a shearing strength equal to V. If not, it will be necessary to use a pair of diagonal stiffeners as shown in part (c) of the figure, or a reinforcing or doubler plate in contact with the web over the connection area.

The ultimate shearing strength of the column web $(0.55F_ytd_c)$ must be equal to V or stiffening is required. From this information the required web thickness can be determined. In the expression developed, A_{bc} equals the planar area of the connection web (d_bd_c). If M_p is assumed to be in foot-kips, the following expression, from Sec. 2.5 of the "Commentary on AISC Specification" can be developed:

$$0.55F_ytd_c = \frac{M_p(12)}{0.95d_b}$$

$$t = \frac{23M_p}{A_{bc}F_y}$$

Should the shearing strength of the column web be insufficient, the diagonal stiffeners shown in part (c) of Fig. 22-19 can be used. These stiffeners act like the diagonals of a truss to carry the excess shear. The flange force V must be resisted by the web and the stiffener. An expression for the required area of the stiffener A_{st} is developed as follows:

$$\frac{M_p}{0.95d_b} = 0.55\,F_y\,td_c + F_yA_{st}\cos\theta$$

$$A_{st} = \frac{1}{\cos\theta}\left(\frac{M_p}{0.95d_bF_y} - 0.55td_c\right)$$

A similar discussion can be made for the elastic design of rigid knee connections and the AISC formula recommended in Sec. 1.5.1.2 of the "Commentary on AISC Specification."

(a)

(b)   (c)

FIG. 22-19

22-5. CONCLUSION OF TEXT

The author has attempted to include in this textbook only the elementary phases of structural steel design. His main purpose has been to try to interest the student in the subject as he feels that the longest step a person can take toward proficiency in any field is to become interested in the subject.

The student needs to realize that this book only begins to present the knowledge now available concerning structural steel design. A person going into this field should study a great deal to familiarize himself with this information and also to keep abreast of the latest developments. The amount of structural research under way at this time far exceeds the work done at any time in the past. Furthermore, steel research projects are being initiated at an ever-increasing rate.

Several current trends are underway in the steel design field and will apparently continue for some time. The designer must concentrate on

these and other developments if he is to progress in the field. These subjects include the following;

   1. Vastly increased computer usage.

   2. Continued development and applications of stronger and stronger
steels.

Verrazano-Narrows Bridge between Staten Island and Brooklyn, N. Y.
(*United States Steel Corporation*)

   3. An increasing trend towards single unit design such as the composite structures and orthotropic systems.

   4. More plastic design applications.

PROBLEMS

   Note: Use A36 steel, the AISC Specification and assume full lateral support
is provided for all of the beams and frames shown. The working loads given
in each case include estimates of the structure weight.

   22-1 to 22-8. Select sections by the elastic and plastic methods for each of
the beams shown.

(Ans. W 24 X 55, with .9-W 21 X 55, W 21 X 44 plastic)

Prob. 22-1

Prob. 22-2

(Ans. W 24 X 55, with .9-W 21 X 55, W 21 X 44 plastic)

Prob. 22-3

Prob. 22-4

(Ans. W 24 X 76, .9-W 24 X 68, W 21 X 55 plastic)

Prob. 22-5

Prob. 22-6

(Ans. W27 X 94, with .9-W27 X 84, W 24 X 76 plastic)

Prob. 22-7

Prob. 22-8

22-9 to 22-15. Select by the plastic method a single rolled section which will be satisfactory for the entire structure for each of the beams shown.

(Ans. W 30 X 108)

PROB. 22-9

PROB. 22-10

(Ans. W21X44)

PROB. 22-11

PROB. 22-12

(Ans. W 27 X 84)

PROB. 22-13

PROB. 22-14

2 k/ft

(Ans. W18×35)
PROB. 22-15

22-16 to 22-18. Select a single rolled section for the beams shown in the accompanying illustrations and draw shear and moment diagrams for the sections selected using the collapse loads used in design. Use plastic method only.

PROB. 22-16

(Ans. W 24 X 76)
PROB. 22-17

PROB. 22-18

22-19 to 22-27. Select a single rolled section for each of the beams shown which will be satisfactory for the entire structure. Then select a section for the span which has the smallest moment and design cover plates as necessary for the other parts of the beam. Compare the weight differences between the two procedures. Use plastic method only.

(Ans. W18 X 35, W14 X 22 with $\frac{1}{2}$ X 6 X 14'-0" PLs)

PROB. 22-19

PROB. 22-20

(Ans. W18 X 40, W16 X 31 with $\frac{1}{2}$ X 4 X 11'-0" PLs)

PROB. 22-21

PROB. 22-22

(Ans. W18 X 35, W16 X 26 with $\frac{3}{8}$ X 4 X 11'-0" PLs)

PROB. 22-23

PROB. 22-24

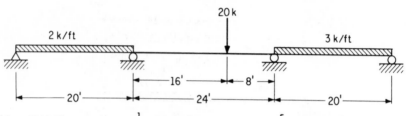

(Ans. W18 X 35, W14 X 22 with $\frac{1}{4}$ X 3 X 9'-0" PLs in span 1 and $\frac{5}{8}$ X 4 X 14'-0" PLs in span 3)

PROB. 22-25

PROB. 22-26

(Ans. W16 X 31, W14 X 26 with $\frac{1}{4}$ X 3 X 18'-0" PLs in span 3)

PROB. 22-27

22-28 to 22-31. Select sections using the plastic method for the frames shown considering moment only. Assume beam and column sizes are the same for each frame.

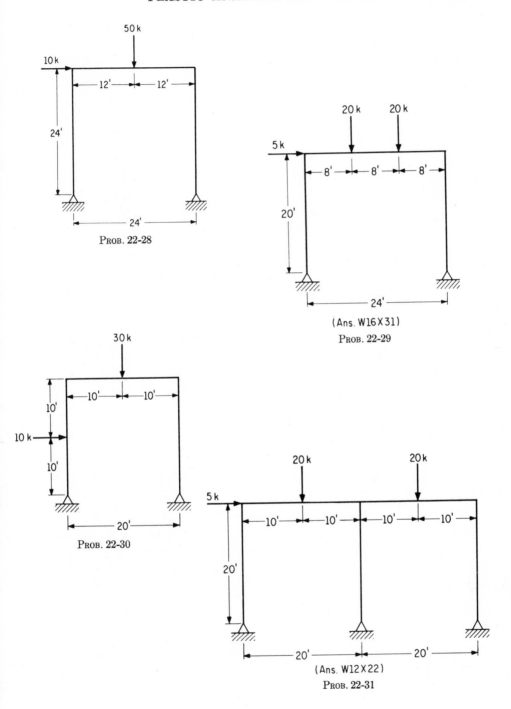

PROB. 22-28

(Ans. W16×31)
PROB. 22-29

PROB. 22-30

(Ans. W12×22)
PROB. 22-31

INDEX